ROUND TABLE Viewpoints

BUSINESS LAW

Selected, Edited, and with Introductions and Summaries by

M. Neil Browne
Bowling Green State University

Nancy K. Kubasek
Bowling Green State University

McGraw Hill **Higher Education**

Boston Burr Ridge, IL Dubuque, IA New York San Francisco St. Louis
Bangkok Bogotá Caracas Kuala Lumpur Lisbon London Madrid Mexico City
Milan Montreal New Delhi Santiago Seoul Singapore Sydney Taipei Toronto

The McGraw-Hill Companies

Higher Education

ROUNDTABLE VIEWPOINTS: BUSINESS LAW, FIRST EDITION

Published by McGraw-Hill, a business unit of The McGraw-Hill Companies, Inc., 1221 Avenue of the Americas, New York, NY 10020.

Roundtable Viewpoints is published by the **Contemporary Learning Series** group within the McGraw-Hill Higher Education division.

1 2 3 4 5 6 7 8 9 0 DOC/DOC 0 9 8

MHID: 0-07-352729-7
ISBN: 978-0-07-352729-1
ISSN: 1942-9592

Managing Editor: *Larry Loeppke*
Senior Managing Editor: *Faye Schilling*
Senior Developmental Editor: *Jill Peter*
Editorial Coordinator: *Mary Foust*
Editorial Assistant: *Nancy Meissner*
Production Service Assistant: *Rita Hingtgen*
Permissions Coordinator: *Lenny J. Behnke*
Senior Marketing Manager: *Julie Keck*
Marketing Communications Specialist: *Mary Klein*
Marketing Coordinator: *Alice Link*
Senior Project Manager: *Jane Mohr*
Design Specialist: *Tara McDermott*
Cover Graphics: *Kristine Jubeck*

Compositor: Hurix Systems Private Limited
Cover Image: Royalty-Free/Corbis

www.mhhe.com

CONTENTS IN BRIEF

CONTENTS

CORRELATION GUIDE

The *Roundtable Viewpoints* series offers varying perspectives on important issues and provides readers with balanced and fair coverage of a topic to form their own opinion or to support their research. These readers are designed to address a number of different issues regarding a subject area. Each issue question is relevant to the topic and guides readers through the readings.

Roundtable Viewpoints: Business Law is an easy-to-use reader that presents issues on important topics in business law. For more information on *Roundtable Viewpoints* and other *McGraw-Hill Contemporary Learning Series* titles, visit www.mhcls.com.

This convenient guide matches the issues in **Roundtable Viewpoints: Business Law** with the corresponding chapters in three of our best-selling McGraw-Hill Business Law textbooks by Kubasek et al., Barnes et al., and Brown/Sukys.

Roundtable Viewpoints: Business Law, 1/e	**Dynamic Business Law by Kubasek et al.**	**Law for Business, 10/e by Barnes et al.**	**Business Law with UCC Applications, 12/e by Brown/Sukys**
Issue 1: Are Courts Strangling Businesses with Tort Suits?	**Chapter 8:** Torts	**Chapter 6:** Intentional Torts **Chapter 7:** Negligence and Strict Liability **Chapter 29:** Management of the Corporate Business	**Chapter 5:** Criminal Law **Chapter 6:** Tort Law **Chapter 12:** Legality
Issue 2: Should An Employer Be Able to be Fired for Any Reason?	**Chapter 4:** Alternative Dispute Resolution **Chapter 6:** International and Comparative Law **Chapter 42:** Employment and Labor Law **Chapter 43:** Employment Discrimination	**Chapter 9:** The Nature and Origins of Contracts **Chapter 23:** The Agency Relationship—Creation, Duties, and Termination **Chapter 25:** Employment Laws	**Chapter 12:** Legality **Chapter 33:** The Principal and Agent Relationship **Chapter 34:** Agency Operation **Chapter 35:** Employment Law **Chapter 36:** Labor-Management Relations Law **Chapter 40:** Government Regulation of Corporate Business
Issue 3: To What Extent Should the Board of Directors Be Free to Make Business Decisions?	**Chapter 39:** Corporations: Directors, Officers, and Shareholders	**Chapter 29:** Management of the Corporate Business	**Chapter 39:** Corporate Governance

Roundtable Viewpoints: Business Law, 1/e	Dynamic Business Law by Kubasek et al.	Law for Business, 10/e by Barnes et al.	Business Law with UCC Applications, 12/e by Brown/Sukys
Issue 4: When is Someone Acting on Your Behalf?	**Chapter 33:** Agency Formation and Duties **Chapter 34:** Liability to Third Parties and Termination	**Chapter 23:** The Agency Relationship—Creation, Duties, and Termination **Chapter 25:** Employment Laws **Chapter 24:** Liability of Principals and Agents to Third Parties	**Chapter 33:** The Principal and Agent Relationship **Chapter 34:** Agency Operation
Issue 5: Should Employers Be Able to Force Employees into Arbitration?	**Chapter 4:** Alternative Dispute Resolution	**Chapter 2:** Dispute Settlement	**Chapter 4:** Alternative Dispute Resolution **Chapter 36:** Labor-Management Relations Law
Issue 6: Should the Law Allow a Business to Withhold Information from Consumers?	**Chapter 45:** Consumer Law	**Chapter 9:** The Nature and Origins of Contracts **Chapter 46:** Consumer Protection Laws	**Chapter 6:** Tort Law **Chapter 19:** Warranties and Product Liability **Chapter 20:** Consumer Protection
Issue 7: Should Homeowners Be Able to Do What They Want with Their Property?	**Chapter 8:** Tort Law **Chapter 49:** Real Property	**Chapter 33:** Personal Property and Bailments **Chapter 34:** Real Property	
Issue 8: Should the Government Be Able to Take Your Property for Purpose of Job Creation?	**Chapter 5:** Constitutional Principles **Chapter 49:** Real Property	**Chapter 4:** Business and the Constitution **Chapter 33:** Personal Property and Bailments **Chapter 34:** Real Property	**Chapter 23:** Real Property
Issue 9: Who Should Be Sued When Many People Are Involved in a Securities Fraud?	**Chapter 7:** Crime and the Business Community **Chapter 41:** Corporations: Securities and Investor Protection	**Chapter 31:** Securities Regulation **Chapter 29:** Management of the Corporate Business	**Chapter 15:** Discharge and Remedies **Chapter 40:** Government Regulation of Corporate Business **Chapter 41:** Professional Liability
Issue 10: What Should You Be Able to Keep When You Go Bankrupt?	**Chapter 32:** Bankruptcy and Reorganization	**Chapter 44:** Bankruptcy	**Chapter 32:** Bankruptcy

PREFACE

The law is continually evolving. Hence, to effectively study the law is to study not just the rules that currently govern society, but to consider the areas where the law is currently in flux. In this **Roundtable Viewpoints**, we have chosen ten legal issues that are currently being debated among those interested in the study of business law. The issues are ones that ordinarily might arise in a Business Law or Legal Environment of Business classroom, but would not be covered in depth in the ordinary textbook.

Reading the business law or legal environment textbook gives students a sense of the rules that currently govern business. Incorporating discussions of the issues raised in this book, and giving students the opportunity to explore these issues in depth gives them a much more accurate perception of the depth and fluidity of the law, and a much better understanding of the actual complexity of the law.

Structure of This Book. This book is organized into ten issues, each of which relates to at least one chapter of a standard business law or legal environment of business textbook. Some issues would actually be applicable to more than one chapter, so the chapter with which an instructor would use a particular issue will depend upon the structure of the course. For example, the issue, "Should states be able to use the power of eminent domain to take private property from one private party and transfer it to another private party for the alleged public purpose of economic redevelopment?" fits nicely into a constitutional law chapter because it involves an interpretation of the takings clause of the Fifth Amendment, yet it also fits in nicely in a property chapter when one is discussing the extent to which the government should determine the use of private property. Both public and private law issues are included.

Every important legal issue, at some point or another, is addressed by the court. Therefore, for each of the issues in this book, we provide not just a set of articles addressing the issue, but also a relevant case. In many instances, just to reinforce the lack of rigidity in the law, we include both the majority opinion and the dissenting opinion. As professors of law well know, often the reasoning from today's dissenting opinion forms the basis for next year's majority opinion.

Each issue begins with an introduction that provides the students with an idea of what the writers of the various articles are attempting to accomplish. The introduction is followed by the relevant case and articles. Marginal challenge questions appear alongside the articles and cases to stimulate the students' thought as they are reading the articles. The articles are followed by sections designed to encourage further student reflection: the issue summary, issue highlights, and critical thinking questions. The section closes with a list of resources that students may delve into if they wish to explore the issue in more depth.

ACKNOWLEDGMENTS

The authors wish to recognize the contributions of four phenomenal research assistants who contributed to the development of this text: Lauren Biksacky, Rachel Childers, Allison Smith, and Daniel Tagliarina. Their assistance was crucial in our collecting articles that would be of interest to today's students.

GUIDED TOUR

ISSUE 1

Are Courts Strangling Businesses with Tort Suits?

For years tort reform has been a recurrent theme for debate in Congress and among the public. Advocates of tort reform argue that the current tort system allows outrageous punitive damage awards that are unwarranted and unduly harm businesses. Opponents of tort reform argue that punitive damages are necessary to punish those who have committed egregious wrongs, as well as to deter others from engaging in similar harmful behavior. At the forefront of tort reform efforts are proposed caps on the amount any party may receive in punitive damages from a tort case. The articles in this chapter provide a mere snapshot of some of the perspectives regarding the desirability of punitive damage caps.

In their article, "Medical Malpractice Reform and Insurer Claims Defense: Unintended Effects?" Ambrose and Carroll examine how punitive damage caps affect medical malpractice lawsuits. As the United States experiences another medical malpractice insurance crisis, many parties again push for tort reforms, including caps on punitive damages. In light of this crisis, Ambrose and Carroll investigate how capping punitive damage awards will affect defense expenses that insurance companies face in light of medical malpractice litigation. Ambrose and Carroll found that caps on punitive damages tend to be correlated with higher losses and defense costs, seemingly indicating that capping punitive damage awards does not reduce defense costs or losses for medical malpractice insurers. However, some other tort reforms might offset some of the losses insurers occur under punitive damage caps. Ambrose and Carroll conclude by considering the important implications of tort reforms on medical malpractice. They want to strike a balance between ensuring that injured parties are justly compensated and that a deterrent effect still exists to prevent poor medical treatment from occurring.

Instead of focusing on medical malpractice, in the second article Rubin and Shepherd discuss accidental deaths. Rubin and Shepherd believe the purpose of the tort liability system is to create incentives to reduce risk, and thus ask if tort reforms affect the ability of torts to decrease the accidental death rate. While the authors find that tort reform, in general, actually leads to a higher accidental death rate, they did find that specific tort reforms are correlated with a reduction in the incidence of accidental deaths. In particular, capping non-economic damage, such as punitive damages, does lead to a decrease in the

ISSUE INTRODUCTIONS

Designed to introduce the issue to the reader, the issue introduction states an issue question, provides history, current events, a list of the upcoming article selections for the issue, and relevant information about the issue to help facilitate discussion.

ISSUE SUMMARY

The articles in this chapter can best be understood as addressing a broader question than how we should modify the employment-at-will doctrine. Each author featured in this chapter was indirectly answering the question: Who should the law protect? Each author had a different answer: employees who are whistleblowers; gay, lesbian, and bisexual employees; employees who are asked to perform illegal activities; and even employers who are at risk for wrongful termination lawsuits. Each author focused on a different group of people.

Why is the author's focus significant? Consider a different issue. Consider environmental law. What happens when we focus on the needs of corporations? We lessen restrictions on pollution. What happens when we focus on the needs of farmers? We lessen restrictions on the use of water. What happens when we focus on the needs of future generations? We do everything possible to conserve the planet's resources. Depending upon our focus, we shift our goals, our priorities, and our laws.

Think again about the employment-at-will doctrine. When we focus on employees, how do our laws change? We probably create more exceptions to the doctrine to prevent wrongful termination. What happens when we shift our focus to a select subset of employees? We probably create narrow exceptions to protect a small and very specific group of employees. How does the law change when we focus on employers' needs? We most likely restrict the number of exceptions to the doctrine so that employers can hire and fire at will.

When you read arguments about the law, ask yourself: On which group of people is the author focusing? Does the author provide any justification for that focus? What are the implications of the author's choosing one group as opposed to the myriad of other groups available? Whether you agree with an author's argument will probably be linked to how you feel about the author's focus.

ISSUE SUMMARIES

Issue summaries appear at the end of each issue text. The summary brings the readings together, offers concluding observations, and suggests new directions for the student to take to further explore the issue.

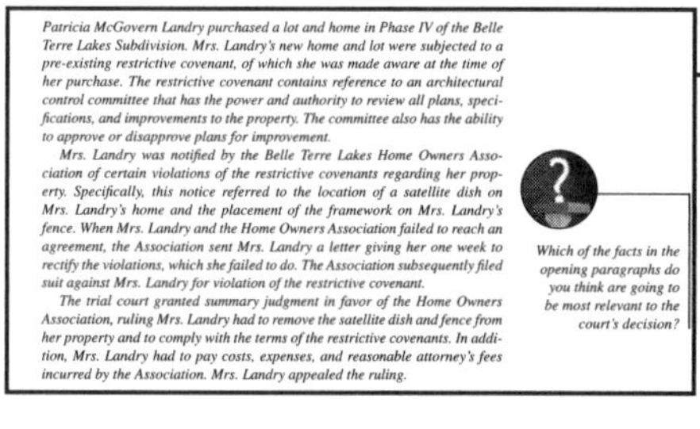

Patricia McGovern Landry purchased a lot and home in Phase IV of the Belle Terre Lakes Subdivision. Mrs. Landry's new home and lot were subjected to a pre-existing restrictive covenant, of which she was made aware at the time of her purchase. The restrictive covenant contains reference to an architectural control committee that has the power and authority to review all plans, specifications, and improvements to the property. The committee also has the ability to approve or disapprove plans for improvement.

Mrs. Landry was notified by the Belle Terre Lakes Home Owners Association of certain violations of the restrictive covenants regarding her property. Specifically, this notice referred to the location of a satellite dish on Mrs. Landry's home and the placement of the framework on Mrs. Landry's fence. When Mrs. Landry and the Home Owners Association failed to reach an agreement, the Association sent Mrs. Landry a letter giving her one week to rectify the violations, which she failed to do. The Association subsequently filed suit against Mrs. Landry for violation of the restrictive covenant.

The trial court granted summary judgment in favor of the Home Owners Association, ruling Mrs. Landry had to remove the satellite dish and fence from her property and to comply with the terms of the restrictive covenants. In addition, Mrs. Landry had to pay costs, expenses, and reasonable attorney's fees incurred by the Association. Mrs. Landry appealed the ruling.

Which of the facts in the opening paragraphs do you think are going to be most relevant to the court's decision?

CHALLENGE QUESTIONS

Each issue contains challenge questions, in the form of marginal notes, designed to stimulate critical thinking and discussion. The challenge questions are thought-provoking and relevant to the issue and its selections.

ISSUE HIGHLIGHTS

- To bring a successful § 10(b) suit by a private party, the private party must prove that the defendant: (1) made a material misrepresentation or omission; (2) knowingly and intentionally committed misrepresentation or omission; (3) the misrepresentation or omission is related to the purchase or sale of a security; (4) the plaintiff erroneously relied upon the misrepresentation or omission; (5) the plaintiff suffered economic loss due to the misrepresentation or omission; and (6) the misrepresentation or omission is the direct cause of the loss.
- To be held liable under § 10(b), according to the Supreme Court, a third party must be guilty of all of the elements of securities fraud.
- Plaintiffs are increasingly relying upon Rules 10b-5(a) and (c) to try to recover damages from a broader range of defendants under the concept of scheme liability.
- The Securities and Exchange Commission (SEC) favors the application of scheme liability to third parties.

ISSUE HIGHLIGHTS

Highlights appear at the end of each issue and help to identify important information and details about the issue. The main points covered in the readings are recapped in the issue highlights.

CRITICAL THINKING

Much of legal reasoning, which includes most arguments about legal issues, involves arguments by analogy. In that American jurisprudence is based on legal precedent, legal arguments tend to make analogies between facts patterns and case specific information to argue when specific precedents apply. It is this process of applying precedent to new situations that builds American law. Accordingly, assessing the quality of legal analogies is key to determining the strength of many legal arguments. As a critical thinker, asking how strong the analogy is between past cases and the issue at hand is a crucial first step towards evaluating the strength of an argument.

The case and articles excerpted in this chapter are no exception. Starting with the Supreme Court case *Stoneridge*, included in this chapter, we see how reasonable people can disagree based on different assessments of the strength of a legal analogy. Much of Justice Kennedy's majority opinion rests on the assessment that the Court's earlier ruling in *Central Bank* bars scheme liability where the third party did not actively make a misrepresentation that was relied upon by other parties. However, in his dissent, Justice Stevens argues that Justice Kennedy misses key points in his application of the legal analogy between *Central Bank* and *Stoneridge*. According to Stevens, the facts of *Central Bank* are too different to apply directly to *Stoneridge*. Depending on how one assesses the analogy between *Central Bank* and *Stoneridge* will determine how one views the Court's ultimate ruling in *Stoneridge*. While the legal analogy is not the only argument presented by the Court, it is the focus of the Court's argument.

CRITICAL THINKING

Found at the end of each issue, this essential feature provides key strategies for using critical thinking skills in discussing the issues and forming an educated and well-thought-out opinion.

ADDITIONAL READING RESOURCES

Bernard S. Black, Brian R. Cheffins, *and* Michael Klausner, "Liability Risk for Outside Directors: A Cross-Border Analysis," *Eur. Financial Mgmt. J.*, 11, 153–171 (2005).

Lisa Fairfax, "Spare the Rod, Spoil the Director? Revitalizing Directors' Fiduciary Duty Through Legal Liability," *Houston L. Rev.*, 42, 393–456 (2005).

Jonathan R. Macey *and* Maureen O'Hara, "The Corporate Governance of Banks," *Econ. Pol. Rev.*, 9: 1 (2003).

Troy A. Paredes, "Corporate Governance and Economic Development," *Regulation*, 28: 1, 34–39 (2005).

David Rosenberg, "Galactic Stupidity and the Business Judgment Rule," *J. Corp. L.* 32: 301 (2006).

Mark R. Schwartz, Thomas W. Dunfee, *and* Michael J. Kline, "Tone at the Top: An Ethics Code for Directors?", *J. Bus. Ethics*, 58: 1–3, 79–100 (2005).

Lynn A. Stout, "The Mythical Benefits of Shareholder Control," *VA L. Rev.* (2006).

Duane Windsor, "Corporate Social Responsibility: Three Key Approaches," *J. Mgmt. Stds.*, 43: 1, 93–114 (2006).

Adam Winkler, "Corporate Law or the Law of Business: Stakeholders and Corporate Governance at the End of History," *L. & Cont. Problems*, 67 (2004).

ADDITIONAL READING RESOURCES

This feature encourages further research relevant to each issue. Many perspectives frame each issue, and these resources provide additional material related to the topic being discussed.

INTRODUCTION

If we desire respect for the law, we first must make the law respectable.
Justice Louis Brandeis

The law that governs the interactions between buyers and sellers is called *business law*. As Justice Brandeis implies above, business law is dynamic. While it possesses a stable core of principles and expectations, it evolves. This evolution is a response to new knowledge and new aspirations in different historical settings.

The formation and evolution of business law occurs only because there is respect in legal discussions for multiple points of view. Regardless of how certain a legislator, lawyer, or legal commentator may be about a certain regulation, right, or responsibility, only the most foolishly dogmatic would fail to acknowledge that "other reasonable people may well disagree."

This acceptance by lawyers of the inevitable foment surrounding debate is incredibly beneficial to the development of an improved legal framework for business. Conversation among people with different conclusions enlightens all who will listen; it raises new questions that bring light to that component of our viewpoint that had been hidden by the vigor of our enthusiasm for a particular conclusion.

This particular book is a compelling exhibit of what we can learn when we open ourselves to multiple points of view about a legal question. But even more, it serves as an illustration of the supplement to learning provided by encounters with alternative viewpoints. Many of us recall the insecurity and challenge we felt when one of our teachers first presented us with contending viewpoints about an important question and then asked us to form our own judgment. That daunting task alerts us to the necessity of weighing and evaluating contending viewpoints.

As with this volume, this developmental challenge works best when the reader cannot take the easy way out by simply looking at credentials of the author and then choosing whichever set of credentials seems the most prominent. But, as we attempted to do in this book, the full force of the challenge hits our consciousness once we realize that credentials offer very little in terms of the quality of the reasoning. Instead, the reader must weigh the effects of the ambiguity, the questionable assumptions, the relative worth of the evidence, and the quality of the analogies, and only then make a decision about the best answer to the question being debated.

ISSUE SUMMARIES

The first issue relates to one of the most recurring debates in both the state and federal legislatures: whether we need tort reform. Advocates of tort reform argue that the current tort system allows outrageous punitive damage awards that are unwarranted and unduly harm businesses. Opponents of tort reform argue that punitive damages are necessary to punish those who have committed egregious wrongs, as well as to deter others from engaging in similar harmful behavior. This section provides a selection of articles addressing this question.

The second issue explores a topic that is often shocking to students when they first encounter it: the employment-at-will doctrine. Upon first encountering the doctrine many students express disbelief. They will ask, "You mean someone can be fired because the boss does not like them?" The articles in this section discuss the implications of various proposed modifications in the doctrine in terms of the stakeholders affected by such modifications. The reader will be able to tell from the reasoning in these articles that the so-called public policy exceptions are always up for grabs in terms of whether they should be expanded or limited.

Issue 3 revolves around the desirability and extent of the business judgment rule. The basic idea of owners having some control over the managerial decisions made on behalf of their firm is rather simple. But who should fall under the protection of the business rule and in what situations is very much in conflict among jurisdictions and legal commentators. Business leaders need some space to make decisions that may not appear to be in the long run interest of the firm, but at the same time property owners need protection from unrestricted executive decisions.

The fourth issue contains several perspectives about the extent to which someone is acting on behalf of another such that this latter person is legally liable for the act. Two selections focus on the concept and application of the idea of apparent agency. When does such an agency take place? What are the standards for holding a principal liable in such an agency situation? The remainder of the selections examine the scope and existence of agency in particular business scenarios.

Issue 5 is an emerging issue in employment law. Employers often ask prospective employees to agree as a condition of employment to take any subsequent legal disagreement with the employer to arbitration. By agreeing to arbitration, employees give up their right to have their alleged harm adjudicated in the courts. The employer is trying to reduce costs and find an efficient system of resolution. But the arbitration clause severely limits the opportunities of potential litigants to seek significant compensation for employer abuses of substantive rights. The selections in this part of the book tend to focus on the controversies surrounding the desirability of mandatory arbitration in alleged discrimination cases.

The sixth issue involves the struggle between buyer and seller over who should have what information about the nature of the good or service being exchanged. If the consumer is to be sovereign and make rational decisions consistent with his or her best interests, then full knowledge about the good or service in question is highly beneficial. But firms often see such information as theirs; they know that sharing certain information would be both costly and destructive of profits. The articles in this section present arguments about the extent to which sellers should be required by the government to divulge any information about the product that would affect sales.

Property rights are certainly one of the most important institutions of the American economic and legal systems. However, the concept of ownership is not always straightforward, as we can see from Issues 7 and 8. The articles for Issue 7 address the question of the extent to which homeowners' associations, private, quasi-governing bodies, can restrict individual's ownership rights. The question of when homeowners' associations can restrict the use of property is especially contentious when the homeowners wish to use their property in a way that is socially beneficial, but are prohibited from doing so by the association.

Issue 8 takes the question of interference with homeowners' rights even further, by addressing the question of the extent to which the government can use its power of eminent domain to take an individual's private property for the purpose of furthering economic development. How one resolves this issue is determined to a large extent by whether one believes the term *public use* should be broadly or narrowly defined.

When Enron collapsed, many of those directly responsible for the fraud did not have sufficient funds to repay the shareholders for all the money they lost. Understandably, this situation led many to ask the question of whether anyone else not directly involved in the fraud could be held liable. The idea of holding third parties who aided and abetted in the perpetuation of securities fraud is known as scheme liability. The viability of scheme liability as a method for shareholder recovery is the focus of the ninth set of articles. Regardless of what the courts say today, shareholders may still continue to try to urge the courts to accept a theory of scheme liability whenever there are large losses caused by corporate fraud and the perpetrator does not have the resources to compensate the injured shareholders.

The final question is one that is being increasingly discussed as we face declining economic conditions. Issue 10 asks what rights debtors should have when they file for bankruptcy. A related question to be considered is whether one should respond to this issue in the same manner when the debtor is an individual as opposed to being a corporation.

The ten issues that provide the focus for discussion in this book are simply illustrative of the exciting flavor of business law. Our effort to ask critical thinking questions again and again is a stimulus to the necessary evaluative stance that turns disagreement into a personal reasonable opinion. We believe that it will be especially helpful to provide a critical thinking framework that readers can use to sort through the reasoning in each reading.

What follows is offered as a guide to deep thinking in the face of disagreement about what business law should be in a particular area of commercial practice.

GUIDE TO CRITICAL THINKING

Any critical thinking includes the application of evaluative standards to assess the quality of the reasoning being offered to support the conclusion. And there is no better context in which to develop critical thinking skills than in the study of the laws that affect business. Critical thinking skills learned in the study of business law will be easily transferred to the decisions of business stakeholders.

Legal reasoning is like other reasoning in some ways and different in others. When people, including lawyers and judges, reason, they do so for a purpose. Some problem or dilemma bothers them. The stimulus that gets them thinking is an ISSUE. It is stated as a question because it is a call for action. It requires us to *do* something, to think about answers.

Which answer best accomplishes a particular business objective? Here is where critical thinking is essential to business success. Some answers can get the decision maker into trouble; others will advance the intended purpose. Each answer is called a CONCLUSION.

There are many forms of critical thinking, but they all share one characteristic—they focus on the quality of someone's reasoning. Critical thinking is active; it challenges each of us to form judgments about the quality of the link between a set of reasons and the conclusion supposedly derived from them.

The following structure for critical thinking is a thoroughly tested method used by successful market decision makers. Every time you read a legal argument, try to follow this pattern of careful thinking.

ISSUE

In almost any legal conflict, finding and expressing the issue is an important step in forming our reaction. The issue is the question that caused the disagreement in the conflicting viewpoints.

Next identify the author's reasons and conclusion.

REASONS AND CONCLUSION

Authors do not form legal conclusions based on whim. They have support for their decisions. That support consists of their reasons. When we ask someone *why* a person formed a particular conclusion, we are showing our respect for reasons as the proper basis for any assertion. We want a world rich with opinions so we can have a broad field of choice. But we should agree with only those legal arguments that have convincing reasons supporting the conclusion. To ask "why?" is our way of saying, "I want to believe you, but you have an obligation to help me by sharing the reasons for your conclusion."

Apply critical thinking to the reasoning.

EVALUATION OF THE REASONING

A person's reasoning, once it has been laid before us by following the steps discussed here, is a message that we may either accept or reject.

Here is a small sample of some especially useful critical thinking tools for thinking about business law:

- Look for potential ambiguity in the reasoning. "Ambiguity" refers to a lack of clarity in a word or phrase in the reasoning. Many words have multiple meanings; until the intended meaning is discovered, we cannot tell whether we wish to agree or disagree with the reasoning.
- Ask whether the analogies used in the decision are strong. When judges follow particular precedents, they are saying that the key similarities between the facts in the precedent and those in the case at hand are so similar, that it makes sense to apply the same rule of law in both. Are there key differences in the factual situations that raise questions about the quality of that analogy?
- Check the quality of the judge's reasoning. Does the judge use evidence to support the opinion that is both abundant enough and reliable enough that we should agree with the reasoning?
- Think about the extent to which important missing information prevents you from being totally confident about the judge's reasoning. Is there important missing information that you would need to have before making up your mind?
- Consider the possibility of rival causes. When the judge claims that one action caused another, think about whether some alternative cause may not have been responsible.

ISSUE 1

Are Courts Strangling Businesses with Tort Suits?

For years tort reform has been a recurrent theme for debate in Congress and among the public. Advocates of tort reform argue that the current tort system allows outrageous punitive damage awards that are unwarranted and unduly harm businesses. Opponents of tort reform argue that punitive damages are necessary to punish those who have committed egregious wrongs, as well as to deter others from engaging in similar harmful behavior. At the forefront of tort reform efforts are proposed caps on the amount any party may receive in punitive damages from a tort case. The articles in this chapter provide a mere snapshot of some of the perspectives regarding the desirability of punitive damage caps.

In their article, "Medical Malpractice Reform and Insurer Claims Defense: Unintended Effects?" Ambrose and Carroll examine how punitive damage caps affect medical malpractice lawsuits. As the United States experiences another medical malpractice insurance crisis, many parties again push for tort reforms, including caps on punitive damages. In light of this crisis, Ambrose and Carroll investigate how capping punitive damage awards will affect defense expenses that insurance companies face in light of medical malpractice litigation. Ambrose and Carroll found that caps on punitive damages tend to be correlated with higher losses and defense costs, seemingly indicating that capping punitive damage awards does not reduce defense costs or losses for medical malpractice insurers. However, some other tort reforms might offset some of the losses insurers occur under punitive damage caps. Ambrose and Carroll conclude by considering the important implications of tort reforms on medical malpractice. They want to strike a balance between ensuring that injured parties are justly compensated and that a deterrent effect still exists to prevent poor medical treatment from occurring.

Instead of focusing on medical malpractice, in the second article Rubin and Shepherd discuss accidental deaths. Rubin and Shepherd believe the purpose of the tort liability system is to create incentives to reduce risk, and thus ask if tort reforms affect the ability of torts to decrease the accidental death rate. While the authors find that tort reform, in general, actually leads to a higher accidental death rate, they did find that specific tort reforms are correlated with a reduction in the incidence of accidental deaths. In particular, capping non-economic damage, such as punitive damages, does lead to a decrease in the number of accidental deaths. Accordingly, capping punitive damages does not lead to more accidental deaths, and punitive damage caps might be necessary to create a more efficient tort system.

When discussing punitive damages, it is important to remember that juries are typically the ones who have to make the initial decision regarding if punitive damages should be awarded, and if so, what the appropriate amount of damages should be. Viscusi's article in this chapter examines the role of juries in creating large punitive damage awards. Viscusi argues that there are no clear guidelines for directing juries how best to assess punitive damages. Moreover, juries tend not to follow specific mathematical models for damages on the rare occasion that these specific instructions are given. The Supreme Court suggested in *State Farm v. Campbell* that punitive damage awards probably should not exceed nine times the compensatory damages. Viscusi examines the impact of adopting the suggesting single-digit multiplier rule, as well as if punitive damages were capped to an amount equal to the compensatory damages. In the end, Viscusi concludes that the suggested caps would limit the amount of punitive damages, but it is important to also consider the rationale for punitive damages instead of simply focusing on cutting costs by capping punitive damages.

Viscusi offers a quantitative analysis of actual jury awards of compensatory damages, and then assesses how proposed caps would affect these awards. In the fourth article Greene, Coon, and Bornstein also examine juries' role in assessing punitive damages. However, Greene, Coon, and Bornstein conduct a study with various test groups portraying jurors to see what influence various caps on punitive damages had on the overall amount of damages awarded. The authors found that limits on punitive damage awards do tend to limit the punitive damages given, while not increasing the amount of compensatory damages. Nonetheless, when punitive damage awards were completely barred, the jurors would increase the compensatory damages to make up for their inability to assess punitive damages. Greene, Coon, and Bornstein tentatively surmise that some limits on punitive damages might be useful for limiting punitive awards while not increasing compensatory damages, but this does not mean that the ethical and policy questions surrounding punitive damages have been answered.

In *State Farm v. Campbell*, the Supreme Court enters the debate regarding punitive damages. The Supreme Court was ruling on an objection to a punitive damage award of $145 million when the compensatory damages were only $1 million. The majority opinion argues that there is a tradition in the law of double, triple, and quadruple damages, but these are all limited compared to the damages that were 145 times the compensatory damages in this case. While not legally binding, the Supreme Court suggested a single-digit multiplier for damage awards if the award is to make it through the appeals process. The majority remanded the case so a lower court could figure out the correct amount of punitive damages. Justice Ginsburg wrote a dissenting opinion. Ginsburg argues that there is a much longer tradition of the Court's not getting involved in determining proper damage amounts. She argues that the $145 million punitive award is probably excessive, but it is not the place of the Court to determine what the proper damages are. Rather, states, via their courts and legislatures, are better equipped for making decisions regarding proper damage amounts.

The articles in this chapter approach the dilemma surrounding punitive damages in a variety of ways. One thing the articles collectively highlight is that punitive damages can have effects on a number of other issues, as well as be affected by a number of other issues. Accordingly, any discussion of punitive damages needs to be aware of the potential impact punitive damage caps will have on these related areas. Also, as several of the authors indicate, questions regarding punitive damage caps must consider whether the caps are effective, as well as if the caps are indeed good policy given the intended purposes of imposing punitive damages. When reading this chapter, be sure to think about whether punitive damages are an effective idea, as well as if they are an overall good policy decision. Consider who benefits and who might lose in the various scenarios discussed.

ISSUE ARTICLES

Jan M. Ambrose and Anne Carroll, "Medical Malpractice Reform and Insurer Claims Defense: Unintended Effects?" 32 *Journal of Health Politics, Policy and Law*, 843 (2007).

Paul H. Rubin and Joanna M. Shepherd, "Tort Reform and Accidental Deaths," 50 *Jounal of Law and Economics,* 221 (2007).

W. Kip Viscusi, "Tort Reform and Insurance Markets," 7 *Risk Management and Insurance Review*, 9 (2004).

Edith Greene, David Coon, and Brian Bornstein, "The Effects of Limiting Punitive Damage Awards," 25 *Law & Human Behavior*, 217 (2001).

State Farm Mutual Automobile Insurance Company v. Campbell et al., 538 U.S. 408 (2003).

ARTICLE 1.1

Medical Malpractice Reform and Insurer Claims Defense: Unintended Effects?

Jan M. Ambrose and Anne Carroll

INTRODUCTION

The United States has recently experienced its third medical malpractice insurance crisis, a period characterized by deterioration in insurer financial performance, a significant increase in premium levels, and often a corresponding decrease in coverage availability. The combined ratio for medical malpractice rose rapidly from 115 percent in 1998 to 165 percent in 2002 (Hartwig and Wilkinson 2003),[1] signifying a striking increase in underwriting losses. These losses occurred despite the fact that direct premiums written rose by nearly 40 percent over the same period (Nordman, Cermak, and McDaniel 2004). In addition, several notable insurer exits took place. In 2001, the nation's largest malpractice insurer, St. Paul, withdrew from the market. Other large insurers that left the market include PHICO and Frontier Insurance Group (Mello 2006).

The authors call for government intervention in the medical malpractice market; is there an alternative place for government intervention that might be superior?

The recent crisis has once again created pressure for government intervention in the medical malpractice market with the aim of improving the availability and affordability of insurance coverage. This type of intervention is not new to the medical malpractice market; a number of states responded to earlier malpractice crises in the mid-1970s and mid-1980s by enacting various tort reforms and by directly intervening in insurance markets with government-sponsored insurance mechanisms. Tort reforms tend to focus on placing some type of limits on damages, attorney fees, legal process, or the way in which liability is shared across parties. Government sponsored insurance mechanisms typically take the form of joint underwriting associations (JUAs) or patient compensation funds (PCFs).

Clearly, the ability of these actions to reduce the cost of medical malpractice claims and thereby improve the availability and affordability of medical malpractice insurance coverage is of great interest to policy makers. Underlying the success of interventions to reduce costs is the premise that reforms have the intended effect on the behavior of all involved parties: physicians, plaintiffs, lawyers, and insurers. This article examines the effect of reforms on the claims defense efforts of medical malpractice insurers. While some evidence exists that certain reforms may reduce losses and premiums,[2] previous research has not examined the extent to which these reductions may be enhanced or offset if tort reforms and government insurance mechanisms specifically affect the claims defense expense component of medical malpractice premiums as well.

Claims defense expenses are categorized as "loss-adjustment expenses" in insurer financial reports; the mean ratio of these expenses to premiums earned for medical malpractice averaged 32 percent during the period 1991–2002.[3] Claims defense expenses represent all expenses that an insurer incurs as a result of adjusting a claim, litigated or not, including costs associated with claims investigation, medical examinations, expert witnesses, fees and salaries for claims adjusters and others working for the defense of a claim, and defense-attorney fees. While insurance company reporting does not allow for a specific breakdown of expenses across these categories, a significant portion of these expenses is associated with the defense of litigated claims. Evidence in some states shows that the costs of defending claims have been rising at a faster rate than the claims themselves. Black et al. (2005) investigated closed claims in Texas during the period 1988–2002 and found that mean and median payouts per large malpractice claim rose 0.1–0.5 percent per year, while defense costs per large claim paid rose 4.2–4.5 percent per year during the same period. Studies examining closed claims data in Washington (Smego, Barclay, and Slavich 2005) over the period 1994–2004 and in Illinois for the period 1980–1999 (Shapo 2001) found similar results.

Medical malpractice reforms may be one factor affecting defense expenses if the reforms influence how aggressively insurers choose to defend claims. If tort reforms and other interventions affect the resources that insurers devote to defending claims, claims defense expenses may systematically change. In a competitive environment with pricing flexibility,[4] insurers will pass expected changes through their rating structures, and any change in claims defense expenses will have an obvious, direct effect on premium levels. An indirect effect is also possible if more- or less-aggressive claims defense efforts could lead to respectively lower or higher payouts for claims. If reforms work as intended to control payouts and lower expenses, premiums will be more affordable and insurers will be willing to make coverage available as their costs become more predictable. A healthy medical malpractice insurance market is beneficial to all. Physicians can afford to practice in the specialty and geographic region they prefer. Patients have access to the care they require, and there is an insurance mechanism in place to compensate them in the event of malpractice.

If reforms have some unintended effects, public-policy goals may be compromised. For instance, if reforms cause claims defense expenses to increase either absolutely or disproportionately relative to payouts, then we would expect premium levels to increase or insurer profitability to decrease, changes which might bring about affordability or availability problems such that patient access or compensation issues would develop. If claims defense expense increases offset payout decreases, premiums may not systematically change, but a question of resource allocation may arise if incentives to defend claims increase to the point that claims defense expenses are higher and payments to victims lower than optimal. In fact, many policy makers have criticized the malpractice system in the United States for having high overhead costs relative to payouts to victims. Studdert et al. (2006) found that for every dollar spent on patient compensation, $0.54 went to administrative expenses, including defense costs and contingency fees charged by the plaintiffs' attorneys. Through their effect on claims defense efforts, reforms may alter the efficiency of the malpractice system in allocating premium dollars to patients. As an integral part of premiums, if claims defense expenses are affected by reforms, the general welfare of physicians and patients may also be affected in regard to access and availability. Therefore, how malpractice reforms operate on claims defense expenses is an important health policy consideration; our article will help provide some insight to policy makers.

We begin the article with a discussion of the general nature of malpractice reforms, how they might affect insurers' claims defense expenses, and what links previous studies have found between these reforms and medical malpractice insurance performance measures. We then construct a framework to test the relationship between claims defense expenses and the presence of reforms and subsequently present the empirical results and our conclusions.

MALPRACTICE REFORMS AND THEIR EFFECTS

Medical malpractice reforms can be classified broadly into two groups: those that focus on changes to tort law within the legal system and those that involve government sponsorship of insurance mechanisms.

Tort Reforms

The variety of tort reforms passed by states following the medical malpractice insurance crises of the 1970s, 1980s, and most recently the late 1990s and early 2000s, seeks to reduce malpractice claims costs directly or indirectly by changing the incentives and behavior of the parties involved. We categorize these tort reforms into four groups: those that limit damages, those that limit contingency fees, those that alter the legal process, and those that alter liability rules. We describe each reform and its original intent, followed by our hypothesis regarding the reform's direct or indirect, intended or unintended effect on claims defense expenses. We also highlight the findings of previous research related to the impact of a particular reform on claim payouts or premiums; however, we can only infer what this evidence might imply about claims defense expenses, as no study to date has specifically examined the relationship between malpractice reforms and claims defense expenses.

Damage Limits

In terms of limiting damages, the most common reform is to put a cap on noneconomic damages. Because these damages are difficult to value and are often perceived to be awarded by juries at unpredictably high levels, such caps place limits on the dollar amount a plaintiff may receive for pain and suffering.[5] Punitive awards are another category of damages capped or even prohibited by some states. The intent of the imposition of either type of cap is to decrease the size of a damage award directly; a cap may also reduce claim frequency by decreasing the willingness of plaintiff or attorney to pursue a claim because the expected judgment will be lower. The effect that these caps have on claims may also have an impact on the resources that insurers devote to defending claims. Clearly, to the extent that damage caps deter patients from making a claim in the first place, claims defense expenses are expected to be lower. Furthermore, if damages are known to be limited, defense counsel may not need to produce as much evidence or testimony regarding the extent of those damages.[6] Additionally, the plaintiff may be more likely to settle if recovery is limited, thereby saving the insurer the expense of a jury trial. However, if the limit on damages gives physicians less incentive to take care, the damage-cap reform may inadvertently cause claims frequency, along with claims defense expenses, to increase.

There is some evidence that noneconomic damage caps reduce claims payouts (Danzon 1984, 1986; Sloan, Mergenhagen, and Bovbjerg 1989; Viscusi and Born 1995, 2005), but evidence of the effect of noneconomic damage caps on premiums is mixed. Zuckerman, Bovbjerg, and Sloan (1990), Danzon, Epstein, and Johnson (2003), and Thorpe (2004) found that these caps lower premiums, while Sloan (1985), Viscusi et al. (1993), and Viscusi and Born (1995, 2005) found no effect. Evidence on punitive damages is similar. In Viscusi and Born (2005), punitive damage reforms had a significant negative effect on losses; however, premiums were lower only in states that did not allow punitive damages. The suggestion that noneconomic damage limits may reduce claims payments without necessarily translating to lower premiums implies two possible scenarios. Claims defense expenses could be relatively higher in states with damage limit reform, certainly an unintended effect of such reform, or insurers could be exercising market power by retaining the savings as profit rather than passing these savings on to policyholders in the form of lower premiums.

How would one argue that a reduction of claims payouts from noneconomic damage caps is not necessarily a positive effect?

FRAMEWORK FOR ANALYSIS

The purpose of this study is to empirically examine the effects that both tort reforms and government insurance mechanisms have had on medical malpractice claims defense expenses in the recent malpractice crisis. In constructing our model, we consider the relationship between claims defense expenses and claims. Regardless of the hypothesized effects of reforms on claims defense expenses, the resources insurers devote to defending and settling claims are not independent of the size of the claims themselves. Claims defense expenses are, in large part, variable rather than fixed in nature, so that as the size of a claim increases or decreases, the claims defense expenses should increase or decrease accordingly. The larger the claim, the more likely that the marginal cost of increased defense efforts will be outweighed by the marginal benefit of obtaining lower claim amounts. The larger the expected claim, the more effort defense attorneys will expend in trying to limit damages paid. Because claims defense expenses are influenced by the size of losses themselves and both expenses and claims may be affected by tort reforms, our model reflects this interdependency. In particular, we posit that losses incurred are a function of tort and government reform measures and other factors and that claims defense expenses are a function of losses incurred, tort and government reform measures, and other factors.

$$\text{Losses Incurred}_{it} = f\,(\text{Reforms}_{it}, \text{Other Factors}_{it}) \qquad (1)$$

$$\text{Claims Defense Expenses}_{it} = f\,(\text{Losses Incurred}_{it}, \text{Reforms}_{it}, \text{Other Factors}_{it}) \qquad (2)$$

The unit of observation is states, indexed as *i*, during the years 1998–2002, indexed as t.[7]

We are principally interested in estimating equation 2. Hence, we use an instrumental variables approach in which losses incurred are first estimated from equation 1 and then the estimated value of losses incurred is used on the right-hand side of equation 2 to approximate claims defense expenses.[8] In this way, we hope to capture the independent effect that tort reform has on claims defense expenses. To illustrate, consider noneconomic damage caps. Prior research has found that noneconomic damage caps lower losses. This effect is captured in the first equation. We expect that lower losses will result in lower claims defense expenses; thus we include the estimated effect of lower losses incurred from the first equation as an explanatory variable in the second equation. In the second stage, the variable for the reform of noneconomic damage caps therefore captures the effect of the cap on claims defense expenses, holding constant its effect on losses.

Specifically, equation 2 is estimated in the following form:

$$\begin{aligned}&\ln \text{Medical Malpractice}\\ &\quad = f\,(\ln \text{Losses Incurred}_{it}\ [\text{estimated}]\\ &\quad \text{Claims Defense Expenses}_{it}\\ &\quad \text{Tort Reforms}_{it}\\ &\quad \text{JUA}_{it}\\ &\quad \text{PCF}_{it}\\ &\quad \text{Provider Market Characteristics}_{it}\\ &\quad \text{Insurance and Legal Market Characteristics}_{it}\\ &\quad \text{Economic Variables}_{it})\end{aligned}$$

The dependent variable is the natural log of medical malpractice claims defense expenses aggregated across all insurers in a state.[9] Similar data from self-insured entities is not available. Key variables of interest on the right-hand side of the equation are JUA, PCF, and the tort reform variables: noneconomic damage caps, attorney fee limits, punitive damage limits, modified collateral source rule, modified joint and several liability doctrine, mandatory pretrial screening, and statute of limitations.[10] With the exception of statute of limitations, which is coded as the maximum number of years a plaintiff has to file a case, each of these variables takes the value 1 if that fund or reform existed in a state for a given year and 0 otherwise. . . .

Table 1 Tort and Government Reform Variable Definitions and Summary Statistics

Variable Name	Definition	Mean	Standard Deviation
Limit on Noneconomic Damages	1 if there is a dollar limit on noneconomic damages, 0 otherwise	0.444	0.498
Limit on Punitive Damages	1 if there is a dollar limit on punitive damages, 0 otherwise[a]	0.360	0.481
Modified Collateral Source Rule	1 if evidence that claimant has been compensated for damages from other sources is permitted or required, 0 otherwise	0.580	0.495
Limit on Attorney Fees	1 if there is a limit on attorney fees, 0 otherwise	0.460	0.499
Modified Joint and Several Liability Doctrine	1 if the joint and several liability doctrine is abolished for some or all of damages, 0 otherwise[b]	0.688	0.464
Mandatory Pretrial Screening	1 if it is mandatory that the case be heard by a bearing or screening panel before going to trial, 0 otherwise	0.260	0.440
Statute of Limitations	The maximum number of years an adult claimant has to file a claim	4.122	2.251
Patient Compensation Fund (PCF)	1 if there is a PCF, 0 otherwise	0.200	0.401
Joint Underwriting Association (JUA)	1 if there is a JUA, 0 otherwise	0.240	0.428

[a]If punitive damages for medical malpractice were not allowed in a state, we considered this a limit of zero.
[b]"Joint and several liability doctrine is abolished for some or all damages" generally means that damages are apportioned according to degree of fault.

Table 2 Log Loss-Adjustment Expenses Equation Results

Variable Name	**Coefficient**	**Absolute *t*-statistic**
Log Estimated Losses Incurred	0.566	5.18***
Tort and Government Reforrn		
Limit on noneconomic damages	0.350	3.44***
Limit on punitive damages	0.317	3.45***
Modified collateral source rule	–0.186	1.65
Limit on attorney fees	0.261	2.85***
Modified joint and several liability doctrine	–0.099	0.92
Mandatory pretrial screening	–0.323	2.83***
Statute of limitations	0.015	0.62
Patient compensation fund	–0.209	1.88*
Joint underwriting association	0.130	0.97
Provider Market Characteristics		
General surgeons per capita	–5.459	1.28
Ob-gyns per capita	7.651	2.19**
Inpatient surgeries per capita	0.010	0.77
Legal and Insurance Market Characteristics		
Lawyers per capita	0.041	0.67
Mean delay ($t - 1$)	0.020	0.55
Percent jury trials	1.280	3.77***
Market share of top three medical malpractice insurers	0.003	0.84
Direct premiums earned	2.21E-6	4.05***
Economic Characteristics		
Real per capita income	–0.004	2.66**
Model Statistics		
F-statistic	76.730***	
R^2	0.912	

*** Significant at 1% level
** Significant at 5% level
* Significant at 10% level

RESULTS

Results for the claims defense expense equation are shown in table 2. First, and not surprisingly, losses incurred are associated with higher claims defense expenses. The coefficient suggests a sizable variable component to claims defense expenses.

Of the tort reform variables, several have a significant effect on insurers' claims defense expenses. Interestingly, limits on both noneconomic and punitive damages are associated with higher claims defense expenses, a presumably unintended effect of both caps. This result provides evidence that insurers are perhaps more inclined to let a case move forward to trial if they have a reduced risk of paying higher damage awards. Although counterintuitive, attorney fee limits are also associated with higher claims defense expenses. If fee limits reduce the number of smaller claims not worth attorneys' time, this outcome could be possible and would not necessarily be contrary to the reform's intent. With a greater proportion of larger claims, claims defense expenses simply may be higher because they vary with losses, as previously noted. Mandatory pretrial screening exhibits a significant negative relationship with claims defense expenses, suggesting that this reform apparently is successful in reducing the number of claims going all the way to trial. . . .

The results for the first-stage equation, equation 1, which estimates losses incurred as a function of reforms and other factors, are not presented here but do warrant some discussion because together, losses incurred and claims defense expenses form the basis for premium determination.[11] Several of the reform variables were found to have a significant impact on losses incurred. Contrary to expectations and the findings of Viscusi and Born (2005), limits on punitive damages showed a positive relationship with losses incurred ($p = 0.001$). If this form of recovery is limited in a state, then perhaps juries tend to compensate for that limitation with greater compensatory damages. Collateral source offsets were negatively associated with losses incurred ($p < 0.001$), indicating that such offsets do reduce claims, a finding that is consistent with those of Danzon (1984, 1986). The existence of a PCF ($p < 0.001$) was negatively related to claims incurred, suggesting that these funds may help keep premiums more affordable in these states, a result that supports the findings of Viscusi and Born (2005). A longer statute of limitations was associated with higher losses incurred ($p = 0.047$), a result concurrent with Danzon (1984). No other reform variables were significant at traditional levels. These results show that certain tort reforms, in this case punitive dollar limits and PCFs, tend to affect losses and claims defense expenses in a similar way. Notably, however, our results reveal that most other tort reforms affect claims defense expenses and losses incurred differently (if they have an effect at all), indicating the potential offsetting effect that reforms may have on losses and expenses. This underlines the importance of specifically examining the behavior of the claims defense expense component of premiums in the wake of malpractice reforms.

CONCLUSIONS

The goal of medical malpractice reform is to improve availability and affordability of malpractice insurance. Most reforms seek to directly reduce damages or to reduce the likelihood that a case goes to trial with the cost savings directly contributing to lower premiums. Reforms may also have indirect effects, intended or not, on the behavior of all participants in the medical malpractice process. In particular, because claims defense expenses comprise such a significant portion of premiums, the importance of understanding how malpractice reform may affect insurers' claims defense efforts is crucial to policy makers if they are to achieve their goals. If, in some adverse way, a reform changes incentives for insurers to defend claims, loss payments or claims defense expenses conceivably might increase and force premiums up. Furthermore, if incentives for claims defense effort are altered, liability may not be apportioned optimally across parties, thus interfering with the more general societal goals of deterring medical errors and adequately compensating injured patients. Previous research has not directly examined the relationship between reforms and claims defense expenses; this study addresses the gap in the research.

We find that tort and government reforms in the medical malpractice market do have a significant effect on the resources that insurers devote to defending malpractice claims. Specifically, damage limits (both punitive and noneconomic) and attorney fee limits are associated with greater levels of spending on claims defense expenses. To the extent that previous research has found an insignificant effect of either type of damage limits on premiums but a negative effect on claims, the results found here provide a consistent explanation. If damage limits reduce claims but the reduction is offset by an increase in claims defense expenses, one would expect a negligible impact on premiums. This, however, is not likely the result policy makers desire when enacting damage limits, because it works at cross-purposes to the goal of affordable premiums. If physicians leave or limit their practices due to the perception of high premiums, patients could be harmed by the decrease in access to care. In fact, Mello et al. (2005) found some evidence showing that this is a valid concern; in Pennsylvania, rising liability costs had notable effects on specialists' decisions to reduce or eliminate high-risk aspects of their practices. However, physicians may benefit if the additional resources devoted to defending claims prevent the payment of claims in which no medical error occurred on the part of the physician, but without claims-level data, we cannot ascertain that this is the case. The impact of attorney fee limits on patients is potentially more problematic. Our study finds suggestive evidence that attorneys may not be taking small cases in states with fee limits. While a decrease in expenses and the weeding out of nuisance suits are desirable and intended effects of this reform, some patients with valid claims may be unable to access compensation through the legal system, which clearly would not be an acceptable outcome.

Mandatory pretrial screening and PCFs are both associated with lower expenses on claims defense. In the case of pretrial screening, this outcome is one of the goals of that reform. If these lower defense expenses translate to lower premiums, physicians will be better off. Patients also might benefit if pretrial screening makes the disposition of cases more efficient by increasing the probability of recovering damages (particularly for smaller claims) and/or speeding up the resolution of cases. However, the effect on patients cannot be directly tested with our particular data set. In the case of PCFs, our results suggest an unintended moral hazard effect in which some claims are not defended vigorously enough by attorneys to achieve the optimal level of legal liability. Physicians are interested in protecting their reputations and clearly have a stake in insurers spending a lot of energy defending claims on their behalf. However, they are also interested in lower premiums, and our results from the first-stage equation for losses incurred suggest that states with a PCF are likely to have lower premiums. Patients would likewise benefit if affordable premiums would improve or ensure access to care as a result.

This study demonstrates that malpractice reform has a significant impact, albeit sometimes in an unintended way, on the claims defense spending of insurers. Thus, the research can help policy makers assess how reforms have performed against the goals of affordability and availability of insurance coverage and, in turn, patients' access to care. However, our results also suggest that the effects of reforms on claims defense expenses may change the allocative efficiency of the medical malpractice system. If insurers spend more on defense as a result of tort reform, does that lead to injured patients receiving inadequate compensation? Could the extra defense spending induced by certain tort reforms reduce the deterrent incentives for medical negligence? These questions cannot be answered definitively with the data presented here but are worthy of future investigation.

REFERENCES

American Medical Association (AMA). 2004. State Laws Charts I and II. Available by request from the Advocacy Resource Center of the AMA. October 11. www.ama-assn.org/ama/pub/category/4134.html.

American Tort Reform Association (ATRA). n.d. ATRA Issue Pages. www.atra.org/issues/index.php?issue=7338 (accessed May 26, 2005).

Black, B., C. Silver, D. A. Hyman, and W. M. Sage. 2005. Stability, Not Crisis: Medical Malpractice Claim Outcomes in Texas, 1998–2002. *Journal of Empirical Legal Studies* 2:207–259.

Danzon, P. 1984. The Frequency and Severity of Medical Malpractice Claims. *Journal of Law and Economics* 27:115–148.

———. 1986. The Frequency and Severity of Medical Malpractice Claims: New Evidence. *Law and Contemporary Problems* 49 (2):57–84.

Danzon, P., A. J. Epstein, and S. Johnson. 2003. The "Crisis" in Medical Malpractice Insurance. Paper prepared for the Brookings-Wharton Conference on Public Policy Issues Confronting the Insurance Industry, Washington, DC, January 8–9, 2004.

FindLaw. n.d. FindLaw. www.findlaw.com (accessed June 2005).

Hartwig, R. P., and C. Wilkinson. 2003. Medical Malpractice Insurance. Insurance Information Institute Insurance Issues Series. June. server.iii.org/yy_obj_data/binary/729103_1_0/Medmal.pdf.

Mello, M. M. 2006. Understanding Medical Malpractice Insurance: A Primer. Robert Wood Johnson Foundation Research Synthesis Report No. 8. January. www.rwjf.org/publications/synthesis/reports_and_briefs/issue8.html.

Mello, M. M., D. M. Studdert, C. M. DesRoches, J. Peugh, K. Zapert, T. A. Brennan, and W. M. Sage. 2005. Effects of a Malpractice Crisis on Specialist Supply and Patient Access to Care. *Annals of Surgery* 242:621–628.

National Association of Insurance Commissioners (NAIC). 1999–2003. *NAIC Profitability Report*. Kansas City, KS: NAIC.

National Conference of State Legislatures. 2002. State Medical Liability Laws Table. October 16. www.ncsl.org/standcomm/sclaw/statelaws1.htm (page has since been updated to reflect newer data).

Nordman, E., D. Cermak, and K. McDaniel. 2004. Medical Malpractice Insurance Report: A Study of Market Conditions and Potential Solutions to the Recent Crisis. Presented to the National Association of Insurance Commissioners' Property and Casualty Committee. September 12. www.naic.org/documents/topics_Med_Mal_Rpt_Final.pdf.

Shapo, N. S. 2001. Medical Malpractice Claims Study. Springfield: Illinois Department of Insurance, Casualty Actuary Section. www.idfpr.com/DOI/Reports/Med_Mal_Report/2001_med_mal_text.pdf.

Sloan, F. A. 1985. State Responses to the Malpractice Insurance "Crisis" of the 1970s: An Empirical Analysis. *Journal of Health Politics, Policy and Law* 9:629–646.

Sloan, F. A., P. M. Mergenhagen, and R. R. Bovbjerg. 1989. Effects of Tort Reforms on the Value of Closed Medical Malpractice Claims: A Micro-analysis. *Journal of Health Politics, Policy and Law* 14:663–689.

Smego, L. M., D. L. Barclay, and E. Slavich. 2005. Medical Malpractice Closed Claim Study: Claims Closed from July 1, 1995, through June 30, 2005. State of Washington, Office of the Insurance Commissioner. October. www.insurance.wa.gov/special/wic/MedMalDataCallOct2005.pdf.

Studdert, D. M., M. M. Mello, A. A. Gawande, T. K. Gandhi, A. Kachalia, C. Yoon, A. L. Puopolo, and T. A. Brennan. 2006. Claims, Errors, and Compensation Payments in Medical Malpractice Litigation. *New England Journal of Medicine* 354:2024–2033.

Thorpe, K. 2004. The Medical Malpractice "Crisis": Recent Trends and the Impact of State Tort Reforms. Web exclusive, *Health Affairs*, January 21. content.healthaffairs.org/cgi/reprint/hlthaff.w4.20v1.

Viscusi, W. K., and P. Born. 1995. Medical Malpractice Insurance in the Wake of Liability Reform. *Journal of Legal Studies* 24:463–490.

———. 2005. Damages Caps, Insurability, and the Performance of Medical Malpractice Insurance. *Journal of Risk and Insurance* 72:23–43.

Viscusi, W. K., R. J. Zeckhauser, P. Born, and G. Blackmon. 1993. The Effect of 1980s Tort Reform Legislation on General Liability and Medical Malpractice Insurance. *Journal of Risk and Uncertainty* 6:165–186.
Zuckerman, S., R. R. Bovbjerg, and F. Sloan. 1990. Effects of Tort Reforms and Other Factors on Medical Malpractice Insurance Premiums. *Inquiry* 27:167–182.

END NOTES

1. The combined ratio is incurred claims and incurred underwriting expenses divided by premiums earned. A ratio less than 100 percent indicates profitable underwriting performance.
2. The term "losses" is used in the insurance context to mean claim payments, not in the accounting context to mean the difference between revenues and expenses. "Losses" and "claims" are synonymous and are used interchangeably in this article.
3. Computed from National Association of Insurance Commissioners (NAIC) data on defense and cost-containment expenses in Nordman, Cermak, and McDaniel (2004).
4. In some states, rate regulation may limit insurers' ability to adjust their rates.
5. The dollar limit of the cap varies by state but typically falls in the \$250,000–\$750,000 range.
6. In the case of noneconomic damages, additional evidence would be required to establish the extent of the plaintiff's pain and suffering. In the case of punitive damages, additional evidence demonstrating that the physician (or other provider) acted recklessly and with malice or deceit would be necessary.
7. We exclude Washington, DC, from the analysis. For computational reasons, 4 observations drop out, leaving us with 246 observations.
8. The variables for other factors used to estimate equation 1 are general surgeons per capita, ob-gyns per capita, internists per capita, inpatient surgeries per capita, lawyers per capita, mean delay ($t - 1$), percent jury trials, the market share of the top three malpractice insurers, direct premiums earned, real per capita income, unemployment rate, percent of population uninsured, percent of population older than age sixty-five, percent of population with earned bachelor's degrees, five-year treasury note rate, and the governor's political party. The five-year treasury note rate is particularly important. Because medical malpractice losses incurred are long tail, taking several years to be paid out, the funds set aside in reserve will have time to earn investment income. In this way, we take into account the effect that investment cycles have on the malpractice market, given that these cycles are frequently mentioned as contributors to medical malpractice crises.

9. Data for loss-adjustment expenses and losses incurred comes from the NAIC profitability reports (1999–2003). These reports present data on a statewide basis.
10. Sources for data on reform variables include the National Conference of State Legislatures (2002); American Tort Reform Association (ATRA n.d.); American Medical Association (2004); state statutes found at FindLaw (n.d.).
11. The results for equation 1, the losses incurred equation, may be obtained from the authors.

ARTICLE 1.2

Tort Reform and Accidental Deaths

Paul H. Rubin and Joanna M. Shepherd

1. INTRODUCTION

Classical law and economics analysis of tort law treats torts as externalities. A well-functioning legal system creates incentives for potential tortfeasors to internalize the costs of the externalities by making injurers liable for damages if a tort actually occurs. This leads to efficient behavior under many circumstances (Brown 1973; Landes and Posner 1987; Shavell 1987, 2004). As a result, any tort reform that reduces the scope of liability could increase accident risk as potential tortfeasors internalize fewer costs.[1]

What is an externality?

However, this premise depends on numerous assumptions. These include the following: damages are pecuniary, not nonpecuniary; injurers and victims are strangers, and not in any preaccident contractual relationship; victims as well as injurers have incentives to take optimal precautions; the system operates costlessly; and actions of tortfeasors are harmful, not protective.

As modern liability has expanded to include product liability and medical malpractice and as the system has moved toward strict liability, these assumptions are increasingly subject to challenge. Damages are now equally pecuniary and nonpecuniary, so nonpecuniary damages (such as pain and suffering) are about one-half of all damage payments (Tillinghast-Towers Perrin 2002). For products liability and malpractice, victims and injurers are in a preinjury contractual relationship. The system is very costly to operate, with estimates of costs and fees of up to 54 percent of total spending (Tillinghast-Towers Perrin 2003). Only $ .22 of every dollar that goes through the tort system is returned to consumers for compensation for economic damages. Liability for many types of accidents is strict, with negligence of victims increasingly less important in determining damages and liability.

Most important, many defendants in modern tort suits are actually engaged in reducing, not increasing, accident risk; this applies to makers of many products (medicines, protective equipment) and to physicians. For example, the American Association for Justice (AAJ) Web site lists "litigation groups," that is, "voluntary networks of AAJ members sharing an interest in a particular type of case."[2] As of June 13, 2007, there were 11 such groups; of these, 33 were directly related to health care providers, including categories such as birth trauma, health care disability, medical negligence, and pharmacy liability. Thus, 40 percent of the litigation groups represent health-related providers; the share of health spending in the economy is about 15 percent.

These factors operate together to challenge the very basis of tort law (Calfee and Rubin 1992). Because injurers and victims are often in a preinjury contractual relationship, victims will pay for potential damage payments ex ante in the form of higher prices. The ex ante payments must cover not only pecuniary damages but also nonpecuniary damages and administrative costs. As prices increase, consumers become less willing to pay for the goods and services covered by tort law. And because many of these goods and services would reduce risk, increasing tort liability may actually lead to increased, not reduced, accident risk.

In addition, unpredictable and high liability costs may make it difficult or expensive for potential injurers to obtain insurance for their own liability (Priest 1991). If liability insurance becomes very costly or is unavailable, suppliers may decide to stop supplying the goods and services altogether. Again, if these goods and services are risk reducing, increasing tort liability may increase accidents.

In contrast, tort reforms that decrease tort liability may make risk-reducing products more available and affordable, leading to a reduction in accidents. In addition, tort reform may induce some accident victims to take more precautions because the amount of compensation in the event of an accident will be reduced. Increased victim precaution could also reduce accidents.

In this paper, we test whether tort reforms are associated with increases or decreases in accidents. Many aspects of the tort system and tort reform have been studied in detail.[3] The general findings are that tort reform reduces the number of lawsuits and amount of damages and has improved the profitability of insurance companies. Although no studies have examined the impact of tort reform on accidents, it is generally agreed by most economists that "if the liability system has a real purpose today, it must lie in the creation of incentives to reduce risk" (Shavell 2004, p. 268). If it does not reduce risk, then there is a real question about the social purpose of the modern American tort system.

Thus, to evaluate the merits of the tort system and decide on the benefits of tort reform, it is necessary to examine the relationship between tort reform and accidents. Section 2 explores the theoretical relationship between specific tort reform and accidents. Section 3 tests the relationship by investigating the association between tort reform and accidental death rates. Section 4 discusses implications and concludes.

2. THE RELATIONSHIP BETWEEN TORT REFORM AND ACCIDENTS

2.2. Specific Tort Reforms

In the empirical section of this paper, we examine the relationship between accidental death rates and several different tort reforms: caps on noneconomic damages, caps on punitive damages, a higher evidence requirement for punitive damages. . . . We now describe each tort reform and the possible effects of the reforms on death rates.

Noneconomic damages are damages for nonpecuniary losses such as pain and suffering, loss of consortium, emotional distress, and other intangible losses. Nonpecuniary losses are real losses. However, in general they do not increase the marginal utility of wealth, and so consumers do not generally purchase insurance against this class of losses. Moreover, this class of damages involves no direct economic loss and has no precise value. Because of the intangibility of the losses and the lack of guidance from the courts on the value of the losses, jury awards for noneconomic damages are highly erratic. Proponents of tort reform claim that noneconomic damage caps would make the damages more predictable and reduce the excessive size of the awards, promoting both more efficient deterrence and ease of settlement. Moreover, reducing the unpredictability of damage awards may make provision of insurance easier and cheaper, and so some providers may be better able to purchase such insurance. This may also lead to increased supplies of risk-reducing goods and services.

Punitive damages are awarded not to compensate plaintiffs but to punish defendants for intentional and malicious conduct and to deter future conduct. Punitive awards are infrequent but have increased in frequency and size in recent years. As in the case of caps on noneconomic damages, proponents of tort reform claim that caps are needed to make punitive damages more predictable and less excessive. Again, this should improve the settlement process and achieve more efficient deterrence. In most states, reforms to punitive damages have taken one of two forms: caps on punitive damages or higher evidence requirements before punitive damages are awarded. (The U.S. Supreme Court has also limited punitive damages, finding that in most cases a "single digit multiplier" is appropriate, so that punitive damages cannot in general be larger than nine times actual damages; State Farm Mutual Automobile Insurance Co. v. Campbell et al., 538 U.S. 408 [2003]). . . .

3. EMPIRICAL EVIDENCE OF THE RELATIONSHIP BETWEEN TORT REFORM AND ACCIDENTAL DEATHS

. . .We provide two empirical analyses. First, we compare state death rates before and after tort reform and compare death rates in tort reform states to death rates in non-tort-reform states. Then we use panel data regressions to more systematically examine the relationship between tort reform and death rates. We also examine the sensitivity of our regression results to alternative specifications. . . .

3.1. Death Rates before and after Tort Reform

Table 1 displays a comparison of death rate trends in the years before and after the enactment of certain tort reforms.[4] The table shows that death rates decreased in the years that five of the seven tort reforms were enacted.[5] For three of these reforms, death rates were increasing in the years prior to enactment but began decreasing the year after.

The table also reveals that tort reform states experienced larger than average decreases (or smaller than average increases) in accidental, non-motor-vehicle death rates in the years after five of the reforms were enacted. Prior to three of the reforms, the tort reform states had the opposite relationship with the average; they had experienced smaller than average decreases (or larger than average increases) in the years before the reforms were enacted.

This analysis controls for no other factors affecting death rates. The relationship between tort reform and death rates is tested more systematically in the next section.

Table 1 Trends in Accidental, Non-Motor-Vehicle Death Rates before and after Tort Reforms

	Median % Change in Rates		Median % Change Difference in Rates		
Tort Reform	**Year before Tort Reform**	**Year after Tort Reform**	**Year before Tort Reform**	**Year after Tort Reform**	**Times Enacted**
Cap on noneconomic damages	3.37	4.72	1.76	−2.56	15
Cap on punitive damages	1.07	−1.94	−.2	−2.47	20
Higher evidence standard for punitive damages	.08	−.5	.29	−.36	32
Product liability reform	−.94	1.17	.03	.31	25
Collateral source reform:					
Offset awards	.82	1.31	−.27	2.90	18
Adonil evidence	2.17	−2.85	.57	−2.39	17
Prejudgment interest reform	−.4	−4.7	.86	−2.24	14
Joint and several liability reform	−1.2	1.11	.77	2.7	38

Note. The first column reports the change in death rates from 2 years to 1 year before each tort reform is enacted. The second column reports the change in death rates from the year before to the year after each tort reform is enacted. The third and fourth columns present the difference in the death rate changes between tort reform used non tort reform states. Specifically, we calculated the average percentage change in death rates in the year before and after each tort reform and then compared the change in death rates in each tort reform scale to this average.

3.2. Panel Data Regressions

Although the preceding analysis suggests an impact of some tort reforms on accidental deaths, it controlled for no other factors affecting death rates. To explore the relationship between tort reform and death rates more systematically, we use a state-level panel data set from 1981–2000.[6] . . .

We use the results from the primary regression . . . to estimate real-world magnitudes of the relationship between tort reforms and death rates; the results of these computations are presented in Table 2.[7] As the table shows, the percentage changes in accidental deaths range between 2 and 5 percent, depending on the associated tort reform. However, even modest percentage changes translate into a substantial number of lives saved: we estimate that tort reforms are associated with almost 2,000 fewer deaths in the year 2000.[8] Computed over all states and years that had each reform, tort reforms are associated with approximately 24,000 fewer deaths.[9]

3.3. Sensitivity Analysis

We also examine the sensitivity of the tort reform coefficients to a range of alternative specifications. . . .

We also test whether the decrease in accidental deaths happened before the enactment of tort reform and thus cannot be attributed to tort reform. Estimations that include 1-year and 2-year leads result in a majority of statistically insignificant lead and lag coefficients, which suggests that accidental death rates did not begin decreasing in the years before tort reform.

Table 2 Real-World Magnitudes of the Relationship between Tort Reform and Death Rates

Tort Reform	Annual Death Rates (%)	Number of Deaths in 2000	Deaths across All Years
Cap on noneconomic damages	−3.54	−333	−5,242
Higher evidence standard for punitive damages	−2.57	−982	−11,798
Product liability reform	−3.83	−1,267	−16,841
Prejudgment interest reform	−4.88	−647	−9,060
Collateral source reform:			
Offset awards	+4.71	+938	+14,160
Admit evidence	+2.43	+294	+4,468
Net effect		−1,998	−24,314

Note. Values presented are average changes. These computations are based on the coefficients from the primary regression (Table 3) and the average annual populations and average annual death rates in the states that had each reform. The sums of the individual reforms differ by one from the net effects owing to rounding.

Next we test whether tort reforms in one state affect death rates in another, nearby state. Interstate effects in the same direction as the state effects could be evidence of a broader regional force driving the relationship between tort reform and accidental deaths, or they could be evidence of spillover effects—perhaps people across the border will travel into the tort reform state to gain more access to medical care. Interstate effects in the opposite direction from state effects could be evidence of doctors moving to nearby tort reform states, which would decrease death rates in the tort reform states and increase death rates in the doctors' original states. In an estimation that includes dummy variables indicating whether any other state in the region[10] has each tort reform, although most coefficients are insignificant, the interstate effects are opposite to the state effects for three tort reforms and in the same direction as the state effects for one tort reform.

Finally, we estimate a separate regression to determine whether stricter caps with lower dollar limits have a stronger effect on death rates than more lenient caps with high dollar limits.[11] The coefficient on the amount of the cap on noneconomic damages is positive and significant.[12] This indicates that a cap with a lower dollar limit, or a more stringent cap, is associated with lower death rates.[13]

4. CONCLUSIONS

The U.S. tort system is a more significant economic factor than the tort system of any other country. It is estimated that the U.S. tort system costs about 2.3 percent of the gross domestic product (GDP); for no other country was the amount more than 1.3 percent of the GDP (Italy), and the average for all Organisation for Economic Co-operation and Development countries was .9 percent (Rubin 1995, using data from Tillinghast-Towers Perrin). It is an extremely expensive system and can be justified only if it provides substantial deterrence.[14] Our paper suggests quite the opposite: tort reforms are actually associated with increases in the number of accidental deaths.

Although the theoretical predictions about the relationship between tort reform and accidents is mixed, our empirical evidence suggests that several tort reforms—caps on noneconomic damages, a higher evidence standard for punitive damages, product liability reform, and prejudgment interest reform—are associated with decreases in accidental death rates. In contrast, reform of the collateral source rule is associated with increases in accidental death rates. Next we estimate that the tort reforms adopted in the states between 1981 and 2000 are associated with approximately 24,000 fewer deaths. The results are robust to several alternative specifications.

What other reforms might be consistent with the results of this study?

Our results suggest that certain reforms are needed to make the current tort system more effective. Proponents of tort reform should concentrate on caps on noneconomic damages, a higher evidence standard for punitive damages, product liability reform, and prejudgment interest reform. . . .

APPENDIX

Variables and Sources

Death Rate Data. Data on death rates are from the Centers for Disease Control and Prevention (2005).

Tort Reform Variables. Tort reform data are from the American Tort Reform Association. Most data are compiled in ATRA (2005). We made some updates and corrections to this data using ATRA Issues Pages. . . .

Unemployment Rate. Unemployment rate data were collected from U.S. Department of Labor, Bureau of Labor Statistics, Local Area Unemployment Statistics. . . .

Income. Per capita income data were obtained from U.S. Department of Commerce, Bureau of Economic Analysis, Regional Economic Accounts, State Annual Personal Income (http://www.bea.gov/bea/regional/spi/). The nominal data were changed into real data using a consumer price index series (with 1983/1984 as the base year); see U.S. Department of Labor, Bureau of Labor Statistics, Consumer Price Index. . . .

Demographic Variables. Age, gender, race, and population data were compiled from U.S. Census Bureau, Population Division, Population Estimates. . . .

Per Capita Alcohol Consumption. This variable is the per capita ethanol consumption from beer, wine, and spirits for each state. It is obtained from National Institutes of Health, National Institute on Alcohol Abuse and Alcoholism, Per Capita Ethanol Consumption for States, Census Regions, and the United States, 1970–2004 (Gallons of Ethanol, Based on Population Age 14 and Older). . . .

Hospital Beds per Capita. Data on per capita beds in hospitals that are American Hospital Association members (excluding nursing homes) are compiled from American Hospital Association (2007, table 6).

Legal Services per Capita. This variable is the per capita number of employees engaged in legal services. Legal services include all for-profit and nonprofit establishments that are headed by members of the bar and are engaged in offering legal advice or legal services. The data are available from the U.S. Census Bureau, USA Counties. . . .

Voting Data. The data on voting in presidential elections are from Leip (2004).

REFERENCES

Brown, John Prather. 1973. Toward an Economic Theory of Liability. Journal of Legal Studies 2:323–49.

Calfee, John E., and Paul H. Rubin. 1992. Some Implications of Damage Payments for Nonpecuniary Losses. Journal of Legal Studies 21:371–411.

Congressional Budget Office. 2004. The Effects of Tort Reform: Evidence from the States. http://www.cbo.gov/ftpdocs/55xx/doc5549/Report.pdf.

Landes, William, and Richard Posner. 1987. The Economic Structure of Tort Law. Cambridge, Mass.: Harvard University Press.

Priest, George L. 1991. The Modern Expansion of Tort Liability: Its Sources, Its Effects, and Its Reform. Journal of Economic Perspectives 5:31–50.

Rubin, Paul H. 1995. Fundamental Reform of Tort Law. Regulation 4:26–33.

Shavell, Steven. 1987. The Economics of Accident Law. Cambridge, Mass.: Harvard University Press.

———. 2004. Foundations of Economic Analysis of Law. Cambridge, Mass.: Harvard University Press.

Tillinghast-Towers Perrin. 2003. U.S. Tort Costs: 2002 Update. http://www.towersperrinxom/tp/getwebcachedoc?webc=TILL/USA/2003/200302/Tort_Costs_2002_Update_rev.pdf.

Wooldridge, Jeffrey M. 2003. Introductory Econometrics. 2d ed. Cincinnati: South-Western College Publishing.

END NOTES

1. If liability is excessive, tort reform might be efficient, but in most cases it would still lead to increased risk.
2. American Association for Justice, Member Resources: Litigation Groups. . . .
3. It is common to use state data to examine various effects of tort reform on variables of interest. Congressional Budget Office (CBO) (2004) provides a useful summary of this research.
4. Because some states enacted the same tort reform more than once (that is, the second reform was enacted after the first was found unconstitutional), there may be more reforms enacted than states with each reform.
5. The conclusions are the same if the mean percentage change is used instead of the median percentage change.
6. Some of the variables are not available after 2000.
7. The magnitudes are computed by comparing the number of accidental deaths in states with each type of tort reform to what this number would have been had there been no tort reform. The percentage difference in death rates between tort reform states and non-tort-reform states is 100(exp(B)–1), where /3 is each coefficient estimate (Wooldridge 2003, p. 226). For example, in 2000 there were 9,098 deaths in states with caps on noneconomic damages, but there would have been approximately 9,431 deaths if there had been no caps (9,098 is a 3.53 percent decrease from 9,431). Similarly, in 2000 there were 37,296 deaths in states with higher evidence standards for punitive damages, 31,860 deaths in states with product liability reform, 12,615 deaths in states with prejudgment interest reform, 20,855 deaths

in states with reforms that allow courts to offset awards by the amount of collateral source payments, and 12,400 deaths in states with reforms that permit the admissibility of evidence of collateral source payments. To compute the total increase or decrease in deaths, we did the same calculations on the number of accidental deaths across all states and years that had each tort reform, instead of just 2000 deaths.

8. The 95 percent confidence intervals for the increase or decrease in deaths associated with each tort reform in 2000 are as follows: cap on noneconomic damages (96–577 fewer deaths), higher evidence standard for punitive damages (313–1,664 fewer deaths), product liability reform (561–1,989 fewer deaths), prejudgment interest reform (288–1,016 fewer deaths), collateral source reforms that offset awards (424–1,439 more deaths), and collateral source reforms that allow admission of evidence of collateral source payments (18 saved and 599 more deaths).
9. The 95 percent confidence intervals for the increase or decrease in deaths associated with each tort reform for all years are as follows: cap on noneconomic damages (1,512–9,069 fewer deaths), higher evidence standard for punitive damages (3,760–19,979 fewer deaths), product liability reform (7,450–26,438 fewer deaths), prejudgment interest reform (4,032–14,229 fewer deaths), collateral source reforms that offset awards (6,397–21,728 more deaths), and reforms that allow admission of evidence of collateral source payments (279 saved and 9,096 more deaths).
10. We use the standard regional categories: South, Northeast, Midwest, and West.
11. For the variable measuring the amount of the cap on noneconomic damages, states with no caps are assigned values equal to $1 more than the highest cap ($ 875,001). This variable is meant to represent the maximum amount a potential tortfeasor would expect to pay in damages. Thus, for states with no caps, this variable could actually take on values near infinity. To be more realistic about how much potential tortfeasors expect to pay, and to not bias the results by assigning huge values to no-cap states, we assign values that are only slightly higher than those of the cap states. Assigning even larger values does not change the sign or significance of the results.
12. The coefficient (standard error) on the amount of the cap on noneconomic damages is .00000006(.00000003) (significant at the 5 percent level).
13. We do not have a variable measuring the amount of the cap on punitive damages because the state rules vary widely and apply in different situations and with different conditions.
14. "Thus, the use of the liability system will be socially worthwhile if and only if the savings from accident reduction it brings about exceed its administrative costs" (Shavell 2004, p. 284).

ARTICLE 1.3

Tort Reform and Insurance Markets

W. Kip Viscusi

TORT REFORM TARGETS

The tort liability crisis in the mid-1980s witnessed a dramatic increase in insurance premiums and denials of insurance coverage. In an effort to provide greater stability to insurance markets and to reduce liability costs, most states enacted some kind of tort reforms in the 1980s. These reforms often took the form of damages caps and limitations on liability.

Recent increases in insurance premiums have stimulated interest in enacting some kind of tort reform. Unlike the 1980s liability crisis, current problems seem to stem less from denials of coverage than from increases in premium rates. However, as with the liability crisis of the mid-1980s, the focus has been on lines of insurance such as general liability, products liability, and medical malpractice. These lines have continued to exhibit premium increases. Medical malpractice premiums increased by 8.7 percent in 2001 and by 9.5 percent in 2000, and product liability premiums jumped by 42.6 percent in 2001, after exhibiting a decline of 10.4 percent in 2000.[1]

Proposed reforms have focused primarily on two damages components: noneconomic damages, such as pain and suffering, and punitive damages. Are reforms of either of these components of damages sensible? Whether reforms are desirable hinges on two different sets of concerns. First, to what extent are reforms warranted based on the criteria for these damage components and the performance of the courts with respect to these damages awards? Second, which types of reforms will best foster insurance market performance while at the same time maintaining the constructive role that such damages components may play in the judicial system? As I will show in this article, punitive damages and noneconomic damages share common limitations and should be prominent targets of reform, but the character of the reforms that have been proposed to date often are not ideal. Past proposals have been designed strictly with respect to the narrow objective of reducing insurance costs, which is not necessarily equivalent to fostering sound insurance market performance. . . .

WHY JURIES DON'T DO WELL: PUNITIVE DAMAGES

The problems with punitive damages are in many respects similar to those with respect to pain and suffering. If juries decide to award punitive damages because of reckless or malicious behavior, then there is no structure given to them by the punitive damages instructions to enable them to assess the awards in a meaningful manner. As a result, there is evidence that juries have a very consistent sense of when behavior is particularly egregious, but they are less able to map these concerns into dollar values of awards.[2]

From a law and economics perspective, one could establish punitive damages that generated optimal deterrence amounts by setting total damages equal to the harm that has been caused divided by the probability of conviction. The total of the compensatory award plus the punitive award should be such that when multiplied by the probability of conviction it just equals the harm inflicted. Thus, in situations in which there is a 50 percent chance of conviction, the total penalty should consequently be double the value of the harm, which is typically the compensatory award.[3]

Whereas, the underlying theory for setting optimal levels of punitive damages is straight-forward, there is a considerable gap between the theory and actual practice. This optimal deterrence approach is not included in any existing punitive damages instructions. One barrier to adopting this approach may be that many people do not believe that it is reasonable to boost the penalty level simply because the probability of conviction is low. Should, for example, taxpayers be subject to a doubling of penalties if the Internal Revenue Service chose to cut in half the number of auditors for that state? In an experimental test of jury instructions modeled on the law and economics approach to optimal punitive damages, I found that juries either will not or cannot implement these instructions.[4] Indeed, even when given precise numerical instructions that involve little more then addition and multiplication, jurors tended to ignore these instructions and chose instead to focus on the same kinds of anchoring influences and other criteria that currently govern punitive damages awards in situations where optimal deterrence instructions are not given.

What assumptions are those who support caps on punitive damages making?

Jurors make a variety of systematic errors. Juries are sensible with respect to judgments regarding fault, but juries are very bad at mapping these concerns into dollar penalty amounts. Another difficulty is that of hindsight bias. Jurors perform very poorly in taking themselves back to the informational conditions before the accident and making judgments as to what the defendant did or did not know at that point in time. By assuming the party that caused the accident had superior knowledge before the accident that the adverse outcome would occur, jurors tend to overstate the extent to which there is deliberate disregard for safety in such situations. Such biases are particularly acute when the company has done a risk analysis and chosen a product design that could have been safer, albeit at a perhaps much greater cost. Jurors also may succumb to anchoring effects in which the plaintiff's attorneys provide numerical guidance to jurors as to what the punitive damages amount should be so as to provide a numerical crutch for juries to select a dollar penalty amount. Such guidance could be the advertising budget for the firm, the profits the firm would make in that state over the next decade, or some other accounting measure that bears no relationship whatsoever to any sound theory of punitive damages.

One possible remedy of the difficulties with respect to punitive damages is to transfer greater authority over setting these amounts to judges and to restrict jurors to deciding when punitive damages are warranted. My evidence with respect to the comparative performance of judges and jurors indicates that judges are less prone to the kinds of biases that contaminate juror behavior. Judges are better at risk assessment, less prone to hindsight bias, and generally are more likely to perform in a manner that is consistent with efficient incentives for deterrence.[5] . . .

EMPIRICAL ASSESSMENT: PUNITIVE DAMAGES

. . . To date, I have been able to identify 63 blockbuster awards of $100 million or more, many of which are for personal injury or environmental torts.[6] Very few of these major awards are for medical malpractice or related problems such as pharmaceutical liability, so that for medical malpractice insurance, restrictions on noneconomic damages will loom as a more important concern than restrictions on punitive damages.

Of the 63 blockbuster punitive damages awards, 60 have been by juries, with only three resulting from bench trials. The general sense that the problems of excess punitive damages awards can be traced to jury behavior is not mistaken. The total of these 63 blockbuster awards is for $214.4 billion, of which $210.5 billion has been awarded by juries and $3.9 billion has been the result of bench trials.

Table 1 provides a summary of the 11 punitive damages awards that have been for at least $1 billion. The only bench trial that led to a billion dollar punitive damages award was a light cigarettes class action in Illinois. This 2003 trial took place in a plaintiff-oriented venue—Madison County, Illinois. An ongoing concern with respect to class actions is whether plaintiffs search out favorable forums for these cases that would have dimmer prospects if litigated elsewhere. The roster of billion dollar punitive awards for jury cases also includes several cigarette cases, as well as environmental damages cases such as that pertaining to the Exxon Valdez oil spill, and a personal injury case stemming from a rear impact crash that produced nonfatal burn injuries among occupants of a General Motors vehicle.

While the punitive damage amounts are substantial, the cost of these punitive awards usually is borne by the defendant companies rather than an insurer.

Awards often are not covered by insurance, in part due to restrictions in some states prohibiting insurance of punitive damages. In addition, the defendants in such blockbuster award cases usually are large companies, which may self-insure. Though it is also true that many of these awards are reduced or overturned on appeal, the prospect of large awards may induce settlements, including for cases that have not yet gone to trial but in which a similar

Table 1 Summary of Punitive Damages Awards of at Least $1 Billion

Case Name	**Year of Decision**	**Punitive Damages Award ($ millions)**	**Compensatory Damages Award ($ millions)**	**Ratio of Punitive Damages to Compensatory Damages**
Bench Punitive Awards *Miles v. Philip Morris Inc.* (Illinois)	2003	3,100.00	7,100.00	0.4
Jury Punitive Awards *Cowart v. Johnson Kart Manufacturing Inc.* (Wisconsin)	1999	1,000.00	24.00	41.7
Grefer v. Alpha Technical Services Inc. (Louisiana)	2001	1,000.00	56.13	17.8
Hayes v. Courtney (Missouri)	2002	2,000.00	225.00	8.9
Pennzoil Co. v. Texaco Inc. (Texas)	1985	3,000.00	7,530.00	0.4
Boeken v. Philip Morris Inc. (California)	2001	3,000.00	5.54	541.5
In re: New Orleans Tank Car Leakage Fire Litigation (Louisiana)	1997	3,365.00	2.00	1,682.5
Exxon Corp. v. Department of Conservation and Natural Resources (Alabama)	2000	3,420.00	87.70	39.0
Anderson v. General Motors Corp. (California)	1999	4,775.00	107.60	44.4
In re: The Exxon Valdez (Alaska)	1994	5,000.00	287.00	17.4
Bullock v. Philip Morris Inc. (California)	2002	28,000.00	0.65	43,076.9
Engle v. R.J. Reynolds Tobacco Co. (Florida)	2000	145,000.00	12.70	11,417.3

Source: Adapted from Table 1 of Hersch and Viscusi (2003).

punitive damages award is anticipated. Moreover, the potential for appeal may be limited. In the case of the $10 billion total award in *Miles v. Philip Morris Inc.*, during the appeals process the company must post a bond of $12 billion to cover the award amount of $10.2 billion plus interest. As of this writing, posting this amount is not feasible for the company, and it is seeking to have the bond amount reduced, thus far without success.

WHAT LEGAL REFORMS MAKE SENSE?

. . . With respect to punitive damages, the most forceful reform effort has been that undertaken by the U.S. Supreme Court in 2003. In the *State Farm v. Campbell* case, the Court offered its most definitive guidance to date with respect to the appropriate level of punitive damages awards. In the normal course of events, the Court would not expect punitive awards to exceed the value of the compensatory damages award, and at the maximum such punitive damages awards should not be more than nine times greater than the compensatory damages award.

How effective would such limits be in restraining punitive damages awards can be ascertained by examining two different sets of case data shown in Table 2. The first set of results consists of a comprehensive sample of 63 blockbuster punitive damages awards of $100 million or more, while the second data set consists of a nationally representative state court sample of cases in 1996. As is evident from the first row in the table, the total dollar magnitude of the blockbuster awards greatly exceeds the tally for the state court sample. In each

Table 2 What Legal Reforms Make Sense?

Effect of Ratio Limits on the Amount of Punitive Damages Awards

Ratio Limit	Blockbuster Awards	State Court Sample, 1996
9	$14.2 billion	$104.5 million
1	$6.6 billion	$15.1 million
Total	$214.4 billion	$245.9 million

The Share of Punitive Damages Cases Affected by Ratio Limits

	Percentage of Cases Under the Limit	
Ratio Limit	**Blockbuster Awards**	**State Court Sample, 1996**
9	43	96
1	8	71

instance, imposing a ratio limit that the punitive award cannot be more than nine times the value of the compensatory damages award has a significant restraining effect, but the influence is much greater for the blockbuster awards that drop from $214.4 billion to $14.2 billion once this limit is imposed. In contrast, the state court awards are reduced by just over half of their amount by such a limit. If, however, the limit imposed is that the punitive award cannot exceed the compensatory damages award, the amount of blockbuster awards is reduced even further to $6.6 billion, and the total punitive awards in the state court sample drops to only $15.1 million.

The bottom panel of Table 2 indicates the fraction of awards that would be permitted to continue if these restraints were imposed. The blockbuster awards are affected to a much greater extent, as only 8 percent of such awards would be permitted if the magnitude of the punitive award could not exceed the compensatory damages award. However, for the state court sample, in which the awards tend to be less extreme, 71 percent of the awards would survive the test that the punitive award could not exceed the compensatory damages award. Thus, the share of cases affected by such a limit would be less than the majority for the state court sample, even though the total magnitude of awards that would be eliminated by this strict guideline would be considerable.

WILL LEGAL REFORMS MATTER?

To assess how various kinds of legal reforms will affect insurance markets, Patricia Born and I have examined the influence of several reform variables on measures of insurance market performance.[7] The focus of our analysis was on medical malpractice insurance over the 1984–1991 period. Using a comprehensive data set on individual insurance companies by state by year, we found a variety of results that are instructive with respect to the effect of reform efforts on this line of insurance. . . .

The role of various punitive damages reforms for medical malpractice is significant but less influential, in part because medical malpractice has not been the main area in which punitive damages have played a dominant role. What does appear to matter is whether punitive damages are insurable in that particular state. States that prohibit the insurability of punitive damages or that prohibit punitive damages altogether have lower levels of losses, controlling for other aspects of insurance. These limits on insurability will in fact reduce medical malpractice losses, but not as much as would noneconomic damages reforms. As with the noneconomic damages limits, however, the effects of such restraints also tend to be concentrated among the firms that otherwise would have experienced the largest losses. Once again, it is the loss extremes that tend to be affected most by punitive damages limits, which is consistent with the general sense that these awards contribute to the substantial volatility of losses in the absence of some form of restraint.

WHY SHOULD INSURERS CARE?

Most liability reforms generally reduce the losses incurred by insurers, which is a change that insurers generally welcome. But what if such policies were taken to the extreme by abolishing tort liability altogether? Losses would be reduced, but there would be no market for insurance. The potential puzzle consequently is why insurers should have such a strong interest in cost reducing efforts and why trade associations acting on behalf of insurers, such as the Alliance of American Insurers, have often supported various tort reform efforts given that such reforms reduce the potential market for insurance.

One major reason for this support is that insurance markets are not perfectly flexible and do not adapt in the same way as would be expected in an idealized economic model. Rather, insurance is a highly regulated market in which there is substantial price inflexibility due to this regulation.

To demonstrate the influence of price inflexibility, I will examine the data from 1981–1984 period of intense price competition that took place before the major tort liability crisis that occurred from 1984–1986. For this time period I will analyze what I believe is a unique data file based on the Insurance Services Office (ISO) ratemaking files for product liability bodily injury coverage. The unit of observation is the individual insurance policy written for a particular company. The sample size is quite large, ranging roughly from 7,000 to 11,000 policies for any particular year. . . .

Table 3 provides regression results for a series of insurance equations. The first regression focuses on the determinants of the natural logarithm of the manual rate for the particular five-digit class of products sold in the state. The manual rate serves as the price guideline set by the state insurance commissioners for each product group, though insurance underwriters are permitted to deviate from the manual rate, such as for firms with particularly good loss ratios.

The first explanatory variable in the manual rate equation is the natural logarithm of the product loss for that product i in the previous period f - 1 divided by the exposure level, which is the dollar value of the sales covered by insurance.[8] This variable captures the losses per unit of coverage of insurance being written. As one would expect, increases in losses per unit of coverage raise the manual rate.

Similarly, states in which policies have a high loss amount per unit of exposure also have higher manual rates for that product in the state. High wage levels, which in turn will increase the cost associated with losses, have a positive effect on the manual rate as well. The equation also includes a measure of the Treasury bill rate as well as a series of 37 product group dummy variables to control for product-specific differences in insurance rates.

The main variable of interest in the manual rate equation is that for regulation. States in which there is insurance regulation have lower manual rates than states that do not. Indeed, this result is true not only for regulation

Table 3 Regression Results for Insurance Equations

	Ln(Manual Rate)[a]	**Ln(Premium Rate)**[b]	**Ln(Exposure)**[b]	**Ln(Premiums)**[b]	**Ln(Loss Ratio)**[b]
Independent Variables (Standard Errors in Parentheses)					
Intercept	9.645*	–5.892*	14.171*	–7.396*	–6.271*
	(0.140)	(0.160)	(0.318)	(0.324)	(0.400)
Ln(Manual Rate)	—	0.677*	–0.782*	0.113*	—
		(0.006)	(0.014)	(0.013)	
Ln(Product Loss$_{it-1}$/ Product Exposure$_{it-1}$)	0.169*	0.067*	0.036*	0.104*	—
	(0.024)	(0.003)	(0.006)	(0.006)	
Ln(State Loss$_{it-1}$/ State Exposure$_{it-1}$)	0.008*	–0.001	0.220*	0.223*	—
	(0.003)	(0.003)	(0.008)	(0.007)	
Ln Wage	0.204*	–0.196*	1.035*	0.837*	0.761*
	(0.040)	(0.042)	(0.093)	(0.085)	(0.114)
Regulation	–0.129*	0.309*	–1.628*	–1.356*	–0.242*
	(0.030)	(0.031)	(0.070)	(0.064)	(0.086)
Ln Real Treasury Bill Rate	0.404*	0.048	0.088	0.517*	–1.098*
	(0.059)	(0.063)	(0.068)	(0.126)	(0.175)
Adj. R^2	0.35	0.51	0.24	0.15	0.06
N	28,350	27,759	27,762	27,759	43,063
Detailed Insurance Regulation Variables					
Modified/Prior Approval	–0.128*	0.297*	–1.418*	–1.145*	–0.065
	(0.031)	(0.033)	(0.073)	(0.066)	(0.089)
Flex Rating	–0.119*	0.320*	–1.369*	–1.072*	–0.430*
	(0.032)	(0.034)	(0.075)	(0.068)	(0.092)
File & Use/Use & File	–0.133*	0.311*	–1.874*	–1.612*	–0.270*
	(0.031)	(0.032)	(0.071)	(0.065)	(0.087)

[a]The regression equation also includes a set of 37 product group dummy variables.

[b]The regression equation also includes a set of 41 product group dummy variables.

*Indicates coefficients that are statistically significant at the 5% level, two-tailed test.

overall, but also holds for each of the three different forms of regulation that are distinguished in the bottom panel of Table 3-modified prior approval or prior approval states, states with flex rating in which prior approval is required for large rate changes, and file & use/use & file states in which approval is required either before or after instituting a new rate. In every instance, the results with respect to the manual rates are consistent with the price restraining effects of regulation.

The regression results for the premium rate equation have somewhat different implications. The measure of insurance prices that will be used here is the ratio of premiums to the number of exposure units for the particular product, thus being a measure of actual prices charged rather than simply the price guidance under the manual rate. What is evident in these results is that regulation does not have a price restraining effect in terms of actual prices charged. Rather, the effect of regulation is to boost the actual price charged for insurance. Thus, we observe a result opposite of what might be intended, but an effect that is in line with economic theory. . . .

It is noteworthy that the 1981–1984 period is generally considered as a period of intense price competition in which insurers lowered prices. These results indicate that insurers in regulated states lowered their prices to a lesser extent. An explanation for this effect is that regulation boosts the adjustment costs associated with subsequently increasing prices. Firms will consequently decrease prices in regulated states less during periods of price competition because of the greater costs of raising prices when market conditions change. Thus, insurance regulation has led to downward price rigidity during periods of intense price competition. Regulation has not simply restrained manual rates, which is the intended effect of insurance regulation.

As one would expect, these various interferences with the functioning of markets have ramifications for other aspects of insurance market performance. Because insurance regulation leads to higher premium rates actually being charged for insurance, one would expect the quantity of insurance purchased to be reduced by regulation. That quantity effect did occur, as is shown by the results for the log insurance exposure variable, which reflects the dollar volume of sales that is being covered by insurance. The combined influence of insurance regulation on prices and quantity is reflected in the premium regressions. As is shown by the results in Table 3, insurance regulation decreases the total value of premiums written in the state.

For this time period, insurance regulation does reduce the loss ratio of insurers, where the inverse of the loss ratio is the usual measure of insurer profitability. This influence on loss ratios is a significant effect for all forms of regulation other than prior approval or modified prior approval regulation. In situations in which regulation leads to quantity rationing, one would expect firms to respond to the constraint by restricting coverage to exclude the higher risks and to provide coverage to the more favorable risks. The result is that insurance should become more profitable, thus lowering loss ratios because the mix of risks insured by the firm has changed.

Because insurance regulations induce price inflexibility, it is difficult for insurers to respond to changing and increasing liability costs. Insurance ratemaking tends to be based on observed frequencies of risk occurrences. Risks that vary substantially over time and are difficult to estimate as well as risks that are increasing over time will tend to pose particular problems for the ratemaking process. The same kinds of difficulties posed by legal uncertainties created by punitive damages and pain and suffering awards have also been identified as instrumental factors in undermining insurance market responses to terrorism risks, as demonstrated in recent work by Cummins and Lewis (2003) and Doherty, Lamm-Tennant, and Starks (2003). What these articles have shown is that uncertainty in the key parameters pertaining to terrorism risks, rising costs, and unpredictable costs have greatly impeded insurance market responses to this class of hazards. These problems are identical to caused by the punitive damages and noneconomic damages awards.

A major reason why these complications are so fundamental is that the insurance market functioning is grounded in classical statistics based on actual insurance experiences rather than a Bayesian approach that can respond more quickly to judgmental shifts in risk.[9] This link to actual insurance experience is especially acute in regulated states where rates must be justified based on past performance indices.

POLICY PRESCRIPTIONS

Noneconomic damages have been at the forefront of reform efforts largely because of their major role for medical malpractice insurance. Punitive damages are potentially more explosive and pose a greater threat both to insurers as well as to the companies that are defendants in these cases. The era of million dollar awards has now given way to an era of billion dollar awards. These highly publicized billion dollar verdicts may increasingly serve to anchor awards in future liability cases.

In the case of punitive awards, the U.S. Supreme Court has been the primary institution imposing more structure on these awards, thus filling a void that tort reform has not addressed. How the guidelines for punitive awards specified in *State Farm v. Campbell* will actually influence the punitive awards that are observed is not yet clear, but certainly there will be some evident future restraint resulting from this decision.

Both noneconomic damages and punitive damages share common difficulties that cannot be fixed easily. Rigid caps on these awards limit costs but do not solve the underlying problem with these awards. Put simply, juries have been given an impossible task in setting those damages levels. The guidelines provided in the jury instructions provide no firm guidance for setting these award amounts in a reliable, predictable manner. It would be desirable to have additional structure at the award stage rather then arbitrary discipline after the fact. The ideal solution is to have juries or judges set those awards in a responsible manner rather than to respond after the fact by imposing caps on award levels. From the standpoint of insurance market performance, the major need is for increased stability and predictability of awards levels. The more narrowly framed objective of keeping awards low is not necessarily in insurers' interest since it eliminates a potential market for insurance.

Can you think of any changes in the way the authors did their study that would have improved the quality of the results they obtained?

Thus, in many respects the focus of reforms on rigid caps, which in the extreme case would totally eliminate these award components, may be misdirected if the objective is to foster a sound environment for insurance underwriting. Having stable and predictable awards for noneconomic damages and punitive damages should be the objective. Improvements of that nature would benefit the insurance industry by providing an opportunity to write coverage for a major class of financial risks that firms face. Reforms that provide for the scheduling of noneconomic damages, coupled with provision for attorney's fees, would not only protect the interests of plaintiffs and provide for the kind of stable and predictable losses that are amenable to being insured, but would also receive greater support from the plaintiff's bar. Reform proposals that would cap noneconomic damages at low levels will impinge on the plaintiff's ability to cover legal fees, which in turn will also affect the adequacy of the award in addressing the economic losses associated with the case.

The need to make allowances for attorney's fees in reforms of punitive damages is not necessary because the provision for noneconomic damages and compensatory damages would generally provide adequate compensation. The U.S. Supreme Court decision may do a great deal to limit the most dramatic outliers in punitive damages awards. Additional fine tuning of punitive damages reforms ideally should reflect the underlying potential rationales for punitive damages and not be concerned solely with cost reduction.[10]

REFERENCES

Cummins, J. D., and C. M. Lewis, 2003, Catastrophic Events, Parameter Uncertainty, and the Breakdown of Implicit Long-Term Contracting: The case of Terrorism Insurance, *Journal of Risk and Uncertainty*, 26(2–3): 153–78.

Doherty, N. A., J. Lamm-Tennant, and L. Starks, 2003, Insuring September llth: Market Recovery and Transparency, *Journal of Risk and Uncertainty*, 26(2–3): 179–200.

Hersch, J., and W. K. Viscusi, 2004, Punitive Damages: How judges and juries perform, *Journal of Legal Studies*, 33(1), 1–58.

Insurance Information Institute, 2003, The Fact Book 2003 (New York: Insurance Information Institute).

Polinsky, A. M., and S. Shavell, 1998, Punitive Damages: An Economic Analysis, *Harvard Law Review*, 111(4): 869–962.

Schmit, Joan T., S. Travis Pritchett, and L. Paige Fields, 1988, Punitive Damages: Punishment or Further Compensation? *Journal of Risk and Insurance*, 55(3): 453–66.

Sunstein, C. R., R. Hastie, J. W. Payne, D. A. Schkade, and W. K. Viscusi, 2002, *Punitive Damages: How juries decide* (Chicago: University of Chicago Press).

Viscusi, W. K., 1993, The Risky Business of Insurance Pricing, *Journal of Risk and Uncertainty*, 7(1): 117–39.

Viscusi, W. K., 1999, How Do judges Think About Risk? *American Law and Economics Review*, 1(1–2): 26–62.

Viscusi, W. K., 2001a, jurors, judges, and the Mistreatment of Risk by the Courts, *Journal of Legal Studies*, 30(1): 107–42.

Viscusi, W. K., 2001b, The Challenge of Punitive Damages Mathematics, *Journal of Legal Studies*, 30(2): 313–50.

Viscusi, W. K., and P. H. Born, 2002, Damages Caps, Insurability, and the Performance of Medical Malpractice Insurance, Working Paper.

END NOTES

1. These statistics are from the Insurance Information Institute (2003), pp. 73–74.
2. For a series of experimental studies of jury behavior with respect to punitive damages, see Sunstein et al. (2002).
3. For a detailed advocacy of this approach, which dates back to Jeremy Bentham, see Polinsky and Shavell (1998). Also see Schmit, Pritchett, and Fields (1988) more generally for discussion of the rationales for punitive damages.
4. *See* Viscusi (2001b) for a report on the performance of a large sample of adult respondents.
5. *See* Viscusi (1999, 2001a, 2001b) for a comparison of the performance of judges and juries.
6. This compilation is drawn from Hersch and Viscusi (2003).
7. The most recent of our efforts is Viscusi and Born (2002).
8. The average losses experienced under each of these policies represents the losses to date and the additional losses expected to occur for policies written in that year. The loss projections are made using the ISO development factors. The value of losses is highest in 1983 and 1984, which was just before the emergence of the perceived liability crisis.
9. In Viscusi (1993), I examine the role of classical statistics and insurance market volatility in affecting insurance markets.
10. Among these potential factors is whether there should be a regulatory compliance defense in punitive damages cases. If firms are, for example, in compliance with specific government health and safety regulations with respect to their product, then presumably their safety decisions should not be designated as being reckless by jurors.

ARTICLE 1.4

The Effects of Limiting Punitive Damage Awards

Edith Greene, David Coon, and Brian Bornstein

THE EFFECTS OF LIMITING PUNITIVE DAMAGE AWARDS

Cries for reform first sounded in the 1970s and continue to the present day. The target of this attack is a tort liability system that many people (including insurance, medical, and pharmaceutical executives as well as legislators and judges) perceive as capricious, unpredictable, and out of control (see, e.g., Chookaszian, 1997; Ellis, 1989; Parliman & Shoeman, 1994). Much of the criticism centers on concerns about the perceived excessiveness and unpredictability of jury damage awards. This uncertainty is generally believed to produce inefficiency in terms of businesses' planning for risk-producing activities and in predicting the outcome of a case and negotiating a settlement (Baldus, MacQueen, & Woodworth, 1995).

Despite evidence that effectively undermines the concerns about extravagant awards (e.g., Daniels & Martin, 1995; Koenig & Rustad, 1993; Ostrom, Rottman, & Goerdt, 1996; Saks, 1992), tort reformers have ushered in a number of reform packages that they suggest will rein in runaway juries and effectively reduce their awards. Indeed, nearly every state legislature has enacted some version of tort reform including measures that cap or limit jury damage awards, elevate the standard of proof necessary for the awarding of damages, bifurcate punitive damages trials, allocate a portion of the punitive damage award to the state, and amend the standard of review for excessive verdicts (Hurd & Zollers, 1994; Kershaw & Pernini, 1997; Koenig & Rustad, 1993).

Can you think of any factors other than the rising cost of malpractice verdicts that might have contributed to the increasing cost of insurance premiums?

For several years in the late 1980s and early 1990s, the tort reformers seemed to be winning the war. A second phase of the battle may now be underway, however. In the past few years, the highest courts in at least eight states have struck down all or parts of these tort reform measures (Glaberson, 1999), and dozens of new challenges are making their way to state supreme courts across the country. State courts are invalidating parts of the tort reform packages that did not pass state constitutional muster and, in particular, those that effectively enable the legislature to interfere in a jury's evaluation of the evidence and assessment of damages. . . .

PROPOSALS TO CAP PUNITIVE DAMAGE AWARDS

Some states impose an absolute upper limit on the amount of money that can be awarded as punitive damages. For example, Alabama imposes a $250,000 cap. Other states (e.g., Florida) impose a maximum permitted ratio under which punitive damages may be awarded in some ratio to the compensatory damages (typically two or three times, although punitive awards in Colorado may not exceed the compensatory award). Still other states (e.g., Nevada) simultaneously impose both kinds of limits. Finally, in some states (e.g., Nebraska, New Hampshire, Louisiana, Washington), jurors are not allowed to award any punitive damages (Hurd & Zollers, 1994; Koenig & Rustad, 1993).

Caps on punitive damage awards are widely perceived to be the most important of all legislative tort reforms (Weiler, 1991), yet they are also highly controversial. Galanter and Luban (1993) argue, for example, that punitive damages should be linked to the heinousness of the wrongful act and have nothing to do with the amount of compensatory damages awarded to an injured party. Thus, they oppose proposals that explicitly cap the punitive award at some multiple of the compensatory award. Owen (1994) suggests that such arbitrary methods of measurement deprive the decision maker of the ability to tailor the punishment to fit the particular wrongdoer and the wrongful act. Reform proponents, on the other hand, claim that these caps will reduce the size, variability, and unpredictability of punitive damage awards. Perhaps not surprisingly, little of this debate has been enlightened by empirical investigation.

By definition, of course, caps will effectively control the maximum amount that can be awarded in punitive damages (Robbennolt & Studebaker, 1999). However, we suspect that there may be a cost to this accomplishment in the form of higher and more variable compensatory damage awards in situations in which the punitive damage award is artificially limited. The present study examines that notion.

Why might jurors inflate their compensatory damage award when punitive damages are limited? The task of assessing damages involves multiple and seemingly conflicting goals. Jurors must first focus on the plaintiff and determine an appropriate compensatory award to that plaintiff regardless of its impact on the defendant.[1] Suppose, for example, that a plaintiff is injured in an accident because his car's brake pads—ostensibly repaired by the defendant—had failed. In theory, it should not matter whether the defendant is a small locally owned automobile repair shop or the Ford Motor Corporation. Jurors should award compensatory damages that fully and fairly repay the plaintiff for his losses related to the defective brake pads. Jurors may then turn to the defendant and assess punitive damages against that defendant with little regard for the plaintiff or his needs. If the defendant opted to forego adequate testing in the interests of saving money, that defendant should be assessed a reasonable punitive damage award.

What kinds of errors in judgment might the judge make that could potentially be just as problematic as the errors common to jurors?

Unfortunately, jurors' instructions do not make these distinctions and directions clear (Greene & Bornstein, in press). Rather, the instructions tend to explain the intended function of each kind of award but tend not to clearly guide jurors in how to address these complementary functions. The instructions make no distinction, for example, between the plaintiff and defendant focus that implicitly underlie the two kinds of damage awards. Under these circumstances, defendant-focused concerns can cross over into the assessment of compensatory damages and plaintiff-focused concerns can cross over into the assessment of punitive damages (Anderson & MacCoun, 1999).

We suspect that this crossover might be especially likely to happen in situations in which punitive awards are capped and jurors' ability to adequately punish and deter the defendant is effectively thwarted. Anderson and MacCoun speculate that jurors manage such conflicts through a process of equifinality (Heider, 1958) whereby multiple pathways to a goal exist and when one pathway to a goal is obstructed, another is used. Thus, we suspect that when punitive damage awards are capped (or are not an option), jurors may use their compensatory damage award (the economic component of which is typically not capped) as a means of imposing punishment or promoting deterrence toward the defendant.

We further suspect that this crossover effect would be more prominent in situations in which the defendant's conduct has been especially malicious (as opposed to less reprehensible) and in which punishment and deterrence may be particularly appropriate. Jurors who hear evidence of egregious conduct on the part of the defendant and who have scant or no opportunity to award punitive damages would be especially likely to feel that their ability to punish and deter has been thwarted. These jurors might be likely to augment their awards for compensatory damages. The present study tested these hypotheses. . . .

METHOD

Materials

Trial Summaries

. . . Finally, where appropriate, they [the mock jurors] were informed about any cap or limit that had been placed on their punitive damage award. The limits we used were as follows: (a) Dollar Limit, in which punitive damages were not to exceed $200,000; (b) Proportional Limit, in which the punitive damage award could not exceed the compensatory damage award; and (c) No Limit. (In reality, caps can be either explicit, e.g., jurors in Colorado are explicitly instructed that their punitive damage award cannot exceed their compensatory award or implicit, e.g., jurors in Florida are not told about limits imposed on their awards. We suspect that even if jurors are not directly instructed that punitive damages are capped at a certain level, they may nonetheless have this expectation from information available in the media, conversations with others, or from general knowledge of tort reform legislation.) Jurors in a fourth condition (No Punitive Damages) served as a control condition and were not given the opportunity to award punitive damages. These jurors were neither instructed nor questioned about punitive damages. We were particularly interested in comparing the compensatory awards from the three conditions in which punitive awards were allowed (including the two conditions in which they were capped) to the compensatory awards decided by this control group. . . .

RESULTS

Punitive Damage Awards

Caps on punitive damages would obviously be expected to have their most direct effect on assessments of punitive damages. . . .

As expected, the mean punitive damage award in the No Limit condition . . . was significantly higher than both the Proportional . . . and the Dollar Limit conditions . . . that did not differ from each other.

Also as expected, the mean punitive award assessed against a defendant whose conduct had been highly reprehensible . . . was greater than the punitive award assessed against a defendant whose conduct was only mildly reprehensible. . . .

Total Award

The highest compensatory awards came from jurors who were not given the opportunity to award punitive damages. This finding suggests that jurors may not make the distinctions between compensatory and punitive damages that the

Table 1 Mean Compensatory Awards as a Function of Punitive Damage Limit, Transformed and Nontransformed Amounts[a]

	Mean Compensatory Award	
Punitive damage Limit	**Transformed**	**Nontransformed (in thousands)**
No limit	5.47^{a} (.73)	\$1,015 (2,241)
Proportional limit	5.38^{a} (.78)	\$732 (988)
Dollar limit	5.33^{a} (.65)	\$489 (613)
No punitive award	5.79^{b} (.72)	\$1,630 (2,487)

Note: Analyses were conducted on transformed awards only. Means with different superscripts are significantly different ($p < .01$).

[a]Standard deviations are given in parentheses.

Table 2 Mean Deviation Values for Compensatory Awards as a Function of Punitive Damage Limit and Defendant Reprehensibility, Transformed and Nontransformed Amounts[a]

	Mean Deviation Value	
Condition	**Transformed**	**Nontransformed (in thousands)**
Low reprehensibility		
No limit	5.89[a] (.29)	$1,124 (1,991)
Proportional	5.88[a] (.36)	$1,007 (828)
Dollar limit	5.59[b] (.34)	$526 (478)
No punitive award	6.32[c] (.26)	$2,598 (2,535)
High Reprehensibility		
No limit	6.01[a] (.28)	$1,427 (1,961)
Proportional	5.70[b] (.27)	$595 (351)
Dollar limit	5.56[b] (.26)	$439 (325)
No punitive award	5.98[a] (.24)	$1,095 (633)

Note: Analyses were conducted on transformed deviations scores only. Means with different superscripts are significantly different ($p < .01$).

[a]Standard deviations are given in parentheses.

law intends (Greene, 1989) but rather, that they may reason more holistically and award amounts that they believe constitute a sufficient *total* award. By this reasoning, when jurors are unable to punish and deter the defendant by way of a punitive damage award, they may do so by increasing the size of the compensatory damages they award to the plaintiff. Thus, the compensatory award in the No Punitive Award Condition would approximate the total (compensatory plus punitive) award in the No Limit Condition.

Jurors' Intentions in Awarding Damages

. . . So, although jurors perceive the compensatory award (but not the punitive award) to be the appropriate vehicle for repayment and the punitive award (but not the compensatory award) to be a means of punishing the defendant, we are not particularly sanguine that jurors are adhering to the law's objectives. That the deterrence goal was not a prominent feature of the punitive damages decision is perhaps not surprising. Because we gave no information about the defendant's financial condition, it may have been difficult for mock jurors to use the punitive award as a means of deterrence. In addition, others (Hastie,

Table 3 Mean Total Award as a Function of Punitive Damage Limit, Transformed and Nontransformed Amounts[a]

	Total Award[b]	
Punitive Damage Limit	**Transformed**	**Nontransformed (in thousands)**
No limit	5.81[a] (.73)	$2,593 (7,379)
Proportional	5.53[b] (.78)	$993 (1,296)
Dollar limit	5.53[b] (.51)	$597 (640)
No punitive award	5.79[a] (.72)	$1,630 (2,487)

Note: Analyses were conducted on transformed awards only. Means with different superscripts differ significantly, $p < .02$.
[a]Standard deviations are given in parentheses.
[b]Total award in No Punitive Award Condition consisted of compensatory award only.

Table 4 Mean Ratings of Award Objectives for Compensatory and Punitive Awards, as a Function of Question Type on a 1–10 Scale[a]

	Award Type	
Question Type	**Compensatory**	**Punitive**
To what extent is your (compensatory/punitive) damage award intended to:		
Make up for losses incurred by the plaintiff?	6.89[a] (1.72)	5.86[a] (2.01)
Punish the defendant?	5.90[b] (1.91)	6.15[b] (1.98)
Deter the defendant and similar others?	5.84[b] (1.93)	5.98[a] (1.97)

Note: Within each Award Type, means with different superscripts differ significantly ($p < .05$).
[a]Standard deviations are given in parentheses.

Schkade, & Payne, 1999) report that punishment plays a much larger role in mock jurors' thoughts about punitive damages than does deterrence.

DISCUSSION

Much of the rhetoric concerning tort reform has occurred in the absence of empirical investigation. That situation has begun to change in the very recent past, however, as social scientists have begun to assess some of the effects of statutorily imposed attempts to reform punitive damages assessments (Anderson & MacCoun, 1999; Robbennolt & Studebaker, 1999). The present study complements the results of other recent studies in showing that there are unexpected effects of one important and highly controversial legislated reform: the limiting of punitive damage awards.

Our data show that jurors who were not given the opportunity to award punitive damages in three kinds of cases (personal injury, products liability, and insurance bad faith) augmented the amount that they awarded in compensatory damages. Jurors who had no option to award punitive damages apparently inflated their compensatory damage award to serve punitive ends.[3] In fact, our data show that the compensatory damages awarded by these jurors were statistically equivalent to the total amount (compensatory plus punitive) awarded by jurors whose punitive damage awards were not limited in any way.

We found no effects of other limitations of punitive awards (absolute dollar limit or proportional limit) on compensatory damages. So, for example, the compensatory awards from jurors with a $200,000 limit on punitive damages were not higher than those from jurors with no limit on punitive damages. This finding is especially remarkable given that the caps we imposed on punitive damages were more restrictive than is typically the case and would have, we suspected, resulted in more crossover into compensatory awards than is typically the case. And yet, we found no augmentation of compensatory awards even when punitive damages were restricted to $200,000. It appears from these data that as long as jurors are given the opportunity to award some money for purposes of punishment and deterrence, they do not feel the need to increase their compensatory award to meet those objectives. One might test this hypothesis by lowering the cap on punitive damages even further to see if, and at what point, jurors start to augment their compensatory awards.

We wondered if jurors would be likely to inflate their compensatory award when punitive awards were disallowed (or severely limited) and when the defendant had acted in a highly reprehensible manner. We reasoned that jurors would want to punish the defendant for his egregious conduct and that the only means available to them was through the compensatory award. But, like other researchers (Anderson & MacCoun, 1999; Cather et al., 1996), we found no effect of defendant reprehensibility on the amount of the compensatory damage award. One explanation of this null finding is that our reprehensibility manipulation, although successful, was relatively weak: recall that the mean punitive awards in response to less reprehensible and more reprehensible conduct differed by only $30,000. (Recall also that our manipulations were identical to those used by Cather et al. Finally, it is worth noting that there is no absolute standard that equates with egregious or reprehensible behavior, so our notion of reprehensible conduct may not have been perceived as such.) Had the defendant's behavior been clearly reckless or intentional, we might have seen an effect of defendant reprehensibility on compensatory awards when punitive awards were capped or disallowed. In those situations, jurors might feel especially desirous of condemning the defendant's conduct, yet they would have no vehicle but the compensatory award to allow them to do so.

Next, we turn to the variability in compensatory damage awards. Recall that Robbennolt and Studebaker (1999) found differences in compensatory award variability as a function of the cap on punitive damages. So did we. In fact, our pattern of results is very similar to theirs. We found that capping the punitive damage award generally reduced the variability in compensatory damage awards.

Finally, we examine the effects of our manipulations on the punitive damage awards. As expected, mock jurors assessed higher punitive damages against the more errant defendants and when their awards were not limited. These findings suggest that in setting punitive damages, jurors are indeed attentive to the egregious nature of the defendant's conduct and that limitations on punitive damages obviously result in reduced awards of that type.

Summarizing our quantitative findings, we find both good news and troubling news. The good news is that mock jurors in our study, like those in Cather et al. (1996), seemed to appropriately compartmentalize their decision making about compensation and punishment/deterrence in three civil tort cases. They did not augment their compensatory damage awards when their punitive awards were limited. They were also not more likely to augment the compensatory award when the defendant's conduct was highly reprehensible (vs. less reprehensible), although this finding may be an artifact of a weak manipulation of defendant's conduct. By contrast, mock jurors were attentive to the reprehensibility of the defendant's conduct when they assessed punitive damages, as the law would intend them to be. Finally, limiting the punitive damage award reduced the variability in the compensatory award as well as the mean punitive award. These findings provide some tentative support to the notion that limiting the punitive damage award will decrease the size and variability of damage awards generally. We found no evidence for the hypothesized crossover effect, at least in the conditions where punitive damages were capped. Mock jurors did not "compensate for the constraint" (Anderson and MacCoun, 1999) in their punitive damage decision making by inflating their compensatory award.

The troubling news is this: when jurors were not allowed to award punitive damages, they inflated the level of their compensatory awards. This finding, consistent with Anderson and MacCoun's data, suggests that jurors who have no option to award punitive damages may nonetheless find an alternative avenue for punishing the defendant. These findings support the notion that jurors may have an overall impression of what an injury is worth and, rather than concerning themselves with the damage components as an accountant might, instead search for a sum that is felt to be appropriate (Kalven, 1958).

There are obvious limitations to the conclusions of our study. Although we examined the impact of caps in three kinds of cases and found no differential effects of our manipulations in these three causes of action, all of our summaries were greatly abbreviated and lacked some degree of legal realism and vividness. We did not include some information that could have affected awards (e.g., concerning the defendant's financial status, the conditions that trigger liability for punitive damages). In particular, requests or counterrequests for damages by the parties in these cases might have moderated our findings by serving as anchors for resulting awards. Further, our mock jurors were college students. Although students and jury-pool subjects tend to make decisions in similar ways (Bornstein, 1999), we cannot be sure to what extent the effects of our independent variables would hold with a different population. Finally, our participants did not deliberate. Jury discussions about damages can be complex and motivated by subtle attempts at persuasion and compromise (Greene, 1989). Obviously, our mock jurors missed this opportunity.

With these caveats in mind, we briefly ponder the policy implications of our findings. Our data tentatively support the assumption that limitations on punitive damage awards may reduce the size of punitive awards and the variability of compensatory awards without simultaneously inflating the size of the latter. This sanguine finding, in conjunction with the fact that legislative caps simplify courts' review of the amount of the awards in additur/remittitur (Baldus et al., 1995), might argue for the implementation and continued use of damage caps.

However, we note the concerns of others (e.g., Baldus et al., 1995; Galanter & Luban, 1993) that legislative caps raise serious ethical and policy questions. Because of inconsistencies across states in laws limiting punitive damages, similarly injured plaintiffs may receive radically different compensation in different locales. Further, serious inequities may exist in how tortfeasors are dealt with. Wildly malicious defendants may escape significant sanction in some jurisdictions but not others. Because legislative caps may bear little relation to the amount of money required to actually punish and deter, they may undercut the very premise of punitive damages (Baldus et al.). Therefore, we advocate for further empirical research along these lines, tempered by careful and thoughtful applications of the research findings in setting future policy.

REFERENCES

Anderson, M. C., & MacCoun, R. J. (1999). Goal conflict in juror assessments of compensatory and punitive damages. Law and Human Behavior, 23, 313–330.

Baldus, D., MacQueen, J. C., & Woodworth, G. (1995). Improving judicial oversight of jury damages assessments: A proposal for the comparative additur/remittitur review of awards for nonpecuniary harms and punitive damages. Iowa Law Review, 80, 1109–1267.

Bornstein, B. H. (1999). The ecological validity of jury simulations: Is the jury still out? Law and Human Behavior, 23, 75–91.

Cather, C., Greene, E., & Durham, R. (1996). Plaintiff injury and defendant reprehensibility: Implications for compensatory and punitive damage awards. Law and Human Behavior, 20, 189–206.

Chin, A., & Peterson, M. (1985). Deep pockets, empty pockets: Who wins in Cook County jury trials. Santa Monica: Rand Corporation.

Chookaszian, D. (1997, July 28). Tort reform: Reining in punitive damages will make American business more competitive. Forbes, 7/28/97, p. 166.

Daniels, S., & Martin, J. (1995). Civil juries and the politics of reform. Evanston, IL: Northwestern University Press.

Ellis, D. D. (1989). Punitive damages, due process, and the jury. Alabama Law Review, 40, 975–1008.

Galanter, M. & Luban, D. (1993). Poetic justice: Punitive damages and legal pluralism. American University Law Review, 42, 1393–1463.

Glaberson, W. (1999). State courts overturn laws limiting suits and awards. New York Times, 7/16/99, p. A1.

Greene, E. (1989). On juries and damage awards: The process of decision making. Law and Contemporary Problems, 52, 225–246.

Greene, E., & Bornstein, B. (2000). Precious little guidance: Jury instructions on damages. Psychology, Public Policy, and Law, 6.

Hans, V. P., & Ermann, M. D. (1989). Responses to corporate versus individual wrongdoing. Law and Human Behavior, 13, 151–166.

Hastie, R., Schkade, D. A., & Payne, J. W. (1999). Juror judgments in civil cases: Effects of plaintiff's requests and plaintiff's identity on punitive damage awards. Law and Human Behavior, 23, 445–470.

Heider, F. (1958). The psychology of interpersonal relations. Hillsdale, NJ: Erlbaum.

Hurd, S. N., & Zollers, F. E. (1994). State punitive damages statutes: A proposed alternative. Journal of Legislation, 20, 191–212.

Kalven, H. (1958). The jury, the law, and the personal injury damage award. Ohio State Law Journal, 19, 159–178.

Kershaw, A. E., & Pernini, D. M. (Winter 1997). Geressy v. Digital—Using statistical analysis to curb excessive jury awards. Employee Relations Law Journal, 23, 55–65.

Koenig, T., & Rustad, M. (1993). The quiet revolution revisited: An empirical study of the impact of state tort reform of punitive damages in products liability. The Justice System Journal, 16, 21–44.

MacCoun, R. J. (1996). Differential treatment of corporate defendants by juries: An examination of the "deep-pockets" hypothesis. Law and Society Review, 30, 121–161.

Ostrom, B. J., Rottman, D. B., & Goerdt, J. A. (1996). A step above anecdote: A profile of the civil jury in the 1990s. Judicature, 79, 233–241.

Owen, D. G. (1994). A punitive damages overview: Functions, problems and reform. Villanova Law Review, 39, 363–413.

Parliman, G. C., & Shoeman, R. J. (1994). Punitive damages: A discussion of judicial and legislative responses to excessive jury awards. Employee Relations Law Journal, 20, 177–1988.

Robbennolt, J. K., & Studebaker, C. A. (1999). Anchoring in the courtroom: The effects of caps on punitive damages. Law and Human Behavior, 23, 353–373.

Saks, M. J. (1992). Do we really know anything about the behavior of the tort litigation system—and why not? University of Pennsylvania Law Review, 140, 1147–1292.

Texas Civil Practice and Remedies Code (1999). Section 41.008. Retrieved from Lexis-Nexis on World WideWeb, 6/7/00.

Wasserman, D. T., & Robinson, J. N. (1980). Extra-legal influences, group processes, and jury decisionmaking: A psychological perspective. North Carolina Central Law Journal, 12, 96–159.

Wilson, T. D. (1985). Strangers to ourselves: The origin and accuracy of beliefs about one's own mental state. In J. H. Harvey & G. Weary (Eds.), Attributions in contemporary psychology, New York: Academic Press.

Weiler, P. (1991). Medical malpractice on trial. Cambridge, MA: Harvard University Press.

END NOTES

1. A number of studies have shown that corporate defendants pay greater compensation than individual defendants in both actual (Chin & Peterson, 1985) and simulated trials (Hans & Ermann, 1989; Wasserman & Robinson, 1980) although what might appear on the surface as a deep-pocket effect may actually be a defendant-identity effect (MacCoun, 1996). Wealthy defendants were not necessarily at a disadvantage, unless they were corporations as well.
2. This amount is statutorily imposed on punitive damage awards in Texas (although Texas juries also have the option to award twice the amount of economic damages plus an amount equal to noneconomic damages if that sum is more than $200,000, Texas Civil Practice and Remedies Code, 1999) and is apparently the lowest upper limit at which punitive damages are capped. We also note that this amount is considerably lower than the mean punitive damages awarded when these case materials were used for a different purpose (Cather et al., 1996). Thus, we were fairly certain that by using this low ceiling, we would cause jurors to feel that their ability to effectively punish and deter the defendant had been restricted. This situation would allow us to test the possibility that limiting punitive damages would affect judgments of compensatory damages. To what extent our data are dependent on the low cap we opted to impose is, of course, an empirical question.
3. Interestingly, jurors who had no option to award punitive damages did not tell us that they intended the compensatory award to punish and deter, however. It may be that they augmented their compensatory awards without clearly distinguishing compensatory goals from punitive

goals. Perhaps they lacked awareness of the factors that influenced their awards (Wilson, 1985). Alternatively, their responses may be explained by demand characteristics. They may simply have inferred that compensatory damages are supposed to compensate and that punitive damages are supposed to punish.

ARTICLE 1.5

State Farm Mutual Automobile Insurance Co. v. Campbell et al.

Although investigators and witnesses concluded that Curtis Campbell caused an accident in which one person was killed and another permanently disabled, his insurer, State Farm Mutual Automobile Insurance Company (State Farm), contested liability, declined to settle the ensuing claims for the $50,000 policy limit, ignored its own investigators' advice, and took the case to trial, assuring Campbell and his wife that they had no liability for the accident, that State Farm would represent their interests, and that they did not need separate counsel. In fact, a Utah jury found Campbell to be 100 percent at fault for the accident and returned a judgment for over three times the policy limit. State Farm refused to appeal. The Utah Supreme Court denied Campbell's own appeal, and, after initial refusal, State Farm paid the entire judgment. The Campbells then sued State Farm for bad faith, fraud, and intentional infliction of emotional distress. The trial court's initial ruling granting State Farm summary judgment was reversed on appeal. On remand, the court denied State Farm's motion to exclude evidence of dissimilar out-of-state conduct. The case was then separated into one phase for fault and one phase for damages. In the first phase, the jury found unreasonable State Farm's decision not to settle. Before the second phase, the Supreme Court refused, in BMW of North America, Inc. v. Gore, 517 U.S. 559, to sustain a $2 million punitive damages award which accompanied a $4,000 compensatory damages award. The trial court denied State Farm's renewed motion to exclude dissimilar out-of-state conduct evidence. In the second phase, which addressed, inter alia, compensatory and punitive damages, evidence was introduced that pertained to State Farm's business practices in numerous States but was not directly related to the Campbells' complaint. The jury awarded the Campbells $2.6 million in compensatory damages and $145 million in punitive damages, which the trial court reduced to $1 million and $25 million respectively. Applying Gore, the Utah Supreme Court reinstated the $145 million punitive damages award. State Farm appealed.

JUSTICE KENNEDY

We address once again the measure of punishment, by means of punitive damages, a State may impose upon a defendant in a civil case. The question is whether . . . an award of $145 million in punitive damages, where full compensatory damages are $1 million, is excessive and in violation of the Due Process Clause of the Fourteenth Amendment to the Constitution of the United States. . . .

Had you been on the jury in this case, would you have voted for the award that was handed down by the original jury? Why or why not?

II

We recognized in *Cooper Industries, Inc. v. Leatherman Tool Group, Inc.,* 532 U.S. 424, 121 S.Ct. 1678, 149 L.Ed.2d 674 (2001), that in our judicial system compensatory and punitive damages, although usually awarded at the same time by the same decisionmaker, serve different purposes. . . . Compensatory damages "are intended to redress the concrete loss that the plaintiff has suffered by reason of the defendant's wrongful conduct." . . . By contrast, punitive damages serve a broader function; they are aimed at deterrence and retribution. . . .

While States possess discretion over the imposition of punitive damages, it is well established that there are procedural and substantive constitutional limitations on these awards. . . . The Due Process Clause of the Fourteenth Amendment prohibits the imposition of grossly excessive or arbitrary punishments on a tortfeasor. . . . The reason is that "[e]lementary notions of fairness enshrined in our constitutional jurisprudence dictate that a person receive fair notice not only of the conduct that will subject him to punishment, but also of the severity of the penalty that a State may impose." [*Gore*], at 574, 116 S.Ct. 1589; *Cooper Industries, supra,* at 433, 121 S.Ct. 1678. . . . To the extent an award is grossly excessive, it furthers no legitimate purpose and constitutes an arbitrary deprivation of property. . . .

Although these awards serve the same purposes as criminal penalties, defendants subjected to punitive damages in civil cases have not been accorded the protections applicable in a criminal proceeding. This increases our concerns over the imprecise manner in which punitive damages systems are administered. We have admonished that "[p]unitive damages pose an acute danger of arbitrary deprivation of property. Jury instructions typically leave the jury with wide discretion in choosing amounts, and the presentation of evidence of a defendant's net worth creates the potential that juries will use their verdicts to express biases against big businesses, particularly those without strong local presences." *Honda Motor, supra,* at 432, 114 S.Ct. 2331; see also *Haslip, supra,* at 59, 111 S.Ct. 1032 (O'CONNOR, J., dissenting). . . . Our concerns are heightened when the decisionmaker is presented, as we shall discuss, with evidence that has little bearing as to the amount of punitive damages that should be awarded. Vague instructions, or those that merely inform the jury to avoid "passion or prejudice," . . . do little to aid the decisionmaker in its task of assigning appropriate weight to evidence that is relevant and evidence that is tangential or only inflammatory.

In light of these concerns, in *Gore, supra,* we instructed courts reviewing punitive damages to consider three guideposts: (1) the degree of reprehensibility of the defendant's misconduct; (2) the disparity between the actual or potential harm suffered by the plaintiff and the punitive damages award; and (3) the difference between the punitive damages awarded by the jury and the civil penalties authorized or imposed in comparable cases. *Id.,* at 575, 116 S.Ct. 1589. We reiterated the importance of these three guideposts in *Cooper Industries* and mandated appellate courts to conduct *de novo* review of a trial court's application of them to the jury's award. 532 U.S. 424, 121 S.Ct. 1678. Exacting appellate review ensures that an award of punitive damages is based upon an " 'application of law, rather than a decisionmaker's caprice.' " *Id.,* at 436, 121 S.Ct. 1678 (quoting *Gore, supra,* at 587, 116 S.Ct. 1589 (BREYER, J., concurring)).

III

Under the principles outlined in *BMW of North America, Inc. v. Gore,* this case is neither close nor difficult. It was error to reinstate the jury's $145 million punitive damages award. We address each guidepost of *Gore* in some detail.

While the author of the opinion claims the case is not difficult, is it possible to make the argument that in fact it is difficult to apply at least one of the three factors?

A

"[T]he most important indicium of the reasonableness of a punitive damages award is the degree of reprehensibility of the defendant's conduct." *Gore,* 517 U.S., at 575, 116 S.Ct. 1589. We have instructed courts to determine the reprehensibility of a defendant by considering whether: the harm caused was physical as opposed to economic; the tortious conduct evinced an indifference to or a reckless disregard of the health or safety of others; the target of the conduct had financial vulnerability; the conduct involved repeated actions or was an isolated incident; and the harm was the result of intentional malice, trickery, or deceit, or mere accident. *Id.,* at 576–577, 116 S.Ct. 1589. The existence of any one of these factors weighing in favor of a plaintiff may not be sufficient to sustain a punitive damages award; and the absence of all of them renders any award suspect. It should be presumed a plaintiff has been made whole for his injuries by compensatory damages, so punitive damages should only be awarded if the defendant's culpability, after having paid compensatory damages, is so reprehensible as to warrant the imposition of further sanctions to achieve punishment or deterrence. *Id.,* at 575, 116 S.Ct. 1589.

Applying these factors in the instant case, we must acknowledge that State Farm's handling of the claims against the Campbells merits no praise. The trial court found that State Farm's employees altered the company's records to make Campbell appear less culpable. State Farm disregarded the overwhelming likelihood of liability and the near-certain probability that, by taking the case to trial, a judgment in excess of the policy limits would be awarded. State Farm amplified the harm by at first assuring the Campbells their assets would be safe from any verdict and by later telling them, postjudgment, to put a for-sale sign on their house. While we do not suggest there was error in awarding punitive damages based upon State Farm's conduct toward the Campbells, a more modest punishment for this reprehensible conduct could have satisfied the State's legitimate objectives, and the Utah courts should have gone no further.

This case, instead, was used as a platform to expose, and punish, the perceived deficiencies of State Farm's operations throughout the country. The Utah Supreme Court's opinion makes explicit that State Farm was being condemned for its nationwide policies rather than for the conduct directed toward the Campbells. 65 P.3d, at 1143. . . . This was, as well, an explicit rationale of the trial court's decision in approving the award, though reduced from $145 million to $25 million. . . .

A State cannot punish a defendant for conduct that may have been lawful where it occurred. . . . Nor, as a general rule, does a State have a legitimate concern in imposing punitive damages to punish a defendant for unlawful acts committed outside of the State's jurisdiction. Any proper adjudication of conduct that occurred outside Utah to other persons would require their inclusion, and, to those parties, the Utah courts, in the usual case, would need to apply the laws of their relevant jurisdiction. . . .

. . . Lawful out-of-state conduct may be probative when it demonstrates the deliberateness and culpability of the defendant's action in the State where it is tortious, but that conduct must have a nexus to the specific harm suffered by the plaintiff. A jury must be instructed, furthermore, that it may not use evidence of out-of-state conduct to punish a defendant for action that was lawful in the jurisdiction where it occurred. . . . A basic principle of federalism is that each State may make its own reasoned judgment about what conduct is permitted or proscribed within its borders, and each State alone can determine what measure of punishment, if any, to impose on a defendant who acts within its jurisdiction. *Id.*, at 569, 116 S.Ct. 1589. . . .

For a more fundamental reason, however, the Utah courts erred in relying upon this and other evidence: The courts awarded punitive damages to punish and deter conduct that bore no relation to the Campbells' harm. A defendant's dissimilar acts, independent from the acts upon which liability was premised, may not serve as the basis for punitive damages. A defendant should be punished for the conduct that harmed the plaintiff, not for being an unsavory individual or business. Due process does not permit courts, in the calculation of punitive damages, to adjudicate the merits of other parties' hypothetical claims against a defendant under the guise of the reprehensibility analysis, but we have no doubt the Utah Supreme Court did that here. 65 P.3d, at 1149. . . . Punishment on these bases creates the possibility of multiple punitive damages awards for the same conduct; for in the usual case nonparties are not bound by the judgment some other plaintiff obtains. *Gore, supra,* at 593, 116 S.Ct. 1589 (BREYER, J., concurring). . . .

The Campbells have identified scant evidence of repeated misconduct of the sort that injured them. Nor does our review of the Utah courts' decisions convince us that State Farm was only punished for its actions toward the Campbells. Although evidence of other acts need not be identical to have relevance in the calculation of punitive damages, the Utah court erred here because evidence pertaining to claims that had nothing to do with a third-party lawsuit was introduced at length. . . . In this case, because the Campbells have shown no conduct by State Farm similar to that which harmed them, the conduct that harmed them is the only conduct relevant to the reprehensibility analysis.

B

Turning to the second *Gore* guidepost, we have been reluctant to identify concrete constitutional limits on the ratio between harm, or potential harm, to the plaintiff and the punitive damages award. . . . We decline again to impose a bright-line ratio which a punitive damages award cannot exceed. Our jurisprudence and the principles it has now established demonstrate, however, that in practice, few awards exceeding a single-digit ratio between punitive and compensatory damages, to a significant degree, will satisfy due process. In *Haslip,* in upholding a punitive damages award, we concluded that an award of more than four times the amount of compensatory damages might be close to the line of constitutional impropriety. 499 U.S., at 23–24, 111 S.Ct. 1032. We cited that 4-to-1 ratio again in *Gore.* 517 U.S., at 581, 116 S.Ct. 1589. The Court further referenced a long legislative history, dating back over 700 years and going forward to today, providing for sanctions of double, treble, or quadruple damages to deter and punish. *Id.,* at 581, and n. 33, 116 S.Ct. 1589. While these ratios are not binding, they are instructive. They demonstrate what should be obvious: Single-digit multipliers are more likely to comport with due process, while still achieving the State's goals of deterrence and retribution, than awards with ratios in range of 500 to 1, *id.,* at 582, 116 S.Ct. 1589, or in this case, of 145 to 1.

Nonetheless, because there are no rigid benchmarks that a punitive damages award may not surpass, ratios greater than those we have previously upheld may comport with due process where "a particularly egregious act has resulted in only a small amount of economic damages." . . . The converse is also true, however. When compensatory damages are substantial, then a lesser ratio, perhaps only equal to compensatory damages, can reach the outermost limit of the due process guarantee. The precise award in any case, of course, must be based upon the facts and circumstances of the defendant's conduct and the harm to the plaintiff.

In sum, courts must ensure that the measure of punishment is both reasonable and proportionate to the amount of harm to the plaintiff and to the general damages recovered. In the context of this case, we have no doubt that there is a presumption against an award that has a 145-to-1 ratio. The compensatory award in this case was substantial; the Campbells were awarded $1 million for a year and a half of emotional distress. This was complete compensation.

The harm arose from a transaction in the economic realm, not from some physical assault or trauma; there were no physical injuries; and State Farm paid the excess verdict before the complaint was filed, so the Campbells suffered only minor economic injuries for the 18-month period in which State Farm refused to resolve the claim against them. The compensatory damages for the injury suffered here, moreover, likely were based on a component which was duplicated in the punitive award. Much of the distress was caused by the outrage and humiliation the Campbells suffered at the actions of their insurer; and it is a major role of punitive damages to condemn such conduct. . . .

The remaining premises for the Utah Supreme Court's decision bear no relation to the award's reasonableness or proportionality to the harm. They are, rather, arguments that seek to defend a departure from well-established constraints on punitive damages. While States enjoy considerable discretion in deducing when punitive damages are warranted, each award must comport with the principles set forth in *Gore.* Here the argument that State Farm will be punished in only the rare case, coupled with reference to its assets (which, of course, are what other insured parties in Utah and other States must rely upon for payment of claims) had little to do with the actual harm sustained by the Campbells. The wealth of a defendant cannot justify an otherwise unconstitutional punitive damages award. *Gore,* 517 U.S., at 585, 116 S.Ct. 1589. . . . The principles set forth in *Gore* must be implemented with care, to ensure both reasonableness and proportionality.

C

The third guidepost in *Gore* is the disparity between the punitive damages award and the "civil penalties authorized or imposed in comparable cases." *Id.,* at 575, 116 S.Ct. 1589. We note that, in the past, we have also looked to criminal penalties that could be imposed. *Id.,* at 583, 116 S.Ct. 1589; *Haslip,* 499 U.S., at 23, 111 S.Ct. 1032. The existence of a criminal penalty does have bearing on the seriousness with which a State views the wrongful action. When used to determine the dollar amount of the award, however, the criminal penalty has less utility. Great care must be taken to avoid use of the civil process to assess criminal penalties that can be imposed only after the heightened protections of a criminal trial have been observed, including, of course, its higher standards of proof. Punitive damages are not a substitute for the criminal process, and the remote possibility of a criminal sanction does not automatically sustain a punitive damages award.

Here, we need not dwell long on this guidepost. The most relevant civil sanction under Utah state law for the wrong done to the Campbells appears to be a $10,000 fine for an act of fraud, 65 P.3d, at 1154, an amount dwarfed by the $145 million punitive damages award. The Supreme Court of Utah speculated about the loss of State Farm's business license, the disgorgement of profits, and possible imprisonment, but here again its references were to the broad fraudulent scheme drawn from evidence of out-of-state and dissimilar conduct. This analysis was insufficient to justify the award.

IV

An application of the *Gore* guideposts to the facts of this case, especially in light of the substantial compensatory damages awarded (a portion of which contained a punitive element), likely would justify a punitive damages award at or near the amount of compensatory damages. The punitive award of $145 million, therefore, was neither reasonable nor proportionate to the wrong committed, and it was an irrational and arbitrary deprivation of the property of the defendant. The proper calculation of punitive damages under the principles we have discussed should be resolved, in the first instance, by the Utah courts.

The judgment of the Utah Supreme Court is reversed, and the case is remanded for further proceedings not inconsistent with this opinion.

It is so ordered. . . .

JUSTICE GINSBURG, DISSENTING

Not long ago, this Court was hesitant to impose a federal check on state-court judgments awarding punitive damages. In *Browning-Ferris Industries of Vt., Inc. v. Kelco Disposal, Inc.,* 492 U.S. 257, 109 S.Ct. 2909, 106 L.Ed.2d 219 (1989), the Court held that neither the Excessive Fines Clause of the Eighth Amendment nor federal common law circumscribed awards of punitive damages in civil cases between private parties. *Id.,* at 262–276, 277–280, 109 S.Ct. 2909. Two years later, in *Pacific Mut. Life Ins. Co. v. Haslip,* 499 U.S. 1, 111 S.Ct. 1032, 113 L.Ed.2d 1 (1991), the Court observed that "unlimited jury [or judicial] discretion . . . in the fixing of punitive damages may invite extreme results that jar one's constitutional sensibilities," *id.,* at 18, 111 S.Ct. 1032; the Due Process Clause, the Court suggested, would attend to those sensibilities and guard against unreasonable awards, *id.,* at 17–24, 111 S.Ct. 1032. Nevertheless, the Court upheld a punitive damages award in *Haslip* "more than 4 times the amount of compensatory damages, . . . more than 200 times [the plaintiff's] out-of-pocket expenses," and "much in excess of the fine that could be imposed." *Id.,* at 23, 111 S.Ct. 1032. And in *TXO Production Corp. v. Alliance Resources Corp.,* 509 U.S. 443, 113 S.Ct. 2711, 125 L.Ed.2d 366 (1993), the Court affirmed a state-court award "526 times greater than the actual damages awarded by the jury." *Id.,* at 453, 113 S.Ct. 2711;[1] cf. *Browning-Ferris,* 492 U.S., at 262, 109 S.Ct. 2909 (ratio of punitive to compensatory damages over 100 to 1).

It was not until 1996, in *BMW of North America, Inc. v. Gore,* 517 U.S. 559, 116 S.Ct. 1589, 134 L.Ed.2d 809, that the Court, for the first time, invalidated a state-court punitive damages assessment as unreasonably large. . . .

In *Gore,* I stated why I resisted the Court's foray into punitive damages "territory traditionally within the States' domain." 517 U.S., at 612, 116 S.Ct.

1589 (dissenting opinion). I adhere to those views, and note again that, unlike federal habeas corpus review of state-court convictions under 28 U.S.C. § 2254, the Court "work[s] at this business [of checking state courts] alone," unaided by the participation of federal district courts and courts of appeals. 517 U.S., at 613, 116 S.Ct. 1589. It was once recognized that "the laws of the particular State must suffice [to superintend punitive damages awards] until judges or legislators authorized to do so initiate system-wide change." *Haslip,* 499 U.S., at 42, 111 S.Ct. 1032 (KENNEDY, J., concurring in judgment). I would adhere to that traditional view.

I

The large size of the award upheld by the Utah Supreme Court in this case indicates why damages-capping legislation may be altogether fitting and proper. Neither the amount of the award nor the trial record, however, justifies this Court's substitution of its judgment for that of Utah's competent decisionmakers. In this regard, I count it significant that, on the key criterion "reprehensibility," there is a good deal more to the story than the Court's abbreviated account tells.

Ample evidence allowed the jury to find that State Farm's treatment of the Campbells typified its "Performance, Planning and Review" (PP & R) program; implemented by top management in 1979, the program had "the explicit objective of using the claims-adjustment process as a profit center." App. to Pet. for Cert. 116a. "[T]he Campbells presented considerable evidence," the trial court noted, documenting "that the PP & R program . . . has functioned, and continues to function, as an unlawful scheme . . . to deny benefits owed consumers by paying out less than fair value in order to meet preset, arbitrary payout targets designed to enhance corporate profits." *Id.,* at 118a-119a. That policy, the trial court observed, was encompassing in scope; it "applied equally to the handling of both third-party and first-party claims." *Id.,* at 119a. . . .

Evidence the jury could credit demonstrated that the PP & R program regularly and adversely affected Utah residents. Ray Summers, "the adjuster who handled the Campbell case and who was a State Farm employee in Utah for almost twenty years," described several methods used by State Farm to deny claimants fair benefits. . . . Expert testimony noted by the trial court described these tactics as "completely improper." . . .

Regarding liability for verdicts in excess of policy limits, the trial court referred to a State Farm document titled the "Excess Liability Handbook"; written before the Campbell accident, the handbook instructed adjusters to pad files with "self-serving" documents, and to leave critical items out of files, for example, evaluations of the insured's exposure. *Id.,* at 127a–128a (internal quotation marks omitted). Divisional superintendent Bill Brown used the handbook to train Utah employees. *Id.,* at 134a. While overseeing the Campbell case, Brown ordered adjuster Summers to change the portions of his report indicating that Mr. Campbell was likely at fault and that the settlement cost was correspondingly high. *Id.,* at 3a. The Campbells' case, according to expert testimony the trial court recited, "was a classic example of State Farm's application of the improper practices taught in the Excess Liability Handbook." *Id.,* at 128a. . . .

To further insulate itself from liability, trial evidence indicated, State Farm made "systematic" efforts to destroy internal company documents that might reveal its scheme, App. to Pet. for Cert. 123a, efforts that directly affected the Campbells, *id.,* at 124a. For example, State Farm had "a special historical department that contained a copy of all past manuals on claim-handling practices and the dates on which each section of each manual was changed." *Ibid.* Yet in discovery proceedings, State Farm failed to produce any claim-handling practice manuals for the years relevant to the Campbells' bad-faith case. *Id.,* at 124a-125a.

State Farm's inability to produce the manuals, it appeared from the evidence, was not accidental. Documents retained by former State Farm employee Samantha Bird, as well as Bird's testimony, showed that while the Campbells' case was pending, Janet Cammack, "an in-house attorney sent by top State Farm management, conducted a meeting . . . in Utah during which she instructed Utah claims management to search their offices and destroy a wide range of material of the sort that had proved damaging in bad-faith litigation in the past-in particular, old claim-handling manuals, memos, claim school notes, procedure guides and other similar documents." *Id.,* at 125a. "These orders were followed even though at least one meeting participant, Paul Short, was personally aware that these kinds of materials had been requested by the Campbells in this very case." *Ibid.*

Consistent with Bird's testimony, State Farm admitted that it destroyed every single copy of claim-handling manuals on file in its historical department as of 1988, even though these documents could have been preserved at minimal expense. *Ibid.* Fortuitously, the Campbells obtained a copy of the 1979 PP & R manual by subpoena from a former employee. *Id.,* at 132a. Although that manual has been requested in other cases, State Farm has never itself produced the document. *Ibid.*

"As a final, related tactic," the trial court stated, the jury could reasonably find that "in recent years State Farm has gone to extraordinary lengths to stop damaging documents from being created in the first place." *Id.,* at 126a. State Farm kept no records at all on excess verdicts in third-party cases, or on bad-faith claims or attendant verdicts. *Ibid.* State Farm alleged "that it has no record of its punitive damage payments, even though such payments must be reported to the [Internal Revenue Service] and in some states may not be used to justify rate increases." *Ibid.* Regional Vice President Buck Moskalski testified that "he would not report a punitive damage verdict in [the Campbells'] case to higher management, as such reporting was not set out as part of State Farm's management practices." *Ibid.* . . .

State Farm's "policies and practices," the trial evidence thus bore out, were "responsible for the injuries suffered by the Campbells," and the means used to implement those policies could be found "callous, clandestine, fraudulent, and dishonest." *Id.,* at 136a; see *id.,* at 113a. . . . The Utah Supreme Court, relying on the trial court's record-based recitations, understandably characterized State Farm's behavior as "egregious and malicious." *Id.,* at 18a.

II

The Court dismisses the evidence describing and documenting State Farm's PP & R policy and practices as essentially irrelevant, bearing "no relation to the Campbells' harm." . . . It is hardly apparent why that should be so. What is infirm about the Campbells' theory that their experience with State Farm exemplifies and reflects an overarching underpayment scheme, one that caused "repeated misconduct of the sort that injured them," *ante,* at 1523? The Court's silence on that score is revealing: Once one recognizes that the Campbells did show "conduct by State Farm similar to that which harmed them," *ante,* at 1524, it becomes impossible to shrink the reprehensibility analysis to this sole case, or to maintain, at odds with the determination of the trial court, see App. to Pet. for Cert. 113a, that "the adverse effect on the State's general population was in fact minor," *ante,* at 1525.

Evidence of out-of-state conduct, the Court acknowledges, may be "probative [even if the conduct is lawful in the State where it occurred] when it demonstrates the deliberateness and culpability of the defendant's action in the State where it is tortious. . . ." *Ante,* at 1522; cf. *ante,* at 1521. . . . "Other acts" evidence concerning practices both in and out of State was introduced in this case to show just such "deliberateness" and "culpability." The evidence was admissible, the trial court ruled: (1) to document State Farm's "reprehensible" PP & R program; and (2) to "rebut [State Farm's] assertion that [its] actions toward the Campbells were inadvertent errors or mistakes in judgment." App. 3329a (Order Denying Various Motions of State Farm to Exclude Plaintiffs' Evidence). Viewed in this light, there surely was "a nexus" between much of the "other acts" evidence and "the specific harm suffered by [the Campbells]." *Ante,* at 1522.

III

When the Court first ventured to override state-court punitive damages awards, it did so moderately. The Court recalled that "[i]n our federal system, States necessarily have considerable flexibility in determining the level of punitive damages that they will allow in different classes of cases and in any particular case." *Gore,* 517 U.S., at 568, 116 S.Ct. 1589. Today's decision exhibits no such respect and restraint. No longer content to accord state-court judgments "a strong presumption of validity," *TXO,* 509 U.S., at 457, 113 S.Ct. 2711, the Court announces that "few awards exceeding a single-digit ratio between punitive and compensatory damages, to a significant degree, will satisfy due process." *Ante,* at 1524.[2] Moreover, the Court adds, when compensatory damages are substantial, doubling those damages "can reach the outermost limit of the due process guarantee." *Ibid.;* see *ante,* at 1526 ("facts of this case . . . likely would justify a punitive damages award at or near the amount of compensatory damages"). In a legislative scheme or a state high court's design to cap punitive damages, the handiwork in setting single-digit and 1-to-1 benchmarks could hardly be questioned; in a judicial decree imposed on the States by this Court under the banner of substantive due process, the numerical controls today's decision installs seem to me boldly out of order.

* * *

I remain of the view that this Court has no warrant to reform state law governing awards of punitive damages. *Gore,* 517 U.S., at 607, 116 S.Ct. 1589 (GINSBURG, J., dissenting). Even if I were prepared to accept the flexible guides prescribed in *Gore,* I would not join the Court's swift conversion of those guides into instructions that begin to resemble marching orders. For the reasons stated, I would leave the judgment of the Utah Supreme Court undisturbed.

END NOTES

1. By switching the focus from the ratio of punitive to compensatory damages to the potential loss to the plaintiffs had the defendant succeeded in its illicit scheme, the Court could describe the relevant ratio in *TXO* as 10 to 1. See *BMW of North America, Inc. v. Gore,* 517 U.S. 559, 581, and n. 34, 116 S.Ct. 1589, 134 L.Ed.2d 809 (1996).
2. *TXO Production Corp. v. Alliance Resources Corp.,* 509 U.S. 443, 462, n. 8, 113 S.Ct. 2711, 125 L.Ed.2d 366 (1993), noted that "[u]nder well-settled law," a defendant's "wrongdoing in other parts of the country" and its "impressive net worth" are factors "typically considered in assessing punitive damages." It remains to be seen whether, or the extent to which, today's decision will unsettle that law.

ISSUE SUMMARY

From medical malpractice to accidental death rates, punitive damages are related to a number of other issues. While trying to determine what the appropriate caps and guidelines should be for punitive damages, if any are appropriate in the first place, one should not lose sight of the intention underlying punitive damages. Compensatory damages are intended to assess the place of the victim and try to return him or her to the position he or she would have been in if not for the harm suffered. Conversely, punitive damages are intended to examine the specifics of the defendant and punish the defendant for the wrong that occurred. In addition to serving as punishment, punitive damages are intended to act as deterrence to prevent the defendant and other similarly situated parties from committing the same type of wrong as was at issue in determining the punitive damage award. These two goals, punishment and deterrence, should not be forgotten when discussing potential reforms to how punitive damages are assessed. The authors in this chapter are all aware that determining which punitive damage caps work is not the same as advocating for specific policies regarding punitive damages.

One important consideration in determining the appropriate level of punitive damages is maintaining the purpose of punitive damages while controlling for intended and unintended effects. The articles in this chapter suggest that punitive damages have many effects on other issues, some of which can be predicted and others that may come as a surprise. It seems as if any potential reform needs to consider multiple possibilities and try to create a system that best serves the public as a whole, and one that is hopefully more consistent than the present system.

ISSUE HIGHLIGHTS

- Total losses from tort cases are positively correlated with caps on punitive damages, calling into question the wisdom of capping punitive damages to limit overall awards.
- Caps on punitive damages are correlated with increased defense spending by medical malpractice insurers, which has potential ramifications for allowing injured parties to receive just compensation.
- Caps on punitive damages are associated with a decrease in the accidental death rate, suggesting that caps on punitive damages do not negatively affect the deterrence effect of punitive damages.
- Juries are given inadequate instructions as to how best to assess punitive damages against a defendant.
- Imposing a ratio limit on punitive damages has the greatest impact on blockbuster punitive damage awards, but still would affect some non-blockbuster decisions.

- In a study of various punitive damage caps, as long as jurors could assess some punitive damages the jurors did not raise the compensatory award to allow for a higher overall award.
- When punitive damages were completely barred, jurors tended to increase the compensatory damage award to function both as compensation and as punishment.
- A majority of the Supreme Court has suggested that punitive damage awards should be limited to a single-digit multiplier of the compensatory damage award if the overall award is to avoid judicial scrutiny.
- A minority of the Supreme Court has argued that states, and not the Court, should determine what appropriate punitive damage awards in tort cases are.

CRITICAL THINKING

An important part of assessing any argument is identifying significant ambiguity in the reasoning. Ambiguity is those moments when a word or phrase is used without having one clear meaning. The problem with ambiguity is that it impairs clarity because the ambiguous word or phrase could have multiple possible meanings, and these various meanings could drastically change the point being made. If one party cannot clearly tell what the other meant, there is a potential problem with understanding. The ambiguity is particularly egregious when the word or phrase is critical to a person's main point.

When discussing the efficacy of punitive damage caps, the phrase "punitive damage caps" is a potential significant ambiguity. As was demonstrated by Viscusi in his article, capping punitive damages to either nine times the compensatory damages or capping punitive damages to a level equal with the compensatory award can have radically different effects on the total level of damages. Given these different outcomes, ambiguity in a discussion of punitive damages can lead to confusion as to what the potential ramifications are. A cap of nine times the compensatory damages is not the same as a cap of one times the compensatory damages, and this ambiguity should be cleared up in discussions to keep everyone on the same page.

Also, Greene, Coon, and Bornstein's study included in this chapter discusses multiple types of punitive damage caps. In their findings, jurors tended not to alter the compensatory damages in light of punitive damage caps that limited the total damages that could be given. However, when punitive damages were completely forbidden, the jurors would increase the compensatory damages to function as punitive damages. Given that some caps seem to work, but absolute bans do not, being specific with what types of punitive damages are being discussed is critical to aid in understanding. Furthermore, if Greene, Coon, and Bornstein are correct, jurors need to be able to give some punitive damages or else they will raise the compensatory damages. What is not known is the level at which jurors start to raise compensatory damages to correct for caps on punitive damages. Accordingly, specific language regarding what punitive damage caps are being discussed is needed to reliably use studies such as Viscusi's or Greene, Coon, and Bornstein's.

While the authors in this chapter typically identified what they meant by punitive damage caps, a common theme in many of the articles was the potential impacts of punitive damage caps. Some of these impacts are intended, while others are unintended. Given the potential widespread effects of punitive damage caps, it is important to clear up ambiguity in any discussion of punitive damage caps. Also, as many of the authors acknowledged, there are significant policy implications resting on studies of punitive damage caps. If policymakers misinterpret what type of punitive damage caps a study or expert was discussing, the results could be disastrous. Even in less serious situations, ambiguity hampers understanding and should be avoided whenever possible. When communicating, make sure ambiguous words and phrases are clearly explained. When reading, check to see if authors explain what is meant by ambiguous words or phrases. When ambiguity still exists, be careful about accepting any conclusions without full understanding. Now, skim over the articles you read in this chapter and see if the authors explained what they meant when they said punitive damage caps. Also, are there other words or phrases used that constitute significant ambiguity?

ADDITIONAL READING RESOURCES

Anthony J. Sebok, Punitive Damages: From Myth to Theory, 92 *Iowa Law Review,* 957 (2007).

Brian H. Bornstein, Richard L. Wiener, Robert Schopp & Steven L. Willborn (eds), *Civil Juries and Civil Justice: Psychological & Legal Perspectives* (2007).

David A. Soley, Robert Y. Gwin, and Ann E. Georgehead (eds.), *Business Torts Litigation* (2nd ed. 2005).

Linda L. Edwards and J. Stanley Edwards, *Tort Law for Legal Assistants* (3rd ed. 2003).

Luke Ledbetter, "It's the [Tort System], Stupid": Consumer Deductibles: How to More Equitably Distribute the Risks of Medical Malpractice and Adequately Compensate Victims Without Statutory Damage Caps, 6 *Appalachian Journal Law*, 51 (2006).

Michael P. Murphy, "Would a Noneconomic Damages Cap Be Unconstitutional, and is One Necessary in Iowa?" 53 *Drake Law Review*, 813 (2005).

Robert S. Peck, *Violating the Inviolate: Caps on Damages and the Right to Trial by Jury*, 31 DAYTON L. REV 307 (2006).

Vanessa Ruggles, The Ineffectiveness of Capped Damages in Cases of Employment Discrimination: Solutions Toward Deterrence, 6 *Conn. Pub. Int. L. J.* 143 (2006).

W. Kip Viscusi & Patricia H. Born, Damage Caps, Insurability, and the Performance of Medical Malpractice Insurance, 72 *J. of Risk & Ins.* 23 (2005).

For more information check these cites:

http://home.uchicago.edu/~gbecker/Businessweek/BW/2003/09_15_2003.pdf

http://www.brann-light.com/Pub-TWL/punitive_dam.htm

http://www.consumeraffairs.com/news03/med_mal.html

http://www.justice.org/PressRoom/FACTS/products/howproductliability-reformwouldharmlowincomeamericans.aspx

http://www.rand.org/pubs/research_briefs/RB9028/index1.html

ISSUE 2

Should An Employee Be Able to Be Fired for Any Reason?

Suppose you work for Jones & Co., a small accounting firm. Jones decides that he does not like the way you organize his files. Can he fire you? Alternatively, imagine Jones begins to feel the stress of a slowing economy, and he wants to free up money within his company. Can he fire you? Say Jones just really doesn't like your personality. Can he fire you? If you are an at-will employee, then the answer is probably *yes* in all three scenarios, even though that answer may not seem fair to you. The prevailing employment doctrine in America is the employment-at-will doctrine. Under the doctrine, employers may terminate employees for any legal reason. Granted, there are exceptions to the rule, but the exceptions are not clear-cut. This chapter explores differing opinions about how the employment-at-will doctrine should be modified to create or change exceptions to the doctrine.

The first article in this chapter will introduce the employment-at-will doctrine and related legal concepts. The following articles offer answers to the issue posed in this chapter: Should an employee be able to be fired for any reason? Jones argues that the doctrine should be modified to offer more protection to whistleblowers. Baumgarten thinks that the doctrine in Georgia should be modified to recognize a public policy exception. Scialdone urges Ohio legislators to modify the doctrine to provide more protection to gay, lesbian, and bisexual employees. Rand, unlike the previous authors, argues that the doctrine in Maine should be modified to protect employers from wrongful termination suits.

This section's readings begin with How At-Will Employment Is Changing, an article that defines at-will employment, explains exceptions to the employment-at-will doctrine, and discusses how various courts are approaching modifications to the at-will employment doctrine. For example, you will learn that some states now recognize an "implied contract" that prevents employers from firing employees without just cause. Other courts still enforce the at-will employment doctrine, which allows employers to hire and fire at will. As you will read, there are many situations in which the assumption that an employee is an employee at-will can be negated through public policy exceptions, contracts (both implied and explicit), and guarantees made by employers.

In the second article of this chapter, Jones argues that the whistleblower exception to the common law doctrine of employment-at-will must be interpreted broadly for public policy reasons—to encourage employees to report the illegal and corrupt activities of their organizations without fearing retaliatory termination. Jones explains the employment-at-will doctrine, the whistleblower exception, and how various states have interpreted, expanded, narrowed, and even ignored the whistleblower exception. As a reaction to the stigma, ostracization, and retaliation that whistleblowers face, Jones also proposes more far-reaching, cultural protections for whistleblowers.

In the third article in this chapter, Baumgarten delves deeply into one of the states that Jones could have used as evidence of the consequences of not recognizing the whistleblower exception to the employment-at-will doctrine: Georgia. Baumgarten argues that Georgia, as one of only two states in the country that does not recognize the public policy exception, should join the rest of the country by drastically altering its interpretation of the employment-at-will doctrine. Baumgarten provides proposed legislation, and discusses the advantages of creating the exception through legislative, rather than judicial, action.

In the fourth article in this chapter, Sexual Orientation-Based Workplace Discrimination: Carving a Public Policy Exception to Ohio's At-Will Employment Doctrine, Scialdone argues that Ohio should recognize a public policy exception to the at-will employment doctrine when employees are discriminated against or terminated based upon sexual orientation. Scialdone reviews existing statute and case law in Ohio, examining the courts' varying interpretations of the public policy exception. Scialdone concludes that the existing statute and case law do not provide adequate protection for gay, lesbian, and bisexual employees in Ohio.

The final selection in this chapter is about Maine, a state that does prohibit employers from firing at-will employees based upon sexual orientation. In Employment at Will in Maine: R.I.P.?, Katy Rand presents an argument on behalf of the employment-at-will doctrine as a necessary protection for businesses. She also argues that employment at-will is not threatened by civil rights statutes; rather, employment at-will is eroded when those civil rights statutes are expanded to groups that do not require or need protection. When almost every employee qualifies as a protected employee, Rand contends that employers are forced to keep unproductive employees far too long so that the employers can build a case for for-cause termination, just in case that terminated employee becomes a discrimination plaintiff. Rand is concerned about the interests of employees and shareholders as well, whom she claims are harmed by the inefficient and unproductive workplaces that result when the employment-at-will doctrine is compromised.

As you can see already, reasonable people disagree about when and how the employment-at-will doctrine should be modified. Though the employment-at-will doctrine exists in each state, the exceptions to the doctrine and resulting interpretations differ by state. Numerous advocates see needs for new and varying exceptions; other advocates see the need to restrict the number of exceptions to the doctrine. As you read this chapter, ask yourself what each author is trying to accomplish by modifying the employment-at-will doctrine. Do the authors present convincing arguments for their goals?

ISSUE ARTICLES

"How At-Will Employment Is Changing," *HR Focus* (October 2007), Vol. 84 Issue 10, 1–15.

Julie Jones, "Give a Little Whistle: The Need for a More Broad Interpretation of the Whistleblower Exception to the Employment-At-Will Doctrine," 34 *Texas Tech Law Review*, 1133 (2003).

Nancy Baumgarten, "Sometimes the Road Less Traveled is Less Traveled for a Reason: the Need for Change in Georgia's Employment-At-Will Doctrine and Refusal to Adopt to the Public Policy Exception," 35 *Georgia Law Review*, 1021 (2001).

Frank Scialdone, "Sexual Orientation-Based Workplace Discrimination: Carving a Public Policy Exception to Ohio's At-Will Employment Doctrine," 11 *Law & Sexuality* 193, (2002).

Katy Rand, "Employment At Will in Maine: RIP?" 22 *Maine Bar Journal,* 12 (2007).

ARTICLE 2.1

How At-Will Employment Is Changing

More workplace litigation and other factors are challenging at-will employment. The trend puts into peril the employer's right to hire and fire "at will" in the absence of contractual or other limitations.

What is happening, and how can organizations protect the at-will employment relationship?

AT-WILL, DEFINED

How does the author signal immediately what the perspective of the article will be?

Employment at will is the "default" legal rule of the employment relationship. That is, it generally applies to any private-sector employee who is not covered by a collective bargaining agreement and who does not have an enforceable contract of employment. Employees retained at will may be discharged for any legal reason.

At-will employment frequently is challenged on various allegations that it is an "excuse" for unfair termination. Despite regular attacks, the courts usually uphold the concept.

There are some restrictions at the state level on at-will employment. Montana abolished at-will employment through legislation, while Puerto Rico and the Virgin Islands have "just cause'' statutes requiring that employers identify the cause and reasoning behind terminations subject to scrutiny by the courts. In Colorado, workers enjoy a "rebuttal presumption,'' where the courts have held that if an employee works for an indefinite period without a contract spelling out terms and conditions, he or she is presumed to have rights against termination. South Dakota has a statute stipulating that a "hiring at a yearly rate is presumed to be for one year'' and requires the employer to prove sufficient grounds for termination before the end of that year. (The accompanying table provides information on how states approach at-will employment.) . . .

EXCEPTIONS TO THE RULE

The public policy exception is the most widespread exception to at-will terminations. Violations of public policy laws and protections are not just a reason to throw out a termination; they can cause awards of punitive damages to be paid by an employer.

Examples of public policy exceptions to at-will terminations include employees who report or testify about the employer's illegal activity, refuse to commit crimes on behalf of the employer, decline to work in unsafe conditions or request safety inspections of the workplace, or need leave to perform legal duties such as jury duty and military service.

In many states, courts are ruling against employers when workers demonstrate they were discharged for exercising a right clearly established under such laws as the Family and Medical Leave Act, the Civil Rights Act, the Americans with Disabilities Act, the Fair Labor Standards Act, and Sarbanes-Oxley.

Workers also have raised causes of action in some states for wrongful discharge where they are terminated for refusing to violate professional codes of ethics, especially if these are legislatively endorsed.

In many jurisdictions, it also is against public policy to discharge an employee not only for filing a workers' compensation claim, but also for intending to file one or for filing a claim against a former employer.

Whistleblowing is protected by legislation in many states—under certain conditions. Often the infraction reported must be serious and involve regulations or laws pertaining to public health, safety, or general welfare—and the whistleblowing must be done out of a good-faith concern over the wrongful activity, rather than from a motive such as malice, spite, jealousy, or personal gain. Nuclear safety, Medicare fraud, falsification of medical records, and misuse of public funds have been found to be sufficient public-policy concerns to invoke the protection of whistleblower laws.

Why is it necessary to be very careful about defining whistleblowing?

Retaliatory discharge claims are a second exception to at-will terminations. States use different criteria to determine whether a retaliatory discharge claim is sufficient to offset employment at will. In some jurisdictions, the public policy needed to support a claim must be based on constitutional or statutory provisions.

A third exception is where a contract of employment is implied by statements or actions by the organization or its managers. Such actions include oral promises made to employees or statements made in company policies and employee handbooks.

Vague and general terms are usually too indefinite to create an implied contract. Offers of "permanent" or "lifetime" employment, for example, promises of a position "as long as performance is satisfactory" are not enough to create an employment contract.

In most states, the receipt of an annual or monthly salary does not provide a definite term of employment. An economically motivated reduction in force is just cause for termination even if an employee has an implied contract of lifetime employment.

HANDBOOK CHALLENGES

Courts in most states have taken the position that company manuals or handbooks—even promises made during employment interviews—may constitute "implied contracts.'' Both substantive and procedural contractual protections have been implied from manuals.

Where this rule has been adopted, employers can structure handbooks and manuals to accomplish their objectives, but they cannot defeat legitimate employee expectations by arbitrarily departing from announced policies even though they were under no obligation to institute the polices in the first place.

If the provisions in a manual or personnel policy guide are indefinite, vague, or lack specific contractual terms, however, the manual will not establish contractual rights. The same is true if the language merely declares the employer's general approach to the issues addressed.

An employee's subjective understanding or mere expectation is insufficient to create a binding term of employment. The employee must still identify an oral or written assurance of job security or procedural protection. The court will look to the totality of the circumstances to aid in determining whether a contract exists.

GOOD-FAITH COVENANT

The implied covenant of "good faith and fair dealing'' applicable to at-will employment is recognized by many states. The covenant provides that neither party will do anything that would injure the right of the other to receive the benefits of the arrangement.

Whether the covenant is implied in a particular case depends on the existence of employer representations that have caused employees to reasonably believe they have job security and will be treated fairly. Implied contractual obligations may even coexist with express provisions that seem to negate them where the common expectations of the parties' relationship dictate.

A covenant of good faith and fair dealing does not create a duty on behalf of an employer to terminate its employees only for just cause, however, or to otherwise modify the employment-at-will arrangement.

Courts that decline to recognize contract actions for breach of an implied covenant of good faith and fair dealing reason that such covenants would be wholly inconsistent with the very nature of at-will employment. Some of those courts, however, concede that there could be a cause of action where the employee is deprived of constitutional or statutory rights contrary to public policy or where contractual agreements guarantee the employees may not be fired without "just cause.''

State court decisions are aligning more with the just-cause provisions hammered out over the past half century of litigation and arbitration in the unionized workplace.

PRESERVING AT-WILL

In light of these challenges, what can employers do to preserve at-will status? An employer generally can protect its right to discharge at will by stating in its hiring application that employment can be terminated with or without cause or notice at any time and disavowing any representation to the contrary made by anyone other than designated top company officials.

An employer also can clearly and prominently state in its personnel manual that the handbook does not constitute an express or implied contract or reserve either the right to unilaterally review and change policies and procedures or the right to terminate employees at will. . . .

At-Will Employment Cases: How the States React

State	Implied Contract	Public Policy	Good Faith
Alabama	Yes	No	No
Alaska	Yes	Yes	Yes
Arizona	Yes	Yes	Yes
Arkansas	No	Yes	No
California	Yes	Yes	Yes
Colorado	Yes	Yes	No
Connecticut	Yes	Yes	Yes
Delaware	Yes	Yes	Yes
D.C.	Yes	Yes	No
Florida	No	No	No
Georgia	No	No	No
Hawaii	Yes	Yes	No
Idaho	Yes	Yes	Yes
Illinois	Yes	Yes	No
Indiana	Yes	Yes	No
Iowa	Yes	Yes	No
Kansas	Yes	Yes	No
Kentucky	Yes	Yes	No
Louisiana	No	No	No
Maine	Yes	No	No
Maryland	Yes	Yes	No
Massachusetts	Yes	Yes	Yes
Michigan	Yes	Yes	No
Minnesota	Yes	Yes	No
Mississippi	No	Yes	No
Missouri	No	Yes	No

(continued)

(continued)

State	Implied Contract	Public Policy	Good Faith
Montana	Yes	Yes	Yes
Nebraska	Yes	Yes	No
Nevada	Yes	Yes	No
New Hampshire	Yes	Yes	Yes
New Jersey	Yes	Yes	Yes
New Mexico	Yes	Yes	No
New York	Yes	No	No
North Carolina	Yes	Yes	No
North Dakota	Yes	Yes	No
Ohio	Yes	Yes	No
Oklahoma	Yes	Yes	No
Oregon	Yes	Yes	No
Pennsylvania	Yes	Yes	No
Rhode Island	No	No	No
South Carolina	Yes	Yes	No
South Dakota	Yes	Yes	No
Tennessee	Yes	Yes	No
Texas	Yes	Yes	No
Utah	Yes	Yes	Yes
Vermont	Yes	Yes	No
Virginia	Yes	Yes	No
Washington	Yes	Yes	No
West Virginia	Yes	Yes	No
Wisconsin	Yes	Yes	No
Wyoming	Yes	Yes	Yes

Note: North Carolina: No cases of clear expression.

(Source: BNA)

ARTICLE 2.2

Give a Little Whistle: The Need for a More Broad Interpretation of the Whistleblower Exception to the Employment-At-Will Doctrine

Julie Jones

I. INTRODUCTION

Recent corporate corruption causes one to ask whether the legal system affords employees who blow the whistle on employers' illegal activities the protection necessary to ensure a system of accountability without resorting to a system of tattling or the potential for "crying wolf" situations. The visibility of whistle-blowers has increased with the recent exposure of corruption within WorldCom, the FBI, and Enron. *Time* magazine named three women who blew the whistle on these organizations as the 2002 Persons of the Year: Coleen Rowley of the FBI, Cynthia Cooper of WorldCom, and Sherron Watkins of Enron. Although these three women were not the first to blow the whistle on businesses engaged in corrupt activities, the media and society have scrutinized their high profile employers; and thus, the acknowledgment of these three women illustrates the profound impact of whistleblowing in society. Nonetheless, whistleblowing is not for the faint of heart, and these three women are examples of the consequences of blowing the whistle on wrongful activities in an employment situation. The following high-profile stories exemplify the role of the whistleblower in society and business as well as the stigma attached to whistleblowers.

Coleen Rowley worked for the FBI. She and her Minneapolis office strongly believed that the FBI should keep a probing eye on Zacarias Moussaoui, a man later implicated as a co-conspirator in the attacks of September 11. Unfortunately, her pleadings to the FBI to investigate Moussaoui were ignored. A few months after the attacks, she and several others went to Washington D.C. for interviews by the House and Senate Intelligence Committees concerning their knowledge of Moussaoui's questionable activities, including enrolling at a flight school. Prior to the interview, Rowley made notes about issues she wanted to discuss at the meeting. These notes became a thirteen-page memo she presented to the director of the FBI and two members of the Senate Committee on Intelligence. Rowley never intended for anyone else to read the memo, yet she quickly became the interest of the media. She was then called to Washington D.C. to openly testify about her warnings to the FBI. Rowley's message to the Committee was clear: "The bureau could be great . . . if only it put the goal of protecting Americans above the goal of protecting itself. . . ."

Cynthia Cooper worked her way up the WorldCom ladder. She became the vice president of internal audit. She reported to the audit committee that the board of WorldCom "had been playing dirty with its accounting practices." According to Cooper, the company had inflated its profits by $ 3.8 billion to cover a decline in earnings. Cooper asked Arthur Anderson, the company's accounting firm, about WorldCom's taking of $ 400 million out of its reserve account and adding that amount to its earnings. According to Anderson, this maneuvering of money was not a problem. Anderson told Cooper that she should back away from her inquiries. Cooper believed she might lose her job over her questioning of the company's financial practices. She had even begun to remove personal items from her office. Concerned that Anderson's auditing practices had been called into question during the Enron incident, Cooper directed her team to redo the audit.

Sherron Watkins was the vice president of Enron. When Andrew Fastow, Enron's former Chief Financial Officer, asked her to find some assets within the company to sell off, Watkins noticed bookkeeping problems. When she asked about these nebulous arrangements, no one could or wanted to provide an explanation. Watkins was aware of employees who had questioned the CEO of the company and had been in trouble for doing so. Enron subsequently filed for bankruptcy.

Whistleblowers face a double-edged sword: on one hand they may be viewed as a nuisance to the employer, but on the other hand the whistleblower may be faulted for not telling her superiors about the problem.

> To many . . . the word "whistleblower" represents heroes who risk their lives or careers for the benefit of society. On the other hand, critics perceive them to be nothing short of "tattletales," "snitches," or "industrial spies" who toss out employee loyalty for furtherance of their own political, ethical, moral, or personal agendas.[1]

What are the financial pressures that prevent more people from being "whistleblowers"?

. . . One likes to think that everyone maintains a high level of integrity, yet the clarity of this ideal becomes cloudy when one is walking a narrow fence between putting bread on the table and unemployment. In an attempt to ease the struggle between the good of earning a living and the evil of illegal activity, employees now enjoy more protection from employers who wrongfully terminate employment in response to the employee's reporting of her employer's illegal activity.

The term "whistleblower" originates from the English bobbies' habit of blowing their whistles to indicate that a person is in the process of committing a crime. As used in an employment context, the term "whistleblower" refers to a person " 'who, believing that the public interest overrides the interest of the organization he serves, publicly 'blows the whistle' if the organization is involved in corrupt, illegal, fraudulent, or harmful activity.' " Whistleblowing is an employee's disclosure of his supervisor's or employer's illegal activities to management or law enforcement officials. The objectives of whistleblowing are "to expose, deter, and curtail wrongdoing."[2] Whistleblowing can be an advantageous method of policing employers' activities.

While in theory, whistleblowers provide a necessary and commendable check on an employer's activities, the reality is that employers often retaliate against whistleblowers for the whistleblower's reporting of illegal activities. To make matters worse, society frowns upon whistleblowers because their act of reporting illegal activities makes them "essentially a tattletale, a traitor, a squealer, a turncoat, a rat—all pejorative terms for someone who informs on his co-workers or criticizes the organization which provides his livelihood." These terms are less than complimentary of a person who attempts to put a stop to unlawful activities. Why does society vilify the employee's attempt to do a good deed more than the employer's illegal activity when the whistleblower's motivation is to protect society from the illegal activities of the employer?

Employers justify retaliating against whistleblowers as a necessity "to enforce employee loyalty, to avoid disruptions of employee morale, to preserve internal company security and procedures, or to avoid public embarrassment of the employer." However, the employer's retaliation can severely damage the whistleblower's career. Not only is there a possibility that the employer will terminate a whistleblower's employment, but future employers may resist hiring a person who blew the whistle at a previous job.

An interesting issue regarding whistleblowing arises in employment-at-will situations. Employment-at-will means that the employer can discharge the employee for any reason and the employee can leave for any reason unless there is an express agreement which provides otherwise. Therefore, according to a strict application of the at-will employment doctrine, an employer could terminate a whistleblower without facing liability for the termination. The strict application of employment-at-will, however, disregards the whistleblower's legitimate and respected desire to enforce laws and regulations. To cope with this conflict, many states have created a public policy exception to the employment-at-will doctrine for whistleblowers whose employment has been terminated.

The roots of whistleblower protection run as deep as the American Civil War. In the period since early labor laws, whistleblower protection has become a significant facet of employment. Many states recognize a whistleblower exception to the common law doctrine of at-will employment, but the extent of this protection varies among states.

This comment argues that the whistleblower exception to employment-at-will must be broadly interpreted to foster a more encouraging environment in which employees will feel comfortable sharing information about an employer's illegal activities. . . . This communication of information between employees and authorities is a necessary check on employers in order to curtail an employer's temptation to take advantage of his superior position in the company. . . .

II. EMPLOYMENT-AT-WILL DOCTRINE

Employment-at-will is an integral component of the American labor system. . . . The doctrine of employment-at-will was one of the departures America made when it separated from Great Britain. While employment-at-will is still a viable doctrine, many changes have been made to the notion that employment is terminable for any reason or no reason at all. These changes have evolved over time and have contributed to the dilution of the employment-at-will doctrine.

The employment-at-will doctrine was rigorously followed from the late nineteenth century up to the 1960s. In the 1960s, however, the government began to focus on issues related to quality of life and individual liberties. Although employment-at-will served the goal of encouraging successful businesses, many wrongfully terminated employees had no legal recourse when terminated for reporting their employers' wrongful activities. As a result, courts have moved away from strict adherence to the employment-at-will doctrine. Courts and legislatures have created exceptions to the employment-at-will doctrine. Court-created exceptions to employment-at-will include the following three approaches: (1) a contract-based cause of action, (2) an implied covenant of good faith and fair dealing, and (3) a public policy exception. The public policy exception is the most common exception to employment-at-will. According to the public policy exception, if an employer terminates an employee and a court finds that the termination violates public policy, then the employee may assert a cause of action against the employer for wrongful discharge. The public policy exception first appeared in the 1963 case *Petermann v. International Brotherhood of Teamsters.* This case provided the foundation for the future creation of a cause of action for terminated whistleblowers.

In *Petermann,* an at-will employee refused to follow his employer's request that he falsely testify to a legislative investigative committee. The employer terminated the employee. The defendant in the case argued that because Petermann was an employee at-will, the employer could terminate Petermann's employment at any time for any reason or for no reason at all without incurring liability for wrongful termination. The court disagreed with the defendant's argument and stated that in order to promote the public policy against perjury, the court must " 'deny the employer his generally unlimited right to discharge an employee whose employment is for an unspecified duration, when the reason for the dismissal is the employee's refusal to commit perjury.' " The court held that the employer wrongfully discharged Petermann. The court reasoned that "to hold that one's continued employment could be made contingent upon his commission of a felonious act at the instance of his employer would be to encourage criminal conduct upon the part of both the employee and employer and would serve to contaminate the honest administration of public affairs." After the *Petermann* decision, the public policy exception developed quickly. . . .

In essence, the public policy exception holds that if terminating an employee would be contrary to public policy, then the employer cannot fire the employee. . . .

Since the early 1970s, federal and state statutes have diluted the employment-at-will doctrine. Recognizing the harshness of the application of the employment-at-will doctrine, "the courts have abandoned their former strict allegiance to the doctrine and have commenced to carve out far-reaching exceptions curtailing the employer's wide latitude to discharge." This erosion of the employment-at-will doctrine does not mean, however, that applying the public policy exception is precise or unambiguous. As a result, no uniformity exists among jurisdictions in the way in which they interpret the public policy exception.

III. THE WHISTLEBLOWER EXCEPTION TO EMPLOYMENT-AT-WILL

. . . Whistleblowers play an important role in law enforcement by acting as a means to police employers' business practices. Therefore, the legal system should provide sufficient protection for whistleblowers. Although the employee's reporting of his employer's wrongful activities appears to fall within the pejorative term of "tattletaling," the employee should be validated rather than reviled. Furthermore, the employer's wrongful acts should not be marginalized simply because an employee blows the whistle and exposes the wrongdoing.

One must examine how the whistleblower exception developed in order to understand the spectrum of interpretation which surrounds the exception. The range of interpretation of whistleblower statutes raises questions concerning what the whistleblower exception really stands for. Some states broadly interpret the exception while other states maintain a narrow interpretation.

A. Creation of the Whistleblower Exception

Whistleblowing is one type of public policy exception to employment-at-will. The foundation of the whistleblower exception to employment-at-will emerged as early as the *Petermann* case. Although *Petermann* did not specifically refer to a whistleblower exception, it does reflect the recognition of exceptions to employment-at-will. States that recognize a whistleblower exception to at-will employment realize "the desirability of protecting workers who are willing to speak out against dangerous conditions and illegal activity carried on by co-workers or employers."

The creation of the whistleblower exception was not without reluctance. It took some time before courts were comfortable encroaching upon employer autonomy by allowing a whistleblower exception to at-will employment. Over time, however, some courts recognized the importance of "striking a balance between the competing interests of employer discretion, employee security and public policy." Employees argue for more protection to enforce the laws, and employers argue for less protection because whistleblower complaints cost money and waste resources. Yet, the public interest in ensuring that corporations follow the law outweighs the employer's interest in having control. The law of retaliatory discharge is a necessary remedy "to preserve employees' ability to assert their rights and to promote the interests of the public." Although this balance of the public's interest over the employer's interest favors protection for employees who blow the whistle, not all states have recognized the whistleblower exception to at-will employment. Many states have recognized this exception, but the extent of this exception varies from state to state.

B. Interpretation of the Whistleblower Exception

The extent which the whistleblower exception protects employees at-will depends upon a court's interpretation of the exception. Some courts maintain a narrow exception to the employment-at-will doctrine for whistle-blowers while other courts interpret the whistleblower exception more broadly. An examination of court decisions in several different states sheds light on courts' interpretations of the whistleblower exception.

1. No Recognition of Whistleblower Exception

As recently as August 2002, courts in Virginia held the state does not recognize a whistleblower exception to employment-at-will. Several Virginia cases reflect the Virginia Supreme Court's position. In *Dray v. New Market Poultry Products, Inc.,* Dray inspected the production lines at New Market Poultry Products. After noticing her efforts to prod the other employees to follow proper sanitary rules failed, Dray reported these problems to management, who ignored the deficiencies. Dray then reported the violations of the sanitary rules to on-site governmental inspectors, who confirmed there were unsanitary conditions. In response, Dray's supervisor told her "'that she would be fired if she ever again brought plant sanitary deficiencies to the attention of the . . . governmental inspectors.'" Nevertheless, Dray and quality control inspectors continued to notice problems on the production lines. Believing that Dray had informed the government inspector of newly discovered adulterated poultry products in violation of her supervisor's warning, the employer terminated Dray's employment. Although the court was aware of other jurisdictions which had created exceptions to the employment-at-will doctrine, the court declined to adopt those exceptions. The court held "in the present case, the plaintiff seeks to mount a generalized, common-law 'whistleblower' retaliatory discharge claim. Such a claim has not been recognized as an exception to Virginia's employment-at-will doctrine, and we refuse to recognize it today." . . .

Although the Virginia Supreme Court has held it will not recognize a generalized whistleblower exception to employment-at-will, the court appears to have left the door slightly ajar for future expansion of a whistleblower exception. The courts . . . recognized a narrow public policy exception to employment-at-will in situations where an employee reports an employer's violation of a public policy set forth in a specific state statute and the employee is a member of the class the statute is intended to protect. The courts do not explicitly state they will never recognize a whistleblower exception to employment-at-will. Perhaps future cases involving whistleblower protection will force the Virginia courts to reassess their current narrow interpretation of exceptions to employment-at-will.

2. Broad Approach

New Jersey is an example of a state that offers broad protection for whistleblowers. The Conscientious Employee Protection Act (CEPA) offers protection for whistleblowers in New Jersey. The New Jersey Supreme Court recognized the purpose of the CEPA is to "protect and encourage employees to report illegal or unethical workplace activities and to discourage public and private sector employers from engaging in such conduct." The court also noted CEPA "should be construed liberally to effectuate its important social goal."

What does New Jersey emphasize in its reasoning that Virginia gives little attention to?

New Jersey is one of the few states where courts recognize the whistleblower statute should be broadly interpreted and applied to protect employees who report misconduct of their employers. The court recognizes that protecting whistleblowers has a positive impact on social and public policy. In addition, the New Jersey Supreme Court does not distinguish between different classes of employees protected by the CEPA, but rather notes the Act applies to both public and private employers and employees.

In *Pierce v. Ortho Pharmaceutical Corp.,* the New Jersey Supreme Court noted it "has long recognized the capacity of the common law to develop and adapt to current needs. The interests of the employees, employers, and the public lead to the conclusion that the common law of New Jersey should limit the right of an employer to fire an employee at will." This broad interpretation of the whistleblower exception for public and private employees in New Jersey is quite a contrast from states which protect only public employees. This refreshingly broad interpretation is logical because the New Jersey courts do not draw a line between different classes of employees deserving protection.

3. Narrow Approach

a. Wisconsin • The Supreme Court of Wisconsin has maintained a very narrow whistle-blower exception to employment-at-will. In *Hausman v. St. Croix Care Center,* the defendant nursing home employed the plaintiff. The plaintiff

(Hausman), along with several other employees of the nursing home, felt that several residents of the nursing home were not receiving proper care. Hausman reported her concerns to the director of nursing, but no action was taken to resolve the problems. Because the director of nursing ignored Hausman's complaints, Hausman reported her concerns to the nursing home's administrators. Again, Hausman's complaints fell on deaf ears, and no action was taken to alleviate the problems. Hausman then reported the problems to the Regional Ombudsman who was responsible for "identifying, investigating, and resolving complaints made by or on behalf of providers of nursing home care." He found Hausman's concerns to be legitimate, which resulted in an investigation by the Bureau of Quality Compliance. The investigators from the Bureau of Quality Compliance did not interview Hausman or the other employees who voiced concerns, and they did not issue any citations. The nursing home suspended Hausman and then terminated her employment. The court recognized "the question of whether compliance with an affirmative legal command that causes an employee to report abuse of nursing home residents constitutes an exception to the employment-at-will doctrine is one which this court has not previously faced." The court reasoned that there are exceptions to the employment-at-will doctrine and discussed the plaintiff's request that the court "redefine the public policy exception to the employment-at-will doctrine to include actions for wrongful termination based on particular whistleblowing activities of a discharged employee." However, the court refused to expand the whistleblower exception. It noted "admittedly, adoption of such a wide-ranging whistleblower exception would advance the public interest by encouraging employees in diverse industries to report conduct that threatens the public's health, safety, and welfare. Such a wide extension of existing law by this court, however, would be contradictory to our established precedent."

b. Texas • Texas courts have also grappled with the whistleblower exception to employment-at-will. These courts have made clear that they will not expand the state legislature's exceptions to employment-at-will. *Sabine Pilot Service, Inc. v. Hauck* held that only a narrow exception to the employment-at-will doctrine exists in Texas. In this case, Hauck worked as a deckhand for Sabine Pilot Service. Displayed on the boat which Hauck worked on was a sign stating that pumping bilges into the water was illegal. One of Hauck's daily chores as a deckhand was to empty the bilges into the water. However, he refused to continue pumping the bilges into the water after learning that his work was illegal. Shortly thereafter, Sabine terminated Hauck's employment. Hauck argued his termination resulted from his refusal to engage in the illegal activity. Sabine countered that it fired Hauck for failing to complete other duties assigned to him. The court held that although Texas courts have faithfully followed a strict interpretation of employment-at-will, public policy required the court to recognize a very narrow exception to the doctrine.

In *Johnston v. Del Mar Distributing Co.,* a Texas appellate court agreed that a public policy exception to employment-at-will is necessary but refused to create a private whistleblower exception. The court recognized that state law protects governmental employees from termination for reporting illegal activities of their employers, but since the legislature specifically worded the statute to cover governmental employees only, private employees are not protected from termination after reporting an employer's wrongful activities. . . .

Finally, in *Austin v. HealthTrust, Inc.,* the Texas Supreme Court argued that although these legislative decisions guide Texas courts' reasons for declining to create a common law whistleblower exception to the employment-at-will doctrine, the court would continue to defer to the state legislature the responsibility of creating protections for employees against whom employers have retaliated.

Because Texas courts argue the state legislature has the duty of creating whistleblower protection, legislators have a perfect opportunity to enact legislation which protects both public and private employees. Expanding the narrow whistleblower exception would contribute to more equitable treatment of employees at-will.

IV. EFFECTIVENESS OF THE WHISTLEBLOWER EXCEPTION TO EMPLOYMENT-AT-WILL

The reality of the efficacy of whistleblower protection statutes is rather bleak. While whistleblower statutes purportedly protect the whistleblower, many employees continue to face retaliation and harsh consequences as a result of blowing the whistle on employers' wrongful activities. Whistleblowers become the target of blame when their employers' businesses fail or receive negative attention from media and society. Employers, other employees, and even society can become harsh critics of the whistleblower who appears to be unfaithful to the employer. This critical judgment of a whistleblower's speaking out against his employer's wrongful activities is unwarranted because the employer, not the employee, is the person engaging in the wrongful or illegal act. The employer who has committed the illegal act is to blame, yet the whistleblower becomes a scapegoat for the employer when the employer receives negative attention.

A whistleblower needs not only legal protection from being fired, but also protection against the harsh criticisms of his reputation. Of course, regulations and statutes cannot govern a person's opinion about whistleblowers. Therefore, a change in society's opinion about whistleblowers is needed to help erase the stigma attached to whistle-blowing. Not only would this encourage whistleblowing, it would also serve to protect a person who blows the whistle. Although other employees may continue to respond negatively to their co-workers' whistleblowing, an increase in protection for whistleblowers and a better awareness of the reasons a person may blow the whistle would contribute to wider acceptance of the beneficial role whistleblowers play in the business world.

A. Effect of Whistleblower Exception on Whistleblowers

A whistleblower faces much attention when he decides to expose his employer's wrongdoings. Since co-workers and peers often ridicule whistleblowers, the decision to blow the whistle is difficult and must be carefully evaluated in light of the consequences the person may experience. In order to determine what changes can be made to encourage whistleblowing, one must understand the reaction to and the treatment of whistleblowers.

1. Treatment of Whistleblowers

a. The Decision to Blow the Whistle • The stories of the three women named as the *Time* Persons of the Year are examples of the hostility whistleblowers often experience. Each woman worked for a high-profile, well-respected company or government agency. After recognizing their employers had engaged in wrongful activities, such as manipulating bookkeeping numbers or ignoring obvious warnings to monitor a potential terrorist, these women attempted to correct the appalling errors their employers had knowingly made. While many people at first glance would agree their reporting of these wrongful activities was the right course of action, the real response to these women's actions is quite telling of how people truly feel about whistleblowing. . . .

These women represent the hardships employees face when they choose to blow the whistle on their employer's illegal activities. In fact, two of these women say that if they had it to do all over again, they would not blow the whistle. Even though whistleblower protection laws prevent termination of whistleblowers, these employees still experienced retaliation. Many whistleblowers ultimately suffer from alcoholism or depression. Statistics also indicate some whistleblowers have even attempted suicide after they blew the whistle on their employers and experienced the resulting hostility. These are serious consequences to endure for uncovering someone else's wrongdoings. . . .

b. The Fallout After the Whistle is Blown • Another important question one must consider when examining whistleblower protection is whether blowing the whistle effects changes in businesses. At the FBI, the Director has said "'the level of cooperation [between the field agents and headquarters] is much better'" as a result of Rowley's exposing the communication pitfalls within the FBI. This appears to be what Rowley desired: increased communication so potential threats to security could be prevented. In reality, the FBI has promoted several officials who held leadership positions just prior to the September 11 attacks. According to a former Justice Department official, " 'they have basically promoted the exact same people who have presided over the . . . failure.' " In addition, the FBI promised it would upgrade its computer system so that searches could be more easily conducted. However, the FBI has failed to fulfill this pledge. Although the potential for the FBI to increase the efficiency of its operations so the safety and security of the public at large is not jeopardized, the FBI has seemingly dismissed Rowley's warnings about Moussaoui and has, therefore, left people wondering whether the FBI can put its pride aside and focus on protecting the public.

Likewise, WorldCom owned up to its mistakes after Cooper blew the whistle on fraudulent accounting tactics. The company appointed a new CEO, Michael Capellas, to lead WorldCom out of the mire of corporate fraud and bankruptcy. Although the company faces extraordinary fines, it has retained many of its large accounts and has even gained a few new clients. Capellas expresses very high expectations for WorldCom to re-emerge as a viable and competitive company. Other long-distance companies and critics, however, "aren't so quick to forget the past." Although the company appears to be getting its feet back on solid ground, Bernie Ebbers, the former CEO of WorldCom, has not been charged with anything.

Enron has suffered tremendously from its off-balance-sheet partnerships. Once perceived as a great innovative and modern company, Enron now faces claims of $ 400 billion dollars from investors and employees. Currently, only the former Chief Financial Officer, Andrew Fastow, faces criminal charges. Enron continues to operate under bankruptcy protection, but the likelihood of its re-emergence as a successful company is very doubtful.

The life of the whistleblower is not enviable. Whistleblowers are targets of great criticism and even hatred. This harsh treatment could be alleviated if the legal system would lead the way in shaping society's impressions of whistleblowers by imposing more protection for them.

2. Whistleblower Exception is not an Effective Means of Protecting Whistleblowers

Even though the number of state whistleblower statutes has increased, they have proven to be very ineffective in encouraging whistleblowing or preventing retaliation. The statutes provide a facade of protection for whistleblowers, yet they have not effectively contributed to an increase in whistleblowing or a decrease in retaliation against employees who blow the whistle. Employers' and society's negative views of whistleblowers are two key factors which fuel the plight of the whistleblower. . . .

Due to financial difficulties a whistleblower experiences when bringing actions against his employer, employees are discouraged from bringing valid actions. In addition, since whistleblowers are often seen as tattletales or complainers, whistleblowers may be less likely to bring an action against an employer because of this stigma. Many employees hold loyalty as the highest ideal: they will remain faithful to their employer at all costs.

B. A Proposed Solution for Increasing the Efficacy and Value of Whistleblowing

The recognition of three whistleblowers as the 2002 Persons of the Year has hopefully awakened courts and state legislatures to the need for additional protections for whistleblowers. Whistleblowing plays a significant role in an employment setting because it can provide a measure of accountability between employees and employers. If employers know that one of their employees could report their illegal activities and the whistleblower would be protected against termination, then perhaps employers would be more diligent in following standards and rules in fear of becoming unwilling public figures chastised for engaging in illegal activities.

To ensure this system of accountability is effective, employees must have assurance that they will not be subject to termination by the employer. The legal system must take note that the source of this assurance should be legislation which is judicially enforced. Legislatures need to adapt "their approaches to whistleblowing in order to maximize its benefits and minimize its potentially negative consequences." Since many legislatures have created different groups of people who come within the realm of whistleblower protection laws, confusion may arise as to which classes of employees come within a particular state's whistleblower statute. State legislatures must be conscious of the fact that distinguishing between different classes of people deserving protection from termination can be problematic. Saying that one particular type of employee is more worthy of protection than another employee simply by virtue of his field of employment raises questions about fairness. Both public and private employees should have whistleblower protection so that they will feel confident and willing to expose their employers' illegal activities.

V. CONCLUSION

Whistleblowing has recently emerged in the spotlight of the corporate world. The passage of the Sarbanes-Oxley Act of 2002 by Congress indicates that people may be more inclined to take whistleblowing seriously. In the past, whistleblowers have chosen to follow a lonely road because few or ineffective protections existed for them. Whistleblowing in an employment-at-will setting, although merely one area of employment where whistleblowers find little support, represents how the law and society tend to view these "tattletales" and how the legal system must effect changes in whistleblower protection laws to defend whistleblowers. With the creation of more exceptions to the employment-at-will doctrine, one might argue employment-at-will may soon disappear altogether. Still, the creation of many of these exceptions is a necessary first step in providing the protection employees deserve and should be considered more important than maintaining the employment-at-will doctrine, a doctrine which is contrary to the idea that people should adhere to the rules and if they do not follow the law, then they must accept responsibility for their actions.

The law should not penalize whistleblowers for having the courage to speak out against their employers who engage in illegal activities. With the creation of broader whistleblower protection, employers will feel a sense of responsibility and accountability, and employees will have the ammunition to step up and fight for what is right without fearing threats to their careers.

The legal system as a whole must take charge of this mandate for increasing protections for whistleblowers. Working together in a concerted effort, the legal system can lead society in forming a more positive and encouraging environment for blowing the whistle on employers' illegal activities.

END NOTES

1. Joan Corbo, Kraus v. New Rochelle Hosp. Med. Ctr.: *Are Whistleblowers Finally Getting the Protection They Need?,* 12 HOFSTRA LAB. & EMP. L.J. 141, 141 (1994).
2. Elletta Sangrey Callahan & Terry Morehead Dworkin, *The State of State Whistleblower Protection,* 38 AM. BUS. L.J. 99, 100 (2000).

ARTICLE 2.3

Sometimes the Road Less Traveled Is Less Traveled for a Reason: The Need for Change in Georgia's Employment-at-Will Doctrine and Refusal to Adopt the Public Policy Exception

Nancy Baumgarten

I. INTRODUCTION

Imagine that after years of hard work, you are finally given the opportunity to hold an exciting job—you have been hired as a security guard for a major power company. You learn subsequently that a construction superintendent is engaging in criminal activities. Just as you are about to reveal these illegal acts, your employment at the company is terminated. You bring an action against your former employer for wrongful and malicious discharge, but the court grants summary judgment in favor of the company that fired you.

Imagine now that you obtain another job in a convenience store. Your employer requests that you submit to a "Psychological Stress Evaluation" test, which seeks to analyze the truthfulness of your answers to questions by measuring voice stress. Upon completion of the test, you are discharged from the store. You bring a suit for wrongful termination against your former employer, alleging that your employer made known to others that your termination resulted from your test, causing you great embarrassment and suffering. The court dismisses your case for failure to state a claim upon which relief can be granted. The court reasons that "[w]here the plaintiff's employment is terminable at will, the employer, with or without cause and regardless of the motives involved, can discharge the employee without incurring liability."

Now imagine that you are pregnant. This joyful news, however, is coupled with the devastation you experience upon learning that your job has been terminated. You bring an action against your former employer alleging wrongful discharge because of your physical condition. The court, however, grants summary judgment to the employer because there are no public policy exceptions to the termination of at-will employees on grounds of gender or pregnancy related issues.

Finally, imagine that after faithfully working for a company for twenty years in the area of safety management, you are terminated from your position. You bring a claim alleging that your termination violated the Federal Age Discrimination in Employment Act (ADEA). The court dismisses your complaint for failure to state a cognizable claim. Since the Georgia General Assembly never explicitly enacted a legislative exception for the discharge of employees on the basis of age, the court denies you the chance to uncover the truth behind your termination.

Unfortunately, the cases "imagined" above were not hypotheticals, but rather realities faced by four discharged employees in the state of Georgia over the course of the last quarter century. In each of these cases, the court did not even give these individuals a chance to prove their allegations; instead their cases were either dismissed on the pleadings or at the summary judgment stage. In each case, the plaintiff had no claim because of Georgia's unwavering adherence to an at-will employment doctrine that favors employers and the state's obstinate refusal to adopt an exception that could have potentially given all four former employees a chance to bring claims in our courts.

Georgia's employment-at-will doctrine stipulates that if an employer and employee enter into an employment relationship for an unspecified period of time, the relationship is terminable at the will of either party. This doctrine permits an employer to terminate the relationship "for good cause, for no cause or even for cause morally wrong, without being thereby guilty of legal wrong." Georgia has codified this doctrine:

If a contract of employment provides that wages are payable at a stipulated period, the presumption shall arise that the hiring is for such period, provided that, if anything else in the contract indicates that the hiring was for a longer term, the mere reservation of wages for a lesser time will not control. An indefinite hiring may be terminated at will by either party.

Throughout the past twenty years, the employment-at-will rule has been significantly limited in its application and scope throughout the country. Criticizing its harshness to employees as well as its outdated nature, many courts have adopted common-law exceptions to the rule. The exceptions designed to eliminate some of the rule's harsh and arbitrary effects fall into the following categories: (1) the implied contract, (2) the covenant of good faith and fair dealing, and (3) the public policy exception.

The theory used by most courts to modify the employment-at-will doctrine is the public policy exception, which is the subject of this Note. This exception is recognized where an employee's discharge is in violation of public policy. The theory rests upon the underlying sentiment that "basic public policy overrides the freedom of contract embodied in the traditional at-will rule."

Most states recognize the public policy exception. As of 1995, five states had refused to recognize this exception to the employment-at-will doctrine. They included Florida, Mississippi, New York, Alabama, and Georgia. Today, however, Georgia and Alabama remain the only two states that still refuse to recognize this exception to the employment-at-will doctrine. While taking the "road less traveled" is often the noble and difficult path, this Frostian notion does not apply to the employment-at-will doctrine. As comedian Jerry Seinfeld has noted, "sometimes the road less traveled is less traveled for a reason." This Note contends that it is time for Georgia to join the rest of the nation and recognize the public policy exception. . . .

II. THE PUBLIC POLICY EXCEPTION

The claim available under the public policy exception is commonly referred to as "retaliatory discharge," "wrongful discharge," or "discharge in derogation of public policy." It prevents employers from undermining clearly defined public policy goals defined by society and the legislature. It also seeks to prevent employers from abusing their power in the at-will employment relationship.

What would employers call a so-called "retaliatory discharge"?

The public policy/retaliatory discharge exception originated in the California case of *Petermann v. Teamsters Local 396*. In Petermann, an employee alleged that his employer discharged him for testifying truthfully before a legislative committee instead of committing perjury, as he was encouraged to do. The employee was held to have a cause of action for unlawful termination contrary to the state's public policy. Because the discharge allegedly occurred in response to the employee's refusal to perform an act that would violate a criminal statute, the Petermann court recognized a new cause of action: unlawful termination contrary to the public policy of California.

Given the apparent "lawless" nature of the at-will doctrine, the need for this exception is evident. . . .

The public policy exception is a fair doctrine because it balances the protections offered to the employee, employer, and society at large. Employees have job security because they will not be discharged for reasons which contravene public policy. Employers maintain the freedom to make decisions with regard to their corporate structures as long as their conduct does not violate public policy. And society benefits through the creation of a more stable employment market, the maintenance of public policies and values, and the elimination of litigation by dissatisfied employees.

Both the strength and the weakness of this exception lie in the amorphous concept of "public policy." While this characteristic has created a flexible doctrine capable of application in a wide variety of situations, it has also resulted in an exception that is virtually indefinable. It has consequently been argued that determining what constitutes "public policy" is the Achilles' heel of the doctrine itself.

Since the difficulty in defining public policy has created most of its problems, courts have identified sources from which to justify this exception, which include constitutions, statutes, administrative regulations, the common law, and general notions of right and wrong. The use of nonlegislative sources to discern public policy has generated controversy. Due to the vagueness of the public policy exception, some courts leave the development of the exception to legislatures. Courts adhering to this view typically reject judicial decisions as appropriate sources of public policy. This may, however, ultimately deny an employee a cause of action simply because the public policy was not expressed by a legislature.

In 2001, Georgia and Alabama are the only two states which do not recognize the public policy exception in its full form. The rest of the country recognizes the public policy exception through either common or statutory law.

Although no uniform set of elements has been established for the public policy exception, Professor Henry H. Perritt Jr. has offered the following four element test in an attempt to establish some guidelines for the courts:

1. Clarity: The existence of a clear public policy manifested in a state or federal constitution, statute, or administrative regulation, or in the common law.
2. Jeopardy: That dismissing employees for the conduct like that of the plaintiff would jeopardize the public policy.
3. Motivation: That the plaintiff's dismissal was motivated by conduct related to the public policy.
4. No justification: That the employer lacked overriding legitimate business justification for the dismissal.

There are several situations in which the public policy exception may arise. These include: (1) an employee's refusal to commit an unlawful or illegal act; (2) an employee's fulfillment of a public obligation; (3) an employee exercising a right or privilege; (4) an employee exposing some wrongdoing by the employer; and (5) an employee performing some act that public policy would support or refusing to perform some act in opposition to public policy.

III. A SAMPLING OF GEORGIA CASE LAW REGARDING THE EMPLOYMENT-AT-WILL DOCTRINE AND THE REFUSAL TO ADOPT THE PUBLIC POLICY EXCEPTION

Although as early as 1936, Georgia courts were advancing the notion that "an indefinite hiring may be terminated at will by either party," a survey of Georgia case law in the employment context reveals a pro-employer undercurrent, especially in wrongful discharge cases.

A. *In Land v. Delta Air Lines, Inc.*

Mr. Land was employed by Delta Airlines as a freight service agent. When he was discharged for an on-the-job injury which resulted in his incapacity to work, he filed suit against Delta for wrongful discharge. Land claimed that Delta made an oral contract with him that his employment would last for the remainder of his life or until he decided to retire.

The court determined that the evidence offered by Land failed to prove the existence of a lifetime employment contract. Relying on Georgia's statutory codification of the employment-at-will doctrine, the court ruled that the plaintiff did not have a cause of action.

B. *Goodroe v. Georgia Power Company*

Mr. Goodroe was hired as a security officer by the Georgia Power Company in 1975. He brought an action against his former employer claiming that he had been discharged in 1976 without cause. He also claimed that there had been a conspiracy against him that led to his discharge. When the defendant answered that the employment was at will and could consequently be terminated by either party at any time and for any reason, Goodroe amended his complaint. He alleged that Georgia Power terminated him because he was about to uncover criminal activities.

The Court of Appeals affirmed the lower court's grant of summary judgment for the employer. Even though Goodroe urged the court to find an exception to the employment-at-will doctrine, the court refused to do so because the statute did not provide for the exception.

C. *Evans v. Bibb Company*

Mr. Evans brought an action for wrongful discharge against Bibb Company, alleging that he had been wrongfully discharged for trying to pursue his rights under Georgia's Worker's Compensation Act. In line with Georgia's precedent, the Court of Appeals affirmed the lower court's decision that an at-will employee may not bring an action for wrongful discharge.

As in Goodroe, Evans urged the court to adopt a public policy exception. The Georgia Court of Appeals refused to do so, recognizing that other states have adopted the public policy exception; however, due to the lack of express statutory provisions allowing a retaliatory discharge claim, the court would not create such a remedy. Echoing the explanation in the Goodroe case, the court stated that "[c]ourts may interpret laws, but may not change them."

D. *Mr. B's Oil Company, Inc. v. Register*

Ms. Register, who had been hired to work in a convenience store owned by Mr. B's Oil Company, was required to take a "Psychological Stress Evaluation" ("PSE") shortly after beginning work. The purpose of this test was to use voice stress as a means of analyzing the accuracy of an employee's answers to specific questions. When Register was terminated after taking the PSE, she brought suit against her employer for wrongful termination. The Court of Appeals reversed the lower court's refusal to dismiss the case for failure to state a claim, leaving Register without any cause of action. This was despite the fact that she further alleged that the employer had told others the circumstances of her termination, which resulted in great embarrassment and suffering.

While this case again displayed Georgia's firm adherence to the employment-at-will doctrine, Judge Benham strongly opposed Georgia's refusal to adopt the public policy exception. He opined that Georgia's adherence to the employment-at-will rule was "much too harsh, and the more enlightened view is that adopted by other states." Moreover, he stressed that the Georgia courts have recognized the inadequacies of the employment-at-will doctrine, even though they had not recognized the public policy exception.

E. *Borden v. Johnson*

A former at will employee brought an action against her former employer for wrongful discharge on the basis of her pregnancy. The Court of Appeals affirmed the lower court's grant of summary judgment for the employer on the grounds that the employee failed to show that her discharge violated a public policy recognized by the legislature.

The court explained further that the legislature has created some 'public policy' exceptions to the at-will employment doctrine in Georgia. The court cited statutes that prohibit the discharge of an employee because his wages have been subject to garnishment for any one indebtedness; criminalize the discharge of employees due to age; give an employee who has been discharged for attending a judicial proceeding in response to a court order a cause of action to recover damages and attorney's fees; and finally, provide an employee discharged due to a handicap a chance to initiate a civil action against his former employer.

Since the employee's pregnancy and the consequent discharge were not covered by any of the statutorily defined exceptions created by the legislature, the plaintiff in Borden did not have a valid claim for relief.

IV. THE NEED FOR CHANGE IN GEORGIA

The foregoing survey of Georgia cases reveals that absent a specific legislative exception to the employment-at-will doctrine, the courts will refuse to recognize the public policy exception. The courts do not feel, however, that Georgia plaintiffs are without a cause of action. Rather, courts refer employees to federal statutes for wrongful discharge.[1]

A. A Federal Remedy May Not Always Be Available for a Plaintiff

While the notion of an available federal remedy is reassuring, it inevitably raises the question of whether federal law reaches employer conduct that would undermine Georgia public policy. Title VII provides:

It shall be unlawful employment practice for an employer

(1) to fail or refuse to hire or to discharge any individual, or otherwise to discriminate against any individual with respect to his compensation, terms, conditions, or privileges of employment, because of such individual's race, color, religion, sex, or national origin. . . .

While this statute provides a remedy for certain forms of employment discrimination, it offers no protection in some situations commonly covered by the public policy exception, such as the employee's refusal to perform an illegal act. Title VII, moreover, has significant limitations. First, the term "employer" is defined as "a person engaged in an industry affecting commerce who has fifteen or more employees for each working day in each of twenty or more calendar weeks in the current or preceding calendar year. . . ." Accordingly, a plaintiff who is employed by an employer with less than fifteen employees would not be protected by the federal statute.

Furthermore, in order to claim a violation of Title VII, the charge must "be filed within one hundred and eighty days after the alleged unlawful employment practice occurred. . . ." A Georgia plaintiff, unaware of this filing requirement, may miss the opportunity to bring a cause of action under federal law against his or her employer. A plaintiff would be especially likely to miss the federal deadline if a Georgia plaintiff brought an action in state court prior to bringing an action in federal court. By the time the case is dismissed in state court, it is highly likely that the one hundred and eighty day limitation will have passed.

Another significant limitation to federal recovery can be found in Title VII. This limitation is described as follows:

[Title VII] shall not apply to an employer with respect to the employment of aliens outside any State, or to a religious corporation, association, educational institution, or society with respect to the employment of individuals of a particular religion to perform work connected with the carrying on by such corporation, association, educational institution, or society of its activities.

Thus, federal statutes prohibiting unlawful employment practices do not apply to all situations. Even if a plaintiff falls within the parameters of Title VII, there are still significant limitations on the recovery under federal law. . . .

Even when the Title VII requirements are met, recovery is limited. One limitation applies to punitive damages. Punitive damages are recoverable only if the defendant acted with malice or reckless indifference to the federal rights of the individual and are not recoverable from governmental entities. A second limitation is the cap placed on the amount of compensatory and punitive damages that an employee may recover. Had the plaintiff been entitled to bring a state cause of action, the stringent requirements and caps of federal relief might not exist.

It is important to realize that when Title VII was enacted, Congress did not intend for it to be the sole remedy available for employees discharged wrongfully. The statute itself provides:

Nothing in this subchapter shall be deemed to exempt or relieve any person from liability, duty, penalty, or punishment provided by any present or future law of any State or political subdivision of a State, other than any such law which purports to require or permit the doing of any act which would be an unlawful employment practice under this subchapter.

This section shows that the federal statute would not preempt state statutes or laws purporting to provide remedies for employees, so long as they do not violate Title VII.

B. The Public Policy Exception Is in Line with Georgia's Policies in Other Areas of Law

Georgia should adopt the public policy exception to the employment-at-will doctrine because such an exception conforms with Georgia's policies in other areas of law. Consider Georgia contract law, where it is firmly established that "a contract to do an immoral or illegal thing is void." While violations of public policy may not always be considered "immoral or illegal," there is an underlying current of a sense of "wrong" inherent in such violations. In Georgia, parties have the freedom to contract as they wish. Therefore, contracts typically will not be voided as against public policy, "except where the case is free from doubt and where an injury to the public interest clearly appears." The courts have adopted the rule that a contract is not contrary to public policy unless it has been declared so by the General Assembly, the consideration of the contract is against good morals or law, or the contract has been executed in order to effect an illegal or immoral agreement.

Why does the author argue that the law should be consistent with other Georgia law?

Georgia's courts are willing to invalidate contracts on the ground that they violate public policy. If these violations are recognized in contract law, by extension public policy grounds should be recognized in the employment context because employment is contractual. It is true that when the employment-at-will doctrine applies, there is no express contract between the employer and employee for a specific length of employment. Nevertheless, there is an individual providing services for an employer in exchange for compensation, an implied form of a contractual relationship. It is indeed ironic that Georgia does not uphold an immoral or illegal contract agreement, but does uphold an immoral termination of an employment "contract.". . .

V. PROPOSAL FOR CHANGE IN GEORGIA THROUGH LEGISLATIVE MEANS

. . . Given the Georgia courts' insistence that a change to the employment-at-will doctrine should come from the legislature, it is more likely that a successful public policy exception will eventually be implemented, if at all, in Georgia through legislative action. A legislative, as opposed to a judicial exception, has distinct advantages. A judicially created exception, such as the public policy exception, may provide little guidance to "facilitate an acceptable compromise between ensuring employees' rights and affording employers predictability."

This can often result in the opening of a "Pandora's Box" of potentially frivolous litigation.

The legislature can offer more consistency in developing a suitable limitation for the exception. The Georgia legislature should consider four principal issues regarding the creation of wrongful discharge legislation: (1) the protections and standards that should govern terminations of employment relations; (2) the act's coverage and whether or not economic motivations and layoffs should be covered; (3) the common law remedies and statutory damages available to terminated employees; and (4) the procedural and dispute resolution methods that the act should utilize. In addition, consideration should be given to the appropriate sources for defining and determining public policy.

An effective statute would need to balance a limitation of the discretion of courts with the flexibility needed for application to new situations. One proposed statute reads as follows:

The Public Policy Exception to the Employment-at-Will Doctrine

(1) For a claim for damages to be recognized for the public policy exception, all of the following criteria must be met:

(a) Where the exception is a logical and clear extension of articulated legislative intent to protect an employee's right; and

(b) Where the exception is of at least equally serious import as a statute; and

(c) The complaint has been brought within two years from the time of dismissal.

(2) Any party can request arbitration and such arbitration shall be allowed only with the consent of the other party. If a party refuses to arbitrate and loses the case in the courts, that party shall be liable for all court costs incurred.

(3) Remedies for a wrongful termination action based on a public policy exception shall be limited to:

(a) Backpay: Such backpay shall be reduced by an amount which could have been made had the claimant made reasonable attempts to procure other employment.

(b) Frontpay: (i) Such frontpay shall not be extended for more than a period of two years; and (ii) Shall be reduced by any amount received as a result of future employment enabled by the claimant's termination or such an amount had the claimant made reasonable attempts to procure future employment.

(c) Attorney fees: Such fees shall be recoverable from the employer in a successful action by the claimant.

(d) Reinstatement shall be an option only if both parties agree.

(4) Only in cases of egregious behavior on the part of the employer shall punitive damages be awarded.

Such a statute could serve as a guide for the Georgia legislature. The adoption of another state's public policy exception statute would bring with it the advantage of affording Georgia's courts the wisdom and experience of that state's judicial decisions interpreting, applying, and explaining the statute in concrete situations. Georgia is in an enviable position when it considers adoption of the public policy exception at such an advanced stage in the development of the doctrine. The entire nation offers examples from which Georgia can choose the best approach for its state policy. The availability of such a vast expanse of data should allay any fears that the Georgia legislature and courts may have about the adoption of this exception.

VI. CONCLUSION

The time has come for Georgia to adopt the public policy exception to the employment-at-will doctrine. Georgia cannot afford to shut the door on plaintiffs fired for unjust causes, leaving them without a remedy at the state level. Federal relief may not always be an option for a plaintiff, and employees in Georgia are not entitled to the same protections afforded by forty-eight of the other states in the country. . . .

Furthermore, Georgia should realize that adopting this exception would bring employment law in line with Georgia's policies in other areas. Consistency throughout the different substantive arenas of Georgia law is indeed important. Failure to provide such consistency undermines the strength of Georgia's support of public policy measures in other areas.

If the Georgia legislature enacts a statute implementing this exception, then it has the great advantage of models in many other states from which to garner guidance. A study of the other states' systems can alleviate any fears that Georgia may have that an exception would end up swallowing the rule.

END NOTE

1. Id. It is significant to note that while Borden v. Johnson does suggest the possibility of federal statutory remedies, it never provides an example of such a statute.

ARTICLE 2.4

Sexual Orientation-Based Workplace Discrimination: Carving a Public Policy Exception to Ohio's At-Will Employment Doctrine

Frank Scialdone

I. INTRODUCTION

Ohio's at-will employees have few protections against workplace discrimination based on sexual orientation. Currently, there are no federal or Ohio statutes that specifically prohibit private or public workplace sexual orientation-based discrimination. With no statutory protections, Ohio employees subjected to this type of discrimination must rely on alternative ways to obtain legal recourse. One of those ways is to argue that sexual orientation-based discrimination in the workplace violates public policy and is therefore an exception to Ohio's doctrine of at-will employment.

Without direct state or federal statutory enactments, the public policy exception may be an increasingly effective means to obtain legal recourse in some regions. There are several indications that Ohio has a sufficiently clear public policy against employment practices that discriminate on the basis of sexual orientation.

First, one state court has specifically held that Ohio has a clear public policy against employers who discriminate on the basis of sexual orientation in violation of a municipal ordinance. Moreover, a federal district court in Ohio has likewise found that clear public policy can be established on the basis of a city ordinance prohibiting sexual orientation discrimination.

Second, while federal and state legislators have been slow to enact legislation against discrimination based on sexual orientation, smaller municipalities have increasingly enacted this type of legislation. Importantly, three of Ohio's ten largest cities have laws that prohibit workplace discrimination on the basis of sexual orientation, as do several suburban and rural municipalities.

Third, the Supreme Court of Ohio's adoption of the Code of Professional Responsibility, Judicial Code of Conduct, prohibits bias on the basis of sexual orientation in the performance of judicial duties, which is applicable to the entire state judiciary.

Fourth, although Governor Bob Taft recently removed "sexual orientation" from a fifteen-year-old executive order that prohibited employment bias within the state government, he has publicly declared that the deletion is only to ensure that "all Ohio citizens have equal employment opportunity" vis-a-vis state jobs. . . .

Before you read the reasoning in this essay, what is incomplete or potentially flawed about these reasons?

II. BACKGROUND

A. Ohio Employment Laws and Sexual Orientation Discrimination

. . . Without a statute or an executive order prohibiting private or public employment discrimination on the basis of sexual orientation, many aggrieved employees have consequently argued that sexual orientation as the sole basis of termination is a violation of the Equal Protection Clause of the Fourteenth Amendment to the United States Constitution. In a recent case, *Glover v. Williamsburg Local School District Board of Education*, the United States District Court for the Southern District of Ohio, while recognizing that gays and lesbians are not a suspect class, held that "state action which discriminates against homosexuals and is motivated solely by animus towards that group" necessarily violates the Equal Protection Clause, because a "desire to effectuate one's animus against homosexuals can never be a legitimate governmental purpose." Because very few actions can be proven to be motivated "solely by animus" toward homosexuals, and because the equal protection argument only applies to government actions, most Ohio citizens have no legal recourse against employment discrimination on the basis of sexual orientation.

Aggrieved employees fired on the basis of sexual orientation have also sought legal recourse by arguing that this type of wrongful discharge violates Ohio public policy. One of the benefits of this approach is that it potentially provides a legal option to all Ohio citizens. To date, there have been three cases—two reported and one unreported—that address the public policy exception to at-will employment involving sexual orientation discrimination.[1] Interestingly, the cases yield differing results. These three cases and the argument for the recognition of the existence of a public policy prohibiting sexual orientation discrimination in the workplace are the focuses of this Article and are treated in Parts III and IV, respectively.

B. At-Will Employment in Ohio and the Public Policy Exception

In Ohio, the doctrine of at-will employment provides that an employer can terminate an employee "for any cause, at any time whatsoever, even if done in gross or reckless disregard of any employee's rights."[2] The Supreme Court of Ohio softened this harsh rule by creating a tort-based public policy exception to the employment-at-will doctrine. The employer's wrongful discharge, however, must violate a "sufficiently clear" public policy.

The Supreme Court of Ohio first embraced a public policy exception to at-will employment in the 1990 case of *Greeley v. Miami Valley Maintenance Contractors, Inc.* In Greeley, the court recognized a limited public policy exception allowing recovery only "when an employee is discharged or disciplined for a reason which is prohibited by statute."

In 1994, the Supreme Court of Ohio in *Painter v. Graley* significantly expanded the sources from which a public policy exception could be established. The Painter court held that the public policy sufficient to justify an exception to the employment-at-will doctrine is not limited to public policy expressed by the General Assembly in the form of statutory enactments. The existence of such a public policy may be discerned by the Ohio judiciary based on sources such as the constitutions of Ohio and the United States, legislation, administrative rules and regulations, and the common law.

The Painter court also provided direction for lower courts to determine whether an employee's wrongful discharge violated public policy, suggesting that the lower courts might find the analysis formulated by Villanova Professor Henry H. Perritt useful in developing case law in this area. Professor Perritt's analysis requires a plaintiff-employee to establish:

1. That clear public policy existed and was manifested in a state or federal constitution, statute, or administrative regulation, or in the common law (the clarity element);
2. Dismissing employees under circumstances like those involved in the plaintiff's dismissal would jeopardize the public policy (the jeopardy element);
3. The plaintiff's dismissal was motivated by conduct related to the public policy (the causation element); and
4. The employer lacked any overriding legitimate business justification for the dismissal (the overriding justification element).

In subsequent cases, the Supreme Court of Ohio has noted that the "clarity" and "jeopardy" elements of the tort of wrongful discharge in violation of public policy are questions of law to be determined by the courts. . . .

The cases following Painter indicate that Ohio courts have primarily, but not exclusively, recognized a public policy exception to the at-will employment doctrine based on statutory sources. In *Kulch v. Structural Fibers, Inc.*, the Supreme Court of Ohio recognized a public policy exception based on the Occupational Safety and Health Act (OSHA) provision that prohibits retaliation against employees who file OSHA complaints. The court also relied on other statutory provisions favoring safety in the workplace. In *Collins v. Rizkana*, the court again held that "a cause of action may be brought for wrongful discharge in violation of public policy based on sexual harassment/discrimination."

In Stephenson v. Litton Systems, Inc., the Ohio Court of Appeals for Montgomery County recognized a public policy that favors removing drunk drivers from state roads. In Stephenson, an employee was terminated after notifying the police that her supervisor was going to be driving while intoxicated. The court based its finding of sufficient public policy on the "sweeping enactments by the General Assembly" designed to discourage drunk driving, and, in part, on the existence of a police drunk driving hotline that was well publicized at the time. . . .

In *Simonelli v. Anderson Concrete Co.*, the Court of Appeals for Franklin County held that firing an at-will employee for consulting an attorney could serve as a basis for the public policy exception. Based on a federal district court case in Iowa, the court reasoned that the "legislative recognition of the power of the state judiciary to regulate the legal profession . . . the fact that lawyers, as guardians of the law, play an important role in the preservation of society; [and] the adoption by the Iowa Supreme Court of the Code of Professional Responsibility, which articulates the public policy that citizens of the state are entitled to access to professional legal services" provided a basis for the public policy exception to the employment-at-will doctrine. The court further noted "that a consultation with a lawyer is so fundamental to our system of justice that an employer's discharge of an employee for consulting a lawyer would violate public policy."

III. OHIO CASE LAW: THE PUBLIC POLICY EXCEPTION AND SEXUAL ORIENTATION

A. *Greenwood v. Taft, Stettinius & Hollister* (1996)

In *Greenwood v. Taft, Stettinius & Hollister,* a plaintiff-attorney employed by a Cincinnati-based law firm brought a wrongful discharge action against his former employer. The plaintiff alleged that he was terminated for being homosexual and for working on behalf of a homosexual cause. The Court of Appeals for Hamilton County held that a Cincinnati ordinance prohibiting employment discrimination based on sexual orientation was insufficient to support a public policy exception to the employment-at-will doctrine. The court stated that a sufficient public policy exception "must be of uniform statewide application; it cannot be fragmentary, as with a single municipal ordinance." Unfortunately, in Greenwood, the plaintiff could not contend that his dismissal was in violation of the Ohio Code of Professional Conduct because he did not raise the argument at the trial level.

In 1996, the Supreme Court of Ohio denied a motion for a discretionary appeal. Justice Pfeifer dissented because he believed that the case involved "a matter of great public or general interest." He opined that the case presented novel legal questions that deserved answers, such as:

Can an employer in Ohio fire an employee based upon his sexual preference? Does the Code of Professional Responsibility enunciate a public policy that lawyers should not be fired because of the clients they choose to represent? Does the recently adopted Disciplinary Rule prohibiting discrimination based on sexual orientation provide the requisite public policy? These questions remain unanswered by the court.

B. *Mier v. Certified Oil Co.* (1997)

In 1997, the Franklin County Court of Common Pleas held that Ohio has a clear public policy against employers who discriminate on the basis of sexual orientation in violation of a municipal ordinance. In Mier, the plaintiffs, who were employed by the defendant in Columbus, Ohio, alleged that they were terminated because they are lesbians, in violation of section 2331.03 of the Columbus City Code. Section 2331.03 prohibits employment discrimination on the basis of sexual orientation. The court stated that the violation of section 2331.03 is sufficient to give rise to a public policy exception to the doctrine of at-will employment and therefore denied the defendant's motion to dismiss. . . .

The Mier court went on to reject the Greenwood court's contention that "public policy which warrants an exception to the employment-at-will doctrine must be of uniform, statewide application; it cannot be fragmentary, as with a single municipal ordinance." According to the Mier court, the Greenwood decision invented a new standard for determining the sufficiency of public policy and ignored existing precedent. The court also rejected the Greenwood court's reasoning that because municipal ordinances are subject to revision, repeal, or findings of unconstitutionality, an ordinance cannot constitute a sufficient source of public policy. The court posited:

If this argument were accepted, it would follow that statutes also cannot give rise to a sufficiently clear public policy since they too are subject to repeal, revision, or findings of unconstitutionality. Nevertheless, the Supreme Court has repeatedly found the public policy exceptions to the employment-at-will doctrine can be based upon statutes.

C. *Das v. Ohio State University* (2000)

Most recently, in *Das v. Ohio State University*, a federal district court in Ohio asserted that a plaintiff may bring a claim for sexual orientation discrimination under the Ohio public policy exception based on a city code. The plaintiff, Das, argued that she was terminated because of her sexual orientation in violation of Columbus City Code, and thus in violation of Ohio public policy. The Das court recognized that the Painter decision allowed exceptions to the at-will employment doctrine if the violation of public policy based on an acceptable source was "of equally serious import as the violation of statute." The court found that municipalities are given the power, under Section 3, Article XVIII of the Ohio Constitution, to adopt anti-discrimination legislation as long as it is not in conflict with state statute. The court determined that the Columbus code was not in conflict with any state statutes; therefore, it was a valid source for the public policy.

The court ultimately determined that there was not enough evidence to prove that Das was fired because of her sexual orientation, and consequently affirmed her employer's motion for summary judgment. Notwithstanding this finding, the court stated that it "does not turn a blind eye to the fact that persons of gay, lesbian, and bisexual orientation are often discriminated against in the workplace." The court clearly left the door wide open for future sexual orientation discrimination claims to be brought under the Ohio public policy exception to at-will employment, at least in Columbus.

IV. PROS AND CONS OF A PUBLIC POLICY EXCEPTION TO AT-WILL EMPLOYMENT

Numerous municipalities, in both urban and rural locales in many different areas of the state, have enacted ordinances prohibiting workplace discrimination on the basis of sexual orientation. One compelling indication that a public policy against workplace discrimination on the basis of sexual orientation should be recognized is that three of the ten largest cities in Ohio have ordinances that prohibit employment discrimination on the basis of sexual orientation. Cleveland, Columbus, and Toledo all have laws that prohibit workplace discrimination on the basis of sexual orientation. Further, many mid-size and smaller municipalities throughout the state also have similar ordinances.

As you read these pros and cons, can you think of any advantages or diadvantages that the author missed?

Another indicator that a "sufficiently clear public policy" against sexual orientation-based discrimination exists in Ohio is that the state, in 1974, repealed a law criminalizing consensual sodomy. In a dissenting opinion to Ohio ex rel. *Grant v. Brown*, Justice Stern stated:

The recent amendments to R.C. Title 29, which decriminalize all private sexual activity between consenting adults, indicate an express public policy to tolerate the existence of different sexual life styles in this state. Insofar as the Criminal Code in Ohio is now concerned, no distinction is drawn between heterosexual and homosexual activities.

However, the majority in Brown, in a brief 4-3 decision, ruled that although homosexual acts between consenting adults are not prohibited by law, "the promotion of homosexuality as a valid life style is contrary to the public policy in the state." In Brown, a relator tendered articles of incorporation for the Greater Cincinnati Gay Society, Inc., a nonprofit corporation, to the Secretary of State. The Secretary of State refused to accept the articles because they "appeared to be contrary to public policy since homosexuality as a 'valid life style' has been, and is currently defined by statute, as a criminal act."

The Brown majority rejected the argument that there was no animus against homosexuals in the Ohio Criminal Code, despite the fact that no statute existed that defined homosexuality as a criminal act. The court noted that the Secretary of State had broad discretion in the matter, and without further discussion found that the promotion of homosexuality was against public policy. Acknowledging that homosexual acts between consenting adults were no longer offenses under the Criminal Code, the court without discussion found that the promotion of homosexuality is against Ohio public policy.

The Brown majority opinion was not well reasoned with regard to the proposition that homosexuality, even at that time, was against Ohio public policy. As Justice Stern's dissent highlighted, past judicial decisions failed to support the majority's contention. In fact, according to Justice Stern, "nowhere in the recorded decisions of the Ohio Supreme Court has any justice ever used the term "homosexual' or "homosexuality,' let alone discuss the policy implications of such a life style." The majority merely made a naked statement without further analysis.

Today, the Brown decision is unequivocally devoid of force as a statement about whether Ohio has a public policy against discriminating in employment on the basis of sexual orientation. The Brown decision is over twenty-five years old, and Ohio public policy unquestionably has changed over time. Moreover, Brown addressed what the court characterized as the "promotion of homosexuality," not whether it was against public policy to fire or discriminate against an employee on the basis of sexual orientation. The Secretary of State has since allowed the incorporation of pro-gay organizations, such as the Ohio Human Rights Bar Association and various Stonewall affiliate organizations including Stonewall Cleveland and Stonewall Columbus. The Supreme Court of Ohio itself has since adopted the Ohio Code of Judicial Ethics that expressly prohibits a judge from discriminating or showing bias on the basis of sexual orientation in his or her duties. In short, times have changed, both legally and socially.

Ohio courts, under Painter, may recognize a code-based public policy exception to at-will employment that is of equal importance and authority as a statute. Employees who are members of a profession governed by a professional code of ethics may be able to make a viable argument that a professional code is sufficiently clear public policy. An ethical rule that prohibits discrimination on the basis of sexual orientation may be a suitable source of public policy because it is aimed at serving the interests of the public and is applied throughout a state.[3]

Similarly, in an area with a regional prohibition, such as a city or county ordinance, against sexual orientation discrimination in the workplace, one could conceivably argue that an employee who is fired on the sole basis of sexual orientation should be able to carve out a sufficiently clear public policy. First, there is a statewide policy that governs sexual orientation discrimination by lawyers. Second, the prohibition "by law" would be found in the regional ordinance, as well as supported by the numerous regional ordinances that further the notion of a statewide public policy.

Canon 3 of the Ohio Code of Judicial Conduct provides a more general statement of public policy. Canon 3 states:

A judge shall perform judicial duties without bias or prejudice. A judge shall not, in the performance of judicial duties, by words or conduct manifest bias or prejudice, including but not limited to bias or prejudice based upon . . . sexual orientation . . . and shall not permit staff, court officials, and others subject to the judge's direction and control to do so.

While the judicial code clearly states to the public the standard of conduct expected by the profession from itself, Canon 3 can reasonably be understood as an expression of a more general, statewide embodiment of a public policy against discriminatory employment practices based on sexual orientation under the common law. One of the sources of public policy underlying the Painter decision is the common law. The Code of Judicial Conduct, which governs Ohio's judges, the administrators of the common law, plainly embodies a public policy against sexual orientation discrimination. The Ohio Supreme Court, in pronouncing the ethical rules that govern the legal profession, has not only codified the rules that govern the entire profession but has also set an example of a public policy of tolerance and nondiscrimination.

Probably one of the most damaging setbacks to the argument for the recognition of a public policy exception to at-will employment on the basis of sexual orientation is Governor Taft's executive order that replaced a sixteen-year-old policy specifically protecting gays and lesbians working for state agencies from workplace discrimination and providing a clear statement of public policy prohibiting workplace discrimination on the basis of sexual orientation. . . .

The Taft executive order, at the very least, removed a readily available statement of statewide policy against sexual orientation-based discrimination in the workplace. However, if the public statements of the Taft administration are taken seriously, the policy of discriminating on the basis of sexual orientation should still be in place, even after Taft's removal of the reference to "sexual orientation" in the order. After all, if Governor Taft is "opposed to discrimination against any person for any reason," as has been stated by his administration to the media, then the newly revised executive order certainly protects gays and lesbians who are discriminated against in the workplace.

Although the legislature has repealed laws prohibiting sodomy, Ohio's civil rights statutes do not include sexual orientation among their protections. In fact, as the Greenwood court pointed out, "while R.C. 4112.02 prohibits discrimination based on "handicap,' that term is defined specifically to exclude homosexuality, bisexuality, and other sexual disorders or dysfunctions." Further, the Ohio ethnic intimidation statute does not include a penalty for crimes motivated by sexual orientation.

V. CONCLUSION

Ohio's at-will employees have minimal express state and federal protections against workplace discrimination based on sexual orientation. Currently, the public policy exception to the at-will employment doctrine holds promise for an employee who has been wrongfully terminated on the basis of sexual orientation to establish a viable cause of action against an employer. As explained in this Article, support for a sufficiently clear public policy against discriminatory employment practices based on sexual orientation can be found in the common law, numerous municipal ordinances, the Supreme Court's adoption of The Code of Professional Responsibility, the repeal of state sodomy laws, and the publicly stated intent of Governor Taft's executive order.

END NOTES

1. See Greenwood v. Taft, Stettinius & Hollister, 663 N.E.2d 1030 (Ohio Ct. App. 1995).
2. Phung v. Waste Mgmt., Inc., 491 N.E.2d 1114, 1116 (Ohio 1986) (quoting Peterson v. Scott Constr. Co., 451 N.E.2d 1236, 1239 (Ohio Ct. App. 1982)) (holding that public policy does not require that there be an exception to the employment-at-will doctrine, absent a sufficiently clear public policy warranting a cause of action).
3. Id. The Colorado court in fact expressed that the scope of ethics codes as sources for public policy should be limited to those situations where the "ethical provision [is] designed to serve the interests of the public rather than the interests of the profession." Id. (brackets in original).

ARTICLE 2.5

Employment at Will in Maine: R.I.P.?

Katy Rand

A month before starting law school, I received a copy of *Taliento v. Portland West Neighborhood Planning Council* in the mail along with directions to read the case and digest it before law school orientation, where we (or, I would later learn, the one unfortunate soul called upon) would "discuss" it. I ambled my way through the legal jargon and put the case down, understanding only one thing: in Maine, as in all but one other state, employment is presumed to be "at-will," meaning that employers are free to discharge employees at any time and without just cause, unless an employment contract provides otherwise.

In short, employers can terminate employees "for good cause, for no cause or even for bad cause." With no legal training whatsoever, but with a background in management, I found the rule inherently fair. After all, more than a few employees under my supervision walked off the job with no notice and for "no cause" or "bad cause" and I was left scrambling to fill their shifts, with no remedy against the employee.

With law school and a few years of practice behind me, I understand the employment-at-will doctrine as something more than a "what's good for the goose" rule balancing the rights of employers and employees. The employment-at-will doctrine is vital to the free market economy and critical for preserving employers' rights to make unbiased and often unpopular business decisions, unswayed by the threat of litigation. The doctrine discourages judges and juries from second-guessing discharge decisions that appear unwise or unfair, and gives employers the freedom they need to make independent business judgments without interference from courts.

What makes the author think that the doctrine is important to a free enterprise market economy?

Unfortunately for employers and for employees who inevitably and indirectly will bear the costs of increased litigation, the doctrine is slowly being eroded across the country and recently, in Maine. A recent Maine Supreme Judicial Court ("Law Court") decision, *Whitney v. Wal-Mart Stores,* though not purporting to address or alter the doctrine of employment at will, has produced a destructive, if unintended, effect on it. As the doctrine of employment at will is whittled away by the courts, employers are becoming increasingly limited in their ability to terminate employees for valid business reasons that discharged employees perceive as unjust. If Maine continues on this course, employers in the state can expect to lose their right to fire for "no reason" or for a "bad reason," and to have their business decisions scrutinized by the courts. As Maine struggles to attract and retain businesses, it cannot afford to lose employment at will.

CERTAIN STATUTES LIMIT EMPLOYMENT AT WILL

The doctrine of employment at will does not, of course, shelter employers from liability from *every* employment decision. Congress and the state legislature have, through statute, identified a number of "bad reasons" for which employees may not be terminated—namely, race, sex, age, religion, disability, national origin, and, now in Maine, sexual orientation. Nor may employers fire employees because they "blow the whistle" or in retaliation for the exercise of rights protected by the civil rights statutes. These laws protect activity society seeks to encourage, or at least not discourage, as opposed to protecting status.

Because these civil rights laws limit the reasons for which employers may fire employees, they necessarily erode the doctrine of employment at will. But to the extent that they protect desirable behavior or classes of individuals that have been subject to oppression and for whom there is still a real risk of unfair treatment, these laws reflect society's judgment that the infringement on employer freedom is justified. In short, civil rights laws, properly focused, do not threaten the doctrine of employment at will. They do threaten that doctrine, however, when their protections are extended too broadly to individuals who do not need protection.

Employment at will is a bedrock principle of employment law in Maine, and one that the Law Court has been faithful to over the years, repeatedly declining plaintiffs' invitations to recognize exceptions to the doctrine that have taken hold in other states. However, a recent decision, *Whitney v. Wal-Mart Stores,* holds that the definition of disability is so expansive as to include most of the population and threatens the continued existence of employment at will in Maine. Given Maine's long tradition respecting employers' and employees' freedom to contract, it seems unlikely that either the Legislature that drafted the definition of "disability" or the *Whitney* majority intended to modify or overrule well-settled employment law. Read together, however, the statute and recent decision do just that.

COMMON LAW EXCEPTIONS TO EMPLOYMENT AT WILL

Although employment at will is the default rule in Maine, as in nearly all other states, employers and employees are free to agree that termination will be only for cause or that some procedure or method must be followed before an employee may be terminated. As with any other contract case, the question in employment contract cases is generally whether the parties agreed—or what, exactly, they agreed to. The Law Court historically has guarded employment at will closely, holding that "[p]arties may provide that an employer is not free to discharge an employee without cause, but the intent to do so must be *clearly stated.*" Thus, in Maine, unlike in some other states, an employment contract for a definite duration or to terminate only for cause or pursuant to certain procedures cannot be implied.

The Law Court has not always stood so firmly in its stance against implied employment contracts. In *Terrio v. Millinocket Community Hospital,* the plaintiff contended that her termination was in breach of her employment agreement, established in large part by her employer's oral promises that she was secure in her job for "the rest of (her) life" and that she would be employed until "normal retirement age." After reciting the general employment-at-will rule "that a contract of employment for an indefinite length of time is terminable at will by either party," the Court characterized the issue as "whether a contract of employment for a definite term arose from the total factual circumstances. . . ." In concluding that the jury was entitled to interpret the employer's comments as "evidence of a specific oral promise of employment for a definite term," the Court emphasized that the comments were made "in the context of her long service in a position of substantial responsibility (from which she would normally have retired in less than seven years). . . ." The Law Court's recognition in *Terrio* that an employment contract could arise from circumstances and conduct surrounding oral promises arguably amounted to adoption of an implied in-fact model of employment agreement formation. That model did not survive in Maine, however.

Seven years later, in *Larrabee v. Penobscot Frozen Foods,* two former employees alleged that they "expressly or impliedly promised to work for the Defendant . . . [and that in] exchange for [their] promises, the Defendant expressly or impliedly promised to pay the Plaintiffs a specified wage and to refrain from discharging them in bad faith or without good cause." Relying on the classic formulation of the employment-at-will rule as recited in *Terrio*—"a contract of employment for an indefinite length of time is terminable at the will of either party"—the trial court granted Defendant's motion to dismiss the breach-of-contract claim on the ground that the plaintiffs did not allege that their employment contract had a definite duration. . . .

To the extent that the implied contract theory could be said to have survived *Larrabee,* subsequent cases have put it to rest. In *Libby v. Calais Regional Hospital,* the plaintiff alleged that an employee handbook, outlining specific termination procedures, constituted an employment contract which her employer breached when it terminated her without following those procedures. The Court recognized that an employee handbook could constitute an employment contract sufficient to change the employment relationship from "one terminable at will to one terminable only by its express terms." However, the Court said the handbook "must clearly state an intent to impose restrictions upon the employer's right to discharge the employee." The handbook at issue in *Libby* provided a method of discharging employees and therefore implied that discharge would be only for cause. It did not, however, expressly restrict the hospital's right to discharge employees at will, and therefore did not, according to the Court, limit the hospital's right to terminate the plaintiff. Justices Hornby and Roberts dissented, viewing the question of whether the handbook constituted a contract to terminate only for cause as a jury question.

In *Bard v. Bath Iron Works,* the Law Court put the nail in the implied-contract coffin. The plaintiff in *Bard* claimed that a "Rules and Regulations" pamphlet he received at the beginning of his employment created an implied contract providing that he could be discharged only if found to have violated one of the rules and regulations. The Court again said that a contract creating an exception to the employment-at-will rule "must expressly restrict the employer's common-law right to discharge the employee at will and clearly limit the employer to the enumerated method or methods of terminating the employment." With no such express restriction in the pamphlet, the employer was entitled to summary judgment. . . .

Thus, the Law Court has repeatedly been asked to make more flexible the rule that any restriction of an employer's right to terminate employees at will be clearly and expressly stated, and has repeatedly declined to do so. Employers can control the "express" and "clear" promises they make, whether orally or in their personnel policies and handbooks, and therefore can avoid inadvertently converting an at-will employment relationship into one terminable only for cause.

The Law Court has thus far been similarly staunch in its refusal to recognize a cause of action for breach of an implied covenant of good faith and fair dealing in the employment context. Relying on the implied-contract cases discussed above, the Court has almost consistently rejected this cause of action on the ground that it does not "recognize implied promises in employment contracts of indefinite duration."

WRONGFUL DISCHARGE IN VIOLATION OF PUBLIC POLICY

The law court has also resisted recognizing a cause of action in tort for wrongful discharge in violation of public policy, despite the fact that a number of states have recognized a public policy limitation on the employment-at-will doctrine, holding that an at-will employee may be terminated for any reason or no reason, but not for a reason that contravenes public policy.

In *Larrabee,* which was decided before the enactment of Maine's Whistleblower Protection Act, the Court rejected plaintiff's claim that her termination, which she claimed was motivated by ill will, could give rise to the tort of wrongful discharge. The Court left open the possibility that it would recognize "such a cause of action when the discharge of an employee contravenes some strong public policy," but held that the case presented "nothing more than a purely private dispute."

Three years later, in *Pooler v. Maine Coal Products,* the plaintiff, who was fired for refusing to drive a truck assigned to him and that he contended was unsafe, claimed that he was terminated in violation of the Whistleblower Protection Act ("WPA") and also that his termination constituted wrongful discharge in violation of public policy. The trial court instructed the jury on the elements of the WPA but declined to give the plaintiff's requested instruction on wrongful discharge. The Law Court held that the trial court's failure to give a wrongful discharge instruction was not error because the elements of a wrongful discharge tort, if the Court were to recognize it, were the same as the WPA claim. Both, the Court reasoned, required a showing of some potential violation of the law or threat to safety. Similarly, in *Bard* the Court declined to recognize the tort of wrongful discharge where the employee also contended that his termination violated the WPA. "[W]here a statutory right and remedy are provided," the Court reasoned, "there is no need to recognize a redundant tort."

Thus, the Law Court has so far been unwilling to recognize a cause of action for wrongful discharge, at least when the "public policy" that the employee claims his termination contravened is embodied in a statute providing its own private cause of action and remedy. Indeed, the Law Court generally has been friendly to the doctrine of employment at will, resisting whatever urge has led so many other states to recognize exceptions to the doctrine such as the implied-contract and wrongful-discharge theories. However, recent developments in the area of Maine disability discrimination law have the profound, even if unintended, effect of significantly undermining at-will employment in Maine.

MAINE HUMAN RIGHTS ACT'S DEFINITION OF 'DISABILITY' AND WELCOME CLARIFICATION FROM THE HUMAN RIGHTS COMMISSION

Since the Rehabilitation and Americans with Disabilities acts were passed in 1973 and 1990, respectively, individuals with disabilities have been among the groups protected from employment discrimination. In 1971, Maine passed the Maine Human Rights Act ("MHRA"), also prohibiting discrimination on the basis of, among other things, disability. The MHRA's legislative history confirms that the law was written to address discrimination against classes of persons historically subjected to stereotyping and disparate treatment, including, in the employment context, where such treatment was based on factors unrelated to their ability to perform a particular job. Before the MHRA's enactment, Governor Kenneth M. Curtis created a Task Force on Human Rights to investigate and propose solutions to the problem of discrimination in Maine. The Task Force's report to the Governor confirms that its focus was upon traditionally marginalized groups or classes of people, rather than on unfair treatment of individuals generally. This focus mirrors that of Congress when it passed the ADA, the MHRA's federal counterpart respecting the disabled, which identifies the individuals with disabilities whom the law protects as a "discrete and insular minority."

When the Legislature first enacted the MHRA in 1971, the statute prohibited disability—then "handicap"—discrimination, but provided no definition of the operative term. In 1975, the Legislature added a definition of "physical or mental handicap," which was subsequently amended to replace the word "handicap" with "disability." Unfortunately, the definition that the Legislature adopted was, on its face, much broader than what the legislative history, discussed above, suggests the Legislature intended. "Physical or mental disability" includes "any disability, infirmity, malformation, disfigurement, congenital defect or mental condition caused by bodily injury, accident, disease, birth defect, environmental conditions or illness. . . ." Thus, the definition standing alone covers just about every medical condition imaginable, regardless of its severity, duration, or effect on the individual.

In 1985, the Maine Human Rights Commission ("Commission") proposed a rule that would narrow this statutory definition so that it mirrored the definition contained in the ADA and applied only to individuals who were substantially limited in one or more major life activities. While considering the proposed rule, the Commission received comments from many individuals and organizations. Every one of them was "supportive of the Commission's effort to clarify its interpretation of the phrase 'physical or mental handicap' as referring to serious impairments of more than temporary duration." Thus, in 1985 there was a clear consensus that the MHRA's definition of "physical or mental disability" needed to be reigned in. The Commission therefore adopted Employment Regulation 3.02(C)(1), providing that an individual with a physical or mental disability "means any person who has a physical or mental impairment which substantially limits one or more of such person's major life activities, has a record of such impairment, or is regarded as having such an impairment." For the next nearly twenty years, this regulation mandated an effects-based assessment of disability and therefore limited the class of individuals entitled to protection to those the Task Force on Human Rights set out to protect.

WHITNEY V. WAL-MART: EVERYONE IS A MEMBER OF A PROTECTED CLASS

In *Whitney v. Wal-Mart,* a Wal-Mart tire-lube manager with high blood pressure and heart disease brought a note to work from his doctor restricting him to working no more than forty-five hours per week. Whitney's supervisors informed him that his management position required him to work between forty-eight and fifty-two hours per week and that, if he could not work those hours, non-salaried management positions might be available to him. After applying unsuccessfully for several such positions, Whitney secured a position in another store. He then sued Wal-Mart, arguing that his demotion amounted to disability discrimination.

Wal-Mart moved for summary judgment on the ground that Whitney was not substantially limited in any major life activity, therefore not "disabled" and not entitled to protection under the MHRA. Magistrate Judge Kravchuk agreed and recommended summary judgment in Wal-Mart's favor. Judge Hornby, in turn, certified the case to the Law Court, asking for guidance on the validity of the Commission rule and whether MHRA disability discrimination plaintiffs, like ADA plaintiffs, are required to show substantial limitation of a major life activity in order to qualify as disabled under the statute. After reviewing the legislative history of the MHRA, the Law Court held, four to three, that the Commission's 1985 rule was inconsistent with the plain meaning of the statute, which unambiguously defined "disability" without any reference to major life activities or substantial limitations.

The Law Court was faced with an undeniably difficult statute to interpret, but the majority of the justices found the MHRA's definition of "physical or mental disability" unambiguous, making deference to the Commission's rule unnecessary and, in the court's view, inappropriate. Leaving the correctness or incorrectness of the Law Court's decision aside, its effect is to sweep a large portion, if not all, of the population into a protected class.

The notion that an employer may not terminate an employee because she has a scar on her face or walks with a limp (a "disfigurement" and an "infirmity," respectively) has surface appeal. Some may even argue that these are acceptable exceptions to the employment-at-will doctrine—that, just as an employer may not discriminate on the basis of race, it may not discriminate on the basis of minor impairments and cosmetic disfigurements like those now covered by Maine law. In practice, however, protecting such a large class of individuals dramatically limits an employer's ability to terminate an "at-will" employee. While the problematic terminations are not going to be because of minor impairments, those impairments put employees under the MHRA's protection, enabling them to claim pretext. Thus, any employee with the mildest impairment who perceives his or her termination as unfair or unwise—and, as the reader can imagine, most terminated employees believe their terminations were undeserved—and alleges or believes that the real reason for the termination was his or her "disability," can haul the employer into court to defend its decision.

A recent Law Court case illustrates the problem created by the statute's definition of disability and *Whitney's* interpretation of it. In *LePage v. Bath Iron Works Corp.,* the plaintiff, Daniel LePage, claimed that his employer's refusal to issue him a firearm after a psychological examination revealed that he had "aggressive tendencies" constituted disability discrimination. The Law Court found that the claim was time-barred, and therefore did not reach the question whether his "personality profile traits" constituted a disability post-Whitney. Had the Court reached the question, however, it may well have concluded, based upon the statutory definition of disability, that LePage's "aggressive tendencies" constituted a "mental condition" under the MHRA, or that he was at least regarded as having such a condition, and that he was therefore protected under the Act.

Even if the Law Court were able to read the statute in such a way as to conclude that LePage was not disabled—a doubtful proposition in light of the Court's characterization of the statute as unambiguous in *Whitney*—that conclusion would come only after long and probably expensive litigation. The requirement that BIW arm its security guards was mandated by the federal government as one of many post-9/11 security reforms, leaving the employer with no alternative but to litigate with Mr. LePage the issue of whether his "civil rights" were violated when he was not allowed to carry an automatic weapon due to his aggressive personality. Neither the Maine Legislature . . . nor the *Whitney* majority could possibly have intended this absurd result.

Faced with the fact that nearly every employee in the state is now a potential discrimination plaintiff, an employer must be able to articulate a reason, and a good one, for terminating any employee. This is so because if the articulated reason is perceived as unfair or unwise, the employer faces the very real risk that a jury or court will reject the employer's stated reason, or attribute some ulterior motive to the employer's failure to provide a reason and conclude instead that the employee was terminated because of his disability. Employers must "build a case" against employees they want to terminate even for cause, ensuring that every infraction is documented, every counseling session reduced to writing to be used as evidence that the employer's motive was pure. Further, because it takes time to document infractions and repeatedly counsel employees for misconduct, employers are often forced to keep unproductive and even disruptive employees on the payroll far longer than they should while they build a defense to an anticipated lawsuit.

EROSION OF EMPLOYMENT AT WILL HURTS MORE THAN EMPLOYERS

Are there also other people who benefit from the erosion of the doctrine besides the employees themselves?

Why should anyone other than employers and lawyers who represent employers be concerned? Because, as both studies and current events confirm, when employment at will is eroded, employees suffer.

The cost to employers who have lost the unfettered right to terminate employees is fairly easy to identify. Employers who fear lawsuits will keep inefficient employees on the payroll and those employees will contribute less than their co-workers—perhaps even less than the cost of their retention. To recoup or avoid the loss that occurs when they are forced to keep employees on against their will, employers will either pass along the added labor costs to employees through decreased compensation or decrease the number of new employees they hire. Alternatively or simultaneously, employers will raise prices and become less completive or return less to their shareholders. And, as anyone who has worked with unproductive or disruptive employees knows, they affect the morale, and thus productivity, of others as their continued employment undermines their coworkers' trust in their employer to maintain an equitable workplace.

In 1995, labor market economists Richard Vedder and Lowell Gallaway examined the effect that wrongful-termination litigation had on job opportunities and income growth for workers across the country and in California. Their findings were notable, if not surprising.

Using regression analysis of data covering the period between 1970 and 1989, Vedder and Gallaway estimated that, by 1989, "growth in the application of the wrongful-termination notion had depressed the compensation of workers in the United States below the estimated time trend by 7.47 percent." Using 1993 employment data for the individual states, Vedder and Gallaway calculated that the loss of jobs between 1970 and 1990 as a result of wrongful-termination in those states that had recognized it was approximately 1.325 million.

Perhaps even more troubling is Vedder and Gallaway's finding that lower income individuals are the ones most likely to experience loss in job opportunities and income because risk-averse employers are less likely to offer employment to marginal applicants, who tend to be less educated, low income, and, in California at least, minority. Indeed, Vedder and Gallaway opine that the erosion of employment at will has had the ironic effect of increasing income inequality.

University of Chicago law professor Thomas J. Miles has also examined the effect of employment-at-will exceptions on the labor market and, like Vedder and Gallaway, found that the exceptions do have real effects on employer behavior. Specifically, Miles noted that temporary employment rose a statistically significant 15 percent in the presence of an employment-at-will exception. As erosion of the employment-at-will doctrine raises the costs of terminating permanent employees, employers are encouraged to limit their risk by substituting temporary workers. The result is fewer employees with long-term employment prospects.

The situation in France, where employment is presumed to be for an indefinite term and employers are not free to terminate at will, confirms that employment law has a profound effect on both employer behavior and the economy. The unemployment rate in the United States in March of 2006 was 4.7 percent, while the 2005 unemployment rate in France was nearly twice that, at 9.5 percent. Since May of 2003, the U.S. economy has created nearly four million new jobs and, according to Commerce Department figures, the American economy grew at a rate of 3.4 percent during the second quarter of 2005.

France's economy, on the other hand, grew by only 0.1 percent that quarter and only 0.4 percent in the first quarter of 2005. Although France's rejection of employment at will means employees enjoy great protection and job security, "French employers and the French economy as a whole pay the price." . . .

AN EASY FIX: AMEND THE STATUTE

There is no reason to believe that the Maine legislature intended to undermine employment at will—long the rule in Maine—when it drafted such a broad definition of disability. Nor is there any reason to believe that the Law Court intended to take Maine employment law in a new direction or otherwise undermine a consistent history favoring the contractual freedom of employers and employees when it decided *Whitney.* However, the unintended consequence of the statutory definition and Law Court decision is essentially to eviscerate employment at will. The MHRA currently protects anyone with a health condition, as opposed to the historical victims of discrimination. The law is out of step with the policy underlying the MRHA.

The problem created by the broad definition and *Whitney* is not difficult to remedy. [Maine's statute should] be amended to cover only those individuals whom society recognizes as disadvantaged (as compared to the population at large) members of a class for which there is a recognized history of discriminatory treatment.

Maine cannot afford to lose jobs, and employees cannot afford to shoulder the increased costs that will inevitably accompany restrictions on employment at will. Legally correct or not, the Law Court's interpretation of 5 M.R.S.A. § 4553(7-A) in *Whitney* constitutes bad policy calling for a legislative solution.

CONCLUSION

Employment at will, once firmly established, has been eroded in Maine. By defining the class of "disabled" individuals so broadly as to include people with the most minor of impairments [Maine has] handed every terminated and disgruntled employee a potential cause of action. As a result, Maine courts can expect an increase in the number of employment-related lawsuits, Maine businesses can expect increased costs of managing their workforce and litigating terminations, and Maine employees can expect to bear at least a portion of the increased cost of doing business in the state. Employers and employees alike would benefit from, and should demand, legislative action limiting the scope of the term "disability" in the MHRA.

ISSUE SUMMARY

The articles in this chapter can best be understood as addressing a broader question than how we should modify the employment-at-will doctrine. Each author featured in this chapter was indirectly answering the question: Who should the law protect? Each author had a different answer: employees who are whistleblowers; gay, lesbian, and bisexual employees; employees who are asked to perform illegal activities; and even employers who are at risk for wrongful termination lawsuits. Each author focused on a different group of people.

Why is the author's focus significant? Consider a different issue. Consider environmental law. What happens when we focus on the needs of corporations? We lessen restrictions on pollution. What happens when we focus on the needs of farmers? We lessen restrictions on the use of water. What happens when we focus on the needs of future generations? We do everything possible to conserve the planet's resources. Depending upon our focus, we shift our goals, our priorities, and our laws.

Think again about the employment-at-will doctrine. When we focus on employees, how do our laws change? We probably create more exceptions to the doctrine to prevent wrongful termination. What happens when we shift our focus to a select subset of employees? We probably create narrow exceptions to protect a small and very specific group of employees. How does the law change when we focus on employers' needs? We most likely restrict the number of exceptions to the doctrine so that employers can hire and fire at will.

When you read arguments about the law, ask yourself: On which group of people is the author focusing? Does the author provide any justification for that focus? What are the implications of the author's choosing one group as opposed to the myriad of other groups available? Whether you agree with an author's argument will probably be linked to how you feel about the author's focus.

ISSUE HIGHLIGHTS

- "Employment at-will" means that employees hired at will may be discharged for any legal reason.
- Employment at-will is the default legal rule of the employment relationship, applying to any private-sector employee who is not covered by a collective bargaining agreement.
- A "whistleblower" is an employee who chooses to alert management and/or law enforcement officials that her employer is involved in corrupt, illegal, fraudulent, or harmful activity.
- *Petermann v. International Brotherhood of Teamsters* (1963) is the case that introduced the public policy exception to the employment-at-will doctrine because the court decided that it was against public interests to

allow employers to make employment contingent upon the commission of a felony.

- In *Painter v. Graley* (1994), the Ohio Supreme Court established a four-pronged test to determine whether termination of an employee violated a public policy. The test requires the employees to prove the clarity element, the jeopardy element, the causation element, and the overriding justification element.
- In 1995, labor market economists Richard Vedder and Lowell Gallaway calculated that the loss of jobs between 1970 and 1990 as a result of the wrongful-termination concept in those states that had recognized it was approximately 1.325 million.
- University of Chicago law professor Thomas J. Miles found that temporary employment rose a statistically significant 15 percent in the presence of an employment-at-will exception.

CRITICAL THINKING

As you were reading this chapter, you may have noticed a somewhat puzzling conflict. Four different authors each looked at employment laws in America, and each author came to a different (though sometimes similar) conclusion. You may have wondered why. After all, if the authors are examining the same basic material, why did they not all arrive at the same conclusion?

One way to explain divergent conclusions is to examine the authors themselves. Who are these people? How do they see the world around them? What are their goals? Believe it or not, you can answer some of these questions without a face-to-face interview. You can find the answers in the authors' writing.

Let's review each author's conclusion. Jones believes there should be more protection for whistleblowers. Baumgarten thinks that Georgia should adopt a public policy exception to the employment-at-will doctrine. Scialdone urges Ohio to prevent discrimination based on sexual orientation by using the public policy exception to the employment-at-will doctrine. Rand argues that Maine should protect businesses by allowing fewer exceptions to the employment-at-will doctrine. Here we have four distinct conclusions, all based on study of American statute and case law.

How can we explain these differing conclusions? We need to identify the authors' assumptions. Assumptions are unstated beliefs that connect an author's reasons to her conclusion. Let's use a simplified example. Argument: Oranges contain lots of vitamin C; therefore, you should eat oranges. What is missing? The missing step is an assumption—that you should eat lots of vitamin C. Without the assumption, the reason ("oranges contain lots of Vitamin C") does not lead to the conclusion ("you should eat oranges"). If we told you that maggots contain vitamin C, you probably would not rush to the conclusion that you should eat maggots—unless you held a certain assumption (that we should eat lots of vitamin C). When we add the assumption, then it becomes clear why we should eat oranges (because we should eat lots of vitamin C, and oranges contain lots of vitamin C).

You may be wondering though, "What do I do after I've found an assumption?" You should ask, "What is the justification for that assumption?" Is there any proof that we should eat lots of vitamin C? Assumptions need to be backed by evidence. Just as you would not accept an author's reasons if he had no evidence of their validity, you would not accept an author's assumptions if he had no evidence to support those assumptions. If an author's assumptions are not supported by evidence, then the author's argument falls apart. Remember, assumptions are connective tissue; the author needs those assumptions to lead us from his reasons to his conclusion.

Now let's try to identify a couple of assumptions made by the authors featured in this chapter. The author's assumptions will tell us about the authors and how they see the world around them. Think about Jones, Baumgarten, and Scialdone. All three are arguing for more exceptions to the employment-at-will doctrine. All three are arguing for more protection for employees. Why? All three are making a basic assumption: The purpose of the law is to protect the weak from the powerful. Jones, Baumgarten, and Scialdone see a world in which employers have lightning bolts, and employees need to be protected by more than rain-soaked cardboard boxes. In the view of these three authors, the law should provide the needed protection; the law should build a shelter over the employees' heads.

Rand holds a quite different assumption: The purpose of the law is to promote the economic health of the state. In Rand's view, employees are holding employers at knife point, threatening lawsuits on a daily basis. As a result, Rand sees a situation that will cause employers to flee the state, leaving the economy devastated. If the employment-at-will doctrine were modified to protect employers from wrongful termination suits, then the law would promote an environment in which businesses would be eager to operate. Rand wants the courts and legislature to create that business-friendly environment.

So far we've identified two assumptions made by the authors featured in this chapter. There are many more assumptions waiting to be identified. You should look for assumptions whenever you read arguments like the ones found throughout this book. Don't stop after identifying the assumptions, though. Remember, our job isn't done yet. We need to ask whether that authors have any evidence to support their assumptions.

Let's look again at the assumptions we identified in this chapter. Is there any evidence that the purpose of the law is to protect the weak from the powerful? A strong analogy could be drawn to existing legislation and case law that protect minorities from discrimination. Based on precedent, you could say that the law tries to protect the weak. Is there any evidence for the second assumption, that the purpose of the law is to promote the economic health of the state? Again, a strong analogy could be drawn to existing state and case law that except businesses from rules and regulations when compliance would impose an undue hardship on the business. Based on precedent, you could say that the law tries to protect businesses.

When two assumptions conflict and there is evidence for both assumptions, what do you do? You ask yourself, "Which assumption has the most convincing evidence?" Are you more convinced that the law is supposed to protect the weak or the economy? In part, your answer will depend upon your own personal assumptions about the world around you. When you have decided which evidence is more convincing, you will be better prepared to decide which arguments to accept and which arguments to reject. Remember: Assumptions tie an argument together; but when an author holds unjustified or unsupported assumptions, the argument crumbles. You can improve your critical thinking skills by demanding that assumptions be supported by evidence.

ADDITIONAL READING RESOURCES

Autor, David H., "Outsourcing at Will: The Contribution of Unjust Dismissal Doctrine to the Growth of Employment Outsourcing," *J. Labor Econ.* 21:1, 2003.

Autor, David H., William R. Kerr, and Adriana D. Kugler, "Does Employment Protection Reduce Productivity? Evidence from US States," *The Econ. J.* 117:521, F189–F217, June 2007.

Bowman, James S., and Jonathon P. West, "Lord Acton and Employment Doctrines: Absolute Power and the Spread of At-Will Employment," *J. Bus. Ethics* 74:2, 119–130, August 2007.

Callahan, Elletta Sangrey, "Employment at Will: The Relationship between Societal Expectations and the Law," *Amer. Bus. L. J.* 28:3, 455–482, Sept. 1990.

Kugler, Adriana D., "How Do Firing Costs Affect Worker Flows in a World with Adverse Selection?" *J. Labor Econ.* 22:3, 2004.

Miles, Thomas J., "Common Law Exceptions to Employment At Will and U.S. Labor Markets." *Journal of Law, Economics, and Organization*, Vol. 16, No. 1, 74–101, 2000.

Moss, Scott A., "Where There's At-Will, There Are Many Ways: Redressing the Increasing Incoherence of Employment At-Will," *U. of Pitt. L. Rev.* 67:2, Winter 2006.

Roehling, Mark V., "The Employment At-Will Doctrine: Second Level Ethical Issues and Analysis," *J. Bus. Ethics* 47:2, 115–124, Oct. 2003.

Schwab, Stuart J., "Life-Cycle Justice: Accommodating Just Cause and Employment at Will." *Michigan Law Review.* 92:8,1993.

For more information, check these sites:

http://www.bls.gov/
http://www.dol.gov/
www.bls.gov/opub/mlr/2001/01/art1full.pdf [*last viewed on 6/9/08*]
http://www.cato.org/pubs/regulation/reg18n1e.html [*last viewed on 6/9/08*]
http://www.workinglife.org/blogs/view_post.php?content_id=7979 [*last viewed on 6/9/08*]

ISSUE 3

To What Extent Should the Board of Directors Be Free to Make Business Decisions?

Imagine that you own stock in American Corporation, a consumer goods superstore. You open the newspaper to check American Corporation's stock value, only to discover that the value has dropped 60% overnight. Shocked, you begin to search for a cause. You find that the board of directors invested hundreds of millions in a start-up company that has flopped. Then, you find that the start-up company was owned by a member of the board of directors. You're outraged, but is there anything you can do about the board of directors' error? The answer to that question depends upon whether the board of directors is protected by the business judgment rule, the focus of this chapter.

We begin this chapter with a lecture that will introduce and define the business judgment rule. Then, you will read an argument against the application of the business judgment rule to directors of nonprofit organizations. The third selection in this chapter is an excerpt of a decision made by the District Court for the Southern District of New York. The court was asked to determine whether the business judgment rule protected a board of directors from claims that they breached their fiduciary duty to the corporation's shareholders. The final article in this chapter describes the application of the business judgment rule to executives of broadcast television networks.

In the first selection of this chapter, Branson will introduce the business judgment rule in two different forms—the Delaware version and the American Law Institute version. Branson will explain the five key elements of the business judgment rule: (1) a decision was made; (2) the decision was an informed one; (3) the decision maker did not have any conflicts of interest related to the decision; (4) there was a rational basis for the decision; and (5) the decision maker acted in good faith. In addition, Branson will describe the bases for, purposes of, and implications of the business judgment rule.

In the second article in this chapter, Lee asks whether the business judgment rule should apply to directors of nonprofit organizations. Because nonprofit directors act as trustees for the nonprofit organizations they lead,

Lee argues that nonprofit directors should be held to the ordinary negligence standard of care, which is more stringent than the standard of care demanded by the business judgment rule. Lee addresses five reasons generally given to support the business judgment rule, and then explains why each reason fails to transfer from the corporate world to the nonprofit world. Lee concludes by explaining the public policy reasons for using a negligence standard, rather than the business judgment rule, to measure decisions made by nonprofit directors.

The third selection is this chapter is taken from a decision made by the District Court for the Southern District of New York. In *Patrick v. Allen*, the plaintiff owned stock in a corporation. He found that the board of directors had been leasing land owned by the corporation to an elite golf club for a break-even price. The plaintiff then found that many of the members of the board were also members of the same golf club that was leasing the corporation's land. The plaintiff brought suit against the board of directors because the board was not acting in the best interests of the company. The board members claimed they were protected from suit by the business judgment rule. As you will read, the court decided that the board members were not acting as disinterested parties and were therefore not protected by the business judgment rule.

In the final selection of this chapter, Baynes asks whether television executives who make decisions about the negative portrayal of minorities on television are protected by the business judgment rule. Baynes premises his argument on the idea that broadcast executives must make fully informed decisions that take into account profit maximization as well as possible regulatory responses, including the broadcasters' public interest mandate, if they wish to be protected by the business judgment rule. Baynes argues that, in recent history, broadcast executives have not met the requirements to be protected by the business judgment rule.

As Lee and Baynes show, the business judgment rule does not apply to all directors and executives in the same way. The business judgment rule, as described by Branson and the District Court, requires that directors be informed, disinterested, rational, and seeking the best outcomes for their respective organizations. Think again about our opening example with American Corporation. As you read this chapter, ask yourself what the board of directors must have done to be protected by the business judgment rule. Under what circumstances could you, as a shareholder, sue the board of directors for breaching their fiduciary duty?

ISSUE ARTICLES

Branson, Douglas M., "The Indiana Supreme Court Lecture: The Rule that Isn't a Rule: The Business Judgment Rule," 36. *Valparaiso University Law Review,* 631 (2002).

Denise Ping Lee, "The Business Judgment Rule: Should it Protect Nonprofit Directors?" 103 *Columbia Law Review,* 925.

Stuart K. Patrick v. Herbert Allen et al., 355 F. Supp.2d 704 (2005).

Baynes, Leonard M., "Racial Stereotypes, Broadcast Corporations, and the Business Judgment Rule," 37 *University of Richmond Law Review,* 819 (2003).

ARTICLE 3.1

The Indiana Supreme Court Lecture: The Rule That Isn't a Rule—The Business Judgment Rule

Douglas M. Branson

I. INTRODUCTION

The much misunderstood business judgment rule is not a "rule" at all. It has no mandatory content. It involves no substantive "do's" or "don'ts" for corporate directors or officers. Instead, it is a standard of judicial review, entailing only slight review of business decisions. Alternatively, it could be called a standard of non-review, entailing no review of the merits of a business decision corporate officials have made.

In what sense is the business judgment rule a rule, despite what he author says?

Various commentators' comments to the contrary, mostly based upon one celebrated (or lamented) Delaware decision,[1] strictly speaking, the standard of care applicable to corporate directors remains due care. As the Model Business Corporation Act and the Indiana statute phrase it, a director is to discharge her duties "with the care an ordinarily reasonably prudent person in a like position would exercise under similar circumstances." The standard of conduct is not "slight care," or "gross negligence," or anything other than due care.

But who cares? Many do, because in the modern era the number of temporal occasions at which the business rule *ex ante* becomes the yardstick for directors in shaping their decision-making processes, or *ex post* the yardstick by which courts and litigants review (or do not review) directors' decisions, have multiplied. The uses to which the rule may be put, and the temporal stages at which it may be encountered, either in transactional settings or in litigation, have proliferated, often to the detriment of those who would be critical of corporate conduct.

The business judgment rule is multi-faceted. Most generally, the business judgment rule acts as a presumption in favor of corporate managers' actions. Stronger still, the rule provides a safe harbor that makes both directors and their actions unassailable if certain prerequisites have been met. In litigation, the rule is a means for conserving judicial resources, thereby permitting courts to avoid being mired down in rehashing decisions that are inherently subjective and ill suited for judges, as opposed to business men and women. Last of all, the rule is the law's implementation of broad economic policy, built upon economic freedom and the encouragement of informed risk taking.

Newer uses to which the business judgment rule may be put include the means by which boards of directors adopt takeover defenses and by which, after the fact, courts review the adoption of those defenses when disgruntled shareholders pursue litigation. Another newer use is as a means by which corporations and their attorneys evaluate and, based upon that evaluation, recommend that courts dismiss derivative litigation.

Yet another use to which the business judgment rule may be put is as a teaching tool. I impress upon law students their future roles as "process engineers." By placing a premium upon the process that directors follow to reach a decision, rather than the resulting decision itself, the business judgment rule serves as a vibrant illustration of process engineering and the attorney's role in it. Moreover, the business judgment rule and the roles it may play are not limited to the corporate boardroom. The business judgment rule and good process are a part of "institutions law," useful to the attorney advising a neighborhood association, a PTA, or a faculty or faculty committee, as well as a corporation's board of directors.

Apropos of the business judgment rule's currency, prior to 1990 no Indiana decision parsed the business judgment rule. Subsequent to 1990, no less than four Indiana appellate court decisions have dealt with various elements of the rule. And, except for Delaware, the Indiana experience would be representative of the experience in most of the incorporating jurisdictions in the United States.

One last curiosity to be noted before delving into the rule itself is that, despite the vastly increased invocations of the rule in the modern era, the business judgment rule remains uncodified. With one exception, it is purely a product of judge-made law. It also remains an exclusively American legal construct, again with one exception. The exception is Australia, which in 1999, based upon a well-known United States formulation of the rule, enacted the first, and to this author's knowledge, the only statutory version of the business judgment rule. . . .

II. DO NOT CONFUSE POLICY BASES OR THE EFFECT OF THE RULE WITH THE RULE ITSELF

Courts are among the major perpetrators of this common error. "Courts," one venerable court stated, will not review "an honest mistake of business judgment." This economium is a statement of the result of the rule, not the rule itself.

A similar statement is that "directors of a commercial corporation may take chances, the same kind of chances that a man would take in his own business." This statement describes more a policy basis for the rule rather than the rule itself, or the rule stated in any helpful analytical way.

Yet another court recited, in a manner similar to the venerable court first quoted above: "ordinarily neither the directors nor the other officers of a corporation are liable for mere mistakes or errors of judgment."

III. COMMON FORMULATIONS OF THE RULE

There are really only two formulations of the rule with wide currency: the Delaware business judgment rule and the American Law Institute (ALI) formulation.

Although not without its critics, the ALI formulation seems to be a good one and has been adopted by the highest courts of several states. It states:

(c) A director or officer who makes a business judgment in good faith fulfills the [duty of care] if the director or officer:

(1) is not interested in the subject of his business judgment;

(2) is informed with respect to the subject of the business judgment to the extent the director or officer reasonably believes to be appropriate under the circumstances; and

(3) rationally believes that the business judgment is in the best interest of the corporation.

In shorthand, a director and her decision are protected from legal attack if: first, she and her colleagues made a judgment or decision; second, the decision makers were free from disabling conflicts of interest; third, they exercised some (not necessarily reasonable) care in informing themselves about the matter decided; and fourth, they had a rational (not necessarily reasonable) basis for the decision they made.

One function of the rule is as a conservator of judicial resources. If the rule required "reasonable" care or a "reasonable" basis for every decision, courts would have to hold plenary hearings (trials) because it is in those fora that questions of reasonableness are decided. The rule would not serve its function. Instead, if other prerequisites are present (proactive directors making a decision, freedom from conflicts of interest, and so on), the defending directors need demonstrate only some (slight) care and only a rational (plausible) basis for the decision made.

Delaware courts state the rule more succinctly and in the language of a "presumption." Thus, the business judgment rule is "a presumption that in making a business decision the directors of a corporation acted on an informed basis, in good faith and in the honest belief that the action taken was in the best interests of the company."

Delaware courts look for the same elements as do other courts: a judgment or decision, some care, and good faith (absence of conflicts of interest or base motive). The difference is, because of the use of presumption, in Delaware, a plaintiff shareholder has the burden of going forward. The challenging shareholder must demonstrate that the collegial body (the board) was infected by conflicts of interests on the part of a critical group (although perhaps less than a majority) of directors. Or the shareholder might offer credible proof that the directors merely rubber-stamped the Chief Executive Officer's (CEO's) decision, and thus had not made a judgment or decision of their own.

By contrast, the ALI version is a safe harbor. The directors have the burden of establishing the presence of the rule's elements. Once they do so, however, the payoff is greater. The director will have sailed into an impregnable harbor. On the other hand, presumptions may be upset, meaning perhaps that the directors will have to go through the ordeal of a trial in order to vindicate themselves. . . .

IV. FURTHER POLICY BASES FOR THE RULE

. . . The business judgment rule now more than ever is necessary to encourage truly independent persons to serve as directors. Persons of reason, intellect and integrity would not serve if the law exacted from them a degree of prescience not possessed by others." Once on the board, a strong business judgment rule is necessary to encourage those independent directors to engage in the type of informed risk taking that is essential to business success.

Returning to the judicial point of view, courts are ill-equipped to review business decisions. Those decisions often involve intangibles, intuitive insights or surmises as to business matters such as competitive outlook, cost structure, and economic and industry trends. Business decisions often come down to matters of touch and feel not susceptible to systematic analysis.

Courts may also buttress their non-involvement with a statutory argument. Corporate statutes universally provide that it is the board of directors, and not the court, who is to manage or supervise the management of the corporation's business and affairs.

Last of all, as previously mentioned, a policy behind the rule is conservation of the judicial resource. The business judgment rule is a filter that enables courts to easily screen out non-meritorious challenges to the actions of directors and executives.

V. RELATIONSHIP TO THE STANDARD OF CONDUCT

The standard of conduct is due care. It is not slight care or gross negligence. With that established, the business judgment rule may be the *de facto* standard of conduct in cases in which directors are proactive, making a judgment or decision, that may be a deliberative decision to take no action, as opposed to cases of complete nonfeasance.

The last policy reason leads nicely to a hypothetical showing how the rule and the standard of conduct might play off one another. After a shareholder suit is filed, the directors and the corporation might file a motion for summary judgment. They could attach thereto an affidavit by the Chief Financial Officer stating that she had prepared and distributed a written report on the pros and cons of the decision to be made, an affidavit by a director stating that the board met and received an oral report from another senior executive or outside consultant, and a copy of the board resolution, certified by the corporate secretary as a true and correct copy of the resolution contained in the minutes of the board meeting. The court would examine such affidavit evidence. The business judgment rule requires only some care, so the court need not review the decision-making process on a plenary basis. The court might then grant the defense motion. . . .

VI. COMPONENTS OF THE RULE—THERE MUST HAVE BEEN A DECISION OR JUDGMENT

Sometimes it is said that there must be an *independent* judgment or decision. Rubber-stamping the CEO's or controlling shareholder's wish or command will not do. One of the classic cases involved a shareholder contention that, when the directors of the Chicago Cubs baseball club voted to uphold majority owner P.K. Wrigley's decision to have no lights and therefore no night baseball, those directors were merely implementing Wrigley's inveterate belief that God meant baseball to be a game played in the daytime. According to the plaintiff minority shareholder, the reasoning given by the directors—that night baseball would ruin the neighborhood surrounding Wrigley Field—was pretextual. Nonetheless, the Illinois court afforded business judgment rule protection to the Chicago Cubs' board of directors and its decision.

A decision to make no decision is also a judgment or decision for purposes of the rule's application. Veteran directors, though, say that boards often act by consensus and that consensus builds by a process of accretion. A requirement that matters be put to motions and votes encourages confrontation. It forces boards to act like legislative bodies or, worse yet, like faculty meetings at colleges and universities.

The business judgment rule's emphasis on the process leading to formal judgments also constitutes make-work for lawyers who, as process engineers, come to have a larger role than they should have in the board room. Similarly, critics of the modern business judgment rule say that insistence on formal decisions places a premium on play acting and on paper trails. It does not improve the quality of decisions that are made.

VII. COMPONENTS OF THE RULE—THE JUDGMENT OR DECISION MUST BE AN INFORMED ONE

Again, the requirement is some care, not due care. This is what the Supreme Court of Delaware meant in *Smith v. Von Gorkom* when it stated that "we think the concept of gross negligence is also the proper standard for determining whether a business judgment reached by a board of directors was an informed one." That is, the statement upon which arch-conservative commentators rest their argument that in the modern era, the standard of conduct has changed across the board to gross negligence or slight care, rather than due care. . . .

VIII. COMPONENTS OF THE RULE—ABSENCE OF DISABLING CONFLICTS OF INTEREST

Conflicts that disable and those that do not are at the antipodes of a spectrum. At the disabling antipode are direct pecuniary interests of the director, her family or associates, or an affiliate of the director, in the judgment or decision for which the rule's protections are sought. . . .

When a critical mass of directors also wore second hats as well-paid, long term consultants, hired and fired by the controlling shareholder, their decision was held not entitled to business judgment rule protection. Bank directors who circumvented local banking laws by forming a "competing loan company" were not entitled to the rule's protection for that decision because they accepted management fees from the loan company.

Few universal principles may be stated. One may be that so-called structural bias, that is, the predilection of directors to favor those of the same social or economic class, such as fellow directors or senior managers, in the eyes of most courts does not disable. The argument is frequently made in the context of special litigation committees' recommendations that derivative suits not go forward against fellow directors. The "there but for the grace of God go I" motivation that may lurk behind a decision that litigation is not in the corporation's best interests, while real, is not, generally speaking, legally cognizable. Nonetheless, out of an abundance of caution, and also a subliminal recognition of the structural bias problem, most boards staff special litigation committees with new "expansion" directors who can in no way be alleged to have any connection with the wrongdoing alleged and against whom the structural bias argument has less force.

Another universal principle is that if a single decision-maker seeks the protection of the business judgment rule she must, "like Caesar's wife, be above reproach."[2]

A sub-species of the conflict of interest species is the dominated director case. Rather than a discernable pecuniary interest, what is alleged is that the director is beholden generally to a controlling shareholder or CEO, thus being disabled by his lack of independence. A plaintiff making such an argument faces an uphill battle. Courts are loathe to find that an otherwise reputable business person is not his or her own person. Courts would rather rely on an identifiable pecuniary interest to ground a finding that a particular decision maker was disabled. Nonetheless, the cases do succeed from time to time. A five person board staffed by outside counsel, inside counsel, and a corporate employee, all of whom were beholden to the controlling shareholder, who occupied the fourth board slot, was found by the Ohio Supreme Court to have been dominated.

By contrast, if counsel and other advisers scrub the board clean, removing all inferences of conflicts or of board domination, and then those non-executive, independent directors, convening in executive session, run the decision-making process from start to finish, their decision is entitled not only to business judgment rule protection, but also to *heightened* business judgment rule protection. What that means analytically is hard to say, and it may only be a word choice for emphasis. The result though is clear. The decision made will be very nearly unassailable if the rule's other elements are met.

IX. COMPONENTS OF THE RULE—A RATIONAL BASIS FOR THE DECISION

Directors could be free of disabling—indeed, all—conflicts or domination, gather voluminous information, digest, and make not only an unwise, but an off-the-wall decision. Under the ALI version, such a decision would not be entitled to business judgment rule protection. A decision to put a man on Mars, or to accept not only a lower but clearly inferior bid for the company, might be judgments lacking a rational basis.

On this score, some judges and commentators say that directors are not liable unless their decision or judgment was manifest folly. Others say that directors' decisions are unassailable unless they amount to a gross abuse of discretion. Those phrasings may be too permissive. By contrast, the statement that "all directorial decisions must have a sound business purpose" goes too far in the other direction. . . .

X. COMPONENTS OF THE RULE—UMBRELLA REQUIREMENT (BROODING OMNIPRESENCE) OF GOOD FAITH

In a transactional setting, an attorney advising a board might run through the rule's elements as a checklist: judgment or decision, absence of disabling conflicts, some care, and a rational basis. She would then do well to pause, raise her head, and sniff—loudly and several times. All good lawyers apply a "smell test." Even if all of the law's formal requirements have been met, if the deal under consideration does not feel right, or smell right, they do not do the deal, or at least they advise postponement until they dig down to the source of their olfactory concern.

In the business judgment rule context, the umbrella requirement of good faith is a surrogate of sorts for a smell test. It also has particular utility in two more delimited areas.

One is when the decision-making process has been infected by illicit motives other than pecuniary conflicts. Revenge, spite, jealousy, or other base motives may be behind a decision. In such a case, lack of good faith would be the proper means by which to attack the decision.

Another is knowing approval of illegal conduct. Directors who approved forgiveness of indebtedness by a political party when the forgiveness was tantamount to an illegal campaign contribution were not entitled to protection, even though they had no personal conflicts and they had a rational basis for the decision made.

A recent decision stated that directors who knowingly or deliberately withhold material information from the board in order to mislead shareholders lack good faith. Under such circumstances the shroud of protection otherwise afforded by the business judgment rule would fall to the ground.[3] Another recent case held that a cryptic and peremptory refusal of a derivative action plaintiff's demand, in a case of obvious wrongdoing, constituted a lack of good faith. The court could thus look into the merits of demand denial itself.[4]

The good faith requirement is something of a catch-all. It also demonstrates the flexibility of the business judgment rule. For example, in a dominated directors' case, a court could alternatively find that the directors rubber-stamped the decision of a controlling shareholder and made no judgment or decision, that the directors lacked independence, or that the directors lacked the required good faith. In nearly every business judgment rule case, then, judges have a number of "outs," although in their wisdom judges may choose not to use them. This is as it should be because, first and foremost, the business judgment rule is a judicial construct, born out of judges' realizations about limitations on their abilities, about conservation of the judicial resource, and about their proper role in business cases.

XI. PRESUMPTION OR PREREQUISITE?

Delaware courts—and courts in jurisdictions that follow Delaware law—phrase the business judgment rule as a "presumption" that "in making a decision, the directors of a corporation acted on an informed basis and in good faith."

What is the "bursting bubble" theory of presumptions?

The most frequent understanding of presumption is the Thayerian, or "bursting bubble," theory of presumptions. That is to say, a party's proof of circumstances A, B, and C (here, a judgment or decision, by duly elected directors who exercised some care) leads to a presumption of the ultimate fact, D (here, that reasonable care was in fact exercised). If the opposing party can poke a hole in the foundational facts (conflict of interest, were woefully under-informed, and so on), then the bubble bursts and the presumption of the ultimate fact dissipates or, indeed, evaporates altogether. This theory of presumption predominates in American law and is the version the Federal Rules of Evidence adopted.

When Delaware and other courts use the language of presumption, they seem blissfully unaware of what the law of evidence teaches us about presumptions. Perhaps they are articulating some other non-Thayerian view of presumption when, in a case or two, they have referred to the business judgment rule as a "powerful presumption."

I doubt it. Instead I think that Delaware jurists have given the bursting bubble theory very little thought. And, that lack of deliberation is of no moment in Delaware. Delaware courts require more than a pin prick—indeed, much, much more—before finding that the presumption of due care set up by application of the rule vanishes.

For example, in *In re Walt Disney Company Derivative Litigation,* the Delaware chancellor reviewed the payment of a $ 140 million severance package to a crony of CEO Michael Eisner who had served less than a year as corporate president and who had demonstrated a singular lack of accomplishment (many would say outright malfeasance) in the position. Nonetheless, the directors approved a "no fault" termination, triggering payment of the severance. The directors who approved included Eisner, three corporate officers beholden to Eisner, the principal of the grammar school Eisner's children attended, the president of the university Eisner's children attended, Eisner's personal architect, and Eisner's personal attorney. If ever a plaintiff pricked and burst a bubble on lack-of-independence grounds, the plaintiffs did in *Disney.* Nonetheless, the Delaware Court refused to review the merits of the no fault termination decision, applying the business judgment rule.

Delaware courts' lack of deliberation on the use and misuse of presumptions may be of little significance in Delaware but could affect outcomes elsewhere. The courts of many states, including Indiana, look to Delaware case law in processing corporate law cases. Blending the Delaware business judgment rule with the accepted wisdom about presumptions, other state courts could come to a result opposite that which Delaware courts would reach, holding corporate directors over for trial on breach of duty of care allegations.

The American Law Institute states its version of the rule as a safe harbor rather than a presumption. Although the ALI version has been criticized as a movement from "presumption to prerequisite," the ALI version offers greater protection and clarity than the presumption formulation of the business judgment rule because the ALI version requires a greater quantum of proof by directors. . . .

XII. CONCLUSION

. . . That then is the business judgment rule—a rule that is not a rule. It is a great law school teaching tool. In the non-academic world, properly applied, the rule permits courts to accord to boards of directors the proper amount of deference to board decisions. Last of all, the rule provides a schematic for any advisor counseling any collegial group, and not just a board of directors, to reach a judgment or decision that in all likelihood will be a sound one.

END NOTES

1. *Smith v. Van Gorkom*, 488 A.2d 858 (Del. 1985) (discussed further throughout).
2. *Kahn v. Tremont Corp.*, 694 A.2d 422, 430 (Del. Ch. 1997) (quoting *Lewis v. Fuqua*, 502 A.2d 962, 967).
3. *Potter v. Pholad*, 560 N.E.2d 388, 395 (Minn. Ct. App. 1997)
4. *Harhen v. Brown*, 710 N.E.2d 224, 234-36 (Mass. Ct. App.), *rev'd*, 730 N.E.2d 859 (Mass. 2000).

ARTICLE 3.2

The Business Judgment Rule: Should It Protect Nonprofit Directors?

Denise Ping Lee

INTRODUCTION

Following the collection of over $ 1.5 billion[1] in donations by over 200 nonprofit organizations [n2] for victims of the World Trade Center tragedy, an important question rose to the forefront of our generous public's mind: How much of that money truly arrived in the form of assistance to those in need and how much eventually disappeared through mismanagement and greed?

Public scandals involving nonprofits have graced the news quite frequently, though perhaps still less than what would be expected from a sector growing at the rate of almost three times its for-profit counterpart. From the recent American Red Cross debacle over the mismanagement of its Liberty Fund, to the United Way scandal in 1992 involving the former-President William Aramony and his penchant for limousines and Concorde flights, the American public has had many occasions to be disappointed by organizations supposedly created to "do good." When these types of events occur and the public is left with its charitable coffers plundered, the puzzling question always remains: Where was the board of directors throughout the incident, and to what level of care should its members be held responsible? For those directors or officers who engage in self-dealing, their actions will frequently constitute a breach of their duty of loyalty under a justifiably stringent fairness standard. Yet the more difficult question lies in determining the standard by which to judge the actions of those remaining directors who, despite the absence of personal financial gain, may have failed to adequately supervise the organization's affairs, thereby breaching their duty of care.

Historically, nonprofit directors were regarded as trustees with a correspondingly strict standard of care in their management of a public trust. Trustees, as remains the case today, were expected to exercise reasonable care and skill, whereby findings of ordinary negligence resulted in personal liability. As the nonprofit landscape changed over the years, however, legislatures and courts began replacing trustee precepts with corporate governance principles, often with little or no alteration. Through this process, nonprofit directors in some jurisdictions gradually came to benefit from the substantial leeway courts allow corporate directors in their management decisions, which enjoy the protection of the common law business judgment rule. For a variety of reasons justifiable in the business context, the rule precludes courts from second-guessing directors' decisions as long as they are rational, not self-interested, and made in good faith on an informed basis. In essence, the business judgment rule only punishes instances of gross negligence, as opposed to the trustee standard, which attaches liability for ordinary negligence.

It is highly questionable whether nonprofit directors warrant the extraordinary latitude bestowed upon for-profit directors when, in theory at least, the mission statements of their respective organizations lie at opposite ends of the spectrum. Despite this fact, courts have inched toward the rule's acceptance in the nonprofit context, but still have not definitively determined whether the rule should apply or, alternatively, whether ordinary negligence should suffice to constitute a breach of the nonprofit director's duty of care.

Mindful of this uncertainty, this Note argues against application of the business judgment rule to nonprofit directors because its safe harbor protection would further impair the already severely limited accountability found in nonprofit organizations today. Indeed, the considerable differences between nonprofits and their for-profit counterparts, not limited to organizational structure and market incentives, would defeat the purpose of the rule and only lead to more disappointing management lapses similar to those mentioned previously. In its place, this Note proposes that judicial review of nonprofit director actions be based on ordinary negligence, thereby aligning the corporate duty of care standard, defined as one of a reasonable person, with a commensurate level of judicial review.

I. NONPROFITS, THEIR ROLE IN SOCIETY, AND THE EVOLUTION OF THE DIRECTOR'S STANDARD OF CARE

A. Background on Nonprofits

1. The Nonprofit Economy

Nonprofits have become an important part of the economy by any standard. Comprising over 1.5 million organizations,[2] nonprofits employ nearly 8.6 million workers,[3] earn nearly [*929] $ 700 billion annually, and have operating expenditures of $ 548 billion, equivalent to 7.5% of the country's gross domestic product. Moreover, the total number of nonprofits has been expanding at an astonishing rate, with no clear end in sight. Tax-exempt nonprofits organized under section 501(c)(3) of the Internal Revenue Code increased by 58.2% between 1989 and 1998—far exceeding the growth rate of for-profit corporations.[4]

The world of nonprofits has changed significantly over time; some have continued to operate as small, neighborhood charitable organizations, while others have transformed themselves into large, quasi-business operations, similar to their behemoth corporate counterparts. As with any group of this size, nonprofit activities vary widely, with organizations ranging from traditional charities, such as neighborhood soup kitchens and the Red Cross, to hospitals run in a manner similar to for-profit hospitals, to even the National Football League. Contrary to popular belief, private philanthropy is not the main source of nonprofit revenue; rather, over forty percent of nonprofit revenue is derived from fees for services performed. Although the size of the nonprofit sector has been rapidly increasing, financial support from the government has been falling over time, thereby causing nonprofits to become more "market-oriented in their operations, but at the price of posing questions about the legitimacy of the special tax and other privileges that they enjoy."

2. What Is a Nonprofit?

A nonprofit is generally defined as an organization "barred from distributing its net earnings, if any, to individuals who exercise control over it, such as members, officers, directors, or trustees."[5] This characteristic—referred to as the "nondistribution constraint"—does not prohibit a nonprofit from earning a profit, but merely disallows the distribution of any profit earned. Similar to the state laws governing for-profit corporations, most nonprofit statutes permit nonprofits to be formed "for any lawful purpose," not necessarily a strictly charitable one. Despite this similarity to for-profit corporations, nonprofits are distinguished by "the absence of stock or other indicia of ownership that give their owners a simultaneous share in both profits and control." Thus, nonprofits have no real owners, though some may argue that, theoretically, they belong to the public trust. In some cases, nonprofits are made up of "members," whose position may be similar to that of shareholders with respect to voting power. Although this characteristic seems to make nonprofit governance similar to for-profit governance, such a depiction is misleading because state statutes tend to give nonprofits "complete freedom in establishing criteria for membership and in determining what rights . . . the members are to have." . . .

[A] distinction that has been made in classifying nonprofits is between donative and commercial nonprofits. A donative nonprofit receives most or all of its income through grants or donations: "Organizations for the relief of the needy, such as the Salvation Army, the American Red Cross, and CARE, are perhaps the most obvious examples." Commercial nonprofits, in contrast, receive most of their income by charging fees for their services: "Many nursing homes, most hospitals, and the American Automobile Association would clearly fall within this latter category."

3. The Law Governing Nonprofits

The rapid development of the nonprofit sector has caught many legislatures unprepared. As a result, "nonprofit corporation law is poorly developed and varies in significant respects from one state to the next." In most states, nonprofit corporation statutes closely parallel those governing business corporations and may be even more permissive. One example of the greater leeway given to nonprofits is the frequent allowance of self-perpetuating boads.

The responsibility of enforcing nonprofit law generally rests solely with the state attorney general, whose task is to protect the public interest. Unfortunately, the monitoring of nonprofits is frequently understaffed and lowly prioritized, given the many tasks that the attorney general's office must juggle with limited resources and time. Thus, nonprofit law is empty rhetoric in many respects, including the laws governing the fiduciary duties of directors. Nonprofit directors are given the privilege of acting essentially "free from supervision," which allows them greater leeway to breach their fiduciary duties. Unlike business corporations, which provide for shareholder derivative suits, standing for suits against nonprofits is extremely limited, and few parties are able to sue even if they have legitimate grievances. Even the two groups most likely to take a strong interest in the nonprofit—namely its donors and beneficiaries—have been denied standing. . . .

For these reasons, nonprofit governance poses significant problems. The nondistribution constraint "is often poorly policed and . . . as a consequence, the managers of nonprofits often find, and take advantage of, the opportunity to profit at the expense of the organization." Because many nonprofit boards are entirely autonomous and self-perpetuating, which by definition is the case when they have no voting members, directors can frequently misuse revenues and privileges due to the lack of monitoring. Another danger particularly relevant to the nonprofit context is the possibility that the charitable character of the organization will be "usurped by being used as fronts for illicit interests." The most frequently pursued claims against nonprofit directors allege some sort of self-dealing, but other claims may exist in cases of mismanagement, neglect, improper (but disinterested) decision making, and failure to comply with the corporation's internal laws. Given the lack of sufficient monitoring by state attorneys general, the board of directors is often the only governing body in a position to oversee the proper management of the nonprofit corporation. Furthermore, even in cases where the attorney general might choose to intervene, the board has an insider's perspective that tends to be more effective in detecting misbehavior. Having such a pivotal role makes the contours of the board's duty of care all the more important.

Why would the business judgment rule be any more appropriate for one business than for another?

II. THE RATIONALE BEHIND THE BUSINESS JUDGMENT RULE AND ITS INAPPLICABILITY TO NONPROFITS

This section analyzes the reasons frequently espoused in favor of the business judgment rule in the corporate context and discusses whether these reasons retain their potency when carried over to the nonprofit arena. The most frequently cited justifications of the rule include: (1) promoting risk-taking and allowing shareholders to voluntarily undertake risk; (2) encouraging competent directors to serve; (3) preventing judicial second-guessing; (4) allowing directors sufficient leeway in managing the corporation; and (5) permitting more effective market mechanisms to manage director behavior. Upon analyzing each of these justifications in relation to nonprofits, this Note concludes that allowing nonprofit directors the protection of the business judgment rule is not warranted because it would result in an unacceptable tradeoff in the balance between encouraging director service and maintaining an acceptable liability standard.

A. Risk-Taking

The primary argument articulated in defense of the business judgment rule is the need to encourage risk-taking activities on the part of corporate actors. Without the rule, many fear that directors and officers would become excessively cautious, aware that decisions that are subsequently determined to have been improper could expose them to substantial personal liability. Modern portfolio theory dealing with diversification of risk is also relevant to this rationale, as shareholders may be said to undertake the risk of bad business judgments voluntarily and rationally in the hope of higher returns. By picking and choosing firms that run the gamut from low-to high-risk profiles, diversified shareholders are able to maximize their returns while minimizing much of the risk associated with the more volatile components of their portfolios. In the corporate context, the business judgment rule functions quite well: It grants broad director discretion and allows each corporation to pursue its own course and risk level, while giving ultimate power to shareholders to choose firms appropriate to their appetite for risk. Without the rule, judges in a sense would be making the choice of an appropriate risk level for all investors by forcing corporations to behave similarly based on a reasonable standard of caution. The business corporation model functions especially well because shareholders who grow dissatisfied with director management and risk levels can easily sell their stock in the open market and invest in companies more suited to their desired level of risk.

The argument in favor of encouraging risk-taking is considerably weaker, however, when carried over to the nonprofit arena. Nonprofit organizations should be more cautious in preserving their resources because their obligation to donors and patrons is not to maximize profits, but rather to distribute funds to those in need or to provide services to its members or the general public. Significant risk-taking is rarely something [*947] bargained for when dealing with nonprofit corporations, and most people would assume that their donations are not going toward risky projects that may fail to serve the nonprofit mission. In a similar vein, some courts hold directors of financial institutions to a higher standard of care than directors of nonfinancial institutions because of the nature of the business and a general discomfort with the "notion of banks as entrepreneurial risk-takers." One important bank function is managing other people's money, a function that "places bank directors and officers in something close to a genuine fiduciary or trust relationship with their depositors." This line of reasoning could also be applied to charitable nonprofit directors, who are given the important function of collecting other people's money, in a quasi-contractual relationship with the donor, and distributing as much of the original value as possible to the proper beneficiaries. . . .

Risk-taking as a rationale for the business judgment rule in the nonprofit context is further weakened by its inapplicability to the investment concerns of donors and patrons. Modern portfolio theory does not apply in the nonprofit world because donors and patrons do not own equity interests in the organizations to which they contribute and, therefore, receive no direct benefit from risky activities that possibly lead to higher returns. Even beneficiaries are not certain to receive the benefit of risky activities, since there is no contractual arrangement guaranteeing a portion of the returns. Once a contribution has been made to a nonprofit, donors can only hope that their contribution will not be squandered on risky projects that do not further charitable undertakings. Unlike their shareholder brethren, donors are not privileged with the exit option of selling their nonprofit stock either to reap the returns or to manifest their dissatisfaction. Donors are arguably able to punish the organization by deciding never to donate to that particular organization again. But ascertaining whether a nonprofit has acted improperly is extremely difficult, and, even if it were possible, it always occurs too late—donors have already lost their contribution. With few reporting requirements, nonprofits benefit enormously from the frequently prohibitive cost of accessing information that would aid donors' decisions on future giving. Rarely would it be worth the time and money for donors to investigate thoroughly, given that they have no right to residual returns from any recovery.

B. Encouraging Competent Directors to Serve

The second most frequently cited argument in favor of the business judgment rule is the need to encourage competent individuals to serve as directors. Because directors generally earn relatively low wages for their positions, some fear that qualified directors would be reluctant to serve without the protection of the rule. This argument has even been made in the corporate context despite the fact that many directors are paid quite handsomely for the insignificant amount of time they spend discharging their duties. The argument seems much more compelling, however, in the context of nonprofit directors, who are not likely to earn anything at all. However, a thorough examination of the differences between nonprofit and for-profit boards leads to the conclusion that the same rationale of encouraging competent directors to serve would bolster support for discarding the business judgment rule.

First, nonprofit boards tend to be self-perpetuating, since most nonprofits do not have members with the power to vote for directors. This peculiarity of the nonprofit structure calls for a stricter standard than that applied under the business judgment rule because there is a greater risk in nonprofits that incompetent directors will be impossible to remove. The rule works properly in the for-profit context because competent directors are encouraged, and incompetent directors are continually subject to shareholder voting and proxy fights—mechanisms that are commonly used to remove poorly performing directors.

Second, directors of nonprofits are typically uncompensated, with the exception of directors serving on private foundation boards. This seems to be the best argument in favor of applying the business judgment rule, or perhaps an even lower standard of review, since many nonprofit directors are receiving no monetary gain whatsoever. Yet, many states already have separate statutes protecting uncompensated directors from personal liability so as to encourage these directors to serve. The problem of uncompensated directors being subject to liability is best dealt with legislatively rather than judicially, so that each state provides the proper incentives according to its situation and the desires of its voting public. Even without these statutes, a host of other mechanisms are in place to minimize the possibility that directors will be forced to pay out-of-pocket, such as limited standing, courts' discretion in punishing only the most deserving cases, indemnification provisions, and directors' and officers' insurance. For these reasons, the fear of discouraging competent directors from service is largely obviated through other means. . . .

Third, nonprofit boards tend to be larger than those of business corporations, with an average size of greater than thirty members, compared with thirteen for businesses. "Nonprofit directors and trustees are selected for many reasons: they represent constituent groups, have special [*952] skills, are sources of funding, bring recognition to the organization through their prominence, or represent the community or sources of support." The larger board size likely leads to individual nonprofit directors having less information and feeling less personal responsibility for decisions than their for-profit counterparts. . . .

The arguments in favor of stricter standards are buttressed by the distressing fact that, for now, nonprofit boards are largely ineffective in providing oversight. Known for their looser practices and sometimes sloppy administrative procedures, nonprofits are often filled with board members that have had "few other institutional, board, corporate, or legal experiences," as opposed to the majority of corporate directors who have had such experiences. This means that while corporate board members understand what is expected of them in carrying out their directorial duties, the same cannot be said for nonprofit board members. For this reason, it is imperative that the business judgment rule not allow nonprofit boards an even further incentive to shirk their duties. Nonprofit boards are created to govern, and it makes little sense to apply a liability rule to attract directors that ultimately serves to undermine the purpose of the board.

C. Judicial Second-Guessing

Why might judges be in a better position than some business executives to assess the propriety of particular business decisions?

A third argument in favor of the business judgment rule contends that courts and judges are ill-equipped to second-guess business decisions; thus, a stricter level of scrutiny would lead to economically inefficient levels of liability since the benefit of hindsight may lead to excessively punitive judicial review. One court has suggested that failing to respect decisions made in good faith by disinterested directors would "invite courts to become super-directors." Nonetheless, this argument is most persuasive when dealing with complicated business decisions that judges may be unable to understand fully. When carried over to the nonprofit context—especially in relation to donative nonprofits—the argument is much weaker because charitable decision making tends to be less complex and easier for judges to comprehend than business decisions. Unlike for-profit directors, who perhaps have MBAs or law degrees, directors of many donative nonprofits do not have specific educational training with respect to their duties;[6] therefore, it is difficult to argue that a learned judge could not evaluate the substance of a nonprofit decision and determine its reasonableness.

Even with regard to commercial nonprofits, where decision making can be quite complex, the judicial inadequacy argument is difficult to sustain. Corporate directors, whether for-profit or nonprofit, should not be entitled to special protection against judicial second-guessing when similarly situated professionals are not. Lawyers, doctors, accountants, and all other professionals are subject to ordinary negligence review, and courts have never questioned their ability to second-guess decisions after the fact. The negligence standard is one based on a "reasonable person," which by definition should be interpretable and reviewable by judges. Though the standard has always resisted mechanical interpretation, it has remained an integral part of our civil liability system. If the problem lies with the standard itself, then perhaps it should be discarded in all areas, not just in judicial review of director actions.

D. Avoiding Shareholder Management of the Corporation

Another frequently cited rationale for implementing the business judgment rule is that it allows directors, rather than shareholders, to manage the corporation's affairs. The theory is that without the hurdle imposed by the business judgment rule, shareholders would litigate more frequently in order to influence the managerial decisions of directors. However, this argument is necessarily founded upon the fact that corporate shareholders have standing to sue. Nonprofits function in an entirely different context: Standing is extremely limited, and the usurpation of the board's power is less of a problem. Because nonprofits do not have shareholders with an equity interest in the corporation, the only group that might be interested in managing the affairs of the corporation would be the general public, including donors and beneficiaries. Although a similar agency problem exists in the nonprofit context as in the for-profit context between the general public, as residual claimant, and the directors as agents, standing limitations in the nonprofit context prevent the possibility of donor or patron management. The attorney general, as the main enforcer of the public's rights, continues to be the primary source of litigation against nonprofits, and donors and beneficiaries are rarely, if ever, granted that same privilege. Thus, any heightened standard of care would only be enforceable by the attorney general, thereby avoiding excessive control over directors by donors or beneficiaries. Arguably, without the business judgment rule, there might be more governmental control of nonprofit organizations through the attorney general; but . . . the attorney general is likely to focus on issues of greater perceived importance rather than attempting to influence the general management of numerous nonprofit organizations. . . .

E. Market Mechanisms Lacking in the Nonprofit Sphere

Last, but not least, in the corporate context, implementing an ordinary negligence standard, by not granting the safe harbor protection of the business judgment rule, is arguably less necessary to curb director misbehavior, due to the many self-enforcing market mechanisms that control corporate conduct just as effectively as litigation or more so. The corporate structure, including ownership rights and a fiercely competitive corporate environment, allows for many methods of control beyond litigation. Effective constraints that serve to manage director behavior in the for-profit context include strong competition both in product markets and in the market for managerial talent. In the for-profit context, having to compete on an organizational level (against other businesses providing similar products or services) and on a personal level (for directorial jobs and prestige) causes directors to be more diligent in their duties, for fear of being ousted from their positions. . . .

This leads to the single most important reason why the business judgment rule should not be applied to nonprofits: The nonprofit sector lacks comparable market mechanisms to control director misbehavior. The only means of ensuring an adequate level of care on the part of nonprofit directors is through statutory standards, litigation, and judicial review. "For nonprofit organizations, directors' legal accountability, not market forces, is the principal line of defense against director failure." A standard of care penalizing only gross negligence would virtually eliminate accountability, leaving directors to do as they please, unfettered by other shackles.

In comparison to for-profits, nonprofits generally do not encounter strong product market competition for the services they provide, although competition is increasing in certain sectors and among commercial nonprofits that charge for their services. Even with the trend toward greater competition, nonprofits face far less competition than business corporations, and, even so, competition in the nonprofit sphere has less of an impact on director behavior because the emphasis is not placed on the bottom line. Furthermore, "in a world in which managerial performance is not based on easily observable criteria (like profits or share prices)," the nonprofit market for skilled managerial talent is not as effective in inducing directors to behave properly.

More significantly, the lack of nonprofit ownership eliminates numerous accountability benefits that go hand-in-hand with ownership rights, including the "election of directors, calling of special meetings, and removal of directors with or without cause." The fact that directors cannot own shares in nonprofits further exacerbates the situation by extinguishing the possibility of aligning the incentives of the director with the nonprofit organization. . . .

The aforementioned market mechanisms serve an invaluable function in the for-profit context by effectively controlling director behavior, and, therefore, may counterbalance the negative repercussions of implementing a gross negligence standard of review in that context. There is little possibility, however, of creating a true "market" in the nonprofit sector. Thus, the prospect of ex ante control over director conduct is unlikely, leaving essentially only one control mechanism: ex post judicial evaluation of director decisions. Although this mechanism is inevitably less effective than a self-enforcing system, it is nonetheless vital to the nonprofit sector if we are to have any assurance of accountability among nonprofit directors. . . .

CONCLUSION

Nonprofit directors work in an environment quite different from that of their corporate peers. Unfortunately, the law has tended to overlook the particular needs of nonprofits and has instead outfitted nonprofits with a corporate suit that does not quite fit. Without fully contemplating the negative consequences of applying the business judgment rule to nonprofit directors, state courts have done and could further do much damage to the accountability provided by the nonprofit director's standard of care, one that is already far lower than might be expected. This Note has argued that the adoption of the business judgment rule for nonprofits does not make sound public policy sense if society seeks to encourage directors to discharge their duties faithfully. The significant differences that nonprofits face in organizational structure and in the market that surrounds them lead to severely undesirable consequences when a gross negligence standard of review is applied. Subject to negative repercussions only when reckless indifference is proven, nonprofit directors are given great latitude to mismanage nonprofit corporations whose existences are founded upon a public trust, whereby numerous privileges are afforded nonprofits at the public's expense.

One step forward in the process of implementing proper standards for nonprofits . . . would be to discard the business judgment rule in the nonprofit context, and, in its place, apply an ordinary negligence standard of review. This would be crucial to moving the director's duty of care beyond purely theoretical perimeters to a new rubric of better-delineated, higher accountability standards. Nonprofit governance plays a unique and important role in protecting the public trust, and, until now, it has done a fairly poor job of sustaining this burden. The societal interest in the proper administration of charitable organizations demands a more stringent standard of care in exchange for the numerous benefits bestowed upon these organizations. Only by these means will the public regain its faith in the capacity of nonprofit directors to dutifully put an end to the many wolves in sheep's clothing, lurking in the nonprofit sphere.

END NOTES

1. David Whelan, September 11 Charities Have Raised $ 1.5-Billion and Distributed $ 476-Million, Chron. Philanthropy, Dec. 21, 2001.
2. National Center for Charitable Statistics
3. This employment figure does not include religious workers or volunteers, which are estimated to be another one million paid employees and 7.3 million volunteers.
4. The growth rate for all U.S. firms from 1992 to 1997 was seven percent
5. Henry B. Hansmann, The Role of Nonprofit Enterprise, 89 Yale L.J. 835, 838 (1980).
6. Andre P. Juneau, Common Liability Risks of Nonprofit Directors & Officers: Good Intentions & Unfamiliar Roles May Create Problems for Board Volunteers, Texas Association of Nonprofit Organizations 1 (Summer 2001).

ARTICLE 3.3

Stuart K. Patrick v. Herbert Allen et al.

What would it mean for a director to be "disinterested"?

Stuart K. Patrick, a shareholder in Real Property Owners, Inc. brings action against RPO's board of directors for their actions in directing the company. He alleges that the board of directors is in breach of their fiduciary duties because for the past 48 years RPO has been leasing their sole property, a 174 acre piece of land in New York to Deepdale Golf Club, an elite 250 member club, for millions of dollars under the fair market value for the property. In fact, they lease the property to Deepdale at break-even prices. Not surprisingly, many of the directors of Real Property Owners, Inc. are also members of the Deepdale Golf Club. The directors argued that their decisions as directors were shielded from judicial review by the business judgment rule and that the complaint failed to state a claim for either breach of fiduciary duty or waste. The court found that the shareholder sufficiently alleged that, because of the directors' status as members of the golf club to which the corporation leased its property, they were not disinterested directors with respect to the transactions involving the golf club. Thus, the court cannot conclude that the business judgment rule protected the directors' decisions concerning the golf club and the property.

WILLIAM H. PAULEY III, DISTRICT JUDGE:

Stuart K. Patrick ("Plaintiff" or "Patrick"), a shareholder and former director of Real Property Owners, Inc. ("RPO"), brings this diversity action against the directors of RPO (collectively, "Defendants"). Patrick alleges that Defendants breached their fiduciary duties to RPO and its shareholders and committed corporate waste by mismanaging RPO's lone asset: a 174-acre property in Nassau County that has been leased to Deepdale Golf Club at break-even rent for the past 48 years.

Presently before this Court is Defendants' motion to dismiss the Complaint . . . Defendants argue that their decisions as directors are shielded from judicial review by the business judgment rule and that the Complaint fails to state a claim for either breach of fiduciary duty or waste. For the reasons set forth below, Defendants' motion to dismiss is granted in part and denied in part.

Background

Deepdale is an exclusive golf club in North Hills, New York, with approximately 250 members and an initiation fee of nearly $ 100,000. Deepdale's members include prominent figures in sports, entertainment, fashion and finance. In 1947, Deepdale Golf Club was located on the former Vanderbilt Estate in Lake Success. At that time, members of Deepdale formed RPO as a privately traded New York corporation and organized it "as a real estate business, a real estate agency, and a real estate brokerage business" to purchase the tract occupied by Deepdale. RPO sold that property to private investors in 1954. Two years later, RPO purchased the Grace Estate in North Hills (the "Property") and leased it to Deepdale. A December 2000 appraisal valued the 174-acre Property at $ 35–40 million.

Since acquiring the Property, RPO has leased it exclusively to Deepdale. The arrangement began by an oral agreement requiring Deepdale to pay annual rent equaling the Property's real estate taxes and liability insurance costs. In 1976, the parties executed a written lease for the period from March 1, 1976 through February 28, 1977, with a provision that it could be extended for consecutive one-year terms by written agreement. Such an agreement was executed for the 1977-78 term. Although Deepdale has continued to use the Property and pay rent to RPO since 1978, no subsequent agreement or lease has been executed. Currently, the annual rent is $ 330,000 - an amount sufficient only to cover the real estate taxes and insurance costs associated with the Property. Plaintiff alleges that the fair market annual rent for the Property is at least $ 6 million, which would require Deepdale to increase its annual dues substantially.

At RPO's inception, most of its shareholders were members of Deepdale. Over time, as non-members inherited or privately purchased RPO shares, the corporation's shareholders became more diversified. In 1976, with approximately 14,000 shares outstanding, RPO embarked on a private offering of an additional 1,000 shares. In order to sell the entire allotment, RPO sold shares to non-members, including Deepdale employees. At present, only 35% of RPO shareholders are Deepdale members.

Plaintiff has never been a member of Deepdale. He was on the RPO board of directors from 1989 through June 2004.

The Complaint alleges that from 2000 through 2002, Plaintiff pushed for a higher rent and urged the full board to consider selling the Property, but defendants Allen and Kramer refused to entertain any alteration of the status quo. For instance, when Patrick suggested that RPO raise the rent to $ 500,000, Allen and Kramer rejected his proposal outright. Similarly, in March 2002, Bayswater Development, LLC indicated its intent to purchase the Property for $ 35 million. Allen and Kramer refused to meet with Bayswater and indicated that they would vote their shares against any such a sale. Like Allen and Kramer, the newer directors have refused to consider any changes because, according to Plaintiff, their loyalties are "hopelessly" divided between RPO and Deepdale.

On January 27, 2004, Patrick filed this action against the balance of the then-existing RPO board pursuant to . . . [statute that] permits a director of a corporation to sue another director for, *inter alia,* mismanagement and waste of corporate assets. The Complaint alleges that Defendants breached their fiduciary duties and committed corporate waste by failing to extract a reasonable rent from Deepdale and "by failing to allow the RPO board to negotiate in good faith for a possible sale of the Property." The Complaint also alleges that Defendants Allen and Kramer breached their fiduciary duties by "offering to purchase additional shares so as to entrench their unlawful scheme and acquire such shares at an unfairly low price."

Discussion

Defendants move pursuant to Rule 12(b)(6) to dismiss the Complaint for failure to state a claim. Defendants contend that their decisions regarding the Property and Deepdale are shielded by New York's business judgment rule and that Plaintiff has not sufficiently alleged a breach of fiduciary duty or corporate waste. . . .

Business Judgment Rule

Defendants argue that Plaintiff's claims are foreclosed by operation of the business judgment rule because the claims challenge the decisions of RPO's directors.

New York law governs this action since RPO is a New York corporation. New York's business judgment rule creates a presumption that a corporation's directors act in good faith and in the best interests of the corporation. The rule is designed to "bar judicial inquiry into actions of corporate directors taken in good faith and in the exercise of honest judgment in the lawful and legitimate furtherance of corporate purposes." When the rule applies to a board's business decision, a court will defer to the directors unless "no person of ordinary sound business judgment would say that the corporation received fair benefit." In contrast, when circumstances remove a corporate decision from the scope of the rule, "the burden falls upon the board to demonstrate that its actions were reasonable and/or fair."

The business judgment rule will not protect a decision that was the product of fraud, self-dealing or bad faith. Directors may benefit from the rule "only if they possess a disinterested independence and do not stand in a dual relation which prevents an unprejudicial exercise of judgment." "It is black-letter, settled law that when a corporate director or officer has an interest in a decision, the business judgment rule does not apply. When a shareholder attacks a transaction in which the directors have an interest other than as directors of the corporation, the directors may not escape review of the merits of the transaction."

Therefore, in an action seeking to hold a director liable, a court must first determine whether the business judgment rule applies. While the rule generally removes directors' decisions from court review, it "does not foreclose the courts from making an initial inquiry as to the status of those members of the board who are charged with misfeasance."

A. Defendants' Interest in the Transactions

A director is considered interested in a transaction if the director stands to receive "a direct financial benefit from the transaction which is different from the benefit to shareholders generally."

Plaintiff maintains that Defendants are interested parties with respect to RPO's transactions involving Deepdale and the Property because they stand to benefit personally in a manner other than as RPO shareholders. Plaintiff argues that, through their decisions to retain the Property and lease it to Deepdale at below-market rent, Defendants enjoy dramatically reduced dues and fees as Deepdale members.

Defendants do not dispute that the long-standing relationship between PRO and Deepdale yields benefits for Deepdale members, including themselves. Nonetheless, they argue that a recent New York state court decision, *Shapiro v. Rockville Country Club, Inc.*, compels the conclusion that Defendants are disinterested and warrants the application of the business judgment rule.

Like this action, *Shapiro* involved a corporation that leased valuable property for minimal rent to a country club known as Rockville Links. Shareholders who were not members of Links brought a derivative suit against directors who were club members. In granting the defendants' motion for summary judgment, the court held that the corporation's directors were disinterested with respect to the lease transactions despite being members of Links. The court reasoned that the directors

> received the same benefit that is conferred upon all of those who are shareholders of [the corporation] and members of Links, reduced dues and fees. These same benefits were available and provided to those Plaintiffs who were previously members of Links and would be available to any of the Plaintiffs if they chose to become a member of Links.

Defendants argue that they are disinterested "because Deepdale membership is shared widely among RPO shareholders and is available to all." However, neither the Complaint nor the documents to which it refers suggest that membership in Deepdale was available to all RPO shareholders. To the contrary, the Complaint depicts Deepdale "as an extremely exclusive golf club" with only 250 members and a six-figure initiation fee. The Complaint identifies ten members of Deepdale - all of them prominent figures in sports, entertainment, fashion, and finance. Given these allegations, there is no reasonable basis to infer that membership is available to RPO's less affluent shareholders, such as the groundskeepers, bartenders and waitresses at Deepdale.

Therefore, Plaintiff has sufficiently alleged that, because of Defendants' status as Deepdale members, they are not disinterested directors with respect to the transactions at issue. **As such, at this early stage of the proceedings, this Court cannot conclude that the business judgment rule protects Defendants' decisions concerning Deepdale and the Property.**

Which facts are especially significant in terms of shaping the court's judgment?

ARTICLE 3.4

Racial Stereotypes, Broadcast Corporations, and the Business Judgment Rule

Leonard M. Baynes

I. INTRODUCTION

The major networks have received a great deal of criticism for the absence of, and stereotyping of, people of color who appear on their prime-time television shows. Many more African American characters appear on television series today than at any other time in television's previous history. African Americans comprise an ever larger and growing segment of the viewing audience. Black households watch an average of seventy hours of television per week as compared to fifty hours for viewers overall.

Although today's portrayals of African American characters, at first glance, seem fair and responsible, upon closer examination, one realizes that certain stereotypes still exist. For instance, in sitcoms the African American characters are more often than not portrayed as the buffoon. Dr. Camille Cosby conducted a study for the American Psychological Association and found that ethnic minorities were still "negatively stereotyped as criminals, dangerous characters, or victims of violence." Dr. Cosby found that "negative television imageries of African-Americans instruct African-Americans to hate themselves . . . [and] instruct other ethnic people to dislike African-Americans."

The situation is even worse for the other major minority groups in the United States. For example, the networks have a lot of work to do with respect to the portrayal of Latinos on television. Too few depictions of America's fastest growing minority exist on television today. Many of these depictions are still very negative. There are hardly any portrayals of Asian Pacific Americans or Native Americans on television, and many of those have also been stereotypical.

This article analyzes whether the broadcast executives who have made decisions as to minority representation on television have violated their duty of care or are protected by the business judgment rule. Executives of major broadcast corporations operate in somewhat unique and complicated environments. These executives have to be concerned not only with profit maximization, but also with the regulatory environment, and their related public interest mandate. These executives also have to monitor their activities closely to ensure that they do not run afoul of any current or future regulatory constraint or liability. Like other executives, they have to worry about maximizing profits. For broadcast executives, the road to profit maximization is rather circuitous. These broadcast corporations earn their income based on the number of (and the prices of) commercials they sell for their broadcast programming. . . .

The federal government actually owns the frequencies through which broadcasters transmit their signals. The Federal Communications Commission ("FCC") now allocates licenses to broadcasters through a competitive bidding process, whereby the highest bidder gains an eight to ten year license to operate its frequency in the airwaves. Technically, the broadcaster does not own the frequency and is obligated to operate its facilities in the "public interest, convenience, and necessity." The concept of "public interest" is very elastic and has no clear definition. Broadcast licenses theoretically can be revoked or not renewed, but the FCC has very infrequently revoked broadcast licenses.

The broadcast executives have to be aware and mindful of FCC regulations, and also the threat (albeit somewhat limited) of license revocation for failure to comply with such regulations. The broadcasters also have to operate in the public interest, a concept which is ill defined. However, some of the public interest contours [*825] were clearer in a more regulated environment. Since the courts have invalidated (and the FCC has repealed) some of these rules, the exact scope of the public interest requirement is less clear, but such uncertainty makes it much more difficult for the broadcasters. As a consequence, the broadcasters may inadvertently compromise their public interest mandate.

Unlike many other corporations, broadcasters have a great deal of exposure to the public. Ninety-eight percent of the U.S. population has at least one television in their home. In many parts of the country, there are several broadcasters in one geographic market. These broadcasters air programming sometimes twenty-four hours a day, seven days a week.

Broadcasters are in a unique situation when it comes to the business judgment rule and the fiduciary duty of care because the corporate executives have to balance each of these interests, i.e., profit maximization, the regulatory environment, their public interest mandate, and their image and reputation in the community. Each of these interests is rationally related to the corporate executives' duties to the shareholders.

Why is this industry special in terms of the boundaries of the business judgment rule?

The *Smith v. Van Gorkom*[1] case teaches us that the board of directors and the senior executives of the corporation have to make fully informed decisions. The broadcast executives may lose the protection of the business judgment rule if they fail to consider each of the above factors, and, therefore, may be liable for a violation of the duty of care. So if the broadcast executives have never made a deliberate decision as to whether to have minority programming, they would not be protected from liability under the business judgment rule. If they made a decision not to broadcast minority programming for discriminatory reasons, they would not be protected from liability under the business judgment rule. If they failed to consider profit maximization in their decision making, they also could be found to violate their duty of care. And if they made a decision that was not fully informed—like focusing solely on profit maximization and not other factors like the regulatory environment, their public interest mandate, and their image and reputation in the community—they would not be protected from liability by the business judgment rule. . . .

II. THE DUTY OF CARE AND THE BUSINESS JUDGMENT RULE

The shareholders of corporations elect a board of directors to manage the corporation. In turn, the board may elect officers as is specified in the corporate bylaws. The officers, senior executives, and members of the board of directors of a corporation owe a duty of care to shareholders and the corporation. Both the directors and officers of a corporation are required to perform their duties in good faith and with the degree of care that an ordinarily prudent person in a like position would use under similar circumstances. A director, in performance of his or her duties, shall be fully protected by relying upon the records of the corporation and upon the information, opinions, reports, and statements of the corporation's officers and employees. In some jurisdictions, officers also benefit from relying on information from employees. In any event, breaches of fiduciary duty are tempered by the business judgment rule, which protects corporate decisions against after-the-fact substantive review by a court, unless the corporate action was the result of misconduct going to the good faith of the decision, principally as a result of fraud, illegality, irrationality, conflict of interest, or gross negligence.

Mere errors of judgment and honest mistakes are insufficient as grounds for breach of the duty of care. These specific negligent acts are protected by the business judgment rule because the power of the board members and senior managers is discretionary. Traditionally, courts generally do not want to interfere with the corporate executives' discretion. They do not want disgruntled shareholders to second-guess important decisions. Conversely, they want the corporate executives to be able to operate in an environment where they feel safe to take the necessary business risks. Therefore, if directors make fully informed, good faith decisions, without a conflict of interest, courts employ a presumption that they have exercised due care, which is rebuttable by a showing that the decision had no rational basis.

Corporate executives may lose the benefit of the business judgment rule, however, if they fail to base their decisions at least partially on a goal to maximize profits. . . .

Because statutes governing corporations charge the board with managing the corporation, the board of directors ought to be respected. Conversely, both corporate executives and directors may violate the duty of care and lose the protection of the business judgment rule in those cases where directors and senior executives have been inactive in corporate management. For example, in Francis v. United Jersey Bank, Mrs. Pritchard was the largest shareholder and a member of the board of directors of a reinsurance company. After her husband died, she drank heavily and was bedridden. During this time, her sons, who were also board members, withdrew large sums of money from the corporation in the form of "loans." Mrs. Pritchard failed to obtain and read the annual statements of the financial condition of the company that would have disclosed that her sons were misappropriating funds from the corporation.

The court found that Mrs. Pritchard breached her duty by being derelict in her responsibilities. The Francis court set out minimum standards for board members and senior executives. The court stated that business executives must:

> acquire at least a rudimentary understanding of the business of the corporation. Accordingly, a director should become familiar with the fundamentals of the business in which the corporation is engaged. Because directors are bound to exercise ordinary care, they cannot set up as a defense lack of the knowledge needed to exercise the requisite degree of care. If one "feels that he has not had sufficient business experience to qualify him to perform the duties of a director, he should either acquire the knowledge by inquiry, or refuse to act." . . .

The question presented here as to whether the networks lose the protection of the business judgment rule and, therefore, have breached their duty of care centers on the type and quality of the decision-making processes the networks follow in determining their programming of minority-themed televisions shows or lack thereof. The broadcast executives will lose the benefits of the business judgment rule if their decisions were irrational, not fully informed, or failed to properly monitor [n386] the diversity of their broadcast schedules, violating the Communications Act. They will be protected by the business judgment rule if they made stupid decisions or well-considered nondiscriminatory decisions to broadcast their current all-white program line-up. This author believes, given the publicly available evidence of the broadcast executives' actions, that they have either made an irrational decision or one that was not fully informed.

III. ANALYSIS OF WHETHER BROADCAST CORPORATIONS' DECISION MAKING VIOLATES THE DUTY OF CARE

. . . The premise of this article is that the senior executives of the broadcast corporations would be protected by the business judgment rule only if they make fully informed decisions that take into account profit maximization as well as possible regulatory responses, including the broadcasters' public interest mandate. Regulation and the public interest doctrine are rationally related to the goal of profit maximization. If the broadcast executives failed to consider each of these factors in their decision making, then they may very well have violated the duty of care. In addition, the broadcast executives have a social responsibility to eradicate harmful media stereotypes. This section explores each of these factors.

A. Profit Maximization or Advertising Discrimination

1. Profit Maximization

Dodge v. Ford Motor Co[2] • Teaches us that senior corporate executives have to make rational decisions. In Dodge, the board failed to consider the maximization of shareholder profits. The court found that the board abused its discretion by failing to award dividends to the shareholders.

In the context of creating television shows, broadcasters always seemed to guess wrong, at least when it comes to the popularity of shows with mostly minority casts. Broadcasters have historically believed that many minority-focused shows would be unpopular with the general viewing audience. From I Love Lucy and I Spy, to The Cosby Show, broadcasters have often been hesitant in broadcasting these shows. However, when these shows were successful, they reaped the benefits in terms of awards and profits. Of course, hesitancy and caution are often virtues, but one wonders whether these particular attributes have to do more with the races of the character and actors than with the content of the shows.

In other circumstances, broadcast executives just replicate successful formats; that is why many of the television shows of the 1990s consisted of white, successful, single people working and playing in New York City. It is not particularly creative, but it is a very cautious and disciplined response to a proven and popular format. After The Cosby Show, however, there were very few attempts to duplicate the format. For the most part, after The Cosby Show ended its run, there has been an absolute absence of sophisticated African American situation comedy on broadcast television. Instead, in the mid-1990s, there was a resurgence of outdated stereotypes like Homeboys in Outer Space on the new networks like UPN and The WB.

How does one explain this? As in other formats, why didn't the very successful African American comedy, The Cosby Show, spawn many imitators? Did the broadcasters even consider what they were doing or were they blind to the possibilities of that format? To this author, it seems that the broadcasters were asleep at the switch as to the possible future success of the Cosby-like format. Indeed, if they followed what they normally do—copying successful formats—they could have saved themselves from the grief that they are now incurring because of their policies, or lack thereof. . . .

Broadcast executives were not paying attention to the market. They failed to try to maximize their audience size, which would have maximized their profit. Many minority focused and themed shows were successful crossover hits in the past; therefore, there is no excuse for failing to develop those kinds of programs in the present. To some extent, you may not have to raise the issue of discrimination and regulatory issues concerning the breach of the duty of care since it appears that the broadcasters may have failed to take care of their primary business, i.e., maximizing profits. They have failed to maximize audience size, which is related to their profitability. Such failure is a breach of the duty of care.

These market anomalies, however, beg the question—why? Why have these executives not seen these opportunities? Are they always blind? Or are they just blind when it comes to issues of race? One explanation for this blindness may be that the broadcasters have been passively complicit in discrimination by advertisers towards minority broadcast audiences.

2. Advertising Discrimination

In the case of the broadcast industry, profit maximization depends on the quantity and the price of the commercials sold. However, advertisers often say they are looking for the right demographics and will often pay higher advertising rates for a younger, more affluent—and most likely white—audience. This search for the right demographics may conflict with the fact that African American viewership is almost double their size of the population. This "search" for the "right audience demographics" seems reminiscent of past advertiser practices in refusing to place spots on The Nat "King" Cole Show; East Side, West Side; or even to some extent I Spy because of fear of Southern boycotts of their products. This author wonders whether the "search" is merely a pretext designed to avoid advertising on programs that have large minority viewership. . . .

The question then becomes: How does this advertising discrimination relate to the business judgment protections that are afforded to corporate officers and directors? The officers and directors of broadcast corporations will argue that they are protected by the business judgment rule and that they have acted rationally by trying to maximize profits. If evidence of discrimination is found . . . then officers and directors would not be protected by the business judgment rule. Discrimination is illegal, and illegal conduct is not protected. Moreover, even violations of public policy might not be protected by the business judgment rule. . . .

Discrimination is illegal and against public policy. The business judgment rule does not protect directors and officers if they have engaged in some sort of illegality as to their decision and duties. If the broadcasters have in fact passively participated in discrimination against minority-themed programming, then their decisions are unprotected by the business judgment rule. Also, the broadcast executives could in fact be liable for breach of the duty of care.

B. Have the Broadcast Executives Made Rational and Fully Informed Decisions?

It appears that broadcasters have made two distinct, but related, decisions as to the issue of minority programming. The first decision relates to the smaller number of shows with predominately minority casts, and the second relates to the small number of shows with integrated casts. In making these decisions, a director in performance of his or her duties "shall . . . be fully protected in relying . . . upon the records of the corporation and upon [the] information, opinions, reports, or statements . . . of the corporation's officers and employees." In some jurisdictions, officers also benefit from relying on information from employees.

1. Minority-Focused Programming

Television programming and schedules are approved and given the "green light" by the president of the entertainment division of the networks. The concepts, the themes, and location in the schedule are all approved at this level. This approval includes the decision, or non-decision, concerning minority-focused programming. Of course, the officer who ultimately makes this approval relies on her creative staff to develop concepts, schedules, and formats. Presumably, the officers—the president or vice president of the entertainment division—advise the board of what the prime-time programming will be and the expected audience shares and ratings. Thus, the board and the officers who head the entertainment division will argue that they relied on the information, opinions, reports, and statements of the corporation's officers and employees in reaching their decision. Therefore, they will claim that they are protected by the business judgment rule. However, Van Gorkom teaches us that board members and officers do not receive this protection if they have no reasonable basis to rely on the parties when they know that the parties are uninformed. In the case of minority-focused programming, the creative people and the heads of the entertainment divisions have been just as uninformed as the CEO in Van Gorkom. In that case, neither the president of the corporation nor the board of directors were fully informed about the intrinsic value of their corporation. In addition, the officers and directors in Van Gorkom failed to read the merger agreements before approving the deal. The board relied exclusively on the CEO who was also ill informed. . . .

It does not appear that either the directors or senior officers of broadcast corporations have considered the size of the minority market or how profitable minority-themed shows have been. In addition, it does not appear that the creative people in developing these shows considered the minority market. Therefore, as in Van Gorkom, the broadcast directors cannot rely on the uninformed advise of their underlings. Thus, this author does not believe that they will benefit from this statutory protection. In the case of shows with all-white casts, it also appears that the board and senior officers should not benefit from this statutory protection.

2. Integrated Programming

In terms of programming with integrated casts, the board and the officers who head the entertainment division will argue that they relied on the information, opinions, reports, and statements of the corporation's officers and employees in reaching their decision. Therefore, they will claim that they are protected by the business judgment rule. Furthermore, many of the casting decisions are delegated to casting directors.

As scripts develop, casting directors stay in touch with writers and producers. Specific descriptions of characters are sent to agents and posted on the Internet. Rene Balcer, the executive producer of the NBC crime drama Law & Order said that "the story dictates who's going to be what." Balcer indicated that "there is a phenomenon that if you don't specify race in a script, nine times out of [ten] a white person will be cast—that if you want a person of color you write it down and if you want a white person you don't write it." How is the decision being made if race is not specified in 90% of the casting decisions? That's not a decision. Based on Van Gorkom and Francis, the directors and officers can not rely on this non-decision. The historical and present absences or stereotypes of people of color suggest that the networks never have made a fully informed decision on these matters. Again, if you somehow can show that this failure to make an informed decision was made in bad faith, the corporation would not be able to indemnify or eliminate liability for their misfeasance. . . .

There is also a dearth of minority directors employed by the major networks. A recent Directors Guild of America study showed that, of "the 40 most popular series of the 2000-2001 season, . . . 80% of drama and comedy episodes . . . were directed by white males." African American males directed 3% of these popular series, Latino males 2%, and Asian American males about 1%. The fact that there are so few writers and directors of color and that most of those who are African American work on minority-themed shows, helps to explain why there are under-representations and stereotypes still on television. The low percentage and, in some cases, the absence of people of color at the casting and program conception stage lends itself to a breach of the duty of care.

C. Have the Broadcast Executives Taken into Account Possible Regulatory Responses?

The FCC regulates the broadcast corporations. Thus, as part of their fiduciary duty, the board of directors and senior officers have an obligation to monitor and oversee regulatory developments and to ensure that the corporation is in compliance with present and future regulatory mandates set forth by the FCC. Broadcast corporations have an obligation to broadcast in the public interest. By failing to have diverse programming, broadcast corporations may be in violation of FCC case law. A regulator may impose harsh regulations that might be costly and affect these corporations' profitability. Therefore, concern for regulation is rationally related to the corporate executives' goal to maximize profits. . . .

The broadcast executives' failure to monitor may lead to additional regulation. Several members of Congress have been concerned about the issue of negative minority media stereotypes. In the 107th Session of Congress, Congressmen Eliot Engel introduced legislation to amend the Communications Act, requiring the Federal Communications Commission to establish an office on victims of media bias. This office would function "as a clearinghouse for complaints, grievances, and opinions relating to radio, television, and cable television . . . and their depictions of victims of media bias." It would also collect and analyze data on media portrayals and conduct an annual conference designed to focus attention on the images of media bias. Some foreign countries handle the problems of negative media stereotypes by actually regulating the content of their broadcasters. This proposed legislation, therefore, is a good first step because having access to information often provides evidence of disparity. Further, some FCC officials, some members of Congress, and some academics are thinking about these issues and advocating proposals to deal with the situation. Thus, any decision that broadcast executives make cannot be fully informed unless it takes into account that non-action may lead to increased regulation, which may lead to a decrease in profitability.

D. Have Broadcast Executives Violated Their Public Interest Mandate?

1. Public Interest, Convenience, and Necessity

Even if the proposed legislation or regulation is not enacted, broadcasters may have violated their public interest obligations. The federal government owns the electronic spectrum through which the broadcast signal travels. The FCC awards licenses to broadcasters in trust, and as fiduciaries, for the American public.

. . . Not having anyone of color in the new fall season when people of color comprise almost thirty percent of the population seems to be prima facie evidence of discrimination. Moreover, having characters of color disproportionately depicted in stereotypical ways may also be discriminatory. By broadcasting programs with an insufficient number of people of color, or by stereotyping them, the broadcast executives may have inadvertently violated their public interest mandate and, therefore, may have lost the protection of the business judgment rule.

2. Large Percentages of the U.S. Populations Still Hold Stereotypes

Even if broadcasters are not legally obligated to broadcast diverse programming and the executives have not breached their fiduciary duty, broadcasters have a social responsibility to do so. In doing so, they will help to eradicate stereotypes, which this author believes is within the public interest mandate of the broadcasters. People of color have historically known that there is a correlation between media portrayals and status in society. There is a long history of concern and comment by prominent people of color concerning how they are depicted. They realize that the stereotypes can affect one's ability to succeed in society.

On the other hand, whites often do not have to worry as much about their stereotypes for several reasons. First, whites are the dominant group in society and they often set the order and tone for things. There are very few negative stereotypes of whites as a whole. Whites often are seen more as individuals rather than as members of a group. Therefore, if there is a negative stereotype about whites, it would be rationalized away. It also might be considered isolated to some specific group of whites—such as those that live in trailers, those that are from Appalachia, and those that might have certain southern European origins. But again, those stereotypes do not apply to all whites as a class or group, just to some particular subcategories.

These days, most whites are not the classic racists who, like George Wallace, will block a school house door to prevent African American kids from entering. It is estimated that only 20% of whites hold these traditional racist views.[3] Whites are more likely to have more ambivalent feelings on race issues and individuals of different races.[4] On the one hand, they admire Colin Powell and his accomplishments; they are astonished over Michael Jordan's ability to play basketball; they love and are comforted by Oprah Winfrey's compassion and understanding; their kids listen to hip-hop music; and they often work side by side with people of color. However, many whites still have stereotypical views of people of color. . . .

The electronic media has a very strong influence over the cultural, political, social, and racial attitudes of our society. This influence comes about because of the electronic media's near-omnipresence in the lives of our citizens. Ninety-eight percent of U.S. homes have a television set; forty-nine percent have more than one set. The average family watches over seven hours of television a day. The absence and the stereotyping of people of color by the mass media is a source of concern for all. The depictions of people of color by the media have to be presented in non-stereotypical ways to avoid the perpetuation of harmful stereotypes.

3. Broadcast Media Stereotypes Are Against Public Policy

The jurisprudence of the Supreme Court of the United States demonstrates that eradicating stereotypes is in the public interest. The Court has consistently criticized and warned about negative racial stereotypes. In *Brown v. Board of Education*, for example, the plaintiffs introduced psychological evidence showing that African American children were harmed by segregation in that it made them think less highly of themselves. . . .

Even more recently, the Supreme Court has spoken disapprovingly of the use of stereotypes in a variety of cases, ranging from affirmative action, to voting rights, to jury selection. Justice O'Connor, in her dissent in *Metro Broadcasting, Inc. v. FCC*,[5] stated that race-based assignments "embody stereotypes that treat individuals as the product of their race, evaluating their thoughts and efforts—their very worth as citizens—according to criterion barred to the Government by history and the Constitution. . . .

These Supreme Court cases show evidence of the Court's disapproval of the use of racial stereotypes in decision making. However, all these cases dealt solely with situations where the government is using invidious racial stereotypes in its decision-making. In the context of broadcast invisibility and stereotypes, it is the broadcasters who are the bad actors. However, we cannot stop there in our analysis because the broadcasters are awarded their licenses from the federal government. The broadcasters do not own the spectrum; they merely have a right to use the government's property. The spectrum for which they hold the license is still owned by the federal government. As a consequence, broadcasters hold the licenses as trustees for the public. Broadcasters, therefore, have certain responsibilities to operate pursuant to the public trust and in the public interest. As such, it is incumbent upon broadcasters to provide programming that is representative, yet non-stereotypical.

4. Broadcast Media Stereotypes Influence Behavior

How can a stereotype be against public policy?

Historically, people of color have either been absent or stereotyped by the media. . . .

These negative portrayals and stereotypes have an especially profound effect on children. Research suggests that children devote the greatest proportion of their leisure time to watching television. Many children spend more time watching television than attending school. African American children have been found to watch nearly twice as much television as whites.

Children are more vulnerable to media images because they lack real world experience and the necessary basis for comparison. Often ideas, stereotypes, and roles put forth by the television industry do not reflect the real world. As a result, young children may have difficulty distinguishing "between symbolic and social reality." A recent study suggests that these stereotypes impact negatively on the self-concept of African American children. The television roles in which African Americans are cast communicate to black children the negative value that society places on them. The negative images of minorities in the media impact how children perceive minority characters. "Children more often associate positive qualities, such as financial success and intelligence, with white characters." They associate negative qualities, "including lawbreaking and laziness, with minority characters." Seventy-one percent of the children surveyed believed that the role of the boss is typically played by a white character, while 59% noted that the criminal is typically played by African Americans. . . .

IV. CONCLUSION

Generally, the business judgment rule provides strong protection for officer and director against liability for breaching the duty of care. They lose the business judgment protections in those cases where they have made an illegal decision, they made no decision on something that they should have addressed, or they have failed to make a rational decision or a fully informed one. Of course, the officers and directors of broadcast corporations have to be concerned about maximizing profit. But it appears that they have not been concerned about maximizing profits since historically many television shows with primarily minority characters have made a profit. Many have won prestigious awards. Many times the broadcast executives were misinformed about the public's acceptance of some of these shows. Moreover, since the broadcasters operate in a heavily regulated environment, concerns over regulation and their public interest mandate are rationally related to profit maximization. The broadcasters would have to monitor their programming in order to avoid regulatory problems. They have appointed vice presidents of diversity and diversity boards are just now setting up the infrastructure that will allow them to satisfy their duty to monitor this important aspect of their broadcasting. Each of these interests is rationally related to the corporate executives' duties to the shareholders. So the broadcast executives have to consider profit maximization, regulatory oversight, and their public interest mandate in their decision-making process in order to be afforded the protection of the business judgment rule. . . .

The officers and directors of broadcast corporations have to monitor the company and make a fully informed decision to be protected by the business judgment rule. Given the vast gulf in racial attitudes held by whites and African Americans, any television program that employs only members of one racial group as writers and directors is likely to be distorted. Historically, the broadcast company produced television shows with all white writers, directors, and producers. Even now, there is a dearth of minority writers, directors, and producers of television shows.

The officer and directors of broadcast corporations have made an uninformed decision. Not having people of color in the room while program ideas and scripts are hashed out is very similar to the Van Gorkom board of directors who failed to be informed about the intrinsic value of their company or even read the merger documents. These actions are a breach of the duty of care and should not be protected by the business judgment rule.

END NOTES

1. 488 A.2d 858 (Del. 1985).
2. 170 N.W. 668 (Mich. 1919).
3. Mass Media and Reconciliation, A Report to the Advisory Board and Staff, the President's Race Initiative 9 (1998).
4. Howard Schuman et al., Racial Attitudes in America: Trends & Interpretations 7 (1997).
5. 497 U.S. 547, 602 (1990).

ISSUE SUMMARY

When should people be protected from unethical corporations? Though we have not explicitly asked that question, it has been at the heart of both the first and second chapters. In the first chapter, we asked when employees should be protected from termination by their employers. In the second chapter, we asked when stakeholders should be protected from losses resulting from decisions made by the directors of corporations and companies. In various forms, we have been asking questions aimed at a much broader question: When should people be protected from unethical corporations?

You may have noticed that our broader formulation of the issue is quite ambiguous. What is an unethical corporation? In the first chapter, each author had a different version of unethical conduct by employers. According to the various authors, an unethical employer could be one who discriminates against employees based on sexual preference, or one who retaliates against whistleblowers, or even one who terminates employees without cause. According to the authors in the second chapter, an unethical corporation could be one that pursues business ventures based on the personal interests of the directors, or one that fails to pay enough attention to public interests.

Clearly, there is no consensus about what constitutes ethical or unethical conduct. As a reader, your opinions about each author's argument will be influenced by whether you agree with the author's definition of ethical conduct. To help you decide what decisions are ethical and unethical, consider the WPH Framework for Business Ethics.[1] The WPH Framework is a set of three questions designed to help business managers make ethical decisions. Ask yourself:

1. If every decision affects particular groups of stakeholders, *whom* would this decision affect?
2. If every decision moves me toward an ethical goal, what is the *purpose* of this decision?
3. If I need a set of guidelines, *how* am I going to make ethical decisions?

The WPH Framework walks business managers through three quick questions to help them determine how to make ethical decisions. Think about the authors in this chapter. If the authors were asked to answer the questions posed by the WPH Framework, what would they say? Who are the most important stakeholders in the minds of the authors? In the authors' minds, what should our goals be? How should we achieve those goals? Do you agree with the authors' opinions? Does your agreement or disagreement affect your opinion of the authors' arguments?

As you continue reading, ask yourself how the authors' arguments tie into the broad question: When should people be protected from unethical corporations?

How many different definitions of ethical conduct can you find? Keep a list of the different definitions you find. Not only will the list help you learn about the myriad of opinions held by other people, but those definitions will also encourage you to think more deeply about your definition of ethical conduct. Why is your personal definition better than all those held by the authors featured in this book? You will likely find that your thinking is enriched by attempts to integrate numerous arguments, to analyze their merit, and even to challenge the merit of your own conclusions.

ISSUE HIGHLIGHTS

- The Delaware business judgment rule requires that a business director act with due care—"with the care an ordinarily reasonably prudent person in a like position would exercise under similar circumstances."
- The American Law Institute business judgment rule states that a director who makes a business judgment in good faith fulfills her duty of care if she is not interested in the subject of her business judgment, she is informed with respect to the subject of the business judgment to the extent she reasonably believes to be appropriate under the circumstances, and she rationally believes that the business judgment is in the best interests of the corporation.
- The ordinary negligence standard requires that people, including business directors and nonprofit trustees, exercise the same level of care that a reasonable person would be expected to exercise in a similar situation.
- While a nonprofit organization *can* earn a profit, it can*not* distribute its net earnings, if there are any, to individuals who control the nonprofit, such as members, officers, directors, or trustees.
- Five reasons frequently given to support the business judgment rule are: (1) The rule promotes risk-taking; (2) The rule encourages competent directors to serve; (3) The rule prevents judicial second-guessing; (4) The rule allows directors sufficient leeway when managing the corporation; and (5) The rule permits more effective market mechanisms to manage director behavior.
- In *Dodge v. Ford Motor Co.*, the court ruled that senior corporate executives have to make rational decisions, which includes considering the maximization of shareholder profits.

CRITICAL THINKING

When people attempt to persuade others, they typically provide reasons to support their conclusions. If we want you to believe that hybrid vehicles are better than standard gasoline-powered vehicles, we may provide reasons about the cost of gas, the environmental effects of pollution produced by vehicles, or even the appearances of the different vehicles. If we were to tell you that hybrid vehicles produce only 10% as much carbon monoxide as standard vehicles, how would you react? As a critical thinker, you should ask a key question: How reliable is that evidence?

Not all evidence is created equally. Some evidence comes from unreliable sources. For example, we could have found our data on a random high school student's blog. Some evidence is based on small sample sizes that prevent application of the evidence to larger populations. For instance, we could have performed a test using one hybrid vehicle and one standard vehicle. Some evidence is based on faulty methodology. We could have used outdated and unreliable technology when measuring the amount of carbon monoxide created by the vehicles. When someone presents evidence to you, do not forget to ask: How reliable is that evidence?

Let's reconsider the final selection from this chapter, Baynes's argument. Baynes argues that broadcast executives must meet a test to be protected by the business judgment rule, and that broadcast executives have not met the test. Baynes provides evidence that broadcast executives have not met the test, but let's look again at that evidence. We want to know where Baynes got his evidence, and we want to know whether Baynes is giving us reliable evidence.

Baynes writes that broadcast executives have not paid sufficient attention to profit maximization because they did not attempt to create minority-focused television programs (see section III.A.1). Baynes's reasons are:

1. "Broadcasters have historically believed that many minority-focused shows would be unpopular with the general viewing audience. [. . .] However, when these shows were successful, they reaped the benefits in terms of awards and profits."
2. "Broadcast executives just replicate successful formats;" "[a]fter *The Cosby Show*, however, there were very few attempts to duplicate the format."
3. "Many minority focused and themed shows were successful crossover hits in the past; therefore, there is no excuse for failing to develop those kinds of programs in the present."

What do you see when you read those reasons? Do you see any problems? Normally, we would have rephrased Baynes's reasoning in our own words, but there is something about Baynes's writing that needs to be emphasized. How many times does Baynes give a specific number? How many times does Baynes hide behind the general terms "many" and "a few"? How many times does Baynes name names? How many times does Baynes refer in general to collective "broadcasters" or "shows"?

You may be wondering why it matters whether Baynes's writing is specific or vague. Quite simply, we cannot evaluate Baynes's evidence when we do not know what the evidence is. Look again at the three reasons listed above. What is missing? What is Baynes not telling his readers? Let's examine his reasons one at a time.

Reason one: "Broadcasters have historically believed that many minority-focused shows would be unpopular with the general viewing audience. . . . However, when these shows were successful, they reaped the benefits in terms of awards and profits." After reading that reason, we have several questions for Baynes: (1) Which broadcasters believed minority-focused shows would be unpopular? (2) How do you know what the broadcasters thought? (3) How many of the shows that broadcasters believed would be unpopular were, in fact, popular and successful?

You might be thinking that those questions sound mean or nit-picky. Remember that critical thinking questions are in no way mean-spirited or tedious. Our questions are designed to evaluate Baynes's evidence in a spirit of fairness. Before we know whether Baynes's argument is a convincing one, we need to know whether he has provided reliable and convincing evidence.

Think about question (1). Baynes told us about "broadcasters" in general. We need to know how many broadcasters Baynes is describing. For Baynes's historical argument to hold water, we need to know that Baynes is not describing a few hand-selected broadcasters while passing them off as the majority of broadcasters. Question (2) follows from (1). How does Baynes know about these broadcasters? Are we reading hearsay passed through five sets of ears? We need to know whether Baynes's information came from a reliable source. Question (3) is a question designed to find out whether Baynes is being fair in his analysis of the information. Is Baynes intentionally overlooking situations in which broadcasters correctly predicted that minority-focused shows would be unpopular (or popular)? How frequently were the broadcasters wrong? Without the answers to our questions, we cannot determine whether Baynes is giving us correct, reliable information.

Reread reason two: "Broadcast executives just replicate successful formats;" "[a]fter *The Cosby Show*, however, there were very few attempts to duplicate the format." What questions come to your mind? A few that we would like to ask Baynes are: (1) How frequently do broadcast executives replicate successful formats? (2) How many attempts are "very few"? (3) How many times did broadcasters replicate successful minority-focused shows besides *The Cosby Show*?

Again, our questions for Baynes are both reasonable and fair. Baynes is making a blanket statement about standard practices for broadcast executives (replicating successful formats). We need to know whether Baynes's statement is an accurate representation of the decisions made by broadcast executives. In addition, we need to know what Baynes means when he says that broadcast executives made "very few" attempts to replicate successful minority-focused programming. Is the number so small that most people would agree with Baynes's thinking? Or is the number small in only Baynes's opinion? Finally, we need to know whether Baynes is intentionally omitting relevant information. If broadcast executives did attempt to replicate successful minority-focused shows, we need to know before we can evaluate Baynes's claims.

Finally, let's consider Baynes's third reason: "Many minority focused and themed shows were successful crossover hits in the past; therefore, there is no excuse for failing to develop those kinds of programs in the present." This reason is vague, at best, which leads us to yet more questions for Baynes: (1) How many shows are "many"? (2) Is there anything about the shows that would suggest that successful shows in the past would be successful today?

Because Baynes's reason is so vague, we are not being unfair by asking Baynes for additional information. We need to know how many minority-focused shows were successful before we can expect broadcast executives to see the potential profits flowing from such programming. We also need to know why those shows were successful in the past. Baynes seems to believe that because the shows were successful in the past, similar shows would be successful today; but society has morphed over time, and the public interest in such shows may have dwindled. Does Baynes have any evidence that the past shows would be successful in today's market?

After considering only three of the many reasons in Baynes's argument, we have listed three questions we would like to ask him. We're fairly certain you've thought of other questions to ask as well. While we have our list of questions, you're probably wondering, "What do I do now?" You'll be relieved to know that you don't need to go searching for the answers to our questions (unless you want to do so). Baynes wrote the argument; Baynes gave us what he considered good evidence; Baynes has the duty to convince us that his evidence is reliable. If we had the opportunity to talk to Baynes, then we would have a duty to ask him fair questions during a civil conversation; but, as you know, we don't have Baynes available for questioning.

So, you're probably wondering yet again, "Then what do I do?" Look at our list of questions. Think about the reason you're asking each question. If Baynes were to answer the question a certain way, would your opinion about his argument change? Depending upon the answers to the questions, would you be more or less likely to find Baynes's argument convincing? If so, then you will probably withhold judgment about whether to accept Baynes's conclusion. You cannot evaluate the merit of his argument without more information about his reasons.

Look again at Baynes's argument. Pick a reason from the argument, and then imagine you are having a conversation with Baynes. What would you want to ask regarding that reason? Why would the question be important? How might Baynes answer your question? Would his answer have the potential to change your thoughts about his argument? If so, what are you going to do when Baynes is unavailable to answer your question?

ADDITIONAL READING RESOURCES

Bernard S. Black, Brian R. Cheffins, *and* Michael Klausner, "Liability Risk for Outside Directors: A Cross-Border Analysis," *Eur. Financial Mgmt. J.*, 11, 153–171 (2005).

Lisa Fairfax, "Spare the Rod, Spoil the Director? Revitalizing Directors' Fiduciary Duty Through Legal Liability," *Houston L. Rev.*, 42, 393–456 (2005).

Jonathan R. Macey *and* Maureen O'Hara, "The Corporate Governance of Banks," *Econ. Pol. Rev.*, 9: 1 (2003).

Troy A. Paredes, "Corporate Governance and Economic Development," *Regulation*, 28: 1, 34–39 (2005).

David Rosenberg, "Galactic Stupidity and the Business Judgment Rule," *J. Corp. L.* 32: 301 (2006).

Mark R. Schwartz, Thomas W. Dunfee, *and* Michael J. Kline, "Tone at the Top: An Ethics Code for Directors?", *J. Bus. Ethics*, 58: 1–3, 79–100 (2005).

Lynn A. Stout, "The Mythical Benefits of Shareholder Control," *VA L. Rev.* (2006).

Duane Windsor, "Corporate Social Responsibility: Three Key Approaches," *J. Mgmt. Stds.*, 43: 1, 93–114 (2006).

Adam Winkler, "Corporate Law or the Law of Business: Stakeholders and Corporate Governance at the End of History," *L. & Cont. Problems*, 67 (2004).

For more information, check these sites:

http://www.theconglomerate.org/2005/04/the_german_busi.html (A blog entry about the business judgment rule in Germany) [*Last visited: July 5, 2008*]

http://home.law.uiuc.edu/~ribstein/ribsteinalces.pdf (Larry E. Ribstein, *The Business Judgment Rule in Good and Bad Times*) [*Last visited: July 5, 2008*]

http://www.expertlaw.com/library/employment/business_judgment.html (William R. Hopkins, *Rethinking the Business Judgment Rule in Discrimination Cases: Is There a Clear Line between Protecting an Employer's Business Judgment and Fully Allowing Plaintiff's Evidence of Pretext?*) [*Last visited: July 5, 2008*]

http://papers.ssrn.com/sol3/papers.cfm?abstract_id=711122 (Lyman P.Q. Johnson, *Corporate Officers and the Business Judgment Rule*) [*Last visited: July 5, 2008*]

ISSUE 4

When Is Someone Acting on Your Behalf?

The first time you toured an apartment, who showed you around the rental property? Was it the landlord herself? Or did the landlord send someone else in her place? As you toured the property, you probably asked some questions. You may have even attempted to negotiate a better price for yourself. If you were wheeling and dealing with the landlord, then you could be fairly certain that you would get the better, negotiated price. If, however, you were speaking to someone sent by the landlord, would the landlord have to honor the negotiated price? The answer probably depends on whether the person sent by the landlord was acting as the landlord's agent. In this chapter, you will learn more about the definition of an agency relationship, as well as how we determine whether an agency relationship exists.

The first article in this chapter introduces the legal definition of an agency relationship, as well as the liability attached to individuals involved in the agency relationship. The second selection in this chapter is a piece of case law from the Court of Appeals of South Carolina, in which the court was asked to determine whether apparent agency existed. In the following article, Heinrich examines how the Illinois courts determine whether apparent agency exists between a hospital and a doctor practicing in the hospital. Continuing to explore the doctrine of apparent agency, the fourth selection describes how the Florida courts have limited the application of the doctrine of apparent agency to franchises. The fifth article in this chapter turns its attention to current technology, asking whether agency law has caught up to the growing field of Internet commerce. The sixth selection in this chapter is an excerpt from a decision by the Superior Court of Connecticut in which the court was asked to determine whether an agency relationship existed between a specific Boy Scout troop and a local council. The seventh selection in this chapter reports the results of a ruling by the California Superior Court in which the court found that retail stores and online sellers do not possess an agency relationship simply because they share the same name. In the final selection in this chapter, O'Neill describes how the courts determine whether a member of a religious organization is acting as an agent of that organization.

In the first article in this chapter, Wade argues that courts must streamline the law by choosing between two legal concepts: agency by estoppel and apparent (or perceived) agency. Wade carefully defines concepts related to agency before explaining how agency by estoppel and apparent agency are related. Wade argues that both concepts apply to situations in which a principal holds someone out as his agent; the only difference between the concepts is the level to which a third party must rely on the principal's representations of the agency relationship. For the purposes of creating a uniform standard for tort law, Wade argues that the two concepts need to be streamlined.

In the second selection in this chapter, the Court of Appeals of South Carolina applied one of the concepts discussed by Wade: apparent agency. In the case, the plaintiffs sued the defendant for unpaid rent after the defendant broke her lease and moved out of the plaintiffs' property. The defendant argued that the plaintiffs were estopped from suing her because the plaintiffs had allowed her to believe that another person served as the plaintiffs' agent—a person who had given the defendant permission to break the lease. The court ruled that there was probable cause for a jury to find that apparent agency did exist.

In the third selection in this chapter, Heinrich explores more case law related to apparent agency. According to the Illinois Supreme Court, a plaintiff must prove three things to prove that apparent agency existed between a doctor and hospital: (1) the hospital or its agent acted in a manner that would lead a reasonable person to conclude that the physician was an employee or agent of the hospital; (2) the hospital had knowledge of the acts of the agent that created the appearance of the authority, where there were such acts, and acquiesced in them; and (3) the plaintiff acted in reliance on the conduct of the hospital or its agent. In this case, the Appeals Court found that the plaintiff had not met the three-pronged test and therefore had not proven that apparent agency existed.

In the fourth article in this chapter, Hennessey scolds Florida courts for limiting the doctrine of apparent agency when applied to franchises. Hennessey begins by examining how the Florida courts have treated the doctrine of apparent agency in the past, then turns to the *Orlando Executive Park* case. Hennessey argues that apparent agency exists to protect consumers by allowing consumers to place their faith in franchises that appear to represent reliable national chains. The court, however, found that apparent agency could not be established by the use of brand names, logos, architecture, or uniforms when the franchise contract (to which consumers do not have access) says that the franchisor has no control over the franchisee.

Next, we change our focus from apparent agency to contemporary applications of agency law. In the fifth article in this chapter, Furnari defines Internet commerce before explaining how agency law relates to Internet transactions. Furnari explains that the basic element of trust created during a face-to-face business transaction is missing from Internet commerce, leading consumers to rely heavily on connections between lesser-known sellers and more trusted businesses. By applying traditional advertising and agency principles to Internet transactions, Furnari argues that more companies may soon be liable under the doctrine of apparent agency. Furnari argues that, as the number of Internet transactions increases, courts will need to determine how traditional legal concepts will apply to the internet.

The sixth article in this chapter is a piece of case law from the Superior Court of Connecticut. A specific Boy Scout troop built a rope bridge and invited the local population to cross the bridge. A young boy, not a member of the troop, fell from the bridge and broke his arm. When the boy's family sued the local Boy Scout council, the council argued that no agency relationship existed between the council and the troop. The court examined the precedent and the facts of the case, finding that it could not determine conclusively that an agency relationship did not exist and therefore could not grant the request for summary judgment.

The seventh selection in this chapter describes a ruling by the California Superior Court with regard to the alleged agency relationship between Barnes & Noble retail stores and the online seller barnesandnoble.com. The issue was whether an agency relationship was indicated when the retail stores passed out coupons for the online seller. The court determined that an agency relationship requires that the agent have the power to bind the principal. In this case, the retail stores possessed no power over the creation or use of the coupons and could not bind the online seller in any way, indicating the lack of an agency relationship.

In the final selection in this chapter, O'Neill describes how the courts have defined agency relationships between religious orders and their members. Specifically, O'Neill argues that the courts have unnecessarily narrowed the definition of an agency relationship. O'Neill describes a nun who took a vow of poverty, but was given permission to work outside the order as a nurse if all of her wages were turned over to the order. When the IRS requested the nun's taxes, she argued that she had been employed as an agent of the order and that the order should therefore pay the taxes. The court applied a strict definition of agency that required that the principal have daily control over the agent's action, which the order did not have over the nun. O'Neill argues that the rules need to be expanded to allow members of religious organizations to perform good works without fear of the IRS.

As you can tell, agency law can be applied to a very broad range of situations involving franchises, nonprofit organizations, landlords, religious organizations, online businesses, medical doctors, and more. Think back to the opening paragraph and the example involving a landlord. Based on what you've read so far, do you think the landlord would be forced to honor an agreement made by someone she sent in her place? Under what circumstances would the landlord have to honor the agreement? If you can't answer those questions right now, keep them in mind as you read. You should gain a better understanding of agency law as you work your way through this chapter.

ISSUE ARTICLES

Wade, Chad P., "The Double Doctrine Agent," 42 *Valpariso University Law Review*, 341 (2007).

Thomas and Linda Genovese v. Joseph Bergeron and Theresa Bergeron, 327 S.C. 567 1997 S.C. App. LEXIS 102.

Heinrich, Elizabeth, "Selected Recent Court Decisions—Malpractice: Vicarious Liability Under Apparent Agency: *James v. Ingalls Memorial Hospital*," 24 *American Journal of Law and Medicine*, 514 (1998).

Hennessey, William, "Agency Law: Extending the Common Knowledge Doctrine," 47 *Florida Law Review*, 147 (1995).

Furnari, Nancy R. "Are Traditional Agency Principles Effective for Internet Transactions, Given the Lack of Personal Interaction?" 63 *Albany Law Review*, 537 (1999).

Eric Bahre v. Long Rivers Council Inc., Boy Scouts of America, 1994 Conn. Super. LEXIS 1904 (Connecticutt Superior Court July 19, 1994).

"No California Nexus for Barnesandnoble.com by Stores Distributing Coupons. Sales & Use Tax Alert," 12/15/2007, Vol. 17, Issue 22.

O'Neill, Bridget R., "*Schuster v. Commissioner:* An Appropriate Agency Test for Members of Religious Orders Working Under Vows of Poverty?" *Wisconsin Law Review*, 111(1988).

ARTICLE 4.1

The Double Doctrine Agent

Chad P. Wade

I. INTRODUCTION

> *[W]hatever a man sui juris may do of himself, he may do by another; and as a correlative of the maxim, that what is done by another is to be deemed done by the party himself. "Qui facit per alium, per seipsum facere videtur."*[1]

Although the law of agency is relatively new compared to other areas of law, agency law is the foundation upon which many forms of business organizations are built. Agency provides the starting point for many of the laws governing partnerships and corporations. Furthermore, agency law continues to grow in prominence as laws governing relatively new entities, such as limited liability companies, expand and existing business entities seek to maximize efficiency through cooperation. An understanding of agency law "is of great assistance, if not prerequisite, to an understanding of the laws of partnership and corporations" because in "no other field of law is the close interrelation of business practice and the rules of law more apparent.

In a world of growing conglomerates and entities in search of "synergies," it will become increasingly difficult to determine who has the ability to affect an organization's legal relationships and how those relationships can be affected. Agency law answers these questions. Some relationships are straight forward—the product of clear and direct communication by a principal to an agent regarding what and how a task should be done. Of greater concern, however, are the individuals who have the ability to affect an organization's legal relationships despite the fact that neither agency nor agreed authority exists. It is in these situations that business entities run the greatest risk of being caught unprepared for the consequences of actions taken by individuals unauthorized by the entities themselves. Further adding to the problem, courts' application of the doctrines of apparent authority, apparent agency, and agency by estoppel are inconsistent and confusing, at best. Such powerful doctrines must be carefully drafted and tailored to ensure that they accomplish their respective goals without unduly interfering with business' unending drive for economic efficiency. . . .

II. LEGAL BACKGROUND OF AGENCY THEORY

A. Establishing an Agency Relationship

The first step in determining if a principal is liable for the acts of another under agency law is to establish whether an agency relationship exists between the two parties.

1. Actual Agency

Agency is a legal concept which requires the existence of specific elements; therefore, mere intention to create an agency relationship is irrelevant if the elements of agency are absent. While a court may consider what titles parties give to their relationships, principals cannot escape liability for the acts of a person that fulfills the requirements of agency by simply classifying them by a different title.

Actual agency requires a "manifestation of consent by one person to another that the other shall act on his behalf and subject to his control, and consent by the other so to act." In other words, there are three requirements for an agency relationship. The first requirement is a manifestation of consent by the "principal" to allow the "agent" to act on the principal's behalf. While the *Restatement Second* does not provide a definition for "manifestation," the *Restatement Third* specifically illustrates that a "person manifests assent or intention through written or spoken words or other conduct."

Second, in order for an agency relationship to exist, the "agent" must consent to act on behalf of the "principal." Although both parties must consent to the relationship, consent is not required to be stated in a contract or other legal writing. In some cases, an agency relationship is established by examining the relationship of the parties and implying an agency relationship although no written agreement classifies the relationship as an agency.

The third requirement to establish an agency relationship is that the "principal" must possess a right of control over the "agent." Although the "principal" does not need to actually exercise control over the "agent," the principal simply needs to have the right to exercise control. Furthermore, the "principal" neither needs to have complete control over every moment of the agency relationship nor for the control to be effective at all times.

The absence of any one of these three elements generally prevents courts from finding an actual agency relationship. . . .

2. Perceived Agency

In tort cases, a third party may hold a pseudo principal liable for the torts of a pseudo agent if the pseudo principal has intentionally or negligently held out the pseudo agent as his actual agent and the third party has relied on that manifestation. The *Restatement Second* refers to this concept as "apparent agency." However, for purposes of this Note, "apparent agency" will be referred to as "perceived agency." The difference in terminology is made because of the confusion between the concepts of apparent agency and apparent authority, and the similarity of their respective spellings only exacerbates the problem.

Would a perceived agency be more likely to be a basis for a legal dispute than would be an actual agency?

Perceived agency is a form of [agency that] focuses on the principal's interactions with the third party, rather than focusing on the principal's interactions with the agent. The requirements of perceived agency, as laid out in section 267 of the *Restatement Second,* are two-fold.

The first requirement is an intentional "holding out" by the perceived principal that someone is his agent. *Crinkley v. Holiday Inns, Inc.,* clearly illustrates the "holding out" requirement. In *Crinkley,* hotel guests were assaulted by a group dubbed the "Motel Bandits." The plaintiffs sued the franchisor, Holiday Inn, for inadequate security under the theory that the operator of the hotel was a perceived agent of Holiday Inn, Inc. The court held that perceived agency was a question for the jury and that a reasonable jury could find that Holiday Inn had held out the franchisee as its agent to the third party.

The second requirement of perceived agency is actual, reasonable reliance by the injured third party on the manifestations of agency by the perceived principal. *Miller v. McDonald's Corp.,* illustrates the reliance required under the doctrine of perceived agency. In *Miller,* the plaintiff suffered injuries while dining at a McDonald's restaurant. McDonald's Corporation was the franchisor of the restaurant; however, the restaurant was owned and operated by a company called 3K Restaurants ("3K"). The plaintiff sued McDonald's Corporation on the theory that, even absent an actual agency relationship, McDonald's Corporation should be held liable because 3K was its perceived agent. [n]The court agreed holding that summary judgment for McDonald's Corporation was improper because there was evidence to support a jury finding that the plaintiff relied upon McDonald's Corporation's holding out of 3K.

While *Miller* demonstrates the level of reliance required for perceived agency, the *Restatement Second* enumerates several other key aspects of the doctrine. First, the manifestations or "holding out" of the perceived principal do not have to be intentional. In some cases courts use perceived agency when the perceived principal appears to have taken insufficient steps to inform the public of the non-agency relationship. Further, courts only require "ordinary knowledge" of business relationships (i.e. franchises) by third parties seeking to assert perceived agency. The second key aspect of the doctrine of perceived agency is that it requires actual and reasonable reliance on the manifestations by the perceived principal. The third and final key aspect of perceived agency as laid out in the *Restatement Second* is that there is no requirement of a change of position. . . .

B. Authority to Bind a Principal

After establishing an agency relationship, the agent must possess the authority to act in order to bind the principal. *Restatement Second* sets forth four types of authority: actual; apparent; incidental; and inherent. Conversely, the *Restatement Third* only recognizes actual and apparent authority, while incorporating incidental and inherent authority into several other sections. Equally important to the question of who can bind a principal is the question of how a person can bind the principal.

1. Actual Authority

Actual authority is authority for an agent to act based upon manifestations by the principal to the agent. As previously stated, an agency relationship requires that the principal maintain the right to control the acts of the agent performed on the principal's behalf. Actual authority is created when the principal exercises that right of control by manifesting consent for the agent to act in certain ways. However, the manifestations do not have to be explicit. If the manifestations to the agent specify how the agent should act, the actual authority is called "expressed actual authority." Alternatively, actual authority may be inferred by the agent from the context in which the authority was granted. This type of actual authority is referred to as "implied actual authority." The distinguishing factor between actual authority and other types of authority is that it is based on the manifestations from the principal to the agent. Further, because actual authority is based solely on the manifestations of the principal, it is not contingent upon the principal's unexpressed wishes or mental state. Under actual authority, the agent is not assumed to know everything that the principal knows. . . .

2. Apparent Authority

The second type of authority, apparent authority, arises through manifestations by the principal to a third party. There are several ways for an agent to attain apparent authority. Direct communication from the principal to the third party would qualify as creating apparent authority; however, that is not the only way in which apparent authority may be created. Manifestations may also come from the principal telling the agent to misinform the third party of the agent's authority. Further, the authority may be created by the principal placing the agent in a position which would lead third parties to believe that the agent has such authority. Once the principal has made a manifestation, apparent authority requires that the third party reasonably believe that the agent has authority, and that the belief be traceable to the principal's manifestations. A principal may not be bound by apparent authority if the third party's belief that the agent had authority was unreasonable. Further, an agent cannot bind a principal by tricking the third party into believing that the agent has authority.

The *Restatement Third* retains the doctrine of apparent authority unchanged from the *Restatement Second.* However, the *Restatement Third* provides a deeper analysis of the issue. Namely, the *Restatement Third* points out some unique attributes to apparent authority which are not present in actual authority. For example, apparent authority may exist even after the agency relationship has been terminated. Also, the exercise of apparent authority by an agent may create a cause of action for the principal against the agent. . . .

3. Incidental Authority

The third type of authority, incidental authority, is the authority for an agent to perform the tasks which are concomitant to accomplishing the authorized act. The doctrine of incidental authority provides an agent with authority, even though the principal's manifestations are not sufficiently clear or all encompassing. The illustrations for *Restatement Second* . . . provide clear examples of what type of actions are considered to be within an agent's incidental authority. The *Restatement Third,* on the other hand, simply incorporated incidental authority into its definition of actual authority, thereby eliminating the need for a separate section on the issue.

4. Inherent Authority

The scope and reach of the fourth type of authority, inherent authority, have been relatively limited. In fact, to date, only one court of last resort, the Indiana Supreme Court, has adopted the doctrine. However, a few intermediate courts have used the doctrine to bind a principal. Inherent authority binds a principal in cases where no actual or apparent authority exists and the elements of estoppel are not present. The doctrine was created for two reasons: "the need to ensure fairness for the parties dealing with the agent and the goal of promoting the general commercial convenience of all parties involved." However, with growing concerns for the doctrine's seemingly boundless possibilities, the drafters of the *Restatement Third* decided to eliminate the section and absorb some of its concepts into other areas.

C. An Alternate Theory for Binding a Principal: Estoppel

Beyond the "traditional" concepts of agency and authority, both the *Restatement Second* and *Restatement Third* contain a section on estoppel. In agency law, estoppel is viewed as a net that allows courts the freedom to hold a principal liable in cases where the agent is lacking either an agency relationship or authority to bind the principal. Estoppel can also be used to prevent a principal from denying an agency relationship or authority; however, estoppel is preempted by all other doctrines contained within the *Restatements.* In order for estoppel to apply, therefore, courts must be sure that no other doctrines within the *Restatements* apply. . . .

Under the *Restatement Second,* an individual is estopped from denying an agency relationship if he intentionally or carelessly caused a belief in a third person that one is acting on his behalf or, knowing of the belief, failed to correct the mistake and caused the third party to change position in reliance on that belief. As at least one jurisdiction in Texas has noted, estoppel is closely related to several other agency doctrines. However, to say that the doctrines are equivalent would be incorrect. Apparent authority, for example, is analytically similar to estoppel; however, estoppel, as defined in both the *Restatement Second* and *Third,* does not necessarily require that the third party's belief be directly traceable to the principal in order to apply. For instance, in order for there to be a claim of apparent authority, the third party's belief must be traceable to a manifestation on the part of the principal. Estoppel, on the other hand, does not require as close a fit between the third party's belief and the principal.

Hoddeson v. Koos Bros . . . was the first case to use agency by estoppel to confer liability. In *Hoddeson,* Ms. Hoddeson entered a furniture store owned by Koos Brothers to make a purchase. While in the store, Ms. Hoddeson was approached by a man who appeared to work for Koos Brothers. The man then proceeded to take notes, presumably recording her order, as Ms. Hoddeson selected furniture to purchase. At the end of the discussion, Ms. Hoddeson paid for the furniture and left the store. After waiting for a period of time past the expected delivery date, Ms. Hoddeson went back to the store to inquire what was causing the delay. When she returned, Koos Brothers' employees informed her that they had no record of the transaction. It was assumed that the man who had helped her had not been a member of the sales staff at all. The court remanded the case based on a lack of evidence and findings by the lower court to hold that the "apparent" salesman was an agent with any kind of authority to bind the furniture store. However, the court held that under a theory of estoppel, regardless of whether the salesman had authority, the furniture store could not escape liability by disavowing an agency relationship where it had failed to adequately protect its customers from people falsely pretending to be salesmen. . . .

The law of agency embodies concepts from several areas of law including, but not limited to, torts and contracts. As a result, there has been much confusion over which doctrines apply in different circumstances. However, while the *Restatement Third* is a useful tool to help guide courts in evaluating agency problems, it is a secondary source and as such should not stand in the way of a court's ability to find a result that is equitable and just.

III. ANALYSIS

The doctrine of perceived agency embodies characteristics similar to estoppel. Thus, what is the significant difference between estoppel and perceived agency? As a corollary, should courts retain both doctrines? An examination of cases interpreting these doctrines shows . . . respectively, [the difference is] is the reliance required by each doctrine. Under perceived agency, a plaintiff is only required to show that he justifiably relied upon the manifestations of the principal when dealing with an agent. By comparison, under the doctrine of agency by estoppel, a plaintiff is required to show that he was justified in relying upon the principal's manifestations and that he changed his position based upon that reliance. It is clear that there is a need for an agency doctrine which protects third parties who rely on manifestations by a principal that another is their agent. However, the doctrines must be flexible enough to protect consumers, while not discouraging business from working together in new and creative ways. Requiring detrimental reliance in cases of third party reliance where no agency relationship exists will do just that. . . .

Why is agency related to the idea of estoppel?

A. Restatement Second: A Confusion of Doctrines by the Courts

1. Employer—Employee Relationships

One of the two broad circumstances in which courts have applied agency by estoppel or perceived agency is when the third party believed the person was an employee of the principal and, therefore, believed the person to be an agent of the principal. Although only moderately common, this situation has the capability of arising in an enormous number of settings. . . .

a. Salesmen: Attempts to Define a Doctrine • The seminal case for using estoppel to hold a business responsible for the acts of an apparent salesman is *Hoddeson v. Koos Bros.* The *Hoddeson* court remanded the case, making no finding as to whether the furniture store was actually estopped from denying the agency relationship. However, the court reasoned that agency by estoppel may be appropriate in these types of cases. Although the court's reasoning followed that of the *Restatement Second,* sections 8b and 267, noticeably missing from the court's discussion was the degree of reliance required. The court only indirectly mentioned the degree of reliance by stating that the principal should be estopped if the acts of the perceived agent would lead a person of "ordinary prudence and circumspection to believe that the imposter was . . . the proprietor's agent." . . .

b. Independent Contractor Physicians: Uncertainty in Choosing a Doctrine • Courts' treatment of the relationship between hospitals and their independent contractor physicians varies by jurisdiction. Most jurisdictions use perceived agency to confer liability on hospitals; however, a minority of jurisdictions, most notably Illinois, rejected perceived agency in favor of using agency by estoppel. Because of the additional requirement of change of position, it is much harder for a plaintiff to prevail in jurisdictions that use agency by estoppel.

Williams v. St. Claire Medical Center and *Gasbarra v. St. James Hospital* demonstrate the different ways courts have examined the relationship between a hospital and its independent contractor physicians. . . .

In applying the doctrine of perceived agency to the facts, the *St. Claire Medical Center* court recognized that, by failing to give the plaintiff notice that the anesthesiologist was not an employee of the hospital, it held him out as such. Further, in discussing the plaintiff's reliance, the court stated that the plaintiff's belief that the anesthesiologist was an employee of the hospital was justifiable, omitting any discussion of change of position. By contrast, Illinois has rejected the use of perceived agency in the context of hospital liability.

In *Gasbarra,* the plaintiff sought recovery for the malpractice of a physician that resulted in the death of her child. In a supplemental opinion, the court discussed the plaintiff's agency claim. The court found that no actual agency relationship existed, and without mention of perceived agency, rejected the plaintiff's claim for agency by estoppel. In finding that there was no merit to the plaintiff's claim for agency by estoppel, the court stated that the plaintiff failed to provide any evidence in the record that suggested she changed her position based on a belief that the emergency room physicians were employees of the hospital. In other words, the plaintiff failed to show evidence that if she had known the physicians were not employees of the hospital she would have chosen to take her child to another hospital. Accordingly, requiring change of position in this context makes it much harder for plaintiffs to hold hospitals vicariously liable for the acts of their independent contractor physicians.

2. Franchisor-Franchisee Relationships

Despite the fact that Illinois courts have used agency by estoppel and rejected perceived agency in one context, no jurisdiction has been willing to apply agency by estoppel to franchisor-franchisee relationships. Franchisor-franchisee relationships are present in a wide variety of business enterprises . . . Furthermore, as the Oregon Court of Appeals reasoned in *Miller v. McDonald's Corp.,* "[t]he crucial issues are whether the putative principal held the third party out as an agent and whether the plaintiff relied on that holding out."

Courts consider a variety of factors to find that a franchisor has "held out" a franchisee as its agent. Among those factors courts have most notably deliberated are the effects of a franchisor's national advertising and a franchisee's use of the franchisor's name and insignia on signs and other displays in the store. As to the question of reliance, courts have almost uniformly announced and applied the requirement of justifiable reliance rather than detrimental reliance/change of position.

Little v. Howard Johnson Co. is [a] case often cited as an example of a court requiring detrimental reliance/change of position in perceived agency analysis. The belief that the court required detrimental reliance/change of position is based on the court's statement, "[h]ere, plaintiff has failed to offer any documentary evidence that she was harmed as a result of relying on the perceived fact that the franchisee was an agent of defendant." Taken by itself, the court's statement appears to suggest that detrimental reliance/change of position is required. However, when viewed in light of the facts of the case, another reading emerges.

Little involved a restaurant customer slipping and falling on an icy sidewalk. Arguably, the conditions which caused the plaintiff's injury were completely unrelated to the aspects of the restaurant that the franchisor would have promoted, as uniform to the franchise, to encourage patronage to member franchisees. When considered in conjunction with the surrounding facts, the court's language requires that the instrument which injures a plaintiff must be part of the holding out by the franchisor upon which the plaintiff relied. In many cases, this requirement is inherently fulfilled, as in the case *Miller v. McDonald's Corp.*

In *Miller,* the plaintiff was injured from biting into a sapphire that was inside her sandwich. In finding a perceived agency relationship, the court recognized that McDonald's use of uniform menus, food production methods, and service standards, constituted a holding out of the franchisee as McDonald's agent. While not discussed in the case, it is self-evident that the instrumentality which caused plaintiff's injury, the food, was part and parcel of the representations made by the franchisor and relied upon by the plaintiff. It may be, as King suggests, that requiring a close fit between the instrumentality of injury and the manifestations by the principal would fulfill a detrimental reliance requirement in cases where the plaintiff is injured by instrumentality that is not part of the principal's manifestation. However, in cases like *Miller,* findings that the plaintiff was injured by an instrumentality which was part of the principal's manifestations fail to bring a court any closer to determining whether the plaintiff has detrimentally relied. Therefore, combining those two concepts runs the risk of further muddling an already cloudy area of agency law.

Beyond *Miller* and *Little,* courts from a wide range of jurisdictions have explicitly stated that the only reliance required to hold a franchisor liable for the acts of a franchisee is justifiable reliance. In doing so, courts have equated enticement with reliance and found franchisors liable based solely on the plaintiff's testimony that they chose to do business with the franchisee because they thought they were dealing with the franchisor. However, noticeably lacking in all of the franchisor-franchisee cases is any evidence that the plaintiffs have given up an alternative opportunity they would have taken had they known the business was not run by the franchisor. Further, without such evidence, it is unclear how a plaintiff can claim that he was injured by the franchisor's representations. . . .

B. Restatement Third: Attempting to Streamline the Law

As previously discussed, the *Restatement Third* contains similar language to the *Restatement Second* in the areas of perceived agency and agency by estoppel.

As a result, courts in jurisdictions where the *Restatement Third* is adopted will have a choice of which doctrine to use when faced with agency cases involving employer-employee and franchisor-franchisee relationships.

1. Employer-Employee Relationship Under Restatement Third section 7.07

Under this analysis, the first question would be, did the principal hold out the agent as its employee? Secondly, did the plaintiff rely on the holding out of the principal? Finally, was the plaintiff's reliance reasonable and justifiable? If the answer is "yes" to all three questions, then the principal is liable, but, if the answer is "no" to any of these factors, the principal is not liable.

2. Franchisor-Franchisee Relationships Under Restatement Third section 7.07 Comment f

Courts routinely relied on the *Restatement Second* to impose liability upon franchisors for the misdeeds of their franchisees. In order to fall within the reach of [this rule] an attorney will have to give an employer-employee basis for asserting vicarious liability. Because franchisees are not generally considered employees of franchisors, practitioners will have to draw their complaints carefully, asserting that the tortious acts of the franchisee employee should be imputed to the franchisor, because the franchisor held out all employees of the franchisee as employees of the franchisor.

Applying this idea to the facts of *Miller v. McDonald's,* the plaintiff would have to draw her complaint carefully, asserting that McDonald's Corporation held out all workers at McDonald's restaurants as being employed by McDonald's Corporation; and, as such, McDonald's Corporation should be vicariously liable for the acts of all McDonald's employees. Once that is established, the court could use the same analysis as it would under *Restatement Second* to impute liability upon the franchisor. . . .

IV. CONCLUSION

Although the doctrines of perceived agency and agency by estoppel operate in substantially the same manner, they differ in the level of reliance required to apply them. The law of agency could operate with only one of the doctrines, as they both apply to situations where a principal is somehow responsible for the beliefs of an innocent third party.

END NOTE

1. Joseph Story, Commentaries on the Law of the Agency (1882).

ARTICLE 4.2

Thomas Genovese and Linda Genovese v. Joseph Bergeron and Theresa Bergeron

Thomas Genovese and Linda Genovese (landlords) brought this action against Theresa Bergeron (tenant) to recover unpaid rent and property damages. The tenant entered into six consecutive one-year leases with the landlords whereby the landlords agreed to rent to the tenant a residence in the Shipyard Plantation on Hilton Head Island.

Doris Warner managed the property for the landlords throughout the period during which the tenant rented the property. In December 1993, the tenant informed Warner she had been offered employment in New York and she desired to terminate the lease with the landlords. Because the lease required the landlords' permission before the tenant could sublease the property, the tenant requested that Warner ask the landlords whether she could either sublease the property or terminate the lease. Warner informed the tenant the landlords did not want her to sublease the property and the landlords were considering selling the property. Warner told the tenant she could vacate the premises. The tenant complied with Warner's request to put her desire to terminate the lease in writing and to indicate she planned to vacate the property.

At trial, the landlords moved for a directed verdict on their unpaid rent claim. In opposition to the landlords' directed verdict motion, the tenant argued there was sufficient evidence for a jury to conclude Warner had the apparent authority to release the tenant from her obligations under the lease. The trial court directed a verdict in favor of the landlords and awarded them $ 10,400 in unpaid rent. The jury awarded the landlords $2,000 for property damage caused by the tenant. The tenant appeals.

LEGAL BACKGROUND

. . . Apparent authority to do a particular act is created as to a third person by written or spoken words or any other conduct of the principal which, reasonably interpreted, causes the third person to believe the principal consents to have the act done on his behalf by the person purporting to act for him. The principal must either intend to cause the third person to believe the agent is authorized to act for him, or he should realize his conduct is likely to create such belief.

Under the doctrine of apparent authority, a principal is bound by the acts of its agent when it has placed the agent in such a position that persons of ordinary prudence, reasonably knowledgeable with business usages and customs, are led to believe the agent has certain authority and they in turn deal with the agent based on that assumption. Agency may be implied or inferred and may be shown directly or circumstantially by the conduct of the purported agent exhibiting a pretense of authority with the knowledge of the alleged principal. The apparent authority of an agent results from conduct or other manifestations of the principal's consent, whereby third persons are justified in believing that the agent is acting within his authority. Such authority is implied where the principal passively permits the agent to appear to a third person to have the authority to act on his behalf. . . .

OPINION BY: J. HOWELL GOOLSBY

Why is it not determinative in this case that there IS an agency relationship?

The tenant argues the trial court erred in directing a verdict on the unpaid rent issue because she presented sufficient evidence of apparent authority to survive a directed verdict motion. We agree.

Apparent authority to do a particular act "is created as to a third person by written or spoken words or any other conduct of the principal which, reasonably interpreted, causes the third person to believe the principal consents to have the act done on his behalf by the person purporting to act for him." The principal must either intend to cause the third person to believe the agent is authorized to act for him, or he should realize his conduct is likely to create such belief.

Generally, agency is a question of fact, so that if there are any facts tending to prove an agency relationship, it then becomes a question for the jury.[1]

It is undisputed that Warner was the landlords' agent. At issue, then, is the extent of Warner's agency. Bergeron testified he gave Warner broad authority to manage the property. For instance, as the rental property manager for the landlords throughout the five-year period during which the tenant occupied the property, Warner managed the lease, received rent payments, and ordered necessary repairs to the property. Warner also prepared the rental agreements between the landlords and the tenant for their signing and negotiated the terms with the tenants. The landlords always dealt with the tenant through Warner and there were no contacts between the landlords and the tenant except through Warner.

When the tenant requested in writing whether she could terminate the lease or be allowed to sublet the property, Warner told the tenant the landlords were thinking about selling the property, and the landlords did not want the tenant to sublease it, so the tenant could vacate the property. The landlords did not communicate their opposition to this arrangement between the tenant and Warner until they filed this lawsuit.

Viewing the evidence in the light most favorable to the tenant, as we are required to do, we find there is some evidence in the record for a jury to conclude that, under the doctrine of apparent authority, the conduct of the landlords in clothing Warner with so much authority to manage the property would allow a reasonably prudent person in the tenant's position to believe Warner had the authority to release the tenant from her obligations under the lease. The apparent authority of an agent results from . . . conduct . . . or other manifestations of the principal's consent, whereby third persons are justified in believing that the agent is acting within his authority. . . . Such authority is implied where the principal passively permits the agent to appear to a third person to have the authority to act on his behalf.[2]

Why does the court look at the facts in a manner most favorable to the tenant?

REVERSED AND REMANDED

END NOTES

1. Gathers v. Harris Teeter Supermarket, Inc., 282 S.C. 220, 317 S.E.2d 748 (Ct. App. 1984).
2. 3 AM. JUR. 2D Agency § 79, at 584 (1986).

ARTICLE 4.3

Selected Recent Court Decisions—Malpractice: Vicarious Liability Under Apparent Agency: James v. Ingalls Memorial Hospital

Elizabeth Heinrich

The Appellate Court of Illinois for the First District held that a hospital can not be held vicariously liable for the negligence of its physicians under an apparent agency theory, when the patient:

1. knows or should know that the physician is an independent contractor and
2. has not acted in reliance on the existence of an agency relationship between the hospital and the physician.

The court found that where a plaintiff has signed a consent form which clearly stated that the physician is an independent contractor, she can not reasonably argue that she believes an agency relationship exists. The court found that this case was controlled by the test set forth by the Illinois Supreme Court *in Gilbert v. Sycamore Municipal Hospital*. Using this test, the court clarifies the plaintiff's burden in proving the vicarious liability of a hospital.

The plaintiff, Kayla James, is a minor child, and the action was brought on her behalf by her mother, Lasonia James. The mother alleged that the physician who treated her daughter was negligent in not transferring her to another hospital after she was admitted twenty-two weeks pregnant and leaking amniotic fluid. Her baby survived but suffers severe visual impairment and neurological damage as a result of premature birth. The plaintiff argued that the defendant, Ingalls Memorial Hospital, should be held vicariously liable for the negligence of the physician. The trial court found that there was no actual or apparent agency relationship between the physician and the hospital and therefore granted summary judgment for the hospital. The plaintiff appealed, arguing that the existence of an agency relationship was a question of fact for the jury.

The appellate court agreed that the existence of an agency relationship is normally a jury question, but found that in this case only one reasonable conclusion could be drawn and thus summary judgment was appropriate. The court acknowledged that under Gilbert, a hospital can, in some circumstances, be found vicariously liable for a physician's negligence. To prove apparent agency under the Gilbert test, the plaintiff must show:

1. The hospital or its agent acted in a manner that would lead a reasonable person to conclude that the physician alleged to be negligent was an employee or agent of the hospital;
2. The hospital had knowledge of the acts of the agent which created the appearance of the authority, where there were such acts, and acquiesced in them; and
3. The plaintiff acted in reliance on the conduct of the hospital or its agent. . . .

The court found that where, as here, the plaintiff has signed a consent form stating that the physician is an independent contractor, it would be very difficult to prove that the plaintiff did not know that no agency relationship existed between the physician and the hospital. The court distinguished this case from one in which the independent contractor relationship was known between the physician and the hospital but unknown to the plaintiff. . . .

The court acknowledged that there is no Illinois precedent as to the impact of an independent contractor disclaimer on a consent form . . . The court felt that the plaintiff had failed to show that the hospital held itself out as having an agency relationship with the physician. Thus, because clear statements had been made in the consent form that there was no agency relationship and no evidence suggested that anyone had ever indicated otherwise, the court found that the plaintiff had not provided any reasonable basis for finding that an apparent agency relationship existed between the physician and the hospital.

Furthermore, the court found that this was not a case in which the plaintiff acted in reliance on her understanding of the relationship between the hospital and the physician. The court pointed to deposition testimony by the plaintiff that clearly indicated that the relationship between the physician and the hospital was not a factor in her decision to go to that hospital. The court rejected statements by the plaintiff to the contrary that were provided after the fact.

Why is the plaintiff's degree of reliance on an agency relationship between the hospital and physician an important question in this decision?

This decision indicates that a disclaimer of the relationship between physician and hospital in a consent form, while not dispositive, will in many cases provide strong evidence for a finding that a hospital should not be held vicariously liable. Thus, a hospital wishing to avoid vicarious liability should not only be concerned with representations it makes in its promotional materials but should also provide their patients with specific disclaimers. Conversely, plaintiffs wishing to show apparent agency should be prepared to show specific action by the hospital or physicians that form the basis for their understanding of the relationship between them.

ARTICLE 4.4

Agency Law: Extending the Common Knowledge Doctrine

William T. Hennessey

Mobil Oil Corp. v. Bransford, *648 So. 2d 119 (Fla. 1995).*

Respondent was assaulted by an employee at a gasoline station owned by petitioner but leased to a franchisee. He filed suit against petitioner arguing that petitioner had effectively established an apparent agency relationship with the franchisee station operator. As proof that petitioner had represented the station as its agent, respondent alleged that petitioner's products were sold in the station, that its trademarks and logos were used throughout the station, and that the station's employees were required to wear uniforms bearing petitioner's corporate logos. The trial court granted petitioner's motion for summary judgment, holding that respondent had failed to offer facts sufficient to support a claim of apparent agency. Reversing the trial court, the Fourth District Court of Appeal held that petitioner might be liable under a theory of apparent agency because petitioner owned the station property and prominently displayed its signs and logos there to induce customers to patronize the station. The Florida Supreme Court granted review, and in reversing the decision of the district court, held that respondent failed to allege the level of representation necessary to create an apparent agency relationship.

Why is the common knowledge doctrine less certain than it sounds as a basis for making decisions in apparent agency cases?

Traditionally, courts have applied the master-servant analysis of agency law to determine if a franchisor could be held liable for the acts of a franchisee. However, the widespread growth of advertising and corporate franchising presented courts with relationships which appeared to transcend the traditional notions of master and servant, and principal and agent. Injured plaintiffs argued that the defendant corporation should be estopped from denying liability under the theory of apparent agency, because it "represented" to the public that the franchisee was its agent through the use of advertising and display of corporate logos.

Initially, Florida courts were receptive to this argument. In *Economy Cabs, Inc. v. Kirkland*, the Florida Supreme Court extended the doctrine of apparent agency to the franchise context. The plaintiff in *Economy Cabs* brought suit against a cab company contending that it was liable under the doctrine of respondeat superior for the negligence of the driver of a cab which she believed the company owned. The cab company argued that the cab in question was independently owned by a third party; therefore, the driver could not be considered its employee.

The *Economy Cabs* court held that under these facts, the law will presume as to the plaintiff, and the public generally, that the defendant cab company operated the cabs which bore its name. The court reasoned that corporations should not be permitted to "parade under a flag of truce" to earn a profit and then deny liability for damages inflicted. The court found that third parties who own taxicabs, but operate them "in the name of the company, at the call of the company, and under the colors of the company will be treated as the company."

Although the presumption enunciated by the *Economy Cabs* court could have been logically extended to most franchise relationships, courts were reluctant to do so in many situations.[1] Most notably, very few recoveries were allowed in oil company cases because of what commentators have referred to as the "common knowledge" doctrine. Courts held that no one could reasonably believe that a service station operator was the employee of the oil company because it was a matter of common knowledge that the signs and the uniforms worn by employees merely announced that the oil company's products were for sale at the station.

The Florida Second District Court of Appeal implicitly adopted the common knowledge doctrine in *Cawthon v. Phillips Petroleum Co.* In *Cawthon*, the plaintiff brought suit against an oil company for injuries that occurred in an accident after an employee at a service station negligently repaired his automobile. The oil company argued that the owner of the service station was an independent contractor, and that the signs and advertisements merely indicated that the station carried the oil company's products for sale.

On appeal, the *Cawthon* court held that in order for the theory of apparent agency to apply, the injured party must not only have been misled by the franchisor, but also must have relied on that misrepresentation to his detriment. The court found that service station signs and advertisements only show that the oil company's products are sold at the station, and not that the service station is an agent for the oil company with respect to any standard of service or car repair. Thus, the court found that it was unreasonable to assume that these advertisements conferred upon the service station an apparent agency relationship with the oil company.

After *Cawthon*, the question remained whether Florida courts would extend the common knowledge doctrine into other franchise situations, or whether oil company cases were somehow different. Addressing these and other issues in *Orlando Executive Park v. Robbins*, the Florida Supreme Court adopted a three-prong test for apparent agency. The plaintiff in *Orlando Executive Park* was attacked by an unidentified man while she was a guest at an independently owned Howard Johnson's motel. Similar to the plaintiffs in *Economy Cabs* and *Cawthon*, she brought under an apparent agency theory.[2]

Howard Johnson's principal argument was that it lacked any power to control the franchisee. "Rejecting this argument, the *Orlando Executive Park* court agreed with the district court's finding that while Howard Johnson's control over the operation of the motel may be relevant to a claim of actual agency, it has no relevance to the theory of apparent agency. The *Orlando Executive Park* court held that three elements are necessary to establish an apparent agency relationship:

1. a representation by the principal;
2. reliance on that representation by a third person; and
3. a change of position by the third person in reliance upon such representation to his detriment.

The *Orlando Executive Park* court found that the district court had set out the proper standard for analyzing the element of representation. The district court reasoned that there was sufficient evidence for a jury to reasonably conclude that the uniformity of signs, building design, and color scheme satisfied the element of representation because they easily led persons to believe that each hotel was under common ownership or conformed to common standards of service. To the extent *Cawthon* and other oil company cases suggested that signs and advertising alone are never sufficient to create an apparent agency relationship, the *Orlando Executive Park* court limited them to their facts, and disapproved extending their language into other cases. In affirming the decision of the district court, the *Orlando Executive Park* court held that the existence of an agency relationship is ordinarily a question for the jury, and that it can be proved by the facts on a case-by-case basis.

The instant court retreated from the broad language espoused in *Orlando Executive Park* which suggested that advertising and display of corporate logos alone can create an apparent agency. The instant court stated that the only relevant fact in *Orlando Executive Park* was that the franchisor actually operated several components within the motel. The instant court found that this fact alone demonstrated to the public that the franchisee was in substantial control of the premises. Adopting the common knowledge doctrine, the instant court reasoned that in today's world, it is well understood that the use of franchise logos or other methods of advertising does not necessarily translate into actual or apparent control by the franchisor over any substantial part of the franchisee's business.

Disagreeing with the district court in *Orlando Executive Park*, the instant court held that in order to create an agency relationship with a franchisee, the franchisor must have apparently or directly participated in managing or controlling the acts of the franchisee. In deciding that petitioner lacked any power to control the franchisee, the instant court found it important that the contract itself expressly stated that the franchisee was an independent businessman and that nothing in the contract was to be interpreted as creating a right in petitioner to exercise control over the franchisee.

The instant court agreed with the *Orlando Executive Park* court that the elements necessary to prove an apparent agency are that there has been a representation by a purported principle; a third party has relied on that representation;

and the third party has changed position in reliance on that representation. However, the instant court found that respondent failed to allege the minimum level of representation necessary to satisfy the first of these elements. The instant court held that respondent alleged no genuine representation by petitioner, but merely assumed that such a representation was implicit in the use of petitioner's products and symbols throughout the station.

In a strong dissent, Justice Shaw agreed with the majority that the underlying issue in the instant case was whether petitioner had control over the quality of customer service at the station. However, Justice Shaw found that service was a matter of extensive contractual agreement, pointing out that provisions in the contract required exemplary customer service and were enforceable by petitioner. Justice Shaw also noted there was testimony that petitioner's representatives monitored the station regularly and were at times on the premises discussing business operations. Justice Shaw would have affirmed the decision of the district court because he found that the record contained vast evidence supporting respondent's claims that an apparent agency relationship existed, and that summary judgment was therefore inappropriate.

Retreating from the principal holding espoused by the court only twelve years earlier in *Orlando Executive Park*, the instant court held that signs and logos alone are not sufficient to create an apparent agency relationship. Instead, the instant court examined the contract itself to determine if petitioner had any power to control the franchisee. The district court in *Orlando Executive Park* had flatly rejected this analysis, holding that control was not relevant to the theory of apparent agency.

Apparent agency is based on the "appearance" of an agency relationship and is determined by representations made by the principal to third parties. Typical consumers who happen upon a business franchise are not parties to the contract and therefore should not be limited in their recovery by its terms. Many consumers, in fact, believe that when they visit local franchises they are patronizing large national corporations which will stand behind their products and their service. The *Economy Cabs* court boldly stated that a corporation should not be permitted to "parade under a flag of truce" to earn a profit and then deny liability for damages inflicted. That court found that one of the fundamental principles of our legal system is that for every wrong, the law affords a remedy. . . .

Why is the court's reasoning in Economy Cabs *important for this decision?*

The instant court could easily have decided this case by following the reasoning of *Cawthon* and other oil company cases. Courts throughout the nation have consistently and uniformly rejected extending liability to oil companies for the torts of their franchisees. However, by limiting itself to the issue of representation, the instant court was required to either accept or reject the notion that the use of signs, logos, and corporate uniforms could be sufficient to create an apparent agency relationship. In rejecting the principal holding of *Orlando Executive Park*, the instant court ignored not only common sense but also explicit provisions in the contract which clearly indicated that petitioner was using these representations to distinguish its product and foster public confidence in its service stations.

Thus, rather than leaving a well-settled doctrine undisturbed, the instant court chose to address *Orlando Executive Park,* finding that the holding in that case was misleading and invited unnecessary confusion. In so doing, however, the instant court may have made a sweeping change to the doctrine of apparent agency in Florida. If the holding of the instant case is extended beyond oil company cases and into other franchise situations, the instant court may have eliminated injured plaintiffs' most successful and potent argument. By examining the terms of the contract, the instant court would apparently allow a franchisor to effectively absolve itself from liability by carefully drafting provisions disclaiming any power to control the franchisee. This outcome clearly would contradict the policy behind the theory of apparent agency by binding third party consumers to the terms of an unfamiliar contract, and easily could lead to unconscionable results in the future.

END NOTES

1. Robert W. Emerson, *Franchisors' Liability When Franchisees Are Apparent Agents: An Empirical and Policy Analysis of "Common Knowledge" About Franchising*, 20 HOFSTRA L. REV. 609, 639 n.112 (1992).
2. Orlando Executive Park, Inc. v. P.D.R., 402 So. 2d 442, 445 (Fla. 5th DCA 1981). The plaintiff claimed that the franchisor and franchisee owed her a legal duty to exercise reasonable care for her safety while she was a guest on the premises.

ARTICLE 4.5

Are Traditional Agency Principles Effective for Internet Transactions, Given the Lack of Personal Interaction?

Nancy R. Furnari

I. INTRODUCTION

While no one can question the fact that the law is constantly changing, there are some general principles of law that have remained relatively stable over time. These principles may be applied to different types of fact patterns than in earlier years, but generally their underlying premises remain the same. How can the rapidly advancing world of technology affect these deeply imbedded principles of law? Judges, practitioners, and laymen are continuously forced to reevaluate the legal ramifications of everyday activities as the law changes. But what happens when the law does not catch up with the technology of the times?

Agency law is a category of law that has remained relatively constant over the years. Even though agency law has different interpretations in different jurisdictions, the underlying principles are similar. However, with the rapid expansion of Internet transactions, these well settled principles may not be as effective as they are for the traditional personal transactions people have engaged in throughout the years.

While there has been virtually no case or statutory law on the effect of impersonal Internet transactions on traditional agency principles, it is wise to take a look at the issues soon to arise. To fully understand these issues, it is first necessary to understand how the Internet functions.

"An internetwork or an Internet is a network of networks." The entire World Wide Web is built largely upon the notion of hyperlinking, whereby a consumer jumps from one site to the next. Each site leads to many other sites, all of which are interconnected in some way. An individual may be searching for flowers one minute and the next minute she may be entering into a highly complex contract to buy a car. One site leads to another, and then another, and so on. Moreover, people browsing the Internet may simply enter in a search term at a search engine's web site and, almost instantly, a list of thousands of sites may appear on the screen. The structure and function of the Internet, with all of the advertisements and hyperlinks, lead consumers to transactions they may not have entered into, or even considered, had they been faced with the personal, one-on-one communication traditionally associated with the buyer-seller relationship. . . .

It is the notion of an interlinked community that makes the World Wide Web such a dynamic and thriving environment. Hyperlinking is what the Web is all about . . . no site is an island. So how does a person know where one advertisement or company begins and another ends? When there are multiple icons and banners on a page, how does the average consumer separate one from the other? Sure, one may know that Colgate and Crest are not the same entity and are not part of the same business conglomerate, but what about those many "no-name" companies, companies that either share a web page or have hyperlinks to one another? And what about a "no-name" company that shares a page with a well-known company or is linked with one? One question of real significance is whether a consumer has purchased something from a "no-name" company because he thought it was related to, or part of, the familiar company name. This question raises issues involving agency relationships.

A group of leading business users has suggested that:

> "Governments need to clarify the legal definitions, practices and structures that pertain to commercial activities in an electronic environment, and to seek multilateral agreements on critical legal matters, especially the laws regarding . . . agency . . . Where appropriate, governments should adjust existing laws and regulations so that they apply to "intangible" as well as "material" product environments."[1]

While some jurisdictions have recognized the risk of consumer confusion in this area, many others have not. Even among those states that have recognized the risk and have developed some protective measures, none have adequately addressed the specific legal ramifications, such as agency relationships, that may result from consumer confusion.

II. INTERNET COMMERCE: A DIFFERENT WAY OF TRANSACTING

A. What Is Internet Commerce?

To understand the fundamental issues that arise from Internet commerce, it is necessary to understand what Internet commerce actually is. Various scholars, practitioners, and businesspeople have defined Internet commerce in a number of ways. The most common definition, and the one most relevant to this Comment is, "the buying and selling of products and services over the Internet." A broader definition of Internet commerce refers "to all forms of commercial transactions involving both organizations and individuals, that are based upon the electronic processing and transmission of data, including text, sound and visual images." Internet commerce "includes advertising, trading, and aftersales, as well as online exchange over both private and public networks." The differences in the consumer market today, as compared to just a decade ago, are seen in both the products and services available, as well as how they are bought and sold.

Until fairly recently, individuals who wanted to take advantage of the highly complex world of the Internet had to learn numerous systems to make full use of the resources available. Today, it is much simpler. Consumers and others browsing the Internet have virtually everything done for them, without even having to think. A web browser or other program does most of the thinking for the consumer. While the Internet transactions are still interactive, they can be characterized as more passive than the average personal, paper transactions. There is virtually no human interaction or negotiating; all a consumer has to do is point and click.

B. Foreseeable and Unsettled Ramifications of Impersonal Internet Transactions

Although the Internet has become a widely used medium for many daily activities and responsibilities, and is flooded with information and advertising, there are still comparatively few transactions for value over the Internet, compared to the total number of transactions for value in the world. This may account for the absence of relevant statutes and case law on the issues of consumer confusion in Internet transactions, and the possible agency relationships that may be formed through apparent authority as a result of this confusion. . . .

However, one of the major elements of consumer purchases is missing in Internet transactions. This is the face-to-face contact that has formed the basis of so many transactions. With that element missing, the key element of trust is also missing. Can it reasonably be said that consumers transacting over the Internet place the same amount of trust in a seller on the Internet as they do with a merchant with whom they have discussed the matter in person? One of the advantages of the traditional face-to-face transactions is that goods are usually exchanged in a physical place. A consumer has a fairly reliable sense that she will have some recourse if there is a problem with the transaction. She has a "store" to go to or she at least has some idea of where to begin looking to reach the seller. This same advantage is not always present with Internet transactions.

Why would the absence of face-to-face contact during an Internet purchase affect the application of agency law?

Internet commerce, especially information commerce, may lack the "packaging to help identify the sender after the goods are delivered." Some of these sales may be of significant value and others may be minimal. Confusion as to liability arises here. For instance, "providers of information on the World Wide Web might choose to charge a fraction of a penny to each person accessing their pages. Browsers may be configured to pay these charges, up to a predefined limit, without ever troubling the user." Does giving the browsers the right to charge for the seller's services create some type of agency relationship?

III. TRADITIONAL AGENCY PRINCIPLES

In general, the basic premise behind agency principles "is to enable a person, through the services of another, to broaden the scope of his activities and receive the product of another's efforts, paying such other for what he does but retaining for himself any net benefit resulting from the work performed." Liability may be found through an agency relationship based on the laws of contract.

Fundamental agency principles have been laid out in many states and throughout the country with a high degree of consistency. "An agency is a fiduciary relationship which results from a manifestation of consent by one person to another that the other shall act on his behalf and subject to his control, and the consent by the other to act."[2]

An agency relationship maybe established by conduct or by a written or oral contract. Actual and apparent authority both stem from an agent's power. An agent or apparent agent holds a power to alter the legal relations between the principal and third persons and between the principal and himself. While actual authority is the result of the principal's consent manifested to the agent, apparent authority is the result of consent manifested to a third party.

A. Actual Authority

An agency relationship may be formed through actual authority. Actual authority is created when the principal manifests its consent to an agent, rather than to a third party, as is the case with apparent authority. Such authority may either be express or implied. Express authority occurs when a principal directly authorizes an agent to perform a specific act or acts. However, an agency relationship may also be created in a broader, but more discrete way. Authority may be "implied or inferred from the words used, from customs and from the relations of the parties." A situation may give rise to such implied authority where the principal acts toward the agent in such a way that reasonably creates the appearance of authority. Thus, when referring to an agent's actual authority, the ""scope of [such] authority" includes not only the actual authorization conferred upon the agent by his principal, but also that which has apparently or impliedly been delegated to him."[3]

B. Apparent Authority

As stated above, an agency relationship may be created by apparent authority. Here, as opposed to actual authority, the agent may actually not have express or implied authority. Rather, apparent authority occurs in a situation where a third party believes in good faith that the agent had such authority. This situation usually arises when the a third party is misled by the acts of the principal. An agency relationship may be established:

> by words or conduct of a principal, communicated to a third party, that gives rise to an appearance and reasonable belief by the third party that an agency has been created and the agent possesses the authority to enter into a transaction . . . Such apparent authority may exist even if the principal did not actually subjectively

> intend to create an agency relationship as long as the third party's reliance upon the principal's statement or conduct is reasonable.[4]

The manifestation may be made directly to the third party or through advertising. In order to invoke the doctrine of apparent authority . . . the harm incurred by the injured party must have been caused by the one appearing to be a servant or other agent. . . .

Apparent authority must be occasioned by facts that a person learns which persuade him to believe that authority exists. If one dealing with the agent knows that the agent is acting only for his own benefit, or learns of a change in circumstances from which he should realize that the principal no longer desires the agent to act for him, he cannot bind the principal by contracting with the agent. Generally, a principal may be estopped from denying the authority of his agent if:

1. acts of commission or omission, instructional or negligent, by the principal create the appearance of authority in his agent;
2. the third party acts in reliance upon such appearance of authority, reasonably and in good faith and
3. the third party changes his position to his detriment in reliance upon the appearance of authority.

IV. APPARENT AUTHORITY AS IT APPLIES TO ADVERTISING

The case and statutory law among jurisdictions, is not well settled with regard to the advertiser-advertising agency relationship. If this is so in an area like agency, where long standing principles have been established in our comfortable "paper world," how are we to deal with these advertiser-advertising agency relationships in the global and unfamiliar world of Internet Commerce and the transactions that arise from it?

The recognition of an agency relationship between two parties carries with it the possibility for liability on the part of the principal to third parties for harm caused to them by someone acting as their agent. In the case of apparent authority, such liability may attach to a party when he represents that another is his agent in such a manner that it is reasonable for a third party to believe that the purported agent actually has authority to act on the party's behalf, even if he actually does not have such authority. In other words, if the principal does not give an "agent" authority to act on his behalf, but a consumer has reason to believe that the principal has granted the agent such authority, the principal may be liable to the consumer for the acts of the agent, even if he did not give the agent authority to act on his behalf. Apparent authority has been found through the use of advertisements, particularly when such advertisements are made on a national level. In *Gizzi v. Texaco,* the court concluded that a question of apparent authority existed where a gas station was neither owned nor operated by Texaco, yet prominently displayed the Texaco insignia and slogan, and where Texaco had engaged in national advertising. Similarly, the court in *Shaw v. Delta Airlines, Inc.*, denied a motion for summary judgment, holding that in cases involving advertisements, whether apparent authority exists is an issue for the trier of fact and should not be rejected by summary judgment. The court, quoting Gizzi, asserted that "manifestations of the principal in creating such authority "may be made directly to the third person, or may be made to the community, by signs or advertising."

In cases of apparent authority, the issue is not the relationship entered into between the alleged principal and agent, it is the actual representations made by the alleged principal to the customer, or other third party. Numerous cases have held or suggested that a company can create the representation of an agency relationship through advertising. Many of these cases cite to the Restatement (Second) of Agency, which provides:

> One who represents that another is his servant or other agent and thereby causes a third person justifiably to rely upon the care or skill of such apparent agent is subject to liability to the third person for harm caused by the lack of care or skill of the one appearing to be a servant or other agent as if he were such.

It has also been noted that "the reality of the situation is that the trade name in franchising is indispensable. Very often it is the name alone which sells the product." John Stuart notes a specific example of how such authority can be perceived and, as a consequence, how one company can be held liable for the acts of another:

> [A] hungry motorist, needing a quick meal in an unfamiliar town, is likely to go into any drive-in that he sees, if the only identifying signs were Bill's Hamburgers or Joe's Tacos. However, this is clearly not the case if, instead the signs read McDonald's or Dairy Queen. The motorist is much more likely to choose the drive-in whose name he recognizes and associates with a particular kind of service and food. The franchisor, by displaying the brand name, is saying to the public that at this particular drive-in you will receive the same kind of food and beverages that you receive at any other drive-in at which this sign is displayed. In short, the franchisor is "holding out" all the franchises as the same.

If the signs are accepted as "holding out" all the retail dealers as the same, reasonable reliance is not far behind. The mass media advertising employed by the franchisors can only help to reenforce the public's reliance on the brand name. It is not hard to believe that there are many people . . . who believe that all service stations or drive-ins or clothes cleaners displaying the same name are run by the same company.

If apparent authority may be created by the use of advertisements on a national level, it may certainly be argued that such authority may be found through advertising that is both national and international in scope, such as advertisements on the Internet.

V. ADVERTISING AND SELLING: THE PURPOSE AND FUNCTION OF ADVERTISING

Advertising is the nonpersonal communication of information usually paid for and usually persuasive in nature about products, services or ideas by identified sponsors through the various media." One of the most basic purposes of advertising is to distinguish one product from the thousands of others like it available on the market. . . .

A sale can be completed through either personal or nonpersonal means. The major difference is that when a sale is personal in nature, the buyer and seller are together through at least some, if not all, of the transaction. With nonpersonal selling, the parties to the transaction can be miles away and may never meet. Two serious disadvantages to the consumer in nonpersonal transactions are the lack of information and visual contact with the seller . . . With nonpersonal transactions a consumer is rarely given the opportunity to ask questions or clarify unclear information or terms.

Due to the increase in nonpersonal transactions—particularly sales over the Internet—and the disadvantages that go along with such transactions, consumers may need more protection than they currently get when engaging in sales through personal transactions.

VI. PSYCHOLOGICAL EFFECTS OF ADVERTISING

Advertisers often take advantage of the subconscious mind of their consumers. Throughout life, people are taught learned responses . . . When one hears that a company is the number one seller in the country, one often associates that with something good. One thinks that it is reliable, that there must be some reason that it is number one. It is human nature to want what is best for yourself, and in response to that, when we hear there is a company or product that is the best, most convenient, and most cost effective, we will also tend to buy from that company. For example, Amazon.com, has been categorized as the largest online bookstore in the world. There is a special association we attach to that, so when we see another, less known company, which has the more popular one with the incredible reputation located right next to the former company, and the words "Sponsored By" before it, we tend to think that the less known company is just as reputable. . . .

Human belief and feelings also factor into the advertising game. Socialization, or programming, gives a person certain beliefs, and these beliefs affect our responses to the stimuli that are presented to us. "Feelings are the actual human emotions that result from the instinctive and learned response reaction to a stimulus." These feelings impact heavily on our memory. When people respond to stimuli, "they relate the present stimuli to past experience, consciously remembering past reactions and their results." People usually want to give the reaction that gives a positive response, and often try to remember, whether consciously or subconsciously, those things they have done in the past that will lead them to that end result. For example, if someone has had a bad experience with an unknown company or supplier and has found it difficult to get a response from them, but has found it easy to get the reaction they want from a well-known company, they may want to continue to associate with the well-known company. So, if a person who has had such an experience sees an advertisement for an unknown company, but sees the approval or sponsorship of a well-known company, they may be more apt to purchase from that unknown company. Whether intentionally or not, those well-known advertisers are sending a message to consumers that they support the other advertiser. . . .

When consumers view one product next to a more reputable one, they make a connection. The association they have with the one product or company is likely to be transferred to the other. So, if consumers were more likely to buy a product from one company, they may also be more likely to buy from a company that is associated with it or even sponsored by it.

As discussed above, "very often it is the name alone which sells the product" and the mass media employed by companies to promote their products can only help to reinforce the public's reliance on the brand name. In addition, "it is not hard to believe that there are many people . . . who believe that all . . . [places] displaying the same name are run by the same company." Although the Internet may be a different world from the markets with which we are familiar, it will be helpful to understand the analogies and similarities by looking at a practical example. If a surfer on the Web were to enter a search for "real estate," he may be directed to a site called "Evans Properties," whose caption reads "something for everyone!" If you click on the hyperlink entitled "Information," you will see an advertisement banner for Amazon.com. This is not uncommon, as one will often see advertisement banners on many web sites. This may or may not create the impression of apparent authority. It may or may not be "common knowledge" these banners are just advertisements and the advertiser is not "holding [itself] out" as connected with the owner of that particular web page. However, if one were to click on the hyperlink entitled "Products," one would see in big bold letters "www.AMAZON.com, Sponsor of: www. EVANSPROPERTIES.com." In addition, on the actual home page of Evan's Properties, one would see:

> Our sponsors are world class. We welcome eTOYS. Evans Properties are brought to you by: Amazon.com, Reel.com and eToys! Order your books, music, videos and toys from this site, on secure servers for the comfort of shopping on-line!

Amazon.com is the world's largest online bookstore. Someone seeing that name may rely on Amazon.com's name and reputation in considering whether to buy or take advantage of other products and services advertised on that web page. Whether or not such advertisements and sponsorship constitute a case for apparent authority, through their representations to consumers, is at least a question of fact for a jury to determine. It also raises the issue whether traditional agency principles are suitable for today's new international medium of advertising and sales.

VII. HOW JURISDICTIONS HAVE ATTEMPTED TO ACCOMMODATE THE INTERNET AND AGENCY LIABILITY PRINCIPLES

A. In General

If we go back in history to the evolution of the transportation industry, when the first roads were paved, the signs weren't automatically prevalent. Later the code of conduct was established, and now it is being enforced. The same analogy may apply with the rules of conducting business over the Internet.

In fact, most jurisdictions have yet to address the issue of conducting business over the Internet and its ramifications.

B. California

Some states have specifically dealt with the problems of consumer confusion in this area, and the possible agency relationship consequences that may follow. California law provides:

> The disclosure of the legal name and address information shall appear on any of the following:
>
> 1. the first screen displayed when the vendor's electronic site is accessed,
> 2. on the screen on which goods or services are first offered,
> 3. on the screen on which a buyer may place the order for goods or services or
> 4. on the screen on which the buyer may enter payment information, such as a credit card account number.
>
> The communication of that disclosure shall not be structured to be smaller or less legible than the text of the offer of the goods or services.

California may be ahead of many other states in consumer protection. For example, New York has no comparable law addressing the topic. Even though California does address the high risk of confusion among Internet consumers, it does not specifically address the issue of agency relationships and the possibility of apparent authority existing if the seller of the product is not clearly identified and businesses are not clearly separated and distinct on the web site.

In addition, there is an absence of case law on the California statute, making it difficult to predict how effective it will be and what modifications are needed to properly address the legal issues arising with respect to advertising and consumer transactions over the Internet. . . .

C. THE IMPACT THE LACK OF CONSENSUS ON JURISDICTIONAL ISSUES MAY HAVE ON AGENCY LAW

"Electronic transactions, where buyers and sellers seal deals in the stroke of key, are undeniably the wave of the future, but their impending proliferation has the legal community scrambling to stay ahead of the game."[5] Thus far, jurisdictions in the United States have failed to adopt a uniform, consistent system for dealing with the issue of whether a court has jurisdiction over an entity that has established itself on the Internet. The World Wide Web, by its name alone, implies an international scope of transacting. We can hardly deal with international issues on the Internet level and the legal impact on the people who engage in transactions on it, without first dealing with these issues among the states of this nation.

The discrepancies with regard to broader legal issues, such as whether a state has personal jurisdiction over people or companies transacting over the Internet, inevitably leaves more specific legal issues, such as agency principles, unsettled. Such discrepancies are widespread and even occur among states that are just miles from each other. For example, in *Zippo Manufacturing Co. v. Zippo Dot Com, Inc.*, the court, applying Pennsylvania law, found personal jurisdiction over the defendant because the defendant was not merely advertising over the Internet, it was conducting "electronic commerce." The court reached this conclusion by coupling the advertising with several contracts the defendant entered into over the Internet with citizens of Pennsylvania.

While traditional agency principles may be similar from state to state, laws regulating the sale of goods and services tend to vary a little more. Professor Fred Miller of the University of Oklahoma, who is the executive director of a committee working to make changes to the Uniform Commercial Code (UCC)—which governs the sale of goods—sees electronic transactions as one of the "biggest areas of revision in the UCC." Miller has also expressed that "“face-to-face transactions” . . . are becoming a thing of the past," giving yet another reason to modify the focus of current law. . . .

D. IS THERE A SOLUTION?

Explain to the author why other states may not have followed California's example.

While California is off to a good start in addressing the consumer issues that are sure to arise, and are currently arising over the Internet, its efforts alone are not enough. While it is unclear why other states have not followed California's lead, the truth is, these consumer issues are now a reality. Even if other states did adopt statutes similar to the ones in California, what would be the result? Because the Internet is both intranational and international, it is easy to conceive a wide array of inconsistencies and confusion that could arise because of the different laws that may develop in the different states.

While the following proposal may not be a perfect solution to this problem right now, something needs to be done. The federal government needs to step in and establish some guidelines and regulations for the legal issues arising from consumer transactions over the Internet. Another issue that arises is how to deal with this on an international level. But before we can do that, we must come up with some comprehensive legislation dealing with the legal issues, such as the creation of agency relationships over the Internet, within the United States.

VIII. CONCLUSION

As transactions and advertising over the Internet become more and more prevalent, the law as it exists in many areas, such as agency, must change to accommodate the new issues that are arising. Advertising is a powerful tool and many consumers rely on the reputation of companies, and the images and feelings their products evoke, when deciding whether to purchase a product or service. As personal, face-to-face transactions become a thing of the past and "big name" companies put their world-known logos next to the name of an "unknown" company while advertising their support of the company, consumer confusion increases. Many consumers may reasonably believe the two companies are related or are one and the same and, in turn, reasonably rely on such representation. As traditional agency principles dictate, the question is not whether the alleged principal and agent entered into an agency relationship, but whether the principal has created the representation to a third party that such a relationship exists and whether the third person—here the consumer - justifiably relied on that representation to his or her detriment. It is has been established that such apparent authority can be created through the use of advertisements, especially when those advertisements are national in scope. It has also been found that apparent authority can be created through the Internet, especially when advertisements are used. Given the current case law and traditional agency principles applied in that case law, there is a threat that the finding of apparent authority, and in many cases liability attaching by reason of that apparent authority, may become much more prevalent because of the easy accessibility to advertisements and products over the Internet. This may or may not be justifiable, but under current principles of law, it is nevertheless a reality. Whether or not these principles need to be changed is an issue for both the courts and the legislature to address, and without such a change, well-known companies may be subjecting themselves to liability by supporting and sponsoring less-known companies, whether or not they intend to do so.

END NOTES

1. Organisation for Economic Co-operation and Development, Electronic Commerce: Opportunities and Challenges for Government 16 (1997).
2. *Custom Management Corp. v. New York State Tax Comm'n*, 539 N.Y.S.2d 550, 551 (App. Div. 1989).
3. *Angerosa v. White Co.*, 290 N.Y.S. 204, 208–09 (App. Div. 1936)
4. *Hoysradt v. Nilles Ford-Mercury, Inc.*, 563 N.Y.S.2d 956, 957–58 (App. Div. 1990).
5. Jones, supra note 84.

ARTICLE 4.6

Eric Bahre v. Long Rivers Council, Inc., Boy Scouts of America

Local Boy Scout Troop 260 constructed a rope bridge at a Craft Fair held in the Town of Suffield Center Green, in Suffield, Connecticut. The general public was invited to use the rope bridge. The plaintiff, Eric Bahre, age nine, fell while crossing the rope bridge, breaking his arm. The plaintiff seeks to hold the defendant, the Long Rivers Council, liable on a theory of vicarious liability for any negligent acts of local Boy Scout Troop 260.

The Long Rivers Council had no participation in or knowledge of the rope bridge display. However, local Troop 260 was engaged in recruiting and had both Boy Scouts and adult Boy Scout Troop leaders dressed in the official Boy Scout uniform. There were also posters demonstrating the Boy Scout motto, as well as Boy Scout recruiting pamphlets.

The defendant, Long Rivers Council, has moved for summary judgment, asserting that it did not own, maintain, supervise, or control the rope bridge from which the plaintiff fell, and that local Troop 260 and its members were not agents, employees, or servants of the defendant. The plaintiff, Eric Bahre, opposes this motion to the extent that he claims an agency relationship did exist between local Troop 260 and the defendant, Long Rivers Council.

DISCUSSION

. . . The defendant in this case asserts that there is no issue of material fact regarding the existence of an agency relationship between the defendant and Troop 260. Agency is defined as "the fiduciary relationship which results from manifestation of consent by one person to another that the other shall act on his behalf and subject to his control, and consent by the other so to act . . . [1] "Thus, the three elements required to show the existence of an agency relationship include:

1. a manifestation by the principal that the agent will act for him;
2. acceptance by the agent of the undertaking; and
3. an understanding between the parties that the principal will be in control of the undertaking."

The existence of an agency relationship is generally a question of fact. "However, if 'the facts necessary to establish the existence of an agency relationship simply do not exist,' summary judgment is appropriate."[2] . . .

One of the factors listed . . . in assessing whether such a relationship exists is whether the alleged principal has the right to direct and control the work of the agent. In addition, "an essential ingredient of agency is that the agent is doing something at the behest and for the benefit of the principal."[3]

Why are the facts alleged in this paragraph especially important to the decision?

The plaintiff has submitted affidavits and depositions in support of the fact that the Long Rivers Council has the right to control and was benefited by the actions of local Troop 260 at the time of the incident. The premise of the plaintiff's argument is as follows. At the time of the incident, Troop 260 was engaged in recruiting activity and members of the Troop were wearing the official Boy Scout uniform. The Long Rivers Council has certain rules pertaining to recruiting practices and the wearing of the official Boy Scout uniform and those rules can be enforced by the Council and failure to follow such rules can result in a revocation of the local Troop's charter. The plaintiff's argument on this point is that one of the jobs of the Council is to oversee membership of the local Troops because it is important that the Boy Scout program maintains membership. The Council sets membership goals for the Troops and the recruiting activity at the time of the incident was furthering these goals.

PRECEDENT

There have been several cases nationally which address the issue of whether local or national Boy Scout councils can be held liable for the acts of local Troops or Troop leaders. Jurisdictions across the country have found that there is no liability on the part of the Boy Scouts of America or its local council. In *Wilson v. St. Louis Area Council, Boy Scouts of America*, the trial court granted summary judgment in favor of the defendants where the parents of a scout who was killed brought an action against the local council. At the time of the accident, the plaintiff's son was on a trip with the local Boy Scout troop. He was electrocuted when a pipe with which he was playing came in contact with power lines. The Court in that case found that, as a matter of law, the troop leaders were not agents of the local council. That finding was based on the facts that local councils did not direct or control the activities of troops, and that troops were not required to get permission from the local council before participating in an activity. Based on these facts, the Court concluded that " . . . there was no evidence that [the local council] either controlled or *had the right to control* the leaders' activities on the trip . . . "

In *Mauch v. Kissling*, the parents of a deceased scout brought an action against the Boy Scouts of America and its local council for the death of their son. The scout was a passenger when the plane piloted by his troop leader crashed. The court held that there was simply no evidence presented by the plaintiff that either the Boy Scouts of America or the local council consented to or had control of the scout leader's actions. The Court found, furthermore, that there was evidence to the contrary.

In *McGarr v. Baltimore Area Council, Boy Scouts of America, Inc.*, a mother and her scout son brought an action against the troop scout leader and the local council of boy scouts for injuries incurred by the scout when he fell over a cliff while on a scout-sponsored camping excursion. The Court found no error with the trial court's conclusion that the local council was not vicariously liable for the negligence of the scout leader. The Court based this determination on the fact that the local council did not chose or in any way directly supervise the scoutmaster, stating only that " . . . in these circumstances, it is generally held that the council is not vicariously liable for the negligence of the scoutmaster."

In *Davis v. Shelton*, 33 A.D.2d 707, 304 N.Y.S.2d 722 (1969), the plaintiff sought to hold the local council vicariously liable where a scout was injured falling out of a tree. At the time of the injury, the scout was on a camping trip with his troop. The Court upheld the trial court's determination that the local council was not liable, noting that it exercised no supervision or control over the activities of the local troop. . . .

In *M.L. v. Civil Air Patrol*, and *Dunn v. Gracia*, the courts refused to hold either the Boy Scouts of America or their local council vicariously liable for Scoutmasters or other Troop leaders who sexually molested scouts during troop activities. In M.L., the Court found that the plaintiffs did not present any evidence to indicate that the Boy Scouts of America manifested the necessary control over the scout leader support a theory of respondeat superior. In Dunn, the Court declined to decide the question of the existence of an agency relationship. The Court instead found that, assuming an agency relationship had existed, the scout leader's sexual misconduct was, as a matter of law, not within the scope of that relationship. The Court concluded its opinion by reiterating the fact that it chose not to decide whether there was a right to control on the part of the Boy Scouts or its local council.

Though most of the relevant precedent has supported non-liability of local council, there are cases which do not hold that as a matter of law that the Boy Scouts of America or the local council has no liability for the actions of the troop leader. In the only Connecticut case on the issue, *Kosloff v. Fairfield County Council of Boy Scouts of America, Inc*, the plaintiff brought suit against the local Boy Scout council after being injured at a roller-skating event sponsored by the local council. The defendant council moved for summary judgment. That motion was denied due to the fact that the defendant's supporting documentation did not address the plaintiff's argument that the local council had a right to control the individual scout packs or their leaders.

In *Riker v. Boy Scouts of America*, the appellate court upheld a jury verdict against the Boy Scouts of America, Saratoga County Council. In this case, a spectator attending Scout-O-Rama was injured when struck by a falling flag which had been negligently hung by the local Cub Scout pack leader. The Court stated that "... there appears to be no reason why the [local council] should not be held responsible . . . " This conclusion was based on the fact that the event was sponsored and directed by the local council, which charged admission for the event.

OPINION BY: MICHAEL R. SHELDON

While the court finds the reasoning of the aforementioned cases persuasive, none of them directly address the issue at hand. That issue is whether right of control enjoyed by the Long Rivers Council over recruiting activities and the wearing of the official Boy Scout uniform is sufficient or insufficient, to find as a matter of law, that an agency relationship does or does not exist. There are several cases which find no liability on the part of the local council or the Boy Scouts of America. In each of those cases, the court's determination was based not on a concrete rule of law dictating non-liability, but on a lack of evidence with which to find an agency relationship. By pointing to that lack of evidence, those courts have certainly left open the possibility that, if evidence of control or the right to control were presented, vicarious liability could be found. This possibility is seen even more clearly in *Kosloff v. Fairfield County Council of Boy Scouts of America, Inc.*, and *Riker v. Boy Scouts of America*, both of which support the fact that the local council can, under some circumstances, be held vicariously liable for the actions of its troop leaders. . . .

When a summary judgment is not granted here, is the court saying that the plaintiff should win this case?

While the evidence presented by the plaintiff may not be dispositive of the issue of agency, it does create some question as to facts which bear materially on the outcome of this case. Therefore, this Court cannot rule that, as a matter of law, no agency relationship existed between the Long Rivers Council and Local Troop 260. . . .

THE DEFENDANT'S MOTION FOR SUMMARY JUDGMENT IS DENIED

END NOTES

1. Restatement (Second), 1 Agency § 1. *See McLaughlin v. Chicken Delight, Inc.*, 164 Conn. 317, 322, 321 A.2d 456 (1973).
2. *Kosloff v. Fairfield County Council of Boy Scouts of America, Inc.*, 8 CSCR 1094 (1993).
3. *Leary v. Johnson*, 159 Conn. 101, 105–106, 267 A.2d 658 (1970).

ARTICLE 4.7

No California Nexus for Barnesandnoble.com by Stores Distributing Coupons

The California Superior Court determined that mere distribution of coupons by an online seller through marginally related bricks-and-mortar stores did not constitute an agency relationship triggering use tax nexus. Though the activity did meet the state's broad definition of "selling," the stores did not act as agents or representatives of the online seller, barnesandnoble.com. While the decision limits the state's aggressive stance on what constitutes an agency or representative relationship, the controversial definition of selling remains in effect.

In *Barnesandnoble.com LLC v. State Board of Equalization,* the court was legally bound to apply the definition of selling affirmed by the Court of Appeal ruling in a somewhat similar case, *Borders Online LLC v. State Board of Equalization* (2005). However, barnesandnoble.com did not have the overlapping management and coupon reimbursement circumstances of *Borders.* Barnes & Noble retail stores merely placed barnesandnoble.com discount coupons in the stores' shopping bags.

"The decision is important in that it takes away the ambiguity the California State Board of Equalization has tried to inject into the definition of 'agent' and 'representative,'" says David Bertoni, a partner with Brann & Isaacson LLP, in Lewiston, Maine, the firm that represented barnesandnoble.com. "The SBE has been on a path to try to dilute those terms." In fact, language in the decision underscores the court's rebuke of the SBE's overreaching in interpreting those terms: "Here the undisputed evidence shows that Barnes & Noble retail stores passively distributed coupons issued by Plaintiff, much like a person on a street corner might hand out flyers or coupons. The concept of agency requires something significantly more than simply passing out information at somebody else's request."

Rather, the party distributing coupons must possess the authority to bind the principal, an authority the brick-and-mortar stores did not have. On the basis of the coupons alone, the SBE in its earlier determination had found that the plaintiff was a "retailer engaged in business in the state" [and not an agent.] In this case, Barnes and Noble stores:

1. had no input in creating the coupon program;
2. had no authority to adjust the terms of the coupons or to redeem them;

What is the crucial missing element that would have created an agency relationship in this case?

3. could not accept returns of books purchased from the taxpayer with the coupons;
4. did not solicit sales and could not accept orders for the taxpayer;
5. had no authority to accept anything from customers that would be passed on to the taxpayer; and
6. could not speak for or bind the taxpayer on any subject.

ARTICLE 4.8

Schuster v. Commissioner: An Appropriate Agency Test for Members of Religious Orders Working Under Vows of Poverty?

Bridget R. O'Neill

I. INTRODUCTION

Sister Francine Schuster, a Roman Catholic nun, worked for the National Health Services Corps (NHSC) as a nurse midwife at Su Clinica Familiar in Raymondville, Texas. Sister Schuster had obtained permission from her Order, the Adorers of the Blood of Christ (Order), to work as a nurse midwife and, pursuant to a vow of poverty taken as a precondition of her membership in the Order, endorsed all of her paychecks to the Order. On her federal income tax return, she reported that she had received $ 18,771.20 in wages which were not subject to taxation "by reason of taxpayer being agent of religious order."

The Commissioner of Internal Revenue issued a notice of deficiency to Sister Schuster stating that the wages "were taxable to her individually and not to the Order, because she was not working as an agent of a religious order when she earned her wages." Sister Schuster contested the Commissioner's determination and reasserted her claim that she was acting as an agent of her Order when working at the clinic.

The United States tax court ruled that the two factors necessary to tax the personal services income to the principal rather than the individual were missing in the case. First, the principal, in this case the Order, had not agreed with the third-party employer, the NHSC, that Sister Schuster would work for the clinic as the Order's agent. Thus, the NHSC had no legal obligation to pay the Order for Sister Schuster's services. Second, according to the majority of the tax court, the Order lacked the right to direct or control "in some meaningful sense" Sister Schuster's activities. The United States Court of Appeals for the Seventh Circuit rejected the tax court's agency test because it too narrowly restricted the analysis of the agency relationship. Instead, the court applied an agency test established in *Fogarty v. United States* that "consider[s] . . . all the underlying facts." After applying the Fogarty test, the court held that no agency relationship existed and affirmed the decision to tax Sister Schuster. . . .

II. SCHUSTER V. COMMISSIONER

A. Facts

Sister Francine Schuster is a Roman Catholic nun and a member of the Adorers of the Blood of Christ (the Order). The Order was incorporated in the state of Illinois on July 24, 1886 and is a federally tax-exempt religious organization. . . .

As a condition of membership in the Order, Sister Schuster took vows of perpetual poverty, chastity and obedience. Pursuant to her vow of poverty, Sister Schuster executed a "Declaration Concerning Remuneration" in which she agreed "never [to] claim or demand, directly or indirectly, any wages, compensation, remuneration, or reward . . . for the time or for the services or work that I devote for . . . [the Order] during the time I may remain there or elsewhere in the name of or upon commission from said [Order]". She also agreed to "embrace the Father's will as it is expressed in the constitution [of the Order] and as it is mediated through those who exercise authority in our congregation," thereby subjugating her will to that of the Order.

The Order allows members to secure a mission, which is outside employment in an occupation. A Provincial Superior of the Order must approve the mission. Missions are approved if they relate to religious and charitable works within the Order's general purpose. Each member must obtain approval of the Order before accepting and before terminating her employment with the mission. The Provincial Superior has authority to direct members regarding the performance of a mission and to require members to withdraw from the mission. At times, the Order has required members to terminate their missions.

In accordance with their vows, members may not keep any funds earned from their missions and must transfer all such funds to the Order. Members whose missions require them to live away from the Order's convent are required to submit a monthly budget statement of their living expenses. The Order may approve or revise the monthly expenses and pays the expenses as approved. Each member also receives a maximum allowance for personal expenses . . . The amount that each member receives is not related to the amount of wages, if any, received from her particular mission.

Members who wish to withdraw from the Order may do so with or without dispensation from the Roman Catholic Church. Upon withdrawal, members are entitled to receive any personal property owned before joining the Order, any property received by gift or inheritance while a member, and their dowries held when they entered the Order. . . .

Sister Schuster made her vows of poverty, chastity, and obedience . . . At all relevant times, she continued to be an active member of the Order. Sister Schuster, who holds a bachelor of science degree in nursing, received a nurse practitioner traineeship from the federal government. In order to receive the award, Sister Schuster promised to either

1. practice in a "health manpower shortage area" for twelve months after she completed the traineeship, or
2. pay back the full cost of the award plus interest.

After completing her traineeship at the University of Mississippi, Sister Schuster obtained permission from her Order to interview for positions in health manpower shortage areas in order to fulfill the "practice requirement" of her award. Sister Schuster was offered a position as a nurse midwife at Su Clinica Familiar in Raymondville, Texas, in June 1979. At that time, the professional staff members at the clinic (which included nurse midwives) were employed and compensated by the NHSC, a federal program within the United States Public Health Service.

Sister Schuster obtained permission from her Order to accept the position, which the Order determined would "further the purposes of the Order by helping to relieve the suffering of humankind, and by promoting life." Sister Schuster confirmed her acceptance of the position in a letter to the NHSC. Also on July 1, 1979, the Acting Provincial Superior of the Order wrote two virtually identical letters to the NHSC and the clinic stating the following:

Sister Francine Schuster has informed us of your recent phone notification of a current job opening in nurse midwifery at Su Clinica Familiar, Raymondville-Harlingen, Texas.

The Community of the Adorers of the Blood of Christ would like to contract with you for the services of Sister Francine Schuster, ASC, for the position of nurse midwife for one year at Su Clinica Familiar.

If our offer is acceptable, we request that payment for her services be made to the Adorers of the Blood of Christ.

In response to the Order's letter to the clinic, the director of the nurse midwifery service wrote the following:

Consider this letter as formal acceptance of Sister Francine Schuster on our nurse-midwifery staff. She will be beginning on the pay period that starts July 23. Sister Francine's checks will be paid to her and she can endorse them and send them to you. I endorse my checks "paid to the order of the Sisters of St. Mary, Sister Angela Murdaugh." There is no problem with them going through the mail like that.

The NHSC did not respond to the Order's letter.

Sister Schuster began work at the clinic . . . and her wages, contrary to the Order's request, were paid directly to her. She endorsed and sent each check to the Order. On her 1980 federal income tax return, Sister Schuster stated she had received $ 18,771.20 in wages which were not taxable to her because she had received them as an agent for the Order. The Commissioner of Internal Revenue issued a notice of deficiency to Sister Schuster for $ 1,529 in taxes. According to the Commissioner, the income was taxable to Sister Schuster individually and not to the Order, because Sister Schuster was not acting as an agent of the Order while working as a nurse midwife at the clinic. Sister Schuster filed a petition contesting the Commissioner's determination.

B. Issue and Analysis

Why did the author include the Sister Schuster case?

The central issue in Schuster was who should be taxed on the income generated by Sister Schuster's services. Applying the general rule on assignment of income. . . . Sister Schuster earned the income and should not escape taxation notwithstanding her "anticipatory arrangement"—her vow of poverty. However, assignment of income questions are not always resolved by taxing the person who performs the services. . . .

The real issue in Schuster was whether Sister Schuster received her wages as an agent on behalf of her Order or in her individual capacity. If Sister Schuster received the wages in her individual capacity, the wages would be included in Sister Schuster's gross income. . . . On the other hand, if Sister Schuster received the wages as an agent on behalf of the Order, the wages would be included in the Order's gross income. . . . The agency issue's resolution determines how the wages will be taxed. Thus, the disputed issue in Schuster was how to determine when a member of a religious organization under a vow of poverty was acting as an agent of the order while engaged in outside employment.

1. Tax Court: Majority Opinion

The majority of the tax court in Schuster adopted what the Commissioner termed an "agency triangle" test, which requires two factors for personal services income to be taxed to the principal. First, there must be some agreement between the principal and the third-party employer. Second, the principal must have some meaningful control over how the income is earned. In applying the agency triangle test, the majority focused on the relationship between the Order and the federal government. The majority concluded that because the government had no legal obligation to pay the Order, Sister Schuster earned the wages in her individual capacity. According to the majority, personal services income cannot be received "on behalf" of a principal unless the principal owes a duty to the third party to supply an agent to perform the services, thus completing the "agency triangle." The majority found that the Order had no such duty because the Order was not bound to perform the services itself nor to ensure the services were performed. The majority also found that the Order's approval of the midwife position and receipt of Sister Schuster's checks were not sufficient to affect the legal employer-employee relationship between Sister Schuster and the federal government. Sister Schuster and the Order failed the first half of the agency triangle test because the government and the Order did not have a formal agreement.

The tax court also found that the Order lacked control over the earning of the income because the Order did not have the authority to direct Sister Schuster to work as a midwife. According to the majority, the Order could not control the earning of the income unless the Order had some role in the hiring decision. The majority largely dismissed the vow of poverty as a private agreement which did not alter the tax results because the private agreement did not affect Sister Schuster's status as a federal employee. The Court discussed in great detail Sister Schuster's responsibilities and benefits as a federal employee and concluded that her status as a federal employee was inconsistent with an agency relationship between the Order and Sister Schuster. Having failed the "agency triangle" test, the tax court held the wages were taxable to Sister Schuster.

2. Seventh Circuit: Majority Opinion

The Seventh Circuit Court of Appeals rejected the "agency triangle" test adopted by the majority of the tax court as too inflexible. While the appeals court noted that dealings between the order and the third-party employer are important, the court stated that other relevant factors must also be considered. The court relied on the test set forth in *Fogarty v. Commissioner*, which applied six factors to determine whether an agency relationship existed. The test examined first, the degree of control the order exercised over the member; second, the ownership rights to the wages between the member and the order; third, the mission or purposes of the order; fourth, the type of work performed by the member compared with the order's mission or purposes; fifth, the dealings between the member and the third-party employer, including the circumstances surrounding inquiries and interviews and the control or supervision exercised by the employer; and sixth, the dealings between the employer and the order.

After applying the six factors to the facts in Schuster, the court concluded that Sister Schuster was not acting as an agent of the Order when working at the clinic. Although the court acknowledged that Sister Schuster's midwife services were consistent with the Order's mission, the court found that the other factors showed that no agency existed. First, the Order had failed to exercise day-to-day control over Sister Schuster's activities. In addition, the checks had been issued in Sister Schuster's name, which gave her greater control than the Order over the wages. The dealings between the Order and the NHSC also centered on the issuance of the checks to Sister Schuster. The court emphasized that the Order and Sister Schuster should have insisted that the checks be paid to the Order so that the NHSC would have formally recognized the agency relationship. Based on these findings, the court held that Sister Schuster received the wages in an individual capacity and thus was taxable on the wages.

The court's analysis largely ignored the relationship between Sister Schuster and the Order and treated Sister Schuster's adherence to her vows as irrelevant to the agency issue. Instead, the court focused on the formal aspects of the employment relationship. Thus, despite the court's purported rejection of the Schuster test, in reality, the court's application of the Fogarty test did not differ significantly from Schuster's "agency triangle" test.

III. THE AGENCY RELATIONSHIP BETWEEN A RELIGIOUS ORDER AND ITS MEMBERS UNDER FOGARTY AND SCHUSTER

The Schuster court adopted the flexible Fogarty test to allow consideration of all the relevant underlying facts to determine whether an agency relationship existed between a religious order and its member. Similar to the facts of Schuster, the Fogarty case involved the taxation of a Jesuit priest who taught religion at a secular university and had his paychecks deposited in his order's checking account. The Fogarty court intended that courts would emphasize some factors over others to adapt its test to the unique facts of each case. Unfortunately for Sister Schuster, the factors that seemed most relevant to the Schuster court were precisely the same "inflexible" factors taken into consideration in applying the "agency triangle" test. The application of the Fogarty agency test in Schuster shows that, in fact, the test does not provide needed flexibility but instead focuses on the form of the employment relationship rather than the substance of the relationship between the member and the order.

The first factor considers the degree of control that the order exercises over the member. The court in Schuster interpreted this factor of the Fogarty test as requiring the order to exercise day-to-day control over the member. In evaluating the Order's control over Sister Schuster, the majority largely dismissed Sister Schuster's vow of obedience, which required her to subjugate her will to that of the Order, because she remained free to withdraw from the Order at anytime. While it is true that if Sister Schuster had withdrawn from the Order the Order would not have had the authority to control her, it is also true that the possibility of withdrawal at some future date is irrelevant to the question of whether an agency relationship exists in the present.

The majority also noted other aspects of the Order's control. Sister Schuster was required to seek the Order's approval of her monthly expenses. She also needed the Order's permission to interview for and to accept the nurse midwife position. These actions were not sufficient to establish the necessary daily exercise of control required by the majority's interpretation of the Fogarty test. Despite the Order's authority to control Sister Schuster's daily routine pursuant to her vow of obedience, the majority concluded that the Order did not actually exercise day-to-day control and thus Sister Schuster could not be considered an agent of the Order.

Why is the "degree of control" so important in agency decisions?

The majority's analysis of the "degree of control" factor contradicts basic agency law principles. An agency relationship is defined as the fiduciary relation which results when two parties mutually agree that one party shall act on behalf of the other and subject to the latter's control. Courts have consistently interpreted the control requirement as necessitating that the principal retain the right to control the agent whether or not control is actually exercised. The Schuster majority, however, requires the order actually to exercise day-to-day control. As a practical matter, this day-to-day control requirement precludes members from working as agents of their orders in outside employment because third-party employers generally set the daily routine of the workplace. As a matter of agency law, courts do not require actual exercise of day-to-day control. It should be sufficient that the member remains subject to the control of the order without requiring the order to exercise day-to-day control.

Although never expressly stated, the Schuster court's interpretation of the degree of control factor appears to be based on *Kelley v. Commissioner*, cited in Fogarty as the authority for the first factor. In Kelley, a Roman Catholic priest received permission to live away from his order so that he could decide whether he wished to remain a priest. He claimed that income earned from teaching and from selling securities was received as an agent of his order, despite the fact that he retained the money and used it to pay his personal expenses. Kelley argued that he had simply avoided the "unnecessary step" of sending his wages to the order which would then return the funds to him to allow him to pay his expenses. He had also neglected to inform his order about one of his teaching jobs. The tax court concluded that Father Kelley's vows of poverty and obedience lacked substance because he received no instructions or direction from his order, nor did he remit his compensation to the order.

Kelley, however, is clearly distinguishable from Schuster and provides no basis for imposing an actual day-to-day control requirement on religious orders. The majority's analysis in Schuster shows an attempt to prevent egregious cases such as Kelley, but overlooked the reality of Sister Schuster's position and instead focused on what could have happened. For example, Sister Schuster could have kept her wages, ceased communication with the Order, and eventually withdrawn from the Order to marry as Father Kelley did. In that case, if Sister Schuster asserted her vows of poverty and obedience as evidence of an agency relationship, the court would clearly have stated, as the court in Kelley did, that the vows lacked substance.

Under the facts of Schuster, the majority used the possibility of withdrawal to ignore the substance of the Order's actual control over Sister Schuster. A representative of the Order periodically visited Sister Schuster's mission site to ensure her employment remained consistent with the Order's purposes. The Order directed Sister Schuster not to perform work which conflicted with the Order's moral precepts and, accordingly, Sister Schuster warned the clinic she could not dispense artificial contraceptives. The Order approved Sister Schuster's acceptance of a position at the clinic, which was a Catholic charity. The Order retained the right to control Sister Schuster's activities and remained in a position to override any objectionable directives of the employer. Thus, the Order's control was sufficient to establish an agency relationship.

The second factor of the Fogarty test focuses on the ownership rights of the order and the member. In analyzing this second factor, the majority emphasized that the paychecks were issued in Sister Schuster's name and so "clearly [gave] her superior control over the wages." The fact that the paychecks were nominally issued to Sister Schuster, however, does not affect the ownership of the wages and should not affect her agency status. Sister Schuster was contractually and morally bound to turn the wages over to her Order. The majority also stated that Sister Schuster's endorsement of the checks clearly showed her superior ownership. However, under Steinhauser, the order had an enforceable right to any income earned or received by Sister Schuster while subject to her vow of poverty. Thus, if Sister Schuster had broken her vow of poverty, the Order could have recovered any amounts kept by Sister Schuster while she remained a member. The possibility that Sister Schuster could have withdrawn from the Order is irrelevant to the current ownership of the wages. Yet, the court found that the Order's rights did not give the Order ownership of the wages. . . .

The majority's analysis of the ownership of the wages also must be compared to Kelley, the authority for this ownership factor of the Fogarty test. Again, the Schuster court dismissed Sister Schuster's adherence to her vows. But Sister Schuster, unlike Father Kelley, remitted her wages to the Order and did not exercise any further control over the wages. The Order had an enforceable contract right to compel Sister Schuster to turn over the wages despite the fact that the checks were issued in her name. Had Father Kelley's order exercised its right to his compensation, Father Kelley would not have been taxed.

The third and fourth factors of the Fogarty test examined the type of work the member performed and compared the work to the order's mission. These factors establish the scope of the agency relationship. The majority conceded that, as to these factors, Sister Schuster arguably was acting as an agent of the Order. Providing health care services to the clinic's patients was consistent with the Order's purposes to promote education and provide health care. The majority stated, however, that the fifth and sixth factors outweighed the scope of agency factors, rendering "inescapable" the conclusion that Sister Schuster was acting independently.

In evaluating the fifth factor, the dealings between Sister Schuster and the NHSC, the majority emphasized that Sister Schuster had failed to disclose her agency relationship on her NHSC application, during her telephone interview with NHSC, and in her letter accepting the position. She also visited the clinic alone as a prospective NHSC assignee. However, neither the NHSC nor the clinic argued that they did not know that Sister Schuster was a nun. The clinic, a Catholic charity, was certainly familiar with the vows of members of religious orders. The Order wrote to the NHSC disclosing the agency relationship. The NHSC hired and paid Sister Schuster, knowing that the Order would receive all of Sister Schuster's compensation and that Sister Schuster was subject to the control of her religious superiors. The majority's analysis suggests that to act consistently with her agency relationship, Sister Schuster should have immediately disclosed the agency and conditioned her acceptance of the position on the NHSC's acknowledgement of the agency. Presumably, this would have best been accomplished if Sister Schuster had required the NHSC to pay the Order directly.

The majority also focused on the day-to-day control and supervision of Sister Schuster. While working at the clinic, Sister Schuster was supervised and evaluated as were all other clinic employees. The majority concluded that the fact that the clinic exercised day-to-day control over Sister Schuster was "at least, consistent with the conclusion that [while working at the clinic, Sister Schuster] was acting on her own behalf." The majority's conclusion, however, overlooked the Order's right to control Sister Schuster and focused on the formal aspects of the employment relationship.

In analyzing the relationship between the Order and the NHSC, the majority again focused on the party who received the checks. Although the majority conceded that the Order and the clinic had reached an agreement that Sister Schuster would work at the clinic, the absence of an agreement on the method of payment outweighed this agreement. The majority implied that the agency relationship would have been better supported by an agreement between the Order and the NHSC rather than merely Sister Schuster's acceptance of the position (after receiving permission from the Order). Although the majority rejected the tax court's "agency triangle" which required a formal agreement between the Order and the third-party employer, its own analysis strongly suggests that, in essence, such a contract may be required. The Order's disclosure of the agency relationship and of Sister Schuster's vows of poverty and obedience were not sufficient to establish the agency.

The Schuster court's interpretation of the Fogarty test emphasized the formal aspects of the employment relationship and ignored the substance of the relationship between the religious order and its member. Sister Schuster argued that "only two parties are required to create [an agency] relationship." Although the Schuster majority rejected the "agency triangle" theory, which maintained that an agent could not act "on behalf of" the principal unless the principal owed a duty to the third-party employer, the majority's own analysis focused on the relations between the third-party employer and the order. Specifically, the Order's failure to demand direct payments and its failure to exercise daily control over Sister Schuster proved fatal to the showing of an agency relationship. To establish an agency relationship, the court would require that the order exercise day-to-day control over the member and receive the compensation directly, not through the member.

The right to control the member and an enforceable contract right to the wages are insufficient under the Schuster court's analysis of the Fogarty test. The majority's requirements seem equivalent to taxing all members who work outside their orders. Even a formal contract between the order and the third-party employer would not establish that the order actually exercised daily control over the details of the member's work. Rather than providing flexibility to evaluate the agency relationship, the Fogarty test as interpreted by Schuster precludes the finding of an agency relationship unless the order actually exercises daily control.

IV. CLOSER SCRUTINY OF THE AGENCY RELATIONSHIP: AN ATTEMPT TO CLOISTER THE CLERGY?

Under the Fogarty test as interpreted in Schuster, members of religious organizations will never be considered agents of an order while working for a third-party employer who is unrelated to the order. The order must control the daily details of the member's work to satisfy the "actual daily control" requirement. Thus, members of religious organizations who work for secular employers outside their orders will be taxed regardless of whether or not they remit their wages to their orders. Rather than providing a flexible test to examine all the facts surrounding the relationship between a member and an order, Schuster essentially has eliminated the agency exception to the general rule on assignment of income for members of religious orders.

In Sister Schuster's individual case, the result is that Sister Schuster owes $ 1,529 in taxes and has no money to pay the tax judgment. How does the IRS expect to enforce its judgment against Sister Schuster? At trial, Sister Schuster's Order voluntarily agreed to pay any amount that Sister Schuster may owe as a result of the litigation. If the Order had not volunteered, however, the IRS would be in the unenviable position of attempting to collect from the Order on the theory that Sister Schuster fraudulently conveyed the compensation to her Order without paying the taxes. Other than collecting from the Order, the IRS could attempt to garnish Sister Schuster's personal allowance. . . . Given the enforcement difficulties, it is apparent that the IRS did not pursue Sister Schuster to raise tax revenues, as the costs of this litigation must exceed the amount of the tax judgment. . . .

Instead of distinguishing between genuine members of religious organizations and individuals who seek to evade taxation, the Seventh Circuit and the IRS have eliminated the agency exception when the individual is employed outside the religious organization. While the IRS has improved its position for future litigation against tax protesters as a result of Schuster, it has done so at the expense of a "poverty-pledged nun doing corporal works of mercy on behalf of a religious community." [n]By pursuing Sister Schuster, the IRS has attempted to stop taxpayers from resorting to religious schemes and asserting the "agent of a religious order" exemption from taxation.

VI. CONCLUSION

In an effort to ease litigation of fraudulent religious schemes designed to avoid taxation, the IRS has taxed a member of a bona fide religious organization dedicated to promoting health care. The majority's holding in Schuster, that an order must exercise daily control over a member working outside the order for the member to be considered an agent, will no doubt aid the IRS's position in cases where the "religion" amounts to nothing more than paper vows. Rather than attacking the validity of the religion, the IRS can assert that the order does not control the member. However, the IRS's gains come at the expense of taxing a nun who has vowed to live her life in poverty. The Schuster holding establishes a per se rule that members of religious organizations who work outside their orders will never be considered agents. It is impossible for any order to retain the necessary actual control over day-to-day activities of a member who works for a third-party employer. Rather than adopting a flexible test, the Schuster court has restricted the agency analysis and ignored basic agency law principles. The strict test may reduce abuse of the agency exception by tax evaders, but it does so at the expense of genuine members of religious organizations.

ISSUE SUMMARY

The first issue relates to one of the most recurring debates in both the state and federal legislatures: whether we need tort reform. Advocates of tort reform argue that the current tort system allows outrageous punitive damage awards that are unwarranted and unduly harm businesses. Opponents of tort reform argue that punitive damages are necessary to punish those who have committed egregious wrongs, as well as to deter others from engaging in similar harmful behavior. This section provides a selection of articles addressing this question.

Now that you have finished reading the chapter, have you decided what would happen in our introductory example with the landlord? If the landlord sent someone on her behalf to show you the rental property, then you might expect the someone else to be the landlord's agent. As you've likely gathered by now, your expectations alone are not enough to prove that the someone else was indeed the landlord's agent. Would a reasonable person agree with your perceptions? Was something said to make you believe the someone else had authority to bind the landlord?

Part of the complexity surrounding agency law is the recognition that people perceive events differently. Several players were involved in each of the cases discussed in this chapter. There were principals, agents, apparent agents, and third parties. Each individual had a different perception of the nature of the agency relationship and the authority flowing from that relationship.

As you've read, the courts have tried to create standards that ask what a reasonable person would have believed in a similar situation. Can you think of a better standard to determine whether an agency relationship existed? You could demand that a written contract be shown as proof of an agency relationship. You could demand that the principal give verbal authorization for the agent's actions. You could demand that the third party contact the principal to confirm the agent's authority. There would, however, be negative consequences. Think about the purposes of agency law discussed in this chapter. Does agency law, as it exists now, accomplish its purposes—despite the sometimes murky perceptions of the people involved? If you answered "no," how would you like to see agency law change in the future?

ISSUE HIGHLIGHTS

- Actual agency requires a "manifestation of consent by one person to another that the other shall act on his behalf and subject to his control, and consent by the other so to act."
- Apparent (or perceived) agency requires that the perceived principal hold someone out as his agent and that a third party reasonably rely on the manifestations of agency by the perceived principal.

- Actual authority is authority for an agent to act based upon manifestations by the principal to the agent.
- Apparent authority arises when a third party reasonably believes that an agent has authority due to manifestations by the principal to the third party, such as direct communication between the principal and third party, the principal's telling the agent to misinform the third party of the agent's authority, or the principal's placing the agent in a position that would lead third parties to believe that the agent has such authority.
- Incidental authority is the authority for an agent to perform tasks that are instrumental to accomplishing the authorized act.
- An individual is estopped from denying an agency relationship if he intentionally or carelessly caused a belief in a third person that one was acting on his behalf or, knowing of the belief, failed to correct the mistake and caused the third party to change position in reliance on that belief.
- Internet commerce includes "the buying and selling of products and services over the Internet," "all forms of commercial transactions involving both organizations and individuals, that are based upon the electronic processing and transmission of data, including text, sound and visual images," and "advertising, trading, and after-sales, as well as online exchange over both private and public networks."
- The basic premise behind agency principles "is to enable a person, through the services of another, to broaden the scope of his activities and receive the product of another's efforts, paying such other for what he does but retaining for himself any net benefit resulting from the work performed."

CRITICAL THINKING

"What does *that* mean?" We've all been reading an article or book when, out of nowhere, the author throws us for a loop. When was the last time you wanted to call the author to ask, "What in the world was *that* supposed to mean?" Believe it or not, when you experience those exasperated "What does *that* mean?" moments, you're actually practicing a critical thinking move.

One critical thinking tool that you can add to your box is known as *ambiguity*. Ambiguity refers to those situations when a keyword in an author's argument does not have a clear definition, *and* different plausible definitions of the keyword have the potential to change the author's argument in a substantive way. In other words, we're not going through the author's argument picking out every word that he forgets to explicitly define. The word needs to be important to the author's argument. In addition, if we can think of two fair definitions for the word, and those definitions change the author's conclusion, then we've found an ambiguous term.

Let's consider an example:

> Football University is an excellent school. They've got a top-ten division-one football team, a state-of-the-art sports center, fifty full-time physical trainers, and a brand new football stadium.

That argument makes sense, right? Wrong. When you read the argument, do any keywords strike you as ambiguous? Look at the argument. The author is trying to convince you that Football University is an excellent school. What is an "excellent" school, though? Can you think of different plausible definitions? An excellent school could be a university that enhances students' critical thinking abilities. An excellent school could be a university that prepares students for high-paying careers. An excellent school could be a school that excels at sports, such as football. The author doesn't tell us what an excellent school is, and depending upon the definition we plug in, his argument may not work. If an excellent school enhances critical thinking abilities, then the author hasn't convinced us that Football University is an excellent school.

You may be thinking, "Come on. It's obvious that this author doesn't care about critical thinking abilities." Okay. Fair enough. This was a simplified example. You may think you can guess what the author meant by "excellent school," and you may be able to—but that's not *your* job. It is the author's responsibility to define key terms in his argument. As a critical thinker, you will not always be able to guess what an author means by key terms, nor should you have to guess. When an author fails to define key terms in his argument, the author makes it impossible for you to evaluate the merit of the argument completely. Just like those times when you have unanswered questions about the reliability of an author's evidence, your evaluation is put on hold when you have unanswered questions about the meanings of key terms.

Let's think about an example from this chapter. Many of the articles focused on the doctrine of apparent agency. Do you remember when apparent agency exists? Apparent agency exists when a third party reasonably believes that an agent has authority due to manifestations by the principal to the third party. Read that sentence again. Do any of the words seem ambiguous to you? There is one that catches our eyes: *reasonably*. What does it mean for a third party to "reasonably" believe that an agent has authority?

As you read earlier in the chapter, the courts frequently apply a "reasonable person" standard to determine whether the third party was behaving "reasonably." The courts ask what a reasonable person would have done in a similar situation. Does that standard help to clear up the ambiguity surrounding the term *reasonably*? We don't think so. Can you think of at least two different meanings for *reasonably* or *reasonable person*? What about the following:

1. Is a reasonable person a person with a twelfth-grade education who has no exposure to the legal system (apart from a traffic ticket and the occasional episode of *Law & Order*)?

2. Is a reasonable person a person with the same level of education as the third party in the case, and who also has the same exposure to the legal system as the third party?
3. Is a reasonable person a person with the same level of education as the attorney representing the third party in the case?
4. Is a reasonable person a person who searched for "agency law" on the Internet before engaging in business with any agents?

We could keep going, but you hopefully see our point. There are many different ways to imagine a reasonable person in relation to a given situation. Our choice of a definition will change how we evaluate a person's behavior. If a reasonable person is expected to have no knowledge of the legal system, then we will allow third parties to make unsubstantiated assumptions about the authority granted to agents; we will not expect the third parties to know any better. If, however, a reasonable person is expected to have detailed knowledge (or even cursory knowledge) of the legal system, then we might demand that the third party make more conservative assumptions about agents' authority. Without knowing what a reasonable person is though, we cannot even begin to judge a third party's actions.

Look back at the arguments presented in this chapter. What keywords seem ambiguous? When you read the case law excerpts, was it clear what the judges meant? When you read the law review articles, were you certain that you understand what the authors were trying to say? If not, try to think of multiple plausible definitions for those ambiguous keywords. If the different definitions change the arguments in substantive ways, what should you do? You may have to withhold judgment about each argument's merit. You cannot determine how convincing an argument is if you cannot determine what the author is trying to say.

ADDITIONAL READING RESOURCES

Luis Gomez-Mejia, Robert M. Wiseman, *and* Bernadine Johnson Dykes, "Agency Problems in Diverse Contexts: A Global Perspective," *J. Mgmt. Stds*. 42:7, pg. 1507–1517 (2005).

Bryan W. Husted, "Agency, Information, and the Structure of Moral Problems in Business, Organization Studies," 28:2, pg. 177–195 (2007).

Gary J. Miller, "The Political Evolution of Principal-Agent Models," *Ann. Rev. Pol. Sci*., 8: 203–225 (2005).

Barry M. Mitnick, *Positive Agency in Positive Psychology in Business Ethics and Corporate Responsibility* (2005).

T.A. Simpson, "A Comment on an Inherently Flawed Concept: Why the Restatement (Third) of Agency Should Not Include the Doctrine of Inherent Agency Power," *Ala. L. Rev*. 57: 1163 (2005).

Carolyn Hughes Tuohy, "Agency, Contract, and Governance: Shifting Shapes of Accountability in the Health Care Arena," *J. Health Politics, Pol'y, & L.* 28(2–3): 195–216 (2003).

J. Rodney Turner *and* Ralf Muller, "Communication and Co-operation on Projects between the Project Owner as Principal and the Project Manager as Agent," *Eur. Mgmt. J.* 22:3, 327–336 (2004).

Charles Zech, "The Agency Relationship in Churches: An Empirical Analysis", *Am. J. Econ. & Soc.*, 66: 4, 727–746 (2007).

For more information, check these sites:

http://www.wmitchell.edu/academics/curriculum/courses/assignments/Restatement%20Third%20of%20Agency.pdf (*Restatement (Third) of Agency)* [*Last visited: July 6, 2008*]

http://washburnlaw.edu/library/services/researchguides/restatements.php (*Restatements of the Law: Research Guide*) [*Last visited: July 6, 2008*]

ISSUE 5

Should Employers Be Able to Force Employees into Arbitration?

When is the last time you were hired by a new employer? Do you remember how many forms you had to sign? There were eligibility forms, federal tax forms, state tax forms, local tax forms, personal information forms, emergency contact forms, company policy forms, and the list goes on for a mile. How many pages did you sign before you quit reading what you were signing? Do you know whether you signed a mandatory arbitration clause? Do you know whether you signed away your right to take your employer to court if he or she violates your civil rights? In this chapter, we address a growing trend among employers: requiring employees to sign binding arbitration agreements that include giving up the right to pursue civil rights claims in a judicial forum.

The first selection in this chapter is an excerpt from a decision by the U.S. Supreme Court. The Court was asked whether civil rights claims, such as claims of age discrimination, can be subject to a mandatory arbitration clause. Next, Mary Rebecca Tyre Furman takes a closer look at the implications of the Supreme Court's ruling, which affects all employees who want to bring suit against an employer for discrimination. In the third selection in this chapter, the U.S. Court of Appeals for the Fourth District was asked whether mandatory arbitration clauses applied to Title VII sexual harassment claims. The fourth article in this chapter again asks whether mandatory arbitration clauses should apply to Title VII claims; Arnold argues that employees should be able to seek relief in a judicial forum. The final selection in this chapter presents an argument that employees involved in arbitration for Title VII claims need to be protected from employer retaliation just as if they were engaged in judicial proceedings.

The first selection in this chapter is an excerpt from a 1991 decision by the U.S. Supreme Court regarding the limits of mandatory arbitration clauses. The plaintiff signed a mandatory arbitration clause when he was hired by the defendant, but the plaintiff refused arbitration when he was fired by the defendant. The plaintiff claimed he was fired due to his age, and that claims under the Age Discrimination in Employment Act (ADEA) were not bound by the arbitration clause. The Court rejected the plaintiff's arguments, finding that nothing about the ADEA indicated that Congress meant to preclude plaintiffs from using arbitration to resolve ADEA claims.

Following the first selection, Tyre Furman examines how the Supreme Court's ruling affected employees' rights to pursue Title VII claims in court, rather than in arbitration. Tyre Furman walks through case law related to mandatory arbitration, discussing the evolution of the Supreme Court's opinion. Tyre Furman then addresses the reasons why employees might prefer a judicial forum to arbitration. Finally, Tyre Furman explains why the Supreme Court's ruling regarding mandatory arbitration of ADEA claims should not be broadened to encompass Title VII civil rights claims.

Next, you will read a decision by the U.S. Court of Appeals for the Fourth District in which Tyre Furman's concerns are brought to life. The plaintiff quit her job as a waitress at Hooters after she was allegedly sexually harassed by a coworker. The plaintiff had signed a mandatory arbitration clause on her employment contract, but refused arbitration of her Title VII claim. The Court of Appeals ruled that the plaintiff could not be forced to arbitrate her claim because the arbitration agreement created by Hooters was so one-sided as to deny the plaintiff any due process, justice, or fairness in the proceedings.

The fourth article in this chapter continues the discussion started with Tyre Furman. Arnold examines how the U.S. Supreme Court has changed its view of arbitration over time, particularly in relation to Title VII claims. Arnold describes how the Supreme Court has continued to debate the worth of arbitration as an alternative to the judicial forum, as well as the relative merits of each system. According to Arnold, employees should not be forced to waive their statutory right to a trial for Title VII claims.

In the final article in this chapter, Marshall argues that mandatory arbitration clauses chip away at the protections provided by Title VII. Unlike previous authors featured in the chapter, Marshall points out that the participation clause (which protects employees from retaliation when they testify in official proceedings about violations of Title VII) does not apply to employees who are involved in private proceedings, such as arbitration proceedings. Rather than arguing against arbitration in general, Marshall urges Congress to expand the protection provided by the participation clause to all employees involved in Title VII proceedings, whether those be in arbitration or a judicial forum.

This chapter is unique in that we have two distinct opinions presented by multiple authors. The justices who wrote the featured case law excerpts argue that mandatory arbitration clauses can apply to Title VII claims. The authors who wrote the featured law review articles argue that mandatory arbitration clauses should not apply to Title VII claims. As you read this chapter, keep your eyes open for the places where the authors agree. Do the justices see any problems with arbitration of Title VII claims? Do the law review authors recognize any benefits of arbitration? Do not let the seemingly dichotomous opinions trick you into seeing a complex, gray issue as a simple, black-and-white question.

ISSUE ARTICLES

Robert D. Gilmer, Petitioner v. Interstate/Johnson Lane Corporation, 500 U.S. 20 (1991).

Mary Rebecca Tyre Furman, "Arbitration: An Employer's License to Steal Title VII Claims?" 52 Alabama Law Review 1359 (2001).

Hooters of America, Inc. v. Annette R. Phillips, 173 F.3d 933; 1999 U.S. App. LEXIS 6329.

Joseph A. Arnold, "The Circumvention of Compulsory Arbitration: Two Bites at the Apple, or a Restoration of Employees' Statutory Rights?" 33 *Seton Hall Law Review* 1207 (2003).

Marshall, Edward A, "Title VII's Participation Clause and *Circuit City Stores v. Adams,* 1 *Berkeley Journal of Employment & Labor Law*, 71 (2003).

ARTICLE 5.1

Robert D. Gilmer, Petitioner v. Interstate/Johnson Lane Corporation

Why is it an important right for a person to be able to have a judicial forum, as opposed to an arbitration proceeding?

A corporation hired an individual as a manager of financial services. The individual, as required by his employment, registered as a securities representative with several stock exchanges. His registration application included a provision to the effect that he agreed to arbitrate any claim which arose between him and the corporation and which was required to be arbitrated under the rules of the exchanges. A rule of one of the exchanges provided for the arbitration of any controversy between a registered representative and a member organization arising out of the representative's termination of employment. The corporation terminated the individual's employment in 1987, at which time the individual was 62 years of age. After the individual filed an age discrimination charge with the Equal Employment Opportunity Commission, the individual brought suit against the corporation in the United States District Court for the Western District of North Carolina and alleged that the corporation had discharged him because of his age, in violation of the Age Discrimination in Employment Act of 1967 (ADEA). In response, the corporation, relying upon the arbitration agreement and upon the Federal Arbitration Act (FAA) filed a motion to compel arbitration of the ADEA claim, but the District Court, in denying the motion, expressed the view that Congress had intended to protect ADEA claimants from the waiver of a judicial forum. On appeal, the United States Court of Appeals for the Fourth Circuit, in reversing, expressed the view that nothing in the text, legislative history, or underlying purposes of the ADEA indicated a congressional intent to preclude the enforcement of arbitration agreements.

On certiorari, the United States Supreme Court *affirmed*. It was held that the individual's termination-of-employment claim under the ADEA could be subjected to compulsory arbitration because the individual had not met his burden of showing that Congress, in enacting the ADEA, had intended to preclude arbitration of claims under the ADEA, for

1. the individual conceded that nothing in the text of the ADEA or its legislative history explicitly precluded such arbitration,
2. such arbitration was not inherently inconsistent with the statutory framework and purposes of the ADEA,
3. the individual's generalized attacks on the adequacy of arbitration procedures were insufficient to preclude such compulsory arbitration,

4. there was no indication that the individual, an experienced businessman, had been coerced or defrauded into agreeing to the arbitration provision in the application, and

Stevens, J., joined by Marshall, J., dissenting, expressed the view that

1. compulsory arbitration conflicted with the congressional purpose animating the ADEA; and
2. the court's opinion improperly put to one side any concern about inequality in bargaining power between an entire industry and an individual customer or employee. . . .

JUDGES: WHITE, J., delivered the opinion of the Court, in which REHNQUIST, C. J., and BLACKMUN, O'CONNOR, SCALIA, KENNEDY, and SOUTER, JJ., joined. STEVENS, J., filed a dissenting opinion, in which MARSHALL, J., joined.

JUSTICE WHITE delivered the opinion of the Court.

I.

The question presented in this case is whether a claim under the Age Discrimination in Employment Act of 1967 (ADEA) can be subjected to compulsory arbitration pursuant to an arbitration agreement in a securities registration application. The Court of Appeals held that it could, and we affirm. . . .

Interstate terminated Gilmer's employment in 1987, at which time Gilmer was 62 years of age. After first filing an age discrimination charge with the Equal Employment Opportunity Commission (EEOC), Gilmer subsequently brought suit in the United States District Court for the Western District of North Carolina, alleging that Interstate had discharged him because of his age, in violation of the ADEA. In response to Gilmer's complaint, Interstate filed in the District Court a motion to compel arbitration of the ADEA claim. In its motion, Interstate relied upon the arbitration agreement in Gilmer's registration application, as well as the Federal Arbitration Act (FAA). The District Court denied Interstate's motion, based on this Court's decision in *Alexander* v. *Gardner-Denver Co.*, and because it concluded that "Congress intended to protect ADEA claimants from the waiver of a judicial forum." The United States Court of Appeals for the Fourth Circuit reversed, finding "nothing in the text, legislative history, or underlying purposes of the ADEA indicating a congressional intent to preclude enforcement of arbitration agreements." We granted certiorari to resolve a conflict among the Court of Appeals regarding the arbitrability of ADEA claims.

II.

The FAA was originally enacted in 1925, 43 Stat. 883, and then reenacted and codified in 1947 as Title 9 of the United States Code. Its purpose was to reverse the longstanding judicial hostility to arbitration agreements that had existed at

English common law and had been adopted by American courts, and to place arbitration agreements upon the same footing as other contracts. Its primary substantive provision states that "[a] written provision in any maritime transaction or a contract evidencing a transaction involving commerce to settle by arbitration a controversy thereafter arising out of such contract or transaction . . . shall be valid, irrevocable, and enforceable, save upon such grounds as exist at law or in equity for the revocation of any contract." The FAA also provides for stays of proceedings in federal district courts when an issue in the proceeding is referable to arbitration, § 3, and for orders compelling arbitration when one party has failed, neglected, or refused to comply with an arbitration agreement. These provisions manifest a "liberal federal policy favoring arbitration agreements."

It is by now clear that statutory claims may be the subject of an arbitration agreement, enforceable pursuant to the FAA. Indeed, in recent years we have held enforceable arbitration agreements relating to claims arising under the Sherman Act, the Securities Exchange Act of 1934, and the civil provisions of the Racketeer Influenced and Corrupt Organizations Act (RICO).

Although all statutory claims may not be appropriate for arbitration, "having made the bargain to arbitrate, the party should be held to it unless Congress itself has evinced an intention to preclude a waiver of judicial remedies for the statutory rights at issue." In this regard, we note that the burden is on Gilmer to show that Congress intended to preclude a waiver of a judicial forum for ADEA claims. If such an intention exists, it will be discoverable in the text of the ADEA, its legislative history, or an "inherent conflict" between arbitration and the ADEA's underlying purposes. Throughout such an inquiry, it should be kept in mind that "questions of arbitrability must be addressed with a healthy regard for the federal policy favoring arbitration."

III.

What would Gilmer have needed to show about the ADEA for him to have avoided the decision in this case?

Gilmer concedes that nothing in the text of the ADEA or its legislative history explicitly precludes arbitration. He argues, however, that compulsory arbitration of ADEA claims pursuant to arbitration agreements would be inconsistent with the statutory framework and purposes of the ADEA. Like the Court of Appeals, we disagree.

Congress enacted the ADEA in 1967 "to promote employment of older persons based on their ability rather than age; to prohibit arbitrary age discrimination in employment; [and] to help employers and workers find ways of meeting problems arising from the impact of age on employment." To achieve those goals, the ADEA, among other things, makes it unlawful for an employer "to fail or refuse to hire or to discharge any individual or otherwise discriminate against any individual with respect to his compensation, terms, conditions, or privileges of employment, because of such individual's age." This proscription is enforced both by private suits and by the EEOC. In order for an aggrieved individual to bring suit under the ADEA, he or she must first file a charge with the EEOC and then wait at least 60 days. An individual's right to sue is extinguished, however, if the EEOC institutes an action against the employer. Before the EEOC can bring such an action, though, it must "attempt to eliminate the discriminatory practice or practices alleged, and to effect voluntary compliance with the requirements of this chapter through informal methods of conciliation, conference, and persuasion."

As Gilmer contends, the ADEA is designed not only to address individual grievances, but also to further important social policies. We do not perceive any inherent inconsistency between those policies, however, and enforcing agreements to arbitrate age discrimination claims. It is true that arbitration focuses on specific disputes between the parties involved. The same can be said, however, of judicial resolution of claims. Both of these dispute resolution mechanisms nevertheless also can further broader social purposes. The Sherman Act, the Securities Exchange Act of 1934, RICO, and the Securities Act of 1933 all are designed to advance important public policies, but, as noted above, claims under those statutes are appropriate for arbitration. "So long as the prospective litigant effectively may vindicate [his or her] statutory cause of action in the arbitral forum, the statute will continue to serve both its remedial and deterrent function."

We also are unpersuaded by the argument that arbitration will undermine the role of the EEOC in enforcing the ADEA. An individual ADEA claimant subject to an arbitration agreement will still be free to file a charge with the EEOC, even though the claimant is not able to institute a private judicial action. Indeed, Gilmer filed a charge with the EEOC in this case. In any event, the EEOC's role in combating age discrimination is not dependent on the filing of a charge; the agency may receive information concerning alleged violations of the ADEA "from any source," and it has independent authority to investigate age discrimination. . . .

Gilmer also argues that compulsory arbitration is improper because it deprives claimants of the judicial forum provided for by the ADEA. Congress, however, did not explicitly preclude arbitration or other nonjudicial resolution of claims, even in its recent amendments to the ADEA. "If Congress intended the substantive protection afforded [by the ADEA] to include protection against waiver of the right to a judicial forum, that intention will be deducible from text or legislative history." Moreover, Gilmer's argument ignores the ADEA's flexible approach to resolution of claims. The EEOC, for example, is directed to pursue "informal methods of conciliation, conference, and persuasion," which suggests that out-of-court dispute resolution, such as arbitration, is consistent with the statutory scheme established by Congress. . . .

In arguing that arbitration is inconsistent with the ADEA, Gilmer also raises a host of challenges to the adequacy of arbitration procedures. Initially, we note that in our recent arbitration cases we have already rejected most of these arguments as insufficient to preclude arbitration of statutory claims. Such generalized attacks on arbitration "rest on suspicion of arbitration as a method of weakening the protections afforded in the substantive law to would-be complainants," and as such, they are "far out of step with our current strong endorsement of the federal statutes favoring this method of resolving disputes." Consequently, we address these arguments only briefly.

Gilmer first speculates that arbitration panels will be biased. However, "we decline to indulge the presumption that the parties and arbitral body conducting a proceeding will be unable or unwilling to retain competent, conscientious and impartial arbitrators." In any event, we note that the NYSE arbitration rules, which are applicable to the dispute in this case, provide protections against biased panels. The rules require, for example, that the parties be informed of the employment histories of the arbitrators, and that they be allowed to make further inquiries into the arbitrators' backgrounds. In addition, each party is allowed one peremptory challenge and unlimited challenges for cause. Moreover, the arbitrators are required to disclose "any circumstances which might preclude [them] from rendering an objective and impartial determination." The FAA also protects against bias, by providing that courts may overturn arbitration decisions "where there was evident partiality or corruption in the arbitrators. There has been no showing in this case that those provisions are inadequate to guard against potential bias.

Gilmer also complains that the discovery allowed in arbitration is more limited than in the federal courts, which he contends will make it difficult to prove discrimination. It is unlikely, however, that age discrimination claims require more extensive discovery than other claims that we have found to be arbitrable, such as RICO and antitrust claims. Moreover, there has been no showing in this case that the NYSE discovery provisions, which allow for document production, information requests, depositions, and subpoenas will prove insufficient to allow ADEA claimants such as Gilmer a fair opportunity to present their claims. Although those procedures might not be as extensive as in the federal courts, by agreeing to arbitrate, a party "trades the procedures and opportunity for review of the courtroom for the simplicity, informality, and expedition of arbitration." Indeed, an important counterweight to the reduced discovery in NYSE arbitration is that arbitrators are not bound by the rules of evidence.

A further alleged deficiency of arbitration is that arbitrators often will not issue written opinions, resulting, Gilmer contends, in a lack of public knowledge of employers' discriminatory policies, an inability to obtain effective appellate review, and a stifling of the development of the law. The NYSE rules, however, do require that all arbitration awards be in writing, and that the awards contain the names of the parties, a summary of the issues in controversy, and a description of the award issued. In addition, the award decisions are made available to the public. Furthermore, judicial decisions addressing ADEA claims will continue to be issued because it is unlikely that all or even most ADEA claimants will be subject to arbitration agreements. Finally, Gilmer's concerns apply equally to settlements of ADEA claims, which, as noted above, are clearly allowed.

Gilmer also contends that judicial review of arbitration decisions is too limited. We have stated, however, that "although judicial scrutiny of arbitration awards necessarily is limited, such review is sufficient to ensure that arbitrators comply with the requirements of the statute" at issue.

It is also argued that arbitration procedures cannot adequately further the purposes of the ADEA because they do not provide for broad equitable relief and class actions. As the court below noted, however, arbitrators do have the power to fashion equitable relief. Indeed, the NYSE rules applicable here do not restrict the types of relief an arbitrator may award, but merely refer to "damages and/or other relief." The NYSE rules also provide for collective proceedings. But "even if the arbitration could not go forward as a class action or class relief could not be granted by the arbitrator, the fact that the [ADEA] provides for the possibility of bringing a collective action does not mean that individual attempts at conciliation were intended to be barred." Finally, it should be remembered that arbitration agreements will not preclude the *EEOC* from bringing actions seeking class-wide and equitable relief.

An additional reason advanced by Gilmer for refusing to enforce arbitration agreements relating to ADEA claims is his contention that there often will be unequal bargaining power between employers and employees. Mere inequality in bargaining power, however, is not a sufficient reason to hold that arbitration agreements are never enforceable in the employment context. Relationships between securities dealers and investors, for example, may involve unequal bargaining power, but we nevertheless held in *Rodriguez de Quijas* and *McMahon* that agreements to arbitrate in that context are enforceable. As discussed above, the FAA's purpose was to place arbitration agreements on the same footing as other contracts. Thus, arbitration agreements are enforceable "save upon such grounds as exist at law or in equity for the revocation of any contract." "Of course, courts should remain attuned to well-supported claims that the agreement to arbitrate resulted from the sort of fraud or overwhelming economic power that would provide grounds 'for the revocation of any contract." There is no indication in this case, however, that Gilmer, an experienced businessman, was coerced or defrauded into agreeing to the arbitration clause in his registration application. As with the claimed procedural inadequacies discussed above, this claim of unequal bargaining power is best left for resolution in specific cases. . . .

IV.

We conclude that Gilmer has not met his burden of showing that Congress, in enacting the ADEA, intended to preclude arbitration of claims under that Act. Accordingly, the judgment of the Court of Appeals is

Affirmed.

DISSENT

JUSTICE STEVENS, with whom **JUSTICE MARSHALL** joins, dissenting.

Section 1 of the Federal Arbitration Act (FAA) states:

> "[N]othing herein contained shall apply to contracts of employment of seamen, railroad employees, or any other class of workers engaged in foreign or interstate commerce."

The Court today, in holding that the FAA compels enforcement of arbitration clauses even when claims of age discrimination are at issue, skirts the antecedent question whether the coverage of the Act even extends to arbitration clauses contained in employment contracts, regardless of the subject matter of the claim at issue. In my opinion, arbitration clauses contained in employment agreements are specifically exempt from coverage of the FAA, and for that reason respondent Interstate/Johnson Lane Corporation cannot, pursuant to the FAA, compel petitioner to submit his claims arising under the Age Discrimination in Employment Act of 1967 (ADEA) to binding arbitration. . . .

When the FAA was passed in 1925, I doubt that any legislator who voted for it expected it to apply to statutory claims, to form contracts between parties of unequal bargaining power, or to the arbitration of disputes arising out of the employment relationship. In recent years, however, the Court "has effectively rewritten the statute," and abandoned its earlier view that statutory claims were not appropriate subjects for arbitration. See *Mitsubishi Motors* v. *Soler Chrysler-Plymouth, Inc.* Although I remain persuaded that it erred in doing so, the Court has also put to one side any concern about the inequality of bargaining power between an entire industry, on the one hand, and an individual customer or employee, on the other. Until today, however, the Court has not read § 2 of the FAA as broadly encompassing disputes arising out of the employment relationship. I believe this additional extension of the FAA is erroneous. Accordingly, I respectfully dissent.

ARTICLE 5.2

Arbitration: An Employer's License to Steal Title VII Claims?

Mary Rebecca Tyre Furman

INTRODUCTION

Many employers now require an employee to sign a mandatory arbitration agreement before the employee is hired. This practice, along with the erroneous application of the Federal Arbitration Act ("FAA") to statutory claims of individual rights, has undermined the strength of statutes designed to protect individual rights. The statutes which specifically protect employees' individual rights against employer discrimination include, for example, actions arising under Title VII of the Civil Rights Act of 1964 ("Title VII") and the Age Discrimination in Employment Act ("ADEA"). This Comment focuses on Title VII claims.

Before the Supreme Court's decision in Gilmer v. Interstate/Johnson Lane Corporation, the federal circuits inconsistently applied the FAA to employees' statutory claims. The Gilmer decision held that arbitration of an ADEA claim may be compelled pursuant to an agreement in the employee's securities registration application. Lower courts have interpreted Gilmer to allow employers to compel arbitration of employees' statutory claims regarding their civil rights. Although statutory claims are not relinquished completely by the employee, arbitration of these claims cripples their effectiveness and weakens the claims' social value.

This Comment briefly examines the FAA and pre-Gilmer decisions of the Supreme Court. It then touches on the more notorious deficiencies of arbitration which demonstrate why the federal courts are a more appropriate forum for individual rights claims. Finally, this Comment discusses the purpose and intent of Title VII compared to the reasoning in Gilmer.

I. OVERVIEW OF APPLICABLE LAW

To evaluate whether a court should compel arbitration of an employee's statutory claim, one must first examine case and statutory law regarding arbitration. The FAA was first enacted in 1925 and then later reenacted and recodified in 1947, to legitimize agreements between parties to arbitrate future disputes. The FAA states that "a written provision in . . . a contract evidencing a transaction involving commerce to settle by arbitration a controversy thereafter arising out of such contract . . . shall be valid, irrevocable, and enforceable, save upon such grounds as exist at law or in equity for the revocation of any contract." Congressional affirmation of arbitration is the purpose of the FAA.

In 1953, the United States Supreme Court spoke to the issue of arbitration of statutory claims in *Wilko v. Swan*. Wilko involved the arbitration of federal securities laws as codified in the Securities Act of 1933 and the Securities Exchange Act of 1934. The dispute arose when a customer alleged that the broker used false representations to induce him to buy stock. The broker moved to compel arbitration pursuant to the brokerage contract's arbitration provision. The Court looked to public policy considerations and Congress' intent when it refused to apply the FAA to the plaintiff's statutory claim.

The Court believed there was an inherent conflict between the Securities Act and adjudication by arbitration. It found that the Securities Act granted a special right which differed from common law rights. The Court pointed out that disputes regarding quality of a commodity and money due under a contract were traditionally the type of disputes arbitrated, as opposed to arbitrating a complex federal statute. The fact that the arbiter would be applying law to a set of facts without judicial discretion and that there would not exist a complete record of the proceedings convinced the Court that the statutory claim should not be arbitrated. The Court further considered the legislative objectives of the Securities Act. It found that Congress intended the Securities Act to alleviate buyer disadvantages, and that therefore judicial redress was important.

Three decades later, in *Mitsubishi Motors Corp. v. Soler Chrysler-Plymouth, Inc.*, the U.S. Supreme Court was again faced with the question of whether or not statutory claims may be compelled to arbitration. Although this case, like Wilko, did not consider statutory claims of individual rights, its language and reasoning are followed by the Court in later cases examining individual rights. The dispute arose between two corporations (one domestic and one foreign) under the Sherman Antitrust Act. The Court first asked "whether the parties agreed to arbitrate that dispute." The inquiry, the Court explained, is made by examining the contract which contains the arbitration provision and the arbitration provision's coverage. The second part of the inquiry is whether Congress evidenced an intent to preclude arbitration. To ascertain the intent of Congress, the Court explained, it is appropriate for the courts to examine the text and legislative history of the statute.

Applying the two-part inquiry to the agreement, the Court found that the parties had agreed to arbitrate the dispute. When the Court considered the legislative intent to the Sherman Antitrust Act, it stated that out of respect for "international comity," the arbitration clause should be enforced.

In *Alexander v. Gardner-Denver Co.*, the Court addressed the issue of compelled arbitration of individual rights. The Court held that an employee's right to trial before a federal court under the Equal Employment provisions of the Civil Rights Act was not foreclosed by submitting a claim to arbitration. The arbitration provision existed in the collective-bargaining agreements between the employer and the labor union. The employee alleged racial discrimination prohibited by Title VII. The Court applied a two-part inquiry similar to that in Mitsubishi to the parties' "broad arbitration clause covering 'differences arising between the Company and the Union.' " The justices examined the purpose and legislative history of Title VII. The Court found that "there can be no prospective waiver of an employee's rights under Title VII." It noted especially that Title VII concerns "an individual's right to equal employment opportunities," which cannot be abrogated by a collectivebargaining agreement. After Alexander, a majority of federal courts refused to uphold agreements to arbitrate statutory claims.

Seventeen years later, the Supreme Court revisited the question regarding whether an employee could compel arbitration, pursuant to an employee-employer agreement, of a statutory claim which protected individual rights. In *Gilmer v. Interstate/Johnson Lane Corp.*, the Court held that a statutory claim of discrimination based on age (prohibited by the ADEA) could be required to be adjudicated in arbitration instead of a federal court. In so holding, the Court reviewed some provisions of the FAA and its purpose. The Court, citing Mitsubishi, stated that "by agreeing to arbitrate a statutory claim, a party does not forgo the substantive rights afforded by the statute; it only submits to their resolution in an arbitral, rather than a judicial, forum." Turning to whether or not Congress had evinced an intention to preclude arbitration of the ADEA, the Court found that Congress had not. The Court did concede that "the ADEA is designed not only to address individual grievances, but also to further important social policies." But the Court found no "inherent inconsistency between [individual interests and social policies] and enforcing agreements to arbitrate age discrimination claims." While the employee also challenged the adequacy of arbitration procedures, the Court dismissed this generalized attack on arbitration. Since Gilmer, the federal courts have made a distinction between compelling arbitration found in a collective bargaining contract (Alexander) and one found in a contract of employment.

II. ARBITRATION DEFICIENCIES

Before examining why statutory claims against employers involving individual rights should not be compelled to arbitration, one must first examine the deficiencies, in general, of arbitration. Federal courts are preferable forums for employees to have their complaints resolved for multiple reasons:

1. discovery is broader in federal courts;
2. federal judges, as opposed to industry insiders, are more qualified to interpret federal statutory language and meaning;
3. written opinions are needed for consistency in statutory application;
4. federal courts may impose a broad range of remedies; and
5. federal court oversight is more likely to produce broad industry changes.
   While none of these reasons constitutes a substantive right in itself, together they provide the protections which were intended by Congress in drafting the statutes which protect individual rights.

First, discovery in federal court is broader than in arbitration because the Federal Rules of Civil Procedure allow civil litigants a broad range of pretrial discovery. Discovery is especially important in the litigation of individual rights. Often the evidence of discrimination is not in as blatant a form as a memo from the Personnel Director to the CEO stating that he has fired an employee on the basis of that employee's race. Usually, discrimination is invidious, occurring in the form of glass ceilings, promotional and hiring practices, and attitudes of bigotry throughout the employer's company. Therefore, broad discovery is necessary for an aggrieved employee to meet his burden of proof and thereby receive justice.

Second, federal judges are more qualified than industry insiders to adjudicate questions of federal statutory interpretation. First, arbiters are without authority to develop the law. They are hired to resolve a single dispute and are not required to consider public policy. This may lead to an outcome which would be different in a court because the federal court has discretion to interpret the broad public policy set out in Title VII. Second, because arbiters do not answer to Congress or the public, only industry insiders and the litigants (persons without the power to correct rulings through proper legislation) are aware of their rulings.

Would not many of these alleged disadvantages suggest that arbitration should rarely be used for anything?

Arbiters often lack legal training and education. Although it "requires a sound understanding of law in general and of current societal standards," the arbiters are usually industry insiders who normally decide disputes over prices and contracts, instead of individual rights protected by Title VII. Most arbiters are not skilled in statutory interpretation of individual rights, as opposed to federal courts which are the main workhorses for statutory interpretation and are also under the precedent of the Supreme Court.

The third way in which compelled arbitration is not suited to advance the goals of individual rights statutes is that the opinions of the arbiters are neither written nor recorded. There is no way to surmise their reasons for decisions or to insure consistency in future results. Without written opinions, precedents have not properly been set and interpretive guidelines have not been established. These guidelines are needed for proper review of the decisions (if the arbitration decision is appealed). Written opinions are also needed for their deterrent effect on other employers. Without written opinions, employers do not know which activities are considered discrimination and which activities are legitimate practices. Written opinions also give victims of employment discrimination notice of redress and an education as to how discrimination is defined. Finally, written opinions facilitate the development of the law, which has long been recognized as an important aspect of adjudication.

Fourth, federal courts' freedom to administer a wide range of remedies against discrimination is another reason statutory claims brought against employers which regard individual rights should not be adjudicated in arbitration. A federal court may enjoin a discriminatory practice of the employer, but an arbiter may only determine the outcome of the dispute at hand and assess damages. The federal courts have discretion to grant equitable avenues of relief that are not available in arbitration. Federal courts may grant relief to classes of injured employees and not just the plaintiff at hand.

Finally, federal courts should hear these discrimination claims because broad industry discrimination can be eliminated by court oversight. Arbitration and resolution of single complaints cannot affect sufficient changes in an employer's discrimination. This is consistent with the fact that federal courts may impart broader remedies; they also have the ability to oversee that the employers conform to the remedies. Arbiters decide a dispute and are not involved in enforcing the judgment. Federal courts have played an enormous and indispensable role in correcting discrimination in the past and should be afforded that opportunity in present employment discrimination. As the Supreme Court stated in Alexander, "final responsibility for enforcement of Title VII is vested with federal courts."

This discussion does not seek to imply that arbitration is an insufficient forum for many disputes. Arbitration is a legitimate and sometimes helpful forum of alternative dispute resolution. In many cases, contracts to arbitrate should not be discarded lightly. Contracts to compel arbitration that are between an employer and employee are not made with the same amount of bargaining power. The employer usually has the resources and drafts the contract. The future employee signs the contract to get the job, not knowing what rights he is surrendering to arbitration.

III. PURPOSES OF TITLE VII

Title VII of the Civil Rights Act was created to eliminate discrimination in the workplace. Its objectives were twofold:

1. to end workplace discrimination, and
2. to remedy individual injuries.

The first objective evaluates the need to make sweeping changes against discrimination in the American workplace. Arbitration is not an appropriate vehicle to make these widespread changes. The second objective is fulfilled through compensation or reinstatement of an aggrieved employee. To effectively complete these objectives, an employee's Title VII claim should not be subject to arbitration.

Title VII's prohibition against discrimination did not create a new right, but granted a right to enter federal court. The House Committee on the Judiciary stated, "The bill . . . is designed primarily to protect and provide more effective means to enforce the civil rights of persons within the jurisdiction of the United States." This comment evidences Congress's concern regarding the effectiveness of discrimination suits litigated outside of a federal forum. Title VII turned claims that would traditionally be handled (or mishandled) in a state court into claims "arising under" a federal statute. A claim under a federal statute gives the claimant a door to federal court, which is a more impartial forum for adjudication of his claim. This protection was considered necessary because of existing racial turmoil. Federal question jurisdiction is based on a distrust of state courts to impartially and/or precisely adjudicate a particular dispute. It exists "to protect litigants relying on federal law from the danger that the state courts will not properly apply that law, either through misunderstanding or lack of sympathy." This new right to a federal forum is a safeguard against state and local discrimination.

The federal courts are better suited to assure Title VII's purpose of ending workplace discrimination. If the state courts cannot be trusted with these claims of individual rights, then it is even more offensive to Title VII's purpose to have the claims determined in arbitration. The reasons offered in favor of federal anti-discriminatory statutes being adjudicated in a federal forum, rather than that of a state, apply to arbitration as well. Like state court judges, arbiters are not familiar with the statutes in question or the complex judicial decisions which make up their applicable body of law. Arbiters may be swayed by local discriminations and do not have the job security that is provided for federal judges.

IV. GILMER'S APPLICATION TO TITLE VII CLAIMS

The U.S. Supreme Court's reasoning in Gilmer is inappropriate as applied to claims arising under Title VII. These are the major flaws in the Court's opinion in Gilmer:

1. the Court's erroneous assumption that it must adopt a healthy attitude towards arbitration;
2. the Court's mistaken assumption that a statute meant to protect individual rights is comparable to other federal statutes under which claims have been compelled to arbitration;
3. the Court's erroneous finding that Congress had no intention to preclude other forms of dispute resolution; and
4. the Court's short-sighted assumption that litigants may vindicate their statutory claims appropriately in arbitration. . . .

A. The Court's Assumptions Regarding the FAA

The Court begins by giving a brief overview of the FAA. It ends the analysis by quoting *Cone Memorial Hospital v. Mercury,* stating that the FAA's "provisions manifest a liberal federal policy favoring arbitration agreements." The flaw in accepting this view of arbitration is that it is not statutorily mandated. The FAA never states that the policy for enforcing the contracts should be liberal, instead it sets up certain procedures that must be followed in order for an arbitration contract to be binding.

The context of the quote is also important. The Mercury case involved a dispute between a hospital in North Carolina and a contractor in Alabama. The parties had an arbitration agreement in the construction contract in accordance "with the Construction Industry Arbitration Rules of the American Arbitration Association." The dispute arose over delays in construction, and the hospital filed an action to bar the arbitration. When the Court states that "section 2 [of the FAA] is a congressional declaration of a liberal federal policy favoring arbitration agreements," it cites no authority or congressional history for this proposition.

In Mercury, the type of arbitration agreement is far different from an arbitration provision in an employment contract. An arbitration agreement between two commercial entities contains the safeguard of equal or comparable bargaining power. This insures that both sides are relinquishing a similar privilege. On the other hand, an employee (especially in less skilled jobs) may not have any bargaining power. If he does not sign the arbitration contract the next applicant will. The commercial entities also have experience in making these contracts and have access to experts (corporate attorneys) who are conscious of the drawbacks and benefits associated with arbitration. In contrast, a potential employee may not have the experience or understanding to acknowledge the protections he is foregoing. In light of these differences, the Court incorrectly assumed that it should enforce a liberal policy favoring arbitration.

B. The Court's Comparison to Other Statutory Claims

The Gilmer Court stated, "It is by now clear that statutory claims may be the subject of an arbitration agreement, enforceable pursuant to the FAA." The Court lists cases in which it has enforced arbitration agreements arising under statutory claims. The statutes at issue in those cases were the Sherman Antitrust Act, the Securities and Exchange Act of 1934, the civil provisions of the Racketeer Influenced and Corrupt Organizations Act ("RICO"), and the Securities Act of 1933. Each of these statutes concern regulation of businesses and not individual rights. Compelling an arbitration agreement regarding antitrust issues between two corporations under the Sherman Act is quite different than compelling arbitration regarding discrimination between an employee and an employer. As discussed in the previous section, arbitration contracts between corporations and those between employers and employees are inherently different.

It is also unconscionable to assume that the arbitration of commercial disputes is the same as the arbitration of a person's individual rights and civil liberties. The purposes of the Sherman Act, the Securities Acts, and RICO are very different from the purpose of Title VII. The Sherman Act is designed to regulate and ensure competition in the marketplace. The purpose of the Securities Exchange Act and the Securities Act are to regulate the trade of securities and insure investors of reliable information. RICO was conceived to cease organized crime rings and the control they held over certain commodities. Congress' intention behind Title VII is different than that behind these other statutes.

Moreover, the Court, quoting Mitsubishi, stated that "by agreeing to arbitrate a statutory claim, a party does not forgo the substantive rights afforded by the statute." Once again the Court is quoting from a case which dealt with arbitration of a corporate contract (not an employee-employer contract) and a statutory claim that is not an individual right. The Court is correct in pointing out that arbitration agreements do not forgo a litigant's statutory claim. In other words, the same statutes should be applied in both litigation and arbitration. The right to equal employment rights exists whether the claim is arbitrated or not. The problem, however, lies in the fact that arbitration does not provide sufficient protection for this right. The right to a federal forum is just as important as the individual right itself. The federal forum is the only way Congress can guarantee that its purposes and intentions of protecting certain classes of people will be fulfilled.

C. Whether Congress Has Precluded a Waiver of Judicial Forum

Congress' intention to preclude a waiver of judicial forum is demonstrated by Title VII's "inherent conflict" between arbitration and the purposes of Title VII. The Court states that "having made the bargain to arbitrate, the party should be held to it unless Congress itself has evinced an intention to preclude a waiver of judicial remedies for the statutory rights at issue." The burden is now placed on the employee to demonstrate that Congress "intended to preclude a waiver of a judicial forum." There are three ways to show that such an intention exists:

1. the text of the statute;
2. its legislative history; and
3. "an 'inherent conflict' between arbitration and the [statute's] underlying purposes."

The text of Title VII does not expressly preclude an employee-employer contract from waiving the employee's (or employer's) right to a judicial forum. The legislative history of Title VII communicates the statute's purpose, but does not expressly show Congress' intent to preclude a waiver of judicial remedies. But there does exist "an inherent conflict" between arbitration and Title VII's underlying purpose. Title VII was enacted "to protect and provide more effective means to enforce the civil rights of persons within the jurisdiction of the United States." This evidence of Congress' intent exhibits an inherent conflict with arbitration. If Congress intended for Title VII to protect and provide access to federal courts, then this design precludes arbitration.

Arbitration, which takes these claims out of federal courts, is inconsistent with Congress' intent. Therefore, Congress has evinced "an intention to preclude a waiver of judicial remedies" through the "inherent conflict" between arbitration and Title VII.

D. Vindication of Statutory Claims through Arbitration

The Court, quoting Mitsubishi, stated that "so long as the prospective litigant effectively may vindicate [his or her] statutory cause of action in the arbitral forum, the statute will continue to serve both its remedial and deterrent function." First, it must be remembered that Mitsubishi spoke to arbitration between corporate entities. This statement from Mitsubishi, which is being applied by the Court to justify compelling employee/employer arbitration, makes an erroneous assumption that vindication of the claim will preserve the statute's remedial and deterrent function.

To once again examine the weaknesses of arbitration in general, proper vindication of a Title VII claim is not guarded by arbitration as it would be in a federal forum; biased or unknowledgeable arbiters may fail to properly apply Title VII jurisprudence to the matter before them. Vindication of the individual employee's claim does further the other Title VII goals of remedy and deterrence. The limited available remedies of arbitration prevent it from being an effective forum for Title VII claims. Title VII cannot continue to serve its "remedial function" through arbitration. Without remedies such as injunctions, court oversight, and class-wide compensation, employers may continue to discriminate. The employer may maintain its discriminatory practices against its other employees who (for various reasons) do not or cannot bring suit against the employer.

Title VII's ability to deter discriminatory practiccs is diminished by arbitration. Since arbiters' remedies do not include punitive damages or any wide-range/broad-sweeping ability to require change in policy, the deterrent effect of Title VII is weakened. An employer only has to compensate the individual who brought the claim, instead of being punished and therefore deterred. Arbitration does not include the bad publicity that a federal trial brings to the corporate entity.

The Court did not adequately delve into each and every issue raised in compelling arbitration of an individual rights' statute in an employee-employer contract. It failed to discuss whether arbitration clauses in employment contracts are even covered by the FAA, although the issue was raised in Justice Steven's dissent (joined by Justice Marshall). Justice Stevens stated that "arbitration clauses contained in employment agreements are specifically exempt from coverage of the FAA." This argument is warranted since the text of the FAA never references employment contracts. The dissent explores and concurs with the arguments this Comment makes regarding the intent of Title VII.

Can you imagine a situation where this author would be in favor of compulsory arbitration to uphold a statutory right?

CONCLUSION

Title VII is a prophylactic statute intended by Congress to prevent and deter discrimination based on race, color, religion, sex, or national origin. By giving employees who have been discriminated against a door to federal courts, Title VII provides the fairest forum for discrimination suits to be redressed. The majority's decision in Gilmer did not thoroughly address all issues that compelling arbitration of individual rights in employment contracts raises. Furthermore, the decision should not be broadened to include claims arising under Title VII.

ARTICLE 5.3

Hooters of America, Inc. v. Annette R. Phillips

Annette Phillips (defendant employee) quit her job under circumstances of sexual harassment including grabbing and slapping her buttocks by other employees, which she claimed were a violation of her Title VII rights. Plaintiff employer filed suit to compel arbitration in accordance with an agreement between the parties and pursuant to the Federal Arbitration Act. The trial court denied the request to compel arbitration and plaintiff brought an interlocutory appeal.

I. WILKINSON, CHIEF JUDGE

Appellee Annette R. Phillips worked as a bartender at a Hooters restaurant in Myrtle Beach, South Carolina. She was employed since 1989 by appellant Hooters of Myrtle Beach (HOMB), a franchisee of appellant Hooters of America (collectively Hooters).

Phillips alleges that in June 1996, Gerald Brooks, a Hooters official and the brother of HOMB's principal owner, sexually harassed her by grabbing and slapping her buttocks. After appealing to her manager for help and being told to "let it go," she quit her job. Phillips then contacted Hooters through an attorney claiming that the attack and the restaurant's failure to address it violated her Title VII rights. Hooters responded that she was required to submit her claims to arbitration according to a binding agreement to arbitrate between the parties.

This agreement arose in 1994 during the implementation of Hooters' alternative dispute resolution program. As part of that program, the company conditioned eligibility for raises, transfers, and promotions upon an employee signing an "Agreement to arbitrate employment-related disputes." The agreement provides that Hooters and the employee each agree to arbitrate all disputes arising out of employment, including "any claim of discrimination, sexual harassment, retaliation, or wrongful discharge, whether arising under federal or state law." The agreement further states:

> the employee and the company agree to resolve any claims pursuant to the company's rules and procedures for alternative resolution of employment-related disputes, as promulgated by the company from time to time ("the rules"). Company

will make available or provide a copy of the rules upon written request of the employee.

The employees of HOMB were initially given a copy of this agreement at an all-staff meeting held on November 20, 1994. HOMB's general manager, Gene Fulcher, told the employees to review the agreement for five days and that they would then be asked to accept or reject the agreement. No employee, however, was given a copy of Hooters' arbitration rules and procedures. Phillips signed the agreement on November 25, 1994. When her personnel file was updated in April 1995, Phillips again signed the agreement.

After Phillips quit her job in June 1996, Hooters sent to her attorney a copy of the Hooters rules then in effect. Phillips refused to arbitrate the dispute.

Hooters filed suit in November 1996 to compel arbitration. Phillips defended on the grounds that the agreement to arbitrate was unenforceable. Phillips also asserted individual and class counterclaims against Hooters for violations of Title VII and for a declaration that the arbitration agreements were unenforceable against the class. In response, Hooters requested that the district court stay the proceedings on the counterclaims until after arbitration.

How do the various reasons given in this paragraph demonstrate how important ambiguity is in creating a basis for disagreement among parties?

In March 1998, the district court denied Hooters' motions to compel arbitration and stay proceedings on the counterclaims. The court found that there was no meeting of the minds on all of the material terms of the agreement and even if there were, Hooters' promise to arbitrate was illusory. In addition, the court found that the arbitration agreement was unconscionable and void for reasons of public policy. Hooters filed this interlocutory appeal.

II.

The benefits of arbitration are widely recognized. Parties agree to arbitrate to secure "streamlined proceedings and expeditious results [that] will best serve their needs."[1] The arbitration of disputes enables parties to avoid the costs associated with pursuing a judicial resolution of their grievances. By one estimate, litigating a typical employment dispute costs at least $ 50,000 and takes two and one-half years to resolve. Further, the adversarial nature of litigation diminishes the possibility that the parties will be able to salvage their relationship. For these reasons parties agree to arbitrate and trade "the procedures and opportunity for review of the courtroom for the simplicity, informality, and expedition of arbitration."[2]

In support of arbitration, Congress passed the Federal Arbitration Act (FAA). "Its purpose was to reverse the longstanding judicial hostility to arbitration agreements that had existed at English common law and had been adopted by American courts, and to place arbitration agreements upon the same footing as other contracts." When a valid agreement to arbitrate exists between the parties and covers the matter in dispute, the FAA commands the federal courts to stay any ongoing judicial proceedings, and to compel arbitration.

The threshold question is whether claims such as Phillips' are even arbitrable. The EEOC as amicus curiae contends that employees cannot agree to arbitrate Title VII claims in predispute agreements. We disagree. The Supreme Court has made it plain that judicial protection of arbitral agreements extends to agreements to arbitrate statutory discrimination claims. In *Gilmer v. Interstate/Johnson Lane Corp.*, the Court noted that " 'by agreeing to arbitrate a statutory claim, a party does not forgo the substantive rights afforded by the statute; it only submits to their resolution in an arbitral, rather than a judicial, forum.' " Thus, a party must be held to the terms of its bargain unless Congress intends to preclude waiver of a judicial forum for the statutory claims at issue. Such an intent, however, must "be discoverable in the text of the [substantive statute], its legislative history, or an 'inherent conflict' between arbitration and the [statute's] underlying purposes."

The EEOC argues that in passing the Civil Rights Act of 1991, Congress evinced an intent to prohibit predispute agreements to arbitrate claims arising under Title VII. This circuit, however, has already rejected this argument.[3] The Civil Rights Act of 1991 provided that "Where appropriate and to the extent authorized by law, the use of alternative means of dispute resolution, including . . . arbitration, is encouraged to resolve disputes arising under [Title VII]."

III.

Predispute agreements to arbitrate Title VII claims are thus valid and enforceable. The question remains whether a binding arbitration agreement between Phillips and Hooters exists and compels Phillips to submit her Title VII claims to arbitration. The FAA provides that agreements "to settle by arbitration a controversy thereafter arising out of such contract or transaction.. . shall be valid, irrevocable, and enforceable, save upon such grounds as exist at law or in equity for the revocation of any contract." "It is for the court, not the arbitrator, to decide in the first instance whether the dispute is to be resolved through arbitration."[4] . . .

Hooters argues that Phillips gave her assent to a bilateral agreement to arbitrate. That contract provided for the resolution by arbitration of all employment-related disputes, including claims arising under Title VII. Hooters claims the agreement to arbitrate is valid because Phillips twice signed it voluntarily. Thus, it argues the courts are bound to enforce it and compel arbitration.

We disagree. The judicial inquiry, while highly circumscribed, is not focused solely on an examination for contractual formation defects such as lack of mutual assent and want of consideration.[5] Courts also can investigate the existence of "such grounds as exist at law or in equity for the revocation of any contract." However, the grounds for revocation must relate specifically to the arbitration clause and not just to the contract as a whole. In this case, the challenge goes to the validity of the arbitration agreement itself. Hooters materially breached the arbitration agreement by promulgating rules so egregiously unfair as to constitute a complete default of its contractual obligation to draft arbitration rules and to do so in good faith.

Hooters and Phillips agreed to settle any disputes between them not in a judicial forum, but in another neutral forum—arbitration. Their agreement provided that Hooters was responsible for setting up such a forum by promulgating arbitration rules and procedures. To this end, Hooters instituted a set of rules in July 1996.

What could Hooters have done that would have prevented the failure of their efforts to hold Phillips to the arbitration clause?

The Hooters rules when taken as a whole, however, are so one-sided that their only possible purpose is to undermine the neutrality of the proceeding. The rules require the employee to provide the company notice of her claim at the outset, including "the nature of the Claim" and "the specific act(s) or omissions(s) which are the basis of the Claim." Hooters, on the other hand, is not required to file any responsive pleadings or to notice its defenses. Additionally, at the time of filing this notice, the employee must provide the company with a list of all fact witnesses with a brief summary of the facts known to each. The company, however, is not required to reciprocate.

The Hooters rules also provide a mechanism for selecting a panel of three arbitrators that is crafted to ensure a biased decisionmaker. The employee and Hooters each select an arbitrator, and the two arbitrators in turn select a third. Good enough, except that the employee's arbitrator and the third arbitrator must be selected from a list of arbitrators created exclusively by Hooters. This gives Hooters control over the entire panel and places no limits whatsoever on whom Hooters can put on the list. Under the rules, Hooters is free to devise lists of partial arbitrators who have existing relationships, financial or familial, with Hooters and its management. In fact, the rules do not even prohibit Hooters from placing its managers themselves on the list. Further, nothing in the rules restricts Hooters from punishing arbitrators who rule against the company by removing them from the list. Given the unrestricted control that one party (Hooters) has over the panel, the selection of an impartial decisionmaker would be a surprising result.

Nor is fairness to be found once the proceedings are begun. Although Hooters may expand the scope of arbitration to any matter, "whether related or not to the Employee's Claim," the employee cannot raise "any matter not included in the Notice of Claim." Similarly, Hooters is permitted to move for summary dismissal of employee claims before a hearing is held whereas the employee is not permitted to seek summary judgment. Hooters, but not the employee, may record the arbitration hearing "by audio or video taping or by verbatim transcription." The rules also grant Hooters the right to bring suit in court to vacate or modify an arbitral award when it can show, by a preponderance of the evidence, that the panel exceeded its authority. No such right is granted to the employee.

In addition, the rules provide that upon 30 days notice Hooters, but not the employee, may cancel the agreement to arbitrate. Moreover, Hooters reserves the right to modify the rules, "in whole or in part," whenever it wishes and "without notice" to the employee. Nothing in the rules even prohibits Hooters from changing the rules in the middle of an arbitration proceeding.

If by odd chance the unfairness of these rules were not apparent on their face, leading arbitration experts have decried their one-sidedness. George Friedman, senior vice president of the American Arbitration Association (AAA), testified that the system established by the Hooters rules so deviated from minimum due process standards that the Association would refuse to arbitrate under those rules. George Nicolau, former president of both the National Academy of Arbitrators and the International Society of Professionals in Dispute Resolution, attested that the Hooters rules "are inconsistent with the concept of fair and impartial arbitration." He also testified that he was "certain that reputable designating agencies, such as the AAA and Jams/Endispute, would refuse to administer a program so unfair and one-sided as this one." Additionally, Dennis Nolan, professor of labor law at the University of South Carolina, declared that the Hooters rules "do not satisfy the minimum requirements of a fair arbitration system." He found that the "most serious flaw" was that the "mechanism [for selecting arbitrators] violates the most fundamental aspect of justice, namely an impartial decision maker." Finally, Lewis Maltby, member of the Board of Directors of the AAA, testified that "This is without a doubt the most unfair arbitration program I have ever encountered."

In a similar vein, two major arbitration associations have filed amicus briefs with this court. The National Academy of Arbitrators stated that the Hooters rules "violate fundamental concepts of fairness . . . and the integrity of the arbitration process." Likewise, the Society of Professionals in Dispute Resolution noted that "it would be hard to imagine a more unfair method of selecting a panel of arbitrators." It characterized the Hooters arbitration system as "deficient to the point of illegitimacy" and "so one sided, it is hard to believe that it was even intended to be fair."

We hold that the promulgation of so many biased rules—especially the scheme whereby one party to the proceeding so controls the arbitral panel—breaches the contract entered into by the parties. The parties agreed to submit their claims to arbitration—a system whereby disputes are fairly resolved by an impartial third party. Hooters by contract took on the obligation of establishing such a system. By creating a sham system unworthy even of the name of arbitration, Hooters completely failed in performing its contractual duty.

Moreover, Hooters had a duty to perform its obligations in good faith. Good faith "emphasizes faithfulness to an agreed common purpose and consistency with the justified expectations of the other party." Bad faith includes the "evasion of the spirit of the bargain" and an "abuse of a power to specify terms." By agreeing to settle disputes in arbitration, Phillips agreed to the prompt and economical resolution of her claims. She could legitimately expect that arbitration would not entail procedures so wholly one-sided as to present a stacked deck. Thus we conclude that the Hooters rules also violate the contractual obligation of good faith.

Given Hooters' breaches of the arbitration agreement and Phillips' desire not to be bound by it, we hold that rescission is the proper remedy. Generally, "rescission will not be granted for a minor or casual breach of a contract, but only for those breaches which defeat the object of the contracting parties." As we have explained, Hooters' breach is by no means insubstantial; its performance under the contract was so egregious that the result was hardly recognizable as arbitration at all. We therefore permit Phillips to cancel the agreement and thus Hooters' suit to compel arbitration must fail.

IV.

We respect fully the Supreme Court's pronouncement that "questions of arbitrability must be addressed with a healthy regard for the federal policy favoring arbitration." Our decision should not be misread: We are not holding that the agreement before us is unenforceable because the arbitral proceedings are too abbreviated. An arbitral forum need not replicate the judicial forum. "We are well past the time when judicial suspicion of the desirability of arbitration and of the competence of arbitral tribunals inhibited the development of arbitration as an alternative means of dispute resolution."

Nor should our decision be misunderstood as permitting a full-scale assault on the fairness of proceedings before the matter is submitted to arbitration. Generally, objections to the nature of arbitral proceedings are for the arbitrator to decide in the first instance. Only after arbitration may a party then raise such challenges if they meet the narrow grounds set . . . for vacating an arbitral award. In the case before us, we only reach the content of the arbitration rules because their promulgation was the duty of one party under the contract. The material breach of this duty warranting rescission is an issue of substantive arbitrability and thus is reviewable before arbitration. This case, however, is the exception that proves the rule: fairness objections should generally be made to the arbitrator, subject only to limited post-arbitration judicial review as set forth in section 10 of the FAA.

By promulgating this system of warped rules, Hooters so skewed the process in its favor that Phillips has been denied arbitration in any meaningful sense of the word. To uphold the promulgation of this aberrational scheme under the heading of arbitration would undermine, not advance, the federal policy favoring alternative dispute resolution. This we refuse to do.

The judgment of the district court is affirmed, and the case is remanded for further proceedings consistent with this opinion.

Affirmed and Remanded.

END NOTES

1. *Mitsubishi Motors Corp. v. Soler Chrysler-Plymouth, Inc.*
2. *Gilmer v. Interstate/Johnson Lane Corp.*
3. *Austin v. Owens-Brockway Glass Container, Inc.*
4. *AT&T Techs., Inc. v. Communications Workers of America.*
5. *Virginia Carolina Tools, Inc. v. International Tool Supply, Inc.*

ARTICLE 5.4

The Circumvention of Compulsory Arbitration: Two Bites at the Apple, or a Restoration of Employees' Statutory Rights?

Joseph A. Arnold

INTRODUCTION

A successful advertising company hires Jackie on a full-time basis. She quickly establishes herself as a quality employee and her performance evaluations are excellent. Six months after beginning work, Jackie faints on the job and subsequently takes a two-day medical leave of absence. Apparently, Jackie suffered a negative reaction to a change in medication she was taking to control and prevent arthritis. During day two of Jackie's doctor recommended leave, her manager telephones and fires her. He explains that the company cannot employ someone who, due to repeated absence, could potentially threaten the efficiency of the workforce.

Believing she was wrongfully discharged, Jackie files a lawsuit against her employer under the Americans with Disabilities Act of 1990 ("ADA"). It appears, however, that Jackie's employer requires all prospective employees to sign a company arbitration agreement whereby all employee claims are submitted to arbitration. Based on the precedent established by the Supreme Court in *Gilmer v. Interstate/Johnson Lane Corp*. Jackie's employer invokes the arbitration agreement and the trial court dismisses the claim. Under Gilmer, the Supreme Court held that such an agreement is not only enforceable regarding disputes arising out of an employment contract, but also to federal statutory employment claims. As a result of being forced into arbitration, Jackie may not pursue her claim in court and, therefore, is not afforded the benefits of a jury trial, complete discovery, or the protections of the ADA.

In the wake of Gilmer, employees like Jackie who sign arbitration agreements often find themselves with no ability to enforce their federal statutory rights in court. The Civil Rights Act of 1991 . . . is meant to grant victims of intentional discrimination the right to punitive damages and a jury trial. Despite Congress's efforts to strengthen enforcement of Title VII and the ADA, courts have upheld Gilmer and remained loyal to enforcing arbitration agreements.

Whether arbitration effectively resolves civil rights claims, however, is a contentious subject. As compared to litigation, employees can benefit from arbitration because of its comparatively low cost and faster resolution time. Others, however, argue that Congress granted specific protections for employee rights and the court system is the intended forum for the exercise of those rights. If arbitration is not well-suited to handle statutory discrimination claims, the arbitral forum could represent a substantial erosion of Congress's important anti-discrimination initiatives. . . .

I. LABOR ARBITRATION DEFINED: A HISTORICAL PERSPECTIVE

Arbitration is a "simple proceeding voluntarily chosen by parties who want a dispute determined by an impartial judge of their own mutual selection, whose decision, based on the merits of the case, they agree in advance to accept as final and binding." Arbitration is viewed as a highly effective dispute resolution process because it offers a quicker, less expensive, and less formal alternative to litigation.

Due to these benefits, arbitration first gained popularity in the 1920s among business merchants who chose arbitration rather than litigation to handle contractual disputes. The most significant use of arbitration in the twentieth century, however, occurred in the labor context. Participants in the labor and employment setting chose arbitration as an alternative to litigation because it offers a convenient and informal method of dispute resolution in which an employer and a union can quickly resolve disputes. Arbitration, therefore, serves as a "substitute for industrial strife" by avoiding costly, hostile, and unpredictable work stoppages.[1] To achieve these desirable ends, labor arbitrators are essentially charged with the role of "peacemaker," serving as neutral parties to interpret and apply employment and collective bargaining agreements.

The advantages of arbitration make it an attractive and viable forum for the resolution of disputes in the employment relationship. Despite its utility, however, arbitration traveled a rocky path towards judicial acceptance.

II. THE LEGAL STATUS OF ARBITRATION

A. The Federal Arbitration Act and Early Legal Precedent

At common law, agreements to arbitrate were voluntary and revocable by either party. Courts did not favor arbitration early in its development, believing that an agreement to arbitrate operated to divest courts of legislatively-granted jurisdiction and, therefore, was illegal and void. Congress finally voiced its approval of arbitration in 1925, when it passed the Federal Arbitration Act ("FAA"). Section 2 of the FAA renders arbitration agreements "valid, irrevocable, and enforceable." Section 3 provides that a party to an arbitration agreement can move to stay any court proceedings if the issue is covered by an arbitration agreement, and Section 4 permits that party to obtain an order to compel arbitration if the other party refuses to honor the agreement. The FAA, therefore, transformed arbitration from a voluntary dispute resolution tool to a legally binding agreement backed by Congress.

Despite its enactment, courts did not apply the FAA until nearly thirty-five years later, in *Wilko v. Swan*. In Wilko, a securities brokerage firm attempted to compel arbitration of a customer's claim under the Securities Act of 1933. Rather than compel arbitration under the FAA, the Supreme Court declared the arbitration agreement invalid, holding that the right to a judicial forum for enforcement of the Securities Act preempted the enforceability of arbitration agreements under the FAA. . . .

The Supreme Court effectively overruled Wilko when it decided the "Mitsubishi Trilogy." While the Wilko Court refused to apply the FAA to a statutory claim, the Court in *Mitsubishi Motors Corp. v. Soler Chrysler-Plymouth, Inc.* held that the FAA created a presumption of arbitrability favoring all arbitration agreements. In the "Mitsubishi Trilogy," the Court enforced agreements to arbitrate statutory claims based on antitrust, securities, and racketeering laws. In *Mitsubishi Motors Corp. v. Soler Chrysler-Plymouth, Inc.*, decided in 1985, the Court ruled that the FAA allowed for the arbitration of statutory claims unless Congress clearly indicated otherwise in the statutory language. In *Rodriguez de Quijas v. Shearson/Am. Express, Inc.*, the last decision in the trilogy, the Court specifically overruled Wilko, holding that the arbitration agreement precluded a Securities Act claim from being heard in a judicial forum.

For the first time, the Supreme Court officially endorsed arbitration in the labor setting in the "Steelworkers Trilogy" of 1960. In the "Steelworkers Trilogy," the Court created an "irrebuttable presumption" that employer-union disputes were arbitrable and discouraged judicial intervention in employment disputes governed by an arbitration agreement.

B. The Development of Statutory Rights in the Workplace

. . . As the civil rights movement swept across America, the employer-employee relationship witnessed a substantial level of government intervention in the form of federal regulation. The Equal Pay Act of 1963 marked the beginning of a congressional trend towards ending workplace discrimination and creating equal employment opportunities for all Americans. The most influential anti-discrimination measure is Title VII of the 1964 Civil Rights Act, which makes it unlawful for an employer to discriminate with respect to hiring, firing, or other aspects of employment on the basis of race, color, religion, sex, and national origin. In addition, Congress enacted both the Age Discrimination in Employment Act ("ADEA") in 1967 to combat workplace discrimination on the basis of age, and the Americans with Disabilities Act in 1990 to prohibit employment discrimination on the basis of a disability.

Before 1991, Title VII claimants were not entitled to jury trials. Title VII was silent on the issue and in subsequent years, the Supreme Court assumed that the right to a jury trial did not exist. After deciding that Title VII needed a damages remedy, Congress passed the 1991 Civil Rights Act. Under the Act, victims of discrimination under both Title VII and the ADA have the right to a jury trial, compensatory damages, and punitive damages.

C. The Arbitration of Statutory Law Revisited: Post Civil Rights Movement

How did the civil rights movement affect the growth in importance of the compulsory arbitration issue?

. . . Two influential Supreme Court cases addressed the issue of whether statutory employment claims can be compelled to arbitration, and an analysis of both cases frames the debate that still exists today. The arbitrability of statutory claims arose for the first time in the employment context in *Alexander v. Gardner Denver Company*. Harrell Alexander, Sr., employed by Gardner-Denver Co. as a drill operator, believed the company fired him because he was black. After unsuccessfully pursuing a grievance for wrongful discharge in arbitration, Alexander brought a claim for unlawful discrimination under Title VII. The United States Court of Appeals for the Tenth Circuit affirmed the district court's dismissal of the claim, holding Alexander bound by the arbitral decision and therefore precluded from pursuing a Title VII claim in court.

The Supreme Court . . . reversed in favor of Alexander. The Court noted that the consequence of the lower courts' decisions was to "deprive [Alexander] of his statutory right to attempt to establish his claim in a federal court." The Court held that Title VII provides an individual with independent statutory rights, enforcement of which is vested with the federal courts. The Court stated that the arbitral forum was designed to resolve contract rights and was not appropriate for the resolution of federal statutory rights guaranteed by Title VII. . . .

The "Mitsubishi Trilogy" cases, handed down in 1985, 1987, and 1989, represented a strong shift by the court in its views concerning arbitration and the role of the FAA. In the trilogy, the Supreme Court interpreted the FAA as creating a presumption of arbitrability—even when it results in statutory claims being compelled to an arbitral forum. In Gardner-Denver, however, the Court conclusively identified the judicial forum, and not the arbitration process, as the appropriate forum for the resolution of statutory employment discrimination claims. It was, thus, unclear whether the Supreme Court effectively carved out its own exception to the FAA for statutory employment claims.

The Supreme Court resolved its apparent conflict in the 1991 landmark decision in *Gilmer v. Interstate/Johnson Lane Corp.* Gilmer, fired at age sixty-two, filed a lawsuit in federal court alleging he had been unlawfully discharged based on his age in violation of the ADEA. In response, Interstate filed a motion to compel arbitration. Prior to beginning employment, Interstate required Gilmer to register as a securities representative with several stock exchanges. Importantly, the New York Stock Exchange's ("NYSE") application required Gilmer to arbitrate "any dispute, claim, or controversy" arising out of his employment with Interstate. The United States Court of Appeals for the Fourth Circuit, finding "nothing in the text, legislative history, or underlying purposes of the ADEA indicating a congressional intent to preclude enforcement of arbitration agreements," dismissed Gilmer's suit in favor of arbitration.

The Supreme Court affirmed, extending the "presumption of arbitrability" announced in the "Mitsubishi Trilogy" to include statutory employment discrimination claims, specifically ADEA claims. This decision represented the first time the Supreme Court "held that a statutory civil rights claim can be subjected to mandatory arbitration."

The Gilmer decision departs from the Gardner-Denver policy against enforcing mandatory arbitration agreements as applied to statutory claims. The Court, however, did not expressly overrule Gardner-Denver. The Court instead distinguished the case because Gardner-Denver involved a collective bargaining agreement, while Gilmer enforced an arbitration clause in an individual employment contract. In light of that important difference, Gilmer sent a clear message to employers that arbitration agreements in individual employment contracts will result in the arbitration of all claims, even those based on federal statutes.

Gilmer indicates that the Court is comfortable with the resolution of statutory claims in the arbitral forum. A brief analysis of the inner-workings of the arbitral process, however, reveals that arbitration may not be well-suited to carry out statutory law in a fair manner.

III. THE ARBITRATION PROCESS: AN APPROPRIATE FORUM FOR CIVIL RIGHTS?

The numerous benefits of the arbitral process, such as quicker resolution of disputes at lower costs, validate the congressional policy embodied in the FAA favoring arbitration as a legitimate means of alternative dispute resolution.

Nevertheless, despite the advantages of arbitration, it may come at too substantial a cost to employees. Courts continue to debate the adequacy of the arbitration process for the resolution of statutory employment claims. The Gardner-Denver Court, for example, voiced its skepticism of arbitration when it stated that "arbitral procedures, while well suited to the resolution of contractual disputes, make arbitration a comparatively inappropriate forum for the final resolution of rights created by Title VII." The Gilmer Court responded, however, by stating "such generalized attacks on arbitration" are "far out of step with our current strong endorsement of [arbitration]." Gilmer, therefore, rejected the challenges "as insufficient to preclude arbitration of statutory claims." The Gilmer court's dismissal of Gardner-Denver's apprehensions, however, fails to allay the specific concerns surrounding the arbitration process as an appropriate forum for employees' statutory claims. Gilmer aside, a closer analysis reveals important differences between the judicial and arbitral forums, many of which weigh heavily against employee interests.

One of the Supreme Court's principal concerns was that arbitrators may lack the competency that courts have to understand and apply statutory law. Many arbitrators are not judges, or even lawyers, and although they may be experts in a given business area, arbitrators lack the requisite training to handle statutory claims. Furthermore, arbitrators are not bound by the rules of stare decisis, which may result in the overwhelming interjection of an arbitrator's business judgment into a purely legal decision.

Another concern regarding the arbitration process is that there is no uniform law requiring arbitrators to issue written opinions. Professor Leona Green points out two major problems that arise when arbitrators do not provide opinions. First, the absence of opinions hinders any development of certainty and precedent. Without an arbitrator's reasoning, neither employers nor employees receive guidance as to what behavior is actionable. Similarly, other arbitrators have no precedent to rely upon when deciding cases, undoubtedly leading to inconsistent results.

Second, Professor Green posits that the absence of written opinions makes judicial review nearly impossible. Arbitration awards can be vacated for a "manifest disregard of the law," but courts have difficulty deciding whether an arbitrator exercised such disregard without a written opinion to review. Furthermore, arbitrators can avoid being held accountable for their decisions because there are no written opinions to scrutinize.

Although the absence of written opinions serves as one barrier to judicial review of an arbitrator's decision in a civil rights case, a much larger concern is the extremely narrow grounds on which losing parties may appeal arbitration decisions. The FAA, unsurprisingly given its arbitration-friendly genesis, only allows a court to vacate or modify an arbitral award under very limited circumstances. Appeals are not allowed, however, when an arbitrator misinterprets the law, fails to follow stare decisis, or is confronted with a novel legal issue. . . .

Commentators also voice concerns about the adequacy of arbitration for statutory claims because of the limited opportunity for discovery in arbitration. The speed and efficiency of the arbitration process often results in abbreviated periods of discovery, yet full discovery is often needed to pursue claims under Title VII and other anti-discrimination statutes. Additionally, employees are disadvantaged by a limited opportunity for discovery because the relevant information and documentation sought by the employee in the discovery process is, quite often, already in the hands of the employers. In the court system, victims of discrimination may compel the production of such information through the Federal Rules of Civil Procedure. In the arbitral forum, however, employees are not guaranteed the fairness ensured by the Federal Rules. Accordingly, abbreviated and informal discovery can be dangerously unfair to employees.

Generally, parties to an agreement choose arbitration because it is less expensive and often timelier than court proceedings. The preceding analysis, however, suggests that arbitration may not be appropriate when important civil rights statutes are at stake. Although the informality of the arbitral forum aids the peaceful collective bargaining process between unions and management, that same informality can undermine important Congressional protections for employees' individual rights.

IV. POST-GILMER DECISIONS AND THE RESTORATION OF EMPLOYEE RIGHTS

Despite the pro-arbitration climate, modern jurisprudence indicates that the use of mandatory arbitration clauses in employment contracts may be susceptible to attack.

What is so significant about the Gilmer decision?

A. Challenging the Arbitration Clause Itself

In *Wright v. Universal Maritime Service Corp.*, the Untied States Court of Appeals for the Fourth Circuit affirmed a district court ruling and dismissed an ADA claim, compelling the parties to arbitrate pursuant to an arbitration clause contained in the collective bargaining agreement. When the Supreme Court granted certiorari to review the case, the circumstances seemed ripe for the Court to resolve the existing conflict between Gardner-Denver and Gilmer. Although acknowledging that "there is obviously some tension between these two lines of cases," the Court found it "unnecessary to resolve the question of the validity of a union-negotiated waiver."

Instead, the Wright Court scrutinized the language of the arbitration agreement and refused to interpret an arbitration clause as mandating arbitration of a statutorily protected right unless the language included a "clear and unmistakable" waiver. Regardless of the legality of a prospective waiver of a judicial forum for a civil rights claim, the Court ruled that, at the very least, such a waiver should be explicitly established. In this case, the arbitration clause contained in the CBA, which covered "all matters affecting wages, hours, and other terms and conditions of employment," did not explicitly include Wright's federal statutory employment discrimination claim. Accordingly, a unanimous Court vacated the Fourth Circuit's decision.

Wright is significant for a variety of reasons. It would have been easy for the Wright Court to cite developing circuit court precedent and refuse to uphold any union waiver of individual rights. The Court's failure to do so, however, suggests that the Court is hesitant to adopt the circuits' view, thus shrouding those opinions in doubt. Moreover, the Wright decision relies partly on the court's recognition of the importance of the right to a judicial forum, a right specifically discounted in Gilmer. By scrutinizing the language of arbitration agreements, the Court is acknowledging the importance of employees' right to a judicial forum by protecting against unknowing or unclear waivers. Finally, Wright creates a new avenue of attack for employees seeking access to a judicial forum.

The Court, however, significantly limited the application of the "clear and unmistakable" standard by scrutinizing only those arbitration clauses contained in CBAs, and not individual employment contracts. To be more effective, courts should extend the holding to situations involving individual employees. Individual employees need the protection offered by the "clear and unmistakable" standard because of their lack of bargaining power. To safeguard employees from forcibly signing an arbitration agreement as a condition of employment, at a minimum courts should require the waiver of substantive rights to be readily apparent to the employee. Accordingly, the potential force and impact of Wright will not be felt until a future court extends the "clear and unmistakable" principle to a non-unionized employee.

B. The EEOC and the Circumvention of Mandatory Arbitration

The Equal Employment Opportunity Commission ("EEOC") is the administrative body responsible for the enforcement of Title VII, the ADA, and the ADEA. If the EEOC finds that reasonable cause exists to believe that discrimination occurred, it may elect to pursue the claim in federal court. The interplay between EEOC-led suits on behalf of aggrieved employees and mandatory arbitration agreements has placed the courts in a unique position. Questions exist as to how an arbitration agreement affects the EEOC's responsibilities to an individual employee. In *EEOC v. Waffle House, Inc.*, the Supreme Court sought to resolve the confusion.

Believing that Waffle House employee Baker was wrongfully discharged in violation of the ADA, the EEOC filed suit seeking both broad injunctive relief against discriminatory employment practices and appropriate relief for Baker. In response, Waffle House moved to compel arbitration pursuant to Baker's signed application form which contained an arbitration clause. The United States Court of Appeals for the Fourth Circuit held that the EEOC may seek injunctive relief in the federal forum, but that the FAA policy favoring arbitration outweighs the EEOC's right to seek victim-specific relief on behalf of Baker.

In a 6-3 decision, the Supreme Court reversed the Fourth Circuit and ruled that the existence of a mandatory arbitration agreement did not limit the remedies available to the EEOC. The Court stated that the EEOC has the statutory authority to request compensatory and punitive damages, and there is no language suggesting that the presence of an employee arbitration agreement "materially changes" the EEOC's statutory function or rights. The Court concluded that the EEOC has independent statutory authority, is "the master of its own case," and should, therefore, be unaffected by an arbitration agreement to which it is not a party. Accordingly, the EEOC has the discretion to pursue both injunctive and victim-specific relief regardless of whether employees themselves may be precluded from seeking such relief.

In a lengthy dissent, Justice Thomas, joined by Justice Scalia and Chief Justice Rehnquist, suggests that the majority opinion is unprincipled and lacks statutory support. The Justice disagrees "that the EEOC may do on behalf of an employee that which an employee has agreed not to do for himself." Justice Thomas believes that allowing an employee "two bites at the apple—one in arbitration and one in litigation conducted by the EEOC" is inappropriate and in contravention of the FAA. The Justice observes that the end result of the majority's opinion is to discourage the use of arbitration agreements, therefore contradicting the intent of Congress embodied in the pro-arbitration FAA.

Despite the dissenters, the Supreme Court in Waffle House provides another limited avenue for employees with discrimination claims to avoid being compelled to arbitrate. While Wright and Waffle House evidence a growing concern among members of the Supreme Court, the modern landscape of mandatory arbitration has little room for change. For this reason, it is important to propose and examine other potential developments with the hope that employees get their "bite at the apple."

V. EMPOWERING EMPLOYEES TO PRESERVE THEIR RIGHTS

The Supreme Court has taken few steps to alleviate the tension between the FAA's pro-arbitration policy and the concern for proper enforcement of employment anti-discrimination statutes. The Wright decision safeguards employees from hidden and/or vague arbitration agreements, ensuring that such agreements are "clear and unmistakable." Although the "clear and unmistakable" standard is a step in the right direction, it is limited to the labor union context and has yet to be applied to individual employment contracts.

In Waffle House, the Court ruled that the EEOC can pursue victim-specific relief on behalf of employees who have otherwise waived the right to a judicial forum through an arbitration agreement. The Waffle House decision, however, has very little practical significance because of the EEOC's limited resources. Thus, even though Waffle House establishes an opportunity for an employee to circumvent an arbitration agreement, that opportunity is not readily available.

Other avenues exist that may also help employees get their "bite at the apple." The FAA states that an arbitration clause is valid and enforceable "save upon such grounds as exist at law or in equity for the revocation of any contract." Based on this language, courts may scrutinize arbitration clauses using common law contract principles without offending the purpose of the FAA. One such principle is the doctrine of unconscionability.

The most notable example of the unconscionability rationale comes from the United States Court of Appeals for the Ninth Circuit in *Circuit City Stores v. Adams.* The court determined that Circuit City's arbitration clause was procedurally unconscionable because it was a form contract, was drafted by the party with superior bargaining power, and was presented to prospective employees on a take-it-or-leave-it basis. The court also found the agreement substantively unconscionable for the following reasons:

1. the agreement was not bilateral;
2. the agreement limited the relief available to aggrieved employees that was otherwise available under the state discrimination statutes; and
3. the arbitration clause required Adams to split the arbitration fees with Circuit City.

Circuit City shows that courts may closely scrutinize arbitration agreements for terms that unfairly skew arbitration in favor of the employer.

Courts are responsible for determining whether or not a specific dispute is within the scope of the agreement, and they have used that authority when refusing to compel arbitration of statutory claims. The Wright Court's development of the "clear and unmistakable" standard is an example of how courts may construe strictly the scope of an arbitration agreement. New Jersey crafted a standard similar to Wright in *Quigley v. KPMG Peat Marwick, LLP*. The arbitration clause in question required arbitration of "any claim or controversy . . . arising out of or relating to this Agreement or the breach thereof, or in any way related to the terms and conditions" of employment. Although seemingly a broad and inclusive agreement, the court determined that when the waiver of the right to a jury trial in favor of arbitration is involved, the arbitration clause should "clearly state its purpose" and "any waiver of a statutory right "must be clearly and unmistakably established.' "

A "clear and unmistakable" waiver standard will protect employees from signing an unsuspecting waiver and help them to better understand their rights regarding arbitration. This solution, however, is merely short-term patchwork. Employers can easily revamp their arbitration clauses to specifically include statutory claims such as Title VII. A larger problem, however, still exists: even if faced with an explicit arbitration clause, employees must sign the agreement if they want a job.

As the number of employers requiring employees to sign mandatory arbitration agreements increases, the debate on the application of arbitration agreements to statutory claims continues with fervor. A major concern is the conflict between the supposed "voluntary" nature of arbitration and the lack of employee leverage to refuse or renegotiate an arbitration clause. Many courts cite Gilmer with approval as they enforce agreements to arbitrate Title VII and ADA claims. It is important, however, to establish a middle ground where the pro-arbitration Gilmer policy can be preserved while ensuring that the arbitration process is truly "voluntary." After all, "American workers should not be forced to choose between their jobs and their civil rights." . . .

CONCLUSION

. . . The ongoing scrutiny of the arbitration machinery offered throughout this analysis is not intended to cast doubt on its utility and value. When viewed in light of the important civil rights initiatives bestowed upon employers and employees by Congress, however, the potential drawbacks of arbitration appear costly. Congress clearly provided employees victimized by workplace discrimination an opportunity for vindication in federal court. This is not to say that arbitration is never a suitable alternative, but rather that barring the option of a judicial forum limits the overall effectiveness with which these important statutes can be enforced. Although it is impractical to preclude the use of arbitration agreements in employment contracts and CBAs across the board, it is important to tighten the reins on the commandeering use of such agreements by employers. Specifically, resort to arbitration with regard to civil rights claims should be the product of a mutual agreement rather than be forced upon employees as a condition of employment. A way to accomplish this is for courts to enforce anti-retaliation statutes against employers for taking action against an individual for refusing to sign away the statutory right to trial. A retaliation claim does not represent two bites at the same apple, but rather a sensible inroad to the restoration of employee rights guaranteed by Congress.

END NOTE

1. *Steelworkers v. Warrior & Gulf Navigation Co.,* 363 U.S. 574, 578 (1960).

ARTICLE 5.5

Title VII's Participation Clause and *Circuit City Stores v. Adams*

Edward A. Marshall

I. INTRODUCTION

The Supreme Court's recent decision in *Circuit City Stores, Inc. v. Adams* signified not the conception, but the affirmation of a principle [contrary] to the effectiveness of Title VII. For years, a majority of the federal courts of appeals recognized that the Federal Arbitration Act's (FAA) strong presumption in favor of arbitrability extended to pre-dispute arbitration clauses in most employment contracts. In line with this presumption, these courts have discerned nothing in the text, legislative history, or purposes underlying Title VII mandating an exception for the civil rights statute. Indeed, prior to Circuit City only the Ninth Circuit had declined to enforce compulsory arbitration of Title VII claims, reasoning that the FAA's exclusion of "contracts of employment of seamen, railroad employees, or any other class of workers engaged in foreign or interstate commerce" removed all contracts of employment from the ambit of the statute's presumption in support of arbitration. Despite its congruence with the approach taken by a majority of the circuits, the Supreme Court's decision in Circuit City is perhaps the most monumental abrogation of the efficacy of Title VII since the statute's inception.

Numerous commentators and scholars have urged that, by approving the arbitration of employment disputes, Circuit City struck a significant blow to the ability of Title VII to vindicate society's interest in preventing and remedying workplace discrimination. Most of these authors, however, have focused almost exclusively on the disadvantages associated with the arbitration forum, such as the "repeat player" phenomenon and limited discovery, while virtually ignoring the impact of compulsory arbitration on employees' substantive rights under Title VII. This Article confronts one such substantive deprivation, the ability of employers to use compulsory arbitration to unilaterally eviscerate the protection from employer retaliation guaranteed by Title VII's participation clause.

What are the several disadvantages of arbitration for the ordinary plaintiff?

In practice, if not by design, Title VII places the initial burden of enforcing its substantive provisions upon the individual victims of workplace discrimination. Although the Equal Employment Opportunity Commission ("EEOC." or "the Commission"), has the authority to investigate and commence claims on its own initiative, it does so with pronounced infrequency.

Indeed, statistics indicate that the Commission files less than one percent of the total charges filed each year and "even among the cases where it finds reasonable cause, the [Commission] files suit in less than five percent of those cases." Appreciating the substantial role aggrieved employees must play in bringing an employer's discriminatory practices to light, Congress crafted Title VII to provide individual actors with virtually absolute protection from employer retaliation when the employees make charges, testify, or "participate in any manner" in an EEOC investigation or court proceeding (the "participation clause"). As the courts recognize, such "exceptionally broad protection" is necessary to "ensure not only that employers cannot intimidate their employees into foregoing the Title VII grievance process, but also that investigators will have access to the unchilled testimony of witnesses."

Significantly, however, courts have consistently, and somewhat controversially, held that this broad protection from employer reprisal does not attach to employees who act outside the "statutory machinery" of Title VII or file complaints or testify in an employer's own, internal grievance process. This denial of absolute retaliation protection to employees acting outside of the EEOC and the judicial system leaves employees forced into compulsory arbitration—a "private form of justice"—without the protections from reprisal that have long been recognized as essential to the effective enforcement of Title VII. With more employers seeking to impose pre-dispute arbitration agreements on their employees as a result of the Court's decision in Circuit City and more courts willing to hold that Title VII claims fall within the scope of disputes that may be subject to compulsory arbitration, this denial of participation clause protection to employees engaged in internal processes of dispute resolution may substantially impede the effectiveness of Title VII. . . .

II. *CIRCUIT CITY STORES V. ADAMS*: COMPULSORY ARBITRATION UNDER TITLE VII

A. Antecedents to the Circuit City Decision

One can hardly appreciate the effect of Circuit City on the arbitrability of statutory antidiscrimination claims without a clear understanding of the law as it stood before the Supreme Court's 2001 decision. A historical evaluation of the Court's treatment of arbitration of such claims must begin with its unanimous 1974 holding in *Alexander v. Gardner-Denver*, a decision that reflected the Court's strong reservations regarding the ability of arbitration to effectively vindicate society's interest in maintaining a discrimination-free workplace.

1. Gardner-Denver

Gardner-Denver involved allegations by a black employee that he was terminated on the basis of his race in violation of Title VII. Prior to filing a charge with the EEOC, the plaintiff had sought arbitration under the union's collective bargaining agreement, asserting that he was "unjustly discharged." After the employee filed a charge with the EEOC but before the issuance of a "right to sue" letter, the arbitrator under the collective bargaining agreement held that the plaintiff was "discharged for cause." Due to this prior resolution of the plaintiff's claim in arbitration, the district court dismissed his lawsuit, holding that the employee had waived his right to a judicial proceeding under Title VII by resolving his claim in arbitration. The Tenth Circuit affirmed.

The Supreme Court, however, unanimously reversed the dismissal of the plaintiff's suit, holding that, by submitting his complaint to arbitration under a collective bargaining agreement, the plaintiff did not waive his right to resolve the allegations of discrimination in a judicial forum. Beginning by acknowledging the substantial role federal courts play under the statutory framework, and noting that Title VII was silent as to whether an arbitral decision divests the federal courts of jurisdiction, the Court continued:

> We think it clear that there can be no prospective waiver of an employee's rights under Title VII. . . . Title VII's strictures are absolute and represent a congressional command that each employee be free from discriminatory practices. Of necessity, the rights conferred can form no part of the collective-bargaining process since waiver of these rights would defeat the paramount congressional purpose behind Title VII.

The Court further explained that an employee's statutory right to be free from discrimination and any contractual rights to discharge only "for cause," while complementary, were distinct. While it was the arbitrator's prerogative to enforce the terms of the collective bargaining agreement in an effort to maintain industrial peace, such contractually-conferred authority did not permit the arbiter to resolve statutory employment discrimination claims "regardless of whether . . . contractual rights are similar to, or duplicative of, [those] secured by Title VII."

The Court in Gardner-Denver, however, did not end its analysis with a recitation of the differences inherent between rights contractually granted an employee under a collective bargaining agreement and those under Title VII. The Court continued by emphasizing that arbitration, with its less "complete" record, discovery, and evidentiary rules, was an inappropriate forum for resolving statutory discrimination claims. . . .

Due in no small part to this clear assessment of arbitration as an inappropriate forum to resolve Title VII disputes, the circuit courts in the years following Gardner-Denver consistently held that pre-dispute arbitration agreements could not force employees to waive their right to judicial resolution of their claims under Title VII. Thus, although courts continued to approve compulsory arbitration of statutory claims outside the employment context it was no doubt a surprise to the legal community when the Supreme Court, in *Gilmer v. Interstate/ Johnson Lane Corp.*, held that an employee could be compelled to submit age discrimination claims arising under the ADEA to mandatory arbitration.

2. Gilmer

The plaintiff in Gilmer, a manager of financial services for the defendant-employer, was required to register with the New York Stock Exchange (NYSE). The NYSE registration application provided, through reference to NYSE Rules, that claims arising out of the applicant's employment would be subject to binding arbitration. When the plaintiff was fired at 62 years of age and brought suit against his employer alleging age discrimination in violation of the ADEA, the employer filed a motion to compel arbitration. The district court denied the motion, relying principally on the Supreme Court's decision in Gardner-Denver. The Fourth Circuit reversed.

The Supreme Court affirmed the Fourth Circuit's decision, agreeing that the FAA's strong presumption in favor of arbitrability applied to the dispute and that, as such, "the burden is on Gilmer to show that Congress intended to preclude a waiver of a judicial forum" under the ADEA; such intent would be "discoverable in the text of the [statute], its legislative history, or [in] an "inherent conflict' between arbitration and the [statute's] underlying purposes." After noting that Gilmer conceded that neither the text nor the legislative history of the ADEA precluded arbitration of disputes arising under the statute, the Court rejected the plaintiff's argument that the arbitral forum was inconsistent with the purposes underlying the ADEA. The Court began by asserting the general principle that, "by agreeing to arbitrate a statutory claim, a party does not forgo the substantive rights afforded by the statute; it only submits to their resolution in an arbitral, rather than a judicial, forum." It continued by noting that both arbitration and judicial resolution of discrimination claims vindicate the individual complainant's interest as well as the interests of society as a whole. The Court also asserted that compulsory arbitration did not undermine the interest of the EEOC in enforcing the ADEA, because a "claimant subject to an arbitration agreement will still be free to file a charge with the [Commission.]" . . .

While a striking departure from Gardner-Denver's apparent rejection of arbitration as a proper forum for resolving statutory employment claims, the Court's holding in Gilmer, standing alone, was arguably one of little practical importance to most employees. As Justice White, writing for the majority, emphasized, the arbitration clause in question appeared not in an employment contract, but in an application to register with the NYSE. As a result, the majority declined to resolve the more broadly applicable question of whether Section 1 of the FAA, which precludes the application of the statute to cases involving "contracts of employment of seamen, railroad employees, or any other class of workers engaged in foreign or interstate commerce[,]" shielded employment contracts generally from the FAA's strong presumption in favor of arbitrability.

If that question were answered in the affirmative, then employees could avoid compulsory arbitration of statutory employment claims without bearing the arduous burden of demonstrating a textual, historical, or "inherent" conflict between the arbitral forum and the statute in question that the Gilmer Court indicated would show that Congress intended to preclude a waiver of the judicial forum. Free from the "healthy regard for the federal policy favoring arbitration" compelled by the FAA, the courts could reject compulsory arbitration as inconsistent with the congressional goals underlying Title VII, just as the Supreme Court had apparently done years before in Gardner-Denver. The Court, however, determined that Section 1 of the FAA did not exempt all employment contracts from compulsory arbitration in *Circuit City Stores, Inc. v. Adams.*

B. *Circuit City Stores v. Adams*

Why is this case particularly controversial?

Saint Clair Adams, when applying for a job at Circuit City Stores, signed an employment application providing that all claims arising out of his employment would be subject to mutually binding, mandatory arbitration. Two years after being hired as a sales counselor, Adams filed numerous claims in state court alleging employment discrimination in violation of California law. In response, Circuit City filed suit in federal court seeking to enjoin the state action and compel arbitration of Adam's claims pursuant to the FAA. The District Court granted the employer's request. The Ninth Circuit reversed, reasoning that Section 1 of the FAA rendered the statute inapplicable to Adam's case.

The Supreme Court, however, noting that "the Ninth Circuit's conclusion that all employment contracts are excluded from the FAA conflicts with every other Court of Appeals to have addressed the question[,]" held in a five-to-four decision that "Section 1 exempts from the FAA only contracts of employment of transportation workers." Justice Kennedy, writing for the majority, explained that the Court's limited interpretation of the FAA's exclusionary provision was rooted in the text of Section 1 itself. The majority stated that the language in Section 1 demanded application of the statutory canon of "ejusdem generis," which provides that "where general words follow specific words in a statutory enumeration, the general words are construed to embrace only objects similar in nature to those objects enumerated by the preceding specific words." Here, according to Justice Kennedy, that canon required the exclusion of "contracts of employment of seamen, railroad employees, or any other class of workers engaged in foreign or interstate commerce[,]" be construed to "give effect to the terms "seamen" and "railroad employees," and thus, precluded an interpretation that would "exclude all contracts of employment" from the FAA's strong presumption in support of arbitration."

Moreover, the Court rejected the contention that the phrase "any other class of workers engaged in foreign or interstate commerce" mandated a different result. The Court reasoned that, while the phrases "affecting commerce" and "involving commerce" demonstrated congressional intent to use plenary power under the Commerce Clause, the phrase "engaged in commerce" evidenced "a much more limited intent." Nor was the Court persuaded by Adams' argument that the phrase "engaged in . . . interstate commerce" should be interpreted more broadly due to the Court's restrictive interpretation of the Commerce Clause at the inception of the FAA in 1925. Such a "variable standard for interpreting common, jurisdictional phrases[,]" reasoned the Court, "would contradict our earlier cases and bring instability to statutory interpretation."

Notably absent from the majority's analysis in Circuit City was any extended discussion of the policy ramifications of its decision on the resolution of employment discrimination claims. Instead, its conclusions seemed to rest primarily, if not exclusively, on principles of statutory construction. It would be inaccurate, however, to assume that the Court was unaware of the effects compulsory arbitration would have on claimants alleging unlawful discrimination in the employment setting. To the contrary, Justice Kennedy acknowledged the plaintiff's assertions that arbitration was an inappropriate forum to resolve employment disputes, but explained:

> We have been clear in rejecting the supposition that the advantages of the arbitration process somehow disappear when transferred to the employment context. Arbitration agreements allow parties to avoid the costs of litigation, a benefit that may be of particular importance in employment litigation, which often involves smaller sums of money than disputes concerning commercial contracts. These litigations costs to parties (and the accompanying burden to the Courts) would be compounded by the difficult choice-of-law questions that are often presented in disputes arising from the employment relationship[.] The considerable complexity and uncertainty that the construction of 1 urged by respondent would introduce into the enforceability of arbitration agreements in employment contracts would call into doubt the efficacy of alternative dispute resolution procedures adopted by many of the Nation's employers, in the process undermining the FAA's proarbitration purposes and breeding litigation from a statute that seeks to avoid it.

Thus, notwithstanding the clear reservations expressed in Gardner-Denver regarding the inappropriateness of resolving federal anti-discrimination claims in the arbitral forum, the majority in Circuit City unambiguously rejected the Ninth Circuit's more expansive reading of Section 1 of the Federal Arbitration Act, holding that the Act's presumption in favor of arbitration extended to virtually all contracts of employment. What remained unclear, however, was the role the EEOC was to play in the resolution of grievances filed by workers subject to mandatory, binding arbitration of their discrimination claims. That issue was to be resolved the following year in *EEOC v. Waffle House, Inc.*

C. The Waffle House "Exception"

The Supreme Court's holding in Circuit City, while unambiguously extending the FAA's strong presumption in favor of arbitrability to arbitration clauses in "a broad range of employment contracts[,]" left a myriad of unanswered questions. Among these was whether an agreement between an employee and employer to arbitrate employment claims precluded the EEOC from seeking "victim-specific judicial relief, such as back pay, reinstatement, and damages, in an enforcement action" pursuant to its authority under federal employment discrimination laws. The Sixth Circuit held that an arbitration agreement between an employee and employer could not bind the EEOC as a nonparty to the agreement, but the Second and Fourth Circuits took a contrary position, holding that "the policy goals expressed in the FAA required giving some effect to . . . arbitration agreements." Those circuits, in an attempt to "balance" the policies underlying the FAA and those expressed in statutory antidiscrimination laws, held that the EEOC was restricted to seeking "large-scale injunctive relief" when the aggrieved employees were bound by arbitration agreements, as it was only in that circumstance that the EEOC's primary focus was the vindication of broad, public interests, rather than merely the private interests of the arbitration-bound employee.

The Supreme Court rejected this "balancing" approach in *EEOC v. Waffle House, Inc.*, by holding that "the EEOC has the authority to pursue victim-specific relief regardless of the forum that the employer and the employee have chosen to resolve their disputes[.]" In Waffle House, the EEOC brought suit on behalf of Baker, a former Waffle House employee, alleging that he was terminated due to his disabilities in violation of the Americans with Disabilities Act ("ADA"). While recognizing that the suit arose under the ADA, the Court explained that, since the EEOC's enforcement powers under the ADA mirrored those granted under Title VII, "the provisions of Title VII defining the EEOC's authority provide the starting point for our analysis."

The Court began its analysis by acknowledging that the 1972 amendments to Title VII "created a system in which the EEOC was intended "to bear the primary burden of litigation[.]' " With this congressional grant of authority as a backdrop, the Court explained that this congressional intent was not "trumped" by the FAA:

Nothing in the [Federal Arbitration Act] authorizes a court to compel arbitration of any issues, or by any parties, that are not already covered in the agreement. The FAA does not mention enforcement by public agencies; it ensures the enforceability of private agreements to arbitrate, but otherwise does not purport to place any restriction on a nonparty's choice of a judicial forum.

Justice Stevens, writing for the majority, further explained that "if it were true that the EEOC could prosecute its claim only with Baker's consent, or if its prayer for relief could be dictated by Baker, the [appellate] court's analysis might be persuasive." According to the majority, however, "the exact opposite is true"—the ADA establishes the EEOC as "master of its own case and confers on the agency the authority to evaluate the strength of the public interest at stake." Relying on that statutory grant of independent authority, as well as the FAA's failure to expressly bind nonparties to an arbitration agreement, the Court concluded that "the pro-arbitration policy goals of the FAA do not require the [EEOC] to relinquish its statutory authority if it has not agreed to do so." Thus, while the Court in Waffle House left undisturbed an employer's ability to bind employees to resolution of their employment discrimination disputes in the arbitral forum, it simultaneously rejected any limitation on the EEOC's authority to prosecute charges of discrimination in the traditional judicial arena.

III. AN OVERVIEW OF THE TITLE VII RETALIATION CLAUSE: PROTECTED ACTIVITY

In addition to protecting employees from discrimination based on race, color, religion, sex, or national origin, Title VII also prohibits certain forms of employer retaliation. [It] provides, in pertinent part, that:

> It shall be an unlawful employment practice for an employer to discriminate against any of his employees or applicants for employment . . . because he has opposed any practice made an unlawful employment practice by this subchapter, or because he has made a charge, testified, assisted, or participated in any manner in an investigation, proceeding, or hearing under this subchapter. . . .

A. The Participation Clause

Title VII's participation clause protects employees who file charges with, testify, or participate in an EEOC, state administrative, or court proceeding or investigation. The federal judiciary has long recognized these activities as "essential to the machinery set up by Title VII[,]" and, accordingly, extended "exceptionally broad protection" to these activities under the participation clause. Indeed, courts have even held that "protection [under the participation clause] is not lost if the employee is wrong on the merits of the charge, nor is protection lost if the contents of the charge are malicious and defamatory as well as wrong." vel non of the participation clause should not turn on the substance of the testimony. . . .

Given this traditionally rigid distinction between charges and testimony made within the "statutory machinery" of Title VII and those made in "internal," private contexts, it is likely that the vast majority of employee activity in compulsory arbitration—a "private form of justice"—will not be protected under the participation clause. As a result, such activity may only receive the diluted retaliation protection provided by the statute's "opposition clause."

B. The Opposition Clause

In contrast to the narrow range of activities protected under Title VII's participation clause, the opposition clause potentially shields employees from employer reprisal when engaging in a broad array of activities, ranging from internal complaints to outright protest. The retaliation protections under the opposition clause, however, are not inviolate. Instead, to constitute "protected activity" under the opposition clause, an employee's conduct must take a reasonable form, and be directed at employer conduct the employee reasonably perceives to be unlawful.

In defining the contours of a "reasonable" form of activity, the courts have traditionally balanced the employee's right to oppose unlawful employer conduct and the interest of society in enforcement of Title VII against the employer's need to maintain productivity and stability in the workplace. Thus, the courts have found that filing internal complaints in compliance with an employer's established grievance procedures is a reasonable form of employee opposition. On the other hand, an illegal protest, such as an unlawful stall-in, may constitute an unreasonable form of employee opposition. Notably, however, an employee who bypasses the established channels of an employer's complaint procedure to file an internal charge may be lawfully terminated by the employer for an unreasonable form of opposition.

More important for the purposes of this Article, however, the courts have traditionally held that an employee's conduct is not protected under the opposition clause unless the employee is challenging an employer practice he reasonably and in good faith believes to be a violation of Title VII. Though courts have not required that the challenged employer practice actually be unlawful for the employee to receive opposition clause protection, they have recognized that the language of the clause, requiring opposition to "any practice made an unlawful employment practice by this subchapter," only extends to actions by employees who have a reasonable and good faith basis for believing an employer's conduct violates Title VII.

C. The Implications of *Clark County School District v. Breeden*

In *Clark County School District v. Breeden*, a female employee brought suit under Title VII alleging, inter alia, that she had been unlawfully transferred for making an internal complaint regarding perceived sexual harassment by one of her supervisors. According to the plaintiff, during a meeting to evaluate job applicants at which she was present, her supervisor related an instance wherein an applicant had told a co-worker, "I hear making love to you is like making love to the Grand Canyon." When the supervisor commented that he did not understand the meaning of the simile, a co-worker of the plaintiff replied, "Well, I'll tell you later," and both men began to laugh. The Supreme Court, in a unanimous per curiam decision, reversed the Ninth Circuit's holding that genuine issues of fact remained as to whether the plaintiff had engaged in "protected activity" by relating the incident to her employer. . . .

Significantly, the Supreme Court in Breeden determined that no one could reasonably believe that the supervisor's conduct violated Title VII only after surveying over a decade of precedent that established the standard for determining whether a supervisor had engaged in actionable sexual harassment under the statute. According to the Court, this line of cases clarified that activity is sexual harassment in violation of Title VII "only if it is so severe or pervasive as to alter the conditions of [the victim's] employment and create an abusive working environment." Moreover, the Court reiterated that, in order to establish a violation of the statute, an employee must demonstrate not only that she subjectively perceived the behavior as sufficiently severe or pervasive, but also that the conduct was "so objectively offensive as to alter the "conditions' of [her] employment[,]" explaining that "[a] recurring point in [our] opinions is that simple teasing, offhand comments, and isolated incidents (unless extremely serious) will not amount to discriminatory changes in the "terms and conditions of employment.'" It was only with these prior holdings as a backdrop that the Court concluded that "no reasonable person could have believed that the single incident recounted [by the plaintiff] violated Title VII's standard." . . . The implications of the Court's reasoning in Breeden emphatically reinforce[s] the Ninth Circuit's admonition a decade earlier: "Accusations made in the context of charges before the Commission are protected by [Title VII]; charges outside of that context are made at the accuser's peril."

IV. AN ASSAULT ON THE EFFICACY OF TITLE VII

A. Concerns Related to the Arbitral Forum

The great weight of scholarly commentary relating to the inability of Title VII to function effectively under a system of compulsory arbitration has concentrated on the characteristics of the arbitral forum. Authors have urged that, at least without adequate policing by the courts, mandatory arbitration possesses several attributes likely to disadvantage complainants while favoring employers, rendering the arbitral forum inappropriate for the resolution of statutory employment claims. First, critics of compulsory pre-dispute arbitration agreements in the employment setting urge that arbitrators may be biased, either consciously or unconsciously, in favor of "repeat player" employers. These commentators explain that the employer's control over the selection of arbitrators "may produce [a] . . . bias toward the only party who offers arbitrators the prospect of repeat business." Second, critics of mandatory arbitration contend that the limited discovery procedures available in the arbitral forum provide employees inadequate access to the employer-controlled information essential to demonstrate workplace discrimination, creating a "major impediment to successful prosecution of meritorious claims." Third, these critics note that many employers impose fee-splitting agreements, the costs of which will preclude, or at least dissuade, some employees from pursuing the arbitration of their statutory claims. . . .

In addition to these "external" restraints, internal standards adopted by arbitration associations may also alleviate the potential pro-employer bias of arbitration. For example, representatives of the National Academy of Arbitrators, the American Arbitration Association (AAA), the Society of Professionals in Dispute Resolution, and the Labor and Employment Law Section of the American Bar Association have developed the Due Process Protocol for Mediation and Arbitration of Statutory Disputes Arising Out of the Employment Relationship (the "Protocol"). The Protocol attempts to augment judicial efforts to reduce such bias by setting forth standards to help ensure a fairer arbitral forum. Among these standards are recommendations that the arbitration agreement be "knowingly made[,]" that neutral arbitrators preside over hearings, that the employee be permitted to select a representative of his choosing, and that such representative have access to "all relevant information in connection with a claim, despite the limited pretrial discovery utilized in arbitration." Although the Protocol lacks binding effect, the organizations that promulgated the standards have attempted to ensure compliance with the recommendations, and the AAA has reserved the right to refuse to provide arbitrators to programs that fall below the standards set forth in the Protocol.

Despite these judicial and private efforts to eliminate arbitration procedures that inadequately protect the rights of employees, the arbitration process has not been "cleansed" of its pro-employer bias. Perhaps most importantly, courts, in order to preserve the efficiency and cost-effectiveness of the arbitral forum, have upheld arbitration agreements that contain relatively austere discovery rules. Indeed, some courts have even upheld agreements limiting discovery "to one deposition and those documents which are clearly relevant and material to the dispute and for which the party has a substantial, demonstrable need." In the context of employment discrimination, where access to employer-controlled information is frequently essential to the establishing a claim, such limited discovery may seriously impede an employee's chances of prevailing in arbitration. As the Supreme Court noted in Gilmer, however, "by agreeing to arbitrate, a party trades the procedures and opportunity for review of the courtroom for the simplicity, informality, and expedition of arbitration."

These criticisms are not to imply, however, that the new system of compulsory arbitration fails to confer any benefit upon employees. Proponents of mandatory arbitration urge that judicial enforcement of pre-dispute arbitration agreements may provide aggrieved employees with greater access to fora in which to resolve their disputes . . . Judicial resolution of employment claims is inaccessible to many employees due to the difficulty of finding willing counsel and the exorbitant cost of litigation. Indeed, scholars have estimated that, under the current system, as few as five percent of workers with employment claims succeed at obtaining counsel. Since arbitration typically involves significantly reduced expenditure of time and resources by attorneys, the availability of the arbitral forum may significantly increase the probability that particularly aggrieved employees will find their way to an arena for the resolution of their grievances. Thus, while the arbitral forum itself may disadvantage employees, a system of pre-dispute compulsory arbitration . . . "stands a better chance of providing Saturns for average claimants, in place of the rickshaws now available to the many so that a few can drive Cadillacs." . . .

B. Concerns Related to the Inadequate Protection from Retaliation

1. Predictable Effects of the Denial of Participation Clause Protection

Despite congressional steps to provide the EEOC with a more substantial role in initiating Title VII litigation, individual employee action remains the prime vehicle for achieving the statute's goal of the elimination of invidious employer discrimination. In order for Title VII to be effective, employees must make Title VII claims and fellow employees must participate in these claims. Due to the crucial role of aggrieved employees and employee-witnesses in the enforcement of Title VII, the courts have long granted such actors virtually absolute protection from employer reprisal under the participation clause. Denying the same protection to employees forced to bring claims and testify in the arbitral forum may drastically reduce the effectiveness of the statute, especially since compulsory arbitration is likely to proliferate exponentially in the wake of Court's recent decision in Circuit City.

Employer retaliation is a very real and disturbingly pervasive problem in the modern workplace. EEOC records reveal that, over the past decade, the number of retaliation charges filed with the Commission has nearly doubled, rising from 10,499 in 1992 to 20,407 in 2001.[1] Researchers have demonstrated that these allegations of employer reprisal for challenges to allegedly unlawful practices may be well-founded. Studies of sexual harassment victims, for example, demonstrate that between thirty-three to sixty-two percent of women who filed a complaint against a supervisor were subjected to some form of employer retaliation, including lower job evaluations and termination. While little research has been done to verify similar trends in the arbitration context, such employer reprisal is not likely to be a phenomenon relegated to the internal complaint setting. Indeed, prior research has demonstrated that more assertive responses by complainants to perceived workplace discrimination correlates to a higher risk of resulting retaliation. If that is the case, then one would expect a greater probability of employer reprisal if an employee filed a demand to arbitrate than if she lodged a more informal, internal complaint. If aggrieved employees have only the protection of the opposition clause against retaliation, they will be without redress unless they can demonstrate that their perception of unlawfulness comported with "existing substantive law" and that their employer lacked reasonable grounds to disbelieve them.

Perhaps more important than the actual frequency of employer retaliation, however, is the pervasiveness of the fear of retaliation among employees, and the resultant impact from such fear in dissuading employee action to combat workplace discrimination. Indeed, the court's understanding of the deterrent effect fear of reprisal might have on employees' willingness to come forward and report unlawful discrimination led the courts to provide "exceptionally broad protection" under the participation clause. . . .

Moreover, the conclusions of the Fourth Circuit were not merely the products of judicial speculation. Empirical data emphatically support the Glover court's conclusion that fear of employer reprisal greatly inhibits employee opposition to perceived unlawful discrimination. Research focusing on sexual harassment, for example, suggests that as many as eighty percent of women faced with harassment never report the conduct to their employer with the most common reason for the failure to report being fear of retaliation.[2]

Further, it is likely that this unsettling trend of underutilization in the internal complaint context will translate with equally disturbing potency to the arbitration setting. Indeed, despite the benefits commonly associated with arbitration, and contrary to the assertions that the availability of the arbitral forum would increase the number of complainants alleging discrimination, early research suggests that the imposition of compulsory arbitration often results in a decrease of employee claims.[3] While this reduction in claims may be the result of an amicable employee reaction to perceived conciliatory efforts by employers, studies of underutilization in the internal grievance context suggest that fear of employer reprisal is a reason, if not the primary reason, for this reduction.

Clearly, Title VII cannot effectively vindicate society's interest in achieving a workplace free from discrimination if employees are too afraid of employer reprisal to engage or participate in the arbitration forum; a forum that, as a result of Circuit City, may become the only available arena for the adjudication of discrimination claims for much of the American workforce. Yet, with only the austere support of the opposition clause providing redress, employees have a valid reason to fear such employer retaliation. Without Title VII's participation clause, employers may retaliate with impunity, so long as the employee's perception of unlawfulness falls short of what existing precedent deems violative of the statute, or when the employer believes the employee's testimony lacks veracity. Such inadequate protection can only feed the ubiquitous fears of employer reprisal that operate to inhibit employee action vital to the continued effectiveness of Title VII—a statute that relies principally, if not exclusively, on employee action to achieve the enforcement of its egalitarian mandate. . . .

V. CONCLUSION

Despite intensive scholarly commentary on the ramifications of the Court's recent decision in *Circuit City Stores, Inc. v. Adams*, one of the most inimical attributes of the holding has escaped adequate academic response. By allowing employers to foreclose employee access to the courts through pre-dispute arbitration agreements, Circuit City has relegated a growing number of employment discrimination claims to an arena that denies employees the absolute protections from employer reprisal consistently granted to those seeking resolution of their grievances in the judicial forum. This deprivation of unequivocal protection from retaliation may seriously hinder the effectiveness of Title VII, as many employees faced with only the austere guarantees of the opposition clause may be less likely to voice legitimate concerns about employer discrimination, and, as witnesses, may be less forthcoming with testimony against their employers. . . .

Since employees subject to compulsory arbitration are not likely to adequately facilitate the enforcement of Title VII, legislation overruling Circuit City and prohibiting the enforcement of pre-dispute arbitration agreements in the employment context may seem advisable. Advocates of this course of action, however, ignore the potential for compulsory arbitration to supply resolution mechanisms for a far greater number of employees than the judicial forum has been able to provide. Furthermore, they underestimate the ability of courts and private organizations to eventually eradicate the present pro-employer bias in the arbitral arena. Instead, Congress should provide employees involved in arbitration the same unequivocal protections from retaliation presently enjoyed by those seeking judicial resolution of their claims. Such congressional action is necessary to fully realize the benefits of increased access to dispute resolution forums while safeguarding the ability of the Title VII to effectively vindicate society's interest in maintaining a workplace free from invidious employer discrimination.

END NOTES

1. EEOC, Charge Statistics FY 1992 Through FY 2001. . . . In contrast, the total number of charges filed with the Commission (including those alleging retaliation) during the same time period increased less than 12%, from 72,302 in 1992 to 80,840 in 2001.
2. Shirley Feldman-Summers, Analyzing Anti-harassment Polities and Complaint Procedures: Do They Encourage Victims to Come Forward?, 16 Lab. Law. 307, 308 n. 9 (2000).
3. See David H. Gibbs, Employment Survey Says that Major Companies Increasingly Use Tailored Programs and Processes, 19 Alternatives to High Cost Litig. 237, 237.

ISSUE SUMMARY

Mandatory arbitration clauses are becoming more and more common in American business. Credit card companies now include mandatory arbitration clauses in their contracts; banks include the clauses in loan contracts; car dealerships include the clauses. The clauses are popping up left and right—not to mention all of the employers requiring their employees to sign binding arbitration clauses.

As you read in this chapter, a binding arbitration clause is not as simple as agreeing to use arbitration if you believe your employer intentionally miscalculated your overtime or failed to give you a break for six hours. Employers are now, with the help of the U.S. Supreme Court, requiring employees to sign away their rights to a day in court if the employer violates the employees' civil rights.

Understandably, many people disagree with the Court's opinion. You probably noticed the clear division of opinions surrounding this issue, but did you notice any attempts to establish common ground? Marshall acknowledged the merits of arbitration as an alternative to the judicial forum, and even praised arbitration for making it possible for more claims to be heard. Marshall then suggested ways to make arbitration better for employees pursuing Title VII claims.

Can you think of ways to make arbitration better for both employees and consumers? As mandatory arbitration clauses continue to increase in popularity, you are more and more likely to sign a binding arbitration clause. When you do sign one, what protections would you like to be afforded? What conditions do you want the employer or business to meet? How can we embrace the strengths of arbitration without surrendering the protections of the judicial system?

ISSUE HIGHLIGHTS

- Arbitration is a "simple proceeding voluntarily chosen by parties who want a dispute determined by an impartial judge of their own mutual selection, whose decision, based on the merits of the case, they agree in advance to accept as final and binding."
- Section 2 of the Federal Arbitration Act (FAA) renders arbitration agreements "valid, irrevocable, and enforceable." Section 3 provides that a party to an arbitration agreement can move to stay any court proceedings if the issue is covered by an arbitration agreement, and Section 4 permits that party to obtain an order to compel arbitration if the other party refuses to honor the agreement.

- "The Mitsubishi Trilogy" refers to three rulings by the U.S. Supreme Court in which the Court: (1) held that the FAA created a presumption of arbitrability favoring all arbitration agreements; (2) enforced agreements to arbitrate statutory claims based on antitrust, securities, and racketeering laws; (3) ruled that the FAA allowed for the arbitration of statutory claims unless Congress clearly indicated otherwise in the statutory language; and (4) held that an arbitration agreement precluded a Securities Act claim from being heard in a judicial forum.
- "The Steelworkers Trilogy" refers to three cases in which the U.S. Supreme Court: (1) officially endorsed arbitration in the labor setting; (2) created an "irrebuttable presumption" that employer-union disputes were arbitrable; and (3) discouraged judicial intervention in employment disputes governed by an arbitration agreement.
- In *Alexander v. Gardner-Denver Company*, the U.S. Supreme Court ruled that the arbitral forum was designed to resolve contract rights and was not appropriate for the resolution of federal statutory rights guaranteed by Title VII.
- In *Gilmer v. Interstate/Johnson Lane Corp.*, the U.S. Supreme Court ruled that the presumption of arbitrability announced in the "Mitsubishi Trilogy" included statutory employment discrimination claims, representing the first time the Supreme Court "held that a statutory civil rights claim can be subjected to mandatory arbitration."

CRITICAL THINKING

Legal reasoning is unlike any other form of reasoning you may have encountered in the classroom. Scientific reasoning (also known as empiricism) asks for proof that a claim is true (meaning that results have been gathered from a controlled experiment performed by impartial truth-seekers, and the experiment can be replicated by other impartial truth-seekers). Philosophical reasoning asks that an argument follow certain logical rules (such as, if A is not B, and B is C; then A is not C) to be deemed valid. Psychologists often use case studies as proof (if one person behaves a certain way under specified conditions, then other people may behave the same way under the same specified conditions). How would you characterize legal reasoning? Is it similar to scientific reasoning? Philosophical reasoning? The psychologists' reasoning?

Legal reasoning is largely reasoning by analogy. Arguing by analogy requires drawing a similarity between two things, and using that similarity to draw a conclusion about one of those things. Let's consider an example:

> Did you hear? Marcy and Jenna both got married last June, and now Marcy and her husband are getting a divorce. Marcy and Jenna were both so cute with their husbands, and they both wanted the same things—kids, houses, jobs. Jenna and her husband must be getting divorced soon too.

Start by breaking down the argument. What is the author trying to convince you to believe? She wants you to believe that Jenna must be getting divorced soon. Why does the author believe that Jenna is getting divorced soon? The author says that Jenna is just like Marcy, and Marcy is getting divorced. Therefore, in the author's mind, if Jenna is just like Marcy, and Marcy is getting divorced, then Jenna must get divorced too. Do you see a problem with the author's logic?

Analogies can be great tools; they help us connect our thoughts, and they enhance our understanding of the world around us. Analogies have limits though. Analogies are only as good as they are strong. What does that mean? To determine the strength of an analogy, think about the similarities between the two things being compared. In our example, think about what makes Jenna and Marcy similar. They got married at the same time; they want the same things; they were both cute wives.

Now think about the differences between the two things being compared. In our example, how are Marcy and Jenna different? Quite frankly, we don't know. It could be that Marcy and Jenna married two very different men. Marcy and Jenna could have very different temperaments. Marcy and Jenna could have different incomes, leading to different stress levels and lifestyles. Marcy and Jenna could have different support systems, also leading to different stress levels and marital relationships. We don't have enough information to determine whether Marcy and Jenna differ in significant ways.

When you've made your list of similarities and differences, compare the two. Are there more significant similarities or more significant differences? Do you need more information before you can answer the question? If you need more information, then you will not be able to determine the strength of the analogy. If there are more significant similarities than differences, then the analogy may be strong. If there are more significant differences than similarities, then the analogy may be weak. A strong analogy is more likely to convince you to believe the author's argument than is a weak analogy.

You may be wondering, "What does all of this have to do with legal reasoning?" When judges write their opinions, they tend to rely on one primary form of proof: precedent. What is precedent? Precedent is simply an earlier decision made by the same court or a different court. Precedent is an analogy. The logic is that the court ruled one way in a past case, therefore the court should rule the same way in the current case. Your job as a critical thinker is to ask whether the court's analogy is appropriate. Are there enough similarities to make the analogy a strong one? Or is the court relying on a weak analogy to support its argument?

Let's look at an example from this chapter. In the first selection of the chapter, *Gilmer*, the court dismisses several arguments made by Gilmer. One of Gilmer's arguments is that arbitration of an ADEA claim is unfair because the employer has significantly more power than the employee. The Court cites two pieces of case law as precedent to support its finding that unequal bargaining power is not sufficient reason to deem the arbitration unenforceable. The pieces of case law cited are *Rodriguez de Quijas* and *McMahon*.

What do we know about these two cases? From the context of the decision, we know that (1) the cases involved securities dealers and investors; (2) there was unequal bargaining power between the parties; and (3) the court decided to enforce an arbitration agreement in spite of the unequal bargaining power. That isn't much information. Think about the circumstances surrounding *Gilmer.* How is *Gilmer* similar to the information we have about the precedent? Well, there is unequal bargaining power between Gilmer and his employer.

How is *Gilmer* different from *Rodriguez de Quijas* and *McMahon?* We know that *Gilmer* does not involve securities dealers or investors, but *Rodriguez de Quijas* and *McMahon* do. Beyond that, we know nothing. We do not know whether the degree of inequality in the bargaining power is similar in all three cases. We do not know whether the latter two cases involved mandatory arbitration clauses, civil rights claims, or employee-employer relationships. We do not know enough about the cases to determine whether they differ in any significant way.

So now what do we do? You could perform a quick search to read *Rodriguez de Quijas* and *McMahon*. In fact, courts will rarely give you all of the details you need to determine whether the analogies drawn with precedent are appropriate. If you want to determine the strength of the analogies, often you will need to be proactive and seek out the case law yourself. In other situations though, you can leave the questions unanswered. Simply remember that you cannot determine the merit of the reason involving the analogy if you cannot determine the strength of the analogy. In turn, this may mean you cannot determine the merit of the argument as a whole.

In this case, what will you do? If you find and read *Rodriguez de Quijas* and *McMahon*, look for significant similarities and differences. Determine whether the analogy is weak or strong. If you do not read *Rodriguez de Quijas* or *McMahon,* how will your assessment of the Court's reasoning in *Gilmer* be affected? Do you have enough information about the Court's other reasons to form an opinion?

ADDITIONAL READING RESOURCES

Richard A. Bales, "Beyond the Protocol: Recent Trends in Employment Arbitration," *Employee Rights & Employment Pol'y J.*, Vol. 12 (2007).

Richard A. Bales, "Contract Formation Issues in Employment Arbitration," *Brandeis L. J.*, 44, 415–461 (2006).

Richard A. Bales, "The Employment Due Process Protocol at Ten: Twenty Unresolved Issues, and a Focus on Conflicts of Interest," *Ohio St. J. on Disp. Resol.*, 21: 165 (2005).

Debra Berman & Douglas M. McCabe, "Compulsory Arbitration in Non-union Employee Relations: A Strategic Ethical Analysis," *J. Bus. Ethics*, 66: 2–3, 197–206 (2006).

Sandra F. Gavin, "Unconscionability Found: A Look at Pre-Dispute Mandatory Arbitration Agreements 10 Years after *Doctor's Associates, Inc. v. Casarotto*," *Clev. St. L. Rev*. 54: 249 (2006).

Jonnette Watson Hamilton, "Pre-Dispute Consumer Arbitration Clauses: Denying Access to Justice?" *McGill L. J.*, 51: 693 (2005).

Mara Kent, "Forced" vs. Compulsory Arbitration of Civil Rights Claims," *Law & Ineq.*, 23: 95 (2005).

Alan N. Resnick, "The Enforceability of Arbitration Clauses in Bankruptcy," *Am. Bankr. Inst. L. Rev*. 15: 183 (2007).

Angelito Remo Sevilla, "The End of Duffield and the Rise of Mandatory Arbitration: How Courts Misinterpreted the Civil Rights Act's Arbitration Provision," *Cal. L. Rev.*, 93: 323 (2005).

Kiren Dosanjh Zucker, "Retrieving What Was Luce: Why Courts Should Recognize Employees' Refusal of an Employer's Mandatory Arbitration Agreement as "Protected Activity" under Title VII's Antiretaliation Provision," *Lab. Law*, 22: 233 (2006).

For more information, check these sites:

http://www.adr.org/sp.asp?id=29568 (Full text of the Federal Arbitration Act) [*Last visited: July 7, 2008*]

https://www.law.uoregon.edu/org/olr/archives/83/Baker_83_3_861.pdf (Scott Baker, *A Risk-Based Approach to Mandatory Arbitration*) [*Last visited: July 7, 2008*]

http://www.citizen.org/congress/civjus/arbitration/articles.cfm?ID=7332 (Public Citizen) [*Last visited: July 7, 2008*]

http://www.naca.net/binding-mandatory-arbitration/ (National Association of Consumer Advocates) [*Last visited: July 7, 2008*]

http://www.cfpa.org/issues/issue.cfm/issue/MandatoryArbitration.xml (Center for Policy Alternatives) [*Last visited: July 7, 2008*]

ISSUE 6

Should the Law Allow a Business to Withhold Information from Consumers?

If your cell phone were giving you brain cancer, would you want to know? If you developed a brain tumor as a result of using your cell phone, would you sue the cell phone manufacturer? Assume you did sue the company. What would you do if you found out the company knew about the risk to your health but did nothing to protect you? Many companies have been caught in similar situations, having failed to disclose information that could have saved lives. In this chapter, we ask when manufacturers and sellers should be allowed to hide information from consumers.

In the first selection of this chapter, Behrman explores the right to know information, as well as the duty to disclose information. The second article in this chapter focuses specifically on nondisclosure law and the moral obligations associated with nondisclosure. In the third article in this chapter, Meislik argues about the degree to which concealed information is linked to the American obesity epidemic. The fourth article in this chapter is an excerpt from a ruling by the United States Court of Appeals for the Ninth Circuit in which the court upheld a jury's finding that Dow Corning was liable for failing to disclose potential problems with silicone breast implants. In the fifth article in this chapter, Mabry argues that punitive damages must be used as a deterrent in product liability lawsuits. In the sixth article in this chapter, Lee switches gears to mock Apple Computers for their reaction to the unwanted disclosure of information about an upcoming product. The final selection in this chapter, a publication from the Cato Institute, argues that Americans should be left alone to live their own lives—including leaving the government out of the obesity epidemic, smoking, and advertising.

In the first article in this chapter, Behrman engages in a thought experiment about how businesspeople and attorneys should handle information. Behrman argues that wanting to know information does not constitute a right to know that information. Similarly, having information does not necessarily mean one has a duty to disclose that information. Behrman also distinguishes among the various degrees of rights and duties, thinking about extreme situations as well as the mundane.

In the second article in this chapter, Strudler argues that we must view nondisclosure not just as an economic problem, but also as a moral problem.

Strudler details many ways in which Kronman, an economist, was wrong to argue that nondisclosure provides incentives for people to seek more information. Strudler then tackles Scheppele, a social contract theorist. In conclusion, Strudler combines the approaches taken by Scheppele and Kronman, arguing that a moral approach to nondisclosure law must incorporate Scheppele's emphasis on fair dealing and Kronman's emphasis on incentives.

In the third article in this chapter, Meislik confronts the American obesity epidemic head-on. Meislik describes two ways attorneys are battling food companies: for intentionally mislabeling food, and for intentionally failing to disclose nutritional information. Meislik examines recent cases against food companies, revealing how cases for intentional mislabeling have been successful while cases for nondisclosure have failed. Meislik then draws a comparison between the tobacco industry and the fast-food industry, arguing that Big Food should follow in Big Tobacco's footsteps by providing more information to consumers.

The fourth selection in this chapter is an excerpt from a ruling by the U.S. Court of Appeals for the Ninth Circuit. The plaintiff received silicone breast implants, manufactured by the defendant, that later ruptured and caused an autoimmune disorder. The plaintiff sued for compensatory and punitive damages because there was proof that the defendant was aware of significant problems with the breast implants. The defendant had even instructed salesmen to wash the implants immediately before displaying them because the implants leaked. Because the defendant failed to disclose the danger associated with the faulty implants, the jury awarded the plaintiff significant punitive damages.

In the fifth article in this chapter, Mabry argues that manufacturers like Dow Corning should be punished for failing to disclose information about faulty products such as the breast implants. Mabry proposes that courts use punitive damage awards to punish and deter manufacturers. By exploring a history of large punitive damages, as well as the reasons why punitive damages should deter manufacturers from knowingly selling unsafe products, Mabry argues that unlimited punitive damages should be used to protect innocent consumers from profit-seeking manufacturers.

In the sixth article in this chapter, Lee reports that Apple Computers sued a website that published information about an upcoming Apple product that was, until that point, a secret. According to Lee, Apple was wasting their own time for two reasons: (1) the website was protected by free speech, and (2) the website was providing free advertising for Apple.

In the final selection in this chapter, the Cato Institute takes this chapter down an entirely different path from the other authors featured. While the other authors have encouraged more free exchange of information, the Cato Institute argues that people need to be left alone to live their lives. The government does not need to tell people what to eat, what drugs to take, or how to live.

As with all of the issues presented in this book, reasonable people disagree about when companies should be permitted to conceal information. What do you think? As a consumer, would you want companies to reveal more information? If you were running a company, would you want to hide information from consumers? Can you think of a fair balance that protects consumers while allowing businesses to operate?

ISSUE ARTICLES

Behrman, Jack N., "Information Disclosure, the Right to Know, and the Right to Lie," *Essays on Ethics in Business and the Professions* (Englewood Cliffs, NJ: Prentice Hall, 1988).

Strudler, Alan, "Moral Complexity in the Law of Nondisclosure," 45 *UCLA Law Review* 337 (1997).

Alyse Meislik, "Weighing in on the Scales of Justice: The Obesity Epidemic and Litigation Against the Food Industry," 46 *Arizona Law Review*, 781 (2004).

Mariann Hopkins, v. Dow Corning Corporation, 33 F.3d 1116; 1994 U.S. App. LEXIS 23097.

Cynthia R. Mabry, "Warning! The Manufacturer of This Product May Have Engaged in Cover-Ups, Lies, and Concealment: Making the Case for Limitless Punitive Awards in Product Liability Lawsuits," 73 *Indiana Law Journal.* 187 (1997).

Lee, Timothy, "Apple v. Free Speech," *Regulation: A Cato Institute Publication* (2005).

"The Nanny State," *Cato Handbook on Policy*. 6th ed. Cato Institute. http://www.cato.org/pubs/handbook/hb109/hb_109-26.pdf>. (269-273).

ARTICLE 6.1

Information Disclosure, the Right to Know, and the Right to Lie

Jack N. Behrman

How does the withholding of information affect the amount of freedom in a society?

Information—adequate, relevant, timely, understandable—is a precondition of an efficient and free society. Yet it is also a means to power which can be used to reduce or remove freedom. Therefore, the rights to create property in information, to withhold, to disclose, to determine when and how disseminated are critical. The rights to know, to secrecy, and to lie exist but must be greatly circumscribed if freedom is also to exist.

The values our society expects business to support and promote include justice, honesty, truthfulness, stewardship, freedom, equity, dignity of the individual, and respect for privacy. These are found in the creeds of a number of civic organizations in the United States, including the Four-Way Path of Rotary and the Scout's oath. Truthfulness is basic to all communication, to respect for others, and to freedom. From the standpoint of business, it is basic to any disclosure of information to the various parties involved—customers through advertising, stockholders through annual reports, workers through internal communications, the public through press releases, the government through official reporting, and so on. Conversely, business is concerned to have accurate information available to it from those with whom it deals, including suppliers and customers, government agencies, workers, and so on. Both free enterprise and competition are founded on the availability of truthful information. Much business is conducted by (oral and written) promise, which implies a truthful commitment to future compliance. Without promise, business could be conducted only with great difficulty. Competition also requires that participants in the market have all relevant information—else some are making decisions under the "partial duress" of ignorance, giving others an advantage. Of course, since information is not free, there is also a market for information; there is even a cost for information on sources of information. The issue of disclosure and information gathering is complex; it requires careful thought and action to assure appropriate availability.

The matter of "truth in business" is complicated further by the fact that we cannot ever speak "the Truth," for it is hidden from us. We can only speak what we perceive to be the truth and relevant to the issue at hand. In fact, it is not possible even in court to speak "the whole truth and nothing but the truth." The inability to be fully truthful does not justify a cavalier attitude, however, much less an attempt to deceive or to mislead those who cannot protect themselves. A study done at the Harvard Graduate School of Business Administration some years ago reported widespread cynicism among young people about truthfulness in business. A group of children ages 9 to 12 were asked whether they thought advertising commercials told the truth; 24 of the 33 children replied that the commercials were untruthful because companies "just want to make money." It is a serious condemnation of the capitalist system that children do not believe that those seeking to make money will be truthful in its pursuit.

I. THE RIGHT TO KNOW AND THE DUTY TO DISCLOSE

Managers and lawyers readily discern that information is power: The one who has the better information is able to make better decisions. Yet not all have the same information, and if they did, not all could process it equally as well. Different information and different abilities to handle it distinguish the professions and their individual members from those they serve. Information is so valuable that many companies and lawyers go to great lengths to obtain information about what competitors are doing, even to supporting a form of espionage. (In some situations, such as card games, obtaining or passing information may be cheating—as has occurred at bridge tournaments. It is clear that such information provides power—a greater chance of winning or reducing the chance of loss. Competitive information may also be unwanted because damaging, as when a player in a golf tournament gets upset when learning that a close opponent has just shot three birdies.)

Neither business nor profession has a duty to disclose what knows to just anyone. The duty to disclose must be matched by a right to know on the part of the person or entity receiving the information. Therefore, we must determine who has the right to know, what they have the right to know, and when they have the right to know it. These questions lead to related concerns—such as the right to know for what purposes. The desire to know does not constitute a right to know, and the mere possession of information does not imply a duty to disclose even to those who have a right to know. Thus, a publisher does have a duty to disclose information in a report he or she is printing even if asked by those who will later receive the report; this applies also to auditors or psychiatrists. There is, then, a question of who the right, as well as the duty, to disclose.

The problem raised by the issue of duty to disclose has become acute for lawyers and for auditors dealing with information about a company. In one case, the U.S. Court of Appeals in Chicago ruled that under certain circumstances, auditors can be held liable to the investing public for not knowing what they should have known about a company. The case involved fraud, which stockholders argued the auditors should have uncovered. Auditors, in turn, have argued that to comply, they would have to get information from corporate lawyers, who might have to reveal confidential information. The controversy raised the issue of whether auditors could give "unqualified opinions" unless the lawyers gave them full information; while the lawyers have felt they would lose their standing with the company if they had revealed confidential information. The question of what the public stockholders should have the right to know seems to be lost in dialogue. . . .

Is concealment of information similar to lying or primarily different?

II. THE RIGHT TO LIE

Information disclosure is subverted by lying. Is there a right to lie? Certainly there is a right to lie to protect life. The prisoner of war can withhold information from the enemy (or even lie) concerning the movement of troops or other pertinent military activities. This is a right guaranteed in the rules of war under the Geneva Convention. Would anyone have condemned mothers for lying about the age of their babies in Herod's time, when the soldiers had been ordered to kill children less than 2 years of age? Or a parent, for lying about the presence of his or her loved ones, if they were endangered by a threatening intruder? It is carrying truthfulness to an extreme to expect anyone to tell an intruder where someone is hiding, when they know that injury will be the result. Even so, a minister in Germany during World War II asserted that, if harboring a Jew in his home, he would disclose that fact if questioned by the SS or other officials. (Of course, by that public statement he avoided the chance of harboring anyone, and the truthfulness of his assertion was never tested, so we do not know whether he was lying at that very moment.) Similarly, one may even lie to protect one's own life if it is endangered; or, conversely, one may lie in order to sacrifice one's life in favor of another (as in A Tale of Two Cities). Both are understandable and acceptable at times in the community. These examples show clearly that there is a right to lie, but also that it is constrained by the acceptability of the purpose of the lie to others in the society. . . .

Once we move off the extreme cases, it is much more difficult to ascertain the existence of a right to lie. The criteria are the same—protection in extremis and acceptability to the public—but less easy to determine when and how to apply.

It is not acceptable to lie or deceive for the purpose of personal advantage or merely for the advantage of a superior. Thus, the false testimony of a government official in favor of Jimmy Carter's appointment of Burt Lance as director of the Office of Management and Budget, when discovered in later congressional investigations, was considered unacceptable—particularly since the reason for the falsification was that the individual official considered that his job would be at stake if he criticized Lance because he was sure that Lance would be appointed as director anyway . . . Although there is undoubtedly considerable secrecy with reference to domestic government policy, it would not be acceptable to the public for officials to deceive members of Congress or to lie concerning their policy positions or activities. . . .

Similarly, the protection of the currency against speculative attacks is seen as acceptable grounds for lying. No minister of finance would admit that he was going to devalue the currency, even though he may have already planned and scheduled it. In such cases, the expectation of the inquirer is that the truth is not likely to be told, but he does not know what the truth is. Here the inquirers are not deceived even though they are lied to. There is, therefore, a difference between willful and successful deception on the one hand and honest lying, which does not deceive, on the other. For example, one would always expect an FBI or CIA agent to lie in order to protect his or her cover or that of another agent; it is part of the game that is being played. But when lying or deception is not expected, it is all the more successful. For example, a Washington lobbyist was called before a congressional committee to explain a letter he had written to his employer concerning his contact with a certain senator. The senator had denied ever seeing the writer, though the letter implied that he had been interviewed by, and given information to, the lobbyist. The letter written by the lobbyist to his company stated in part: "In response to your concern about the above issue, Senator and I had lunch Wednesday. I can assure you that his position is as follows. . . . "When asked to explain the implication of his meeting with the senator, the lobbyist replied, "That is very simple. I never said that I met the senator nor that we had lunch together; I had lunch Wednesday, and I assumed that the senator had lunch Wednesday; I know his position from other sources. The statement is accurate to the best of my knowledge." All that may be true, but it was certainly a deception, and a willful one.

There are, further, times when people wish to be deceived and are quite happy to be told what they want to hear, even though it is different from the truth. Several editorials concerning Secretary of State Kissinger's diplomatic style observed that he had a knack for telling people what they want to hear—letting different parties proceed on quite different perceptions of what the situation was, simply because he had emphasized those aspects that were pleasing to them.

Thus, when Americans wanted to hear that we had made no commitments to Vietnam, Kissinger said there were none, meaning none written. But General Thieu wanted commitments, so Kissinger said there were "moral" commitments, and gave Thieu oral assurances. He was apparently willing to deceive Congress and the public.

Whether or not deception was really the intent in these cases, that was the perception of many observers. The result was that Congress attempted to limit the secretary of state's freedom of action, against which Kissinger complained bitterly. The point of this discussion is not that lying or deception is wrong; foreign governments, for example, may not have a right to know certain facts; and concealing them may possibly involve lying or deceiving. However, acceptance of such action depends on public approval after the event. It was Congress and the U.S. public that felt deceived—as well as possibly some foreign individuals or governments who had a right to know. While it may be acceptable on the part of a representative of the American public to deceive someone from another country, it is not acceptable to deceive one's own government officials. Yet secrecy frequently hides the facts not only from the enemy but also from those in the United States who need to know. In assessing the effects of secrecy during the Vietnam War, McGeorge Bundy (former national security advisor to President Johnson) argued that the perils of secrecy were greater than the dangers of excessive presidential power, because it hid the facts from those who needed to make well-informed decisions. Of course, one of the issues is whether or not Congress can be trusted with secret information. Is telling Congress, so that it can make better plans, telling the enemy? There is a wry comment that circulated in upper circles of the U.S. intelligence community after a pillorying before Congress: "When is a secret not a secret? When it is disclosed to a Committee of Congress?" One highly placed administration official charged that "the events of the past year have demonstrated Congress' inability to keep secrets. Kiss-and-tell is not a game to play when the national security is at stake."

III. DIFFERENCES IN DEGREE

There are significant differences between secrecy and deception, between deception and lying, between lying and mere nondisclosure, between not disclosing some information and providing all relevant information, and between providing relevant information and telling "the whole truth." Telling the whole truth is required at times, such as in court, when the provider of information does not really understand the relevance of all that he or she may know. The relevance will be determined by someone else—the judge or the jury.

The scope of relevant information may sometimes be decided by the government or by the person who holds the information—as with a doctor or lawyer—but it need not be the whole truth. Nondisclosure of information merely means that relevant information has not been provided. And nondisclosure or "no comment" is certainly not lying, though it may be deceiving. Lying that is expected is also not deceiving; that is, lying is not deceiving when the hearer knows better in fact. In the case of the U-2 incident over Russia, President Eisenhower lied to the Russian government about the flight; he did not deceive, because the Russians had full information at the time. Undoubtedly, the lie was expected, but it did not serve its purpose and had to be corrected, to the embarrassment of the United States. Nor is secrecy always deception, though it very well may be.

In applying ethical criteria to all these distinctions, the basic consideration is the acceptability of the act in terms of the public interests rather than personal interests. Richard Helms, former director of CIA, was given only small punishment for lying before Congress concerning some activities of the CIA and his involvement. He lied on the grounds that answering truthfully would have meant disclosure of important secret operations in the national interest—though the matters about which he was being questioned were not themselves "fraught with national interest." However, when he was indicted for perjury, he let it be known that if he were to be given serious punishment, he would then testify concerning these same secret activities in a way that would damage the national interest. In this instance, he was willing to disclose in order to save his own skin, where previously he was unwilling to disclose ostensibly on the basis of saving the country's skin.

Although these are difficult judgments to make, they must be made, and the criteria are clearly related to the public interest, rather than self-interest. In the final assessment, lying or deception needs to be approved by the relevant public as in the interest of all others—or as acceptable behavior for any individual in similar circumstances. Applying these criteria to companies, or managers on company business, there is probably no justification for lying or deception. Where the inquirer has no right to know, the company can simply offer "no comment" or withhold information.

The decision is more complex for lawyers and doctors, who are privy to information about clients and patients which they obtain only because of their professional relationship. For any third-party inquiry they also have available the reply of "no comment," since the public has no right to pry—only to obtain information through established procedures.

The most difficult question arises for doctors and lawyers when it appears desirable to lie to or deceive patients or clients in order to help them. The issue turns on the exercise of power and responsibility. In principle, neither has the right to remove the responsibility of the clients for themselves, and in many cases, when patients (clients) find out that they have been so served, they become angry at such usurpation. Once again, the crux of the matter concerns the decision as to who is responsible for what to or for whom.

In sum, there is no right to lie or deceive adhering to businesses, companies, managers, or members of a profession in order to protect themselves in the pursuit of their duties. They have a right not to disclose and to make no comment on sensitive issues or when the inquirers have no right to know.

ARTICLE 6.2

Moral Complexity in the Law of Nondisclosure

Alan Strudler

I. INTRODUCTION

Two hundred years ago, Immanuel Kant offered a thoughtful argument that getting drunk in private is morally worse than getting drunk in public. Why did one of the greatest moral and legal philosophers of modern times, who had written on profound topics such as the nature of political authority, the justification of punishment, and the relation between freedom and causation, bother with the casuistry of drunkenness? Kant believed that all moral choice should be made intelligently and therefore thought it important to demonstrate the power of moral principle to illuminate the range of moral choices a person might face. His idea was that principle matters in the details of how people treat each other and themselves, and not only in issues of life, death, and other monumental concerns.

It is easy enough to see the importance of moral principle for the most profound issues the Supreme Court confronts: issues such as affirmative action, abortion, the right to die, free speech, and pornography all provoke concern about respect for individual dignity, autonomy, and rights—concern naturally expressed through appeal to principle. Taking a clue from Kant's reflections on the varieties of drunkenness, one might suppose that the nuts-and-bolts issues of contract and tort dominating the civil docket in municipal and county courts may be just as much matters of principle as are constitutional issues. Indeed, I will argue that neglect of ideas about moral principle undermines some of the best legal analyses of private law.

Why would a society ever encourage a "game" where people are encouraged to tell only part of what they know when that knowledge affects the rights of others?

In this Article, I argue for the necessity of certain moral concepts—including concepts rooted in concerns about treating people fairly and giving people what they deserve—for making sense of a prosaic problem in private law: the scope and limit of [the] duty to disclose information in precontractual bargaining. The problem arises because individuals not in a fiduciary relationship, who bargain over the sale of a good or service, are ordinarily "free to take a sporting view of their relationship with each other." Such negotiators may thus regard themselves as playing a game whose rules allow them not to reveal the truth when doing so would compromise the chance to "win." The law of nondisclosure allows a person to sometimes, but not always, decline to reveal information in a negotiation, even though the bargaining opponent would correctly regard that information as crucial to the deal. . . .

To demonstrate success, it is necessary to pay attention to the moral drama that occurs in bargaining and to the sources of individual negotiators' grievances about exploitation, deception, and betrayal. I maintain that only a principled account has the power to guide one through the moral complexities and tensions of nondisclosure law. I also maintain that it is judicial unwillingness to tolerate individual wrongdoing and judicial insistence that the law serves to compel wrongdoers to express respect for their victims, rather than judicial concern to promote attractive economic or other socially beneficial aims, that drives plausible nondisclosure law. . . .

II. INCENTIVES AND VICTIMS

The seminal economic account of nondisclosure law, due to Anthony Kronman, emphasizes the social advantages of the incentive structure created by a presumption of nondisclosure. Kronman's account, however, is structurally limited; it can accommodate only the forward-looking objective of getting the social incentives correct. As a consequence, any legal system that exemplifies his account excludes something crucial: a capacity to compel the expression of respect and concern for people who are duped—in other words, for any fraud victim. Or so I will argue.

The core of Kronman's account is the idea that law should recognize a presumption of disclosure in precontractual negotiation because that presumption increases the flow of socially valuable information. He makes the familiar argument that in a free market, the more information individuals possess about goods they buy and sell, the more reason society has to think that these goods will go to those who most value them, and hence, the better off society will be. He also recognizes that there may be valid economic reasons to limit this presumption: a blanket requirement of full disclosure would have undesirable results, as it would limit the incentive for producing some socially valuable information. In particular, people would not engage in costly searches to discover new information if there were a requirement of uncompensated disclosure of all information—even information that was produced through a costly search. Kronman argues that law, therefore, does not and should not require disclosure of information that is ordinarily produced only as the result of a costly search. Instead, law should provide incentives to search for such information by granting property rights in the information to those who discover it. . . .

Kronman's economic account of nondisclosure law in fact contains two significant flaws that limit its value as a judicial tool for addressing the claims of litigants in nondisclosure cases. First, it misidentifies the locus of the wrong that occurs when there is a wrongful failure to disclose: it identifies the wrong as the economic harm to society, but can find no place for the distinctive wrong suffered by the victim of nondisclosure. Second, as a consequence of the first flaw, Kronman's account, despite his intentions, fails to identify as wrongful certain cases of nondisclosure that the law identifies as wrongful and that intuitively seems wrongful.

Not Tracking Nondisclosure Law

A theory of nondisclosure must be tested by its ability to predict and otherwise accommodate entrenched and credible law. Kronman puts his theory to this test, using it to attempt to resolve the tension between some well-known cases from decisional law and from various Restatements. The treatment his theory provides for these cases, however, is both strained and implausible, and the theory's failure stems from Kronman's focus on the economic aspects of the cases while ignoring the moral aspects.

While Kronman reproduces a large number of cases, I will limit attention to just two cases Kronman takes from the Restatement of Restitution that I will call Jewelry Store and Bookstore.

> [Jewelry Store:] A, looking at cheap jewelry in a store which sells both very cheap and very expensive jewelry, discovers what he at once recognizes as being a valuable jewel worth not less that $ 100 which he correctly believed to have been placed there by mistake. He asks the clerk for the jewel and gives 10c. for it. The clerk puts the 10c. in the cash drawer and hands the jewel to A. The shopkeeper is entitled to restitution because the shopkeeper did not, as A knew, intend to bargain except with reference to cheap jewelry.
>
> [Bookstore:] A enters a second-hand bookstore where, among books offered for sale at one dollar each, he discovers a rare book having, as A knows, a market value of not less than $ 50. He hands this to the proprietor with one dollar. The proprietor, reading the name of the book and the price tag, keeps the dollar and hands the book to A. The bookdealer is not entitled to restitution since there was no mistake as to the identity of the book and both parties intended to bargain with reference to the ability of each to value the book.

In Jewelry Store, the law favors requiring disclosure, while in Bookstore, the opposite result obtains. The plain tension between the two cases is that in Bookstore, a buyer may exploit the seller's false belief (about the value of a rare book) in order to get a good price, whereas in Jewelry Store, a buyer may not exploit the seller's false belief (that the price tag is correct). Why treat the two cases differently? Kronman's explanation is elegant and simple; it derives from his thesis that law properly recognizes a policy of encouraging costly but socially valuable searches. The bargain in Bookstore was discovered on the basis of such a search; the bargain in Jewelry Store was not. Hence, nondisclosure law properly distinguishes between the two.

Yet reality may not align neatly with Kronman's economic theory. The problem arises because economic advantages might attach to encouraging people to engage in searches for mistagged items in retail stores, including jewelry stores. One may argue, using Kronman's analysis, that unless one allows such incentives, there will be a deterioration in the quality of information that the market possesses about jewelry. By encouraging people, through the offer of economic rewards, to seek out mistagged goods, one increases the prospects that goods are eventually bought and sold at their true market price and hence that goods end up in the hands of those who value them most—an objective of economic theory. There is, then, at least a prima facie case that pursuant to Kronman's account, one should encourage people to discover instances of mistagged goods, something that is achieved with a rule permitting nondisclosure in Jewelry Store. If so, contrary to Kronman's account, economic analysis requires that Bookstore and Jewelry Store be treated the same.

How would a legal economist reply? A legal economist might attempt to bolster the distinction between Bookstore and Jewelry Store by making the plausible empirical conjecture that more socially productive information will come out of the Bookstore rule permitting nondisclosure than would come from a Jewelry Store rule permitting nondisclosure. This seems to be the strategy that Kronman in fact employs. He explains that while "one can easily imagine an expert . . . browsing in secondhand stores in the hope of finding an undervalued masterpiece[, i]t seems less likely . . . that a bargain hunter would spend time searching the display cases of a fine jewelry store [or, in our case, a fine antique store] in the hope of finding" a mislabeled object. Kronman would thus draw the distinction between Bookstore and Jewelry Store on the basis of his contention that productive searches in cases like the former are more likely to involve a deliberate and costly search than are productive searches in cases like the latter; it follows, in Kronman's view, that cases like Bookstore will respond more productively to economic incentives permitting nondisclosure than would cases like Jewelry Store.

If one concedes the premise that cases like Bookstore and cases like Jewelry Store differ in the extent to which they are likely to involve a deliberate and costly search, one need not follow Kronman in the conclusions that he draws. While the premise might establish that a nondisclosure rule is more desirable in Bookstore than in Jewelry Store, it gives no indication why a nondisclosure rule would not be economically desirable in both cases. After all, a nondisclosure rule in each case would seem to produce some economic good. What should matter, in any economic account, for justifying a nondisclosure rule in Jewelry Store is that the rule be economically beneficial; it seems irrelevant that a nondisclosure rule in Jewelry Store may not create as much benefit as do nondisclosure rules that operate in other domains. But Kronman's own analysis suggests that a rule permitting nondisclosure in Jewelry Store would be economically beneficial because it would encourage deliberate and productive searches. Consider the economic consequences of requiring disclosure in cases like Jewelry Store. If a knowledgeable expert happens to discover a labeling error in Jewelry Store under a disclosure regime, an economic account would assert that he has a diminished incentive to bring this error to light. From a purely economic point of view, that lost incentive is undesirable, as it will lessen the prospects that sufficient information is produced to get goods to those who value them most. It seems undeniable that requiring disclosure in Jewelry Store should be expected to produce some benefits, even though one may suspect that the benefits will be paltry.

Because a nondisclosure rule in both Bookstore and Jewelry Store will produce economic benefits, Kronman must move beyond considering economic benefits alone if he wants to distinguish between the cases in economic terms. He might distinguish between the Bookstore and Jewelry Store nondisclosure rules in terms of their comparative balances of costs and benefits, insisting that while judicial adherence to the rule that underlies each case may produce some economic benefits, adherence to the Jewelry Store rule would bring more costs than benefits. He would then have to argue that a nondisclosure rule in Jewelry Store, but not in Bookstore, flunks a cost/benefit test. . . .

How does the analysis here demonstrate a serious problem with cost-benefit analysis?

In reviewing the variety of costs that Kronman must invoke in order to make the argument that a nondisclosure rule in Jewelry Store fails a cost/benefit test, it becomes clear that neither Kronman nor any legal economist could offer legally credible evidence that such a rule would leave storekeepers or society worse off than would a disclosure rule. It is ironic that legal economists, who aspire to place legal analysis on a respectable scientific footing, must, in the end, rest their justification on pure speculation. But legal economists do not stand alone in appealing to pure speculation to reach conclusions they regard as scientific: their utilitarian intellectual ancestors often encountered the same fate. In trying to explain what is wrong with covertly punishing the innocent when doing so would appease, and thus maximize, the utility of a bloodthirsty crowd, utilitarian legal "reformers" would appeal to highly speculative costs, including the risk that a judge would get caught for framing an innocent person. . . .

More specifically, how could one reason about a nondisclosure rule without simply speculating about its economic consequences? One might argue, for example, that jewelers often earn the right to market their goods at prices that they have ascertained as fair and reasonable, and that when one allows individuals to exploit errors in labeling to deprive jewelers of the chance to sell their goods at reasonable market prices, one denies jewelers this right. Hence, insisting on disclosure in Jewelry Store prevents an unfair outcome, one might conclude, no matter what the economic consequences. If one were to make this argument in such a way that it squared with the distinctions the Restatement draws between Jewelry Store and Bookstore, then one would have to argue that the jeweler has done something to acquire stronger property rights in the information about the value of what he sells than the bookstore proprietor. Interestingly, such an argument is in important respects similar to Kronman's: it asserts that disclosure rules should be crafted in response to the value produced by buyers who possess valuable information. It departs from Kronman's account, however, by denying that economic incentives provide the reason for concern about the value in buyer information; instead, it asks whether nondisclosure compromises the rights of a party, and also ask what may be required to vindicate those rights

III. SECRECY AND THE SOCIAL CONTRACT

Writers who invoke social contract analysis typically aim at prescribing the design of social institutions that foster a relation of moral equality among people living under those institutions. Kim Scheppele embraces such an analysis, using it to develop the leading theoretical account of nondisclosure law that uses moral, rather than simply economic, criteria. She tries to unpack an idea often relied upon in judicial opinions about nondisclosure and often mocked by legal economists: the idea that when two parties bargain over a good, fairness requires that they have roughly equal access to information about that good. She further suggests that a duty to disclose will be imposed when this concern for equal access to information is not satisfied. While Scheppele makes an important point by identifying the value of nondisclosure rules in terms of the protection they provide for fair negotiating process, her concerns about equal access to information are out of line with a plausible reading of the law. Moreover, these concerns derive from a demonstrable mistake Scheppele makes about the criteria to use in assessing the fairness of a negotiating process.

Scheppele spells out the idea of equal access to information in terms of her own ingenious system of classifying secrets—information relevant to a bargain but not possessed by all parties to the bargain. Her argument depends crucially on a distinction she draws between deep and shallow secrets:

> Sometimes the targets of the secret know about the potential existence of a secret, even though they do not know the content of the secret itself. . . .When the target suspects that there might be a secret, we find shallow secrets. When the target is completely in the dark, never imagining that relevant information might be had, we find deep secrets.

Thus, according to Scheppele's account, a deep secret occurs when a negotiator possesses information relevant to the negotiation and her bargaining opponent suspects neither the content nor the existence of this information. Scheppele asserts that a decent system of law will prohibit deep secrets in negotiation but will ordinarily allow shallow secrets, because deep secrets undermine equality in a bargaining relationship whereas shallow secrets do not.

What is the idea of "equality" that must be respected in the negotiating process? To interpret equality, Scheppele borrows the idea of "hypothetical consent" from social contract tradition. When crafting a decision, and hence determining what respect for the equality of individuals is required, a judge should ask the complex hypothetical question: "To which disclosure rules would bargainers have given their consent if they had deliberated about the matter under circumstances in which they were uninformed about how the application of the rule would affect them personally?" Because the hypothetical question is asked in circumstances under which the parties lack information about any differences between them, it is asked under circumstances of equality, and hence, the question captures the moral constraints that respect for equality would impose on disclosure rules.

Scheppele recognizes the roots of her approach in John Rawls's book, A Theory of Justice, but she disagrees with Rawls about both the scope and content of the principles derived through the hypothetical consent apparatus. Rawls clearly intended to limit the scope of his theory of justice to the whole structure of society and thus to bar its application to individual actions, practices, or rules within a society. Scheppele believes Rawls was wrong to restrict his theory of justice in this way because doing so deprives decisionmakers of needed guidance on legislative and judicial issues that are smaller than issues about the basic structure of society.

Scheppele also dissents from Rawls on the content of principles of justice. She considers, but rejects, Rawls's own version of his "difference principle," which provides, very roughly, that social and economic benefits should be distributed equally among all members of society, except when an unequal distribution would favor those worst off in society. Scheppele defends a version of the difference principle differing from Rawls's version, but following much of the spirit, if not the detail, of Rawls's account. Scheppele's account insists that justice, and hence respect for equality, requires a guarantee to each individual of a decent minimum (or a "minimum floor"), thus protecting each person from disaster. There are clear implications for nondisclosure. As Scheppele sees it, if one grants a bargainer the right not to disclose deep secrets, then that will place her opponent at a substantial and unreasonable risk; she will be in a bad position for assessing the possible adverse consequences of a deal such that she may not be able to adequately protect herself. Equality, as Scheppele interprets it through the social contract apparatus, therefore requires disclosure of deep secrets.

Before considering its substantive merits, it is worth noticing how Scheppele's account of nondisclosure fundamentally differs from Kronman's account. While Kronman would instruct a judge to craft a disclosure rule so that it advances the welfare of society as a whole, Scheppele's focus is instead on fairness between the parties . . . A judge guided by Scheppele's theory—because of its emphasis on the fairness of what one party in a negotiation does to the other—could at least consistently say that she was ruling for the sake of the plaintiff to vindicate the plaintiff's rights, and not merely for the sake of society more generally. Because a judge guided by Scheppele's account could plausibly claim to use the law to compel expression of respect for a victim of wrongful nondisclosure, the structure of her account at least allows the possibility of an expressive coherence that Kronman's account lacks. Unfortunately, the substantive content of Scheppele's account, including her normative taxonomy of secrets, does not square with plausible nondisclosure law, and so its expressive promise cannot be realized. . . .

Scheppele errs by failing to recognize how respect for the equality of persons is consistent with respect for morally legitimate differences between persons. She borrows moral ideas about justice in the social system and applies them to assess justice between individuals—moral ideas that are not plausibly applied to the negotiation context. As even Rawls agrees, sometimes respect for equality requires that people are treated unequally in important ways. Scheppele's account yields counterintuitive results. In the next part, I will investigate why, contrary to Scheppele's analysis, it is often unfair for nondisclosure rules to require that negotiators get even roughly equal access to information.

IV. CONCLUSION

Despite my criticisms of Scheppele and Kronman, reflection on their writings suggests the direction that an adequate theory of nondisclosure must take. As Scheppele's account provides, principles of nondisclosure must be evaluated in terms of their role in the process of negotiating fairly. Moreover, as Kronman argues, an adequate account of nondisclosure must recognize the value that an individual, by uncovering information, may bring to the bargaining table. He was simply wrong in supposing that the judicial response to uncovering such information should reason in terms of its incentive implications.

ARTICLE 6.3

Weighing in on the Scales of Justice: The Obesity Epidemic and Litigation Against the Food Industry

Alyse Meislik

Why is the extent of the obesity epidemic relevant to whether there is an analogy between the food industry and the tobacco firms as causes of social harm?

I. INTRODUCTION

On Seattle's Queen Ann Hill, a popular restaurant called the 5 Spot features a dessert called "The Bulge," a gooey sugar-coated fried banana with ice cream, macadamia nuts, whipped cream, and two kinds of syrup. Before consuming this decadent concoction, customers must first sign a liability waiver that states in part, "I release the 5 Spot from all liability of any weight gain that may result from ordering and devouring this sinfully fattening treat." This waiver is a spoof of the obesity lawsuits that have suddenly appeared on the landscapes of court dockets across the nation. Although the waiver makes light of the situation, it also reveals the serious nature of the fears confronting the food industry as lawyers begin fighting "Big Food."

As obesity litigation appears in courts around the country, critics issue scores of complaints and ridicule. Some critics say it is "ludicrous" to blame food companies instead of people for their own "nutritional ignorance, lack of will power, genetic predispositions, failure to exercise or whatever else may play a role" in the problem of obesity. Critics also attack the lawsuits as "just another example of a runaway litigation system where litigation attempts to take the place of individual conduct."

Despite the opposition and mockery, and the minimal success in the courtroom, the food industry and the government behave as though the obesity suits are not frivolous. As of August 2003, state lawmakers had filed more than 140 bills aimed at obesity, a figure which has nearly doubled the seventy-two lawsuits that were filed in all of 2002. Moreover, the Food and Drug Administration ("FDA") announced on July 11, 2003, that by January 1, 2006, labels of packaged foods must list the amount of trans fats in foods. Many new studies confirm that trans fats raise blood-cholesterol levels and lower high-density lipoprotein ("HDL"), the "good cholesterol," thus increasing the risk of heart disease and type-2 diabetes. According to FDA estimates, providing information about trans fats on food labels could prevent 7,600 to 17,100 cases of coronary heart disease and 2,500 to 5,600 deaths every year. The outdated labeling requirements enabled food products to be called "low fat" and "saturated-fat free" while still containing trans fats. The agency intends the new mandatory disclosure to "promote consumer awareness and an understanding of the health effects of trans fat as part of an educational program." . . .

II. THE OBESITY EPIDEMIC

. . . The U.S. Surgeon General's 2001 Report on Overweight and Obesity predicts that "left unabated, overweight and obesity may soon cause as much preventable disease and death as cigarette smoking."[1] Overweight and obesity are associated with many health problems, such as an increased risk for coronary heart disease; type 2 diabetes; endometrial, colon, postmenopausal breast and other cancers; and certain musculoskeletal disorders, such as knee osteoarthritis. It is also associated with sleep apnea, urinary incontinence, gallbladder disease, and non-alcohol related fatty liver disease. According to the National Heart and Lung Blood Institute, all adults (aged eighteen years or older) who have a Body Mass Index ("BMI") of twenty-five or more are considered to be at risk for premature death and disability. These health risks increase as individuals become more obese. In fact, obese individuals have a fifty to one-hundred percent increased risk of premature death. According to a recent report by the Surgeon General, approximately 300,000 deaths per year in the United States may be attributable to obesity, a figure not far behind the annual death of 430,000 per year from tobacco.[2]

Childhood obesity is a serious health problem in itself. In most cases, people who eat poorly when they are children continue to eat poorly as adults since "eating preferences formed in childhood tend to persist in adulthood." Overweight adolescents have a seventy percent chance of becoming overweight or obese adults. The chance of becoming overweight or obese adult increases to eighty percent if a child has at least one parent who is overweight or obese. Obese children face more immediate consequences as well. The most immediate—and often most devastating—consequence of being overweight as a child is social discrimination. These children can develop low self-esteem and depression.[3] Moreover, risk factors for heart disease, such as high cholesterol and high blood pressure, occur with greater frequency in overweight children and adolescents than among children with a healthy weight. . . .

C. Addressing Obesity: The Debate Between Personal Responsibility and the Government's Role in Addressing the Problem of Obesity

The implications of obesity make it evident that individual food choices have vast public consequences. The figures above indicate that the U.S. has a compelling interest in reversing the current trend of obesity. Despite the alarming statistics on the prevalence and ramifications of obesity, the government has done little to address the unhealthy eating habits at the core of the problem.

Regardless of the vast public consequences of obesity, many people argue that individual food choices should be a matter of personal responsibility. Others say that people cannot have personal responsibility if they are uninformed. As mentioned by Judge Sweet in *Pelman v. McDonald's*, a line should "be drawn between an individual's own responsibility to take care of herself, and society's responsibility to ensure that others shield" that person. [n]With this in mind, laws should be created in situations where "society needs to provide a buffer between the individual and some other entity." An example of a buffer is Congress's creation of the Fair Packaging and Labeling Act to protect the individual from manufacturers that attempt to deceive consumers. [n]The Act requires packages and labels to include accurate information. Yet, as Judge Sweet stated, it is "not the place of the law to protect them from their own excesses." He further stated that, "as long as a consumer exercises free choice with appropriate knowledge, liability for negligence will not attach to a manufacturer. . . . When that free choice becomes but a chimera" manufacturers should be held accountable for consumer's decisions. [n]Thus, when manufacturers deprive consumers of the opportunity to make informed choices, they may be able to haul manufacturers into court and hold them accountable.

III. OBESITY LITIGATION

As obesity lawsuits sprang up on the court dockets, many people complained about the "frivolous" nature of the lawsuits and debated about whether the courtroom is the proper place to address the obesity epidemic. Sherman Joyce, President of the American Tort Reform Association, argues that legislation and regulation are more appropriate than using the courts as a means of addressing the problem of obesity. Although Joyce's arguments may be true, recourse to the courts is frequently the only way to create social change in the U.S. because Congress is often "beholden to powerful industry lobbies." According to John Banzhaf III, a professor of public interest law at George Washington University, legislation and regulation are preferable to litigation; however, litigation is often necessary to prompt change. Banzhaf believes that lawsuits may be effective for [making helpful social changes, following the mantra: "If you can't regulate, litigate." He maintains that the mere threat of future lawsuits may be enough to persuade restaurants to reveal the potential dangers of the high fat and calorie content in their foods. Overall, Banzhaf's objectives are to apply legal pressures compelling the food industry to change its practices and to generate enough publicity on the issue of obesity to cause social reform.

Recently, several lawsuits against fast food companies and food manufacturers have been filed and many more may be on the way. For the purposes of this Note, the litigation against the food industry will be placed into two categories:

(1) actions against food companies for explicit, false misrepresentations of in formation; and
(2) actions accusing the food industry of misleading consumers through a lack of disclosure.

The first category includes lawsuits against DeConna Ice Cream of Orange Lake Florida (the maker of Big Daddy Ice Cream) and Robert's Gourmet Food Inc. (the maker of Pirate Booty) for misrepresenting products with inaccurate labels. The second category includes court actions against Kraft Foods, McDonald's, Wendy's, Burger King, and Kentucky Fried Chicken for failing to disclose information about its products. Both categories of lawsuits are significant to the war on obesity since they endeavor to make food companies more accountable for the obesity epidemic in America. The focus of this Note, however, is on the second category of lawsuits. At this time, lawsuits falling within the first category have been successful, while those in the second category have been repeatedly defeated.

[Suits in the second category, actions accusing the food industry of misleading consumers through a lack of disclosure, involve a novel theory, and their prospects for success are uncertain. These suits, which are deemed "frivolous" by many critics, have several legal obstacles to overcome, such as failure to establish legal causation, a lack of foreseeability of harm, contributory negligence, and assumption of risk. Although these court actions may face an "uphill battle," they have succeeded in catching the attention of the food industry, the government, and American consumers. As of 2004, none of these suits have reached a jury; however, these lawsuits have raised public awareness about the risks of obesity, heart disease, and other health concerns. The suits have also been catalysts for "Big Food" to change its practices to benefit consumers. The uncertainty and public relations nightmares associated with this type of lawsuit make it the more feared category of the two. These lawsuits are especially menacing to the food industry because of the possibility that they harbor the potential to evolve into litigation similar in scale to that faced by the tobacco industry.

A. *BanTransFats.com v. Oreos*

In 2003, Stephen Joseph filed a lawsuit on behalf of a nonprofit group called BanTransFats.com, Inc. against Kraft, the maker of Nabisco Oreos. The California lawsuit alleged that Oreos contain trans fats, or hydrogenated and partially hydrogenated oils, which are not safe for consumption. The nonprofit group sought to block Kraft from marketing and selling the "trans fat-laden Oreo cookies" to children. The cause of action was based upon a California civil code provision that only protects manufacturers for common consumer products if the products are both "inherently unsafe and . . . known to be unsafe by the ordinary consumer who consumes the product with the ordinary knowledge common to the community."

According to Joseph's website, trans fats are "unsafe and unfit for human consumption." He contends that trans fats "cause serious lowering of HDL (good) cholesterol and a significant and serious increase in LDL (bad) cholesterol; make the arteries more rigid; cause major clogging of arteries; cause or contribute to type 2 diabetes; and cause or contribute to other serious health problems." Joseph's website also cites a 1999 study by Harvard University's Department of Nutrition which estimated that, in the U.S. diet, replacing trans fats with unhydrogenated vegetable oils would prevent approximately 30,000 to 100,000 premature coronary deaths a year.

As soon as the Oreo litigation became public, the case received massive national and international coverage. After the New York Times featured Joseph's story and picture, his suit quickly gained public attention. His website, BanTransFats.com, went from fewer than 500 hits before the story broke to over 75,000 hits two days later. Kraft headquarters received 277 calls and e-mails about Oreos within two days of the release of the lawsuit's details—essentially, a public relations nightmare.

By creating publicity about the dangers of trans fats present in Oreo cookies, Joseph successfully attracted Kraft's attention. During the height of publicity, Kraft responded to the lawsuit by declaring that the company has been "exploring ways to reduce trans fat in Oreos, and those efforts are continuing." On July 1, 2003, Kraft announced that it would conduct an overhaul of its products.

Within a few weeks of filing, and within three days of public disclosure of the lawsuit's subject matter, Joseph voluntarily withdrew the action against Kraft. According to Joseph, "as a result of the publicity, the legal premise for the lawsuit disappeared." The lawyer's legal basis was that the "existence and danger of trans fat was not common knowledge." Once a flood of publicity from the lawsuit informed the public about the dangers of trans fats, Joseph believed he had "scored [his] home run," so he dismissed the suit.

B. Caesar Barber Files Suit Against McDonald's, Wendy's, Burger King, and Kentucky Fried Chicken

In July 2002, Caesar Barber, a fifty-seven-year-old, 270-pound Bronx janitor, filed a class action in a New York court against McDonald's, Wendy's, Burger King, and Kentucky Fried Chicken, claiming that eating regularly at those restaurants made him obese. He also claimed that the restaurants failed to adequately warn him that his steady diet of fast food would lead to health problems, including heart attacks and diabetes. Barber contended that, as a result of the fast food chains' actions, Barber had two heart attacks and is a diabetic.

This lawsuit was the first broad-based legal action filed accusing the fast food industry of contributing to obesity. Samuel Hirsch, Barber's lawyer, argued that the multibillion dollar fast food industry has an obligation to inform consumers about the dangers of eating food from their restaurants. Hirsch maintained that companies profited enormously from consumers who regularly eat their food. He contended that the fast food chains were negligent in selling food high in fat, salt, sugar, and cholesterol despite studies showing a link between consumption of such foods and obesity, diabetes, and numerous other health problems.

Early in 2003, Hirsch discontinued the Barber litigation because he believed he had a stronger case with a lawsuit that focused on children. His apparent strategy was to attract the sympathies of the court through a plaintiff who was a defenseless child, rather than an adult who arguably should have known fast food was bad for him. A focus on children would leave the plaintiffs less vulnerable to claims of personal responsibility. Hirsch also began concentrating his efforts on one company, rather than filing a broad-based action against several fast food restaurants. Consequently, Hirsch brought a suit against McDonald's.

C. Juveniles Take McDonald's to Court

In Pelman, two juvenile customers of McDonald's, with their parents as guardians, sued McDonald's in August 2002, seeking a class action certification and alleging violations of the New York Consumer Protection Act. The plaintiffs alleged that the practices McDonald's uses to make and sell its products are deceptive, and that this deception injured their health. More specifically, they argued that McDonald's used false advertisements to mislead consumers into thinking that its foods are healthier than they are, failed to disclose the potential dangers of eating the food, and neglected to warn consumers that fatty foods can be addictive. The juveniles further asserted that their purchase and consumption of the defendant's products was a significant or direct factor that led them to become overweight and develop other adverse health effects. According to Judge Sweet, the case involved questions of "personal responsibility, common knowledge, and public health," and the "role of society and the courts in addressing such issues."

Although Judge Sweet dismissed the case pursuant to a summary judgment motion, he granted the plaintiffs leave to amend the complaint, setting the stage for future litigation. Before dismissing the matter, Judge Sweet made observations that practically created a roadmap for filing a case against the food industry. His decision described Chicken McNuggets as a "McFrankenstein creation of various elements not utilized by the home cook" and said that it is "hardly common knowledge that McDonald's french fries are comprised" of countless ingredients besides potatoes. He then instructed the plaintiffs that "it is at least a question of fact as to whether a reasonable consumer would know—without recourse to the McDonalds' Web site—that a Chicken McNugget contained so many ingredients other than chicken and provided twice the fat of a hamburger." He even stated: "This argument comes closest to overcoming the hurdle presented to plaintiffs.

If plaintiffs were able to flesh out this argument in an amended complaint, it may establish that the dangers of McDonalds' products were not commonly well known and thus that McDonald's had a duty toward its customers."

The plaintiffs filed an amended complaint asserting four causes of action, but one count was dropped. The allegations focused on the false advertising component of the original complaint. The first count alleged that McDonald's misled the plaintiffs through advertising campaigns and other publicity by suggesting that its products were nutritious and could be a part of a healthy lifestyle even if consumed on a daily basis. The second count provided that McDonald's failed to adequately disclose the fact that some of its foods were substantially less healthy, as a result of processing and ingredient additives, than what was represented in advertising campaigns and other publicity. The third count asserted that McDonald's engaged in unfair and deceptive acts and practices by misrepresenting to the New York Attorney General and to consumers that nutritional information was conspicuously displayed at all of the stores, when, in fact, this information had not been adequately available at a significant number of McDonald's outlets.

Ultimately, in September 2003, Judge Sweet rejected the amended complaint and dismissed the cause of action with prejudice. The court held that the plaintiffs "failed to allege both that McDonald's caused the plaintiffs' injuries or that McDonald's representations to the public were deceptive." Judge Sweet further held that the plaintiffs made "no explicit allegations that they witnessed any particular deceptive advertisement," and failed to provide the court with enough information to determine whether McDonald's products were the cause of the alleged injuries. The case is currently being appealed.

Despite Pelman's dismissal, in early October, McDonald's announced it would be reformulating its Chicken McNuggets recipe in all 13,600 of its U.S. restaurants to make the product leaner. The new all-white-meat six-piece Chicken McNugget meal contains 260 calories, down from 310 calories, and sixteen grams of fat, a twenty percent reduction. McDonald's claims that this change was contemplated for years; however, it seems too coincidental that the change came shortly after the company faced harsh criticism for the unhealthiness of its food, and specifically, that Chicken McNuggets were attacked by Judge Sweet as a "McFrankenstein creation." Thus, even though Pelman was unsuccessful in the courts, the lawsuit most likely was a significant motivating force for McDonald's to offer its customers healthier dietary choices. . . .

IV. DOES THE HISTORY OF THE TOBACCO LITIGATION FORESHADOW THE FUTURE OF OBESITY LAWSUITS' SUCCESS?

In evaluating the future prospects of the obesity lawsuits in achieving their objectives, obesity litigation should be compared and contrasted with the litigation that devastated Big Tobacco. In fact, some scholars have argued that "the history of tobacco litigation is the future of the fast food industry."[4] Despite many Americans' belief that the obesity lawsuits are frivolous, one lesson to be learned from the tobacco litigation is that "what looks frivolous today may turn out to be very serious tomorrow." Tobacco litigation may have expanded the field of products liability, and similar to the tobacco cases, the odds of winning judgments against food companies could significantly increase if hidden manufacturing or marketing strategies are made public through company whistle-blowers or the legal disclosure process. While it is difficult to predict at this time whether plaintiffs in obesity litigation will be victorious, it would be unwise for the food industry to underestimate the ever-expanding threat of this litigation and to fail to take preventative measures.

A. Comparing Big Tobacco and Big Food

1. Obesity Litigation and Tobacco Litigation Share Many Similarities

Obesity litigation strikingly parallels tobacco litigation in many ways. The protagonists of the obesity suits are the same lawyers who successfully engineered the litigation against the tobacco companies, which settled for a total of more than $ 240 billion. The starting point for both movements is also the same: in 1964, the U.S. Surgeon General Luther L. Terry laid the foundation for what would become a national anti-smoking movement by calling cigarette smoking a "health hazard of sufficient importance in the United States to warrant appropriate remedial action." Similarly, in December 2001, Surgeon General David Satcher issued a "call to action" on obesity, and since his statement, the fat-fighting movement has continued to take hold throughout the U.S. In his address, Satcher directly compared the current obesity situation in the U.S. to the health problems attributable to cigarette smoking and stated that obesity "may soon cause as much preventable disease and death as cigarette smoking." Current statistics show that overweight and obesity contribute to the premature deaths of 300,000 Americans annually, a figure not far behind tobacco's yearly death rate of 430,000.[5] Both tobacco products and the foods responsible for causing obesity impose high economic costs on society. . . .

In both the tobacco and obesity litigation, plaintiffs voluntarily used the products, though it is uncertain whether the defenses of contributory negligence and assumption of risk would shield the food industry from liability. In the tobacco cases, juries evaluated the voluntary nature of the plaintiffs' conduct and still assessed liability on Big Tobacco.

The defense of assumption of risk would most likely not apply to the obesity litigation if children are too young to understand and "appreciate" the nature of the risks associated with eating fast food or junk foods. In addition, if the food industry failed to inform parties of risks associated with eating these foods, plaintiffs would not have the requisite knowledge of these risks. Assumption of risk and contributory negligence may also be unavailable if evidence reveals that the food industry intentionally concealed the risks associated with its products. Contributory fault may be unavailable if it is determined that the food industry acted recklessly or intentionally in causing consumers harm.

2. The Food and Tobacco Industries' Similar Methods of Attracting Customers

The advertising campaigns used by both industries share common features. One of the most damaging findings against tobacco companies, which helped to turn the tide of public opinion against this industry, was the targeting of their advertisements to vulnerable groups, especially children. Similarly, the food industry spends billions of dollars a year in advertising, a large portion of which is aimed at children. Advocates worry that children are particularly receptive to advertising pitches for burgers and fries, sugary cereals that are "part of a nutritious breakfast," and soft drinks, since children are unconcerned about health factors and merely motivated by the idea that these foods taste good. Advocates are also concerned that the industry is pouring billions of dollars into ads that target children, knowing in advance the effect that its advertisements and products will have on the "impressionable minds" of children. Advertisers target children with heavy advertising on Saturday morning television programs when many children watch television, creating tie-ins with toys and Disney movies, and attracting parents with playground settings. This targeting of children also includes marketing efforts within the public schools, where children are "a captive audience for marketers," and products are marketed through means such as conventional advertising campaigns, classroom teaching materials, and lunch room franchises. By aggressively marketing unhealthy food products to children, the food industry becomes more vulnerable to obesity lawsuits since children create more compelling cases.

Unlike tobacco, the food industry is not widely recognized as having preyed on unknowing consumers, so it may lack the "diabolical reputation associated with tobacco manufacturers." Even so, opponents of the food industry are slowly working to eliminate this difference. In the tobacco cases, plaintiffs discovered documents revealing that the tobacco industry "had prior knowledge of the dangers of tobacco [and there had been] a long pattern of concealment, denial, and even manipulation of the addictive component of tobacco." This discovery was fatal to the tobacco companies and resulted in previously unimaginable judgments. Likewise, opponents of the food industry hope to transform its public image into an evil, greedy enemy so that it may share a fate similar to Big Tobacco. They have already begun vilifying the fast food and snack industry by engaging in a public information campaign identical to the campaign used against Big Tobacco. Opponents of Big Food are attempting to create a public health scare about the risks involved with poor diets, particularly those high in fat, and create a negative public image of the industry.

Evidence in the tobacco litigation revealed that the tobacco industry intentionally sought to addict young consumers in order to ensure lifetime customers. Even though opponents of the food industry are now arguing that it is doing the same, as of this time, there is no evidence that any food companies knowingly increased the addictive nature of their products or lied about the dangers of their products to consumers. Still, proponents of the obesity suits contend that it is impossible to know at this juncture exactly what the fast food companies know about their products or did to make them more dangerous until the completion of the discovery phase of trial. Those who support the food industry contend that fast food is not addictive like nicotine, and even if fast food is discovered to be addictive, the addictive effects are not as severe as the addictive effect of nicotine.

Researchers are now investigating whether large amounts of fat in combination with sugar can trigger cravings similar to drug addictions. This type of finding could help explain why fast food sales have increased to more than $ 100 billion a year, despite years of warnings to limit fats. The Physicians Committee for Responsible Medicine ("PCRM") claims there is biochemical evidence that the obsession in America with certain unhealthy foods originates more from a physical addiction to these foods than from a lack of willpower. Dr. Neal Barnard, president of PCRM asserts that researchers have found that certain foods are "seductive foods": foods that are "similar to drugs in that they cause the release of opiate-like compounds that stimulate the brain's pleasure center." According to Dr. Barnard, the opiate-like substances in "seductive foods"—foods such as chocolate, cheese, meats, and sugar—seduce people into becoming "hooked" into eating those foods repeatedly. Dr. Barnard also claims that the food industry "intentionally manipulates the addictive qualities of its products" to maximize the addictive qualities of certain products.

Food industry officials, on the other hand, strongly deny the existence of a conspiracy of this nature. As of this time, no one has brought forward actual evidence that any company attempted to make food addictive—most likely, the manufacturers simply aimed to create a pleasing taste for their foods. . . .

B. Differences Between the Tobacco and Food Lawsuits

While the obesity and tobacco litigation have many similarities, they also differ in several ways. A crucial difference is that "food is essential and we cannot live without it, but people can live without tobacco." Even more important, food does have health benefits, but "there is no such thing as a healthy diet of smoking or smoking in moderation." In addition, unlike tobacco users who tend to show loyalty to particular brands, it is hard to prove causation for liability purposes among junk food addicts since they tend to eat unhealthy products from a variety of different sources. Causation also becomes difficult because people who eat unhealthy foods at restaurants often eat poorly at home and live less active lives. Thus, even if fast food consumption does cause obesity, the food industry could prevail based upon evidence that other factors brought about or complicated the plaintiff's illness.

C. The Food Industry Loses Public Support, Increasing Its Chances of a Future Negative Jury Verdict

The negative publicity against the food industry and the movement against obesity appears to have affected public opinion. As a result of the Pelman litigation, supporters of the obesity suits believe there has been a shift in the public's perception "from seeing obesity only as a personal or family responsibility to seeing it as a societal problem with societal solutions." In a 2002 survey by The National Law Journal, twenty-eight percent of potential jurors said they would decide in favor of a smoker who sued a tobacco company, while fifty-three percent said they would decide in favor of the company. In March 2003, the litigation research firm Bowne DecisionQuest discovered that 24.4% of potential jurors would award damages to an obese plaintiff who sued a fast food chain, and 56.4% would side with the company. These statistics present a mere 3.6% difference between jurors' support of plaintiffs in tobacco litigation and their support of plaintiffs in obesity litigation. Thus, if an obesity suit makes it to a jury, it is not implausible that the food industry could be faced with a fate similar to tobacco.

D. Weighing the Likelihood of the Success of Food Lawsuits following on the Heels of Tobacco

It is difficult to predict whether members of the food industry will one day face the same devastation as the tobacco industry with a large verdict in an obesity lawsuit. The tobacco and food litigation share strikingly similar histories: both suits feature plaintiffs who voluntarily used the products, and the methods of attracting consumers are almost the same. After the expansion of tort liability in the tobacco suits, the similar trends among the two industries could foreshadow what may later ensue in obesity litigation. At the same time, the food industry's sheer lobbying power may be enough to shelter the industry from future lawsuits. Additionally, the differences between the industries may be significant enough to preclude a lawsuit from ever achieving success. For example, the fact that food is a necessity and tobacco is purely a luxury with no health benefits may be enough to distinguish them. . . .

V. STEPS TO BE TAKEN BY FOOD COMPANIES TO SHIELD THEMSELVES FROM THE EXPOSURE OF LAWSUITS

Although Professor Banzhaf argues that "after tobacco, you can never say never," there clearly are many obstacles confronting plaintiffs suing the food industry, which still has the ability to protect itself from costly verdicts. As the tobacco industry learned, this could rapidly change. For this reason, the food industry would be wise to heed the ever-increasing threats of litigation and to take appropriate precautions to disclose nutritional information about its products to consumers. Americans are intolerant of fraud, and companies seem to have the greatest exposure to liability when they misrepresent or intentionally conceal information because these actions deny consumers the opportunity to make informed decisions. In fact, some lawyers believe that "the more information you provide, even if [it is] obvious, the less likely you are to face suits." As seen in the onslaught of obesity litigation, information that may seem obvious to many is not obvious to some. For instance, most people know that living sedentary lifestyles while consuming high levels of fat cause people to become unhealthy and overweight; nevertheless, a portion of the population may not realize the existence of this trend.

The obesity lawsuits have not yet been successful in the courtrooms, but they have motivated both the public and private sectors to bring about changes to address the growing trend of obesity. Currently, a plaintiff's chance of prevailing in obesity lawsuits is questionable, but the food industry would be prudent, from an economic and civic responsibility perspective, to protect itself by keeping its customers nutritionally informed. Judge Sweet provided the food industry with advice as to how it may avoid ending up in court while also providing lawyers with a framework for how to bring food companies into court. Food companies should know the risks associated with their products and should comply with their duty to warn consumers of known, foreseeable risks that are not appreciated by their consumers.

Judge Sweet's road map to successful litigation provides that food companies should be held liable under simple product liability and consumer protection theories if they fail to warn consumers that their products are dangerous. For this reason, food companies should include warnings to consumers to eat their products in moderation. This is exactly what is taking place overseas: McDonald's in France already warns its consumers to eat its food in moderation. In an ad campaign in France that promoted McDonald's meals as a part of a balanced weekly diet, a nutritionist was quoted as saying, "there's no reason to abuse fast food or visit a McDonald's more than once a week." Although this type of warning may seem extreme, it is a sound policy for companies to fully disclose nutritional and food-related health information about their products to maximize the consumer's knowledge of the products and any associated risks.

Some critics believe that the threat of litigation will subside as more food companies go "the healthful route" and provide consumers with more informative nutritional labeling. To reduce liability, and as a simple matter of good public relations, restaurants should consider as a prudent measure adding healthier food options to menus and cutting excessive portion sizes. The food industry should also work to devise healthier versions of foods with less trans fats and less fat in general. Along these lines, food companies should continue to modify their marketing strategies and make health information more readily available in a format that the general public can truly understand. Although many food companies make nutritional information available to consumers on the internet, it is advisable and more meaningful to the general public for the food industry to conspicuously post nutritional information near menu boards in restaurants and on packaging of items.

VI. CONCLUSION: THE OBESITY EPIDEMIC IN AMERICA CANNOT BE IGNORED

Although the onslaught of obesity litigation has been criticized as frivolous, obesity remains a public health threat that has grown to epidemic proportions in the U.S. The social, health, and economic implications of obesity are difficult to ignore, and both the public and private sectors must immediately develop sensible policies and programs to address this serious problem. Whether or not the food industry voluntarily confronts this problem, the issue will not quickly disappear in the legislature, courtrooms, or media.

Why is it clear from the behavior of the food industry that they do not think it is frivolous to accuse them of playing a significant role in stimulating obesity?

The food industry, a major player in this epidemic, has a responsibility to confront the obesity problem. It should keep consumers nutritionally informed, create healthier options for consumers, cut portion sizes, modify marketing, and develop health programs that should include making nutrition and food-related health information readily available. The food industry has already begun taking many of these actions and should continue to do so in the future.

The government also has a responsibility to monitor continuously the food industry to ensure that the public is truly informed about healthy nutritional choices and that it is not misled by deceptive practices. It also must continue to police the marketplace so as to eliminate deceptive practices. Recognizing this duty, various government agencies, such as the FDA and IRS, have already taken action. Various state legislatures, likewise, are in the process of enacting bills to stem the tide of obesity. There are many other avenues available to the government for addressing this epidemic, such as increasing nutritional educational programs; advocating and promoting healthier lifestyles; and providing for, and encouraging programs related to, physical fitness. Segments of the food industry should take careful note of the serious lessons learned from the course of events that brought the tobacco industry to its knees. Considering obesity's current status as one of America's most serious health issues, the striking similarities to the tobacco litigation and associated public outcry related to health concerns cannot be ignored. That so many members of the food industry have voluntarily initiated changes to improve the quality of their food choices is a testament to the fact that some of the lessons hit home. These changes must continue. As medical science advances to uncover the secrets of how our bodies process food, Big Food should learn from Big Tobacco's experiences and make responsible changes, which will, in the end, be in everyone's best interest.

END NOTES

1. U.S. Dep't of Health and Human Services, The Surgeon General's Call to Action to Prevent and Decrease Overweight and Obesity (2001). . . .
2. Melissa Healy, War on Fat Gets Serious, L.A. Times, Jan. 3, 2004, at 1.
3. Carol Torgan, Ph.D., Childhood Obesity on the Rise, The NIH Word on Health (June 2002). . . .
4. Franklin E. Crawford, Fit for Its Ordinary Purpose? Tobacco, Fast Food, and the Implied Warranty of Merchantability, 63 Ohio St. L.J. 1165, 1169 (2002).
5. Melissa Healy, War on Fat Gets Serious, L.A. Times, Jan. 3, 2004,

ARTICLE 6.4

Mariann Hopkins v. Dow Corning Corporation

In this diversity action, Mariann Hopkins sued Dow Corning Corporation to recover for injuries suffered as a result of two sets of breast implants manufactured by Dow, which she received in breast reconstruction surgeries in 1977 and 1986. Mariann argues Dow knew of the severe health risks associated with the implants and concealed these dangers from consumers. The jury found Dow liable for Hopkins' injuries and awarded Hopkins $ 840,000 in compensatory damages and $ 6.5 million in punitive damages. Dow appeals. . . .

HUG, CIRCUIT JUDGE:

I. FACTS

On October 4, 1976, plaintiff Mariann Hopkins underwent a bilateral subcutaneous mastectomy for severe fibrocystic disease at St. Mary's Hospital in San Francisco, California. Dr. Karl Bollinger performed the surgery. During the operation, Dr. Bollinger performed reconstructive surgery on plaintiff's breasts utilizing silicone gel implants manufactured by defendant Dow Corning.

Due to subsequent complications, Dr. Bollinger removed the left implant in November, 1976. In June, 1977, Dr. Bollinger inserted a replacement implant in the left breast and replaced the right breast implant in order to achieve symmetry. These implants were also manufactured by the defendant.

In March, 1979, Dr. Stephen Gospe diagnosed plaintiff with mixed connective tissue disease ("MCTD"). MCTD is a rheumatoligical disorder which includes symptoms such as extreme fatigue, weakness, muscle aches and pains, arthralgia, myalgia and arthritis. There is no known cure for this disease.

In January, 1986, plaintiff contacted Dr. Bollinger about further complications from her breast implants. Plaintiff underwent surgery in February to correct the problem. At that time, Dr. Bollinger discovered the implants had ruptured; during the four-hour operation, he proceeded to remove silicone gel that had escaped from the implant. The ruptured implants were sent to Dow for analysis. Several months later, Dow responded to Dr. Bollinger that "examination and testing of both envelopes found no evidence to indicate that any of the damage was manufacture related." Dr. Bollinger informed plaintiff of these results.

None of plaintiff's physicians informed her that the ruptured implant could be responsible for the connective tissue disease from which she suffered. In December, 1987, plaintiff learned from her mother that a possible connection between the ruptured implants and the immune disorder might exist. Shortly thereafter, plaintiff inquired of her physician, Dr. Pelfini, if a possible causal link existed. Dr. Pelfini informed plaintiff that he had never heard of such a connection. In January, 1988, plaintiff visited another of her treating physicians, Dr. Gospe, and inquired the same of him. Dr. Gospe was also unable to provide information regarding a possible causal connection. Plaintiff filed her complaint on December 1, 1988.

The case was bifurcated so that issues regarding liability would be determined first, and if needed, a second trial on damages would be held. The liability phase of the trial began on October 29, 1991. The evidence presented at trial indicated that Dow rushed development of the silicone gel implants, failed to adequately test the implants, and ignored knowledge of adverse health consequences associated with the implants. Plaintiff presented evidence that Dow created a Mammary Task Force charged with getting the new gel implant to market in less than five months. Even after a task force member presented his concerns about "a possible gel bleed situation" Dow ignored proposed design modifications that would reduce the likelihood of leakage. The record indicates that Dow instructed salesmen to wash the implants with "soap and water" in the nearest rest room, and to "dry with hand towels as the implants become oily after being handled and [bleed] on the velvet in the showcase."

The evidence further indicated that in addition to the evidence of silicone leakage, Dow implants experienced a high rate of rupture. Despite proposals by one task force member to implement a "multiple dip" method as a means of ensuring greater uniformity in the envelope, and thereby less likelihood of rupture, Dow adopted the single dip method because it was "easier" and "cheaper." After an incident in which two of the new gel implants "broke during augmentation surgery for the TV taped demonstrations," Thomas Talcott, a Dow engineer, inquired of key Dow employees, "When will we learn at Dow Corning that making a product 'just good enough' almost always leads to products that are 'not quite good enough?'"

There was also evidence that no research concerning the long-term health effects had been conducted. The longest study to address possible adverse health effects of the implants took place over only 80 days and revealed evidence of inflammatory immune response caused by the gel. Dow continued to market these implants until 1987, without the benefit of a lifetime study to demonstrate the safety of its product.

Other evidence at trial indicated that Dow had knowledge of the harmful effects of silicone on the human body. Dow obtained results of a study in which four dogs received silicone gel implants that resembled the implants that Dow was then marketing. The results demonstrated that after six months, the implants appeared to be functioning properly, but that after two years, inflammation surrounding the implants demonstrated the existence of an immune reaction. Dow did not publicly release the results of this research for several years, and when it did ultimately release the results, Dow omitted the negative findings and implied that the implants were safe.

What could Dow have done differently to have avoided this verdict?

Based on these facts, the jury returned a special verdict finding the defendant liable on all plaintiff's theories, including strict liability, breach of warranty, and fraud. The second trial, pertaining to the amount of damages, began on December 11, 1991. The jury awarded plaintiff $ 840,000 in compensatory damages and $ 6.5 million in punitive damages. The district court denied Dow's motion for a directed verdict. The district court also denied Dow's motions for judgment notwithstanding the verdicts and, alternatively, a new trial. Dow appealed. . . .

II. THE DAMAGE AWARD

Hopkins was awarded $ 840,000 in compensatory damages and $ 6.5 million in punitive damages. Dow challenges the size of these awards. Dow contends that the compensatory damage award vastly exceeds actual damages sustained and further contends that the punitive damages award cannot be sustained because it is "grossly excessive," and no understandable relationship exists between actual damages and punitive damages. Hopkins asserts that the record contains ample evidence to support the amount of both the compensatory and the punitive damages awards.

A. Compensatory Damages

The record indicates that expert testimony presented at trial supported a finding that plaintiff had lost $ 404,083 in earnings as a result of her autoimmune disease. Her past medical bills were stipulated to be $ 37,318, and her future medical bills were computed to a present value of $ 31,600. Therefore, Hopkins' out-of-pocket losses amounted to $ 473,001. In addition, the jury apparently awarded Hopkins $ 366,999 in damages for "severe shock to the mental system" and mental pain. Other than a generalized allegation that Hopkins could not have suffered this degree of loss based on her claims, Dow offers no evidence to support its contention that the damages award was excessive. We conclude that the award of compensatory damages was proper.

Was the plaintiff required to demonstrate evidence of causation, or did the court assume causation?

B. Punitive Damages

The evidence presented at trial established that a large number of Dow silicone gel breast implants had been implanted in thousands of women. Each of these women was at risk of encountering the same fate from which Hopkins suffered. Therefore, Dow's conduct in exposing thousands of women to a painful and debilitating disease, and the evidence that Dow gained financially from its conduct, may properly be considered in imposing an award of punitive damages. Moreover, given the facts that Dow was aware of possible defects in its implants, that Dow knew long-term studies of the implants' safety were needed, that Dow concealed this information as well as the negative results of the few short-term laboratory tests performed, and that Dow continued for several years to market its implants as safe despite this knowledge, a substantial punitive damages award is justified. . . .

AFFIRMED.

ARTICLE 6.5

Warning! The Manufacturer of This Product May Have Engaged in Cover-Ups, Lies, and Concealment: Making the Case for Limitless Punitive Awards in Product Liability Lawsuits

Cynthia R. Mabry

I. INTRODUCTION

Punitive damages, also called exemplary or vindictive damages, are "assessed in addition to compensatory damages [to] . . . punish[] the defendant for aggravated or outrageous misconduct and to deter the defendant and others from similar conduct in the future. [This] . . . is an exception to the general rule that damages are aimed at compensating the victim for his injuries." . . .

In America, ever since punitive damages were assessed for the first time in 1784, there has been an outcry against these awards. Today, product manufacturers are among those lobbying for abolishment of exemplary awards. Of course, their special interest is narrowly focused on curtailment of punitive damages in product liability cases. This Article emphasizes the persistent need for assessment of punitive damages in product liability lawsuits, especially when a manufacturer conceals information about the dangerousness of its product knowing that the product causes personal injuries and deaths. . . .

How is it possible that during a fifteen-year period, a company could have eleven punitive damage verdicts totaling $ 17,327,005 issued against them and still be in business?

II. MANUFACTURERS AND CONSUMERS DISAGREE ON THE NECESSITY OF PUNITIVE DAMAGES

A. As Punishment for Making One Defective Product, Manufacturers May Become Liable for Multiple Punitive Awards

As a result of a few highly publicized cases, manufacturers, their lobbyists, and their defense counsel have banded together and protested against punitive awards. Usually, manufacturers and their representatives argue in a choral refrain that punitive damages should be excluded altogether in mass tort cases. They contend that multiple awards threaten their companies' financial stability.

The voices of this chorus began in 1967 when Judge Friendly of the Second Circuit Court of Appeals wrote the majority opinion in Roginsky v. Richardson-Merrell, Inc. At trial, Roginsky was one of hundreds of plaintiffs who filed personal injury claims against Richardson-Merrell, Inc. ("RMI"). Each plaintiff submitted a demand for relief requesting punitive, as well as compensatory, damages. Like many others, Roginsky alleged that MER/29, a drug RMI manufactured, caused him to develop cataracts. He asserted that RMI acted with such negligence that its conduct constituted irresponsibility, justifying the imposition of punitive damages. Apparently the jury agreed. It awarded Roginsky $ 17,500 in compensatory damages and $ 100,000 in punitive damages.

Roginsky's victory celebration was short-lived. On appeal, Judge Friendly applied a "careful scrutiny" standard and concluded that there was insufficient proof that RMI had acted with reckless or wanton disregard for consumers' rights. Therefore, he reasoned, punitive damages were not warranted. Judge Friendly concluded that although RMI had been careless on several occasions, it had conducted premarket tests to ensure MER/29's safety. He also noted that two RMI executives had enough faith in the drug to ingest it themselves. Moreover, Judge Friendly noted that RMI did not attempt to conceal the unhealthy side effects of taking MER/29 when that information became available. In dicta, however, Judge Friendly expressed concern that there were serious consequences of awarding punitive damages in mass product liability cases. To the delight of manufacturers everywhere, Judge Friendly declared that he had "the gravest difficulty in perceiving how claims for punitive damages in such a multiplicity of actions throughout the nation c[ould] be so administered as to avoid overkill."

About thirty years after Roginsky, some advocates of Roginsky still contend that multiple punitive awards in mass tort cases do present a serious problem. One court explained that "[t]he purpose of punitive damages is to sting, not kill, a defendant." Another court decided that absent tort or constitutional law reform, "the time will arrive when [a corporation's] liability for punitive damages imperils its ability to pay compensatory claims and its corporate existence. Neither the company's innocent shareholders, employees and creditors, nor future . . . claimants will benefit from this death by attrition." . . .

Similarly, many asbestos cases have been and continue to be filed against asbestos manufacturers. In 1988, Celotex Corporation lamented that 65,000 asbestos cases were pending against it and that complainants were filing new cases at an alarming rate of 16,000 per month. Two years later, approximately 90,000 asbestos cases were pending in federal and state courts. Product manufacturers opine that the threat of exemplary awards in situations like those "create[] . . . a serious business risk." They argue that without legislative intervention each individual plaintiff in mass product liability cases potentially could recover a substantial award and bankrupt the wealthiest companies. . . .

In any event, the question remains, "How can a Fortune 500 company, making annual revenues of billions of dollars, be deterred from placing a dangerous product on the market?" In some situations, one punitive damage award may be enough to encourage a manufacturer to design a safer product or to recall a defective one. In other cases, it may not. When manufacturers operate with an indifference toward human safety, for the protection of consumers and users, continued reliance upon punitive awards, even when prior awards have been assessed against the manufacturer, is required. Potential bankruptcy should not preclude a trier of fact from assessing punitive damages when a manufacturer intentionally endangers human lives. If punitive awards force such companies out of business, it is good riddance and the public would be much safer. . . .

B. Cessation of Production Should Avert Punitive Awards

In their battle against exemplary awards, manufacturers assert that the future deterrence objective becomes moot when a manufacturer discontinues its wrongful conduct or terminates sale of the defective product. Courts do not agree that this attempt to mitigate losses, after massive destruction has been done, should shield manufacturers from punitive damages. The general rule is that,

> [t]he element of deterrence is still present in an award of punitive damages and to suggest that maximum deterrence may have been attained in the past and that the particular corporate conduct meriting punitive damages may have been discontinued is no answer in every case where such damages are sought.

If they were not caught, some manufacturers would continue to produce unsafe products without abatement. Even when the product that is the subject of litigation is no longer on the market, punitive damages are still necessary to punish companies that brazenly conceal their misconduct and lie to consumers about the safety of their product. Moreover, the second purpose of punitive damages-deterring others from engaging in the same or similar conduct-is still justification for assessing punitive damages after a product is recalled.

C. The Potential Liability for Punitive Awards Makes Manufacturers Leery of Creating New Products and Has Detrimental Effects on the Larger Community

Some manufacturers also claim that the possibility of having to pay excessive punitive awards discourages them from creating new products or causes them to remove lifesaving products from the market. "'Businesses act defensively, avoid innovation as too risky, and devote enormous numbers of personnel and resources to litigation.'"[1] They say that some of these products, like heart valves and other medical devices, are invaluable to the consumer. Moreover, when a product is removed from the market, it has a societal domino effect that begins with the manufacturer downsizing operations. Next, workers are laid off. Then, in the final stages, plants are shut down.

Proponents are not advocating needless eradication of companies or their products. If the products that these manufacturers consider so essential for human life were manufactured properly, neither producers nor suppliers would have to be concerned with punitive awards. In such cases, consumers who filed lawsuits would not be able to prove entitlement to punitive damages and the companies could continue to offer their unmodified products for sale. . . .

III. DEFINITIONS OF PUNISHABLE CONDUCT AND FACTORS FOR QUANTIFYING DAMAGES VARY FROM STATE TO STATE AND FROM COURT TO COURT

Although plaintiffs have no constitutional entitlement to exemplary awards, they do have a right to seek that relief. Contrary to popular belief, however, punitive damages are not recovered in every case in which they are sought. Actually, statistics show that in product liability lawsuits punitive damages are awarded in a minuscule number of cases-only two percent. That is, in only approximately fourteen cases per year do plaintiffs recover exemplary awards. The number of punitive awards is de minimis because these awards are permissible only when the claimant proves that the defendant manufacturer engaged in conduct that is punishable under applicable state law.

To determine whether punitive awards are warranted, states apply similar, but somewhat divergent standards. Customarily, something more than mere negligence is necessary to support an award, but the degree of contumacious conduct that would justify an exemplary award varies from state to state. Generally, the standards fit into one of three categories: "malice-only," "malice or reckless disregard," and "gross negligence." Most states, however, require proof of some kind of willful misconduct such as fraud, oppression, malice, or wantonness.

The manufacturer's lack of regard for human safety is seriously considered in many states. Ohio legislators, for example, require proof of "flagrant disregard" for the safety of persons who may be harmed by the product, while Connecticut and Oklahoma legislators mandate that fact finders look for evidence of "reckless disregard" for human safety. In comparison, Minnesota legislators established a standard of "deliberate disregard" for the safety of others. Finally, the Restatement (Second) of Torts's definition encompasses some of the terms that appear in state statutes. Its description includes adjectives like "outrageous," "evil," and "reckless indifference" for discerning whether a manufacturer's conduct merits punitive relief. . . .

Over the years, judges, through their opinions, and legislators, through statutes, have enumerated other considerations for punitive damage awards.

Criteria have been listed to assist judges and jurors in making determinations regarding the size of punitive damage awards. These elements, some of which are listed in the Restatement (Second) of Torts, include:

1. the nature, extent, and enormity of the wrong committed;
2. the manufacturer's knowledge of the hazard;
3. the amount of profit the manufacturer acquired from its misconduct;
4. the circumstances surrounding the transaction;
5. the manufacturer's wealth;
6. the manufacturer's scienter;
7. the actual damages recovered;
8. the date that the misconduct was terminated; and,
9. the effect and severity of other punishment the manufacturer either received or could receive.

Furthermore, the Supreme Court and at least nine states require consideration of whether the manufacturer intentionally concealed a known danger and the manufacturer's attitude when the cover-up was detected. In California, Kansas, Kentucky, Minnesota, Mississippi, Ohio, Oklahoma, Oregon, and West Virginia, the factfinder may assess punitive damages based on a manufacturer's concealment. Similarly, in three punitive damages decisions, the Supreme Court deemed concealment punishable conduct. In Haslip, the Supreme Court included concealment as a factor to consider in awarding punitive damages.[2] The Gore Court mentioned concealment as conduct that is reprehensible enough to justify punitive liability.[3] Also, in TXO, deceit, a similar factor, was among the elements the Court considered.[4] . . .

IV. PUNITIVE AWARDS STILL SERVE SOCIETAL NEEDS FOR PROTECTING INNOCENT CONSUMERS FROM UNSCRUPULOUS MANUFACTURERS

Consumers and consumer advocates urge continuation of punitive damages because without unlimited potential liability for such awards, many corporations would manufacture unsafe products with reckless abandonment. Some manufacturers consistently operate in such a careless manner that something more than a sting is needed to deter future wrongdoing. Under those extreme circumstances, exemplary awards serve a great societal need.

Manufacturers should be put on notice that they may pay a high penalty if they conceal the dangerousness of a product when they know the products are injuring and killing people. In each instance, the punitive award should be commensurate with the length of concealment, the particular circumstances surrounding the concealment, and the extent and number of injuries and deaths occurring from the first day of concealment through judgment. When manufacturers have engaged in repetitive and purposeful concealment, multiple and huge civil penalties should be assessed.

Several examples of the kind of flagrant deceitfulness and concealment of hazards which merit assessment of punitive awards have been documented. This Part highlights some incidents that demonstrate why continuation of punitive awards is necessary to protect the public from conscienceless manufacturers.

A.H. Robins Co., Inc. ("Robins") purposely caused serious and permanent injuries to millions of women who used its Dalkon Shield-an intrauterine contraceptive device designed to prevent pregnancy. Robins intentionally and knowingly concealed unequivocal evidence that its product was not as safe as Robins steadfastly represented. From the beginning, Robins demonstrated its disregard for women's safety when it marketed the Dalkon Shield without testing it to ensure its safety for human use.

Then, Robins altered the original design and an internal memorandum showed that Robins intentionally withheld information about those changes. This was noteworthy because Robins marketed the Dalkon Shield using a questionable study that was performed on one of the original, unchanged devices. The study Robins publicized indicated that women who used the Dalkon Shield had an extremely low pregnancy rate of 1.1%. One year after Robins began to sell the device, doctors who prescribed it for their patients informed Robins that it was not as effective as Robins had indicated earlier. The actual pregnancy rate was believed to be around 7–8%-much higher than 1.1%.

Physicians notified Robins that many of their patients had become seriously ill while using the Dalkon Shield. Robins's executives ignored the doctors' evidence that the Dalkon Shield caused unwanted pregnancies, septic abortions, severe pelvic infections, excruciating pain, and several deaths. Thousands of women needed hysterectomies to cure or relieve chronic side effects. Despite its knowledge, Robins callously continued sales and advertising without correcting defects in the product or warning women and their physicians about potential problems. One federal court concluded there was evidence of "a pervasive picture of covering up a defective product and continuing to merchandise it by misrepresenting both its efficacy and its safety."[5]

Not only did Robins fraudulently mislead millions of women who used its product, it also deceived doctors by assuring them the device was safe. Despite painful episodes of serious illness, Loretta Tetuan followed her physician's advice and kept a Dalkon Shield in her body from 1971 until 1980. After she sued Robins, the Supreme Court of Kansas decided there was sufficient evidence of Robins's fraud on Dalkon Shield customers and physicians. The jury [returned a] verdict of $ 1.7 million in compensatory damages and $ 7.5 million in punitive damages.

Robins's officials were stubborn. They defied one physician's recommendation to withdraw the Dalkon Shield from the market in 1972. Two years later, the United States Food and Drug Administration ordered Robins to suspend distribution. Still, it took Robins six more years to advise doctors to remove its product from women displaying asymptomatic signs. Even after Robins ceased distribution, it failed to prevent further injury to women who still had the device implanted in their bodies. It refused to recall the product. This is a persuasive example to support the argument that withdrawal of a product should not preclude assessment of punitive awards against the manufacturer.

The Robins cover-up regarding the Dalkon Shield had been implemented years before cessation of production. Roger Tuttle, a Robins attorney in charge of product liability cases, testified that in 1975, Chief Counsel Forrest ordered him to find and destroy documents which memorialized deficiencies in the Dalkon Shield. Forrest informed Tuttle that he had discussed the plan for document destruction with W.L. Zimmer, III, Robins's president. Tuttle, who secretly retained some of the documents which he was supposed to have eliminated, received confirmation that hundreds of documents were burned in a furnace.

Another shocking concealment implicates the entire asbestos industry. Asbestos manufacturers concealed the dangers of asbestos for at least four decades. Ruthlessly, they deceived people, including their own employees, and secreted information about dangerous health risks associated with exposure to asbestos. By the early 1930s, what eventually became a voluminous stack of credible documents detailing the hazards of handling asbestos products started to pile up. Yet asbestos industry officials kept this information from consumers, users, and their own employees. Moreover, as a practice, companies terminated employees who insisted upon warning labels or other safety precautions to lessen the risk of injury.

Johns-Manville Sales Corporation ("Johns-Manville") was one asbestos manufacturer named in many lawsuits. Johns-Manville employers intentionally and deliberately participated in a concerted effort to conceal a known danger. The extent of Johns-Manville's corporate knowledge about the harmful effects of asbestos and its willingness to hide disparaging information was well documented. For instance, Johns-Manville was a member of the Industrial Health Foundation ("IHF"). Between 1936 and 1941, IHF distributed eleven articles about the dangerous nature of asbestos to its members and suggested ways to protect employees who handled the product. As an IHF member, Johns-Manville received a copy of all those articles, so it knew or should have known that asbestos was a lethal product.

Before the trade articles were published, Johns-Manville's concealment was already in full effect. In 1933, three years before the first article was delivered, Johns-Manville knew that its employees were getting sick. Johns-Manville's workers had begun to seek workers' compensation benefits for asbestos-related illness. The company reacted by passing a resolution to settle all claims.

After receiving results of industry-wide studies which revealed that prolonged exposure to asbestos caused asbestosis-chronic lung disease caused by inhaling asbestos particles- Johns-Manville conducted its own study. However, before Johns-Manville's results were released, its general counsel, Vandiver Brown, ordered A.J. Lanza, the scientist who conducted the internal study, to alter his report. While editing the initial report, Lanza had deleted statements that minimized the risks and effects of exposure to asbestos. When Brown became aware that Lanza had redacted information, Brown demanded that Lanza put that information back into the report. Brown wanted to retain those statements because he believed that they "presented an aspect of [Lanza's] survey that was favorable to the industry." Complying with Brown's wishes, Lanza revised his report.

Further evidence of Johns-Manville's concealment appeared in its meeting minutes. After meeting with an asbestos supplier to discuss ways of reducing employee risk, Johns-Manville conducted its own meeting. All participants agreed to adhere to the company's "past policy of keeping this matter confidential."

Dr. Kenneth Smith, one of Johns-Manville's medical directors, disclosed another "hush-hush" policy that affected employees who had contracted asbestosis. Under that directive, company physicians did not tell an employee when x-rays showed the employee was stricken with asbestosis. The preposterous and selfish reason for withholding this vital information was that it would allow the employee to "live and work in peace and the company can benefit by [the employee's] many years of experience."

Brown's response to another asbestos supplier's comment was just as startling. It sounded like conspiracy to deceive the public and to conceal harm. The president of an asbestos supplier was quoted as saying, "the less said about asbestos, the better off we are." Brown's reply was, "I quite agree with you that our interests are best served by having asbestosis receive the minimum of publicity." When the New Jersey Supreme Court affirmed one punitive damage verdict against Johns-Manville, it wrote, "Not only did it fail to warn users of the serious health hazards associated with exposure to asbestos, it actually took affirmative steps to conceal this information from the public. These actions fully warranted the jury's imposition of punitive damages."

Johns-Manville's far-reaching deceit stretched beyond its corporate headquarters and influenced the media. At least one Johns-Manville official strongly suggested that an asbestos trade magazine reporter refrain from publishing negative articles about asbestos. When the same reporter sought feedback on a proposed review of a book that linked asbestos to pneumoconiosis (lung disease), Brown dissuaded her from reviewing the book. He implied that since several of the trade magazine's subscribers would not approve of the book review, it should not be written. Later, Brown intimated that if the industry decided to allow publication of information about asbestosis, manufacturers and suppliers should "warn" magazine editors to use American data that was "milder"-less damaging-than English data.

While this masquerade continued for decades, millions of people who were exposed to asbestos suffered from serious, sometimes fatal, diseases. According to medical experts, there are two progressive, latent, and incurable diseases derived from inhaling asbestos: asbestosis and mesothelioma. Asbestosis is a lung disease that causes the air sacs to constrict so the sufferer's lung capacity and pulmonary function are significantly decreased. Mesothelioma is a fatal tumor of the membrane that lines the walls of the lungs and the abdominal cavity. Further complications, serious ones, develop as side effects of the medication prescribed to relieve the symptoms of asbestosis and mesothelioma. So, in addition to asbestosis and mesothelioma, patients routinely suffer from diabetes, rheumatoid arthritis, and osteoporosis.

Concealment in the asbestos industry remains a modern day phenomenon. In 1996, a jury in a Texas court issued a verdict of punitive damages against a product manufacturer. For fourteen years, Owens-Corning Fiberglas Corporation ("OCF") manufactured Kaylo-a product containing asbestos. OCF's director of product development warned corporate officers, including the president, that asbestos-containing fiberglass products caused lung cancer. Further, at ten-year intervals (in the 1940s, 1950s, and 1960s), executives received correspondence from different physicians detailing the hazards of handling asbestos. Yet OCF continued to conceal a known danger when it published brochures indicating that Kaylo was a nontoxic substance. . . .

Manufacturers hide defects in their products regardless of the devastating impact of the defects on consumers. A prosthetics manufacturer discovered that one component part of its prosthetic knee was too large.[6] For the prosthesis to have worked effectively, correct sizing was critical. If the prosthesis fit properly, it would not protrude and strike the patient's kneecap when the knee was flexed. Rather than notify its sales personnel and medical professionals about its error, Richards Manufacturing Co., Inc. ("Richards") continued to distribute the improperly sized part. Not surprisingly, Richards's ill-sized component part malfunctioned. It caused one recipient to lose a kneecap. A jury awarded him $ 25,000 in compensatory damages and $ 500,000 in punitive damages. Thousands of others, who were arthritic already, suffered agonizing pain and were immobilized. All of this suffering occurred for the sole reason that Richards wanted to protect its competitive edge on the prosthesis market. It feared that if it took the time to refurbish the part, other companies would lure its customers away.

Some manufacturers are just as insensitive when children's lives are at stake. Riegel Textile Corporation ("Riegel") manufactured flannelette, a cotton material used to make children's pajamas.[7] Riegel knew that many children had suffered severe burns and permanent disfigurement while wearing combustible flannelette garments. Riegel also knew that multiple lawsuits had been filed against it for those children's injuries. A high level official in the company sent an internal memorandum to Linton Reynolds, the person in charge of the research department. In the memorandum entitled "Flammability Liability," the official warned, "[w]e are always sitting on somewhat of a powder keg as regards our flannelette being so flammable." The public was not apprised of the dangers that children were subjected to when they dressed for bed.

While Riegel was endangering children's lives, Admiral Corporation ("Admiral") jeopardized the lives of whole families. Admiral sold defective color television sets to unsuspecting customers. A high voltage transformer in the sets was made of flammable paper and wax materials. Premarket testing was woefully inadequate but after only one heat test, Admiral and its project manager knew that the transformer could catch fire in their customers' homes even after the power had been turned off. Admiral's files contained several complaints about defective televisions and reports of ninety-one fires. Ross Siragusa, Jr., the president of Admiral, randomly kept some summaries of claims against Admiral and discarded other summaries.

When her Admiral television set exploded, Zora Gillham sustained third-degree burns that covered 18.5% of her body. During the eighteen months in which she was hospitalized, Gillham underwent seven operations for her burns and ultimately suffered from a series of complications that rendered her an invalid. A jury awarded her $ 125,000 in compensatory damages, $ 50,000 in attorneys' fees, and $ 100,000 in punitive damages.

Like Robins's executives, Admiral executives and subordinate employees deceived purchasers about the safety of Admiral television sets. One customer refused to accept repossession of a set that Admiral repaired after the transformer caught fire. Admiral employees pressured the customer and assured him that it was safe to take the set back into his home.

Finally, one federal district court judge said that "the tobacco industry may be the king of concealment and disinformation."[8] Tobacco company whistleblowers have started to blow smoke rings around the industry. Actually, these whistleblowers have blown the roof off tobacco company headquarters and exposed their innermost secrets about the hazards of smoking cigarettes. Former employees, experts, and the owner of the Liggett Group-a small tobacco company-have disclosed information that had been hidden from the public for more than thirty years. Tobacco company officials knew that smoking cigarettes may become addictive behavior. Moreover, they knew that they could reduce the harmful effects of smoking by decreasing the amount of nicotine cigarettes contained. Until recently, none of the information about the addictive traits of cigarette smoking or about the tobacco manufacturers' efforts to manipulate the nicotine content in cigarettes was shared with the public. To ensure secrecy, some tobacco companies required their employees to sign confidentiality agreements-codes of silence-promising that they would not testify or give interviews about their role in the cigarette business.

Internal documentation that has been released for public perusal shows that tobacco industry executives purposely concealed negative information about cigarettes. Ian Uydess, a former Philip Morris cancer researcher, publicly accused executives of shelving his suggestions for removing poisonous nitrates from tobacco. Philip Morris also silenced scientists who were studying whether nicotine was addictive. Additionally, Uydess alleged that tobacco companies shut down United States laboratories where hundreds of experiments had been conducted. Data regarding sensitive experiments that scientists performed in the United States were transferred to overseas laboratories in Germany and Switzerland where there would be less intrusion from prying lawyers and United States government representatives.

Destruction of documents seems to have been routine at some tobacco companies. At a hearing, another former Philip Morris scientist gave sworn testimony that he shredded data regarding his findings. Dr. William Raymond Morgan tested the level of "tobacco-specific nitrosamine"-a carcinogen-in Virginia Slims cigarettes. He discovered that Virginia Slims cigarettes contained a much higher level of the carcinogen than he had ever witnessed. Morgan testified that his supervisor, Dr. Cathy Ellis, then the manager of the Biochemical Research Division, ordered him to destroy data that he had compiled. Even though Ellis's directive was in complete derogation of a court order, Morgan yielded to her command and shredded the document. Now Ellis is the vice president of research and development.

Tobacco industry officials' disrespect for the law has been pervasive. They conspired against the public and public representatives. On April 14, 1994, top executives from seven tobacco companies testified before the House Subcommittee on Health and the Environment. Before the interrogation began, each executive raised his hand and solemnly gave an oath to tell the truth. Then, one by one, each spoke into a microphone and swore that he believed that nicotine was not addictive. Evidence, released after they testified, showed that those executives lied. Consequently, they may now be subject to criminal prosecution and penalties for perjury as well as punitive damages in civil actions.

Unfortunately, evidence that some attorneys who advise tobacco companies actively encouraged and participated in cover-ups may have been unearthed along with indicia of other corporate misconduct. Tobacco company lawyers, officers of the court, have been accused of deceitful and unethical acts to protect their clients. Reportedly, one attorney coaxed a scientist to revise a report by threatening to withdraw funds that financed the scientist's research project. Other attorneys have hidden a mass of documents containing unflattering information behind a shroud of attorney-client privilege objections. To avoid disclosure of company documents, tobacco company lawyers have been accused of falsely claiming that the documents were privileged when they knew that no privilege barred disclosure. Unlike Robins's counsel, however, tobacco company attorneys did not require destruction of documents.

Tobacco company executives' mayhem is far-flung. Millions of people are addicted to the nicotine contained in cigarettes. Many of them suffer from debilitating illnesses such as lung cancer, heart disease, and emphysema. Some smokers suffer unnatural and painful deaths. Meanwhile, cigarette manufacturers continue to produce cigarettes, conceal the health risks of smoking cigarettes, and even heartlessly gear advertising toward enticing twelve-year-olds to take their first puff.

A complete discussion of the concealment issue must entail consideration of the reasons that manufacturers conceal and destroy information. A few arguments have surfaced. None are persuasive or acceptable.

A paramount concern with manufacturers is fear of losing sales and profits. Some company officials value sales quotas and stock prices more than consumer safety. Undoubtedly, the strong potential of protracted litigation, losing trials, and accompanying legal fees are driving forces in cover-ups. Dow Corning reported that its litigation costs in 1994 alone exceeded $ 200 million. A Robins attorney must have given credence to those concerns because he decided that taking the Dalkon Shield off the market would be viewed as "a 'confession of liability' and Robins would lose many of the pending lawsuits."

Some companies go to great lengths to stave off unwanted publicity. As previously indicated, Vandiver Brown and other asbestos industry personnel manipulated the media and conspired to deprive the public of damaging information about asbestos. Bad press about a product or the company's lack of ethics could sound the death knell for that company.

One writer offered another rationale for covering up product deficiencies or harmful effects of using the product. Once negative information about the product is exposed, there will not be any more speculation about whether the product presents health risks or whether it is dangerous. This implies that concealment allows continuance of production as long as there is a debate about the possibility of harm. On the other hand, if published data unequivocally proves that the product is harmful, it will affect the manufacturers' ability to produce and sell that product.

Other manufacturers do a cost-benefit analysis and consumers lose. A manufacturer could decide that it would be less expensive for it to risk a lawsuit or risk injuring consumers than to redesign the product. Minor repairs can cost millions of dollars. In a letter, one Riegel official wrote that he knew how to produce a safer fabric for children's pajamas but since the flame-retardant chemicals he needed were so expensive, he would not use the chemicals unless federal law required it. While expressing the same concern during a recent congressional debate, Congressman Scott of Virginia complained that corporations continued to sell highly flammable children's pajamas because it was cheaper to make the unmodified pajamas than to reduce flammability.

Ford Motor Company, also, made a horrific cost-benefit determination. It calculated that a certain number of human lives would be lost when Pinto gas tanks exploded upon impact and caused passengers to burn to death. Rather than redesign the gas tanks at a cost of approximately ten dollars per automobile, Ford representatives performed "a cost-benefit analysis balancing human lives and limbs against corporate profits." Similarly, Robins knew that the string attached to the Dalkon Shield was causing severe medical problems for its three million female customers. However, Robins repeatedly ignored the danger signs and refused to use a slower production method to eliminate the problem.

Finally, the ultimate consequence of liability or disclosure that companies may dread is "death" of the company due to a huge vindictive award or several smaller awards. Consequently, the company could go bankrupt. Moreover, if that company's only product is irretrievably defective, it may be forced to go out of business.

In the business world, paramount concerns are guarding the company and protecting its profits. Whether innocent people are physically or emotionally hurt as a result of the concealment is irrelevant. In the delicate balance of business and safety, business comes first. Although these reasons for concealment may appear laudable to corporate representatives, any and all of them justify punitive awards. Of course, there are some inherently dangerous products, like automobiles, that cannot be rendered risk-free. Despite known risks, however, millions of people make an informed choice to use these products every day. Concealment eliminates the freedom of choice that consumers and users are entitled to make regarding whether they should use a certain product. Moreover, when manufacturers like Robins and Johns-Manville conceal negative effects of product use, they deprive the injured person of the opportunity to seek proper care and treatment for the injury that the product causes. It prevents people like asbestos handlers from taking precautions to protect themselves.

Usually, the doors to corporate boardrooms-where decisions to eradicate documents and to hide information are made-are closed to the general public. Thus, cover-ups may, and do, remain undetected for many years-that is, until someone who was behind one of those doors becomes conscientious and discloses corporate wrongdoing. As a result of these disclosures, it is evident that consumers cannot depend upon manufacturers to monitor their own conduct. Therefore, to protect the public, legislatures, judges, and consumers must endeavor to ensure production and sale of safe products. One way of guaranteeing public safety is through granting punitive awards in appropriate circumstances. . . .

V. CONCLUSION

The threat of multiple and substantial punitive awards remains necessary to promote public safety by deterring bad acts by manufacturers. "While punitive damages may not be a logically perfect method of remedying . . . unavoidable flaws in our system of justice, they are a useful surrogate."[9] The kind of flagrant and reprehensible misconduct that the Gore Court described still abounds in the business world. Moreover, administrative and criminal remedies that should be useful deterrents are woefully inadequate to protect consumers. Thus, punitive damages play a vital role in punishing some manufacturers and deterring others from endangering consumers and users.

Manufacturers who hunger for a competitive edge on the market and large monetary profits have turned a blind eye to the human suffering, deaths, and other destruction that their products have caused. Their actions are in complete disregard for human safety and they must be held accountable without arbitrary limits on punitive awards. Accordingly, on a case-by-case basis, punitive damages should be awarded as often as necessary and in amounts large enough to encourage manufacturers to take better care in designing, producing, and marketing products. . . .

In our imperfect world-the real world-manufacturers engage in cover-ups, lies, and concealment of information about their hazardous products. Consequently, innocent consumers and users are maimed and killed. Without the threat of punitive damages, the maiming and killing will continue.

END NOTES

1. Cong. Rec. E681 (daily ed. May 1, 1996) (statement of Dick Thornburg quoting Senator Lieberman).
2. See Haslip, 499 U.S. at 21-22.
3. See Gore, 116 S. Ct. at 1601.
4. See TXO Prod. Corp. v. Alliance Resources Corp., 509 U.S. 443, 462 (1993).
5. Craig v. A.H. Robins Co., 790 F.2d 1, 4 (lst Cir. 1986).
6. See *Vossler v. Richards Mfg. Co.*, 192 Cal. Rptr. 219, 221 (Ct. App. 1983).
7. See *Gryc v. Dayton-Hudson Corp.*, 297 N.W.2d 727, 729 (Minn. 1980).
8. *Haines v. Liggett Group, Inc.*, 140 F.R.D. 681, 683 (D.N.J.), vacated, 975 F.2d 81 (3d. Cir. 1992); Christopher Kilbourne, Tobacco Companies Castigated By Judge—He Orders Release of Studies on Danger, Record, Feb. 7, 1992, at A1. But see Haines, 975 F.2d at 88, 97–98.
9. *Acosta v. Honda Motor Co.*, 717 F.2d 828, 837 (3d Cir. 1983).

ARTICLE 6.6

Apple v. Free Speech?

Timothy B. Lee

Media darling Apple Computer likes secrecy. CEO Steve Jobs likes to keep the company's products shrouded in mystery until they are unveiled at carefully scripted events. But Apple's zeal for privacy is matched only by its customers' appetite for the latest Apple rumors. Mac fans flock to websites like AppleInsider and Think Secret seeking details of upcoming Apple gadgets.

In January, Apple escalated its ongoing battle with the rumor sites when it filed a lawsuit against Think Secret for printing rumors about its forthcoming Mac Mini computer. The lawsuit has been widely reported in the media, who claim that it raises new issues about the limits of free speech in cyberspace. As the *Financial Times* put it, "Blogs have so far operated mostly outside the law, legal experts say. Now Apple, the alternative computer maker, has decided to test the freedom of the blogosphere by suing the operator of one of the company's most influential fan sites."

On closer examination, it's hard to see what the fuss is about. If anything, the incident reveals more about mainstream journalists' condescending attitude toward their upstart online competitors than it does about law or technology.

Think Secret is not a "blog." It is a commercial, advertisement-supported online magazine. It's run by a college student, and is therefore smaller and less polished than online magazines like *Slate* or *Salon*. But the First Amendment's protections aren't limited to slick publications with large staffs. Some of the Founding Fathers, after all, were prolific pamphleteers, hardly more polished than Think Secret.

What is the purpose of the First Amendment?

It's not obvious, then, how this case presents novel legal questions. Apple argues that because its employees are required to sign nondisclosure agreements, Think Secret must have obtained its rumors in violation of contractual obligations. Apple's lawyers, however, would do well to review the famous Pentagon Papers decision. In 1971, The *New York Times* published excerpts from a classified report on the progress of the Vietnam War. The Nixon administration sued, asking for an injunction against publishing further excerpts. In a 5-4 decision, the high court ruled for the *Times*, holding that as long as the *Times* had not itself broken the law in obtaining the documents, it could not be prevented from publishing them unless their publication posed an imminent threat to national security.

Given that Apple has such a weak legal position, why would they even pursue the legal action described in this article?

Steve Jobs might disagree, but it seems clear that leaking news about upcoming Apple products poses a lesser threat to national security than leaking classified military reports. Clearly, if Think Secret did not itself sign a nondisclosure agreement, it can't be censored because its sources did.

Apple also claims that Think Secret violated Apple's trade secrets when it published the information. But that barely passes the straight face test. Not every piece of information can be declared a trade secret. Under the law, trade secrets must have commercial value to the holder of the secret or its competitors. Had Think Secret published schematics or internal Apple documents detailing logistical or technical details of new products, they might have had a credible case. But mere rumors about the features, appearance, and price of an upcoming product do no appreciable damage to Apple's bottom line and are too vague to be of any use to competitors.

ARTICLE 6.7

The Nanny State

Cato Institute

One of the more disturbing trends in government expansion over the last 30 years has been the collection of laws, regulations, and binding court decisions that make up the "nanny state.'' Those laws and regulations represent government at its most arrogant. Their message is clear: politicians and bureaucrats know more about how to live your life, manage your health, and raise your kids than you do. Former president Ronald Reagan once said: "Government exists to protect us from each other. Where government has gone beyond its limits is in deciding to protect us from ourselves.'' Today's policymakers would do well to heed Reagan's words.

What would be some illustration of laws that would make one describe this country as a "naanny state"?

Unfortunately, they haven't. Lawmakers at all levels of government have shown increasing contempt for personal responsibility and an increasing tendency to employ the power of the state to influence behavior. Government today pressures us to avoid risks, even risks that many of us knowingly and willingly take. There seems to be a consensus among nanny-statists that, with enough public service announcements, awareness campaigns, and social engineering efforts, Americans will start behaving as the nannystatists want them to. The largest, most expensive, and most obvious example of government's nanny is America's failed drug war. Though drug use directly harms no one but drug users, we continue to prohibit certain drugs, either because policymakers believe government should protect users from themselves or because they believe drug use has detrimental effects on society at large, or on the "public health.''

The same philosophy that entrenched the government in the drug war has allowed ensuing nanny-state endeavors to blossom. Once we're comfortable with government control over what pharmaceuticals we're permitted to put into our bodies, the case for restrictions, regulations, and controls on tobacco and alcohol isn't difficult to make. And from there, government can cite, and has cited, the "public health'' effects of obesity as reason to extend its tentacles into our refrigerators and onto our dinner plates. In fact, once policymakers have bought the notion of a "public health'' in need of protection and nurturing by government, they can be comfortable giving the state pervasive control over nearly every facet of our lives—from mandating that we wear our seatbelts, to telling us what risks we should allow our children to take, to telling us what foods we should eat and how much and how often we should eat them. . . .

There seems to be no sphere of life in regard to which government doesn't have an opinion about how we should live and doesn't feel obligated to help us live correctly—through excise taxes, tax breaks, regulation, restrictions on advertising, zoning laws, or outright prohibition. Today we have well-funded, well-staffed federal agencies whose sole mission is to discourage Americans from using alcohol and tobacco. Implementing or raising existing excise taxes on both alcohol and cigarettes is again gaining favor in state legislatures, particularly in states facing a budget crunch. In 2004 the U.S. Department of Justice pressed charges against two California pornography producers and has publicly said it plans to press charges against others. . . .

The nanny state's latest crusade makes Americans even more intimate with their government, bringing the state to our mouths, frying pans, and waistlines. Responding to a rash of media reports announcing that Americans, and American children in particular, are getting heavy, nannystatists have called for a host of new government programs, regulations, and measures intended to persuade, encourage, or outright coerce Americans to eat properly and exercise regularly. Some of those measures are relatively innocuous, such as government-sponsored "public awareness'' campaigns. Others are more troubling, including "fat taxes'' on calorie-dense foods, class action litigation against food producers, and restrictions on portion sizes in restaurants. And the most costly obesity-related proposal was never voted on by lawmakers at all. . . .

Lawmakers should respect Americans' control over their own lives. We need to rethink the idea of "public health,'' so that it encompasses only serious threats to public safety, threats such as deadly diseases or chemical or biological terrorism—threats to which no one would willingly expose himself.

To make the argument contained in this paragraph, the author must be making what assumption about how much access to health and financial information the typical American has? Is his assumption valid?

Individual Americans will make better decisions about risk and lifestyle when they and they alone bear the consequences of those decisions. Of course, what makes a good or bad decision is subjective, which is precisely why personal decisions should be beyond the purview of government. More fundamentally, what we eat, drink, or otherwise put into our bodies; what we do with our bodies; the people we choose to sleep with and how we choose to sleep with them; and what health, financial, or safety risks we elect to take simply are not legitimate concerns of the state. Once government simply leaves Americans alone on these matters, responsibility for decisions about risk and vice and their consequences becomes limited to individual Americans. It's only when government gets involved that the costs of risk are dispersed across the rest of the public.

ISSUE SUMMARY

Should people really be allowed to sue fast-food restaurants if they gain weight? You have probably had more than one conversation with friends, family, and associates about the people who sued McDonald's. What do you think? Should the restaurants be held responsible for the health problems the diners are now experiencing? Or should the diners be held responsible for their personal choices to eat fast food?

The selections in this chapter all addressed a central issue: When should a seller be legally allowed to conceal information? The real question at hand is much broader, though: To what extent should people be held responsible for the decisions they make? That is, even if sellers hide some information from people, to what extent should those people be held responsible for their choices?

Consider again the people who sued McDonald's. You can choose to view the people many different ways. Perhaps they were duped by the big, bad corporation, and they need our help. Perhaps they ignored commonsense warnings about the health effects of fast food, and now they're trying to cash in by suing McDonald's. Perhaps they knew they shouldn't have been eating fast food all the time, but they were too lazy to find out just how bad the food really was. Perhaps they knew exactly what they were doing to themselves, and they chose to eat the fast food anyway.

What do you think? How do you see the plaintiffs who sued McDonald's? As a result, how much responsibility do you assign to them? If you believe they were fooled by McDonald's, do you hold the plaintiffs at all responsible? If you believe the plaintiffs are running a scheme, do you hold them mostly responsible? If you believe the plaintiffs knew what they were doing, do you hold them entirely responsible?

How do you see people? If you believe consumers should seek information and protect themselves, then you are unlikely to blame corporations for hiding information. If you believe consumers need help fighting corporations and protecting themselves, then you are likely to require corporations to disclose information. What do you believe? How do your beliefs influence your opinions of the arguments presented in this chapter?

ISSUE HIGHLIGHTS

- Social contract theory argues that when crafting a decision, and hence determining what respect for the equality of individuals is required, a judge should ask the complex hypothetical question: "To which disclosure rules would bargainers have given their consent if they had deliberated about the matter under circumstances in which they were uninformed about how the application of the rule would affect them personally?"

- According to market theory, the more information individuals possess about goods they buy and sell, the more reason society has to think that these goods will go to those who most value them, and hence, the better off society will be. If full information were free, though, no one would want to search for the information because there would be no incentive to find it.
- Punitive damages, also called exemplary or vindictive damages, are aimed at punishing the defendant for aggravated or outrageous misconduct and deterring the defendant and others from similar conduct in the future.
- When determining the appropriate size of punitive damage awards, judges and juries may consider: (1) the nature, extent, and enormity of the wrong committed; (2) the manufacturer's knowledge of the hazard; (3) the amount of profit the manufacturer acquired from its misconduct; (4) the circumstances surrounding the transaction; (5) the manufacturer's wealth; (6) the manufacturer's scienter; (7) the actual damages recovered; (8) the date that the misconduct was terminated; and, (9) the effect and severity of other punishment the manufacturer either received or could receive. Some courts also consider the manufacturer's concealment and/or deceit.

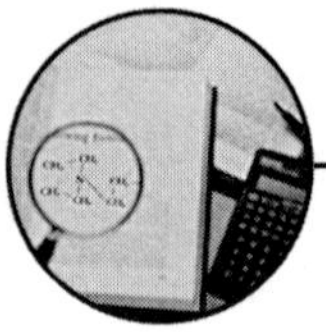

CRITICAL THINKING

Solar power is a renewable energy source. What does that mean to you? Anything? Some might hear that solar power is a renewable energy source and conclude that they should install solar panels on the roof of the house. Some might hear that solar power is a renewable energy source and conclude that they should buy a solar-powered car. Some might hear that solar power is a renewable energy source and conclude nothing at all. What did you think?

Our point has nothing to do with solar power. Our point has to do with information and so-called *facts*. Facts do *not* speak for themselves. People speak for the facts. People manipulate information to suit their needs. The fact that solar power is a renewable energy source means nothing by itself. When a person interprets that fact, then an argument is born.

When you read arguments, do not get stuck thinking about facts only in the author's terms. The author may have interpreted the information one way, but you can interpret the information differently. The author may be thinking about solar panels while you're thinking about a solar car. If your interpretation is just as reasonable as the author's, then the author will need to convince you that his interpretation is more correct than yours if he wants you to accept his conclusion.

Let's think about an example from this chapter. Meislik provides plenty of evidence that the United States is experiencing an obesity epidemic. Assume that you agree with Meislik that an obesity epidemic exists. Now what? Do you jump to the conclusion that fast-food companies should be held responsible?

Can you think of reasonable alternative conclusions that could be drawn from information about America's obesity epidemic? One might conclude: (1) the school systems should force children to develop healthy eating habits; (2) the government should open free gyms for adults to exercise; or (3) the government should begin an aggressive public service campaign to spread information about healthy living habits. Which conclusion seems most reasonable to you? Has Meislik convinced you to agree with her?

Assume you agree with the truth of another one of Meislik's reasons: fast food is very unhealthy. Do you jump to Meislik's conclusion that fast-food companies should be held responsible for the obesity epidemic? Can you think of reasonable alternative conclusions? One might conclude: (1) the government should limit the number of calories that can be served in any fast-food meal; (2) the government should launch an aggressive public service campaign to tell people exactly how much fat is in fast food; or (3) we should go picket outside a fast-food restaurant with signs advertising the calorie content of each dish. Has Meislik convinced you to agree with her conclusion yet?

As you walk through an argument, you will find that most authors' reasons can lead you to other reasonable conclusions. Think back to the first chapter's critical thinking exercise. We asked you to identify the authors' assumptions. When you consider reasonable alternative conclusions, can you see how your assumptions (as well as each author's assumptions) influence the conclusions you form based on the *facts*?

For example, Meislik assumes that people are vulnerable to the cunning of businesses. If Meislik believed the opposite, that people can protect themselves from businesses, then Meislik would not blame businesses for the obesity epidemic. If you see people as individually responsible for their choices and lifestyles, then you are unlikely to agree with Meislik's interpretation of the facts. Remember to ask, "Did Meislik do anything to convince me that she's right?"

Think about some of the other authors featured in this chapter. What information do they provide as evidence? Can you think of reasonable alternative conclusions based on that information? What assumptions might influence your interpretation? When you recognize that no *fact* means just one thing, you open your mind to all of the possible arguments and viewpoints around you. Keep your mind open, ask questions, and think about all of the plausible conclusions you can draw from the information presented by each author.

ADDITIONAL READING RESOURCES

Jean Braucher, "Deception, Economic Loss and Mass-Market Customers: Consumer Protection Statutes as Persuasive Authority in the Common Law of Fraud," *Arizona Law Review*. 48: 829 (2006).

Charles E. Cantu, "Fattening Foods: Under Products Liability Litigation Is the Big Mac Defective?" *J. Food L. & Pol'y*, 1: 165 (2005).

Michael Duffy, "Fraud on the Market: Judicial Approaches to Causation and Loss from Securities Nondisclosure in the United States, Canada and Australia," *Melb. UL Rev.*, 29: 621 (2005).

David P. Graham and Jeremy C. Vest, "Doctors, Drugs, and Duties to Warn: Protections Afforded Medical Device and Drug Manufacturers under the Learned Intermediary Doctrine May Be Threatened," *Def. Counsel J.*, 72: 380 (2005).

Robert W. Gray, "The Applicability of Constructive Eviction, implied Warranty of Habitability, Common-Law Fraud, and the Consumer Fraud Act to Omissions of Material Facts in a Commercial Lease," *J. Marshall L. Rev.*, 38: 1289 (2004).

B. Maron and R. Hauser, "Perspectives on the Failure of Pharmaceutical and Medical Device Industries to Fully Protect Public Health interests," *Am. J. Cardiology*, 100:1, pg. 147–151 (2007).

Melissa Grills Robinson, Paul N. Bloom, and Nicholas H. Lurie, "Combating Obesity in the Courts: Will Lawsuits against McDonald's Work?," *J. Pub. Pol'y & Mkt.*, 24:2, 299–306 (2005).

W. David Slawson, "Contractual Discretionary Power: A Law to Prevent Deceptive Contracting by Standard Form," *Mich. St. L. Rev.* 853 (2006).

For more information, check these sites:

http://www.law.ku.edu/lawrev/schwartz.pdf (Victor E. Schwartz & Cary Silverman, *Common-Sense Construction of Consumer Protection Acts*) [*Last visited: July 8, 2008*]

http://anzhealthpolicy.com/content/2/1/32 (George Thomson & Nick Wilson, *Implementation Failures in the Use of Two New Zealand Laws to Control the Tobacco Industry: 1989–2005*) [*Last visited: July 8, 2008*]

http://works.bepress.com/jacob_kreutzer/1/ (Jacob Kreutzer, *Somebody Has to Pay: Products Liability for Spyware*) [*Last visited: July 8, 2008*]

http://lawandenvironment.typepad.com/law_and_the_environment/2007/02/directors_and_o.html (environmental law blog about asbestos) [*Last visited: July 8, 2008*]

ISSUE 7

Should Homeowners Be Able to Do What They Want with Their Property?

Property rights are certainly one of the most important institutions of the American economic and legal systems. The idea that an individual can own something is fundamental to the functioning of the legal system. However, the definition of own is not as straightforward as one might initially think. Any ambiguity associated with the idea of ownership is hotly debated. The following articles address questions of how entities, not the government, can place limits on an individual's use of his/her property. In other words, should homeowners be able to do whatever they want with their property?

The first piece in this chapter is a case from the Louisiana Court of Appeals for the Fifth Circuit addressing a dispute between a homeowners' association and the homeowner. Explicitly, the question the court faced was "To what extent can the homeowner's association interfere with Ms. McGovern's management of her property?" Although much of the case was determined by specific details of her situation and legal precedent in the state of Louisiana, the majority opinion points to the key idea that the homeowner's association can place limits and regulations on individuals in the community.

The second piece points out a more curious implication of restrictive covenants; they can have significant implications for the environment. To what extent should restrictive covenants be permissible when they interfere with socially beneficial behaviors? As you read this piece, consider a possible question about the argument, what if the restrictive covenants led to socially beneficial behaviors? In what sort of cases are restrictive covenants socially useful and in what situations are they socially harmful?

The last two articles are journal articles addressing two different issues. Rogers addresses how to best understand the role of community associations. He first points out that many traditional ways of viewing community associations fall short because they do not consider the judicial nature of many associations. Rogers instead argues that administrative law is a better way to understand community associations because administrative law works as a better analogue.

Finally, Herman addresses situations where the restrictive covenants limit who can reside in a given community. Herman notes that many private communities may be prohibiting sex offenders from even residing in the community. Although Herman starts from a position where laws such as Megan's Law are acceptable, he does not necessarily believe that private entities should be in the business of regulating where individuals may live.

Collectively, these articles look at restrictive covenants in private communities in very different ways, but all reach a similar issue. Should homeowners be able to do what they want with their property?

ISSUE ARTICLES

Belle Terre Lakes Home Owners Association v. Patricia McGovern, Court of Appeals of Louisiana, Fifth Circuit (2002).

Nancy K. Kubasek, from "The Conflict Between Homeowners' Associations and the Environment," *Real Estate Law Journal* (vol. 33, 2004).

William H. Rogers, from "A Market for Institutions: Assessing the Impact of Restrictive Covenants on Housing," *Land Economics* (vol. 82, 2006).

John J. Herman, from "Not in My Community: Is It Legal for Private Entities to Ban Sex Offenders from Living in Their Communities?" *Widener Law Journal* (vol. 16, 2006).

ARTICLE 7.1

Belle Terre Lakes Home Owners Association v. Patricia McGovern

Patricia McGovern Landry purchased a lot and home in Phase IV of the Belle Terre Lakes Subdivision. Mrs. Landry's new home and lot were subjected to a pre-existing restrictive covenant, of which she was made aware at the time of her purchase. The restrictive covenant contains reference to an architectural control committee that has the power and authority to review all plans, specifications, and improvements to the property. The committee also has the ability to approve or disapprove plans for improvement.

Mrs. Landry was notified by the Belle Terre Lakes Home Owners Association of certain violations of the restrictive covenants regarding her property. Specifically, this notice referred to the location of a satellite dish on Mrs. Landry's home and the placement of the framework on Mrs. Landry's fence. When Mrs. Landry and the Home Owners Association failed to reach an agreement, the Association sent Mrs. Landry a letter giving her one week to rectify the violations, which she failed to do. The Association subsequently filed suit against Mrs. Landry for violation of the restrictive covenant.

The trial court granted summary judgment in favor of the Home Owners Association, ruling Mrs. Landry had to remove the satellite dish and fence from her property and to comply with the terms of the restrictive covenants. In addition, Mrs. Landry had to pay costs, expenses, and reasonable attorney's fees incurred by the Association. Mrs. Landry appealed the ruling.

Which of the facts in the opening paragraphs do you think are going to be most relevant to the court's decision?

JUDGE ROTHSCHILD

In this suit for declaratory and injunctive relief, defendant, Patricia McGovern Landry, appeals from a summary judgment rendered in favor of plaintiff, Belle Terre Lakes Home Owners Association, granting a permanent injunction against her. For the reasons stated more fully herein, we affirm the trial court's judgment and remand for further proceedings. . . .

DISCUSSION

. . . In the present case, plaintiff contended in its petition that appellant violated the provisions of the restrictive covenants applicable to the property by failing to obtain approval for the construction of a fence on the property or for the placement of a satellite dish on defendant's home. Further, plaintiff claimed that both the construction of the fence and the placement of the satellite dish were in violation of the provisions of the covenants.

The trial court concluded that appellant was in violation of Sections 4.13 and 5.09 of the restrictive covenants burdening her property in that she failed to obtain approval of these improvements from the architectural control committee.

Section 4.13 provides that:

> The location of the satellite dishes smaller than 24 inches in diameter shall be approved by the Architectural Control Committee.

Section 5.09 provides that:

> No fence shall be constructed without the prior written consent of the Architectural Control Committee.

By this appeal, appellant first argues that the trial court's finding of lack of prior approval was insufficient to warrant issuing a permanent injunction requiring the removal of the fence and satellite dish from appellant's property, citing Lieber v. Rust, 398 So. 2d 519, 523 (La. 1981). In that case, the court determined that a pier owner was not required to remove his pier for failure to obtain approval of a subdivision's architectural control committee. However, this holding was based on the fact that the pier in question was built on the shore area of a lake which the City of Shreveport had the authority to regulate. The court found that based on this authority, the City specified the location of the pier, and the lack of approval for the placement of the pier by the subdivision was immaterial. We find that the facts of the Lieber case are distinguishable from the facts of the present case where the only restrictions placed on appellant's property were contained in the restrictive covenants. Appellant's first assignment of error is without merit.

Appellant next contends that there exist material issues of fact which preclude summary judgment in this case. Appellant argues that there remains an unresolved question as to whether the prior approval required for the construction of a fence within the subdivision was abandoned by the Home Owners Association for failure to enforce this provision in other instances.

Abandonment, as it relates to building restrictions, is governed by LSA-C.C. art. 782, which provides:

> Building restrictions terminate by abandonment of the whole plan or by a general abandonment of a particular restriction. When the entire plan is abandoned the affected area is freed of all restrictions; when a particular restriction is abandoned, the affected area is freed of that restriction only.

Abandonment of a particular restriction is predicated on a sufficient number of violations of that restriction in relation to the number of lots affected by it. . . . Further, once a violation of a building restriction has been established, the burden shifts to the violator to prove abandonment of a particular restriction. Cook

v. Hoover, 428 So. 2d 836 (La. App. 5 Cir. 1983). To determine whether building restrictions have been waived, there are three areas of consideration; the number of violations, their character and the adverse reaction of property owners to those violations. Mouille v. Henry, 321 So. 2d 377 (La. App. 3 Cir. 1975).

In this case, the Home Owners Association submitted evidence that defendant failed to obtain approval for the construction of the fence. Mrs. Landry admitted that she . . . never obtained approval for the fence from the architectural control committee prior to the construction of the fence. . . .

In support of her claim of abandonment, Mrs. Landry submitted her own affidavit, in which she states that the Home Owners Association did not produce any requests for approvals or approvals from other landowners regarding the construction of their fences and that the developer of the property had constructed numerous other fences throughout the subdivision which appeared to be in violation of the covenants. However, we fail to find that these statements in appellant's affidavit create a genuine issue of material fact. In order to prove abandonment of the restrictions as to fences within the subdivision, Mrs. Landry has the burden of proving a sufficient number of violations of the restrictions applicable to the property. Although she generally referred to other fences in the subdivision, she failed to show that these were in fact violations which had not been approved as required by the covenants. Our review of the record fails to show that appellant produced sufficient factual support to demonstrate that she would meet her evidentiary burden at trial on her defense of abandonment. Absent such factual support, summary judgment was properly granted.

With regard to the satellite dish, appellant contends that an issue of fact exists as to whether she requested approval for the placement of the dish. In her affidavit, Mrs. Landry stated that she was informed by Harold Flynn, a member of the architectural control committee, that approval of the satellite dish would be given if she obtained a letter from the installer of the dish that the present location was the only place a signal could be received. She stated she obtained such a letter and forwarded it to Mr. Flynn. However, the record also indicates that Mrs. Landry admitted in discovery that she never obtained approval for the placement of the satellite dish. Further, the Home Owners Association submitted the affidavit of Mr. Flynn who stated that no approval for the placement of appellant's satellite dish had been given. The record also contains the deposition testimony of the installer of the satellite dish who stated that the dish could be relocated without interference with the signal.

Mrs. Landry's affidavit stating that she requested approval fails to support her claim that she was not in violation of the covenants and in fact, the record clearly shows that no approval was given. Based on our review of the record, we fail to find that Mrs. Landry's affidavit creates an issue of fact as to whether she obtained approval for the placement of the satellite dish as required by the provisions of the restrictive covenants.

Further, although appellant contends that there is a factual question as to whether the denial of approval was exercised reasonably, we find no merit in this contention. The record fails to contain any evidence that approval was denied, and therefore, a determination of reasonableness of such a denial is immaterial to the resolution of this case.

In a case involving a factual situation similar to the present case, the Supreme Court affirmed a trial court's order requiring removal of a satellite dish and a carport where the homeowner violated the restrictive covenants by failing to have his plans for these improvements approved. See, Brier Lake, Inc. v. Jones, 97-2413 (La. 4/14/98), 710 So. 2d 1054, 1061. In the present case, the record shows that appellant failed to obtain approval for the construction of the fence or for the placement of the satellite dish on her home in violation of the restrictive covenant burdening her property. We fail to find the existence of any genuine issues of material fact which would preclude summary judgment in this case. Under these circumstances, we find no error in the trial court's judgment granting judgment in favor of the Home Owners Association. . . .

Was the case of Brier Lake, Inc. v. Jones a good case for the court to rely on in making is decision?

By the next assignment of error, appellant contends that the trial court erred in denying her exception of no right of action. Appellant contends that the articles of incorporation for the Home Owners Association indicate that the association was created to enforce all rights established in Belle Terre Lakes Subdivision, Phases I, II and III. Appellant's property is located in Phase IV of the Subdivision, and appellant contends that the Home Owners Association has no standing to enforce the provisions of the covenant in that subdivision.

However, the provisions contained in the restrictive covenants with regard to the Home Owners Association provide that upon purchase of a lot, a lot owner will become a member of the Home Owners Association. Section 6.1. Further, the covenants state that the Home Owners Association will assist the Architectural Control Committee in policing the restrictions contained therein. Section 6.2. The record in this case clearly shows that appellant became a member of the Home Owners Association when she purchased her property in Phase IV of the Belle Terre Lakes Subdivision. The act of sale to Mrs. Landry referenced the restrictive covenants which empowered the Home Owners Association to enforce its provision. Accordingly, the record supports the trial court's findings that the Home Owners Association by virtue of the provisions of the covenants has the right to police and enforce the terms of the restrictive covenants in Phase IV of the subdivision.

Louisiana courts have held that a homeowners association has a procedural capacity to sue and enforce a subdivision's building restrictions. See, Lakeshore Property Owners Ass'n v. Delatte, 579 So. 2d 1039, 1044 (La. App. 4 Cir. 1991), writ denied, 586 So. 2d 560 (La. 1991). Appellant's argument that the architectural control committee is the only competent party to bring a suit to enforce the building restrictions is without merit. Thus, we find no error of the trial court in overruling appellant's exception of no right of action.

Appellant's final assignment of error concerns the trial court's award of attorney's fees. Appellant contends that the award of attorney's fees is prohibited by federal regulation 47 C.F.R. Section 1.4000. However, as stated herein, we find that the federal regulation is inapplicable to the facts of this case, and thus the prohibition of attorney's fees is not relevant herein.

Attorney's fees are not allowed in Louisiana except where authorized by statute or contract. Brier Lake, Inc. v. Jones, supra, 710 So. 2d at 1061. In the present case, the restrictive covenants contain the following provision allowing the recovery of attorney's fees:

> Section 6.04 Lien Rights. . . . . All expenses, including all reasonable attorneys fees, incurred by the Home Owners Association in . . . enforcing these Restrictions shall be the responsibility of the defaulting Lot Owner . . . and the Home Owners Association shall have the right . . . to recover the costs and expenses owed by such defaulting Lot Owner to recover the costs and expenses owed by such defaulting Lot Owner to the Owners Association, which shall include all attorneys fees incurred by the Home Owners Association in enforcing these Restrictions against the defaulting Lot Owner. . . .

Thus, the specific provisions of this covenant authorizes the recovery of costs, expenses and attorney's fees incurred by the Home Owners Association in the enforcement of the restrictions contained therein. The record shows that the Lot Owner in this case, Patricia McGovern Landry, failed to comply with the terms of the restrictive covenants burdening her property. Under these circumstances, we find no error of the trial court in finding appellant liable for costs, expenses and attorney's fees incurred by the Home Owners Association in connection with this litigation.

CONCLUSION

Accordingly, for the reasons stated herein, the judgment of the trial court ordering appellant Patricia McGovern Landry to remove the fence and satellite dish from her property and to comply with the terms of the building restrictions is affirmed. Likewise, the trial court's judgment holding that the Belle Terre Lakes Home Owners Association is entitled to costs, expenses and reasonable attorney's fees is also affirmed. The case is further remanded to the trial court for a determination of the amount to be awarded. Appellant shall bear all costs of this appeal.

AFFIRMED AND REMANDED

ARTICLE 7.2

The Conflict Between Homeowners' Associations and the Environment

In what some experts see as one of the most stunning transformations of how people live and buy homes, an estimated 50 million people today live in condominiums and common interest developments (CIDs), housing arrangements in which property owners agree to live in accordance with rules established by a homeowners association.[1] Industry trade groups estimate that these associations govern approximately 80 percent of new homes being built today.[2] Real estate experts believe there are approximately 250,000 of these associations functioning today, as compared to fewer than 500 in 1964.[3] As the number of people living in such developments grows, so do the number of conflicts between residents and their governing associations, as property owners challenge the restrictions imposed by the associations.

These conflicts are leading to increased calls for more restrictive legislation to rein in homeowners' associations, as well as more challenges to association actions in the courtroom. In Florida, for example, in early 2004 the state set up a Homeowners Association Task force, a fifteen member panel including consumer advocates, state officials, and real estate executives "to harmonize and improve relations between homeowners and homeowners' associations."[4] The task force was charged with studying whether new legislation was needed to govern homeowners associations.[5] Both Texas and California considered a number of bills to constrain homeowners' associations during 2003.[6]

Can you think of any additional reasons not included by the author that might help to explain the increasing number of suits against homeowners' associations?

The primary restrictions imposed by HOAs that have been challenged by homeowners thus far have been age restrictions, which generally prevent individuals younger than a specified age from residing in developments;[7] pet restrictions, which prohibit residents from keeping animals on their property;[8] and restrictions imposed by design review committees or architectural review standards.[9] As a general rule, these restrictions have been upheld,[10] as long as they are not selectively applied.[11] But we may see a new group of challenges to these restrictions resulting from a conflict between the right of the HOA to establish and enforce aesthetic standards and the right of the residents to engage in practices that protect the environment.

While a growing number of environmentally sound practices may cause conflicts between residents and their HOAs in the near future, this article focuses on one specific environmentally sound practice that may soon generate litigation, and that is the replacement of grass lawns with artificial turf or so-called synthetic grass. This issue is important in any area suffering from drought, and especially in heavily populated areas, such as Las Vegas, Nevada, which is now in the midst of a record five-year drought, as well as being one of the fastest growing metropolitan areas in the country.

THE PRESUMPTIVE VALIDITY OF RESTRICTIONS ON HOMEOWNERS

CIDs are regulated by state statutes, as well as by the common law, in all fifty states. By the year 2000, twenty-three states had adopted the Uniform Common Interest Ownership Act[12] or one of its predecessors, the Uniform Condominium Act, the Uniform Planned Community Act, or the Model Real Estate Act.[13] As noted in the introduction, however, states are increasingly adding a patchwork of regulations to restrict the power of the associations, yet we still see overall similarity among the regulations of these CIDs from state to state.

In most states, there is a presumption of validity applied to restrictions, including architectural standards, enacted by HOAs.[14] This majority position is exemplified by the holding in the case of *Nahrstedt v. Lakeside Village Condominium Association, Inc.*,[15] in which the court stated that the covenants of a particular association are "presumed to be reasonable . . . unless the restriction is arbitrary, imposes burdens on the use of lands it affects that substantially outweigh the restriction's benefits to the development's residents, or violates a fundamental public policy."[16] In *Dolan-King v. Rancho Santa Fe Association,*[17] the California Court of Appeals, citing *Nahrstedt,* further stated that there is still a presumption of reasonableness even if applications are based on subjective as well as objective criteria. Many states refer to the twin requirements of the HOA's making decisions "reasonably and in good faith."[18] Thus it is clear that ordinarily, homeowners have no recourse but to follow the regulations of the association, and when it comes to setting design standards, the courts will ordinarily not interfere with an association's judgment. Restricting the use of artificial turf however, may prove to be one instance where the homeowners' associations' power may not be upheld because such restrictions are unreasonable and violate public policy.

THE UNREASONABLENESS OF RESTRICTIONS ON ARTIFICIAL TURF

Arguably, restrictions on the use of artificial turf fail under the limitation described in *Nahrstedt,* as these restrictions violate public policy by unreasonably prohibiting homeowners from taking actions that are designed to prevent harm to the community. Such restrictions are also directly contrary to public policy as they work in opposition to state legislation. By prohibiting property owners from replacing water guzzling grass with water saving artificial turf, HOAs are unreasonably acting contrary to public policy.

Currently, the west is in the fifth year of a drought that some scientists believe has produced the driest period in the west in the past 1,400 years,[19] and some argue that prehistoric evidence indicates that this drought could last for two decades.[20] Lake Mead, the primary water source for Las Vegas, is less than 60 percent full. Lake Powell, second in size only to Lake Mead among Colorado River lakes, is only at 40 percent capacity.[21]

Droughts, of course, can develop in all regions of the continent, and their effects can be devastating.[22] Since 1980, major droughts and heat waves within the U.S. have resulted in costs exceeding 100 billion dollars, easily becoming one of the most costly weather-related disasters on the continent during that time.[23]

To cope with the current drought,[24] some cities in the West are paying residents to remove water guzzling grass lawns.[25] Other cities are imposing tough watering restrictions and fines of up to $1,000 for violators. Farmers throughout the West are bracing for almost certain cutbacks in water they use for crops.[26] In Carson City, Nevada, where they are starting the summer season with the water table lower than last year because with the drought, water restrictions went into effect in June, restricting odd-numbered addresses to watering on odd-numbered days and even-numbered addresses to watering on even-numbered days. No watering is allowed from 10 a.m. to 7 p.m.[27]

The problems created by the drought are being compounded by the unprecedented growth in the area. Between 2000 and 2003, Phoenix and the rest of Maricopa County added more residents than any other place in the country except Los Angeles County, according to Census Bureau figures. Two other Western communities--Riverside County, Calif., north of San Diego, and Clark County, Nev., home to Las Vegas--followed.[28]

Given the existence of these drought conditions, public policy clearly dictates that property owners should be given every incentive to reduce their use of water. One of the largest uses of water is landscaping. It is typically estimated that 50% of the treated drinking water supplied to cities everywhere in the U.S., and in some foreign countries, is used for outdoor landscape irrigation.[29] And, according to Amy Vickers' *Handbook of Water Use and Conservation,*[30] lawn watering represents one of the biggest non-essential uses of water in many communities.[31] Thus, one of the more powerful weapons in the war against the negative consequences of drought is to reduce the amount of water being used to grow lush, green lawns. And one way to attain that objective is to replace some of these lawns with artificial turf.

Officials are recognizing the usefulness of artificial turf in drought stricken cites. For example, in 2003, Las Vegas, Nevada, unveiled a five-year, $5.5

million plan to reduce water consumption by one-quarter in more than 70 county parks and numerous street medians that included removal of more than 3.1 million square feet of grass, and its replacement with synthetic turf and xeriscape,[32] sustainable landscaping that conserves water and is based on sound horticultural practices.[33] In 2004, the city revealed plans to start using artificial turf on high school playing fields.[34] And homeowners in the city of Las Vegas who want to participate in the city's rebate program for removing grass may replace up to fifty percent of the old lawn with artificial turf under the program.[35]

Artificial turf today is water permeable, which, from a conservation standpoint, makes it comparable to replacing grass with mulch or crushed rock, and superior to replacement with an impermeable covering such as a patio.[36] It also offers a number of additional benefits to the environment. There is no maintenance required, thus eliminating the use of lawn mowers and trimmers, which contribute to air pollution. They do not require the use of pesticides, herbicides, or fertilizers, thereby reducing the amount of toxic chemicals emitted into the environment, including the groundwater. Much of the artificial turf is made from recycled materials, including tires, thereby reducing demand for space in landfills.[37]

In many parts of the country, environmentally conscious homeowners who desire the appearance of a lush, green lawn, or who want a soft surface for their children or pets to play on are turning to synthetic lawns as an environmentally sound way to satisfy those objectives.[38] Thus, the use of artificial turf is one way to meet the public policy objective of reducing use of water for landscaping to help alleviate water shortages created by drought conditions. It is therefore unreasonable for homeowners' associations to prohibit the use of artificial turf, and the courts should refuse to uphold these restrictions.

If you were the judge in a case involving a homeowner challenging an association's restriction against artificial turf, how would you decide the case? Why?

While as of July 2004, there have not been any reported decisions of cases involving resident challenges to HOA restrictions against artificial turf, there has been one case involving another restriction against an environmentally sound activity, the installation of solar panels.[39] In that case, the restriction in question did not directly prohibit the installation of solar panels, but it required there review by an ARC, and placed so many stipulations upon their installation that from a practical perspective, almost no homeowner would be able to install solar panels, and thus the restrictions effectively prohibited the use of solar devices.[40] The court refused to allow the restriction because the state had established by legislation a public policy preference for the use of solar devices.[41] The court distinguished the case before it from cases upholding restrictions by HOAs by stating "these cases, however, are readily distinguishable because no state law established a public policy preference for allowing homeowners to keep animals, have rooftop antennas, or store old vehicles."[42] While no state currently has such a strong mandate for the use of artificial turf as Arizona did for the use of solar energy devices, the message being sent by many municipalities in favor of actions to help reduce water consumption is almost as strong.

CONCLUSION

In some states, this issue may become moot, as states facing droughts may take matters into their own hands and pass legislation making it illegal for homeowners' associations to prohibit the use of artificial turf.[43] However, even if legislatures fail to act on the issue, it seems that homeowners have a strong case to make before the courts that restrictions on the use of artificial turf should not be enforced. Perhaps homeowners associations should prevent this issue from even getting to the courts by thinking reconsidering the needs of the community and removing restrictions against artificial turf from their design guidelines.

END NOTES

a1. **Ms. Kubasek** is a Professor at Bowling Green State University, where she has taught Environmental Law and Business Law for twenty years. She is currently the President of the Academy of Legal Studies in Business. She has published over fifty articles in a broad range of journals, including *The Environmental Law Reporter, Harvard Journal on Legislation, U.C.L.A. Environmental Law Journal, and William & Mary Environmental Law & Policy Review.* She has published several books, the most recent being the 4th edition of *Environmental Law* (Prentice Hall, 2001).

1. Jim Wasserman, *Conflicts Arise From Homes Association Rules,* the Kansas City Star, July 14, 2003.
2. Id.
3. Daniel Yi and Jia-Ru Chong, *Bill Targets Homeowners Associations,* Los Angeles Times, Monday, Sept. 1, 2003.
4. Melissa E. Holsman, *Panel Reviews Homeowner Association Conflicts. . . .*
5. Id.
6. Yi, *supra,* note 3.
7. See, e.g., Ritchey v. Villa Nueva Condominium Assn., 81 Cal. App. 3d 688, 146 Cal. Rptr. 695, 100 A.L.R.3d 231 (1st Dist. 1978) (superseded by statute as stated in Schmidt v. Superior Court, 769 P.2d 932 (Cal.1989)).
8. See, e.g., San Vicente Villas Homeowners Ass'n, Inc. v. Cohen, 2003 WL 22962813 (Cal. App. 2d Dist. 2003), unpublished/noncitable, (Dec. 17, 2003) and review denied, (Mar. 3, 2004) (upholding enforcement of Association prohibition on pets weighing more than 15 pounds); Villa De Las Palmas Homeowners Ass'n v. Terifaj, 121 Cal. Rptr. 2d 780

(App. 4th Dist. 2002), review granted and opinion superseded, 126 Cal. Rptr. 2d 2, 55 P.3d 36 (Cal. 2002) and judgment aff'd, 33 Cal. 4th 73, 14 Cal. Rptr. 3d 67, 90 P.3d 1223 (2004) (enforcing no pet rule); Wilshire Condominium Ass'n, Inc. v. Kohlbrand, 368 So. 2d 629 (Fla. Dist. Ct. App. 4th Dist. 1979); Majestic View Condominium Ass'n v. Bolotin, 429 So.2d 438, 440 (Fla. 4th DCA 1983); Dulaney Towers Maintenance Corp. v. O'Brey, 46 Md. App. 464, 418 A.2d 1233 (1980).

9. During the past decade, fewer than 100 such challenges were filed in court, and approximately 90% were decided in favor of the homeowners' association, according to Ronald H. Rosenberg, as reported in his paper, Design Review by Homeowners' Associations--Beauty is Definitely in the Eye of the Beholder, presented at the 2002 Annual Land Use Conference of The Rocky Mountain Land Use Institute on March 7, 2002. The paper may be found at http:// www.law.du.edu/rmlui/HotTopics/Design-Review/Rosenberg2002DesignReview.rtf.
10. Id.
11. See, e.g., White Egret Condominium, Inc. v. Franklin, 379 So. 2d 346, 352 (Fla. 1979), a case in which an association tried to block the sale of a unit to a purchaser with minor children when other minor children were living in the development.
12. The UCIOA of 1994 is in effect in Connecticut, Conn. Gen. Stat. Ann. §§ 47-200 to -295 (West 1995 & Supp. 2000); and Vermont, Vt. Stat. Ann. tit. 27A, §§ 1-101 to 4-120 (Supp. 2000). The UCIOA of 1982 is in effect in Alaska, Alaska Stat. §§ 34.08.010-.995 (Michie 2000); Colorado, Colo. Rev. Stat. Ann. §§ 38-33.3-101 to -319 (West 2000); Minnesota, Minn. Stat. Ann. §§ 515B.1-101 to 515B.4-118 (West 1990 & Supp. 2001), Nevada, Nev. Rev. Stat. Ann. 116.1101 to .4120 (Michie 1998 & Supp. 1999); and West Virginia, W. Va. Code Ann. §§ 36B-1-101 to - 4-120 (Michie 1997 & Supp. 2000). The Uniform Condominium Act is in effect in Alabama, Ala. Code §§ 35-8A-101 to -417 (1991 & Supp. 2000); Arizona, Ariz. Rev. Stat. Ann. §§ 33-1201 to -1270 (West 2000); Maine, Me. Rev. Stat. Ann. tit. 33, §§ 1601-101 to 1604-118 (West 1999), Missouri, Mo. Ann. Stat. §§ 448.1-101 to. 4-120 (West 2000); New Mexico, N.M. Stat. Ann. §§ 47-7A-1 to -7D-20 (Michie Supp. 1999); North Carolina, N.C. Gen. Stat. §§ 47C-1-101 to -4-120 (1999); Pennsylvania, 68 Pa. Cons. Stat. Ann. §§ 3101-3414 (West 1994); Rhode Island, R.I. Gen. Laws §§ 34-36.1-1.01 to -4.20 (1995 & Supp. 2000); Texas, Tex. Prop. Code. Ann. §§ 82.001 to .164 (Vernon 1995 & Supp. 2001); Virginia, Va. Code Ann. §§ 55-79.39 to .103 (Michie 1995 & Supp. 2000); and Washington, Wash. Rev. Code Ann. §§ 64.34.010 to .950 (West 1994 & Supp. 2001). The Uniform Planned Community Act is in effect in North Carolina, N.C. Gen. Stat. Ann. §§ 47F-1-101 to - 3-120 (1999); and Pennsylvania, 68 Pa. Cons. Stat. §§ 5101-5414 (West Supp. 2001). The Model Real Estate

Cooperative Act is in effect in Virginia, Va. Code Ann. §§ 55-424 to -506 (Michie 1995 & Supp. 2000).

13. The Uniform Common Interest Ownership Act of 1994, 7 U.L.A. 471 (1997), superceded and consolidated these three acts.
14. See James M. Grippando, Note, Condominium Rulemaking—Presumptions, Burdens and Abuses: A Call for Substantive Judicial Review in Florida, 34 U.FLA.L.REV. 219, 227-29 (1982).
15. Nahrstedt v. Lakeside Village Condominium Assn., 8 Cal. 4th 361, 33 Cal. Rptr. 2d 63, 878 P.2d 1275 (1994).
16. Id.
17. Dolan-King v. Rancho Santa Fe Assn., 81 Cal. App. 4th 965, 97 Cal. Rptr. 2d 280 (4th Dist. 2000).
18. See, e.g., Raintree Homeowners Ass'n, Inc. v. Bleimann, 342 N.C. 159, 463 S.E.2d 72 (1995) (Supreme Court of North Carolina upheld the architecture review committees rejection of the homeowners' wish to replace wood shingles with wood-like vinyl siding that had the neighbors' approval because there was no evidence the ARC had acted unreasonably or in bad faith); Villages of Brentwood Homeowners Ass'n, Inc. v. Westermann, 1998 WL 289342 (Tenn. Ct. App. 1998) (Tennessee Supreme Court referred to requirements of an architectural committees "reasonably and in good faith"); Lamden v. La Jolla Shores Clubdominium Homeowners Assn., 21 Cal. 4th 249, 87 Cal. Rptr. 2d 237, 980 P.2d 940 (1999) (California Supreme Court upheld the association, stating that "where a duly constituted community association board, upon reasonable investigation, in good faith and with regard for the best interests of the community association and its members, exercises discretion within the scope of its authority under relevant statutes, covenants and restrictions to select among means for discharging an obligation to maintain and repair a development's common areas, courts should defer to the board's authority and presumed expertise.")
19. Bob Keefe, West Firmly In Drought's Grip; Most Severe Water Shortage In Hundreds Of Years Could Choke Region's Rapid Growth, 6/12/04 Austin Am.-Statesman A17, 2004 WL 57660643.
20. Id.
21. Id.
22. For information about the effects of droughts, see http:// www.drought.unl.edu/risk/impacts.htm.
23. Lott, N., and T. Ross, NCDC Technical Report 2000-02, A Climatology of Recent Extreme Weather and Climate Events. [Asheville, N.C.]: National Climatic Data Center.
24. A drought is a protracted period of deficient precipitation resulting in a water shortage for some activity, group, or environmental sector. For

example, a drought may cause extensive damage to crops, resulting in loss of yield. Drought Outlook And Information Source For 2004. . . .

25. The Southern Nevada Water Authority's Water Smart Landscapes Rebate Program is offering to pay residents $1.00 for every foot of grass they remove and replace with water smart ground cover, including artificial turf. At least half of the replacement, however, must be plant material, so neither artificial turf nor any other ground cover such as mulch or rock can completely replace the grass. . . .

ARTICLE 7.3

A Market for Institutions: Assessing the Impact of Restrictive Covenants on Housing

William H. Rogers

What do you think are the most significant similarities and differences between municipalities and RCAs?

I. INTRODUCTION

There are few features of new housing construction that are becoming as pervasive as residential community associations (RCAs). RCAs, more commonly known as homeowner associations, are private contracts called covenants, which are tied to the land and enable homeowners to provide public goods or to deal with externalities outside of the local government. Some of these RCAs are home to more than 50,000 residents and provide many of the same services that one would expect from a municipality, while the majority of RCAs are the size of subdivision within a municipality. Still, there is a significant legal difference between RCAs and municipalities; covenants are treated as a private contract and municipal incorporations are treated as a public government. This places municipalities under the restrictions of the Avery decision and leaves RCAs open to a variety of institutional forms. This means in part that RCAs, like private corporations, can limit voting rights to non-owning residents such as renters or first mortgage holders. Furthermore, votes can be weighted by the value or size of owned improvements, where the common voting rule is often set beyond simple majority.

The rapid growth of RCAs in the housing market partially[1] implies that flexibility in voting rules is a benefit to single-family housing and zoning by municipal government is incomplete. Still, RCAs are also a lighting rod for criticism and many academics, mostly in the political science fields, are pessimistic about their value. The range of views can be quickly understood by contrasting McKenzie (1994) with Foldvary (1994).

Despite the fact that private covenants are quickly becoming a common feature of improved land, economic study of RCAs is limited, albeit growing. Speyrer (1989), Cannaday (1994), and Hughes and Turnbull (1996a) are the only empirical work on private zoning. While these studies are important, they are also limited in institutional detail and do not correct for spatial autocorrelation. This latter point is especial important because RCAs, being relatively new, are concentrated in areas with new construction.

This paper will investigate the impact of restrictive covenants on single-family housing values in Greeley, Colorado, using a hedonic pricing method. This includes a unique dataset gathered by the author that includes information on the characteristics of individual RCAs. The findings can be summarized in three parts: first, RCAs on average add about 3% or $4,450 to the sale price; second, building restrictions provide no impact on prices and use restrictions increase prices; and finally, the optimal voting decision rule is at an 80% super-majority but voting rights to first mortgage holders significantly reduce prices.

The remainder of the paper is divided into five parts. The next section provides a brief introduction into RCAs, which is followed by a literature review section. Since this study uses a unique dataset, the data portion of the paper is large and detailed. The final two sections summarize the regression model and results.

II. RCAS, RESTRICTIONS, AND RISKS

Ronald Coase's 1960 work, The Problem of Social Costs, (Coase 1960) provides the very familiar framework for when one can expect externalities to be a problem. Externalities in a world of zero transaction costs and fully defined property rights will be internalized through market transactions. However, both a lack of defined property rights and the existence of transaction costs will inhibit efficiency.

Human beings have been dealing with this reality for quite some time and have created various organizations in part to deal with these externalities. National governments and multinational corporations are two sophisticated examples, however, RCAs, while somewhat more humble, are also.

RCAs will attempt to promote efficiency by clarifying and arranging property rights. Negative externalities can be mitigated by removing some of the right to use one's own property and transferring it to the neighbors. For example, in many RCAs, you do not have the right to use your front lawn as a parking lot without the express consent of your neighbors, and because there are significant transaction costs associated with organizing your neighbors to agree on an arrangement, you simply do not bother. This is an example of an efficient outcome if your willingness to pay is less than the sum of the neighbors' willingness to accept. Furthermore, residents who prefer to have more control over personal property and care less about the actions of neighbors will be less likely to move to the restrictive RCA. Therefore, RCAs are able to reduce the negative effects of externalities by adjusting property rights and providing signals to potential buyers.

Of course, zoning boards are given responsibility to reduce externalities through a similar process.[2] Still, RCAs may have an informational advantage over municipal boards because of their small sizes and because there is more flexibility in their institutional formation.

III. PREVIOUS EMPERICAL WORK

. . . The current economic literature is in agreement that, on average, the restrictive covenants do add value to residents by reducing the risk of future externalities. For single-family housing, the estimates range from 2% to 8%. However, Cannaday's study suggests that an optimal level of restrictiveness may exist and some developers have regulated beyond. This implies that not all RCAs are improving housing prices. Furthermore, covenants can be changed in the future by amendments or termination. Therefore, the restrictiveness of the covenant will be affected by the voting rules.

The motivation of this study is to expand the empirical literature by providing more institutional detail about RCA restrictiveness; I will differentiate between use and building restrictions, include voting rules. . . .

IV. DATA

The data is a set of 1,487 single-family house sales and RCAs from Greeley, Colorado, in 2000. Greeley, at about 80,000 residents, is the largest town in Weld County. The single-family sales, including sale price, housing characteristics, and GIS data was gathered from the Weld County Assessors Office and Weld County GIS. All sales were limited to a price range between $50,000 and $500,000 in order to reduce the issue of unlivable house sales or non-arms-length transactions and to remove houses in the upper market. . . .

How do think the results of the study might have been affected by the fact that the study was done in Colorado?

RCA information was gathered at the Weld County Clerk and Recorder, where each covenant must be located and read through in order to build the database. There currently exists no publicly available and useable database for RCAs in Weld County, or anywhere else the author is aware of. . . .

Of the 1,487 sales almost half, or 665 house sales were apart of a RCA. . . .

Covenants in Weld County, Colorado

The scope of this paper is limited to the study of how covenants are used to organize neighborhoods; however, covenants are used to accomplish a broad range of goals. Covenants have been filed in Weld County to restrict the sale date and buyer of a house. Habitat for Humanity, for example, restricts when a recipient of a house may sell or how they may use the house. Some covenants restrict water rights as to irrigation or limit grazing practices. Other covenants require rent control on property or limit future filing of legal suits pertaining to the property.

Covenants which cover multiple housing units vary in detail and scope from one page documents which must be completely enforced by the civil courts to 120-page documents with several self-regulating agents (the homeowner association and architectural committees). Still, there are eight characteristics that can be categorized: use restrictions, architectural restrictions, easements, bureaucratic organizations, assessments, developers' rights, mortgagees' rights, and amendments and terminations. Not every covenant has all eight characteristics; some only have two.

The State of Colorado does include some minor regulation of RCAs. The Colorado Common Interest Ownership Act (2000) (2000 Real Estate Manual) was designed with the recognition that "economic prosperity of Colorado is dependent upon the strengthening of homeowner associations in common interest communities.'' Much of the legislation of the Act is valid "unless otherwise provided by the declarant,'' which makes most HOA organizations legally defendable and leads to some interesting aspects.

First, courts may find the covenant "unconscionable'' at the time it was made and therefore unenforceable. Ellickson (1982) argues that courts are more rigorous in examination of covenants than they are for zoning code. While the Act is not adding any additional restrictions, it does clarify what cannot be considered sufficient evidence of an "unconscionable'' contract.

Secondly, the Act does provide some protection from local governments. Municipal zoning cannot impose additional structure requirements on HOA units that it would not apply on other units. Eminent domain must also be sensitive to property with common interests. If any unit is acquired by eminent domain the compensation must include the unit's allocated interests.

Finally, small HOAs have a cap, which is adjusted to inflation, of $400 for the average annual common expense liability. This does not include insurance premiums or optional user fees.

Voting Rights and Amendments

All residents of a city or county over the age of 18 are given one vote to cast in any election. This is of course true regardless of owning property in the jurisdiction and is protected by the Supreme Court's interpretation of the U.S. Constitution in the Avery decision.[3] By contrast, to be a voting member of the development with a covenant a person must own or have a direct economic interest in property in the development. Depending on the condition of the development and the nature of the covenant, homeowners, developers, and first mortgage holders can all be voting members in the development. The voting membership is not given to each individual. Rather the voting power is divided by the economic interest in the development, much like a corporation.

Barzel and Sass (1990) found condominium associations assigned voting rights in three ways: one-unit-one-vote, voting shares by square feet of the unit, and voting shares by assessed value of the unit. However, in Weld County all associations of single family houses assigned votes via one-to-one-vote; not by one-person-one-vote.

These covenants can be terminated or amended with the approval of the members. Most covenants are valid for 10 to 20 years and then are automatically renewed every 10 or 20 years, while other covenants perpetually "run with the land.'' To terminate or amend a covenant, a majority of members must agree to the change. What constitutes an adequate majority depends on the contract. In Weld County, approved majorities span the entire spectrum from a simple 51% to a surprising 100%.

A single covenant may have different approved majorities depending on the activity. For example, an amendment may require approval of 67% of the units, while a termination requires 75%, and a change to the common property only requires 51%. Majorities can change over time. Some covenants require 90% agreement to any amendment in the first 10 years and 75% afterwards. Out of 220 covenants, in Weld, since the summer of 2003 only ten have been terminated, while there have been almost 100 amendments. For this study, the variable Vote Rule includes the decision rules for amendments at the time of sale.

DEVELOPERS' AND MORTGAGEES' RIGHTS

Developing a subdivision is not a quick process. Developers will sell some completed homes in the subdivision while they continue construction on other homes and property. Risk on this investment increases with the lag in construction time. Therefore, the developer will desire to shorten the development time and maintain property values of the neighborhood until all the homes are sold. In most Weld County covenants, the developer holds voting and direct amendment rights until a specified number of lots are sold and/or a specified period of time has passed. In every contract where the developer held voting rights, three votes were assigned to every lot still owned by the developer.

First mortgage holders also shoulder risk and hold an economic interest in the value of the development. Many covenants are written with the first mortgage holders in mind. Some covenants require all first mortgage holders be given notice of any amendments or termination of the covenant and notice of any changes to the common areas (if any exist). Furthermore, all financial and general meeting records must be presented to the first mortgage holder upon request.

Other covenants give the first mortgage[4] holders voting rights. In every covenant which gives first mortgage holders voting rights, the voting requirements are held separate from the homeowner/developer voting. This does not mean that the homeowners lose their voting rights if they mortgage their homes. Rather the practice is akin to a federal bill passing both the House and the Senate before approval. For example, to pass an amendment a covenant may require 67% of the homeowners' votes and 51% of the first mortgage holders' votes. . . .

VII. CONCLUSION

Residential community associations (RCAs) are growing rapidly in the housing market; some are being developed in unincorporated areas and others, probably the majority are being developed within municipalities. One of the functions they provide is zoning. The rapid growth of RCAs not only implies that they are adding value but also that municipalities are not zoning as completely as homeowners would like.

RCAs are in an advantageous informational position to provide zoning for local externalities because they often are dealing with fewer homeowners than would a municipality. Even large RCAs divide up neighborhoods into smaller villages to provide neighborhood restrictions. RCAs also have the advantage of flexibility in creating voting rules and therefore have more initial flexibility in providing credible restrictiveness.

There are three previous empirical studies on RCAs and restrictiveness that have shown higher housing prices association with restrictions. However, all three are limited in the institutional detail of restrictions and none corrected for spatial autocorrelation. Adding to the literature, this study divides the RCA zoning into use and building restriction as well as adds two variables that measure the variation in voting rules.

Using a semi-log hedonic model and single-family housing data from Greeley, Colorado, this study estimates the impact of voting rules and restrictions. The results are two-fold: first RCAs on average provide about 2% to 3%, or about $2,950 to $4,450 to the house price; secondly, while voting rules for RCAs vary from simple majority to unanimous, the most valuable voting rule is about 80%, mortgagee voting rights hinder housing prices, and use restrictions provide value while building restrictions do not. The total effect of RCAs' institutional characteristics is 3.1% or about $4,600 with mortgagee voting and 6.2% or about $9,200 without.

These results provide additional detail of RCA institutional characteristics and one step closer to a side-by-side comparison of RCAs and municipalities. However, there are three limitations to this study. First, like the previous work, this dataset is limited to one housing market. A national study would require enormous effort. Second, while covenants do provide restrictions and signals to potential buyers, they do not guarantee an adequate measure of restrictiveness, which would require a measure of enforcement. Finally, RCAs also provide public goods; however, this study does not explicitly control for public good provision and the fees collected. I leave these issues for future study.

REFERENCES

. . .Barzel, Yoram, and Tim R. Sass. 1990. "The Allocation of Resources by Voting.'' *The Quarterly Journal of Economics* 105 (3): 745–71.

Cannaday, Roger E. 1994. "Condominium Covenants: Cats, Yesa Dogs, No.'' *Journal of Urban Economics* 35 (1): 71–82.

Coase, R. H. 1960. "The Problem of Social Cost.'' *Journal of Law and Economics* 3 (1): 1–44.

Ellickson, Robert C. 1982. "Cities and Homeowners Associations.'' *University of Pennsylvania Law Review* 130 (June): 1519–80.

Fischel, William A. 1985. *The Economics of Zoning Laws: A Property Rights Approach to American Land Use Controls.* Baltimore: John Hopkins University Press.

Foldvary, Fred E. 1994. *Public Goods and Private Communities*. London: Edward Elgar Publishing Ltd.

Hughes, William T. Jr., and Geoffrey K. Turnbull. 1996a. "Uncertainty Neighborhood Effects and Restrictive Covenants.'' *Journal of Urban Economics* 39 (2): 160–72.

McKenzie, Evan. 1994. *Privatopia*. New Haven, Conn.: Yale University Press. . . .

Speyrer, Janet Furman. 1989. "The Effect of Land-Use Restrictions on Market Values of Single-Family Homes in Huston.'' *Journal of Real Estate Finance and Economics* 2:117–30.

END NOTES

1. RCAs often provide public goods and therefore an increase in housing price may also be due to the net benefit of the public good. This paper is limited to the restrictions and voting rules and therefore the question of efficient public good provision will be left to future study.
2. See Fischel (1985) for an excellent examination of zoning through a property rights approach.
3. Special districts are one notable exception to this decision. These districts are allowed some additional freedoms to alter voting systems. A complete comparison of special districts and community association would likely produce interesting results; however, that comparison is beyond the scope of this study.
4. In no case did a covenant extend rights to second mortgage holders.

ARTICLE 7.4

Not in My Community: Is It Legal for Private Entities to Ban Sex Offenders from Living in Their Communities?

John J. Herman

I. INTRODUCTION

. . . The New Jersey Legislature held hearings and proceeded to pass sweeping new legislation dealing with sex offenders.[1] Known as Megan's Law,[2] the Act requires sex offenders to register with police upon their release from prison.[3] Anyone convicted of sexual crimes is considered a sex offender.[4] Sex offenders are divided into three tiers: Tier One offenders are considered the least threatening and include lesser offenses;[5] Tier Two offenders pose a moderate risk of re-offense;[6] Tier Three offenders are considered the most likely to re-offend and, ultimately, the most dangerous.[7] The presence of a Tier One sex offender in a community requires only police notification.[8] However, the presence of a Tier Three offender requires community-wide notification, often requiring local police or sheriffs to go door-to-door informing the neighborhood of where the offender is residing.[9]

Can you explain the logic for the three tier offender system? Do you agree with that logic?

Many groups decried the passage of these laws, seeing them as an invasion of privacy rights.[10] Like many laws that are invasive or new, court challenges soon followed. Eventually, the matter ended up before the United States Supreme Court. In *Smith v. Doe*,[11] the Court upheld Alaska's sex offender registration statute.[12] The decision was not exhaustive of all arguments, but meant a sex offender registration statute had withstood the ultimate test.

II. THE CURRENT SITUATION

Eleven years after the passage of Megan's Law, every state in the Union has some form of the statute, varying slightly in their specifics.[13] Many states, including Pennsylvania and New Jersey, now make their sex offender registries available online, often through their state police Web sites,[14] indicating a continuing awareness of the problem of sex offenders in our communities.

In this light, a new wave of laws and private agreements are appearing throughout the country.[15] Many cities are now passing ordinances forbidding registered sex offenders from living within a specified distance from anywhere concentrations of children may be found.[16] These lists of places usually include schools and day care centers.[17] Also, many private interest communities are enacting agreements (restrictive covenants) to exclude sex offenders from purchasing or residing within their communities.[18] These developments, particularly the private agreements, are the focus of this article. Putting aside, not lightly, the thorny issues of enforcing such private agreements, the focus is on their viability under existing law and the policy behind them.

These private agreements are not currently regulated by the United States Constitution because they are a form of private action (unless one considers certain arguments).[19] The covenants likely will be attacked on several legal fronts. First, there are arguments that the covenants are illegal restraints on alienation and unreasonable.[20] Second, the Fair Housing Act ("FHA") and its amendments[21] could also be used to argue for the invalidation of the covenants. Finally, some could argue that *Shelley v. Kraemer*[22] prohibits these covenants because court enforcement of them could be state action that discriminates against a group.[23] This landmark United States Supreme Court decision invalidated racially restrictive covenants from being enforced in American courts.[24] The agreements themselves were not prohibited, but enforcement by the courts could constitute state action, thus violating the Constitution.[25] In turn, this could arguably apply to sex offender covenants.

Do you think that Shelley v. Kraemer should apply to make sex offender convenants unconstitutional?

Currently, only one case has addressed the issue: *Mulligan v. Panther Valley Property Owners Ass'n*.[26] Part III of this paper will discuss the case. . . . Part VI will discuss the issue of *Shelley* and other constitutional implications. The New Jersey case, *Panther Valley*, marks an excellent place to begin the discussion.

III. ISSUES SURROUNDING THE ENFORCEABILITY OF COVENANTS BANNING SEX OFFENDERS: *MULLIGAN V. PANTHER VALLEY PROPERTY OWNERS ASS'N*

Panther Valley was filed in 1998 by Elinor Mulligan, a resident of the private community of Panther Valley.[27] She contended that the restrictions adopted by the homeowners association, including one which said that no Tier Three sex offender could reside in the community, were unlawful.[28] The trial court struck down several of the restrictions but upheld the sex offender ban.[29] The case was then appealed.[30]

The New Jersey Superior Court, Appellate Division heard the case on December 11, 2000.[31] . . . The court declined to rule on the amendment issue concerning the sex offender restriction, noting a lack of a sufficient record.[32] It did, however, provide us with an illuminating discussion of the issues surrounding such covenants. . . .

The court commented that the amendment was not overly restrictive on her right to alienate her property because there were only eighty Tier Three offenders in the state, and the compulsion to violate the law was baseless.[33] [n39] The court, however, was more receptive to Mulligan's other public policy arguments.

The first was that simply making a "large segment of the housing market unavailable to one category of individual" was to approach a form of vigilantism.[34] There was no conclusive ruling, but this concern was expressed.[35] The court noted many associations perform quasi-governmental functions and may be treated as governmental actors in some regards.[36] . . .

VI. *SHELLEY V. KRAEMER* AND CONSTITUTIONAL ISSUES

A. *Shelley v. Kraemer* and State Action: Are There Useful Parallels in Racially Restrictive Covenants and Are Private Communities to Be Considered State Actors?

The *Shelley* case became a touchstone of covenant law in that it forbade racially restrictive covenants from being enforced in court.[37] The question is whether the same issues that motivated the *Shelley* decision can be used to invalidate covenants banning sex offenders on constitutional grounds. The obvious distinction is that race is a suspect class subject to strict scrutiny under the law, while classifications involving sex offenders will not be subject to strict scrutiny.[38] However, the arguments are often the same in that those opposing racial covenants usually argued on grounds of public policy, restraints on alienation, and violations of due process and equal protection provisions of state and federal constitutions.[39]

While these arguments were unavailing to the courts that usually considered them, *Shelley* changed that. "[C]ontracts containing restrictive covenants which have for their purpose the exclusion of persons of designated race or color from the ownership or occupancy of real property offend the . . . Fourteenth Amendment to the Constitution of the United States."[40] The discussion of sex offender restrictions may come up in this same light. The lawyers for an offender could argue that while their case is admittedly different in some aspects, the core is the same. Sex offenders, while certainly distasteful, should be able to live where they choose. To allow courts to enforce such restrictions would be to sanction a seemingly less harmful, but ultimately no less invidious, classification.[41]

In regard to private communities being considered quasi-governmental, there is, again, surprisingly little case law on the topic. Courts have "recognized a fiduciary duty of the homeowners association to the homeowner to enforce restrictive covenants."[42] Generally, "this duty has been imposed in recognition of the power held by homeowner associations, the quasi-governmental functions they serve, and the impact on value and enjoyment that can result from the failure to enforce covenants."[43] The first case to comment upon private community associations being quasi-governmental was *Cohen v. Kite Hill Community Ass'n*.[44] The plaintiff in *Cohen* brought suit against the construction of a fence that was not in compliance with a covenant in the regulations.[45] The court analogized the approval of the fence with a zoning board that awarded a variance.[46] It noted the degree to which courts reviewed the award of variances to protect nearby property owners.[47] To protect the private association members from an otherwise unaccountable association, the courts should be available to remedy the award if it is arbitrary or in violation of the declaration,[48] and they should review such an action under a fiduciary duty standard.[49]

The trick to this distinction was determining if the association actually was performing enough quasi-governmental tasks to warrant the comparison. The comparison was predicated on the fact that many associations provided "utility services, road maintenance, street and common area lighting, . . . security services and various forms of communication within the community."[50] In *Panther Valley*, the court noted the record did not indicate whether the association was to be treated as quasi-governmental or not.[51] Therefore, the argument seemingly hinged on this analysis.

In regard to enforcing restrictive sex offender covenants, it would seem as if the lawyer opposing the covenants could approach the case against the association under the guise of a fiduciary duty if his or her client was a member of the association (provided the association could meet the standard to be quasi-governmental). The lawyer would seemingly have to come at it from the opposite angle, however. The seeming trend is that the duty is to enforce the covenants,[52] not to avoid or invalidate them. The argument that would have to be made is that the fiduciary duty generally recognized in giving homeowner associations treatment as quasi-governmental is simply their duty to do right by their members. The argument can be made that to restrict the sale of these homes is not in the interest of the homeowners; it could also be argued that there are freedom of association and other such issues here, especially if the banned sex offender was an existing association member or a close family member the association member wished to help.[53]

The fiduciary duty standard is arguably a matter of public policy. It is included at this point because of the possibility of it allowing the application of the Constitution to these private associations and invoking a whole new array of arguments. The first would be that this heightened duty standard would make sure restrictive sex offender covenants are not passed. Second, it could be argued that if an association is quasi-governmental, the Constitution should apply in full, not just as a heightened duty, and possibly limit an association's ability to create covenants such as those banning sex offenders; whether this argument is viable remains to be seen.

B. *Shelley v. Kraemer* and State Action: No Relief for the Sex Offender in Invalidating Restrictive Covenants

The issue of court enforcement as state action is settled in our law. As discussed, this may have serious implications for the application of private restrictions on sex offenders, both in the context of *Shelley v. Kraemer*[54] and in regarding private communities as quasi-governmental entities. Shelley can be seen to require constitutional scrutiny when there is state action through court enforcement.[55] Additionally, the actions of the associations themselves in acting as a government could warrant constitutional analysis. These are issues which provoke thoughtful reflection, but which ultimately should not stop or deter a private community from enacting such bans on sex offenders in its midst.

One point of contention is whether arguments that invalidate racially restrictive covenants can be used as a useful comparison in arguing against sex offender restrictions being enforced by courts. Most state courts have not extended the reasoning of *Shelley* beyond its strict application to racially restrictive covenants.[56] Some, like Texas, have indicated that the application of *Shelley* may extend to situations where a court enforces a private restrictive covenant.[57] Ramsey dismissed these as a minority view and saw little chance of *Shelley* being applied to sex offender restrictions.[58] These concerns cannot be so lightly dismissed. New problems in the law are always ripe for a split of authority. With even a few states possibly applying the logic of *Shelley* to sex offender restrictions, a thorough discussion of the issues demands its inclusion, even if it is a minority position.

A bold lawyer could argue that the sex offender restrictions are a seemingly less harmful form of discrimination, but that they ultimately have a chilling effect despite the dislike of sex offenders; perhaps criminals in general should be banned. While this argument has some merit, it will fail because it is too far removed from the motivations of *Shelley*. First, the issue of race was (and is) a far more problematic issue for our nation to deal with justly than the residency of sex offenders. Second, the Supreme Court has already upheld sex offender restrictions.[59] Third, while the arguments for both racial and sex offender covenants revolve around public policy, restraints, and other issues, the comparison is shallow when considering the long and noble struggle for equality for all Americans in our nation.

The more complicated issue is the possibility of quasi-governmental actions of private communities being regarded as involving a heightened duty or invoking the full rigor of constitutional scrutiny for sex offender cases. This would admittedly be a step beyond what has to this point been done in the law.[60] However, the area of law surrounding the private associations and their conduct towards sex offenders is itself in its infancy. Some cases have found the actions of private associations to warrant a higher duty to members.[61] The next step would be full review of the private association's actions under the Constitution.

The issue of arguing for a duty to members would only apply in cases where a member opposed the restrictions. Where a member opposed the restrictions, issues could be raised like defining with whom association members could live as a by-product of the sex offender residency restriction. It is perhaps unlikely a court would reverse on the ground of an association owing an individual member any type of duty to permit a family member or other to live in the home. It does raise the issue of living with whom one chooses as a fundamental constitutional right,[62] applicable if the Constitution applies in full to these states.

Some states, like Texas, have concluded "state action exists in enforcing community association restrictive covenants and that constitutional analysis must be undertaken."[63] This is far from a majority of states, but it is worth noting. While they admittedly base this analysis on a logical extension of *Shelley*, the door could be opened to full constitutional analysis if the private association is now seen to act as a public entity.[64] Courts are generally viewed as having a desire to protect individual and fundamental rights, which are possibly threatened by the actions of community associations. It is not unthinkable that a state court would apply the Constitution or the state constitution to these issues because the association is behaving like a public entity.[65]

What does this mean then for restrictive sex offender covenants? In applying the Constitution generally to a community association that is strongly quasi-governmental,[66] the enforcement of these covenants would be open to a new range of arguments. This includes possible violations of procedural or substantive due process or violations of perceived fundamental rights, such as a right to travel where one pleases or live where and with whom one chooses.[67] While these arguments have already been struck down by the Eighth Circuit Court of Appeals and several state supreme courts, they may not be in all.[68]

The decisions reached in those courts were proper; however, at the risk of repetition ad nauseum, the issue is new and ripe for a split of authority. It is wholly conceivable that a different state or federal court could look at these restrictions and decide they violate important fundamental rights that are vital to a free society. It is important to be aware of this possibility and strongly meet these arguments. Otherwise, one risks a zealous advocate blindsiding him or her.

These possible arguments ultimately should not stop a community association from banning residence in its borders by sex offenders. Ultimately, the restrictions are common sense in that they remove sex offenders from target rich environments in large and diverse private communities. Protection of children is simply good policy. Most courts will see extending *Shelley* to sex offenders as overreaching.[69] It is legal as the Constitution should not apply in full to homeowner associations because they are private, no matter how much they act like a public entity.

VII. CONCLUSION

There is no doubt that as long as the government and private community associations are able to do so, they will regulate the presence of sex offenders within their respective jurisdictions. In turn, this will (and is currently starting to in cases like *Miller*) generate a large amount of litigation.[70] These cases could be brought in either federal or state court considering the myriad of issues and sub-issues surrounding these likely cases.[71] There will likely be no definitive ruling that defines the issues for several years. While there likely will be a trend toward enforcing these restrictions,[72] there is again little doubt there will be within these decisions an array of extremes and exceptions, even after the doctrine is ruled fundamentally sound.

These laws are a logical extension of the original Megan's Laws, which proposed to inform the community of the presence of these offenders, recognizing explicitly and implicitly that they are a threat.[73] When towns and private communities move to end this threat, it is the next logical step. When one recognizes there is a possibility of harm or danger to his or her community, and most likely his or her children, one must move to end it. Here, the recognized threat is sex offenders, of whom a community will often be notified; therefore, the prohibition by private communities is simply a proactive step toward removing a threat. If this step is not allowed, it would be a case of a right (notification of certain sexual predators in the community) without remedy (controlling their presence in the community). One would hope that no court would deny a private community (or public municipality) the ability to deal with a recognized threat head-on.

This is not to say that the effects of such laws are not harsh. When one chooses to end another's ability to reside in a community, it is certainly not taken lightly. What is being prevented is perhaps the best way to give the debate clarity. On one hand, you are balancing the removal of one from a private association entirely. The harm being prevented, stopping the sexual abuse of people, especially children, is a powerful goal. Even if just one attack is prevented, it seems worth it when one considers the turmoil caused. Finally, it is the sex offenders' own actions which place them in these restricted groups. Their exclusion is not because of an accident of birth or the color of their skin. When one takes an action, one must be accountable for it, and that is what is occurring with the covenants. Communities which take these steps are aware they could possibly be immersing themselves in a protracted legal battle. They likely feel it is worth the risk, however, in light of the harm.

The aforementioned discussion in many ways makes strong points; it is admittedly a layman's view. It is important, however, to discuss it in conclusion because these points will, in many ways, animate the policy behind the restrictions. It is the common experience all people have that is drawn on, despite legal training, and allows the laws to make sense. Any court will be sensitive to this dynamic; the covenants must still pass muster under existing law, however.

As has been shown, there are possible tough challenges to these private covenants on the grounds of policy, the FHA, and constitutional law. Each one is unavailing when considered in light of existing precedent and common sense. The policy arguments are a bit of a wild card in that they are the most unpredictable.[74] No court will likely give the arguments too much merit. The FHA will have to be interpreted to not only apply to the sex offenders as handicapped, but to overcome the exceptions as well, something which seems unlikely.[75] Finally, constitutional law presents a barrier only if extended to the private communities, which is arguably possible, but unlikely in this context. Therefore, it seems likely private communities can and will put in place and enforce these restrictions. The road to doing so may be hard but worth it in the end.

END NOTES

1. David Ramsey, *Megan's Law and Community Associations: The Case for Banning Sex-Offenders*, 2 CAI'S J. COMMUNITY ASS'N L. 2, 2-3 (1999). It is important to note the author of this article and my reliance on his excellent work in the Community Association Institute's Journal of Community Association Law. Mr. Ramsey is a New Jersey attorney with the firm of Ramsey Berman, P.C. in Morristown, New Jersey. See Posting of Ben Barros to Property Prof Blog, http://lawprofessors.typepad.com/property/2005/10/covenants_again.html (Oct. 3, 2005). He is the author of a covenant banning sex offenders from the private community of Panther Valley in New Jersey. This community is the same one in the only case currently to comment on such private restrictions. *See* Mulligan v. Panther Valley Prop. Owners Ass'n, 766 A.2d 1186 (N.J. Super. Ct. App. Div. 2001). This particular article was written prior to the litigation and is now six-years-old. However, his excellent discussion of the basic issues, especially public policy and the Fair Housing Act/Fair Housing Act Amendments ("FHA/FHAA"), was invaluable to this fledgling law student encountering many of these issues for the first time. Such guidance showed me what to look for and what issues to investigate. The article should be read by anyone interested in the subject.
2. N.J. STAT. ANN. §§ 2C:7-19 (West 2005); Ramsey, *supra* note 1, at 2.
3. *See* New Jersey's Megan's Law, N.J. STAT. ANN. §§ 2C:7-1 to -12 (West 2005).
4. *See* RICHARD J. CODEY & PETER C. HARVEY, ATTORNEY GENERAL GUIDELINES FOR LAW ENFORCEMENT FOR THE IMPLEMENTATION OF SEX OFFENDER REGISTRATION AND COMMUNITY NOTIFICATION LAWS 6 (2005), *available at* http://www.state.nj.us/lps/dcj/megan/meganguidelines1-05.pdf.
5. New Jersey State Police Sex Offender Internet Registry, http://www.nj.gov/njsp/info/reg_sexoffend.html (last visited Oct. 17, 2006).
6. *Id.*
7. *Id.*
8. CODEY & HARVEY, *supra* note 8, at 21.

9. *Id.* at 22, 33-34, 41-43.
10. *See* Robert Hanley, *New Jersey Supreme Court Hears Bitter Legal Argument Over 'Megan's Law,'* N.Y. TIMES, May 3, 1995, at B5.
11. 538 U.S. 84 (2003). In this case, the validity of Alaska's sex offender registration was challenged on the grounds of it violated the Ex Post Facto Clause. *Id.* at 91. The United States District Court for the District of Alaska granted summary judgment for the State, but the United States Court of Appeals for the Ninth Circuit reversed. *Id.* at 91-92. The Supreme Court, on a writ of certiorari, held that the Act was not designed to punish and that its retroactivity to previous offenders registering was in accord with constitutional principles. *Id.* at 93-94.
12. *Smith*, 538 U.S. at 96.
13. Darryl McGrath, *Restrictive Law Makes N.Y. City Off-Limits to Sex Offenders: Many States Grapple with Tighter Controls*, BOSTON GLOBE, Aug. 22, 2005, at A3.
14. *See* New Jersey State Police Sex Offender Internet Registry, . . . ; Pennsylvania State Police Megan's Law Website, (providing basic information including photos and areas of residence).
15. For some discussion of this issue and a different take on some of the issues addressed in this article, see Brett Jackson Coppage, *Comment, Balancing Community Interests and Offender Rights: The Validity of Covenants Restricting Sex Offenders from Residing in a Neighborhood*, 38 URB. LAW. 309 (2006) (discussing issues of covenant enforceability, policy, and constitutional concerns).
16. *See* McGrath, *supra* note 13.
17. *See* McGrath, *supra* note 13.
18. *See* Ramsey, *supra* note 1, at 3.
19. *Id.* at 5-6.
20. *Id.* at 5.
21. 42 U.S.C. §§ 3601-19 (2000). Certain provisions of the FHA were amended by the Fair Housing Amendments Act of 1988, Pub. L. No. 100-430, 102 Stat. 1619 (1988), but for purposes of this paper, the Act and its amendments will be referred to as "FHA."
22. 334 U.S. 1 (1948).
23. *Id.* at 23.
24. *Id.* at 20.
25. *Id.*
26. 766 A.2d 1186 (N.J. Super. Ct. App. Div. 2001). It should be noted that the case here is the only case available on point with this issue. Therefore, New Jersey law may be used to discuss certain aspects of this case regarding the larger scope of enforceability. The discussion here is meant to be nationally-focused, but to whatever extent other states define issues differently from New Jersey, I apologize and hope the reader will forgive this shortcoming.

27. *Panther Valley*, 766 A.2d at 1188.
28. *Id.* at 1189.
29. *Id.* at 1188-89.
30. *Id.* at 1188.
31. *Id.* at 1186.
32. *Id.* at 1192.
33. *Panther Valley*, 766 A.2d at 1192.
34. *Id.*
35. It should be noted that while this court did not rule on the issue, there is a federal district court case that in dicta suggests that dangerous residents can be housed in an area if adequate precautions are taken. *See* Ramsey, *supra* note 1, at 10 (citing Twp. of W. Orange v. Whitman, 8 F. Supp. 2d 408, 420 (D.N.J. 1998)). The same court also said it knew of no grounds on which the municipality or the individual plaintiffs could prevent others with the psychiatric histories and diagnoses [schizophrenia, bipolar disorder, etc] of the Project Live residents or others, such as ex-convicts, who could be predicted . . . to pose a heightened risk of dangerousness, from living in the same communities.Whitman, 8 F. Supp. 2d at 420. They acknowledged Megan's Law but noted it only required notification and did not restrict living arrangements. *Id.* The case may only have limited precedential value, but it shows the issue of sex offender residential restrictions is not settled.
36. *Panther Valley*, 766 A.2d at 1193.
37. Shelley v. Kraemer, 334 U.S. 1, 20 (1948).
38. *See* United States v. Carolene Prod. Co., 304 U.S. 144, 152-53 n.4 (1938). The famous footnote four mentions that strict scrutiny applies where there is a fundamental right implicated or where a class implicates a religious, national, or racial minority. *Id.*
39. *See* Meade v. Dennistone, 196 A. 330, 332 (Md. 1938). The plaintiff argued that such covenants were unenforceable on public policy and federal constitutional grounds. *Id.* The court found these arguments unconvincing. *Id. See also* Nw. Civic Ass'n v. Sheldon, 27 N.W.2d 36, 38 (Mich. 1947). The plaintiff argued on policy grounds, as well as state and federal constitutional grounds. *Id.*
40. Correll v. Earley, 237 P.2d 1017, 1020 (Okla. 1951) (Oklahoma Supreme Court, in its own words, articulated the Shelley standard).
41. These arguments are extensions of common arguments in this field but do not draw from any one particular source.
42. Colorado Homes Ltd. v. Loerch-Wilson, 43 P.3d 718, 721-22 (Colo. Ct. App. 2001) (citing Cohen v. Kite Hill Cmty. Ass'n, 191 Cal. Rptr. 209, 217 (Cal. Ct. App. 1983)).
43. Loerch-Wilson, 43 P.3d at 722.
44. 191 Cal. Rptr. 209 (Cal. Ct. App. 1983).
45. *Id.* at 211.

46. *Id.* at 214.
47. *Id.* at 215 (citing Topanga Ass'n for a Scenic Cmty. v. County of Los Angeles, 113 Cal. Rptr. 836, 843 (Cal. 1974)).
48. *Id.*
49. *Id.* at 217.
50. Cohen v. Kite Hill Cmty. Ass'n, 191 Cal. Rptr. 209, 214 (Cal. Ct. App. 1983) (quoting Wayne S. Hyatt & James B. Rhoads, Concepts of Liability in the Development and Administration of Condominium and Home Owners Associations, 12 WAKE FOREST L. REV. 915, 918 (1976)).
51. Mulligan v. Panther Valley Prop. Owners Ass'n, 766 A.2d 1186, 1193 (N.J. Super. Ct. App. Div. 2001).
52. *See Cohen*, 191 Cal. Rptr. at 217; *Loerch-Wilson*, 43 P 3d at 721-22.
53. These points are drawn from common themes in many cases and writings, but the issue of fundamental rights being argued against these covenants can be seen in *Miller*. Doe v. Miller, 405 F.3d 700. 705-08 (8th Cir. 2005).
54. 334 U.S. 1 (1948).
55. *See* Ramsey, supra note 1, at 6.
56. *Id.*
57. *See* Shaver v. Hunter, 626 S.W.2d 574, 578-79 (Tex. App. 1981); Ramsey, *supra* note 1, at 6.
58. Ramsey, *supra* note 1, at 6.
59. Smith v. Doe, 538 U.S. 84, 105 (2003).
60. Ramsey mentions that the Supreme Court has already ruled on this in Marsh v. Alabama, 326 U.S. 501 (1946). Ramsey, *supra* note 1, at 6. He notes that in Marsh the Court defined a town as "encompassing a wide variety of commercial enterprises, police enforcement, and schools . . . ." *Id.* at 6. The case was admittedly an indication of a possible direction the Court could take. The case, however, dealt with a town owned by an oil company in which the company abridged First Amendment rights. Marsh, 326 U.S. at 502-04. The decision is nearly sixty-years-old and prior to *Shelley*. There was also no reason why the Court, or any other, could not extend the definition of a town to a newer phenomenon or distinguish the case altogether. Ramsey's dismissal of the case as precluding constitutional arguments concerning the applicability of the Constitution to private associations was premature in this case.
61. *See* Cohen v. Kite Hill Community Ass'n, 191 Cal. Rptr. 209, 214-15 (Cal. Ct. App. 1983).
62. *See* Doe v. Miller, 405 F.3d 700, 709-10 (8th Cir. 2005).
63. Ramsey, *supra* note 1, at 6.
64. The applicable test would be the "public function test," which was seen in Marsh. 326 U.S. at 506. The Supreme Court has been less than clear on the test, though in a decision involving a sale of debtor's goods, the Court

did mention police protection and other functions as possibly public. JOHN E. NOWAK & RONALD D. ROTUNDA, CONSTITUTIONAL LAW 562-63 (7th ed. 2004) (citing Flagg Brothers, Inc. v. Brooks, 436 U.S. 149, 163-64 (1978)).

65. *See* Ramsey, *supra* note 1 at 12.
66. This means those associations that behave like towns because they have security, collect trash, etc. *See* Hyatt & Rhoads, supra note 151.
67. *See* Miller, 405 F.3d at 708-09.
68. *See, e.g., id.* at 705; Mann v. State, 603 S.E.2d 283, 285-87 (Ga. 2004); State v. Seering, 701 N.W.2d 655, 670-71 (Iowa 2005) (upholding state sex offender residency restriction statutes).
69. *See* Ramsey, *supra* note 1, at 6.
70. While this article was written, another case was filed in the United States District Court for the Southern District of Ohio. Coston v. Petro, 398 F. Supp. 2d 878 (S.D. Ohio 2005). The plaintiffs claimed Ohio's statute was unconstitutional and sought class action certification, but the case was dismissed due to lack of standing. *Id.* at 882. The case itself probably has little importance right now, but serves to illustrate that this area will likely continue to be a source of litigation for the foreseeable future.
71. Besides the actual issues surrounding the covenants themselves, the problems of procedure seem likely to loom as well. Standing will possibly be an issue in some cases, such as in *Panther Valley*, and jurisdiction between state and federal court is also likely to be messy. The covenants will invoke state law issues as well as federal ones, meaning courts will have to decide if they are proper forums for these battles. In sum, the litigation of these claims is likely to be morass for the foreseeable future.
72. Considering the current cases such as Doe v. Miller, 405 F.3d 700 (8th Cir. 2005) and State v. Seering, 701 N.W.2d 655 (Iowa 2005).
73. *See* Ramsey, *supra* note 1, at 2.
74. *See* Ramsey, *supra* note 1, at 6-8.
75. *See id.* at 8-12.

ISSUE SUMMARY

Overall, the collection of articles presented in this section illustrate the various incarnations of restrictive covenants. This is not to say that the articles lack significant overlap; rather, the articles all address a similar question: Should homeowners be able to do what they want with their property? Further, the articles do seem to reach some common conclusions. First, restrictive covenants are best judged in their individual contexts, but the way in which restrictive covenants should be judged and understood is less than clear. Second, restrictive covenants that govern architecture as opposed to those that restrict residency are very different ideas and probably should be treated differently.

Moreover, it should be clear from the readings that there are many unanswered questions about restrictive covenants. Some of the broader questions that are worthy of reflection are listed below:

1. Why are privately imposed restrictive covenants different from government regulation?
2. Why might individuals be in favor of restrictive covenants? Why might individuals oppose them?
3. What benefits to restrictive covenants grant society? What harm can restrictive covenants cause society?

ISSUE HIGHLIGHTS

- Restrictive covenants are complex and contextual regulations and invite complex questions about their role in the legal system.
- Restrictive covenants can prevent individuals from acting in socially beneficial ways, such as preventing environmentally friendly behaviors.
- There is not yet a clear legal standard or precedent for understanding and judging restrictive covenants.
- Restrictive covenants and community associations function in legislative and adjudicative ways.

CRITICAL THINKING

In the issue summary, we asked you to consider why restrictive covenants might be desirable and why they might be undesirable. One aspect of fully answering this question is understanding the value preferences lying behind each position. Value preferences are one step in the movement from a set of reasons to a conclusion in an argument. Values are positive abstractions that guide an individual's behavior and opinions. However, because values are positive, people hold some values in preference to others in arguments.

Consider the first article and the court case in question. The suit arose from Ms. McGovern's misplacement of her satellite dish and improperly building a fence. Ms. McGovern's behavior violated the architectural standards for the community. So why might the homeowners' association feel the need to develop architectural standards? One reason is that the homeowners' association values unity over individuality. In this case, unity refers to homogeneity of appearance and behavior that limits opportunities for conflict and individuality refers to an individual's desire to express his/her preferences in various ways.

Are there other value preferences that arise in a discussion of restrictive covenants? Does Herman's article about the "Megan's Law" parts of restrictive covenants lead to a different set of values and value preferences than the architectural covenants? Are there common value conflicts that arise between the two situations?

ADDITIONAL READINGS

Country Club Homeowners Association v. Country Club Christian Church. 2003 Mo. App. LEXIS 1365.

Heidi Flinn, *The Necessary Application of the Contract Clause to Cases Involving Restrictive Covenants and Group Family Day Care Homes,* 27 Fordham Urb. L.J. 1793 (2000).

Grandshire Homeowners Association: http://www.grandshire.org/deed/default.htm

Thomas Guernsey, *The Mentally Retarded and Private Restrictive Covenants,* 25 Wm and Mary L. Rev. 421 (1985).

Gerald Korngold, *Resolving the Intergenerational Conflicts of Real Property Law,* 56 Am. U.L. Rev. 1525 (2007).

Motoko Rich, *Homeowner Boards Blur the Lines of Just Who Rules the Roost.* New York Times. 27 July 2003. http://query.nytimes.com/gst/fullpage.html?res= 9B00E3D7113FF934A15754C0A9659C8B63

http://depts.washington.edu/civilr/covenants.htm

ISSUE 8

Should the Government Be Able to Take Your Property for Purpose of Job Creation?

Very few doubt that the economy is an important part of the quality of life for the average citizen in America. However, a still debated question is how much the government should step in to support the economy. In this section, you will contemplate a specific tool that some believe the government should use to affect the economy—eminent domain. Should governments be able to take your property for the purpose of job creation? Should the government have the legal right to transfer private property on the hope that such a transfer would improve the economy?

The six articles in this section all question the appropriate limits on eminent domain. The first piece, *Susette Kelo v. City of New London*, contains the United States Supreme Court's controversial majority, concurring and dissenting opinions about the extent to which a city government could use the power of eminent domain to facilitate economic growth. Does the City of New London have the power, under the "Takings Clause" of the Constitution to transfer land to a private company in hopes of stimulating economic benefits. The majority opinion argues that the City does have such power by discussing the way in which economic benefits are a legitimate public use of the property, and thus can be deemed constitutional under the "Takings Clause." The dissent argues that the majority has abandoned a crucial limitation on government power by equivocating the ideas of public use and public purpose.

Peter Agnetti argues against the decision in *Kelo*. Agnetti points out that the state and government powers may have an interest in the uses of property via tax benefits. In other words, Agnetti sees a large potential for the economic redevelopment justification to be abused to take private property that is not economically blighted. Christensen provides a different argument against the *Kelo* decision was based on an insufficient judicial standard. The Supreme Court's majority opinion relied on a "rational basis" test instead of a "means" or "brightline" test. "Rational basis" and "conceivable reason" tests are too vague to serve as a legitimate and useful judicial standard.

In a slightly different vein, Kubasek discusses a slight variation on eminent domain—the idea of regulatory takings. Regulatory takings arise when the regulations on a piece of real estate change and the owner of the property must comply. Measure 37, an important piece of legislation in Oregon, restricts the use of regulatory takings by mimicking the idea of *ex post facto* where the property owner can develop the land in accordance to the laws at the time of purchase instead of being subject to the new regulations. Measure 37 clones have appeared on the ballots in other states with varying degrees of success. However, as Kubasek points out, the *Kelo* decision may have implications for such legislation.

The fourth article in this section discusses the marketing implications of *Kelo*. According to the authors, the *Kelo* decision opens the door to more drastic conflicts between local government and major sports franchises. Nagel and Southall also suggest the increasing extent to which eminent domain could be providing political "pork" instead of public benefits.

Spaht, however, takes a very different look at the *Kelo* decision and how it affects New Orleans and Louisiana's struggle to rebuild after Katrina and Rita. According to Spaht, *Kelo* offers a potential solution to the "anticommons problem" where a valuable resource is being underused. *Kelo,* Spaht argues, allows the New Orleans government to rebuild parts of the city where residents and property owners have not yet returned.

Overall, the *Kelo* decision and the relationship between eminent domain and economic development is a complicated and controversial one. Value preferences and assumptions about human nature continue to influence how one may answer the question—should governments be able to take your property for the purpose of job creation?

ISSUE ARTICLES

Susette Kelo v. City of New London, Supreme Court of the United States (2005)

Peter M. Agnetti, from "Are You Still Master of Your Domain? Abuses of Economic Development Takings, and Michigan's Return to "Public Use" in *County of Wayne v. Hathcock,*" *St. John's Law Review* (Fall 2005)

Nancy Kubasek, form "Measure 37 Clones Fail at the Ballot Box," *Real Estate Law Journal* (vol. 35, 2007)

Mark S. Nagel and Richard M. Southall, from "A Stadium in Your Front Yard? Eminent Domain and the Potential Sport Marketing Implication of *Kelo v. City of New London,*" *Sport Marketing Quarterly* (September 2007)

William Carlos Spaht, from "Overcoming Another Tragedy in New Orleans: Rebuilding in the Wake of Kelo and Act. No. 851," *Vanderbilt Law Review* (October 2007)

ARTICLE 8.1

Susette Kelo v. City of New London

In 1990 a state agency designated the city of New London, Connecticut (City) a "distressed municipality." In 1996, the Federal Government closed the Naval Undersea Warfare Center, which had been located in the Fort Trumbull area of the City and had employed over 1,500 people. In 1998, the City's unemployment rate was nearly double that of the State, and its population of just under 24,000 residents was at its lowest since 1920. In response to its poor economic condition, the City created the New London Development Corporation (NLDC), a private nonprofit group charged with creating an economic development plan to improve the City. The NLDC's plan involved obtaining 90 acres of land in the Fort Trumbull area of the City and building a new waterfront area to surround the new research facility Pfizer Inc. was building in the city.

The City Council granted NLDC the power to purchase all of the needed land, and then to use the City's power of eminent domain to obtain the rest of the needed land while paying a fair market price for the land. Susette Kelo and others challenged the City's use of eminent domain, arguing that the City's taking violated the Fifth Amendment's "public use" restriction. The Superior Court ruled some of the takings violated the Fifth Amendment, and both sides appealed to the Supreme Court of Connecticut. The court upheld all of the takings as constitutional, and Kelo and the others appealed to the Supreme Court.

JUSTICE STEVENS

III

Two polar propositions are perfectly clear. On the one hand, it has long been accepted that the sovereign may not take the property of A for the sole purpose of transferring it to another private party B, even though A is paid just compensation. On the other hand, it is equally clear that a State may transfer property from one private party to another if future "use by the public" is the purpose of the taking; the condemnation of land for a railroad with common-carrier duties is a familiar example. Neither of these propositions, however, determines the disposition of this case.

As for the first proposition, the City would no doubt be forbidden from taking petitioners' land for the purpose of conferring a private benefit on a particular private party. . . . Nor would the City be allowed to take property under the mere pretext of a public purpose, when its actual purpose was to bestow a private benefit. The takings before us, however, would be executed pursuant to a "carefully considered" development plan. 268 Conn., at 54, 843 A. 2d, at 536. The trial judge and all the members of the Supreme Court of Connecticut agreed that there was no evidence of an illegitimate purpose in this case.[1] Therefore, as was true of the statute challenged in *Midkiff*, 467 U.S., at 245 . . ., the City's development plan was not adopted "to benefit a particular class of identifiable individuals."

On the other hand, this is not a case in which the City is planning to open the condemned land—at least not in its entirety—to use by the general public. Nor will the private lessees of the land in any sense be required to operate like common carriers, making their services available to all comers. But although such a projected use would be sufficient to satisfy the public use requirement, this "Court long ago rejected any literal requirement that condemned property be put into use for the general public." Id., at 244, 81 L. Ed. 2d 186, 104 S. Ct. 2321. . . .

The disposition of this case therefore turns on the question whether the City's development plan serves a "public purpose." Without exception, our cases have defined that concept broadly, reflecting our longstanding policy of deference to legislative judgments in this field.

How are the Berman v. Parker *and* Hawaii Housing Authority_v. Midkiff *cases similar to and different from the* Kelo *case?*

In *Berman v. Parker*, 348 U.S. 26 . . . (1954), this Court upheld a redevelopment plan targeting a blighted area of Washington, D. C., in which most of the housing for the area's 5,000 inhabitants was beyond repair. Under the plan, the area would be condemned and part of it utilized for the construction of streets, schools, and other public facilities. The remainder of the land would be leased or sold to private parties for the purpose of redevelopment, including the construction of low-cost housing.

The owner of a department store located in the area challenged the condemnation, pointing out that his store was not itself blighted and arguing that the creation of a "better balanced, more attractive community" was not a valid public use. . . . Writing for a unanimous Court, Justice Douglas refused to evaluate this claim in isolation, deferring instead to the legislative and agency judgment that the area "must be planned as a whole" for the plan to be successful. . . . The Court explained that "community redevelopment programs need not, by force of the Constitution, be on a piecemeal basis—lot by lot, building by building." Id., at 35. . . . The public use underlying the taking was unequivocally affirmed. . . .

In *Hawaii Housing Authority v. Midkiff*, 467 U.S. 229 . . . (1984), the Court considered a Hawaii statute whereby fee title was taken from lessors and transferred to lessees (for just compensation) in order to reduce the concentration of land ownership. We unanimously upheld the statute and rejected the Ninth Circuit's view that it was "a naked attempt on the part of the state of Hawaii to take the property of A and transfer it to B solely for B's private use and benefit." Id., at 235 . . . (internal quotation marks omitted). Reaffirming *Berman's* deferential approach to legislative judgments in this field, we concluded that the State's purpose of eliminating the "social and economic evils of a land oligopoly" qualified as a valid public use. 467 U.S., at 241–242. . . . Our opinion also rejected the contention that the mere fact that the State immediately transferred the properties to private individuals upon condemnation somehow diminished the public character of the taking. "[I]t is only the taking's purpose, and not its mechanics," we explained, that matters in determining public use. Id., at 244. . . .

Viewed as a whole, our jurisprudence has recognized that the needs of society have varied between different parts of the Nation, just as they have evolved over time in response to changed circumstances. Our earliest cases in particular embodied a strong theme of federalism, emphasizing the "great respect" that we owe to state legislatures and state courts in discerning local public needs. . . . For more than a century, our public use jurisprudence has wisely eschewed rigid formulas and intrusive scrutiny in favor of affording legislatures broad latitude in determining what public needs justify the use of the takings power.

IV

Those who govern the City were not confronted with the need to remove blight in the Fort Trumbull area, but their determination that the area was sufficiently distressed to justify a program of economic rejuvenation is entitled to our deference. The City has carefully formulated an economic development plan that it believes will provide appreciable benefits to the community, including—but by no means limited to—new jobs and increased tax revenue. As with other exercises in urban planning and development, the City is endeavoring to coordinate a variety of commercial, residential, and recreational uses of land, with the hope that they will form a whole greater than the sum of its parts. To effectuate this plan, the City has invoked a state statute that specifically authorizes the use of eminent domain to promote economic development. Given the comprehensive character of the plan, the thorough deliberation that preceded its adoption, and the limited scope of our review, it is appropriate for us, as it was in *Berman*, to resolve the challenges of the individual owners, not on a piecemeal basis, but rather in light of the entire plan. Because that plan unquestionably serves a public purpose, the takings challenged here satisfy the public use requirement of the Fifth Amendment.

Why did the court not think that the fact that the area being taken in Kelo *was not blighted?*

To avoid this result, petitioners urge us to adopt a new bright-line rule that economic development does not qualify as a public use. Putting aside the unpersuasive suggestion that the City's plan will provide only purely economic benefits, neither precedent nor logic supports petitioners' proposal. Promoting economic development is a traditional and long accepted function of government. There is, moreover, no principled way of distinguishing economic development from the other public purposes that we have recognized. In our cases upholding takings that facilitated agriculture and mining, for example, we emphasized the importance of those industries to the welfare of the States in question . . .; in *Berman*, we endorsed the purpose of transforming a blighted area into a "well-balanced" community through redevelopment, 348 U.S., at 33 . . .; [2] in *Midkiff*, we upheld the interest in breaking up a land oligopoly that "created artificial deterrents to the normal functioning of the State's residential land market," 467 U.S., at 242 . . .; and in *Monsanto*, we accepted Congress' purpose of eliminating a "significant barrier to entry in the pesticide market," 467 U.S., at 1014–1015. . . . It would be incongruous to hold that the City's interest in the economic benefits to be derived from the development of the Fort Trumbull area has less of a public character than any of those other interests. Clearly, there is no basis for exempting economic development from our traditionally broad understanding of public purpose.

Petitioners contend that using eminent domain for economic development impermissibly blurs the boundary between public and private takings. Again, our cases foreclose this objection. Quite simply, the government's pursuit of a public purpose will often benefit individual private parties. For example, in *Midkiff*, the forced transfer of property conferred a direct and significant benefit on those lessees who were previously unable to purchase their homes. In *Monsanto*, we recognized that the "most direct beneficiaries" of the data-sharing provisions were the subsequent pesticide applicants, but benefiting them in this way was necessary to promoting competition in the pesticide market. 467 U.S., at 1014.[3] . . . The owner of the department store in *Berman* objected to "taking from one businessman for the benefit of another businessman," 348 U.S., at 33 . . ., referring to the fact that under the redevelopment plan land would be leased or sold to private developers for redevelopment.[4] Our rejection of that contention has particular relevance to the instant case: "The public end may be as well or better served through an agency of private enterprise than through a department of government—or so the Congress might conclude. We cannot say that public ownership is the sole method of promoting the public purposes of community redevelopment projects." Id., at 34. . . .[5]

It is further argued that without a bright-line rule nothing would stop a city from transferring citizen A's property to citizen B for the sole reason that citizen B will put the property to a more productive use and thus pay more taxes. Such a one-to-one transfer of property, executed outside the confines of an integrated development plan, is not presented in this case. While such an unusual exercise of government power would certainly raise a suspicion that a private purpose was afoot,[6] the hypothetical cases posited by petitioners can be confronted if and when they arise. They do not warrant the crafting of an artificial restriction on the concept of public use.[7]

Alternatively, petitioners maintain that for takings of this kind we should require a "reasonable certainty" that the expected public benefits will actually accrue. Such a rule, however, would represent an even greater departure from our precedent. "When the legislature's purpose is legitimate and its means are not irrational, our cases make clear that empirical debates over the wisdom of takings—no less than debates over the wisdom of other kinds of socioeconomic legislation—are not to be carried out in the federal courts."

Midkiff, 467 U.S., at 242. . . . Indeed, earlier this Term we explained why similar practical concerns (among others) undermined the use of the "substantially advances" formula in our regulatory takings doctrine. . . . The disadvantages of a heightened form of review are especially pronounced in this type of case. Orderly implementation of a comprehensive redevelopment plan obviously requires that the legal rights of all interested parties be established before new construction can be commenced. A constitutional rule that required postponement of the judicial approval of every condemnation until the likelihood of success of the plan had been assured would unquestionably impose a significant impediment to the successful consummation of many such plans.

Just as we decline to second-guess the City's considered judgments about the efficacy of its development plan, we also decline to second-guess the City's determinations as to what lands it needs to acquire in order to effectuate the project. "It is not for the courts to oversee the choice of the boundary line nor to sit in review on the size of a particular project area. Once the question of the public purpose has been decided, the amount and character of land to be taken for the project and the need for a particular tract to complete the integrated plan rests in the discretion of the legislative branch." *Berman*, 348 U.S., at 35–36. . . .

In affirming the City's authority to take petitioners' properties, we do not minimize the hardship that condemnations may entail, notwithstanding the payment of just compensation. We emphasize that nothing in our opinion precludes any State from placing further restrictions on its exercise of the takings power. Indeed, many States already impose "public use" requirements that are stricter than the federal baseline. Some of these requirements have been established as a matter of state constitutional law,[8] while others are expressed in state eminent domain statutes that carefully limit the grounds upon which takings may be exercised.[9] As the submissions of the parties and their amici make clear, the necessity and wisdom of using eminent domain to promote economic development are certainly matters of legitimate public debate. This Court's authority, however, extends only to determining whether the City's proposed condemnations are for a "public use" within the meaning of the Fifth Amendment to the Federal Constitution. Because over a century of our case law interpreting that provision dictates an affirmative answer to that question, we may not grant petitioners the relief that they seek.

The judgment of the Supreme Court of Connecticut is affirmed.

It is so ordered.

JUSTICE KENNEDY, CONCURRING

I join the opinion for the Court and add these further observations.

This Court has declared that a taking should be upheld as consistent with the Public Use Clause . . ., as long as it is "rationally related to a conceivable public purpose." *Hawaii Housing Authority v. Midkiff*, 467 U.S. 229 . . .

(1984). . . . This deferential standard of review echoes the rational-basis test used to review economic regulation under the Due Process and Equal Protection Clauses. . . . The determination that a rational-basis standard of review is appropriate does not, however, alter the fact that transfers intended to confer benefits on particular, favored private entities, and with only incidental or pretextual public benefits, are forbidden by the Public Use Clause.

A court applying rational-basis review under the Public Use Clause should strike down a taking that, by a clear showing, is intended to favor a particular private party, with only incidental or pretextual public benefits, just as a court applying rational-basis review under the Equal Protection Clause must strike down a government classification that is clearly intended to injure a particular class of private parties, with only incidental or pretextual public justifications. . . .

A court confronted with a plausible accusation of impermissible favoritism to private parties should treat the objection as a serious one and review the record to see if it has merit, though with the presumption that the government's actions were reasonable and intended to serve a public purpose. Here, the trial court conducted a careful and extensive inquiry into "whether, in fact, the development plan is of primary benefit to . . . the developer [i.e., Corcoran Jennison], and private businesses which may eventually locate in the plan area [e.g., Pfizer], and in that regard, only of incidental benefit to the city." . . .

The trial court concluded, based on these findings, that benefiting Pfizer was not "the primary motivation or effect of this development plan"; instead, "the primary motivation for [respondents] was to take advantage of Pfizer's presence." . . . This case, then, survives the meaningful rational basis review that in my view is required under the Public Use Clause. . . .

My agreement with the Court that a presumption of invalidity is not warranted for economic development takings in general, or for the particular takings at issue in this case, does not foreclose the possibility that a more stringent standard of review than that announced in *Berman* and *Midkiff* might be appropriate for a more narrowly drawn category of takings. . . . This demanding level of scrutiny, however, is not required simply because the purpose of the taking is economic development. . . .

For the foregoing reasons, I join in the Court's opinion.

JUSTICE O'CONNOR, WITH WHOM THE CHIEF JUSTICE, JUSTICE SCALIA, AND JUSTICE THOMAS JOIN, DISSENTING

. . . Today the Court abandons this long-held, basic limitation on government power. Under the banner of economic development, all private property is now vulnerable to being taken and transferred to another private owner, so long as it might be upgraded—i.e., given to an owner who will use it in a way that the legislature deems more beneficial to the public—in the process. To reason, as the Court does, that the incidental public benefits resulting from the subsequent ordinary use of private property render economic development takings "for public use" is to wash out any distinction between private and public use of property—and thereby effectively to delete the words "for public use" from the Takings Clause of the Fifth Amendment. Accordingly I respectfully dissent. . . .

II

The Fifth Amendment to the Constitution, made applicable to the States by the Fourteenth Amendment, provides that "private property [shall not] be taken for public use, without just compensation." When interpreting the Constitution, we begin with the unremarkable presumption that every word in the document has independent meaning, "that no word was unnecessarily used, or needlessly added." . . . In keeping with that presumption, we have read the Fifth Amendment's language to impose two distinct conditions on the exercise of eminent domain: "the Taking must be for a 'public use' and 'just compensation' must be paid to the owner." *Brown v. Legal Foundation of Wash.*, 538 U.S. 216 . . . (2003). . . .

While the Takings Clause presupposes that government can take private property without the owner's consent, the just compensation requirement spreads the cost of condemnations and thus "prevents the public from loading upon one individual more than his just share of the burdens of government." *Monongahela Nav. Co. v. United States*, 148 U.S. 312 . . . (1893); *see also Armstrong v. United States*, 364 U.S. 40 . . . (1960). The public use requirement, in turn, imposes a more basic limitation, circumscribing the very scope of the eminent domain power: Government may compel an individual to forfeit her property for the public's use, but not for the benefit of another private person. This requirement promotes fairness as well as security. . . .

Where is the line between "public" and "private" property use? We give considerable deference to legislatures' determinations about what governmental activities will advantage the public. But were the political branches the sole arbiters of the public-private distinction, the Public Use Clause would amount to little more than hortatory fluff. An external, judicial check on how the public use requirement is interpreted, however limited, is necessary if this constraint on government power is to retain any meaning. . . .

Our cases have generally identified three categories of takings that comply with the public use requirement, though it is in the nature of things that the boundaries between these categories are not always firm. Two are relatively straightforward and uncontroversial. First, the sovereign may transfer private property to public ownership—such as for a road, a hospital, or a military base. . . . Second, the sovereign may transfer private property to private parties, often common carriers, who make the property available for the public's use—such as with a railroad, a public utility, or a stadium. . . . But "public ownership" and "use-by-the-public" are sometimes too constricting and impractical ways to define the scope of the Public Use Clause. Thus we have allowed that, in certain circumstances and to meet certain exigencies, takings that serve a public purpose also satisfy the Constitution even if the property is destined for subsequent private use. . . .

This case returns us for the first time in over 20 years to the hard question of when a purportedly "public purpose" taking meets the public use requirement. It presents an issue of first impression: Are economic development takings constitutional? I would hold that they are not. We are guided by two precedents about the taking of real property by eminent domain. . . .

In [the *Berman* and *Midkiff*] decisions, we emphasized the importance of deferring to legislative judgments about public purpose. Because courts are ill equipped to evaluate the efficacy of proposed legislative initiatives, we rejected as unworkable the idea of courts' "'deciding on what is and is not a governmental function and . . . invalidating legislation on the basis of their view on that question at the moment of decision, a practice which has proved impracticable in other fields.'" Id., at 240–241 . . . (quoting *United States ex rel. TVA v. Welch*, 327 U.S. 546 . . . (1946)). . . . Likewise, we recognized our inability to evaluate whether, in a given case, eminent domain is a necessary means by which to pursue the legislature's ends. . . .

Yet for all the emphasis on deference, *Berman* and *Midkiff* hewed to a bedrock principle without which our public use jurisprudence would collapse: "A purely private taking could not withstand the scrutiny of the public use requirement; it would serve no legitimate purpose of government and would thus be void." *Midkiff*, 467 U.S., at 245. . . . To protect that principle, those decisions reserved "a role for courts to play in reviewing a legislature's judgment of what constitutes a public use. . . . [though] the Court in *Berman* made clear that it is 'an extremely narrow' one." *Midkiff*, supra, at 240, 81 L. Ed. 2d 186, 104 S. Ct. 2321 (quoting *Berman, supra*, at 32, 99 L. Ed. 27, 75 S. Ct. 98).

The Court's holdings in *Berman* and *Midkiff* were true to the principle underlying the Public Use Clause. In both those cases, the extraordinary, precondemnation use of the targeted property inflicted affirmative harm on society—in *Berman* through blight resulting from extreme poverty and in *Midkiff* through oligopoly resulting from extreme wealth. And in both cases, the relevant legislative body had found that eliminating the existing property use was necessary to remedy the harm. . . . Thus a public purpose was realized when the harmful use was eliminated. Because each taking directly achieved a public benefit, it did not matter that the property was turned over to private use. Here, in contrast, New London does not claim that Susette Kelo's and Wilhelmina Dery's well-maintained homes are the source of any social harm. Indeed, it could not so claim without adopting the absurd argument that any single-family home that might be razed to make way for an apartment building, or any church that might be replaced with a retail store, or any small business that might be more lucrative if it were instead part of a national franchise, is inherently harmful to society and thus within the government's power to condemn.

In moving away from our decisions sanctioning the condemnation of harmful property use, the Court today significantly expands the meaning of public use. It holds that the sovereign may take private property currently put to ordinary private use, and give it over for new, ordinary private use, so long as the new use is predicted to generate some secondary benefit for the public—such as increased tax revenue, more jobs, maybe even esthetic pleasure. But nearly any lawful use of real private property can be said to generate some incidental benefit to the public. Thus, if predicted (or even guaranteed) positive side effects are enough to render transfer from one private party to another constitutional, then the words "for public use" do not realistically exclude any takings, and thus do not exert any constraint on the eminent domain power. . . .

The Court protests that it does not sanction the bare transfer from A to B for B's benefit. It suggests two limitations on what can be taken after today's decision. First, it maintains a role for courts in ferreting out takings whose sole purpose is to bestow a benefit on the private transferee—without detailing how courts are to conduct that complicated inquiry. . . . For his part, Justice Kennedy suggests that courts may divine illicit purpose by a careful review of the record and the process by which a legislature arrived at the decision to take—without specifying what courts should look for in a case with different facts, how they will know if they have found it, and what to do if they do not. . . . The trouble with economic development takings is that private benefit and incidental public benefit are, by definition, merged and mutually reinforcing. In this case, for example, any boon for Pfizer or the plan's developer is difficult to disaggregate from the promised public gains in taxes and jobs. . . .

The Court also puts special emphasis on facts peculiar to this case: The NLDC's plan is the product of a relatively careful deliberative process; it proposes to use eminent domain for a multipart, integrated plan rather than for isolated property transfer; it promises an array of incidental benefits (even esthetic ones), not just increased tax revenue; it comes on the heels of a legislative determination that New London is a depressed municipality. . . . But none has legal significance to blunt the force of today's holding. If legislative prognostications about the secondary public benefits of a new use can legitimate a taking, there is nothing in the Court's rule or in Justice Kennedy's gloss on that rule to prohibit property transfers generated with less care, that are less comprehensive, that happen to result from less elaborate process, whose only projected advantage is the incidence of higher taxes, or that hope to transform an already prosperous city into an even more prosperous one.

Finally, . . . the Court suggests that property owners should turn to the States, who may or may not choose to impose appropriate limits on economic development takings. . . . This is an abdication of our responsibility. States play many important functions in our system of dual sovereignty, but compensating for our refusal to enforce properly the Federal Constitution (and a provision meant to curtail state action, no less) is not among them.

* * *

It was possible after *Berman* and *Midkiff* to imagine unconstitutional transfers from A to B. Those decisions endorsed government intervention when private property use had veered to such an extreme that the public was suffering as a consequence. Today nearly all real property is susceptible to condemnation on the Court's theory. In the prescient words of a dissenter from the infamous decision in *Poletown*, "[n]ow that we have authorized local legislative bodies to decide that a different commercial or industrial use of property will produce greater public benefits than its present use, no homeowner's, merchant's or manufacturer's property, however productive or valuable to its owner, is immune from condemnation for the benefit of other private interests that will put it to a 'higher' use." 410 Mich., at 644–645, 304 N. W. 2d, at 464 (opinion of Fitzgerald, J.). This is why economic development takings "seriously jeopardiz[e] the security of all private property ownership." Id., at 645, 304 N. W. 2d, at 465 (Ryan, J., dissenting).

Any property may now be taken for the benefit of another private party, but the fallout from this decision will not be random. The beneficiaries are likely to be those citizens with disproportionate influence and power in the political process, including large corporations and development firms. As for the victims, the government now has license to transfer property from those with fewer resources to those with more. The Founders cannot have intended this perverse result. "[T]hat alone is a just government," wrote James Madison, "which impartially secures to every man, whatever is his own." . . .

I would hold that the takings in both Parcel 3 and Parcel 4A are unconstitutional, reverse the judgment of the Supreme Court of Connecticut, and remand for further proceedings.

END NOTES

1. *See* 268 Conn., at 159, 843 A. 2d, at 595 (Zarella, J., concurring in part and dissenting in part) ("The record clearly demonstrates that the development plan was not intended to serve the interests of Pfizer, Inc., or any other private entity, but rather, to revitalize the local economy by creating temporary and permanent jobs, generating a significant increase in tax revenue, encouraging spin-off economic activities and maximizing public access to the waterfront"). And while the City intends to transfer certain of the parcels to a private developer in a long-term lease—which developer, in turn, is expected to lease the office space and so forth to other private tenants—the identities of those private parties were not known when the plan was adopted. It is, of course, difficult to accuse the government of having taken A's property to benefit the private interests of B when the identity of B was unknown.

2. It is a misreading of *Berman* to suggest that the only public use upheld in that case was the initial removal of blight. *See* Reply Brief for Petitioners 8. The public use described in *Berman* extended beyond that to encompass the purpose of developing that area to create conditions that would prevent a reversion to blight in the future. *See* 348 U.S., at 34–35, 99 L. Ed. 27, 75 S. Ct. 98 ("It was not enough, [the experts] believed, to remove existing buildings that were insanitary or unsightly. It was important to redesign the whole area so as to eliminate the conditions that cause slums. . . . The entire area needed redesigning so that a balanced, integrated plan could be developed for the region, including not only new homes, but also schools, churches, parks, streets, and shopping centers. In this way it was hoped that the cycle of decay of the area could be controlled and the birth of future slums prevented"). Had the public use in *Berman* been defined more narrowly, it would have been difficult to justify the taking of the plaintiff's nonblighted department store.
3. Any number of cases illustrate that the achievement of a public good often coincides with the immediate benefiting of private parties. *See, e.g.*, National Railroad Passenger Corporation v. Boston & Maine Corp., 503 U.S. 407, 422, 118 L. Ed. 2d 52, 112 S. Ct. 1394 (1992) (public purpose of "facilitating Amtrak's rail service" served by taking rail track from one private company and transferring it to another private company); Brown v. Legal Foundation of Wash., 538 U.S. 216, 155 L. Ed. 2d 376, 123 S. Ct. 1406 (2003) (provision of legal services to the poor is a valid public purpose). It is worth noting that in Hawaii Housing Authority v. Midkiff, 467 U.S. 229, 81 L. Ed. 2d 186, 104 S. Ct. 2321 (1984), Monsanto, and *Boston & Maine Corp.*, the property in question retained the same use even after the change of ownership.
4. Notably, as in the instant case, the private developers in *Berman* were required by contract to use the property to carry out the redevelopment plan. *See* 348 U.S., at 30, 99 L. Ed. 27, 75 S. Ct. 98.
5. Nor do our cases support Justice O'Connor's novel theory that the government may only take property and transfer it to private parties when the initial taking eliminates some "harmful property use." Post, at 501, 162 L. Ed. 2d, at 465 (dissenting opinion). There was nothing "harmful" about the nonblighted department store at issue in *Berman*, 348 U.S. 26, 99 L. Ed. 27, 75 S. Ct. 98; . . ., *see, e.g., Strickley*, 200 U.S. 527, 50 L. Ed. 581, 26 S. Ct. 301; . . .; and certainly nothing "harmful" about the trade secrets owned by the pesticide manufacturers in *Monsanto*, 467 U.S. 986, 81 L. Ed. 2d 815, 104 S. Ct. 2862. In each case, the public purpose we upheld depended on a private party's future use of the concededly nonharmful property that was taken. By focusing on a property's future use, as opposed to its past use, our cases are faithful to the text of the Takings Clause. *See* U.S. CONST., AMDT. 5. ("[N]or shall private property be taken for public use, without just compensation"). Justice

O'Connor's intimation that a "public purpose" may not be achieved by the action of private parties, see post, at 500–501, 162 L. Ed. 2d, at 465, confuses the purpose of a taking with its mechanics, a mistake we warned of in Midkiff, 467 U.S., at 244, 81 L. Ed. 2d 186, 104 S. Ct. 2321. *See also Berman*, 348 U.S., at 33–34, 99 L. Ed. 27, 75 S. Ct. 98 ("The public end may be as well or better served through an agency of private enterprise than through a department of government").

6. Courts have viewed such aberrations with a skeptical eye. *See, e.g.*, 99 Cents Only Stores v. Lancaster Redevelopment Agency, 237 F. Supp. 2d 1123 (CD Cal. 2001); cf. Cincinnati v. Vester, 281 U.S. 439, 448, 74 L. Ed. 950, 50 S. Ct. 360 (1930) (taking invalid under state eminent domain statute for lack of a reasoned explanation). These types of takings may also implicate other constitutional guarantees. *See* Village of Willowbrook v. Olech, 528 U.S. 562, 145 L. Ed. 2d 1060, 120 S. Ct. 1073 (2000) (per curiam).
7. A parade of horribles is especially unpersuasive in this context, since the Takings Clause largely "operates as a conditional limitation, permitting the government to do what it wants so long as it pays the charge." Eastern Enterprises v. Apfel, 524 U.S. 498, 545, 141 L. Ed. 2d 451, 118 S. Ct. 2131 (1998) (Kennedy, J., concurring in judgment and dissenting in part). Speaking of the takings power, Justice Iredell observed that "[i]t is not sufficient to urge, that the power may be abused, for, such is the nature of all power,—such is the tendency of every human institution: and, it might as fairly be said, that the power of taxation, which is only circumscribed by the discretion of the Body, in which it is vested, ought not to be granted, because the Legislature, disregarding its true objects, might, for visionary and useless projects, impose a tax to the amount of nineteen shillings in the pound. We must be content to limit power where we can, and where we cannot, consistently with its use, we must be content to repose a salutory confidence." *Calder*, 3 Dall., at 400, 1 L. Ed. 648 (opinion concurring in result).
8. *See, e.g.*, County of Wayne v. Hathcock, 471 Mich. 445, 684 N.W.2d 765 (2004).
9. Under California law, for instance, a city may only take land for economic development purposes in blighted areas. CAL. HEALTH & SAFETY CODE ANN. §§ 33030–33037 (West 1999). *See, e.g.*, Redevelopment Agency of Chula Vista v. Rados Bros., 95 Cal. App. 4th 309, 115 Cal. Rptr. 2d 234 (2002).

ARTICLE 8.2

Are You Still Master of Your Domain? Abuses of Economic Development Takings, and Michigan's Return to "Public Use" in *County of Wayne v. Hathcock*

Peter M. Agnetti

INTRODUCTION

One of the most awesome powers of government is the ability to condemn and take privately owned property through eminent domain.[1] The Fifth Amendment to the United States Constitution restricts the power of eminent domain, prohibiting the taking of private property unless it is for public use.[2] This restraint on government takings is substantively applied to the several states through the Fourteenth Amendment.[3] Many state constitutions similarly limit eminent domain to those takings justified by public use.[4] Notwithstanding constitutional limitations, the power of eminent domain has been widely used by state and federal legislatures for various public purposes, including urban renewal and economic development.[5] Traditionally, eminent domain has been employed to condemn and take private property for improvements such as railroads, utilities, and other infrastructures, and was justified on the theory that the general public would be the beneficiaries of the takings through literal public use.[6] However, with states and municipalities eager to generate higher tax revenues through economic redevelopment, private real property owners nationwide are increasingly finding their non-blighted, middle-class properties appropriated and transferred over to commercial and residential developers for profit-making ventures.[7]

Facilitating the process, the United States Supreme Court has given free reign to state governments to devise legislative takings. The pioneering cases of *Berman v. Parker*,[8] *Hawaii Housing Authority v. Midkiff*,[9] and a Michigan Supreme Court case, *Poletown Neighborhood Council v. City of Detroit*,[10] shifted the understanding of the term "public use" and practically relegated the Public Use Clause to a distant memory.[11] As a result, over the past few decades many state courts and legislatures have come to interpret the state and federal public use clauses in a manner that allows state and municipal governments to condemn and take private property for virtually any reason provided there is a somewhat rationally stated economic benefit in store for the government. . . .[12] Solidifying the demise of federal constitutional protection through the Public Use Clause, the United States Supreme Court, in *Kelo v. City of New London*,[13] held that the taking of private property by a state to promote economic development "unquestionably serves a public purpose," and hence satisfies the public use requirement of the Fifth Amendment.[14] As a result of *Kelo*, the states, through their own constitutional or statutory restraints, are now the sole protectors of private property owners from the threat of eminent domain exercised upon the rationale of economic development.[15]

Despite the *Kelo* precedent and the trend among state legislatures to expand the traditional meaning of the Public Use Clause, several recent state and federal court decisions have successfully reined in expansive executions of eminent domain power.[16] Recently, in *County of Wayne v. Hathcock*,[17] the Michigan Supreme Court has seemingly given hope to private owners of real property by providing a "public use" standard for government takings that are done primarily to benefit other private entities.[18] The court held that Michigan municipalities do not have the power under the state's Public Use Clause to condemn private property for the purpose of transfer to another private party in order to spur economic development, except under exceptional circumstances.[19]

In *Hathcock*, the Wayne County legislature (the "County") sought to condemn the defendants' property in order to develop and establish a 1300-acre business and technology park ("Pinnacle Project") adjacent to the recently expanded Metropolitan Airport.[20] The purpose of the park was to boost the local economy by generating new employment opportunities and a higher tax-base for the local government.[21] The County was able to procure most of the property needed to develop the new park, but still needed to acquire an additional 300 acres to complete its land assembly objective.[22] The County then adopted legislation[23] authorizing the acquisition of the remaining 300 acres desired for the Pinnacle Project.[24] Appraisal-based offers were delivered to the remaining property owners, and although some offers were accepted, the defendants chose not to sell.[25] Unable to secure voluntary sales from the defendants, the County initiated condemnation actions.[26] The trial court, in an unpublished opinion, held that the Pinnacle Project served a valid public purpose under the controlling constitutional jurisprudence, and the Michigan Court of Appeals affirmed.[27]

Who are the primary beneficiaries of an expansion of the definition of public use?

Applying the standard set forth by the dissent in *Poletown*,[28] the Michigan Supreme Court reversed the decision of the lower court.[29] In his dissent in *Poletown*, Justice Ryan explained that there are three elements that "justify[] the use of eminent domain for private corporations: 1) public necessity of the extreme sort, 2) continuing accountability to the public, and 3) selection of land according to facts of independent public significance."[30] Adopting these elements, the *Hathcock* court first reasoned that the Pinnacle Project was "certainly not an enterprise "whose very existence depends on the use of land that can be assembled only by the coordination central government alone is capable of achieving.'"[31] Next, the court stated that because the Pinnacle Project was not subject to sufficient public oversight, there was no guarantee that the venture would contribute the anticipated long term benefits to the local economy.[32] Finally, the court asserted that although enhancement of economic conditions is an appropriate public purpose, the underlying purpose of the Pinnacle Project did not serve the public good independent of the benefits conferred by the private corporations through post-condemnation development.[33]

By overruling *Poletown*, the *Hathcock* court partially restored, at least in Michigan, the definition of "public use" to the rational meaning intended by those who drafted and ratified the public use clauses in the federal and various state constitutions.[34] It is submitted, however, that the requirements test laid out by the Michigan Supreme Court in *Hathcock* still leaves too much discretion with the legislature to take private property unconstitutionally for others' private gain by relying on an economic development rationale. Furthermore, the *Hathcock* decision will likely send reverberations throughout the country, despite the Supreme Court's holding in *Kelo*, because of *Poletown's* vast and strong influence on other states in expanding their own powers of eminent domain.[35]

This Comment asserts that takings that do not fall within one of the limited exceptions and which primarily benefit a private entity at the expense of owners of non-blighted private property not only fail to pass constitutional muster, but also work in an economically inefficient manner so as to threaten perpetually all ownership of real property in the United States. Far from being a discourse on the evils of corporate exploitation, this Comment will examine and criticize the public use requirement of the *Hathcock* court, which revitalized, albeit incompletely, the "dead-letter" of the Public Use Clause in Michigan. Part I will analyze the *Hathcock* checks on government takings and distinguish them from the unfettered discretion given to municipalities by other states and, unquestionably, by United States Supreme Court jurisprudence. Part I also offers ideas on how states can ensure the receipt of the public benefits promised by the private beneficiaries of eminent domain, and will show how the use of eminent domain to eliminate alleged "blight" can manipulatively be used interchangeably with the economic development rationale overruled by *Hathcock* and upheld by *Kelo*. Part I further will propose suggestions for further state restrictions that should be imposed on government condemnations, particularly in the wake of *Kelo's* grant of discretion. Part II briefly advocates the need for meaningful state judicial review of what opportunistic legislatures deem to be a "public use." The Comment concludes with a look at recent public reaction and political responses to economic development takings.

I. *HATHCOCK'S* THREE EXCEPTIONS FOR THE USE OF EMINENT DOMAIN THAT PRIMARILY BENEFITS PRIVATE PARTIES

Although undoubtedly disappointing to state and municipal legislatures looking to give a shot in the arm to the local economy, *Hathcock's* overruling of

Poletown certainly appears to be encouraging news to owners of real property in Michigan.[36] *Hathcock* has refuted the idea that a "generalized economic benefit" to a private corporation is sufficient to satisfy Michigan's Public Use Clause.[37]. . .

The continuous threat of arbitrarily losing one's property because someone else can use it more profitably intuitively promotes economic inefficiency by discouraging the purchase of private property.[38] After all, with no protection from a well-financed developer, it's much less appealing to buy in the first place if the purchase is conditioned on the buyer using the property in a manner that is most financially rewarding to the state. However, *Hathcock* did not completely bar the use of eminent domain for the benefit of another private party. As will be discussed below, there are three exceptions under *Hathcock* that allow for government takings to subsidize a private corporation.

A. The Instrumentalities of Commerce/Public Necessity Exception

In some situations, a public or private project affecting the instrumentalities of commerce cannot be accomplished without the taking of a particular parcel of land. In such cases, eminent domain is needed to provide a resolution.[39] Such projects may include a private railroad or public highway that, due to geographical constraints, needs to run directly through a privately owned piece of real estate.[40] In *Hathcock*, the proponents of the Pinnacle Project could not show that the technology park was unable to be constructed but for the exclusive use of the defendants' private property.[41] As courts have interpreted it, the public necessity exception is a legitimate, widely accepted use of eminent domain.[42] The ability to condemn private property for a genuine public use affecting the instrumentalities of commerce, as traditionally understood, is not in dispute and not within the scope of this Comment.[43] The final two exceptions provided by the court, however, leave considerable room for abuse under the very economic development rationale overruled by the *Hathcock* court.

B. The Public Oversight/Accountability Exception

The *Hathcock* court explained that eminent domain may be used primarily to benefit a private corporation "when the private entity remains accountable to the public in its use of that property."[44] The municipality must put in place "formal mechanisms . . . to ensure that the businesses that . . . [receive the benefit of the condemned] properties . . . continue to contribute to the health of the local economy."[45] The court noted that the Pinnacle Project, like the General Motors manufacturing plant in *Poletown*, was not subject to any public oversight to ensure that the benefits emanating from the property continued to accrue to the community.[46] The court gave some examples of what does and does not constitute public oversight, but left readers and real property owners guessing as to how liberally this exception will be applied by the judiciary.[47]

There are several ways that the public oversight requirement can be accomplished. For instance, one method might be requiring a beneficiary corporation to promise a requisite number of jobs and tax dollars. However, no matter how optimistic such promises may be, they are merely speculative.[48] . . . The court, however, failed to give municipalities that are truly interested in serving the public good through economic stimulation a solution to this dilemma.[49] . . . When weighing the interests of private persons and their residences (or their private commercial real estate) against speculative gains for the community at large, a more exacting standard should be used. . . .

C. The Public Good/Slum Clearance Exception

The final exception addresses the situation where the property itself is in such a condition that condemnation is in the best interest of the public. The *Hathcock* court explained that property may be condemned where "the selection of the land to be condemned is itself based on public concern."[50] That is, the property chosen for condemnation is "selected on the basis of "facts of independent public significance,' meaning that the underlying purposes for resorting to condemnation, rather than the subsequent use of condemned land, must satisfy the Constitution's public use requirement."[51] In *Hathcock*, all of the alleged benefits of the Pinnacle Project, including the new jobs and tax revenue, were to arise after the land was seized by the County and transferred to the private corporations developing the property.[52] Therefore, the Pinnacle Project condemnations did not fit into this seemingly narrow exception. Examples of condemnations that do satisfy this exception are those made in furtherance of slum clearance or removal of "blighted"[53] property.[54] In the process of clearing so called blighted property, the public allegedly accrues the benefits of increased health and safety, even if the property is later transferred to private real estate developers.[55] However, since the Supreme Court's ruling in *Berman v. Parker*, many states have been moving towards very opportunistic interpretations of the word "blight" and the term "public use."[56]

1. Berman's Transformation of "Public Use" to "Public Purpose"

Prior to *Berman*, with a few exceptions, private property could only be taken through eminent domain for traditional public uses, not for "purely private, profit-driven companies."[57] The *Berman* Court, however, interpreted the term "public use" to have a meaning of "public purpose," with such purpose to be determined by the legislature.[58] The public purpose justifying the takings in *Berman* was the removal of blight in the form of slum housing.[59] . . . [T]he rationale has carried forward . . . and the term "blight" has been unjustifiably expanded to meet the goals of economically strapped states and municipalities.[60]

2. Blight Is in the Eye of the Beholder

Even if one subscribes to the theory that the public benefit requirement will suffice in situations of bona fide slum clearance,[61] this exception still leaves the door open to legislative abuse. On its face, this requirement may appear to protect those living in what most would consider non-blighted residential homes. But therein lies the key shortcoming of the *Hathcock* ruling: just as beauty is in the eye of the beholder, the third exception solely depends on what the legislature deems to be blighted property.[62] Just because an area is deemed to be a blight on the community does not necessarily mean it is so. Traditionally, the term "blighted" meant that the property was so run down and dilapidated that its mere presence would constitute a public nuisance.[63] In the past few decades, however, "it has become common for city [and community] leaders to define "blighted' as: "Not developed as nicely as we'd prefer' [or] "not developed by the people we'd prefer.'"[64] Hence, a tax-hungry Michigan city can condemn private property pursuant to the economic development rationale, which was seemingly overruled by *Hathcock*, as long as it is done under the guise of clearing blight.[65]. . .

Unfortunately, the *Hathcock* court did not have the opportunity to address this dilemma directly because the Wayne County legislature did not even attempt to classify the property as blighted, choosing instead to condemn the property solely on the basis of an economic development rationale.[66]

II. THE NEED FOR GREATER JUDICIAL REVIEW

Although *Hathcock* has pleased many commentators for its prohibition on the use of eminent domain for a stated economic development rationale,[67] legislatures can apparently circumvent such a ruling by simply characterizing private property as blighted.[68] A primary way for legislatures to be held accountable to an objective meaning of public use—which includes a definition of blight that incorporates legitimate removal "for the sake of public health and safety,"[69]—is for state courts to cease the abdication of their duty to provide meaningful judicial review of eminent domain used (or rather abused) for the benefit of private entities.[70] Unfortunately, many courts, including the lower courts in the *Hathcock* case, and even the United States Supreme Court in *Kelo*, simply avoid the questions of public use by putting forth the proposition that their hands are tied by the legislature.[71]

Much of the apprehensiveness on the part of the state courts to invalidate economic development takings has come from reliance on United States Supreme Court jurisprudence. The last case prior to *Kelo* in which the Supreme Court directly addressed the federal Public Use Clause was *Hawaii Housing Authority v. Midkiff.*[72] There, the Court upheld the use of eminent domain to redistribute ownership of real property in Hawaii from an oligarchy of landowners to the general public.[73] However, the Court cited *Berman* as guidance for the principle that the role of the judiciary "in reviewing a legislature's judgment of what constitutes a public use, even when the eminent domain power is equated with the police power . . . is "an extremely narrow' one."[74] Likewise, the *Kelo* Court reasoned that the Court's jurisprudence on eminent domain has evolved to a point where now state legislatures are the primary source for construing the definition of public use.[75] This argument, of course, assumes that the legislature's definition of public use or blight is such that the state action would be considered legitimate by the citizens who elected the present government representatives. Given the significant barriers to attacking the findings of fact which lead to condemnation,[76] the public should have greater protection than merely the political process, which is exercised intermittently at the polls. Especially with legislatures armed with *Kelo*, state courts must exercise greater power of review to prevent the abuse of eminent domain being used for economic development, either blatantly or under the guise of blight clearance.

What are the biggest differences between the takings in the slum clearance cases like Hawaii Housing Authority v. Midkiff *and the takings in the economic redevelopement cases?*

CONCLUSION

The *Hathcock* court properly pointed out that there is virtually no limit to eminent domain under the economic development rationale. Moreover, as put by Justice O'Connor in her *Kelo* dissent, "Today nearly all real property is susceptible to condemnation on the Court's theory."[77] A government can always envision a more lucrative use for most privately owned property.[78] With the *Kelo* decision ringing the death knell of the federal Public Use Clause, now only the states have the power to protect private property from abusive takings. However, leaving the door open for legislatures to arbitrarily deem property as "blighted" provides little assurance to real estate owners that their land will not be condemned for some economic purpose under the guise of blight clearance.

Those affected can use the political process to remove the representatives who propose to abuse the power of eminent domain under an economic development rationale. In fact, as a result of the *Kelo* ruling and the rise in abuse by municipal legislatures, public backlash to excessive takings is on the rise and the formation of grassroots efforts to pass statutory protection has begun.[79] The *Kelo* effect should not be underestimated.[80] Politicians are poised to act, demonstrated by the introduction in Congress of two pieces of legislation designed to undo the effect of *Kelo*,[81] and with state legislators moving for constitutional amendments prohibiting eminent domain for private development.[82] *Kelo* has opened the eyes of many politicians, conservative and liberal, to the potential misuses of eminent domain.[83]

The United States Supreme Court can remedially overrule *Kelo* and interpret the federal Public Use Clause literally, thereby allowing an exception for truly blighted property and setting a standard to determine if property is really blighted and not just deemed to be so by an opportunistic legislature.[84] Until it does, however, *Kelo* moves the fight to the states. The ruling in *Hathcock* sets an example for other states to follow in rejecting the economic development rationale. But, like plugging one hole only to gouge out another, because it neglected to address the definition of "blight," *Hathcock* leaves ownership of real property in Michigan essentially in the same position as before: perpetually threatened by the expansion plans of a profitable enterprise that can provide greater tax proceeds to a legislature promising ever more spending to its constituents. In a country that values property rights as much as life and liberty, it is essential that eminent domain be justified by a more legitimate rationale than mere economic development.

END NOTES

1. *See* Dana Berliner, Public Power, Private Gain 1 (2003) . . .; Tony Mauro, Land Case Is a Hot Property, Legal Times, Sept. 20, 2004, at 12. . . .
2. *See* U.S. Const. amend. V (placing two constraints on the power of em inent domain: (1) "no person shall be . . . deprived of life, liberty, or property, without due process of law"; and (2) "nor shall private property be taken for public use, without just compensation"). This second constraint contains the Public Use Clause, which mandates that any taking of private property must be justified with a valid benefit being accrued to the public. *See id.* The analysis of this Comment will concentrate on the taking of private property for a purported "public use" and the various legislative and judicial meanings given to this term.
3. *See* U.S. Const. amend. XIV; Haw. Hous. Auth. v. Midkiff, 467 U.S. 229, 244 n.7 (1984) . . .; *see also* City of Monterey v. Del Monte Dunes at Monterey, Ltd., 526 U.S. 687, 711, 716 (1999).
4. *See, e.g., infra* note 26 (discussing Michigan's constitutional restraints on eminent domain).
5. *See, e.g.*, Berman v. Parker, 348 U.S. 26, 33–36 (1954) . . .; see also Wendell E. Pritchett, *The "Public Menace" of Blight: Urban Renewal and the Private Uses of Eminent Domain*, 21 YALE L. & POL'Y REV. 1, 1–2 (2003). . . .
6. *See* James W. Ely, Jr., *Can the "Despotic Power" Be Tamed? Reconsidering the Public Use Limitation on Eminent Domain*, PROB. & PROP., Nov./Dec. 2003, at 30, 31 . . .; Pritchett, *supra* note 5, at 9 . . .; M. Robert Goldstein & Michael Rikon, *"Public Use' Redefined*, N.Y. L.J., Aug. 25, 2004, at 3 . . .; *see also infra* note 34(discussing the traditional definition of public use).
7. *See* Mauro, *supra* note 1. . . .
8. 348 U.S. 26 (1954).
9. 467 U.S. 229 (1984).

10. 304 N.W.2d 455 (Mich. 1981), overruled by County of Wayne v. Hathcock, 684 N.W.2d 765 (Mich. 2004).
11. *See infra* Part II (discussing the legal analysis provided by the United States Supreme Court for determining if a particular use of eminent domain satisfies the Public Use Clause).
12. *See Midkiff*, 467 U.S. at 241 (holding that the federal Public Use Clause will not prohibit a taking as long as "the exercise of the eminent domain power is rationally related to a conceivable public purpose"); *see also* Berliner, *supra* note 1, at 1 . . .; Ralph Nader & Alan Hirsch, *Making Eminent Domain Humane*, 49 VILL. L. REV. 207, 208 (2004). . . .
13. 545 U.S. __, 125 S. Ct. 2655 (2005).
14. *Id.* at 2664–65.
15. *See id.* at 2668. . . . *But see id.* at 2677 (O'Connor, J., dissenting) (positing that the suggestion by the Court that property owners must rely on the states to determine limits on economic development takings "is an abdication of [the Supreme Court's] responsibility"). "States play many important functions in our system of dual sovereignty, but compensating for our refusal to enforce properly the Federal Constitution (and a provision meant to curtail state action, no less) is not among them." *Id.*
16. *See, e.g.*, Cottonwood Christian Ctr. v. Cypress Redevelopment Agency, 218 F. Supp. 2d 1203, 1229–30 (C.D. Cal. 2002) . . .; Bailey v. Myers, 76 P.3d 898, 904 (Ariz. 2003). . . . Not all state courts, however, have been equally as critical of their legislature's definition of "public use." *See* Kelo v. City of New London, 843 A.2d 500, 520 (Conn. 2004) . . ., aff'd, 545 U.S. __, 125 S. Ct. 2655 (2005); W. 41st St. Realty v. N.Y. State Urban Dev. Corp., 298 A.D.2d 1, 5–7, 744 N.Y.S.2d 121,124 (1st Dep't 2002). . . . Likewise, federal courts now must defer to the central holding of *Kelo* that takings for the purpose of economic development are justified under the federal Constitution. *See* Calhoun Realty, Inc. v. City of Cincinnati, No. 1:03-CV-00198, 2005 WL 2000664, at 2 (S.D. Ohio Aug. 19, 2005). . . .
17. 684 N.W.2d 765 (Mich. 2004).
18. *See infra* Part I (discussing the analysis in *Hathcock*).
19. *See Hathcock*, 684 N.W.2d at 781–83, 787. . . .
20. *See Hathcock*, 684 N.W.2d at 770. . . .
21. *See id.* at 770–71. . . .
22. The County acquired 500 acres through the noise abatement program and an additional 500 acres through solicitation of voluntary sales. *See* Hathcock, 684 N.W.2d at 771.
23. The law was named the Resolution of Necessity and Declaration of Taking. *See id.*
24. *See id.*
25. *See id.* There were a total of nineteen outstanding parcels owned by the defendants. *See id.* The defendants' parcels were dispersed throughout the desired 300-acre area in a checkerboard pattern. *See id.* at 770.

26. *See id.* at 771. . . .
27. *See Hathcock*, 684 N.W.2d at 771–72. The trial court rendered its decision under the analysis of the then-controlling law of Poletown Neighborhood Council v. Detroit, 304 N.W.2d 455, 457 (Mich. 1981), overruled by County of Wayne v. Hathcock, 684 N.W.2d 765 (Mich. 2004). The *Poletown* court held that the City of Detroit was permitted to condemn private residential properties in order to convey those properties to General Motors, a private corporation, for the construction of an assembly plant. See id.; *see also infra* Part I. The Michigan Court of Appeals affirmed on the same grounds but argued that *Poletown* was "poorly reasoned, wrongly decided, and ripe for reversal by [the Michigan Supreme Court]." *See Hathcock*, 684 N.W.2d at 771–72.
28. In his dissent in *Poletown*, Justice Ryan laid out three possible characteristics of a governmental taking for the benefit of a private corporation that would satisfy the constitutional definition of public use. *See Poletown*, 304 N.W.2d at 477–78 (Ryan, J., dissenting).
29. *See Hathcock*, 684 N.W.2d at 788.
30. *Poletown*, 304 N.W.2d at 478 (Ryan, J., dissenting).
31. *See Hathcock*, 684 N.W.2d at 783 (quoting *Poletown*, 304 N.W.2d at 478 (Ryan, J., dissenting)); *see also infra* Part I.A (analyzing the first exception to the general requirement of literal public use when using the power of eminent domain—instrumentalities of commerce).
32. *See Hathcock*, 684 N.W.2d at 784. . . .
33. *See Hathcock*, 684 N.W.2d at 784; *see also infra* Part I.C (analyzing the third exception—public good).
34. For an originalist interpretation of the term "public use," Justice Thomas provided a valuable tutorial in his *Kelo* dissent: "The most natural reading of the [Public Use] Clause is that it allows the government to take property only if the government owns, or the public has a legal right to use, the property, as opposed to taking it for any public purpose or necessity whatsoever." Kelo v. City of New London, 545 U.S. __, 125 S. Ct. 2655, 2679 (2005) (Thomas, J., dissenting). . . . "The Public Use Clause, in short, embodied the Framers' understanding that property is a natural, fundamental right, prohibiting the government from "taking property from A. and giving it to B.'" *Id.* at 2680 (quoting Calder v. Bull, 3 U.S. (3 Dall.) 386, 388 (1798)) (alteration in original).
35. *See* Dean Starkman, *Michigan Upholds Property Rights In Broad Ruling*, WALL ST. J., Aug. 2, 2004, at A6. . . .
36. Property owners in other states should also be encouraged due to *Poletown's* vast influence on other states' expansion of public use to include generalized economic benefits to a beneficiary private corporation. *See supra* note 35 (discussing *Poletown's* national influence). Any optimism, however, must be tapered by the lack of federal constitutional protection. *See Kelo*, 545 U.S. at __, 125 S. Ct. at 2665.

37. *See Hathcock*, 684 N.W.2d at 786. . . .
38. *See* Dana Berliner, *You Can't Go Home Again*, LEGAL TIMES, Oct. 11, 2004, at 42. . . .
39. *See Hathcock*, 684 N.W.2d at 781. . . .
40. *See Hathcock*, 684 N.W.2d at 781 . . .; *see also* Ely, *supra* note 6, at 33 (stating that during the industrial revolution, state and federal courts repeatedly upheld legislation that allowed private railroads "to appropriate private property"). Such takings for the benefit of private entities were rationalized on the theory that railroads, which were analogous to public highways, furthered the "public purpose of improving [interstate] transportation." *See id.* This analogy between private railroads and public highways commenced a line of thinking that "began to conflate public use with the more expansive concept of public interest or public benefit." *See id*; *see also* Thomas W. Merrill, *The Economics of Public Use*, 72 CORNELL L. REV 61, 64 (1986). . . .
41. *See Hathcock*, 684 N.W.2d at 783–84 (explaining that shopping centers, office parks, hotels, and the like do not need eminent domain for their construction, notwithstanding their lack of characterization as instrumentalities of commerce).
42. *See, e.g.*, City of Novi v. Robert Adell Children's Funded Trust, 701 N.W.2d 144, 147 (Mich. 2005). . . .
43. *See, e.g.*, Kelo v. City of New London, 545 U.S. at __, 125 S. Ct. 2655, 2681 (2005) (Thomas, J., dissenting) . . .; Youngstown Sheet & Tube Co. v. Sawyer, 343 U.S. 579, 588 (1952). . . .
44. *Hathcock*, 684 N.W.2d at 782.
45. *Id.* at 784. Unlike the Michigan Constitution, the U.S. Constitution requires no such ""reasonable certainty' that the expected public benefits will actually accrue." *Kelo*, 545 U.S. __, 125 S. Ct. at 2667. The Court in *Kelo* reasoned that "[a] constitutional rule that required postponement of the judicial approval of every condemnation until the likelihood of success of the plan had been assured would unquestionably impose a significant impediment to the successful consummation of many such plans." *Id.* at 2668. Apparently, the *Kelo* Court was more concerned with expediting the taking process than ensuring the purported economic benefits of the plan to the public.
46. *Hathcock*, 684 N.W.2d at 784.
47. *See id.* at 782. As an example of what does not constitute public oversight, the court mentioned a case where the private entity, a power utility, would ""own, lease, use, and control'" the land and the water power emanating from the land. *See id.* (quoting Poletown Neighborhood Council v. City of Detroit, 304 N.W.2d 455, 479 (Mich. 1981) (Ryan, J., dissenting), overruled by County of Wayne v. Hathcock, 684 N.W.2d 765 (Mich. 2004)). As an example of valid public oversight, the court mentioned a case where the state retained control of a petroleum pipeline. *See id.* In

that case: (1) the private beneficiary corporation guaranteed that it would transport petroleum in intrastate commerce; (2) the corporation's plans were subject to directions from the state; and (3) the state was able to enforce those obligations. *Id.* It should be noted that the latter example may fall under the instrumentalities of commerce exception. *See supra* Part I.A.

48. *See* Nader & Hirsch, *supra* note 12, at 220. . . .
49. As discussed in note 47, the examples given by the court for the public oversight exception appear to involve projects that would fall under the first exception, which allows eminent domain to be used to benefit private parties when dealing with instrumentalities of commerce. Assuming the court meant that this second exception is only available for public utilities and the like, the economic development rationale put forth by the County would not be valid even if sufficient public oversight were available. Because the *Hathcock* court was unclear as to whether the second exception could apply to entities other than public utilities, this Comment assumes that this exception may apply to other entities as well and will explore the alternative means available for ensuring public oversight of transfers to these entities.
50. County of Wayne v. Hathcock, 684 N.W.2d 765, 782–83 (Mich. 2004).
51. *Id.* at 783 (quoting *Poletown*, 304 N.W.2d at 478 (Ryan, J., dissenting)).
52. *See id.* at 784. . . .
53. *See infra* Part I.C.2 (discussing traditional and contemporary meanings of the term "blight").
54. *See Hathcock*, 684 N.W.2d at 784.
55. *See id.*; *see also Berman*, 348 U.S. at 32 . . .
56. At least with respect to the United Sates Constitution, *Kelo* eliminates the need for state legislatures to manipulate the term "blight" because economic development has been deemed a public use. *See Kelo*, 545 U.S. __, 125 S. Ct. at 2665. Therefore, only legislatures in states, such as Michigan, with protectively interpreted constitutions need to contrive the meaning of blight to exercise opportunistic eminent domain.
57. *See* Scott Bullock, *Narrow "Public Use,'* NAT'L L.J., Aug. 16, 2004, at 23.
58. *See Berman*, 348 U.S. at 34; *see also Kelo*, 545 U.S. at __, 125 S. Ct. at 2663 (discussing and approving of Berman's deference to the state legislature in its determination of the efficacy of a taking that confiscated both blighted and non-blighted property as part of a community redevelopment program); Bullock, *supra* note 57.
59. *See Berman*, 348 U.S. at 32–33.
60. Incidentally, most of the urban renewal projects did not work out the way the post-New Deal optimists had planned. *See id.* . . . Furthermore, commentators have equated the adverse effect on minority populations of urban renewal projects with, in the uncivilized words of the past,

"Negro removal." *See id.* For a discussion on how urban renewal programs have played a significant role in impeding racial integration by disproportionately relocating minority populations, *see* Pritchett, *supra* note 5, at 6. . . .

61. *See Berman*, 348 U.S. at 28 n. . . . In *Berman*, the buildings in the "Washington, D.C., neighborhood were beyond repair." Berliner, *supra* note 38. . . . Berliner suggests that "the neighborhood probably could have been condemned as a nuisance or hazardous to the public health." *Id.*
62. *See* Editorial, *Let There Be Blight*, WALL ST. J., Apr. 22, 2004, at A18 (explaining that legislatures are quick to characterize choice property as blighted). . . .
63. *See* Jonathan Rauch, *Taking Property: Bush's Landgrab—and the New York Times*,' NAT'L J., July 26, 2002, *available at* http://www.reason.com/rauch/072902.shtml; *see also* Berliner, *supra* note 38 (describing the conditions of the condemned property in Berman).
64. Rauch, *supra* note 63; *see also* Berliner, *supra* note 38 (suggesting that some state legislatures have come to include in their definition of "blight" a building that merely lacks parking or central air conditioning).
65. The *Hathcock* court stated that "*Poletown's* "economic benefit' rationale would validate practically any exercise of the power of eminent domain on behalf of a private entity." County of Wayne v. Hathcock, 684 N.W.2d 765, 786 (Mich. 2004). It seems as though the court's "public good exception," when used to characterize middle-class, non-slum homes as blighted, gives municipal legislatures the same unfettered discretion as does the "economic benefit" rationale. Troublingly, this means that the ability to take private property depends on the definition of blight employed by the government representatives proposing use of eminent domain. . . . As stated above, the modern trend of designating homes that present no public hazard or nuisance as blighted is a legislative alternative to facing litigation on the meaning of the public use clause in the relevant state constitution. . . .
66. *See* County of Wayne v. Hathcock, 684 N.W.2d 765, 775–76 (Mich. 2004). In dictum, however, the court did qualify eminent domain used for the removal of blight as necessarily being "for the sake of public health and safety." *See id.* at 783. . . .
67. *See, e.g.*, Editorial, *Supreme Court Restores Sanctity of Property Rights*, DETROIT NEWS, Aug. 4, 2004, at 10 (praising the Michigan Supreme Court for "turning back the clock and restoring a vital civil liberty" by overruling *Poletown*).
68. *See* Goldstein & Rikon, *supra* note 6 (suggesting that Hathcock will make very little difference in how properties are taken because many abuses of eminent domain are based on findings of blight, not on the economic development rationale). . . .
69. *See Hathcock*, 684 N.W.2d at 783.

70. *See* Goldstein & Rikon, *supra* note 6 (stating that "if the abuses of the use of the power of eminent domain are to be effectively contained . . . the courts have to be given a broader role in the process"). According to Justice O'Connor, the United States Supreme Court did "abdicate" its responsibility in Kelo. *See Kelo*, 545 U.S. at __,125 S. Ct. at 2677 (O'Connor, J., dissenting).
71. *See Hathcock*, 684 N.W.2d at 785; cf. Poletown Neighborhood Council v. Detroit, 304 N.W.2d 455, 475 (Mich. 1981) (Ryan, J., dissenting) ("Notwithstanding explicit legislative findings, this Court has always made an independent determination of what constitutes a public use for which the power of eminent domain may be utilized."), overruled by County of Wayne v. Hathcock, 684 N.W.2d 765 (Mich. 2004). The *Hathcock* court agreed with Justice Ryan's view, but neglected to expand the thought any further. *See Hathcock*, 684 N.W.2d at 785.
72. 467 U.S. 229 (1984).
73. *See id.* at 233. . . .
74. *Id.* at 240 . . .; *see also* Richard B. Tranter, *Defer to Legislatures*, NAT'L L.J., Aug. 16, 2004, at 23. . . .
75. *See Kelo*, 545 U.S. at __,125 S. Ct. at 2664 ("Our public use jurisprudence has wisely eschewed rigid formulas and intrusive scrutiny in favor of affording legislatures broad latitude in determining what public needs justify the use of the takings power.").
76. *See* Goldstein & Rikon, *supra* note 6; *see also* N.Y. Em. Dom. Proc. Law 202 (McKinney 2003). . . .
77. *Kelo*, 545 U.S.at __, 125 S. Ct. at 2677 (O'Connor, J., dissenting).
78. *See* Berliner, *supra* note 38 ("Businesses inevitably generate more jobs than private homes, and big companies pay higher taxes than small companies.").
79. *See Connecticut Tea Party*, WALL ST. J., July 19, 2005, at A14 . . .; *see also* Adam Karlin, *Property Seizure Backlash*, CHRISTIAN SCIENCE MONITOR, July 6, 2005, at 1. . . .
80. *See* Inst. for Justice, Grassroots Groundswell Grows Against Eminent Domain Abuse (July 12, 2005), http://www.ij.org/private_property/connecticut/7_12_05pr.html . . .; *see also* John Tierney, *Making Roberts Talk*, N.Y. TIMES, Sept. 13, 2005, at A31 (explaining how after Justice Souter's endorsement of economic development takings in *Kelo*, a group in Weare, New Hampshire proposed raising local tax revenue by condemning and taking Souter's home so a developer could build a private resort called the "Lost Liberty Hotel").
81. Senator John Cornyn (R-TX) has introduced the "Protection of Homes, Small Businesses, and Private Property Act of 2005," to "prohibit the transfer of private property without the owners' consent if the transfer is for economic development rather than public use." Ronald D. Utt, Kelo Backlash Could Lead to Restoration of Property Rights Lost to

Smart Growth and Eminent Domain Abuses, The Heritage Foundation Web Memo, June 29, 2005, http://www.heritage.org/Research/SmartGrowth/wm781.cfm; *see also* Protection of Homes, Small Businesses, and Private Property Act of 2005, S. 1313, 109th Cong. (2005). Likewise, House Judiciary Chairman James Sensenbrenner (R-WI) plans to introduce the "Private Property Rights Protection Act," which is intended "to restore the property rights of all Americans the Supreme Court took away on June 23." Utt, *supra*; *see also* Private Property Rights Protection Act of 2005, H.R. 3135, 109th Cong. (2005).

82. *See* Inst. for Justice, *supra* note 80 (stating that legislators are assembling support for constitutional amendments in Texas, Florida, Oklahoma, New Jersey, and Michigan).
83. Even Representative Maxine Waters (D-CA), hardly a proponent of conservative ideology, has expressed her displeasure with the *Kelo* ruling, stating that "'government should be in the business of protecting private property.'" Rich Lowry, *"Mad Max" Stands with the Right*, NAT'L REV. ONLINE, Aug. 5, 2005, http://www.nationalreview.com/lowry/lowry200508050737.asp (quoting Rep. Maxine Waters). . . .
84. . . . [T]he Court need not address the problems outlined in Part I.C concerning opportunistic blight designations, and did not address such problems in *Kelo*.

ARTICLE 8.3

Measure 37 Clones Fail at the Ballot Box

Nancy Kubarsek

INTRODUCTION

When Measure 37, a law that gives property owners the right to develop their property under land use laws that were in existence when their property was purchased,[1] was passed by Oregon voters in 2004[2], many environmentalists and slow growth advocates were disappointed[3] and fearful that similar laws would spread across the country.[4] Developers were extremely pleased, and hoped that the success they had attained in Oregon, a state that has traditionally regulated growth very carefully, could be replicated in other western states that have historically been more protective of private property rights.[5] Other states, however, did not rush to adopt "Measure 37 clones" the following year.

Then came the decision in *Kelo v. New London*,[6] a Supreme Court ruling that practically made the relatively obscure term "eminent domain" a household word. It was a decision that sparked legislatures in 46 states to consider legislation covering eminent domain in the year since it was handed down.[7] The decision also led President Bush to pass an executive order "limiting the taking of private property by the Federal Government to situations in which the taking is for public use, with just compensation, and for the purpose of benefiting the general public, and not merely for the purpose of advancing the economic interest of private parties to be given ownership or use of the property taken."[8]

While Measure 37 restricts a very different type of governmental action than the controversial use of eminent domain at issue in the *Kelo* case, some environmentalists feared that property rights advocates, especially those in the western states, had seen the value in conflating the two kinds of actions and using public outrage at the *Kelo* decision to secure passage of legislation that restricts the ability of governments to pass certain kinds of land use regulations.[9] Some environmentalists feared that those in the property rights movement correctly recognized that anger at the abuse of eminent domain might be used to secure the passage of legislation to prevent so-called regulatory takings.[10]

The environmentalists' worst fears have not yet materialized, although property rights advocates did in fact take this approach. Somewhat surprisingly, the approach did not succeed everywhere it was tried, and the 2006 election did not result in the passage of a significant number of so-called Measure 37 clones. However, the proponents of these bills will not be easily discouraged, especially in light of the fact that they did have one success, and at least one very close failure, so we may anticipate seeing many of these measures back on the ballots in many states in future elections.

REGULATORY TAKINGS

Since the landmark United States Supreme Court case of *Lucas v. South Carolina Coastal Commission*[11], there has been increased debate about the concept of a regulatory taking. The high court held in *Lucas* that if a regulation is so restrictive that the property no longer has any economic value to the owner, the property has in effect been taken, even though there has been no physical transfer of title. In such cases, the courts have recognized that the owner of the now valueless property is entitled to compensation just as if there were a physical taking. A mere reduction in the value of property because of a regulation, however, does not entitle the property owner to compensation.

The *Lucas* case seems fair to most people. Mr. Lucas was a very sympathetic plaintiff. After all, he bought the property when his intended use of it for a home was lawful. Many people share the dream of buying a piece of property and building a home on it; they would understandably be devastated if they finally saved up enough money and bought the property for their dream home, only to be told when they got ready to build that the law had changed and they could no longer build anything on their land. The high court was very careful to emphasize in its opinion that the concept of regulatory takings was limited to cases such as the one before it, where a total loss of economic value was caused by the law.

Property rights advocates were not happy with the limited scope of *Lucas*, however, and wanted to expand the definition of regulatory takings to include any diminution of value of property caused by government action. Attempts to broaden the definition of compensable regulatory taking through the court system have not been extremely successful, and so property rights advocates have now begun to take their case to the public, through the referendum process. In October of 2004, they scored their biggest victory to date, securing passage of Measure 34 in Oregon, the state that formerly had the most restrictive land use laws in the country.[12] Land use policies adopted in 1973 had led to the state's being regarded as a model for protecting farmland and other undeveloped land, and restricting most growth to areas that were already developed.[13] In fact, many believe it was probably this state's extensive land use restrictions, along with a very well crafted advertising campaign[14], that led to the passage of Measure 34.

Measure 34 simply provides that landowners are entitled to either exercise development rights that existed before the state implemented its land use regulations, or pay the landowners compensation for the loss in value caused by those restrictions. The law effectively provides compensation for what its supporters would define as regulatory takings, regulations that take away a portion of the value of land.

Not all landowners, of course, were uniformly supportive of Measure 34. Some had purchased farmland because they "knew" that because of the state's restrictive land use regulations, their rural environment would not be disturbed by development. Many of these homeowners now fear that the state will not be able to afford to pay compensation claims and the hills that are now covered with fir trees and pear orchards will soon be covered with Wal-Marts and resort condominiums.[15] The law was publicized as protecting small landowners whose rights to use their property were being arbitrarily taken away by government bureaucrats, but most of the funding to secure passage of the proposal actually came from came from timber companies and real estate interests that stand to profit if large tracts of farmland and forests are unlocked for development, as many expect them to be because the measure did not provide any resources to enable the state to be able to compensate the landowners.[16]

It is too soon to know with any degree of certainty what the long run impact of Oregon's Measure 37 will be, but many state officials and land use planners say that the law is on the brink of wrecking havoc with what was once one of the best systems for reining in sprawl and protecting wide open spaces.[17] The law was immediately challenged by planning advocates who claimed that the law violated the state constitution by benefiting those who bought the land before there restrictions were implemented, but not those who purchased the land afterward.[18] The law was initially struck down,[19] but that ruling was overturned by Oregon's highest court in February of 2006.[20] As the court was determining the fate of the law, most of the claims were put on hold. But now that the law has been finally upheld, the state will likely increase its processing of applications for waivers of restrictions or compensation.

As of the end of October 2006, there had been over $4 billion in claims filed under Measure 37.[21] Because the measure did not provide any funding for compensation, the most likely outcome when all the claims are finally settled is that most of the restrictions will simply be waived, and the Oregon landscape will look very different than it does today.[22]

THE PERCEIVED ABUSE OF EMINENT DOMAIN

The heavily publicized holding in *Kelo v. City of New London*[23] brought to the public's attention an expansion of the use of eminent domain that had been quietly occurring since the Michigan Supreme Court case of *Poletown Neighborhood Council v. the City of Detroit and the Economic Redevelopment Commission.*[24] Eminent domain allows the government to take private property as long as the taking is for public use and the former owner is paid just compensation for the property. Traditional public uses are easy for people to understand, and make sense to most people. Such uses include the property for schools, highways.

In the *Poletown* case, the Detroit Economic Redevelopment Commission had used the power of eminent domain to acquire land being used by its owners for homes and small businesses and turned the land over to General Motors to use for a plant expansion. The court believed that the purpose of the taking, to provide jobs to stimulated moribund economy, constituted public use.[25] Subsequently, we saw increased use of the takings power for economic redevelopment, creating growing public anger because many of these cases resulted in the transfer of private property from one small business or homeowner to a larger business or major corporation. Finally, in 2004, in the case of *County of Wayne v. Edward Hathcock, et al*,[26] the Michigan State Supreme Court overturned the *Poletown* decision, stating that ""Poletown's conception of a public use—that of 'alleviating unemployment and revitalizing the economic base of the community' has no support in the Court's eminent domain jurisprudence. . . ."[27] By this time, however, the controversy had spread to numerous states, and the United States Supreme Court had agreed to step in.

The high court settled the issue with one of the most controversial decisions in recent memory. In *Kelo*, the County invoked its power of eminent domain to acquire forty-six parcels it needed for construction of the Pinnacle Project, a plan to purchase the surrounding land and construct a modern business and technology park abutting the airport that had recently slated for expansion, justifying the taking on grounds of creating jobs and expanding the tax base of the community. The Connecticut Supreme Court upheld the taking, finding that as a matter of first impression, economic development can be a valid public use.[28] The United States Supreme Court agreed with that holding.[29]

REGULATORY TAKINGS ISSUES ON THE BALLOT IN 2006

Regulatory takings proposals were on the ballots in four states during the 2006 elections: Arizona, California, Idaho, and Washington. In general, these measures were touted by their advocates as being designed simply to provide"fair compensation" to those whose property values are reduced by land use regulation, with states being given the option of waiving the waive the land use restriction in lieu of payment. Opponents of these measures point out that the result of such laws' passing would be a sharp reduction in land use regulation because states could not afford the compensation.[30]

One of the major criticisms of most of these initiatives was that they were deceptively advertised as being measures to restrict unfair eminent domain practices, when they were actually much more extensive regulations restricting the more broadly defined regulatory takings. In fact, two other measures that attempted to link the two separate kinds of issues did not even make it to the ballot. A clear "double issue" initiative was struck from the ballot in Oklahoma. The "Protect our Homes Initiative" was an eminent domain initiative

What is a regulatory taking?

that also contained regulatory takings language. The Oklahoma court ruled 6–3 that eminent domain and regulatory taking s are two separate issues, and thus must be addressed in two separate initiatives.[31]

A similar proposal was to have also appeared on the Nevada ballot, but the Nevada State Supreme Court refused to allow the measure on the ballot as it was proposed.[32] The court required the drafters of the initiative to limit the proposal to one issue. The drafters then dropped the regulatory taking issue, leaving only the eminent domain issue on the ballot.

The ballot measure with the biggest potential impact, because of the size of the state in which it was proposed, was California's Proposition 90,[33] officially titled the Government Acquisition, Regulation of Private Property, Initiative Constitutional Amendment. Drafters of this proposition managed to merge both the eminent domain and the regulatory takings issues into one fairly comprehensive proposal. In response to the public concern about *Kelo*, the proposition would have provided that private property could be taken only for a stated public use and not for private use.[34] To make this point even more strongly, the next subsection of the proposal further declared that "property taken by eminent domain shall be owned and occupied by the condemner, or another governmental agency utilizing the property for the stated public use by agreement with the condemner" or be leased to an agency regulated by the Public Utilities Commission or with another entity to which the government has contracted for the performance of some public use project, and all such property can be use only for the stated public use.[35]

These two provisions would have adequately addressed the public concern arising from *Kelo*. Advocates of this proposal could thus justifiably argue that this proposal would prevent the kinds of government actions that led to the government's taking the private property of one business or individual and transferring it to another individual, as situation that had often resulted in a small business or homeowner's losing his property to a big corporation. Had securing passage of an amendment to prevent these abuses of eminent domain been the real intent of the drafters, they would have limited their proposal to these provisions.

The drafters of this proposal went much farther, however, and it was most likely some of these additional aspects of the bill that led to its defeat. The bill did not merely address the traditional taking of private property, but also, following the lead of Measure 37, proved for compensation for "damage to" private property from government actions, specifically including "government actions that result in substantial economic loss to private property. Examples of substantial economic loss include, but are not limited to the downsizing of private property, the elimination of any access to private property and limitations on the use of private air space.

'Government action' shall mean any statute, charter, provision, ordinance, resolution, rule or regulation."[36]

One key difference between this proposal and Measure 37, of course, was that the California law was not retroactive. Whereas the Oregon measure provided compensation for anyone whose property value had been diminished by government regulations after the property had been purchased, the California law would have applied only to new regulations passed after the proposed initiative would have taken effect.

The key arguments put forth by proponents of the act were that the law would stop eminent domain abuse that had occurred in the past when politically connected developers convinced local governments to take individuals property to build developments that would general more tax revenue for the government. It would also stop the government from "taking peoples homes indirectly through regulations" and not giving them compensation, which is not fair treatment of the homeowners.[37] The proponents of the bill argued that the opponents were people who benefited financially from the current rules and were using scare tactics to try to prevent the bill's passage so they could continue to profit from governmental takings of private property.[38] The proponents also claimed that fears of a loss of environmental regulations were unfounded because the law would not allow compensation for any losses caused by existing laws, but only new regulations, and because California already had a full panoply of existing regulations, the enforcement of which would not be affected by the law, California's environmental protections would not be threatened.[39]

Opponents of the initiative claimed that the proponents were trying to pull a "bait and switch" on Californians by claiming that the law was about eminent domain when in the fine print were provisions to allow California's wealthy landowners and corporations to demand huge payouts from taxpayers by claiming that new laws harmed the value of their property or business.[40] They argued that the law could force taxpayers to spend billions of dollars to prevent unwanted development and pass other laws that would protect the environment or consumers by restricting the actions of some property owners or corporations.[41]

The measure failed by a very narrow margin of 47.5% in favor to 52.5% opposed[42] Opponents of the measure were probably assisted when Governor Schwarzenegger wrote an op-ed piece opposing the measure that was referred to by many as a "taxpayer trap."[43]

Idaho's Issue failed by a significantly wider margin of 24–76%[44] The Idaho Measure had provided that "if an owner's ability to use, possess, sell, or divide private real property is limited or prohibited by the enactment or enforcement of any land use law after the date of acquisition by the owner of the property in a manner that reduces the fair market value of the property, the owner shall be entitled to just compensation. . . ."[45]

Proponents of the Measure argued that the law would protect homeowners, farmers, and ranchers from unjust taking of their property, and most importantly would prevent the government from taking someone's home and giving it to another private party or person, as occurred in the *Kelo* case. It would also greatly reduce the number of aggressive government actions that take or diminish the value of people's homes because property owners would have legal recourse against such actions.[46]

Opponents of Measure 2 argued that that the measure was deceptive because it did not provide additional protection to homeowners from eminent domain, but in fact would dismantle local planning efforts that protected quality of life in Idaho. They explained that the first part of the measure merely copied portions of existing law (House Bill 555) that had been enacted by the 2006 Idaho Legislature and signed into law by the governor, and that eminent domain section was included only to distract attention from the initiative's real purpose, which they found to be gutting local planning that protected communities and property values.[47] They further argued that the law was poorly written, contained contradictory provisions, and at minimum would lead to litigation over its provisions, again costing the taxpayers money.[48] Opponents also highlighted the fact that the legislation would restrict the right of communities to zone and rezone property without compensating landowners for economic loss to their property, which would either cost the state potentially millions of dollars, or lead to completely unrestricted growth that would destroy communities.[49]

The opponents rallied a large group of diverse interests to oppose the legislation,[50] and rallying these influential individuals and organizations may have helped prevent passage of the legislation. Opponents of the legislation may have also been aided by the fact that This House is MY Home, the chief proponent of Proposition 2, received $75,000 of its $76,764 in contributions from June 3 to September 30, 2006, from America at its Best, an organization funded primarily by Howard Rich, a wealthy real estate tycoon and political activist in New York.[51] Opponents were thus able to generate a great deal of antagonism for the law by painting the law as an out-of-state, special interest proposition.[52]

Washington's Proposition 933[53] would require government agencies to consider the effects of and alternatives to regulating private property. Compensation would be required when regulations were enforced that damage private property use or value, including regulations prohibiting or restricting property uses that were allowed as of January 1, 1996.[54]

Despite the support of a wide range of organizations,[55] Washington's was defeated by a margin of 42%to 58%. The Washington vote was interesting because it was the only true referendum on regulatory takings; it did not contain an eminent domain restriction like the California, Idaho, and Arizona proposals did.

Only Arizona's Proposition 37, the Private Property Rights Protection Act,[56] managed to gain the voter's approval. According to an analysis by the legislative council of Arizona, the measure restricted the use of eminent domain in the state by excluding from the definition of public use the public benefits of economic development.[57] The measure also provided that a property owner is entitled to just compensation if the value of a person's property is reduced by the enactment of a land use law.[58] The ballot clearly explained, "A "yes" vote shall have the effect of [1] establishing additional rights for individuals whose property is taken by the government for public use (eminent domain), [2] defining "public use," [3] prohibiting the taking of property for economic development, [4] requiring primary residences taken by eminent domain be replaced by a comparable dwelling, [5] requiring compensation for property values reduced by land use laws, [6] requiring attorneys fees' in eminent domain lawsuits, and [7] allowing attorneys' fees in property value reduction lawsuits."[59]

How do the values of those who supported Measure 37 differ from the values of those who opposed the measure?

Supporters of the proposal successfully argued that Measure 207 would prevent the abuse of power, as exemplified by the Kelo decision. They argued that "Proposition 207 addresses government takings, whether by eminent domain or regulation. It prevents the government from taking private property for third-party private development merely to increase tax revenue, and ensures just compensation for property owners in public use takings and when governmental regulation devalues property."[60] They very skillfully tied the measure to protecting Arizonans freedom.[61]

Supporters also had some very good examples with which to appeal to voters' emotion. For example, they cited the treatment of Rita Ulsheimer, who, after struggling with cancer and spousal abuse, bought a humble home where she planned to retire. She particularly liked the awning next to the house that would cover her car from the scorching Arizona sun. But city inspectors demanded she tear down the awning at her own expense because it violated the city code. She was just an innocent victim of government regulators whom, if Measure 207 passed, would receive compensation in such situations where the value of their property was reduced by unnecessary regulations.[62]

Opponents argued that the initiative had been funded "almost entirely by the Illinois-based group Americans for Limited Government" and "should be called the Anti-Neighborhood Preservation and Conservation Act rather than the Private Property Rights Protection Act."[63] They argued that it could require municipalities to compensate property owners for every zoning or land use decision they make and lead to abuse as landowners filed claims every time their was a land use regulation passed, and noted that it would make it difficult to preserve neighborhoods.[64]

Opponents, who included a number of small businesses, conservation groups, public health and safety groups, community and neighborhood groups, planning and historic preservation groups, water and consumer groups, labor organizations, as well as a number of community leaders,[65] were particularly concerned about the environmental effects of the proposal because it would either cost taxpayers an exorbitant amount of money, or make it financially impossible for communities to limit irresponsible development, preserve limited water supplies, and protect open spaces.[66] In particular, they argued that it would Proposition 207 puts at risk important land protection measures including Pima County's Sonoran Desert Conservation Plan which help protect habitat for imperiled species of plants and wildlife.[67] Finally, as in California and Idaho, they argued that it was deceptive and under the guise of preventing eminent domain abuse, snuck in provisions that would primarily benefit land speculators at the expense of neighborhoods.

Proposition 207 was approved by a vote of 65%–35%,[68] a significant margin of victory for its proponents. The measure, however, will face legal challenges, and at this time, it is uncertain how the law will actually be implemented.[69]

THE FUTURE OF MEASURE 37 CLONES

Obviously, no one can foretell what legislation will pass in the future, but it is clear that those who seek compensation for property owners whose land value is diminished are going to continue to try to spread these measures across the country. In California, for example, supporters were on blogs immediately following the election commenting on the narrowness of the loss and hypothesizing that given the huge disparity in advertising expenditures, in the next election, with a little more money devoted to television advertisements, the proposition would surely pass. The future of other similar measures may turn on the effects of Oregon's Measure 37 and Arizona's Proposition 207. It is obviously far too soon to know the impact of Arizona's law. Even though it was passes in 2004, with all the subsequent litigation, the real impact of Oregon's law cannot yet be measured, although in a recent poll, many of those who originally voted for the law have since regretted that decision.[70] It will be interesting to watch how the implementation of these laws unfolds. By the next election, we will have more information about the effects of these laws, and if we see more Measure 37 clones appearing on state ballots, at least voters might have a little bit more information about what they are really voting for if they vote for these measures.

END NOTES

1. Alternatively, the government may purchase the property.
2. The measure passed with 61 percent of the vote. American Society of Land Use Architects, Property Rights on the Ballot, *Most voters uphold land use regulation but limit eminent domain'* Land On Line (Nov. 14, 2006). . . .
3. According to a recent survey only 29 percent of Oregonians would now vote for the measure. American Society of Land Use Architects, "Property Rights on the Ballot *Most voters uphold land use regulation but limit eminent domain'* Land On Line (Nov. 14, 2006). . . .
4. See N. Kubasek, "Oregon's Measure 37: A Harbinger of the Death of Slow Growth," 34 **Real Estate Law Journal** 416 (Spring 2005).for a discussion of this controversial initiative.

5. According to Leonard C. Gilroy, of the Reason foundation, "Measure 37 represents a major advance for the national property rights movement by establishing a system that restores the rights of private landowners that had previously been taken away via regulatory action." Leonard C. Gilroy, Statewide Regulatory Takings Reform: Exporting Oregon's Measure 37 to Other States (April, 2006). . . .
6. 125 S. Ct. 2655 (2005).
7. Correy Stephenson, *'Kelo' One Year Later*, LawyersUSA, August 14, 2006, at 1, 23.
8. *Id.*
9. Dan Whipple, "Give and Takings," Grist, (Oct. 16, 2006). . . .
10. Mary Zeiss Stange, Life, *Liberty and Property Rights*, USA TODAY, Nov. 2, 2006 at 13A.
11. 112 U.S. 2886 (1992).
12. Felicity Barringer, Property Rights Law May Alter Oregon Landscape, New York Times, Nov. 26, 2004, at 1.
13. Associated Press byline," Oregon Property Law is Overturned; A Judge Strikes Down a Rule that Governments Must Pay Landowners if Regulations Lower Values," Los Angeles Times, Oct. 15, 2005, A 14. 13 Figuring prominently in many of the advertisements was 92 year old Dorothy English, who had purchased land in the hills west of Portland in 1953, and wanted to carve out a number of building lots on her 20 acres and make some money to help her enjoy her remaining years. *Id.* Subsequent to the laws passage, she filed a lawsuit demanding $1.5 million in compensation for the loss of value brought about by the change in land use laws governing her property. Laura Oppenheimer, Land Spat Valued at $115 million, The Oregonian, May 19, 2006.
15. Barringer, *supra*, note 12.
16. Baline Harden, *Anti-Sprawl Laws, Property rights Collide in Oregon*, WASHINGTON POST, Feb. 28, 2005, A1.
17. *Id.*
18. Associated press byline, *supra*, note 12.
19. *Id.*
20. Sam Howe Verhovek, Property Rights Law is Upheld in Oregon, LOS ANGELES TIMES, Feb. 22, 2006, 12.
21. Lora Volkert, Oregon: a Glimpse of Idaho's Future, Idaho Business Review, October 9, 2006.
22. According to an article in the Idaho Business Review, as of October 9, 2006, 90 percent of the 3000 claims had been approved, with the government waiving the land use restrictions in each case. Development consistent with these new waivers has not yet commenced, however. Lora Volkert, Oregon a Glimpse of Iaaho's future, IDAHO BUS. REV. OCT. 9, 2006.
23. 125 S. Ct. 2655 (2005).

24. 304 N.W.2d 455 (1981).
25. *Id.*
26. 471 Mich. 445, 684 N.W. 2d 765(2004).
27. *Id.*
28. Kelo, *supra* note 23.
29. *Id.*
30. American Society of Land Use Architects, Property Rights on the Ballot *Most voters uphold land use regulation but limit eminent domain'* Land On Line (Nov. 14, 2006). . . .
31. American Planning Association, Regulatory Takings Ballot Measures Across America, available at http://www.planning.org/legislation/measure37/
32. *Id.*
33. . . .
34. Proposition 90, Government Acquisition, Regulation of Private Property, Initiative Constititutional Amendment Sec.19 (a) (1) (2006). . . .
35. Id. at Sec. (2).
36. *Id.* at Sec. 19 (b) (8).
37. Proposition 90, Government Acquisition, Regulation of Private Property, Initiative Constititutional Amendment, pg. 94, Argument in Favor of Proposition. . . .
38. *Id.*
39. *Id.*
40. Proposition 90, Government Acquisition, Regulation of Private Property, Initiative Constititutional Amendment, pg. 95, Argument Against Proposition. . . .
41. *Id.* To read more arguments against the proposition, see www.NoProp90.com
42. . . .
43. California: No on 90 (even Arnold agrees with that). . . .
44. American Planning Association, Regulatory Ballot Measures Across America. . . .
45. Initiative Used for Limiting Eminent Domain When Used for Economic Development; Defining Land Use Law; and Permitting Just Compensation for Regulatory Takings, Sec. 4 (5). . . .
46. This House is My House. . . .
47. Ben Ysura, Idaho Secretary of state, Idaho Voter's Pamphlet. . . .
48. *Id.*
49. *Prop 2: Chaos for Your Town*, IDAHO MOUNTAIN EXPRESS AND GUIDE, July 14, 2006. . . .
50. Opponents included businesses such as Idaho Association of Commerce & Industry (IACI); Idaho Association of Realtors; Building Contractors of Southwestern Idaho, Inc.; Boise Metro Chamber of Commerce; Greater Pocatello Chamber of Commerce; Coeur d'Alene Chamber

of Commerce; Idaho Falls Chamber of Commerce; Eagle Chamber of Commerce; Rexburg Area Chamber of Commerce; Mini-Cassia Chamber of Commerce; Meridian Chamber of Commerce; Rathdrum Chamber of Commerce; Caldwell Chamber of Commerce; Camas Chamber of Commerce; Lewiston Chamber of Commerce; Twin Falls Chamber of Commerce; Orthopedic Healthcare and Paul Collins, MD; Kull Food Technologies; Intermountain Industries, Inc.; Crusty's Pizza, McCall; Idaho AFL-CIO; Idaho Building Contractors Association; Marshall Thompson, Commercial Printing; Trillium Asset Management; High Country Fusion Company, Inc.; Idaho Forest Owners Association Board, community organizations, such as Idaho Smart Growth; East End Neighborhood Association; Idaho Education Association; League of Women Voters of Idaho; Interfaith Alliance; Idaho Women's Network; Neighbors for Responsible Growth; Moscow Civic Association; Harris Ranch Neighborhood Association; Valley Advocates for Responsible Development; NoSuperWalmart; and Community Voice, city and county associations, conservation associations, such as Greater Yellowstone Coalition; Idaho Conservation League; North Ada County Foothills Association; Sierra Club; Conservation Voters for Idaho; Golden Eagle Audubon Society; Snake River Alliance; Indian Valley Alliance; The Nature Conservancy of Idaho; Land Trust of the Treasure Valley; Wood River Land Trust; and Idaho Rivers United, and a number of prominent individuals, including the governor, former governor, and several other elected officials. Neighbors Protecting Idaho. . . .

51. Josh Israel, In Idaho, It's One for 2, Takings Initiaive Acccountability Project. . . .
52. Prop 2 was placed on Idaho[1]s ballot after Rich paid signature gatherers over $300,000 to collect signatures, and that he poured over $800,000 ((99.7% of the total Prop 2 campaign funding)) into Idaho in an effort to convince Idahoans to support his out-of-state, special interest proposition. Neighbors Protecting Idaho, Idaho Voters Overwhelmingly Reject Prop 2. . . .
53. . . .
54. The complete text of the proposal can be found at. . . .
55. Endorsers of the proposal included: Americans for Limited Government; Bainbridge Citizens United Benton-Franklin Mainstream Republicans; Building Industry Association of Washington; Centralia-Chehalis Chamber of Commerce; Citizens' Alliance for Property Rights; Clark County Citizens United Columbia-Snake River Irrigators Association; Island County Property Rights Alliance; Kitsap Alliance of Property Owners; National Association of Rural Landowners; National Federation of Independent Business – Washington; May Valley Environmental Council; Spokane Pro-America; Walla Walla Local Firefighters Union; Washington Cattlemen's Association; Washington Christmas Tree

Growers; Washington College Republican Federation; Washington Contract Loggers Association; Washington Farm Bureau; Adams County Farm Bureau; Benton County Farm Bureau; Chelan/Douglas County Farm Bureau; Clark/Cowlitz County Farm Bureau; Columbia/Blue Mountain Counties Farm Bureau; Franklin County Farm Bureau; Grant County Farm Bureau; Grays Harbor/Pacific County Farm Bureau; Island County Farm Bureau; King/Pierce County Farm Bureau; Kittitas County Farm Bureau; Lewis County Farm Bureau; Lincoln County Farm Bureau; Mason/Kitsap County Farm Bureau; North Olympic Counties Farm Bureau; Okanogan County Farm Bureau; Skagit County Farm Bureau; Snohomish County Farm Bureau; Spokane County Farm Bureau; Stevens County Farm Bureau; Thurston County Farm Bureau; Walla Walla County Farm Bureau; Wakima County Farm Bureau; Washington Farm Forestry Association; and Washington Fish Growers Association. Learn About 933, www.propertyfairness.com WSFB (accessed 1/12/07).

56. Proposition 207 Amending Title 12, Chapter 8, Arizona Revised Statutes, By Adding Article 2.1; Relating To The Private Property Rights Protection Act. . . .
57. Arizona secretary of State Jan Brewer, 2006 Ballot Proposals and Judicial Performance Review. . . .
58. *Id.*
59. *Id.*
60. *Id.*
61. *Id.*
62. *Id.*
63. *Id.*
64. *Id.*
65. For a list of opponents, *see* Endorsements, Vote No on Proposition 207! . . .
66. *Id.*
67. Effects on the Environment, Vote No on Proposition 207!, . . .
68. Arizona: Proposition 207, Property fairness.org. . . .
69. *Id.*
70. In a recent poll, Oregonians appeared to express regret for the measure, which passed with 61 percent of the vote. Only 29 percent would now vote for it. *Property Rights on the Ballot*, Land Online, Landscape Architecture News Digest, Nov. 14, 2006. . . .

ARTICLE 8.4

A Stadium in Your Front Yard? Eminent Domain and the Potential Sport Marketing Implications of *Kelo v City of New London*

Mark S. Nagel and Richard M. Southall

"There are people that want to stop this project in Brooklyn for, I would argue, either misguided, or myopic, or selfish reasons. We think the project is something that Brooklyn and this city really needs, and (New Jersey Nets' owner) Bruce Ratner is as good a developer as you can find" (Goldstein, 2006, para. 13).—New York Mayor Michael Bloomberg responding to an eminent domain lawsuit claiming part of the land for the New Jersey Nets Brooklyn facility was improperly condemned.

The Fifth Amendment to the United States Constitution explicitly established private property rights, ". . . nor shall private property be taken for public use, without just compensation." When a government agency seizes private land for public use, it exercises its eminent domain powers by condemning land while providing its previous owners with fair market value (Garner et al., 2004). For many years following the United States' founding, such eminent domain powers' utilization was most commonly justified as necessary for extensive public works projects such as the construction of new roads, bridges, dams, or utilities ("Eminent domain history," 2005). However, in 1950, after five years of planning, the District of Columbia utilized eminent domain to condemn blighted real estate it wished to redevelop (*Berman v. Parker*, 1954). Owners of a department store within the redevelopment area argued their property was not blighted and the Fifth Amendment's "Takings Clause" prevented private property from being seized and redistributed to another private party. The Supreme Court unanimously ruled that the land could be condemned and resold to another private party because the redevelopment plan served a public purpose (*Berman v. Parker*).

Extending *Berman*, in 1984 the U.S. Supreme Court strengthened the government's eminent domain powers when it unanimously upheld the state of Hawaii's condemnation and redistribution of private land to other private interests (Hawaii *Housing Authority v. Midkiff*, 1984). Prior to this holding, the vast majority of Hawaiian private real estate was controlled by a small group of owners. The State of Hawaii contended such control caused economic harm to the overall society.

What values do you think are most important to those who support the use of eminent domain to build stadiums? Which are most important to those who oppose such use?

The Court agreed with this reasoning and upheld the state's argument, deeming the redistribution plan served an appropriate public purpose.

The Supreme Court's redefinition of suitable public use permitted a government's legislative branch to utilize redistribution and/or redevelopment as rationale for condemning private property. Some critics argued the *Berman* decision ". . . forged an unholy alliance between cities strapped for cash and entrepreneurs promising economic bounty" (Greenberg, 2005, para. 3). Citing as evidence of such an alliance, from 1998–2002 The Institute for Justice documented over 10,000 eminent domain cases in which local governments attempted to condemn real estate for private redevelopment (Greenberg).

One such instance occurred in 2000, when the city of New London, Connecticut, implemented a redevelopment project to increase tax revenues and improve the economic conditions within its municipality. Although the 115 residential and commercial lots within the 90 acres to be acquired and redeveloped were not "blighted," the city eventually utilized its eminent domain power to acquire 15 parcels owned by citizens who refused to sell to the redevelopment corporation (*Kelo v. City of New London*, 2005). After declining to sell, Susette Kelo and other holdout owners argued the city had misused its eminent domain authority, since seizing one party's private property in order to transfer ownership to another private entity-strictly for the economic benefit of the community-did not qualify as proper public use (*Kelo v. City of New London*, 2005).

On June 23, 2005, the United States Supreme Court (5–4) held for the city of New London. The Court reasoned public benefits, such as economic growth and increased taxes likely to result from the city's redevelopment plans, qualified such condemnation and seizure of private property as a permissible "public use" under the Fifth Amendment's Takings Clause. However, in her dissent, Justice Sandra Day O'Connor noted the potential power legislative branches would now retain due to the Court's ruling:

> Under the banner of economic development, all private property is now vulnerable to being taken and transferred to another private owner, so long as it might be upgraded-i.e., given to an owner who will use it in a way that the legislature deems more beneficial to the public-in the process. To reason, as the Court does, that the incidental public benefits resulting from the subsequent ordinary use of private property render economic development takings "for public use" is to wash out any distinction between private and public use of property-and thereby effectively to delete the words "for public use" from the Takings Clause of the Fifth Amendment (*Kelo v City of New London*, 2005, p. 461).

The case immediately created an uproar among disparate organizations (e.g., Cato Institute, Heritage Foundation, NAACP) across the United States who perceived the decision as threatening any property owner with having their land condemned, seized, and resold by a governmental entity solely to generate increased tax revenues ("Property rights are civil rights," 2005). Although the Supreme Court's decision arguably enhanced legislatures' condemnation powers, by July 2006, the attention generated by the *Kelo* decision resulted in 22 states passing legislation limiting their eminent domain powers (Savin & Hahne, 2006). In addition, numerous other states and municipalities have proposed legislation curtailing their condemnation powers (Savin & Hahne).

Sport organizations, particularly those operating in large facilities, are certainly impacted by the *Kelo* decision and subsequent state and local legislation. Recent redevelopment discussions involving the Dallas Cowboys (Mosier, 2005), Florida Marlins ("SB 4 and Eminent Domain News," 2005), Washington Nationals (Lemke, 2005) and numerous other teams have centered on governments' potential use of eminent domain to acquire land for new facilities, since acquiring adequate contiguous acreage from disparate parcels to build a new stadium can be difficult and potentially expensive, especially in a large metropolitan area. This urban-environment reality resulted in eminent-domain related discussions in nearly half of all new major professional sport construction projects in the 1990s (McGraw, 2005).

Among numerous instances where eminent domain has assisted a team's new-stadium construction, the most notable may have occurred in Arlington, Texas. In 1990, eminent domain was the legal rationale for seizing 13 acres from the Mathes family, who refused to sell their parcel to the Texas Rangers (Bryce, 1997). Although the Mathes were unsuccessful in fighting the eminent domain proceedings' takings portion, they were successful in suing the city, which had failed to provide adequate compensation for the taking. The family was eventually awarded $7.5 million by a Tarrant County jury. The city of Arlington contemplated appealing the ruling, but decided to simply pay the plaintiffs (Bryce).

The *Kelo* decision increases the likelihood a professional team owner will include local government officials, who can potentially exercise eminent domain powers, as part of a public-private coalition that supports building a new revenue-maximizing facility. In some cases, rather than allowing their "city's" team to perform normal due diligence in order to identify a potential building site, local politicians may eagerly utilize eminent domain and provide the franchise with a suitable construction site, thereby easing the team's struggle. Since any new facility is "tangible" evidence of a politician's service to his/her community, a newly re-developed stadium is not just an anchor for a new-urbanism master plan, it is a tailor-made opportunity for "schmoozing" potential campaign donors.

In light of the power the *Kelo* decision provides governments' legislative branches, citizens should maintain vigilant oversight of potential construction plans. Over the past 15 years, sports economists have noted taxpayer-funded facilities' limited economic benefits (Sullum, 2004), and many metropolitan areas have begun to vote "no" to stadium initiatives. This has resulted in some sports owners seeking eminent domain assistance to complete their private or quasiprivate facility projects (McGraw, 2005). Since eminent domain's use "appears" to affect only those landowners whose property is seized, citizens who might be predisposed to vote "no" for tax increases for stadium construction may not realize either the potential impact such legislative activities have upon affected land owners or may have upon them if, or when, their government deems it appropriate to redevelop their land. Since *Kelo* has more broadly defined "public use," legislatures are free to condemn land for private development-if constituents will allow it.

The *Kelo* ruling also potentially presents a municipality with an unusual scenario in which to apply its eminent domain clout. The authors contend, based on the rationale elucidated in *Kelo*, that since a professional sports franchise is a private entity-often one that receives tremendous tax breaks-a local government could potentially utilize eminent domain power to condemn, seize, and resell a professional franchise to a more "suitable" owner, resulting in increased franchise value, improving redevelopment opportunities surrounding the facility in which the team plays, and generating greater tax revenues. Such an eventuality is not as far-fetched as might initially appear. In 1984, after failing to complete an agreement that met the team's financial needs, the state of Maryland initiated eminent domain procedures in an attempt to prevent the Baltimore Colts from leaving ("Historical moments," n. d.). Sensing his tenuous ownership status, Colts owner Robert Irsay secretly commenced the team's now infamous exodus to Indianapolis, Indiana, via Mayflower moving trucks on a snowy March 28th night.

Why might some argue that property oweners in minority neighborhoods are particularly likely to be adversely affected by a broad definition of public use?

Though initially such an eventuality may seem unlikely, when viewed through the lens of continual franchise/league marketing strategies designed to maximize fans' psychic attachment to "their" team by intertwining a city or region's identity with "its" team (Reese, Nagel, & Southall, 2003), the likelihood that face-painted, flag-waving, 12th men-citizens would support their government utilizing eminent domain tactics to prevent "their" team from leaving may someday become a reality.

REFERENCES

Berman v. Parker, 348 U.S. 26 (1954).

Bryce, R. (1997). What price baseball? The Austin Chronicle. Retrieved October 1, 2006, from http://www.austinchronicle.com/issues/vol16/issue42/pols.bushstadium.html.

Eminent domain history. (2005, June 24). Retrieved March 22, 2007, from http://www.pbs.org/now/politics/domain.html.

Garner, B. A., et al. (2004). Black's law dictionary (8th ed.). St. Paul, MN: Thompson.

Goldstein, J. (2006, October 27). Atlantic Yards project abuses uses of eminent domain, suit says. The Sun. Retrieved March 21, 2007, from http://www.nysun.com/article/42433?page_no=2.

Greenberg, G. (2005, January/February). The condemned. Mother Jones. Retrieved March 22, 2007, from http://www.motherjones.com/news/feature/2005/01/01_407.html.

Hawaii Housing Authority v. Midkiff, 467 U.S. 229 (1984).

Historical moments. (n. d.). Retrived October 1, 2006, from http://www.sportsecyclopedia.com/nfl/balticolts/baltcolts.html.

Kelo v. City of New London, 545 U.S. 469 (2005); 125 S. Ct. 2655; 162 L. Ed. 2d 439 (2005).

Lemke, T. (2005, October 6). Landowners must yield to ballpark. The Washington Times. Retrieved October 1, 2006, from http://www.washtimes.com/national/20051006–120902–5838r.htm.

McGraw, D. (2005, May). Demolishing sports welfare. Reason online. Retrieved October 1, 2006, from http://www.reason.com/0505/fe.dm.demolishing.shtml.

Mosier, J. (2005, June 24). Stadium eminent domain imminent for homeowners. Dallas Morning News. Retrieve October 1, 2006, from http://www.dallasnews.com/sharedcontent/dws/news/localnews/cowboysstadium/stories/062505dnmetcondemn.415743ed.html.

Property rights are civil rights. (2005, July 11). Retrieved March 22, 2007, from http://www.opinionjournal.com/diary/?id=110006941.

Reese, J. T., Nagel, M. S., & Southall, R. M. (2003). Legal and marketing implications of ticket transfer policies in the National Football League. Sport Marketing Quarterly, 12(4), 254–255.

Savin, M. D., & Hahne, K. S. (2006). Eminent domain after Kelo. Retrieved March 22, 2007, from http://www.faegre.com/articles/article_2002.aspx.

SB 4 and eminent domain news. (2005, June 23). Retrieved October 1, 2006, from http://newballpark.blogspot.com/2005/06/sb-4-and-eminent-domain-news.html.

Sullum, J. (2004, November 12). The phony economic case for taxpayer-funded stadiums. Retrieved March 23, 2007, from http://www.townhall.com/columnists/JacobSullum/2004/11/12/the_phony_economic_case_for_taxpayer-funded_stadiums.

United States Constitution, Fifth Amendment.

ARTICLE 8.5

Overcoming Another Tragedy in New Orleans: Rebuilding in the Wake of *Kelo* and Act No. 851

William Carlos Spaht

I. INTRODUCTION

During Hurricanes Katrina and Rita, thousands of Gulf Coast residents lost their homes, their possessions, their savings, and some, their lives. Those states hit hardest by the hurricanes have struggled to recover. In places like New Orleans, where hundreds of thousands of residents evacuated and may never return, uncertainty regarding the future of private property has become a fact of life. As the excerpt from Senator McPherson's letter indicates, arguably the single most critical question facing local and state governments trying to rebuild the devastated coast is how to encourage use of abandoned properties to spark the economy.

Michael A. Heller explores this question in an article that analyzes historical situations in which property has gone underused for long periods of time.[1] American property law supports an owner's right to subdivide ownership in her property. According to Heller, however, beneath this seemingly free ability to divide ownership lies a subtle property law doctrine that prevents and abolishes excessive fragmentation and thus ensures that owners have the ability to put property to its most productive use.[2] Heller elaborated on these general anti-fragmentation ideas with a theory he called the "tragedy of the anticommons."[3]

The tragedy of the anticommons is often described by comparison to the tragedy of the commons.[4] In a commons, "multiple owners are each endowed with the privilege to use a given resource, and no one has the right to exclude another."[5] When a commons is created, the given resource is prone to overuse because all parties have unlimited access to it.[6] Anticommons property represents the mirror image of commons property; it is "a property regime in which multiple owners hold effective rights of exclusion in a scarce resource."[7] In an anticommons, the given resource is prone to under-use because owners typically exercise their exclusionary rights and prevent others from using the land.[8] The so-called tragedy of the anticommons occurs when the resource is under-consumed relative to the social optimum.[9] Overcoming an existing tragedy of the anticommons requires bundling property rights, through either government or markets, into the hands of a smaller number of parties who will not prevent one another from using the property.[10]

Heller's theory deserves more attention in light of recent developments in constitutional law and the unique challenges facing governments and property owners in Louisiana after Hurricanes Katrina and Rita. In 2005, the Supreme Court released a controversial opinion in *Kelo v. City of New London* that arguably extended the government's already broad authority to take private property under its eminent domain power provided by the Fifth Amendment.[11] The majority opinion, written by Justice Stevens, defined "public use" to allow governments to take property from individuals and sell it to private owners who intend to build hotels, restaurants, and retail and office space on the property.[12] Claiming that the Court had long rejected a literal definition of "public use," the majority suggested that a taking for any "public purpose" satisfies the Fifth Amendment.[13] In dissent, Justice O'Connor claimed that *Kelo* eviscerated constitutional protections by permitting a government to take property and transfer it to another private owner so long as that government thought that the second owner would put it to a use more beneficial to the community.[14]

Fearing that *Kelo* gave state and local governments too much discretion to take property whenever they so desired, Louisiana passed an amendment to its state constitution that prohibited governments from taking property "for predominant use by any private person or entity" or "for transfer of ownership to any private person or entity" in the fall of 2006.[15] Although the amendment provides some exceptions to the aforementioned rule, it is clearly "part of a national backlash against the outrageous *Kelo* decision."[16] Louisiana was the first of thirteen states in the fall of 2006 to vote on an amendment to its state constitution that would limit a government's ability to use eminent domain to take property purely for the purpose of economic development,[17] just as had been contemplated in areas of New Orleans such as the Ninth Ward.[18] As of January 2007, thirty-four states had passed legislation similar to Louisiana's amendment.[19]

The Louisiana amendment passed by a much smaller margin than many expected, with fifty-five percent voting in favor and forty-five percent opposed.[20] Some believe that the vote was close, not because voters opposed limiting the government's eminent domain powers, but out of fear that the proposed amendment's convoluted language would actually expand the government's ability to take property.[21]

This note analyzes how both *Kelo* and the Louisiana constitutional amendment relate to Heller's theory of the tragedy of the anticommons and explains why Heller's proffered solutions are not the answer for New Orleans, where the underuse of abandoned private property has inhibited the city's recovery from Hurricanes Katrina and Rita. Part II provides a detailed explanation of Heller's theory, the *Kelo* decision, and the Louisiana amendment. Part III clarifies why parts of post-Katrina and Rita New Orleans meet Heller's definition of an anticommons and proposes that *Kelo* offered the government an opportunity to overcome the tragedy. It then evaluates the Louisiana amendment from Heller's perspective to explain why it will likely hinder economic development in New Orleans and identifies some of the shortcomings of Heller's theory so as to explain the passage of the amendment. . . .

II. BACKGROUND

Before analyzing the specific property issues associated with rebuilding New Orleans, one must fully understand the three principal sources undergirding this Note's analysis: Heller's article, in which he explains the tragedy of the anticommons,[22] the *Kelo* opinions,[23] and the Louisiana constitutional amendment passed in response to *Kelo*.[24] This Section provides a detailed description of each.

A. Heller's Theory: The Tragedy of the Anticommons

Heller's theory of the anticommons has been cited as one of the principal justifications for takings by governments under the Fifth Amendment.[25] . . .

1. Heller's Definition of an Anticommons and His Hypothesis

Heller frames his tragedy of the anticommons theory as a foil to the tragedy of the commons.[26] . . . When a commons is created, the given resource is prone to overuse; examples include depleted fisheries and overgrazed fields.[27] The mirror image of commons property, anticommons property is a regime in which multiple owners hold effective rights of exclusion in a scarce resource.[28] Unlike the previous attempts to define an anticommons, Heller's definition recognizes that significant exclusion often has the same detrimental effects on society as does total exclusion.[29] . . .

Because any individual has the power to exclude all others from the property in an anticommons, putting that property to use requires unanimous consent among owners. Such unanimity usually proves difficult to attain; thus, resources either go under-used or go to waste entirely.[30] . . .

2. Overcoming the Tragedy

According to Heller, "avoiding anticommons property is one element that may determine whether countries progress to First World prosperity or spiral downward to Third World despond."[31] So how does a society avoid creating an anticommons? . . . However, the word "begin" limits the hypothesis's usefulness in solving modern crises in our country; most properties have experienced some form of ownership for hundreds of years. In other words, this opportunity to "start" with bundled land and rights has already been lost.

More interesting is the issue pertinent to rebuilding New Orleans: how best to overcome a tragedy of the anticommons once it exists. Heller leaves that question mostly unresolved by explaining what needs to happen without offering a viable solution. He explains that to overcome an existing anticommons, a society must transition to a private property regime that better aligns each owner's interest with efficient use by forcing the private property owner to face the full cost of underconsumption.[32] This transition occurs by consolidating rights into a useable bundle in the hands of a single owner.[33]

In theory, such a consolidation of rights can occur through markets or through governments.[34] By the market route, a property bundler acquires each right from its current holder either legally or illegally, by means such as purchasing.[35] By the government route, governments intervene to redefine and reallocate property rights among individuals by means such as expropriation.[36]

In practice, transitioning to a society in which one owner faces the full cost of underconsumption is difficult. Anticommons property would not be tragic in a world of costless transactions because individuals would trade their initial endowments until resources were in the hands of those who would put them to their highest-valued use.[37] The market route fails in the real world, however, because individuals bargaining for the exchange of resources act inefficiently as a result of transaction costs, strategic behaviors, and cognitive biases.[38] Similarly, governments struggle to overcome the tragedy because it is difficult to calculate compensation and they fear demoralizing potential investors.[39] Heller concludes his description of the anticommons by posing the ultimate question that this Note hopes to answer: "What is to be done?"[40] . . .

Why was there such a strong backlash against the Kelo *decision?*

C. Louisiana's Response: Act No. 851

In response to *Kelo*, Louisiana passed Act No. 851, an amendment to its state constitution, in the fall of 2006.[41] The amendment, an obvious attempt to cabin the wide authority granted by *Kelo*,[42] states that "property shall not be taken . . . by the state or its political subdivisions: (a) for predominant use by any private person or entity; or (b) for transfer of ownership to any private person or entity."[43] This language alone prohibits a sovereign from doing exactly what the local government did in *Kelo*. The amendment goes further, though, and expressly defines "public purpose" as used in § 4 of the Louisiana Constitution, which mirrors the Fifth Amendment to the federal Constitution.[44] . . .

In a final attempt to limit the effects of *Kelo* in Louisiana, the amendment clarifies that "neither economic development, enhancement of tax revenue, or [sic] any incidental benefit to the public shall be considered in determining whether the taking or damaging of property is for a public purpose. . . ."[45] Importantly, the specific arguments made by the New London government defending its taking in *Kelo* included economic development, enhancement of tax revenue, and other benefits that the dissent characterized as incidental.[46] The following section will show that, by responding in such a way to *Kelo*, Louisianans eliminated the possibility of government intervention to help New Orleans overcome its own tragedy of the anticommons.

III. ANALYSIS

This section explores and synthesizes the relationships among the previously described anticommons theory, the *Kelo* case, and the Louisiana constitutional amendment and applies them to the post-hurricanes situation in New Orleans. More specifically, this section first explains why portions of New Orleans qualify as anticommons property. It then describes potential solutions to the city's tragedy contemplated by Heller himself, including the outcome of *Kelo*. Finally, it clarifies the situation in Louisiana as it stands after the constitutional amendment.

A. New Orleans as Anticommons Property

Although there are notable differences between Heller's anticommons examples and the New Orleans situation, the basic circumstances are the same. This section explains why parts of New Orleans meet Heller's definition of anticommons property and then describes the uniqueness of the New Orleans situation, which in some ways clarifies Heller's basic framework.

1. New Orleans fits Heller's Basic Definition of Anticommons Property

Parts of New Orleans qualify as anticommons property under Heller's basic definition: a property regime in which multiple owners hold effective rights of exclusion in a scarce resource, causing the resource to be "underconsum[ed as] compared to the social optimum."[47] A survey conducted in the fall of 2006 showed that New Orleans's population remains roughly sixty percent lower than its pre-storm level.[48] An estimated 454,863 people lived in the city before the storm, whereas only 187,525 lived there in the fall of 2006.[49] Entrepreneurs have flocked to New Orleans to buy as much property as they can while demand and prices are low.[50] These individuals hope to develop their acquired property, encourage rebirth in the city, and sell after increasing the property's value.[51] To promote this activity, the government demolished homes that were flooded beyond repair, hoping that clearing the land would incentivize new building thereon.[52] Nonetheless, redevelopment has been slow, at least in part because those who have the right to exclude these entrepreneurs from property have done so. Essentially, the immediate and unanticipated exodus of long-time residents from the city left some neighborhoods entirely vacant but still privately owned by former residents.[53] These landowners, though absent, possess exclusionary rights and can prevent entrepreneurs from buying their sub-plots and converting them into revenue-generating structures such as hotels, restaurants, and low-income housing.

Many neighborhoods in New Orleans meet Heller's definition of anticommons property because one property owner, often an evacuee, uses her exclusionary rights to prevent the entrepreneur who holds rights to the surrounding land from obtaining rights to the entire parcel and using the land to its full potential.[54] Similarly, just as evacuees prevent entrepreneurs from using the land, entrepreneurs exclude others from using the property by holding onto their accumulations in the hope of initiating a larger project once they secure the remaining parcels. As such, multiple owners, namely evacuees and entrepreneurs, possess exclusionary rights in the large parcel and prevent the use of the property. . . .

Does the author's theory about the anticommons make sense to you?

Unlike in Heller's various examples in which the excluder exercised her rights because of express disagreement over how property should be used, the primary excluding property owner in New Orleans often uses this exclusionary right passively and sometimes unknowingly. Often the owner has relocated to a different city with no plans as to when or whether to return. Thus, a property owner who no longer lives in New Orleans and may never return can hamper the city's redevelopment and economic progress by being unavailable to sell, or agree to a use of, property. Hoping to gain control of the larger plot and initiate a grander money-making project, the party who owns the surrounding land must leave the already acquired land undeveloped.[55] If a single owner could obtain a full bundle of rights to the entire property, that owner could put the property to its "socially optimal" use. Instead, several neighborhoods and whole portions of the city remain entirely deserted, and a tragedy of the anticommons persists. . . .

B. *Kelo* as a Solution to New Orleans's Tragedy of the Anticommons

By giving the government latitude to seize property from private citizens and ensure that such property is used in the public interest, the *Kelo* decision offered a potential solution to the tragedy of the anticommons in New Orleans.[56] When Heller suggested that governments provided a possible solution to such tragedies, he had a *Kelo*-like scenario in mind.[57] Under the authority granted by *Kelo*, the government could take property from private individuals in New Orleans and give it to developers because doing so would serve the public purpose by rejuvenating the local economy. To many, including those in Louisiana who favored the amendment to the state constitution, this was a frightening prospect; it essentially gave the government unlimited authority to take what belonged to someone if doing so would benefit society. Under Heller's theory of the anticommons, however, *Kelo* produced a result that Louisiana residents should have embraced. *Kelo* provided governments with the power to overcome the tragedy of the anticommons by consolidating rights in the hands of a single individual who can put the property to its socially optimal use. At least in the abstract, *Kelo* should have enabled development in New Orleans, just as it did in New London, Connecticut.

The factual similarities between *Kelo* and the current situation in New Orleans are striking. As in New London, the New Orleans economy is struggling and property could be put to a more economically beneficial use if consolidated in the hands of a single owner.[58] Like the developers in *Kelo*, entrepreneurs in New Orleans wait in the wings with plans to rejuvenate the area.[59] Finally, as in *Kelo*, a few individuals have prevented these entrepreneurs and governments from achieving their goals by holding onto their property.[60] Importantly, in *Kelo*, the homeowners who refused to sell, and consequently had their property seized under eminent domain, lived on those parcels; in many of the areas at issue in New Orleans, those landowners who have not sold to developers neither live on their land nor plan to return to it.[61]

Given these factual similarities, it seems probable that, under *Kelo*, a government could use eminent domain to overcome the tragedy of the anticommons in New Orleans. Such takings would serve a public purpose by generating economic development in struggling areas of the city. So long as the government could show that it had some plan for transferring the taken properties into the hands of parties who could put them to a publicly beneficial use, the Fifth Amendment would be satisfied, the rights could be consolidated into a usable bundle for entrepreneurs, and the tragedy of the anticommons would be overcome as they put the property to use.[62]

C. The Current Situation in Louisiana

Heller proposed two possible solutions to an existing tragedy of the anticommons: governments and markets.[63] However, neither governments nor markets acting alone can overcome the tragedy in New Orleans. The amendment to the state constitution ended any possibility that the government could involve itself directly in consolidating property rights. Markets never provided a realistic solution to the tragedy because, in a complex and mobile society where multiple parties possess exclusionary rights in land parcels, high transaction costs prevent efficient bargaining, which, in turn, prevents the consolidation of rights into a usable bundle. The reality of post-hurricane New Orleans ensures that neither of these solutions will succeed independently.

1. Governments Are No Longer a Solution to the Tragedy in Louisiana

The constitutional amendment adopted in Louisiana ended any hope of government using *Kelo*-granted authority to consolidate property rights into a usable bundle.[64] The quick and dramatic response of the Louisiana legislature and citizenry that eliminated this possible solution to the tragedy would not surprise Heller in the least; in fact, he predicted as much. He anticipated that governments would experience difficulty in overcoming the tragedy because of "the cost and administrative complexity of compensation and the fear of demoralizing potential investors by reforming property rights without compensation."[65]

While Heller accurately predicted that government intervention would not succeed in solving the tragedy of the anticommons because of public resistance,[66] his assumption that property owners would act rationally[67] caused him to overlook a major reason for that resistance. Heller focused on compensation and future investors while ignoring the primary reason that people resist government use of eminent domain: the so-called "endowment effect." The endowment effect occurs when sellers demand higher prices than they would be willing to pay to purchase the same item from someone else.[68]

Compensation is always an issue with government takings; however, the problem is especially complicated in New Orleans. With the endowment effect in mind, it is unlikely that landowners in New Orleans would willingly allow the government to take control of their property even in exchange for outrageously high compensation. The people of New Orleans have already lost so much because of the storm that they would likely refuse to give anything they can still call their own to the government, especially because many blame the government for bungling the post-hurricane relief efforts.[69] Similarly, those observing this situation from outside of New Orleans likely fear granting the government such broad eminent domain power because of its potential future impact on their lives—a problem exacerbated by the endowment effect. Put simply, the endowment effect transforms property owners into irrational actors. . . .

2. Markets Are Not a Solution to the Tragedy in Louisiana

Markets likely never offered a viable solution to the tragedy in Louisiana. Heller stated that a society trying to overcome an existing tragedy of the anticommons faces difficulties that usually preclude markets from serving as a solution, including high transaction costs.[70] . . .

. . . In New Orleans, identifying those with whom one must bargain to consolidate rights through the property records should be manageable.[71] Locating those individuals, however, will not be easy. . . . [M]any of New Orleans's property owners no longer live on or near their property. Additionally, most of those displaced by the storm left unexpectedly and without planning, leaving no indication of their intended destinations. . . . [T]hose in New Orleans seeking to overcome the tragedy of the anticommons and put property to its full use must locate individuals who reside throughout the country. In many cases, the transaction costs involved in the location effort alone would be monumental. Add the costs of bargaining with an irrational owner over property that may be one of the only things the owner has left to her name, and it becomes evident that those looking to spark growth in New Orleans cannot rely on markets to overcome the tragedy of the anticommons.

In sum, Heller accurately forecasted many of the difficulties that prevent societies from overcoming an existing tragedy of the anticommons. Because New Orleans cannot overcome the tragedy by either of Heller's proposed methods, the city must resort to unexplored measures if it hopes to fulfill President Bush's promise of being "rebuilt . . . even better and stronger than before the storm."[72] . . .

V. CONCLUSION

The disasters that befell New Orleans during the hurricane season of 2005 revealed the tragedy of the anticommons. Many areas of the city remain undeveloped two years after Hurricanes Katrina and Rita hit the coast. To date, homeowners' exclusionary rights have prevented entrepreneurs from putting a given piece of property to use. As with other anticommons tragedies, property continues to go under-used or completely unused in the afflicted areas of the city. Overcoming the tragedy requires a consolidation of property rights in the hands of one owner so that she can redevelop the land to a socially optimal level.

Because neither of Heller's proffered paths to consolidation is available to New Orleans, the city must resort to unexplored measures to overcome its tragedy. Transaction costs prevent individuals from bundling rights themselves, precluding a purely market-driven solution. *Kelo* gave government the power to eliminate exclusionary rights through eminent domain, and eminent domain was considered in areas such as the Ninth Ward in New Orleans,[73] but an amendment to the state constitution passed in the fall of 2006 ended any possibility of government using this power to bundle rights. Because putting abandoned property to use is a key step in sparking economic progress in New Orleans, the government must enable individuals to overcome the tragedy by attacking the transaction costs that individuals typically encounter in trying to consolidate rights by themselves. . . .

END NOTES

1. Michael A. Heller, *The Tragedy of the Anticommons: Property in the Transition from Marx to Markets,* 111 HARV. L. REV. 621 (1998).
2. Michael A. Heller, *The Boundaries of Private Property*, 108 YALE L.J. 1163, 1165 (1999) ("Hidden within the law, however, is a boundary principle that limits the right to subdivide private property into wasteful fragments.").
3. *Id.* at 1170–72.
4. Heller, *supra* note 1, at 622. *See generally* Garrett Hardin, *The Tragedy of the Commons*, 168 SCIENCE 1243, 1244 (1968) (introducing the concept of the "tragedy of the commons").
5. Heller, *supra* note 1, at 622.
6. *Id.*
7. *Id.* at 668.
8. *Id.* at 624.
9. *Id.* at 677.

10. *Id.* at 640.
11. 545 U.S. 469 (2005); *see* U.S. CONST. AMEND. V ("Private property [shall not] be taken for public use, without just compensation."). *Kelo* remains the authoritative case on eminent domain, as the Court recently denied a petition for writ of certiorari in another takings clause case. Didden v. Village of Port Chester, 173 F. App'x 931 (2d Cir. 2006), cert. denied, 127 S. Ct. 1127 (2007). For a general discussion of eminent domain, see BLACK'S LAW DICTIONARY 562 (8th ed. 2004), which defines eminent domain (also called "condemnation" or "expropriation") as "the inherent power of a governmental entity to take privately owned property . . . and convert it to public use, subject to reasonable compensation for the taking."
12. *Kelo*, 545 U.S. at 474, 480–86.
13. *Id.* at 480.
14. *Id.* at 494 (O'Connor, J., dissenting).
15. LA. CONST. ART. I, § 4 (amended 2006).
16. John Kramer & Lisa Knepper, *Louisiana Ratifies Eminent Domain Reform*, CASTLE COALITION, Oct. 4, 2006, http://www.castlecoalition.org/media/releases/10 4 06pr.html.
17. *Id.*; Mark Ballard, *Property Proposal's Supporters Claim Radio Turned Tide*, ADVOCATE (Baton Rouge), Oct. 2, 2006, at A4.
18. Shaheen Pasha, *Property Grabs and the Gulf*, CNN/MONEY, Oct. 5, 2005, http://money.cnn.com/2005/10/05/news/economy/eminentdomain katrina/index.htm.
19. Linda Greenhouse, *Justices Decline to Take Up New Eminent Domain Case*, N.Y. TIMES, Jan. 17, 2007, at A16.
20. Ballard, *supra* note 17.
21. *See id.* (describing campaign by attorney Paul Loy Hurd of Monroe in the three weeks preceding the vote as aimed at convincing Louisianans that the amendment was a "Trojan Horse" that would expand the government's eminent domain powers because of its vague language).
22. Heller, *supra* note 1.
23. Kelo v. City of New London, 545 U.S. 469 (2005).
24. LA. CONST. ART. I, § 4 (amended 2006).
25. *See, e.g.*, Abraham Bell & Gideon Parchomovsky, *A Theory of Property*, 90 CORNELL L. REV. 531, 533 n.4 (citing Heller's article as one of "[a] number of recent articles [that has] been distinguished by their excellence and the importance of their contributions to the revival of property").
26. For a general discussion of the tragedy of the commons, see Hardin, *supra* note 4.
27. Heller, *supra* note 1, at 622.
28. *Id.* at 668; *see* Kaiser Aetna v. United States, 444 U.S. 164, 176 (1979) (asserting that the right to exclude others is "one of the most essential

sticks in the bundle of rights that are commonly characterized as property"); Wesley N. Hohfeld, *Some Fundamental Legal Conceptions as Applied in Judicial Reasoning*, 23 YALE L.J. 16, 22–23 (1913) (characterizing property as legal relations between and among legal subjects); Thomas Ross, *Metaphor and Paradox*, 23 GA. L. REV. 1053, 1055–56 (1989) (noting that the concept of property has changed from a theory of "thing ownership" to that of a "bundle of sticks").

29. *See* Heller, *supra* note 1, at 667–69 (explaining that the previous definitions of Michelman, Dukeminier, and Krier, which claimed an anticommons existed only when all owners possessed rights to exclude all others, prevented those scholars from identifying a real-world anticommons).
30. *Id.* at 677.
31. *Id.* at 659.
32. *Id.* at 678.
33. *Id.* at 640.
34. *Id.*
35. *Id.* at 640–41 ("In a legal transaction, a property bundler would buy each right from its holder through formal, enforceable contracts. In the storefront example . . . negotiations may only be possible through informal or corrupt channels. Over time, these corrupt channels can be routinized and may replace legal transactions.").
36. *Id.* at 641.
37. *Id.* at 625.
38. *Id.* at 625–26.
39. *Id.* at 679.
40. *Id.*
41. LA. CONST. ART. I, § 4 (amended 2006).
42. *See* Letter to Editor, *We Support Amendment 5*, ADVOCATE (Baton Rouge), Sept. 20, 2006, at B6 ("The proposed amendment . . . was written in response to the Kelo decision. . . .").
43. LA. CONST. ART. II, § 4 (amended 2006).
44. U.S. Const. amend. V; La. Const. art. I, § 4 (amended 2006).
45. LA. CONST. ART. I, § 4 (amended 2006). The amendment makes other changes to § 4 of the Louisiana Constitution that are less relevant to this article. *Id.*
46. *Kelo*, 545 U.S. at 501 (O'Connor, J., dissenting).
47. Heller, *supra* note 1, at 668, 677.
48. Adam Nossiter, *New Orleans Population is Reduced Nearly 60%*, N.Y. TIMES, Oct. 7, 2006, at A9.
49. *Id.*
50. *See* Karen Turni Bazile, *Recovery Forum Held in St. Bernard: Residents Blast Lack of Key Home Advice*, TIMES-PICAYUNE (New Orleans), Feb. 24, 2006, at 1 (describing the St. Bernard Citizens Recovery Committee's plan to encourage growth by buying out destroyed homes

and providing new house construction); Michelle Krupa, *Corps Offers Buyouts in Lakeview; Land Near Breach Used for Protection*, TIMES-PICAYUNE (New Orleans), May 28, 2006, at 1 (describing the outrage of homeowners whose land the Army Corps of Engineers targeted to buy and then use to provide more flood protection to the city); Allen Powell II, *Condo Project in the Works; Plan Also Features 204 Apartments*, TIMES-PICAYUNE (New Orleans), Feb. 25, 2006, at 1 (mentioning that Property One has accelerated its efforts to buy out Belle Promenade and redevelop it because it expects the housing market to "boom in the near future"); Editorial, *Redevelopment by Default?*, TIMES-PICAYUNE (New Orleans), June 11, 2006, at 6 (discussing the guidance needed by "people who've been bought out of flooded neighborhoods); Molly Reid, *Filling in the Spaces: Developers Hope to Jumpstart Neighborhood Recovery By Building Multiple Homes*, TIMES-PICAYUNE (New Orleans), September 9, 2006, at 1 (claiming that the hope of making a profit is the driving force behind individual bargain-seekers, developers, and organizations who are buying up properties in New Orleans); Greg Thomas, *Home Prices Take Off After Katrina; Average Prices Up 21% Throughout N.O. Area*, TIMES-PICAYUNE (New Orleans), Feb. 19, 2006, at 1 (mentioning that investors are attempting to buy property that is ripe for rebuilding).

51. Kathleen M. Howley, *New Orleans House "Flippers' Reap Profit*, SPUR CITY'S REBOUND, June 22, 2006, http://www.bloomberg.com/apps/news?pid=10000103&sid=aDJNcGOCW9rk &refer=us (describing the thousands of homes in New Orleans that have already been "flipped," i.e., bought cheaply after being damaged by the storm, repaired, and resold for a profit).
52. Michelle Krupa & Coleman Warner, *Across South, Displaced Chime In With Own Ideas for Rebuilding N.O.; But Residents Hesitate On the Tough Calls*, TIMES-PICAYUNE (New Orleans), December 3, 2006, at 1 (describing the city's response to relocating those residents who have been bought out of their flooded-out neighborhoods as unorganized and ineffective).
53. William Douglas & Chris Adams, *President Accepts Blame in Big Easy: Bush Praises the City's Progress and Pleads for its Previous Residents to Return,* ORLANDO SENTINEL, Aug. 30, 2006, at A10.
54. *See* Reid, *supra* note 50.
55. *See supra* text accompanying note 54.
56. *See supra* Part I.
57. Heller, *supra* note 1, at 640–41.
58. Kelo v. City of New London, 545 U.S. 469, 472–74 (2005).
59. *Id.* at 473–74.
60. *Id.* at 475.
61. *Id.*

62. *Id.* at 483 (noting that the government's exercise of eminent domain in *Kelo* satisfies the Fifth Amendment because "the City has carefully formulated an economic development plan that it believes will provide appreciable benefits to the community, including . . . new jobs and increased tax revenue").
63. Heller, *supra* note 1, at 640.
64. LA. CONST. ART. I, § 4 (amended 2006).
65. Heller, *supra* note 1, at 679.
66. "Once anticommons property is created, markets or governments may have difficulty in assembling rights into usable bundles. After initial entitlements are set, institutions and interests coalesce around them with the result that the path to private property may be blocked and scarce resources may be wasted." *Id.* at 659.
67. "The tragedy [of the anticommons] is that rational individuals, acting separately, may collectively waste the resource by underconsuming it compared with a social optimum. *Id.* at 677.
68. Christine Jolls, Cass R. Sunstein & Richard Thaler, *A Behavioral Approach to Law and Economics*, 50 STAN. L. REV. 1471, 1484 (1998).
69. *See* David Brooks, Op-Ed., *The Best-Laid Plan; Too Bad It Flopped*, N.Y. TIMES, Sept. 11, 2005, at 414 (arguing that the "government managed to fail at every level" in response to Hurricane Katrina); Christopher Lee & Anushka Asthana, *Damage and Doubts Linger After Katrina; Study Cites Wide Skepticism of U.S. Readiness for This Year's Hurricane Season*, WASH. POST, Aug. 21, 2006, at A13 (stating that seventy percent of those surveyed said most individuals still have not gotten the help they need with housing, health care and restoring their lives; fifty-six percent said that the federal government has not done enough to help state and local governments restore services in the affected areas; and fifty-three percent said that the government's handling of the hurricane had a negative impact on their confidence in government overall); Adam Nossiter, *In the Trail of the Storm: Little Is Left But Stillness*, N.Y. TIMES, June 15, 2006, at A16 (quoting one Katrina victim's experience of the devastation of the hurricanes: "I lost everything, man.").
70. Heller, *supra* note 1, at 679.
71. *See* Fred A. Bernstein, *The New Orleans Market is Poised to Recover*, N.Y. TIMES, Nov. 13, 2005, at 9 (reporting that although property records were unavailable for months after the storm, they are once again available, and the real estate market in New Orleans has exploded over the past year); *see also* Steve Ritea, *Nearly 50 New Orleans Public Schools Devastated*, TIMES-PICAYUNE (New Orleans), Nov. 20, 2005, at 1 (describing the situation that has forced schools to go to City Hall and carefully scrutinize the property records, many of which incurred water damage during Katrina and were sent to Massachusetts to be

freeze-dried); Greg Thomas, *Flooded Property Records Can Be Saved, Official Says; And They'll Be Moved From Court Basement*, TIMES-PICAYUNE (New Orleans), Sept. 13, 2005, at A3 ("Stored in the courthouse basement, which took on nearly a foot of water during Hurricane Katrina, moisture was the biggest enemy to property records. Abstractors, who conduct title searches before a real estate transaction closes, should have access to them within the next few weeks. . . .").

72. *Address to the Nation on Hurricane Katrina Recovery From New Orleans, Louisiana,* 40 WEEKLY COMP. PRES. DOC. 1405, 1407 (Sept. 19, 2005).
73. Shaheen Pasha, *Property Grabs and the Gulf*, CNN/MONEY, Oct. 5, 2005, http://money.cnn.com/2005/10/05/news/economy/eminentdomain katrina/index.htm.

ISSUE SUMMARY

Collectively, the articles in this section may seem somewhat unrelated; however, note the common assumption underlying each of the arguments—private property is an important institution and the government's power to interfere with the institution should be limited. The authors disagree about the extent to which the government should be limited and how public use and public benefit should be defined.

Also, all the authors agree that certain types of eminent domain are clearly within the government's power. Taking private property for highways or public schools is a well-accepted use of eminent domain. One needs to consider why these uses of eminent domain are readily accepted but using eminent domain for economic redevelopment is more controversial.

ISSUE HIGHLIGHTS

- Judicial standards for eminent domain seem to be changing.
- Some uses of eminent domain are generally well accepted by legal scholars and courts.
- The *Kelo* decision has important implications beyond straightforward eminent domain—regulatory takes, as well as economic and political dynamics, seem to be affected as well.

CRITICAL THINKING

Obviously, the decision in *Kelo* and the power of eminent domain are controversial. Given the ambiguity of the language of the "Takings Clause" "private property [shall not] be taken for public use, without just compensation." "Public use" does not have a clear meaning. As the articles demonstrate, some have interpreted public use to refer to the direct ability of the public to use the property taken under eminent domain. Others have interpreted public use to mean something along the lines of something indirectly useful to the public either in the form of job creation, economic redevelopment, or tax revenues.

Another important critical thinking issue that arises in the discussion of eminent domain are issues of value conflicts. Consider what values one would hold to support the broader eminent domain interpretation. What values would one hold to argue against the *Kelo* decision and expansions of eminent domain?

ADDITIONAL READINGS

"Eminent Domain." International Economic Development Council. Available at http://www.iedconline.org/?p=eminent_domain

"Eminent Domain" Expert Law. Available at http://www.expertlaw.com/library/real_estate/eminent_domain.html

Hellegers, Adam. "Eminent Domain as an Economic Development Tool. L. Rev. M.S.U.-D.C.L. 901

Jones, Sonya. "That Land Is Your Land, This Land Is My Land . . . Until the Local Government Can Turn It for a Profit: A Critical Analysis of *Kelo v. City of New London*," 20 BYU J. Pub. L. 139 (2005). Available at http://www.law2.byu.edu/jpl/Vol%2020.1/5Jones.pdf

Mihaly, Marc. "Living in the Past" 34 Ecology L.Q. 1 (2007). Available at http://www.vjel.org/journal/pdf/VJEL10036.pdf

Sightline Institute, Two Years Of Measure 37: Oregon's Property Wrongs, February 2007. Available at http://www.sightline.org/research/sprawl/res_pubs/property-fairness/measure-37-report/two-years-m37-report

ISSUE 9

Who Should Be Sued When Many People Are Involved in a Securities Fraud?

Ever since the public became aware of the major corporate scandals at corporations such as Enron and World Com, the issue of corporate liability for securities fraud has grown in importance. Because these scandals involved multiple parties, and injured huge numbers of people, questions of liability quickly became complex. One method for attributing liability to third parties involved in these scandals was the concept of "scheme liability." Scheme liability involves holding a wide range of third parties legally liable for damages suffered due to false statements and intentional misrepresentations that are used to erroneously boost stock prices. The "scheme" in scheme liability means that a third party aided another party in the other party's fraud, while the third party did not directly make a misrepresentation to the public. Scheme liability is based on § 10(b) of the Securities Exchange Act of 1934 and SEC Rule 10b-5.

While the idea of scheme liability gained much public attention in the aftermath of Enron, the issue had made its way before the Supreme Court prior to Enron's collapse. In 1994 the Supreme Court heard the case *Central Bank v. Interstate Bank*. In *Central Bank* the Supreme Court ruled that third parties must be guilty of all of the elements of securities fraud if the third parties are to be held primarily liable. Furthermore, the Court stated that § 10(b) of the Securities Exchange Act of 1934 and SEC Rule 10b-5 do not automatically extend liability to those who aid a party in its manipulative or deceptive act. The *Central Bank* ruling proved to be far from clear and straightforward and provoked much legal debate regarding the legality of scheme liability. Many of the selections in this chapter discuss the meaning of *Central Bank* and how the Court's opinion helps to shape views regarding the legality of scheme liability.

The first selection in this chapter is from the most recent Supreme Court case to broach this issue. In *Stoneridge Investment Partners v. Scientific-Atlanta, Inc.*, the Supreme Court ruled in a 5–3 opinion that for a third party to be found liable under the concept of scheme liability, the third party must actively engage in the fraudulent behavior. Here, to actively engage in the fraudulent behavior the third party must make a misstatement that the public relies upon in purchasing securities, and this misstatement must affect the price of the securities. Included in this chapter is also Justice Stevens's dissenting opinion, where he argues that Justice Kennedy and the majority are mistaken, and that the requirements for scheme liability are not as stringent as Justice Kennedy insists. The reasoned arguments of both justices help to illustrate the contentious nature of the debate regarding scheme liability, as well as how the Court's opinion is unlikely to conclusively settle the debate.

In his article included in this chapter, Daniel A. McLaughlin argues that § 10(b) of the Securities Exchange Act of 1934 and SEC Rule 10b-5 do not extend scheme liability to third parties. McLaughlin examines legislative history and court precedent to determine that the relevant sections of the Securities and Exchange Act of 1934 do not extend to third parties that do not active make misrepresentations against parties to whom the third parties owe a duty of care. Any application of scheme liability to hold third parties primarily liable, McLaughlin argues, cannot be rectified with Supreme Court precedent. Therefore, scheme liability is never appropriate.

Andrew S. Gold, in his article, discusses the confusion that has ensued in the lower courts since the Supreme Court's ruling in *Central Bank*. While the Court in *Central Bank* stated that third parties may be held primarily liable when all of the conditions of securities fraud are met, the Court failed to clearly explain when these conditions are met. In particular, the Court in *Central Bank* did not address scheme liability, and the lower courts have been split applying either a "bright line" test or a "participation" test. Gold runs through both tests and explains that the participation test, which supports scheme liability, falls short of Supreme Court precedent. Accordingly, Gold believes that the bright line test is the appropriate application of case law and statute to determine when third parties can be liable for securities fraud under scheme liability. For Gold, scheme liability is inconsistent with existing law.

In the next article, much like Gold, Mark Pincus focuses on the disagreement in the lower courts regarding the proper application of scheme liability to third parties. Also like Gold, Pincus indicates that there are two main trends in the lower courts: a narrow reading of § 10(b) of the Securities Exchange Act of 1934 and SEC Rule 10b-5 that excludes scheme liability, and a broader reading that allows for scheme liability. Pincus then argues that much of the disagreement between lower courts preferring one approach to the other is merely semantics. For Pincus, much of the same behavior is disallowed under both the broad and narrow interpretations offered by the lower courts. However, Pincus believes that without a duty of care and an active misrepresentation by a third party, the third party is unlikely to be held liable under scheme liability regardless of which approach the court may take. Despite his limited view of scheme liability, Pincus argues that those who orchestrate and use tax shelters will be found liable under scheme liability.

While the articles and case in this chapter demonstrate a general confusion regarding the application of § 10(b) of the Securities Exchange Act of 1934 and SEC Rule 10b-5, a useful exercise is to consider the intent of these rules. Instead of focusing on the specific meaning of the relevant laws, think about the underlying purpose of scheme liability. When you read the selections for this chapter, ask yourself, "What is it that scheme liability tries to accomplish? Who would the scheme liability benefit? Who would it harm? What are the legal reasons for and against an application of scheme liability to third parties?" By asking the above questions, the desirability (or lack thereof) of scheme liability can illuminate a debate that, as presented here, tends to focus on technical legal questions regarding the applicability of scheme liability. Remember, there is more to the law than rules and procedures, as all legal decisions have an impact on people's lives.

ISSUE ARTICLES

Stoneridge Investment Partners, LLC. v. Scientific-Atlanta, Inc., 128 S.Ct. 761 (2008).

Daniel A McLaughlin, "Liability Under Rules 10b-5(a) & (c)," 31 *Delaware Journal of Corporate Law,* 631 (2006).

Andrew S. Gold, "Reassessing the Scope of Conduct Prohibited by Section 10(b) and the Elements Rule 10b-5: Reflections on Securities Fraud and Secondary Actors," 53 *Catholic University Law Review*, 667 (2004).

Mark S. Pincus, "Circuit Split or a Matter of Semantics? The Supreme Court's Upcoming Decision on Rule 10b-5 "Scheme Liability" and Its Implications for Tax Shelter Fraud Litigation," 76 *Fordham Law Review*, 423 (2007).

ARTICLE 9.1

Stoneridge Investment Partners, LLC. v. Scientific-Atlanta, Inc.

Charter Communications, Inc., a cable operator, engaged in a variety of fraudulent practices to make its quarterly reports appear to meet Wall Street expectations for cable subscriber growth and operating cash flow. Despite the multiple fraudulent practices, Charter executives realized the company would still miss projected operating cash flow numbers. To help meet the shortfall, Charter decided to enter into an arrangement with Scientific-Atlanta and Motorola.

What actions did Scientific-Atlantic and Motorola take that caused the shareholders to attempt to impose liability on them when they had no direct contact with the shareholders?

Scientific-Atlanta and Motorola supplied Charter with the digital cable converter (set top) boxes that Charter furnished to its customers. Charter arranged to overpay Scientific-Atlanta and Motorola $20 for each set top box it purchased until the end of the year, with the understanding that the companies would return the overpayment by purchasing advertising from Charter. The transactions, it is alleged, had no economic substance; but, because Charter would then record the advertising purchases as revenue and capitalize its purchase of the set top boxes, in violation of generally accepted accounting principles, the transactions would enable Charter to fool its auditor into approving a financial statement showing it met projected revenue and operating cash flow numbers.

To hide the connections between the advertisement and the purchases of the set top boxes, the companies drafted documents to make it appear the transactions were unrelated and conducted in the ordinary course of business. Scientific-Atlanta and Motorola had no role in preparing or disseminating Charter's financial statements. And their own financial statements booked the transactions as a wash, under generally accepted accounting principles. It is alleged that Scientific-Atlanta and Motorola knew or were in reckless disregard of Charter's intention to use the transactions to inflate its revenues and knew the resulting financial statements issued by Charter would be relied upon by research analysts and investors.

Stoneridge Investment Partners, LLC. filed a securities fraud class action on behalf of purchasers of Charter stock alleging that, by participating in the transactions, Scientific-Atlanta and Motorola violated § 10(b) of the Securities Exchange Act of 1934 and SEC Rule 10b-5. The District Court granted Scientific-Atlanta's and Motorola's motion to dismiss for failure to state a claim on which relief can be granted. The United States Court of Appeals for the Eighth Circuit affirmed. Stoneridge appealed to the Supreme Court.

JUSTICE KENNEDY

II

Section 10(b) of the Securities Exchange Act makes it

> "unlawful for any person, directly or indirectly, by the use of any means or instrumentality of interstate commerce or of the mails, or of any facility of any national securities exchange . . . to use or employ, in connection with the purchase or sale of any security . . . any manipulative or deceptive device or contrivance in contravention of such rules and regulations as the Commission may prescribe as necessary or appropriate in the public interest or for the protection of investors." 15 U.S.C. § 78j.

The SEC, pursuant to this section, promulgated Rule 10b-5, which makes it unlawful

> "(a) To employ any device, scheme, or artifice to defraud,
> "(b) To make any untrue statement of a material fact or to omit to state a material fact necessary in order to make the statements made, in the light of the circumstances under which they were made, not misleading, or
> "(c) To engage in any act, practice, or course of business which operates or would operate as a fraud or deceit upon any person, "in connection with the purchase or sale of any security." 17 CFR § 240.10b-5.

Rule 10b-5 encompasses only conduct already prohibited by § 10(b). . . . Though the text of the Securities Exchange Act does not provide for a private cause of action for § 10(b) violations, the Court has found a right of action implied in the words of the statute and its implementing regulation. *Superintendent of Ins. of N. Y. v. Bankers Life & Casualty Co.*, 404 U.S. 6, 13, n. 9, 92 S. Ct. 165, 30 L. Ed. 2d 128 (1971). In a typical § 10(b) private action a plaintiff must prove (1) a material misrepresentation or omission by the defendant; (2) scienter; (3) a connection between the misrepresentation or omission and the purchase or sale of a security; (4) reliance upon the misrepresentation or omission; (5) economic loss; and (6) loss causation. . . .

In *Central Bank*, the Court determined that § 10(b) liability did not extend to aiders and abettors. The Court found the scope of § 10(b) to be delimited by the text, which makes no mention of aiding and abetting liability. . . . The Court doubted the implied § 10(b) action should extend to aiders and abettors when none of the express causes of action in the securities Acts included that liability. . . .

The decision in *Central Bank* led to calls for Congress to create an express cause of action for aiding and abetting within the Securities Exchange Act. Then-SEC Chairman Arthur Levitt, testifying before the Senate Securities Subcommittee, cited *Central Bank* and recommended that aiding and abetting liability in private claims be established. . . . Congress did not follow this course. Instead, in § 104 of the Private Securities Litigation Reform Act of 1995 (PSLRA), 109 Stat. 757, it directed prosecution of aiders and abettors by the SEC. 15 U.S.C. § 78t(e).

The § 10(b) implied private right of action does not extend to aiders and abettors. The conduct of a secondary actor must satisfy each of the elements or preconditions for liability; and we consider whether the allegations here are sufficient to do so.

III

The Court of Appeals concluded petitioner had not alleged that respondents engaged in a deceptive act within the reach of the § 10(b) private right of action, noting that only misstatements, omissions by one who has a duty to disclose, and manipulative trading practices (where "manipulative" is a term of art, see, e.g., *Santa Fe Industries, Inc. v. Green*, 430 U.S. 462, 476–477, 97 S. Ct. 1292, 51 L. Ed. 2d 480 (1977)) are deceptive within the meaning of the rule. . . . If this conclusion were read to suggest there must be a specific oral or written statement before there could be liability under § 10(b) or Rule 10b-5, it would be erroneous. Conduct itself can be deceptive, as respondents concede. In this case, moreover, respondents' course of conduct included both oral and written statements, such as the backdated contracts agreed to by Charter and respondents.

A different interpretation of the holding from the Court of Appeals opinion is that the court was stating only that any deceptive statement or act respondents made was not actionable because it did not have the requisite proximate relation to the investors' harm. That conclusion is consistent with our own determination that respondents' acts or statements were not relied upon by the investors and that, as a result, liability cannot be imposed upon respondents.

A

Why did the court believe that reliance by the plaintiff on the defendant's deceptive acts was crucial to a finding of liability?

Reliance by the plaintiff upon the defendant's deceptive acts is an essential element of the § 10(b) private cause of action. It ensures that, for liability to arise, the "requisite causal connection between a defendant's misrepresentation and a plaintiff's injury" exists as a predicate for liability. . . . We have found a rebuttable presumption of reliance in two different circumstances. First, if there is an omission of a material fact by one with a duty to disclose, the investor to whom the duty was owed need not provide specific proof of reliance. . . . Second, under the fraud-on-the-market doctrine, reliance is presumed when the statements at issue become public. The public information is reflected in the market price of the security. Then it can be assumed that an investor who buys or sells stock at the market price relies upon the statement. . . .

Neither presumption applies here. Respondents had no duty to disclose; and their deceptive acts were not communicated to the public. No member of the investing public had knowledge, either actual or presumed, of respondents' deceptive acts during the relevant times. Petitioner, as a result, cannot show reliance upon any of respondents' actions except in an indirect chain that we find too remote for liability.

B

Invoking what some courts call "scheme liability," see, e.g., *In re Enron Corp. Secs. v. Enron Corp.*, 439 F. Supp. 2d 692, 723 (SD Tex. 2006), petitioner nonetheless seeks to impose liability on respondents even absent a public statement. In our view this approach does not answer the objection that petitioner did not in fact rely upon respondents' own deceptive conduct.

Liability is appropriate, petitioner contends, because respondents engaged in conduct with the purpose and effect of creating a false appearance of material fact to further a scheme to misrepresent Charter's revenue. The argument is that the financial statement Charter released to the public was a natural and expected consequence of respondents' deceptive acts; had respondents not assisted Charter, Charter's auditor would not have been fooled, and the financial statement would have been a more accurate reflection of Charter's financial condition. That causal link is sufficient, petitioner argues, to apply *Basic's* presumption of reliance to respondents' acts. *See, e.g., Simpson*, 452 F.3d at 1051–1052; *In re Parmalat Securities Litigation*, 376 F. Supp. 2d 472, 509 (SDNY 2005). . . .

As stated above, reliance is tied to causation, leading to the inquiry whether respondents' acts were immediate or remote to the injury. In considering petitioner's arguments, we note § 10(b) provides that the deceptive act must be "in connection with the purchase or sale of any security." 15 U.S.C. § 78j(b). Though this phrase in part defines the statute's coverage rather than causation (and so we do not evaluate the "in connection with" requirement of § 10(b) in this case), the emphasis on a purchase or sale of securities does provide some insight into the deceptive acts that concerned the enacting Congress. . . . In all events we conclude respondents' deceptive acts, which were not disclosed to the investing public, are too remote to satisfy the requirement of reliance. It was Charter, not respondents, that misled its auditor and filed fraudulent financial statements; nothing respondents did made it necessary or inevitable for Charter to record the transactions as it did.

The petitioner invokes the private cause of action under § 10(b) and seeks to apply it beyond the securities markets—the realm of financing business—to purchase and supply contracts—the realm of ordinary business operations. The latter realm is governed, for the most part, by state law. It is true that if business operations are used, as alleged here, to affect securities markets, the SEC enforcement power may reach the culpable actors. It is true as well that a dynamic, free economy presupposes a high degree of integrity in all of its parts, an integrity that must be underwritten by rules enforceable in fair, independent, accessible courts. Were the implied cause of action to be extended to the practices described here, however, there would be a risk that the federal power would be used to invite litigation beyond the immediate sphere of securities litigation and in areas already governed by functioning and effective state-law guarantees. Our precedents counsel against this extension. . . . Though § 10(b) is "not 'limited to preserving the integrity of the securities markets,'" . . . it does not reach all commercial transactions that are fraudulent and affect the price of a security in some attenuated way. . . .

Petitioner's theory, moreover, would put an unsupportable interpretation on Congress' specific response to *Central Bank* in § 104 of the PSLRA. Congress amended the securities laws to provide for limited coverage of aiders and abettors. Aiding and abetting liability is authorized in actions brought by the SEC but not by private parties. See 15 U.S.C. § 78t(e). Petitioner's view of primary liability makes any aider and abettor liable under § 10(b) if he or she committed a deceptive act in the process of providing assistance. . . . Were we to adopt this construction of § 10(b), it would revive in substance the implied cause of action against all aiders and abettors except those who committed no deceptive act in the process of facilitating the fraud; and we would undermine Congress' determination that this class of defendants should be pursued by the SEC and not by private litigants. . . .

This is not a case in which Congress has enacted a regulatory statute and then has accepted, over a long period of time, broad judicial authority to define substantive standards of conduct and liability. . . . And in accord with the nature of the cause of action at issue here, we give weight to Congress' amendment to the Act restoring aiding and abetting liability in certain cases but not others. The amendment, in our view, supports the conclusion that there is no liability.

The practical consequences of an expansion, which the Court has considered appropriate to examine in circumstances like these, see *Virginia Bankshares, Inc. v. Sandberg*, 501 U.S. 1083, 1104–1105, 111 S. Ct. 2749, 115 L. Ed. 2d 929 (1991); *Blue Chip*, 421 U.S., at 737, 95 S. Ct. 1917, 44 L. Ed. 2d 539, provide a further reason to reject petitioner's approach. In *Blue* Chip, the Court noted that extensive discovery and the potential for uncertainty and disruption in a lawsuit allow plaintiffs with weak claims to extort settlements from innocent companies. *Id.*, at 740–741, 95 S. Ct. 1917, 44 L. Ed. 2d 539. Adoption of petitioner's approach would expose a new class of defendants to these risks. As noted in *Central Bank*, contracting parties might find it necessary to protect against these threats, raising the costs of doing business. *See* 511 U.S., at 189, 114 S. Ct. 1439, 128 L. Ed. 2d 119. Overseas firms with no other exposure to our securities laws could be deterred from doing business here. . . . This, in turn, may raise the cost of being a publicly traded company under our law and shift securities offerings away from domestic capital markets. . . .

C

The history of the § 10(b) private right and the careful approach the Court has taken before proceeding without congressional direction provide further reasons to find no liability here. The § 10(b) private cause of action is a judicial construct that Congress did not enact in the text of the relevant statutes. . . . Though

What classes of parties benefit from what could be seen as the court's strict interpretation of the law in this case?

the rule once may have been otherwise, . . . it is settled that there is an implied cause of action only if the underlying statute can be interpreted to disclose the intent to create one. . . . This is for good reason. In the absence of congressional intent the Judiciary's recognition of an implied private right of action.

> "necessarily extends its authority to embrace a dispute Congress has not assigned it to resolve. This runs contrary to the established principle that 'the jurisdiction of the federal courts is carefully guarded against expansion by judicial interpretation . . .,' *American Fire & Casualty Co. v. Finn*, 341 U.S. 6, 17, 71 S. Ct. 534, 95 L. Ed. 702 (1951), and conflicts with the authority of Congress under Art. III to set the limits of federal jurisdiction." *Cannon v. University of Chicago*, 441 U.S. 677, 746, 99 S. Ct. 1946, 60 L. Ed. 2d 560 (1979) (Powell, J., dissenting) (citations and footnote omitted).

. . . Concerns with the judicial creation of a private cause of action caution against its expansion. The decision to extend the cause of action is for Congress, not for us. Though it remains the law, the § 10(b) private right should not be extended beyond its present boundaries. . . .

Congress thus ratified the implied right of action after the Court moved away from a broad willingness to imply private rights of action. . . . It is appropriate for us to assume that when § 78u-4 was enacted, Congress accepted the § 10(b) private cause of action as then defined but chose to extend it no further.

IV

Secondary actors are subject to criminal penalties, see, e.g., 15 U.S.C. § 78ff, and civil enforcement by the SEC, see, e.g., § 78t(e). The enforcement power is not toothless. Since September 30, 2002, SEC enforcement actions have collected over $10 billion in disgorgement and penalties, much of it for distribution to injured investors. . . . And in this case both parties agree that criminal penalties are a strong deterrent. . . . In addition some state securities laws permit state authorities to seek fines and restitution from aiders and abettors. . . . All secondary actors, furthermore, are not necessarily immune from private suit. The securities statutes provide an express private right of action against accountants and underwriters in certain circumstances, see 15 U.S.C. § 77k, and the implied right of action in § 10(b) continues to cover secondary actors who commit primary violations. *Central Bank, supra*, at 191, 114 S. Ct. 1439, 128 L. Ed. 2d 119.

Here respondents were acting in concert with Charter in the ordinary course as suppliers and, as matters then evolved in the not so ordinary course, as customers. Unconventional as the arrangement was, it took place in the marketplace for goods and services, not in the investment sphere. Charter was free to do as it chose in preparing its books, conferring with its auditor, and preparing and then issuing its financial statements. In these circumstances the investors cannot be said to have relied upon any of respondents' deceptive acts in the decision to purchase or sell securities; and as the requisite reliance cannot be shown, respondents have no liability to petitioner under the implied right of action. This conclusion is consistent with the narrow dimensions we must give to a right of action Congress did not authorize when it first enacted the statute and did not expand when it revisited the law.

The judgment of the Court of Appeals is affirmed, and the case is remanded for further proceedings consistent with this opinion.

It is so ordered.

JUSTICE BREYER took no part in the consideration or decision of this case.

JUSTICE STEVENS, DISSENTING (JOINED BY JUSTICES SOUTER AND GINSBURG)

Charter Communications, Inc., inflated its revenues by $17 million in order to cover up a $15 to $20 million expected cash flow shortfall. It could not have done so absent the knowingly fraudulent actions of Scientific-Atlanta, Inc., and Motorola, Inc. Investors relied on Charter's revenue statements in deciding whether to invest in Charter and in doing so relied on respondents' fraud, which was itself a "deceptive device" prohibited by § 10(b) of the Securities Exchange Act of 1934. 15 U.S.C. § 78j(b). This is enough to satisfy the requirements of § 10(b) and enough to distinguish this case from *Central Bank of Denver, N. A. v. First Interstate Bank of Denver*, N. A., 511 U.S. 164, 114 S. Ct. 1439, 128 L. Ed. 2d 119 (1994).

The Court seems to assume that respondents' alleged conduct could subject them to liability in an enforcement proceeding initiated by the Government, . . . but nevertheless concludes that they are not subject to liability in a private action brought by injured investors because they are, at most, guilty of aiding and abetting a violation of § 10(b), rather than an actual violation of the statute. While that conclusion results in an affirmance of the judgment of the Court of Appeals, it rests on a rejection of that court's reasoning. Furthermore, while the Court frequently refers to petitioner's attempt to "expand" the implied cause of action, . . . a conclusion that begs the question of the contours of that cause of action—it is today's decision that results in a significant departure from *Central Bank*.

The Court's conclusion that no violation of § 10(b) giving rise to a private right of action has been alleged in this case rests on two faulty premises: (1) the Court's overly broad reading of *Central Bank*, and (2) the view that reliance requires a kind of super-causation—a view contrary to both the Securities and Exchange Commission's (SEC) position in a recent Ninth Circuit case[1] and our holding in *Basic Inc. v. Levinson*, 485 U.S. 224, 108 S. Ct. 978, 99 L. Ed. 2d 194 (1988). These two points merit separate discussion.

I

The Court of Appeals incorrectly based its decision on the view that "[a] device or contrivance is not 'deceptive,' within the meaning of § 10(b), absent some misstatement or a failure to disclose by one who has a duty to disclose." *In re Charter Communications, Inc., Securities Litigation*, 443 F.3d 987, 992 (CA8 2006). The Court correctly explains why the statute covers nonverbal as well as verbal deceptive conduct. . . . The allegations in this case—that respondents produced documents falsely claiming costs had risen and signed contracts they knew to be backdated in order to disguise the connection between the increase in costs and the purchase of advertising—plainly describe "deceptive devices" under any standard reading of the phrase.

What the Court fails to recognize is that this case is critically different from *Central Bank* because the bank in that case did not engage in any deceptive act and, therefore, did not itself violate § 10(b). The Court sweeps aside any distinction, remarking that holding respondents liable would "revive the implied cause of action against all aiders and abettors except those who committed no deceptive act in the process of facilitating the fraud.". . . But the fact that *Central Bank* engaged in no deceptive conduct whatsoever—in other words, that it was at most an aider and abettor—sharply distinguishes *Central Bank* from cases that do involve allegations of such conduct. 511 U.S., at 167, 114 S. Ct. 1439, 128 L. Ed. 2d 119 (stating that the question presented was "whether private civil liability under § 10(b) extends as well to those who do not engage in the manipulative or deceptive practice, but who aid and abet the violation").

The Central Bank of Denver was the indenture trustee for bonds issued by a public authority and secured by liens on property in Colorado Springs. After default, purchasers of $2.1 million of those bonds sued the underwriters, alleging violations of § 10(b); they also named Central Bank as a defendant, contending that the bank's delay in reviewing a suspicious appraisal of the value of the security made it liable as an aider and abettor. . . . The facts of this case would parallel those of *Central Bank* if respondents had, for example, merely delayed sending invoices for set-top boxes to Charter. Conversely, the facts in *Central Bank* would mirror those in the case before us today if the bank had knowingly purchased real estate in wash transactions at above-market prices in order to facilitate the appraiser's overvaluation of the security. *Central Bank*, thus, poses no obstacle to petitioner's argument that it has alleged a cause of action under § 10(b).

II

The Court's next faulty premise is that petitioner is required to allege that Scientific-Atlanta and Motorola made it "necessary or inevitable for Charter to record the transactions in the way it did,". . . in order to demonstrate reliance. Because the Court of Appeals did not base its holding on reliance grounds, see 443 F.3d at 992, the fairest course to petitioner would be for the majority to remand to the Court of Appeals to determine whether petitioner properly alleged reliance, under a correct view of what § 10(b) covers.[2] Because the Court chooses to rest its holding on an absence of reliance, a response is required.

In *Basic Inc.*, 485 U.S., at 243, 108 S. Ct. 978, 99 L. Ed. 2d 194, we stated that "reliance provides the requisite causal connection between a defendant's misrepresentation and a plaintiff's injury." The Court's view of the causation required to demonstrate reliance is unwarranted and without precedent.

In *Basic Inc.*, we held that the "fraud-on-the-market" theory provides adequate support for a presumption in private securities actions that shareholders (or former shareholders) in publicly traded companies rely on public material misstatements that affect the price of the company's stock. . . . The holding in *Basic* is surely a sufficient response to the argument that a complaint alleging that deceptive acts which had a material effect on the price of a listed stock should be dismissed because the plaintiffs were not subjectively aware of the deception at the time of the securities' purchase or sale. This Court has not held that investors must be aware of the specific deceptive act which violates § 10b to demonstrate reliance.

The Court is right that a fraud-on-the-market presumption coupled with its view on causation would not support petitioner's view of reliance. The fraud-on-the-market presumption helps investors who cannot demonstrate that they, themselves, relied on fraud that reached the market. But that presumption says nothing about causation from the other side: what an individual or corporation must do in order to have "caused" the misleading information that reached the market. The Court thus has it backwards when it first addresses the fraud-on-the-market presumption, rather than the causation required. . . . The argument is not that the fraud-on-the-market presumption is enough standing alone, but that a correct view of causation coupled with the presumption would allow petitioner to plead reliance.

Lower courts have correctly stated that the causation necessary to demonstrate reliance is not a difficult hurdle to clear in a private right of action under § 10(b). Reliance is often equated with " 'transaction causation.' ". . . Transaction causation, in turn, is often defined as requiring an allegation that but for the deceptive act, the plaintiff would not have entered into the securities transaction. . . .

The Court's view of reliance is unduly stringent and unmoored from authority. The Court first says that if the petitioner's concept of reliance is adopted the implied cause of action "would reach the whole marketplace in which the issuing company does business.". . . The answer to that objection is, of course, that liability only attaches when the company doing business with the issuing company has itself violated § 10(b).[3] . . .

Finally, the Court relies on the course of action Congress adopted after our decision in *Central Bank* to argue that siding with petitioner on reliance would run contrary to congressional intent. Senate hearings on *Central Bank* were held within one month of our decision.[4] Less than one year later, Senators Dodd and Domenici introduced S. 240, which became the Private Securities Litigation Reform Act of 1995 (PSLRA), 109 Stat. 737.[5] Congress stopped short of undoing *Central Bank* entirely, instead adopting a compromise which restored the authority of the SEC to enforce aiding and abetting liability.[6] A private right of action based on aiding and abetting violations of § 10(b) was not, however, included in the PSLRA,[7] despite support from Senator Dodd and members of the Senate Subcommittee on Securities.[8] This compromise surely provides no support for extending *Central Bank* in order to immunize an undefined class of actual violators of § 10(b) from liability in private litigation. Indeed, as Members of Congress—including those who rejected restoring a private cause of action against aiders and abettors—made clear, private litigation under § 10(b) continues to play a vital role in protecting the integrity of our securities markets.[9] That Congress chose not to restore the aiding and abetting liability removed by *Central Bank* does not mean that Congress wanted to exempt from liability the broader range of conduct that today's opinion excludes.

The Court is concerned that such liability would deter overseas firms from doing business in the United States or "shift securities offerings away from domestic capital markets.". . . But liability for those who violate § 10(b) "will not harm American competitiveness; in fact, investor faith in the safety and integrity of our markets is their strength. The fact that our markets are the safest in the world has helped make them the strongest in the world." Brief for Former SEC Commissioners as Amici Curiae 9.

Accordingly, while I recognize that the *Central Bank* opinion provides a precedent for judicial policymaking decisions in this area of the law, I respectfully dissent from the Court's continuing campaign to render the private cause of action under § 10(b) toothless. I would reverse the decision of the Court of Appeals.

III

While I would reverse for the reasons stated above, I must also comment on the importance of the private cause of action that Congress implicitly authorized when it enacted the Securities Exchange Act of 1934. A theme that underlies the Court's analysis is its mistaken hostility towards the § 10(b) private cause of action.[10]. . . The Court's current view of implied causes of action is that they are merely a "relic" of our prior "heady days." *Correctional Services Corp. v. Malesko*, 534 U.S. 61, 75, 122 S. Ct. 515, 151 L. Ed. 2d 456 (2001) (SCALIA, J., concurring). Those "heady days" persisted for two hundred years.

During the first two centuries of this Nation's history much of our law was developed by judges in the common-law tradition. A basic principle animating our jurisprudence was enshrined in state constitution provisions guaranteeing, in substance, that "every wrong shall have a remedy."[11] . . . While it is true that in the early days state law was the source of most of those rules, throughout our history—until 1975—the same practice prevailed in federal courts with regard to federal statutes that left questions of remedy open for judges to answer. . . .

In a law-changing opinion written by Justice Brennan in 1975, the Court decided to modify its approach to private causes of action. *Cort v. Ash*, 422 U.S. 66, 95 S. Ct. 2080, 45 L. Ed. 2d 26 (constraining courts to use a strict four-factor test to determine whether Congress intended a private cause of action). A few years later, in *Cannon v. University of Chicago*, 441 U.S. 677, 99 S. Ct. 1946, 60 L. Ed. 2d 560 (1979), we adhered to the strict approach mandated by *Cort v. Ash* in 1975, but made it clear that "our evaluation of congressional action in 1972 must take into account its contemporary legal context." 441 U.S., at 698–699, 99 S. Ct. 1946, 60 L. Ed. 2d 560. That context persuaded the majority that Congress had intended the courts to authorize a private remedy for members of the protected class.

Until *Central Bank*, the federal courts continued to enforce a broad implied cause of action for the violation of statutes enacted in 1933 and 1934 for the protection of investors. . . .

In light of the history of court-created remedies and specifically the history of implied causes of action under § 10(b), the Court is simply wrong when it states that Congress did not impliedly authorize this private cause of action "when it first enacted the statute." . . . Courts near in time to the enactment of the securities laws recognized that the principle in *Rigsby* applied to the securities laws.[12] Congress enacted § 10(b) with the understanding that federal courts respected the principle that every wrong would have a remedy. Today's decision simply cuts back further on Congress' intended remedy. I respectfully dissent.

END NOTES

1. *See* Brief for SEC as Amicus Curiae in *Simpson v. AOL Time Warner Inc.*, No. 04-55665 (CA9), p. 21 ("The reliance requirement is satisfied where a plaintiff relies on a material deception flowing from a defendant's deceptive act, even though the conduct of other participants in the fraudulent scheme may have been a subsequent link in the causal chain leading to the plaintiff's securities transaction").
2. Though respondents did argue to the Court of Appeals that reliance was lacking, see Brief for Appellee Motorola, Inc., in No. 05-1974 (CA8), p. 15, that argument was quite short and was based on an erroneously broad reading of *Central Bank of Denver, N. A. v. First Interstate Bank of*

Denver, N. A., 511 U.S. 164, 114 S. Ct. 1439, 128 L. Ed. 2d 119 (1994), as discussed, supra, at 3 and this page. The Court of Appeals mentioned reliance only once, stating that respondents "did not issue any misstatement relied upon by the investing public." 443 F.3d at 992. Furthermore, that statement was made in the context of the Court of Appeals' holding that a deceptive act must be a misstatement or omission—a holding which the Court unanimously rejects.

3. Because the kind of sham transactions alleged in this complaint are unquestionably isolated departures from the ordinary course of business in the American marketplace, it is hyperbolic for the Court to conclude that petitioner's concept of reliance would authorize actions "against the entire marketplace in which the issuing company operates." . . .
4. *See* S. Rep. No. 104-98, p. 2 (1995) (hereinafter S. Rep.).
5. *Id.*, at 1.
6. The opinion in *Central Bank* discussed only private remedies, but its rationale—that the text of § 10(b) did not cover aiding and abetting—obviously limited the authority of public enforcement agencies. *See* 511 U.S., at 199–200, 114 S. Ct. 1439, 128 L. Ed. 2d 119 (STEVENS, J., dissenting); *see also* S. Rep., at 19 ("The Committee does, however, grant the SEC express authority to bring actions seeking injunctive relief or money damages against persons who knowingly aid and abet primary violators of the securities laws").
7. PSLRA, § 104, 109 Stat. 757; *see also* S. Rep., at 19 ("The Committee believes that amending the 1934 Act to provide explicitly for private aiding and abetting liability actions under Section 10(b) would be contrary to S. 240's goal of reducing meritless securities litigation").
8. *See id.*, at 51 (additional views of Sen. Dodd) ("I am pleased that the Committee bill grants the Securities and Exchange Commission explicit authority to bring actions against those who knowingly aid and abet primary violators. However, I remain concerned about liability in private actions and will continue work with other Committee members on this issue as we move to floor consideration"). Senators Sarbanes, Boxer, and Bryan also submitted additional views in which they stated that "while the provision in the bill is of some help, the deterrent effect of the securities laws would be strengthened if aiding and abetting liability were restored in private actions as well." *Id.*, at 49.
9. *Id.*, at 8 ("The success of the U.S. securities markets is largely the result of a high level of investor confidence in the integrity and efficiency of our markets. The SEC enforcement program and the availability of private rights of action together provide a means for defrauded investors to recover damages and a powerful deterrent against violations of the securities laws"); *see also Bateman Eichler, Hill Richards, Inc. v. Berner*, 472 U.S. 299, 310, 105 S. Ct. 2622, 86 L. Ed. 2d 215 (1985) ("Moreover, we repeatedly have emphasized that implied private actions provide 'a most

effective weapon in the enforcement' of the securities laws and are 'a necessary supplement to Commission action'"); Brief for Former SEC Commissioners as Amici Curiae 4 ("Liability [of the kind at issue here] neither results in undue liability exposure for non-issuers, nor an undue burden upon capital formation. Holding liable wrongdoers who actively engage in fraudulent conduct that lacks a legitimate business purpose does not hinder, but rather enhances, the integrity of our markets and our economy. We believe that the integrity of our securities markets is their strength. Investors, both domestic and foreign, trust that fraud is not tolerated in our nation's securities markets and that strong remedies exist to deter and protect against fraud and to recompense investors when it occurs").

10. The Court does concede that Congress has now ratified the private cause of action in the PSLRA. . . .

11. Today, the guarantee of a remedy for every injury appears in nearly three-quarters of state constitutions. ALA. CONST., ART. I, § 13; ARK. CONST., ART. II, § 13; COLO. CONST., ART. II, § 6; CONN. CONST., ART. I, § 10; DEL. CONST., ART. I, § 9; FLA. CONST., ART. I, § 21; IDAHO CONST., ART. I, § 18; ILL. CONST., ART. I, § 12; IND. CONST., ART. I, § 12; KAN. CONST., BILL OF RIGHTS § 18; , KY. CONST., § 14; LA. CONST., ART. I, § 22; ME. CONST., ART. I, § 19; MD. CONST., DECLARATION OF RIGHTS, ART. 19; MASS. CONST., PT. I, ART. 11; MINN. CONST., ART. 1, § 8; MISS. CONST., ART. III, § 24; MO. CONST., ART. I, § 14; MONT. CONST., ART. II, § 16; NEB. CONST., ART. I, § 13; N. H. CONST., PT. I, ART. 14; N. C. CONST., ART. I, § 18; N. D. CONST., ART. I, § 9; OHIO CONST., ART. I, § 16; OKLA. CONST., ART. II, § 6; ORE. CONST., ART. I, § 10; PA. CONST., ART. I, § 11; R. I. CONST., ART. I, § 5; S. C. CONST., ART. I, § 9; S. D. CONST., ART. VI, § 20; TENN. CONST., ART. I, § 17; TEX. CONST., ART. I, § 13; UTAH CONST., ART. I, § 11; VT. CONST., CH. I, ART. 4; W. VA. CONST., ART. III, § 17; WIS. CONST., ART. I, § 9; WYO. CONST., ART. I, § 8; *see also* Phillips, *The Constitutional Right to a Remedy*, 78 N. Y. U. L. REV. 1309, 1310, n. 6 (2003) (hereinafter Phillips).

The concept of a remedy for every wrong most clearly emerged from Sir Edward Coke's scholarship on Magna Carta. *See* 1 SECOND PART OF THE INSTITUTES OF THE LAWS OF ENGLAND (1797). At the time of the ratification of the United States Constitution, Delaware, Massachusetts, Maryland, New Hampshire, and North Carolina had all adopted constitutional provisions reflecting the provision in Coke's scholarship. *Del. Declaration of Rights and Fundamental Rules* § 12 (1776), reprinted in 2 W. SWINDLER, SOURCES AND DOCUMENTS OF UNITED STATES CONSTITUTIONS 198 (1973) (hereinafter Swindler); MASS. CONST., PT. I, ART. XI (1780), reprinted in 3 FEDERAL AND STATE CONSTITUTIONS, COLONIAL CHARTERS, AND OTHER ORGANIC

LAWS 1891 (F. Thorpe ed. 1909) (reprinted 1993) (hereinafter Thorpe); MD. CONST., DECLARATION OF RIGHTS, ART. XVII (1776), in *id.*, at 1688; N. H. CONST., ART. XIV (1784), in 4 *id.*, at 2455; N. C. CONST., DECLARATION OF RIGHTS, ART. XIII (1776), in 5 *id.*, at 2787, 2788; *see also* Phillips 1323–1324. Pennsylvania's Constitution of 1790 contains a guarantee. PA. CONST., ART. IX, § 11, in 5 Thorpe 3101. CONNECTICUT'S 1818 CONSTITUTION, ART. I, § 12, contained such a provision. Reprinted in Swindler 145.

12. *See, e.g., Slavin v. Germantown Fire Ins. Co.*, 174 F.2d 799 (CA3 1949); *Baird v. Franklin*, 141 F.2d 238, 244–245 (CA2) ("The fact that the statute provides no machinery or procedure by which the individual right of action can proceed is immaterial. It is well established that members of a class for whose protection a statutory duty is created may sue for injuries resulting from its breach and that the common law will supply a remedy if the statute gives none"), cert. denied, 323 U.S. 737, 65 S. Ct. 38, 89 L. Ed. 591 (1944); *Kardon v. National Gypsum Co.*, 69 F. Supp. 512, 514 (ED Pa. 1946) ("The right to recover damages arising by reason of violation of a statute . . . is so fundamental and so deeply ingrained in the law that where it is not expressly denied the intention to withhold it should appear very clearly and plainly").

ARTICLE 9.2

Liability Under Rules 10b-5(a) & (c)

Daniel A. McLaughlin

I. INTRODUCTION

With a declining stock market and the exposure of a number of far-reaching corporate scandals, plaintiffs' counsel in recent years have understandably sought to cast a broad net in the search for solvent defendants in securities fraud actions. In particular, plaintiffs increasingly invoke subsections (a) and (c) of Rule 10b-5, contending that these longstanding rules permit the maintenance of novel causes of action that are otherwise barred by the traditional barriers to reaching remote defendants in private actions under section 10(b). Specifically, plaintiffs' counsel often seek to use Rules 10b-5(a) and (c) to impose liability for misrepresentations or omissions on defendants who neither made the misrepresentation nor had a duty to disclose any omitted facts, often on the theory that such defendants participated in a "scheme" to cause misrepresentations to be made by another defendant.

In a number of recent cases, district courts have accepted plaintiffs' novel readings of these subsections, treating Rules 10b-5(a) and 10b-5(c) as if they were separate and independent sources of liability from the traditional securities fraud claim brought under Rule 10b-5(b), and further assuming that the contours of such actions were unsettled. More recently, the Securities and Exchange Commission (SEC) has weighed in with amicus curiae briefs filed in the Ninth Circuit supporting this view of "scheme" liability under Rule 10b-5(a). In fact, however, this reading of Rules 10b-5(a) and 10b-5(c) is flatly inconsistent with settled U.S. Supreme Court precedents that draw on the text of the enabling statute, section 10(b) of the Securities Exchange Act of 1934, as well as with Circuit-level precedents regarding causes of action asserted under other "10b"-series rules. Moreover, the Second, Seventh, and Eighth Circuits, as well as a number of federal district courts, have recently reaffirmed that Rules 10b-5(a) and (c) do not alter the longstanding requirements of the implied private right of action under section 10(b) and Rule 10b-5: the defendant must make a misrepresentation, owe the plaintiff a duty to disclose, or carry out a manipulative transaction in the subject security.

II. THE STATUTE AND THE RULE

What is the primary purpose of Section 10(b)?

Section 10(b), enacted in 1934 as part of the original Securities Exchange Act, makes it unlawful "[t]o use or employ, in connection with the purchase or sale of any security . . . any manipulative or deceptive device or contrivance in contravention of such rules and regulations as the [Securities and Exchange] Commission may prescribe."[1] As the Supreme Court has observed, in holding that aiders and abettors are not liable for violations of section 10(b), "[T]he statute prohibits only the making of a material misstatement (or omission) or the commission of a manipulative act. . . . We cannot amend the statute to create liability for acts that are not themselves manipulative or deceptive within the meaning of the statute."[2] "[T]he statutory text controls the definition of conduct covered by § 10(b). . . . It is inconsistent with settled methodology in § 10(b) cases to extend liability beyond the scope of conduct prohibited by the statutory text."[3]

Rule 10b-5, hastily promulgated in 1942 to give the SEC express authority over fraudulent purchases (as well as sales) of securities,[4] is divided into three subsections, which (with exceptions not relevant here) track the language of section 17(a) of the Securities Act of 1933:

> It shall be unlawful for any person, directly or indirectly, by the use of any means or instrumentality of interstate commerce, or of the mails or of any facility of any national securities exchange,
>
> (a) To employ any device, scheme, or artifice to defraud,
> (b) To make any untrue statement of a material fact or to omit to state a material fact necessary in order to make the statements made, in the light of the circumstances under which they were made, not misleading, or
> (c) To engage in any act, practice, or course of business which operates or would operate as a fraud or deceit upon any person,
>
> in connection with the purchase or sale of any security.[5]

What is the relationship between Section 10(b) and Rule 10 b-5?

Plaintiffs' counsel, seizing upon the absence of any reference to a misrepresentation or omission in subsections (a) and (c) of Rule 10b-5, increasingly seek to use those subsections as a means to plead a cause of action against defendants who have neither made any false or misleading public statement nor owed the plaintiffs any duty of disclosure. But the basic elements-a misrepresentation, duty to disclose or the execution of a manipulative transaction-are required by section 10(b) itself, as the Supreme Court has made clear.

III. THE SUPREME COURT DEFINES "DECEPTION" AND "MANIPULATION"

The Supreme Court, in *Ernst & Ernst v. Hochfelder*,[6] expressly held that the subsections of Rule 10b-5 cannot create liabilities beyond those imposed by the statutory text. *Hochfelder* is remembered today mostly for its bottom-line holding: scienter, i.e., an "intent to deceive, manipulate, or defraud," is an element of the section 10(b) cause of action.[7] The Court drew this requirement from the common law of fraud, which was imported into section 10(b) by the use of "commonly understood terminology of intentional wrongdoing"[8] such as the terms "manipulative," "device," and "contrivance"[9] in the statute.

But the Court's holding in *Hochfelder* also required it to resolve an issue raised in that case by the SEC: the contention that scienter is not a requirement of a claim under Rule 10b-5 because only one of the three subparts of Rule 10b-5, on its face, requires proof of scienter. Specifically, the SEC argued, and the Court agreed, that the express terms of Rules 10b-5(b) and 10b-5(c) "could be read as proscribing, respectively, any type of material misstatement or omission, and any course of conduct, that has the effect of defrauding investors, whether the wrongdoing was intentional or not."[10] Nonetheless, the *Hochfelder* Court emphasized that the reach of Rule 10b-5 was limited by the scope of section 10(b):

> The rulemaking power granted to an administrative agency charged with the administration of a federal statute is not the power to make law. . . . Thus, despite the broad view of the Rule advanced by the [SEC] in this case, *its scope can not exceed the power granted the [SEC] by Congress under § 10(b).*"[11]

A year later, in *Santa Fe Industries v. Green*,[12] the Court was called upon to define the phrase "manipulative or deceptive device or contrivance" in section 10(b) in the context of a private action under Rules 10b-5(a) and (c). The plaintiffs in *Santa Fe* challenged a "short-form" merger, which under Delaware law permitted a parent company to compel the plaintiff minority shareholders to accept cash in exchange for their shares.[13] Although the plaintiffs alleged affirmative and intentional misrepresentations, they conceded that they had not relied on them, and thus the Court assumed that the defendants had not made an actionable misrepresentation or nondisclosure.[14] The Second Circuit, in an opinion predating *Hochfelder*, had found—quoting the text of Rule 10b-5(a)-that the plaintiffs had stated the following claim: "that the Delaware procedure as applied to the facts of this case constitutes a 'device, scheme, or artifice to defraud' because of the gross undervaluation by defendants of the shares the minority shareholders are forced to sell."[15] The Second Circuit explicitly rested its decision on Rules 10b-5(a) and (c):

> [An] erroneous assumption is that in order to allege a claim under Rule 10b-5 there must be some showing of misrepresentation or lack of disclosure. . . . But only sub-division [b] of 10b-5 deals with nondisclosure and misrepresentation. The Rule contains two other subdivisions which state explicitly that fraud other than and in addition to a failure to disclose or truthfully represent is also actionable. . . . It must be that the failure to observe this broader scope of Rule 10b-5 led the court below to dismiss the complaint . . . lest there be any lingering doubt on this point, we now hold that in such cases, including the one now before us, no allegation or proof of misrepresentation or nondisclosure is necessary.[16]

Before the Supreme Court, the plaintiffs' "principal argument" was that the merger violated Rules 10b-5(a) and (c).[17] The Court explained, citing *Hochfelder*, that the statute's requirements were controlling.

. . .

Finding no actionable "deception, misrepresentation, or nondisclosure," the Court defined the remaining statutory term—"manipulative"—as follows: manipulative conduct "is 'virtually a term of art when used in connection with securities markets' . . . [which] refers generally to practices, such as wash sales, matched orders, or rigged prices, that are intended to mislead investors by artificially affecting market activity."[19] As discussed in more detail below, courts have followed this definition of "manipulative" as referring to similar types of artificial market activity (i.e., the execution of securities transactions designed to simulate genuine interest in buying or selling at an artificial price). As a result, unless such undisclosed artificial market activity is pleaded and proved, claims under section 10(b) necessarily turn on "deceptive . . . devices or contrivances."[20]

Following the rejection of Rules 10b-5(a) and (c) as sources for liability in the absence of deception or manipulation, the Court went on to clarify the scope of "decept[ion]" under section 10(b) in *Chiarella v. United States*.[21] *Chiarella*, involving trading on material non-public information by an employee of a financial printer, was brought as a criminal action under Rules 10b-5(a) and (c), not 10b-5(b).[22] Even though *Chiarella* unquestionably involved a dishonest and deliberate attempt to trade on information that was unavailable to the market at large, the Court refused to extend the concept of "deception" beyond the basic common law categories of misrepresentation or a duty to disclose, holding that "[w]hen an allegation of fraud is based upon nondisclosure, there can be no fraud absent a duty to speak . . . premised upon a duty to disclose arising from a relationship of trust and confidence between the parties to a transaction."[23] The Court found that the . . . jury instructions, quoting Rules 10b-5(a) and (c), mischaracterized the requirements of a section 10(b) violation, resulting in reversible error.

. . .

> Alternatively, the jury was instructed that it could convict if "Chiarella's alleged conduct of having purchased securities without disclosing material, non-public information would have, or did have, the effect of operating as a fraud upon a seller." The judge earlier had stated that fraud "embraces all the means which human ingenuity can devise and which are resorted to by one individual to gain an advantage over another by false misrepresentation, suggestions or by suppression of the truth."[24]

In short, the *Chiarella* Court expressly held that the need for either a misrepresentation or a duty to disclose is an essential element of liability under Rules 10b-5(a) or (c).[25]

The Court recounted these decisions when it held, in *Central Bank*, that because section 10(b) "prohibits only the making of a material misstatement (or omission) or the commission of a manipulative act," and "does not include giving aid to a person who commits a manipulative or deceptive act," the statute does not reach aiders and abettors.[26] After *Central Bank*, litigation has focused on what types of acts fit the definition of "the making of a material misstatement (or omission)" and "the commission of a manipulative act," mostly with regard to the issue of what constitutes "making" a misrepresentation.[27] In light of the Court's clear and unambiguous holdings in *Santa Fe* and *Chiarella*, however, it is already clear that-under Rules 10b-5(a) and (c), just as under Rule 10b-5(b)-liability under section 10(b) does not extend beyond those three categories: (1) the making of a misrepresentation, (2) an omission or non-disclosure coupled with a duty to speak, and (3) the commission of a manipulative act.

. . .

V. THE MEANING OF "MANIPULATIVE"

One argument made by plaintiffs' attorneys in seeking to use Rules 10b-5(a) and (c) to evade the requirement of pleading and proving a misrepresentation or duty to disclose is to contend that the term "manipulation" can extend to false statements that "manipulate" the market for a security. While some district courts have accepted variants on this argument, recent decisions by the Second, Seventh, and Eighth Circuits have squarely rejected efforts to redefine "manipulation" to cover conduct not involving the use of manipulative securities trades.

In re Global Crossing, Ltd. Securities Litigation[33] involved an effort to hold an outside auditor liable for statements made by the issuer, including some made without specific mention of the auditor. *Global Crossing* was thus, at its core, a garden-variety false statement case (albeit one involving very large losses), in which the plaintiffs sought to attribute issuer statements to the auditor. The court accepted the premise that involvement in the issuance of false financial statements could constitute "manipulation":

> Andersen argues that because plaintiffs failed to allege "tie-in agreements, wash sales, matched orders or rigged prices," they have failed to state [a market manipulation] claim. It is true that plaintiffs fail to assert a market manipulation claim, as those claims are technically understood-they have alleged no illegal trading activity that would artificially cause stock prices to rise. But subsections (a) and (c) encompass much more than illegal trading activity. . . .
>
> The use of the term "manipulative" in section 10(b) itself "connotes intentional or willful conduct designed to deceive or defraud investors by controlling or artificially affecting the price of securities." Plaintiffs allege precisely such manipulative conduct, with precisely such a result. Schemes used to artificially inflate the price of stocks by creating phantom revenue fall squarely within both the language of section 10(b) and its broad purpose, to "prevent practices that impair the function of stock markets in enabling people to buy and sell securities at prices that reflect undistorted (though not necessarily accurate) estimates of the underlying economic value of the securities traded."[34]

The Second Circuit, in *Lentell v. Merrill Lynch & Co.*,[35] a case involving a brokerage firm's liability for its analyst reports, explicitly rejected this position, holding that claims sounding in misrepresentation or omission are not actionable as "manipulation":

> [P]laintiffs cast their claims in terms of market manipulation, pursuant to Rule 10b-5(a) and (c). We hold that where the sole basis for such claims is alleged misrepresentations or omissions, plaintiffs have not made out a market manipulation claim under Rule 10b-5(a) and (c), and remain subject to the heightened pleading requirements of the PSLRA.[36]

A similar conclusion was reached by the Seventh Circuit. The district court in *Foss v. Bear, Stearns & Co.*, rejected an attempt to impose Rule 10b-5(a) and (c) liability on a brokerage firm whose employee opened accounts with securities he allegedly knew to be stolen from the plaintiff estate by its prior administrator.[37] On appeal, the Seventh Circuit affirmed, refusing to apply the label of "manipulation" and instead holding that the absence of a misrepresentation made, or duty to disclose owed, by the brokerage firm to the estate was fatal to the claim: "Foss wants us to call the conduct 'manipulation' rather than 'fraud,' but this is a distinction without a difference. In securities law, manipulation is a kind of fraud; deceit remains essential."[38]

The Eighth Circuit, in a decision discussed in more detail below,[39] likewise rejected a definition of "manipulative" conduct that would swallow the definition of "deceptive" conduct:

> The term "manipulative" in § 10(b) has the limited contextual meaning ascribed in *Santa Fe*. Thus, any defendant who does not make or affirmatively cause to be made a fraudulent misstatement or omission, or who does not directly engage in manipulative securities trading practices, is at most guilty of aiding and abetting and cannot be held liable under § 10(b) or any subpart of Rule 10b-5.[40]

The position of the Second, Seventh, and Eighth Circuits is the only sensible reading of the Supreme Court's repeated emphasis on defining "manipulative" practices to include types of conduct . . . in which the common element is the execution of transactions that upset the market mechanism itself, rather than just the universe of information about the issuer. . . . The Court in *Santa Fe*, in limiting the definition of "manipulative," left little room to doubt that it regarded the term as having a specific meaning:

> Section 10(b)'s general prohibition of practices deemed by the SEC to be "manipulative"—in this technical sense of artificially affecting market activity in order to mislead investors—is fully consistent with the fundamental purpose of the 1934 Act. . . . No doubt Congress meant to prohibit the full range of ingenious devices that might be used to manipulate securities prices. But we do not think it would have chosen this "term of art" if it had meant to bring within the scope of § 10(b) instances of corporate mismanagement such as this, in which the essence of the complaint is that shareholders were treated unfairly by a fiduciary.[42]

The Court cited back to its interpretation of the former Rule 10b-6, which it had described just a month earlier as "an antimanipulative provision designed . . . to prevent stimulative trading by an issuer in its own securities in order to create an unnatural and unwarranted appearance of market activity."[43]

This reading of section 10(b)'s use of the term "manipulative" is consistent with the commonly understood meaning of the term, and with the reasons why the requirements of pleading and proving market manipulation have always been distinct from misrepresentation or omission cases.[44] It is also consistent with Congress' use of the term elsewhere in the securities laws, such as section 9 of the Exchange Act, which is captioned "Prohibition Against Manipulation of Security Prices" and makes it unlawful to "effect any transaction" or "enter an order or orders" in certain circumstances "[f]or the purpose of creating a false or misleading appearance of active trading in any security . . ., or a false or misleading appearance with respect to the market for any such security."[45] It is thus unsurprising that few courts have been willing to create a new class of "manipulation" claims that are little more than "deception lite," alleging damages from reliance on misrepresentations or omissions but satisfying less than all of the required elements of a misrepresentation or omission claim.

VI. ENRON AND "SCHEME" LIABILITY

Aside from recasting the definition of "manipulative" conduct, the main argument made in favor of liability under Rule 10b-5(a) in misrepresentation or omission cases is that a secondary actor can be liable for an issuer's statements by virtue of having participated in a "scheme" to issue such statements. In general, "scheme" liability has been urged in two contexts. First, plaintiffs have sought to impose liability on parties that did business with the issuer, often in ways characterized as "sham" transactions. Sham transactions are those having no other economic purpose or are accompanied by non-public misrepresentations, where the issuer then improperly accounted for the transaction. Second, plaintiffs have sought to impose liability on accountants who were not mentioned in a public statement reporting financial results on the theory that their involvement in the underlying accounting decisions constituted an unlawful accounting scheme resulting in the issuance of false financial information.

As discussed above, the problem with "scheme" liability under Rule 10b-5(a)-and with similar efforts under Rule 10b-5(c)-is that it is inconsistent with the Supreme Court's reading of the language of section 10(b) itself.[46] The opinions accepting "scheme" liability have generally not grappled with the leading Supreme Court cases: few of them cite *Chiarella* at all, and none mention the fact that *Santa Fe* and *Chiarella* have already decided the scope of "deception" under Rules 10b-5(a) and (c). Several of these opinions have also placed undue reliance on dicta in other Supreme Court opinions that found liability under the traditional categories of misrepresentation or duty to disclose.

The Second Circuit, in a recent unpublished opinion, and the Eighth Circuit, in a published opinion, both rejected this theory of liability, and at this writing, an appeal is pending in the Ninth Circuit addressing the question.[47]

. . .

In short, none of the cases adopting "scheme" liability for misrepresentations made by others have offered any substantial justification for departing from the consistent holdings of the Supreme Court regarding the essential elements of section 10(b) liability, nor even acknowledged those holdings. As the Supreme Court recently observed in rejecting another effort to alter the longstanding elements of a section 10(b) claim, "the uniqueness of [this] perspective argues against the validity of its approach in a case like this one where we consider the contours of a judicially implied cause of action with roots in the common law."[75]

. . .

VIII. CONCLUSION

Rules 10b-5(a) and (c) do not impose a different standard for liability than the longstanding standards governing any claim under section 10(b). Recent efforts to create a distinct cause of action under Rules 10b-5(a) and (c) are not supportable in light of the consistent holdings of the Supreme Court construing section 10(b) and in light of recent decisions of the Second, Seventh, and Eighth Circuits declining to apply those rules to allow liability in the absence of one of the three traditional elements of a section 10(b) claim-a misrepresentation, a duty of disclosure, or manipulative securities transactions. As a result-other than statutory methods such as "control person" liability-the sole basis for reaching remote or secondary defendants in cases involving reliance on misrepresentations by an issuer remains pleading and proof that the defendant actually "made" the misrepresentation in question within the meaning of *Central Bank*.

ENDNOTES

1. 15 U.S.C. § 78j(b) (2005) (emphasis added).
2. Cent. Bank of Denver, N.A. v. First Interstate Bank of Denver, N.A., 511 U.S. 164, 177–78 (1994).
3. *Id.* at 175, 177.
4. *See* Ernst & Ernst v. Hochfelder, 425 U.S. 185, 212 n.32 (1976).
5. 17 C.F.R. § 240.10b-5 (2005).
6. 425 U.S. 185 (1976).
7. *Id.* at 193.
8. *Id.* at 214.
9. *Id.* at 199. The Court recently reaffirmed the significance of "the common-law roots of the securities fraud action" in addition to the express statutory requirements. Dura Pharm., Inc. v. Broudo, 125 S. Ct. 1627, 1632 (2005).

10. *Hochfelder*, 425 U.S. at 212 (emphasis added). The Court subsequently confirmed this reading of Rules 10b-5(b) and (c) in *Aaron v. SEC*, 446 U.S. 680 (1980). In *Aaron*, the Court—while reaffirming that scienter was required by the "plain meaning of the language of [s]ection 10(b)," as well as by section 17(a)(1) of the 1933 Act (which uses language identical to Rule 10b-5(a))—held that there is no scienter requirement in sections 17(a)(2) and (a)(3) of the 1933 Act, which use language identical to Rules 10b-5(b) and (c), respectively. *Id.* at 690, 697. The different outcomes in *Aaron* and *Hochfelder* can only be explained by the conclusion that the language of Rule 10b-5 goes beyond the SEC's delegated rulemaking authority derived from section 10(b).
11. *Hochfelder*, 425 U.S. at 13–14 (emphasis added). The Court's subsequent statements that Rule 10b-5 is coextensive with section 10(b), see SEC v. Zandford, 535 U.S. 813, 816 n.1 (2002) (referencing United States v. O'Hagan, 521 U.S. 642, 651 (1997); *Hochfelder*, 425 U.S. at 214), must be read in this light: not to suggest that the subsections of Rule 10b-5 can add to or define the scope of the section 10(b) cause of action, but simply to recognize that the SEC, in enacting the Rule, took the full measure of rulemaking authority granted it under the statute.
12. 430 U.S. 462 (1977).
13. *Id.* at 465–67.
14. *Id.* at 467–69, 474.
15. Green v. Santa Fe Indus., 533 F.2d 1283, 1285 (2d Cir. 1976), rev'd, 430 U.S. 462 (1977).
16. *Id.* at 1286–87.
17. *Santa Fe*, 430 U.S. at 474 n.14.
19. *Id.* at 476 (quoting *Hochfelder*, 425 U.S. at 199).
20. *See infra* Part V.
21. 445 U.S. 222 (1980).
22 *Id.* at 225 n.5 ("Only Rules 10b-5(a) and (c) are at issue here.").
23. *Id.* at 235, 230.
24. *Id.* at 236 (citations omitted).
25. The Third Circuit, citing *Chiarella,* required proof of a duty to disclose on the part of corporate directors in finding liability for the loss of conversion rights by holders of convertible bonds in Pittsburgh Terminal Corp. v. Baltimore & Ohio R.R. Co., 680 F.2d 933, 940–42 (3d Cir.), *cert. denied,* 459 U.S. 1056 (1982).
26. *Cent. Bank,* 511 U.S. at 177–78.
27. The Second Circuit, for example, follows a "bright line" approach to claims involving reliance on a misrepresentation made by an issuer of securities, under which "a secondary actor cannot incur primary liability . . . for a statement not attributed . . . to that specific actor at the time of public dissemination, that is, in advance of the investment decision." Wright v. Ernst & Young LLP, 152 F.3d 169, 175 (2d Cir. 1998),

cert. denied, 525 U.S. 1104 (1999) (citations omitted). *Accord* Shapiro v. Cantor, 123 F.3d 717, 720 (2d Cir. 1997). Several other circuits have taken similar approaches. *See, e.g.*, Fidel v. Farley, 392 F.3d 220, 234–36 (6th Cir. 2004) (following Wright); Ziemba v. Cascade Int'l, Inc., 256 F.3d 1194, 1205–06 (11th Cir. 2001) (same). *See also* Gariety v. Grant Thornton LLP, 368 F.3d 356, 369 (4th Cir. 2004); GSC Partners CDO Fund v. Washington, 368 F.3d 228, 246 (3d Cir. 2004). The proper standards for "making" a misrepresentation, however, are outside the scope of this article.

33. 322 F. Supp. 2d 319 (S.D.N.Y. 2004).
34. *Id.* at 336–37 (citations omitted). *Accord In re* AOL Time Warner, Inc. Secs. & "ERISA" Litig., 381 F. Supp. 2d 192, 217 (S.D.N.Y. 2004) ("[B]oth 10b-5 and *Santa Fe* contemplate manipulation of the securities markets to be practices, acts, misstatements or omissions designed to mislead investors."). The *AOL Time Warner* court's discussion is *dicta*, as the court did not sustain any claim under Rules 10b-5(a) or (c) separate from the main Rule 10b-5(b) claims against an issuer for its own alleged false statements. A number of other decisions have similarly permitted Rule 10b-5(a) and (c) liability either in tandem with Rule 10b-5(b) liability or otherwise in circumstances that could support traditional liability for a misrepresentation or duty to disclose. *See, e.g.*, *In re* Qwest Commc'ns Int'l, Inc. Sec. Litig., 387 F. Supp. 2d 1130, 1146–47 (D. Colo. 2005); SEC v. Santos, 355 F. Supp. 2d 917, 919–20 (N.D. Ill. 2003) (denying motion to dismiss where brokerage firm failed to disclose, in reports to city, its improper payments made to city official in exchange for business); *In re* Royal Ahold N.V. Secs. & ERISA Litig., 351 F. Supp. 2d 334, 371–72, 377–84 (D. Md. 2004) (holding corporate insiders liable for "manipulation" of financial statements); *In re* Salomon Analyst AT&T Litig., 350 F. Supp. 2d 455, 472–74 (S.D.N.Y. 2004) (denying motion to dismiss by CEO for public statements made by an employee allegedly at his direction).
35. 396 F.3d 161 (2d Cir.), *cert. denied*, 126 S. Ct. 421 (2005).
36. *Lentell*, 396 F.3d at 177–78 (citing Schnell v. Conseco, Inc., 43 F. Supp. 2d 438, 447–48 (S.D.N.Y. 1999) (B.D. Parker, J.) (stating that the *Schnell* court "refus[ed] to characterize allegations as market manipulation claims where alleged 'schemes to defraud' consisted largely of an aggregation of material misrepresentations to inflate stock, such as research reports containing misrepresentations of the underlying facts and use of false names to solicit investors")). *Accord In re* Yukos Oil Co. Secs. Litig., No. 04 Civ. 5243, 2006 WL 800736, at *17–18 (S.D.N.Y. Mar. 30, 2006); *In re* Nat'l Century Fin. Enters., Inc. Inv. Litig., No. 2:03-MD-1565, 2006 WL 469468, at *21 (S.D. Ohio Feb. 27, 2006); SEC v. KPMG LLP, No. 03 Civ. 671, 2006 U.S. Dist. LEXIS 1283, at *76–77 (S.D.N.Y. Jan. 13, 2006); Catton v. Defense Technology Sys., Inc., No. 05 Civ. 6954, 2006

U.S. Dist. LEXIS 205, at *16–17 (S.D.N.Y. Jan. 3, 2006); JHW Greentree Capital, L.P. v. Whittier Trust Co., No. 05 Civ. 2985, 2005 U.S. Dist. LEXIS 27156, at *25–26 & n.11 (S.D.N.Y. Nov. 10, 2005); Collier v. Aksys Ltd., No. 3:04CV1232, 2005 U.S. Dist. LEXIS 20300, at *49–54 (D. Conn. Aug. 15, 2005); *In re* Recoton Corp. Secs. Litig., 358 F. Supp. 2d 1130, 1138 n.4 (M.D. Fla. 2005). The plaintiffs in *Lentell* argued that their claims, premised upon misleading analyst reports, were properly pleaded as Rule 10b-5(a) and (c) claims under *In re Enron Corp. Secs., Deriv. & ERISA Litig.*, 235 F.Supp. 2d 549 (S.D. Tex. 2002), discussed below. *See* Joint Brief of Plaintiffs-Appellant at 68–76, Lentell v. Merrill Lynch & Co., 396 F.3d 161 (2d Cir. 2005) (No. 03-7948); Joint Reply Brief of Plaintiffs-Appellant at 31–33, Lentell v. Merrill Lynch & Co., 396 F.3d 161 (2d Cir. 2005) (No. 03-7948).

37. No. 03 C 8338, 2004 U.S. Dist. LEXIS 9304, at *7–10 (N.D. Ill. May 17, 2004), *aff'd*, 394 F.3d 540 (7th Cir. 2005).
38. Foss v. Bear, Stearns & Co., 394 F.3d 540, 542 (7th Cir. 2005) (citing Schreiber v. Burlington N., Inc., 472 U.S. 1 (1985); Santa Fe Indus., Inc. v. Green, 430 U.S. 462, 476–77 (1977)). Despite the discussion of Rule 10b-5(a) and (c) in the various cases cited herein, including its own prior precedent in *SEC v. Coffey*, 493 F.2d 1304 (6th Cir. 1974), the Sixth Circuit recently concluded that there was "very little case law explaining more specifically what types of claims are actionable under these provisions." Benzon v. Morgan Stanley Distribs., Inc., 420 F.3d 598, 611 (6th Cir. 2005). The court in *Benzon*, relying solely upon Affiliated Ute Citizens v. United States, 406 U.S. 128 (1972), the district court decision in *Scholnick v. Schechter*, 752 F. Supp. 1317 (E.D. Mich. 1990), and "[a] plain-language reading of the Rule," concluded that a brokerage firm's compliance with its disclosure obligations did not necessarily dispose of Rule 10b-5(a) and (c) claims arising from mutual fund sales practices, but nonetheless affirmed the dismissal of those claims in the absence of clear authority on the matter. *Benzon*, 420 F.3d at 610–11.
39. [footnote omitted]
40. *In re Charter Commc'ns, Inc., Sec. Litig.*, No. 05-1974, slip op. at 7 (8th Cir. Apr. 11, 2006), http://www.ca8.uscourts.gov/opndir/06/04/051974P.pdf (citations omitted).
42. *Santa Fe*, 430 U.S. at 476–77 (emphasis added).
43. *Id.* at 476 (quoting Piper v. Chris-Craft Indus., Inc., 430 U.S. 1, 43 (1977)).
44. *See, e.g.*, SEC v. U.S. Envtl., Inc., 155 F.3d 107, 112 (2d Cir. 1998); United States v. Russo, 74 F.3d 1383, 1391–92 (2d Cir. 1996) (noting distinction between manipulation and cases requiring a misrepresentation or duty to disclose); United States v. Regan, 937 F.2d 823, 829 (2d Cir.) (same), *amended*, 946 F.2d 188 (2d Cir. 1991), *cert. denied*, 504 U.S. 940 (1992); *Catton*, 2006 U.S. Dist. LEXIS 205, at *16–17; *In re*

Initial Pub. Offering Secs. Litig., 383 F. Supp. 2d 566, 577 (S.D.N.Y. 2005) ("In market manipulation cases, . . . the plaintiff's burden [of pleading loss causation] is somewhat different [from cases involving false statements], because of the nature of the artificial inflation caused by manipulative conduct."). *See also* TSC Indus., Inc. v. Northway, Inc., 426 U.S. 438, 460–63 (1976) (discussing absence of duty of corporation to disclose its transactions in its own stock in absence of actual "market manipulation").

45. 15 U.S.C. § 78i(a)(1) (2005).
46. There are also a number of practical objections to "scheme" liability, particularly in the context of private litigation, including the difficulty of translating the requirements of reliance, materiality, loss causation, and compliance with the statute of limitations and the pleading requirements of Rule 9(b) and the Private Securities Litigation Reform Act into cases where the plaintiff may have been entirely unaware of the conduct and even the existence of the defendant at the time of the plaintiff's investment. These objections are outside the scope of this article.
47. [footnote omitted]
75. Dura Pharm., Inc. v. Broudo, 125 S. Ct. 1627, 1633 (2005).

ARTICLE 9.3

Reassessing the Scope of Conduct Prohibited by Section 10(b) and the Elements of Rule 10b-5: Reflections on Securities Fraud and Secondary Actors

Andrew S. Gold

I. INTRODUCTION

When the Supreme Court decision in *Central Bank, N.A. v. First Interstate Bank, N.A.*[1] rejected aiding and abetting liability for private actions under Section 10(b) of the Securities Exchange Act,[2] it produced a major upheaval in securities law.[3] The *Central Bank* Court upended decades of lower court decisions that recognized aiding and abetting claims,[4] and engendered substantial scholarly criticism.[5] . . .

In the lower courts, however, the actual impact of *Central Bank* has been inconsistent.[6] The *Central Bank* Court stated that secondary actors—for example, a securities issuer's accountant, law firm, or bank—may be primarily liable if all of the elements of securities fraud are met.[7] The Court did not decide when secondary actors meet those elements,[8] and ten years after *Central Bank*, the scope of liability for secondary actors remains unsettled.

High profile cases such as the Enron securities litigation have included substantial claims of wrongdoing by accounting firms, lawyers, and underwriters for allegedly engaging in fraudulent acts in conjunction with a securities issuer.[9] Following *Central Bank*, the question is whether such secondary actors qualify for primary liability based on their participation in an issuer's fraud. In misrepresentation cases (on which this article will focus), lower courts have split into two schools of thought. Courts seeking to determine liability generally apply either a "bright line" test, which requires the secondary actor to actually make a fraudulent statement relied on by investors, or a "substantial participation" test, which only requires substantial participation in the creation of the issuer's statement.[10]

Two recent post-*Central Bank* developments merit particular attention. The SEC, in amicus briefs, has supported a form of the "participation" test, whereby a secondary actor is liable for securities fraud when its participation is such that it can be considered a "coauthor" of the issuer's fraudulent statements, even if they are not attributed to the secondary actor itself.[11] As a result, courts may conclude that the SEC's position merits judicial deference if the statute is ambiguous.[12] For example, the *Enron* court apparently deferred to the SEC's interpretation.[13]

In addition, in *SEC v. Zandford*,[14] the Supreme Court embraced the entirety of Rule 10b-5,[15] including parts (a) and (c), which permit "scheme" and "course of business" liability.[16] A recent proposal suggests that *Zandford* permits a broad reading of primary liability for secondary actors whenever they can be said to participate in a "fraudulent scheme,"[17] thus recasting issues of secondary participation in terms of an overarching primary liability. "Scheme" liability would not require a misstatement by a secondary actor to trigger liability.[18]

What is the relationship between the Central Bank case and SEC v. Zandford?

The SEC's theory, although an elegant reading of *Central Bank* and Section 10(b), cannot be squared with statutory text as the Supreme Court has interpreted it.[19] "Co-authors" do not "make" misleading statements unless they communicate the misrepresentation, the statement is attributed to them at the time, or the actual maker of the statement serves as their agent.[20] Similarly, the *Zandford* case cannot be used to circumvent *Central Bank* in misrepresentation cases without effectively amending Section 10(b).[21] If participation in drafting misrepresentations created primary liability for fraudulent "schemes" or "courses of business," *Central Bank* would be largely emptied of its meaning.[22] The SEC's theory would unduly expand part (b) of Rule 10b-5, and the proposed application of *Zandford* would unduly expand parts (a) and (c). . . .

This article concludes that the "bright line" test is the only interpretation of primary liability for secondary actors that is consistent with the reasoning of *Central Bank*, as it is the only test under which investors can be said to rely on statements made by the secondary actor, such that the secondary actor can be said to "use" or "employ" deceptive devices. Although certain forms of participation by secondary actors may meet this test for primary liability—participation as such, they cannot support a primary claim without conflicting with the text of Section 10(b). . . .

Part II of this Article analyzes *Central Bank* and the lower court decisions that have applied its holding. Part III addresses the SEC's co-authorship test for primary liability. Part IV addresses the impact of *Zandford*. Part V argues for a narrow interpretation of the Section 10(b) private right of action even if the statutory text is considered ambiguous.

II. CENTRAL BANK AND LOWER COURT INTERPRETATIONS OF ITS HOLDING

A. The *Central Bank* Decision

Although private actions are frequently brought pursuant to Section 10(b) of the Securities Exchange Act, this provision does not actually prohibit conduct on its own. Section 10(b) authorizes the SEC to set forth rules making it unlawful:

> For any person, directly or indirectly, by the use of any means or instrumentality of interstate commerce or of the mails, or of any facility of any national securities exchange . . .
>
> To use or employ, in connection with the purchase or sale of any security registered on a national securities exchange or any security not so registered, . . . any manipulative or deceptive device or contrivance in contravention of such rules and regulations as the Commission may prescribe as necessary or appropriate in the public interest or for the protection of investors.[23]

. . . While the Supreme Court has recognized an implied private right of action under Section 10(b) and Rule 10b-5 despite the absence of express textual support,[24] the Court also recognized the lack of evidence that such liability was intended by Congress.[25] . . .

The existence (or non-existence) of congressional intent to create a private action is significant. The more recent holdings on implied rights of action require a determination that Congress intended a private right of action in order for courts to recognize one.[26] . . .

It is against this backdrop that *Central Bank* was decided. The Court reversed a Tenth Circuit ruling that found liability expressly on the basis of aiding and abetting.[27] The *Central Bank* Court relied on the absence of any textual reference to "aiding and abetting" in Section 10(b) to preclude such liability under Rule 10b-5, rejecting an implied right of action beyond the primary liability already established by the Court's precedent.[28] . . .

[W]here the issue is the scope of conduct prohibited by Section 10(b), the *Central Bank* Court explained that "the text of the statute controls."[29] Thus, while a private plaintiff may sue under Section 10(b), it "may not bring a 10b-5 suit against a defendant for acts not prohibited by the text of § 10(b)."[30] . . .

B. The "Bright Line" Test

In the wake of *Central Bank*, a number of lower courts settled on a test for primary liability that requires the secondary actor to engage in a misrepresentation on which a plaintiff relied, rather than merely participate in its creation.[31] This typically means that the statement must be attributed to the secondary actor.[32] Known broadly as the "bright line" test, this theory can be traced to language in *Central Bank* warning that if the Court accepted aiding and abetting liability, it would permit plaintiffs to circumvent the reliance element of the private right of action.[33]

In misrepresentation cases, the reliance requirement supplies a necessary causal link between the alleged deceptive act and a plaintiff's injury: it is integral to primary liability.[34] Unless the secondary actor also "makes" the material misstatement, it is not the secondary actor's actions which have caused the plaintiff's injury from that misstatement, even if the secondary actor indirectly enabled the injury to occur.[35] The deceptive words are typically someone else's words—and therefore the source of liability is typically someone else's action.

In *Basic Inc. v. Levinson*, the Supreme Court concluded that a plaintiff's reliance is a necessary element to proving a Section 10(b) claim based on a misrepresentation.[36] . . .

Courts applying the "bright line" test have focused on this reliance requirement in mandating that the secondary actor must make a misrepresentation rather than merely participate in its creation.[37] . . .

A definition of primary liability that collapses aiding and abetting liability into a subset of primary liability would empty *Central Bank* of all significance.[38] The "bright line" courts thus seek to give meaningful effect to the *Central Bank* holding that Section 10(b) does not cover aiding and abetting, and to ensure satisfaction of the reliance element of a Rule 10b-5 claim.

C. The "Substantial Participation" Test

Other courts have taken a broad view of primary liability, and concluded that secondary actors that participated in a misrepresentation could be liable for securities fraud. For example, in one of the early post-*Central Bank* decisions, the district court in *In re ZZZZ Best Securities Litigation* concluded that an accountant, Ernst & Young, could be primarily liable based on its role in the creation, review, or issuance of allegedly fraudulent statements.[39] The *ZZZZ Best* court concluded that *Central Bank* required a secondary actor to commit deceptive acts, but that Ernst & Young's participation in the misrepresentation was extensive enough to attribute the misstatements to them.[40]

The *ZZZZ Best* court largely relied on pre-*Central Bank* decisions that found primary liability in such contexts.[41] The court also argued, however, that even if the investing public were "not . . . able to reasonably attribute the additional misstatements and omissions to Ernst & Young, the securities market still relied on those public statements and anyone intricately involved in their creation and the resulting deception should be liable under Section 10(b)/Rule 10b-5."[42] This attribution of misrepresentations to secondary actors, with varying degrees of participation required, has since been adopted by a number of courts, including the Ninth Circuit.[43] . . .

D. The Mandate of the Bright Line Test

. . . [T]he text of Section 10(b) requires the "bright line" test. Section 10(b) only covers those who "use" or "employ" a manipulative or deceptive device or contrivance.[44] . . . Even if intent to deceive were present, participation in the creation of a deceptive device is distinct from its use. . . .

The above arguments do not entirely eliminate liability for secondary actors participating in a misrepresentation. Secondary actors may also make primary statements, such as when an accountant certifies a fraudulent SEC filing.[45] . . . The source of the primary liability is that the secondary actor in a sense made the statement relied upon, even though its express utterance comes from the issuer.[46]

A secondary actor may also be liable when it uses the maker of a statement as its agent.[47] In this case, one may rightly say that the principal made the statement, albeit through an "indirect" source.[48] Indeed, recognition of agency liability appropriately gives meaning to the terms "directly or indirectly," found in Section 10(b).[49] Such agency liability, however, would not apply to the typical instance of an accountant, lawyer, or underwriter involved in the disclosure process. To the contrary, these secondary actors are agents of the issuer, not the other way around. . . .

III. THE SEC'S CO-AUTHORSHIP TEST

A recent effort to expand liability to participants emphasizes the degree of a secondary actor's participation.[50] In 1995, Professor Langevoort proposed a "participation" test based on the extent of a secondary party's participation in drafting a misleading statement. As he explained:

> My suggestion is that the notion of participation or involvement in these cases be redefined in terms of proximate causation or a broad notion of "co-authorship." Any person who plays a significant role in the formulation of a disclosure document or other form of publicity that contains a material misstatement or omission should be liable as a primary violator if he or she acted with the requisite degree of scienter and all the other requirements for Rule 10b-5 liability are met. A significant role is one in which the person is invited, expected, or is otherwise in a position to affect the form or content of the disclosure—where the person has the ability to influence its capacity to deceive. This could take the form of drafting, editing, or providing information.[51]

The SEC has since adopted a co-authorship theory. In *Klein v. Boyd*,[52] a Third Circuit panel applied this reasoning to hold a secondary party liable for an issuer's misrepresentation.[53] The Third Circuit granted rehearing en banc, vacating the panel's opinion.[54] As amicus, the SEC filed a brief supporting the co-authorship view.[55] Although the parties settled prior to a decision by the full circuit, this brief was subsequently incorporated into the SEC's amicus brief in the *Enron* litigation.[56]

As with other participation theories, the reliance requirement is fatal to this theory because creation of a misrepresentation alone does not cause deception. In the context of a misrepresentation case, the misrepresentation itself is the deceptive device. The rough draft of the misrepresentation as such, no matter if every word were written by a secondary actor, is not a deceptive device. . . .

The appeal of the co-authorship test is that it superficially appears to fit into the requirements of *Central Bank*. Rule 10b-5, subsection (b), sets forth liability where a party "make[s]" a misleading statement.[57] The *Central Bank* Court, when it noted that secondary actors could be liable, suggested that

Why would the SEC want to expand liability?

parties would be liable if they "make[] a material misstatement" on which a purchaser or seller of securities relies.[58] The *Central Bank* majority's use of the word "make" almost certainly meant to "communicate" or "utter" the misstatement. Nevertheless, it is semantically possible to say that a creator of a statement "makes" the statement.[59]

The SEC argued, in effect, that "creating" a statement is equivalent to "making" a statement.[60] In context, this understanding is implausible. If one asks who made the statements in this article, the answer is the author, not the publisher or an anonymous ghostwriter. . . . In short, the "co-authorship" test is not different in kind from the other participation tests. One who participates a great deal in preparing a misstatement, but does nothing more than participate, cannot be primarily liable.

IV. RULE 10B-5 AND THE *ZANDFORD* DECISION

Another possible means to avoid the ambit of *Central Bank* is to look to subsections (a) and (c) of Rule 10b-5.[61] Because "scheme" and "course of business" liability under those subsections does not require misrepresentations, a secondary actor may arguably be found to commit fraudulent acts by participating in the creation of a misrepresentation without making a misrepresentation himself. The participation would allegedly qualify as part of a scheme or course of business, which acted as a fraud. Since the scheme or course of business is relied upon, reliance on the statements of the secondary actors is unnecessary.

. . . The theory that section (a) and (c) of Rule 10b-5 can expand liability to secondary actors in misrepresentation cases is not new.[62] A new development is the Supreme Court's recent opinion in *SEC v. Zandford*,[63] which endorsed all three subsections of Rule 10b-5.[64]

In *Zandford*, the Court addressed the requirement under Section 10(b) that a manipulative or deceptive act be made "in connection with" the purchase or sale of a security.[65] The respondent broker, Zandford, had defrauded an elderly man, Mr. Wood, who had opened an investment account for himself and his daughter.[66] Zandford misappropriated Wood's money by selling the securities in the account and then transferring the proceeds to his own account.[67]

The SEC claimed that Zandford engaged in a fraudulent scheme in which he made sales of his customer's securities for his own benefit.[68] Zandford defended himself against claims of securities fraud on the theory that the sales themselves were lawful, and that the subsequent misappropriation, although fraudulent, did not have a connection with the sale of the securities.[69] He compared his scheme to a mere theft of cash from an investment account.[70] The Supreme Court disagreed.

According to the *Zandford* court, "the securities sales and respondent's fraudulent practices were not independent events."[71] Instead, the fraud perpetrated by the respondent was directly linked to the sales themselves.[72] In so holding, the Court applied sections (a) and (c) of Rule 10b-5, which address "scheme" and "course of business" liability.[73] It is this latter, unremarkable aspect of *Zandford* which is apparently urged as proof that the Supreme Court recognizes a broad reading of Rule 10b-5 that would include participation theories of liability.

The State Attorneys General amicus brief in the *Enron* litigation noted that *Zandford* had confirmed the existence of "scheme" liability.[74] The brief added that the Court had expressly approved all subsections of Rule 10b-5 when it stated that "the scope of Rule 10b-5 is coextensive with the coverage of § 10(b)."[75] This judicial approval, however, may not expand Section 10(b)'s scope via acceptance of an extensive Rule 10b-5.

As the *Hochfelder* decision makes clear, Section 10(b) controls the proper reading of Rule 10b-5, not the reverse.[76] The real issue posed by adoption of subsections (a) and (c) is what type of "scheme" or "course of business" will satisfy the strictures of Section 10(b). In this regard, *Zandford* is simply not on point.[77] *Zandford* was not a case that tested the limits of subsections (a) and (c) of Rule 10b-5 for secondary actors. Although Rule 10b-5 can be read broadly when all of its subsections are adopted, *Zandford* addressed a different issue under Section 10(b)—the "in connection with" requirement.[78]

Nothing in the *Zandford* opinion suggests that the Court would accept "scheme" or "course of business" liability as a means of regulating secondary actors that assist in the creation of another actor's misrepresentation. Both subsections can readily be understood to prohibit deceptive conduct that does not involve misrepresentations, or even prohibit misrepresentations that are part of a scheme, without also prohibiting participation in misrepresentations.[79] *Zandford* was a unanimous decision,[80] joined by all five justices in the *Central Bank* majority.[81] It is unlikely these justices used *Zandford* as an opportunity to curtail their holding in *Central Bank*.

The key to resolving whether a secondary actor's involvement creates primary liability is the same regardless of which provision of rule 10b-5 is at issue. One must determine what conduct was manipulative or deceptive, and then determine whether the secondary actor used or employed the manipulative or deceptive conduct. In the context of a misrepresentation, the secondary actor's actions will typically be relied upon only in those instances where the secondary actor made an independent statement or the misrepresentation is attributable through the law of agency.[82]

If a secondary actor did not make a misstatement, yet participated in a fraudulent scheme, the defrauded party must still have relied upon some act by the secondary actor. . . . In other words, if it is a misrepresentation that deceived the plaintiff, then subsections (a) and (c) do not expand the potential parties subject to liability.

V. AMBIGUITY IN SECTION 10(B) AND JUDICIAL DEFERENCE

A. The Problem of Ambiguity in Section 10(b)

It is conceivable that courts, including the Supreme Court, will find Section 10(b) ambiguous on the question of liability for secondary actors. Such a finding of ambiguity would be unsurprising.[83] The common law precedent discussed above could encourage this conclusion. Moreover, though the text and relevant Supreme Court precedents are sufficiently clear to preclude a participation theory, participation theories are not absolutely excluded by the statutory language. . . . [A]ny such ambiguity should be construed narrowly, to limit the private action. . . .

VI. CONCLUSION

The absence of statutory text explicitly excluding a participation theory should not encourage the taking of judicial liberties: "Congress' failure to act does not justify further judicial elaboration of the 10b-5 action."[84] And, given recent legislative history, it is hard to say that Congress acquiesced in private actions against secondary actors based on their participation in creating a misrepresentation.[85] Congress showed its ability to reverse *Central Bank* when it amended the Securities Exchange Act to permit the SEC to bring enforcement actions against aiders and abettors.[86] Its failure to do the same for private litigation is noteworthy, and courts should pause before construing Section 10(b) to include secondary actors that participate in fraud without independently committing fraud.[87] . . .

This article concludes that Section 10(b) precludes a participation theory. In light of the text of Section 10(b), the participation theories should generally be rejected, as secondary actors that participate in the creation of a misrepresentation do not typically "use" or "employ" a deceptive device or contrivance. But, if a court nonetheless found the text ambiguous, this ought not to be an invitation to defer to the SEC's broad reading, whatever format the SEC interpretation might take.

The Supreme Court will likely have to resolve the circuit split regarding primary liability for secondary actors in private litigation. Should the Court do so, it will face the same concerns respecting secondary liability as it did in *Central Bank*. The possibility of a de facto aiding and abetting action recast in terms of "participation" is quite real. Judicial restraint counsels a restrictive reading of statutory ambiguity in this context. A narrow interpretation of the scope of conduct prohibited by Section 10(b) for private actions most closely follows the original text of Section 10(b), unadorned by judicial elaboration.

END NOTES

1. 511 U.S. 164 (1994).
2. 15 U.S.C. § 78j (2000); *Central Bank*, 511 U.S. at 191 (rejecting aiding and abetting liability under § 10(b)).
3. *See, e.g.*, Robert A. Prentice, *Locating that "Indistinct" and "Virtually Nonexistent" Line Between Primary and Secondary Liability Under Section 10(b)*, 75 N.C. L. REV. 691, 694–95 (1997) (noting that *Central Bank* "had the potential to effect a sea of change in . . . securities fraud litigation").
4. *Central Bank*, 511 U.S. at 192 n.1 (Stevens, J., dissenting) (citing examples of circuit court decisions from eleven federal circuits). Justice Stevens noted that hundreds of federal court and administrative proceedings recognized aiding and abetting liability prior to the *Central Bank* decision. *Id.* at 192.
5. *See, e.g.*, Alan R. Bromberg, *Aiding and Abetting: Sudden Death and Possible Resurrection*, 27 SEC. & COMMODITIES REG. 133–34, 139–40 (1994); Donald C. Langevoort, *Words From on High About Rule 10b-5, Chiarella's History, Central Bank's Future*, 20 DEL. J. CORP. L. 865, 869 (1995); Prentice, *supra* note 3, at 694–96; James D. Redwood, *Toward a More Enlightened Securities Jurisprudence in the Supreme Court? Don't Bank on It Anytime Soon*, 32 HOUS. L. REV. 3, 6–7 (1995). This is by no means to suggest that the *Central Bank* decision was universally decried, however. *See, e.g.*, Joseph A. Grundfest, *We Must Never Forget that It is an Inkblot We are Expounding: Section 10(b) as Rorschach Test*, 29 LOY. L.A. L. REV. 41, 44 (1995). *Cf.* Robert S. De Leon, *The Fault Lines Between Primary Liability and Aiding and Abetting Claims Under Rule 10b-5*, 22 J. CORP. L. 723 (1997). Professor Fischel argued, well before *Central Bank* was decided, that its result was required by the Court's earlier jurisprudence. *See* Daniel R. Fischel, *Secondary Liability Under Section 10(b) of the Securities Act of 1934*, 69 CAL. L. REV. 80, 82 (1981).
6. *See* De Leon *supra* note 5, at 730–31.
7. *See* Central Bank, N.A. 5. Interstate Bank, N.A., 511 U.S. 164, 191 (1994) (citing Fischel, *supra* note 5, at 107–08).
8. *See* De Leon, *supra* note 5, at 726–29.
9. *See* In re Enron Corp. Sec., Derivative & ERISA Litig., 235 F. Supp. 2d 549, 564 (2002).
10. *See* De Leon, *supra* note 5, at 730–31.
11. *See generally* Amicus Curiae Brief of the Securities and Exchange Commission, Klein v. Boyd, 1998 Fed. Sec. L. Rep. (CCH) P90,136 (3d Cir. 1998), *rehearing en banc granted*, judgment vacated (Mar. 9, 1998) (Nos. 97-1143; 97-1261). . . .
12. *Cf. Enron*, 235 F. Supp. 2d at 588–89.

13. *Id.* at 588. . . .
14. 535 U.S. 813 (2002).
15. 17 C.F.R. § 240.10b-5 (2003).
16. *See Zandford*, 535 U.S. at 819.
17. *See, e.g.*, Amicus Curiae Memorandum of the State Attorneys General Relating to Defendant's Motion to Dismiss at 10, In re Enron Corp. Sec. Litig., 235 F. Supp. 2d 549 (2002) (No. H-01-3624).
18. *Zandford*, 535 U.S. at 820.
19. *See infra* text accompanying notes 50–60.
20. *See infra* text accompanying notes 50–60.
21. *See infra* text accompanying notes 61–82.
22. *See infra* text accompanying notes 61–82.
23. 15 U.S.C. § 78j (2000).
24. *See* Herman & McLean v. Huddleston, 459 U.S. 375, 380 (1983) . . .; Ernst & Ernst v. Hochfelder, 425 U.S. 185, 196 (1976) . . .; Superintendent of Ins. of N.Y. v. Bankers Life & Casualty Co., 404 U.S. 6, 13, n. 9 (1971). The private right of action was first recognized in Kardon v. Nat'l Gypsum Co., 69 F. Supp. 512 (E.D. Pa. 1946).
25. *See Hochfelder*, 425 U.S. at 196 (noting that Section 10(b) "does not by its terms create an express civil remedy for its violation, and there is no indication that Congress, or the Commission when adopting Rule 10b-5, contemplated such a remedy"). *See also* Central Bank, N.A. v. Interstate Bank, N.A., 511 U.S. 164, 173 (1994) (noting that "determining the elements of the 10b-5 private liability scheme has posed difficulty because Congress did not create a private § 10(b) cause of action and had no occasion to provide guidance about the elements of a private liability scheme").
26. *See* Touche Ross & Co. v. Redington, 442 U.S. 560, 577–78 (1979); Transamerica Mortgage Advisors, Inc. v. Lewis, 444 U.S. 11, 15–16 (1979).
27. *See* Central Bank, N.A. v. First Interstate Bank, N.A., 511 U.S. 164 (1994); *see also* First Interstate Bank, N.A. v. Pring, 969 F.2d 891 (10th Cir. 1992).
28. *Central Bank*, 511 U.S. at 176–77.
29. *Id.*
30. *Id.* Technically, the language of Section 10(b) does not prohibit any conduct, except insofar as Rule 10b-5 does so. Section 10(b) creates liability based on actions "in contravention of such rules and regulations as the [SEC] may prescribe." 15 U.S.C. § 78j(b) (2000). Nevertheless, Section 10(b) is not without content. For example, certain limitations on the breadth of Rule 10b-5, such as a scienter requirement for Rule 10b-5 actions, have been found in the text of Section 10(b). *See* Ernst & Ernst v. Hochfelder, 425 U.S. 185, 193 (1976). *See also* Santa Fe Indus., Inc. v. Green, 430 U.S. 462, 472–73 (1977) (pointing out that Section 10(b)

only extends to cases involving manipulative or deceptive conduct). This precedent addresses the conduct "covered" by Section 10(b). *Cf. Central Bank*, 511 U.S. at 175. For a theory that Section 10(b) was originally intended to give the SEC very broad power to regulate the securities markets, *see generally* Steve Thel, *The Original Conception of Section 10(b) of the Securities Exchange Act*, 42 STAN. L. REV. 385 (1990).

31. *See, e.g.*, Wright v. Ernst & Young LLP, 152 F.3d 169, 175 (2d Cir. 1998); Anixter v. Home-Stake Prod. Co., 77 F.3d 1215, 1226 n.10 (10th Cir. 1996); In re JWP Inc. Sec. Litig., 928 F. Supp. 1239, 1256 (S.D.N.Y. 1996); Primavera Familienstiftung v. Askin, 1996 WL 494904, at *6–7 (S.D.N.Y. Aug. 30, 1996); In re Kendall Square Research Corp. Sec. Litig., 868 F. Supp. 26, 28 (D. Mass. 1994).
32. *Cf.* Ziemba v. Cascade Intern'l, Inc., 256 F.3d 1194, 1205, 1207 (11th Cir. 2001) ("In order for [a secondary actor] to be primarily liable under § 10(b) and Rule 10b-5, the alleged misstatement or omission upon which a plaintiff relied must have been publicly attributable to the defendant at the time that the plaintiff's investment decision was made.").
33. *Central Bank*, 511 U.S. at 180 ("Were we to allow the aiding and abetting action proposed in this case, the defendant could be liable without any showing that the plaintiff relied upon the aider and abettor's statements or actions. . . . Allowing plaintiffs to circumvent the reliance requirement would disregard the careful limits on 10b-5 recovery mandated by our earlier cases.") (citations omitted).
34. *See* Basic Inc. v. Levinson, 485 U.S. 224, 243 (1988).
35. *Cf. Wright*, 152 F.3d at 175.
36. *See Basic*, 485 U.S. at 243 ("We agree that reliance is an element of a Rule 10b-5 cause of action.").
37. *E.g., Wright*, 152 F.3d at 175.
38. *See Wright*, 152 F.3d at 175.
39. In re ZZZZ Best Sec. Litig., 864 F.Supp. 960, 964, 976 (C.D. Cal. 1994).
40. *See id.* at 969–70.
41. *See id.* at 970.
42. *Id.* Professor Prentice has argued that this latter reasoning is appropriate in light of the Supreme Court's acceptance of the fraud on the market theory . . ., *supra* note 3, at 747. This reasoning overextends the application of the fraud on the market theory, however. It requires courts to equate the general reliance the market might have placed on a secondary actor's reputation to a reliance on the participant's specific doings. This argument could capture secondary actors that fail to blow the whistle, let alone secondary actors that participate in a fraud. Prentice concedes that a whistle blowing duty was implicitly rejected in *Central Bank. See id.* at 765. This reasoning ignores the requirement that the secondary actor's

fraudulent acts must be relied upon (here, the alleged creation of the misrepresentation)—the actor's mere presence is not a deceptive act.

43. In re Software Toolworks Inc., 50 F.3d 615, 628 n.3, 629 (9th Cir. 1994); McNamara v. Bre-X Minerals, Ltd., 57 F. Supp. 2d 396, 427 (E.D. Tex. 1999); Cashman v. Coopers & Lybrand, 877 F. Supp. 425, 432–34 (N.D. Ill. 1995).
44. 15 U.S.C. § 78j (2000); *see also supra* note 23and accompanying text.
45. *See, e.g.*, DiLeo v. Ernst & Young, 901 F.2d 624, 628 (7th Cir. 1990). . . .
46. Prior to *Central Bank*, the Sixth Circuit had described a "direct contact" test for determining when there is a primary violation. *See e.g.*, Molecular Tech. Corp. v. Valentine, 925 F.2d 910, 917 (6th Cir. 1991). Such a theory can be squared with *Central Bank* to the extent there is deceptive conduct by the secondary actor—not mere reliance on a secondary actor simply because it is the issuer's accountant or law firm. The statute requires a manipulative or deceptive device or contrivance.
47. *See, e.g.*, Suez Equity Investors v. Toronto-Dominion Bank, 250 F.3d 87, 101 (2d Cir. 2001). . . . Agency liability should not be confused with respondeat superior liability, which is secondary liability and incompatible with the holding in *Central Bank*. *Cf.* Fischel, *supra* note 5, at 106–07 n.145. . . . The respondeat superior theory is not based on a showing that an employer made a misrepresentation, but rather shifts responsibility for the misrepresentations of employees. Employers are still potentially subject to liability for misrepresentations made by corporate employees, which Congress addressed through the "controlling person" provision of the Exchange Act, section 20(a).
48. It is debatable whether an alleged conspiracy may fit into this mold. For a broad interpretation of conspiracy liability along these lines, see James D. Cox, *Just Deserts for Accountants and Attorneys After Bank of Denver*, 38 ARIZ. L. REV. 519, 528–32 (1996). It is certainly arguable that under a conspiracy to commit fraud, the fraudulent acts can be attributed to a co-conspirator. However, in the typical case of secondary actors (other than control persons within the corporation), this form of conspiracy would not exist. Accountants, for example, do not generally reach agreements to defraud the public, even in those cases where they knowingly assist in creating a misrepresentation. Also troubling is the possibility of recasting every aiding and abetting claim as a conspiracy claim—a concern recognized by the lower courts. *Cf.* Dinsmore v. Squadron, Ellenoff, Plesent, Sheinfeld & Sorkin, 135 F.3d 837, 843 (2d Cir. 1998). . . . A conspiracy liability premised on tacit agreement to aid someone who is committing fraud would likely run afoul of *Central Bank's* restrictions. If conspiracy liability were viable in this context, it would entail a test sufficiently stringent that the typical aiding and abetting claim would be excluded.

49. In *Central Bank*, the Court rejected an apparent argument by the SEC that Congress's provision for Section 10(b) liability, where the defendant acted "directly or indirectly", provided a textual basis for aiding and abetting liability. *See Central Bank*, 511 U.S. at 176. . . . The language has since been argued as support for an agency theory. *Cf.* Prentice, *supra* note 3, at 730–32; Thomas L. Riesenberg, *Fraud Claims Against Professionals After* Central Bank, INSIGHTS, 9, 14 (Feb. 1995). Professor Fischel notes a plausible alternative meaning for the language, however—"that it allows liability to be imposed upon a defendant even though such defendant does not himself use the jurisdictional means (i.e., mail a letter in interstate commerce)." Fischel, *supra* note 5, at 95 n.83.
50. Langevoort, *supra* note 5, at 891–92.
51. *See id.* at 892. Professor Langevoort appears to recognize that his interpretation is in tension with *Central Bank*, and even in conflict with *Central Bank* dicta regarding primary liability. *See id.* at 891 (stating that holdings that use a broader approach to primary liability "allow for substantial revisionism."); *id.* at 892 (suggesting that the proposed participation test may not be entirely faithful to Justice Kennedy's apparent intent in *Central Bank*).
52. Klein v. Boyd, 1998 Fed. Sec. L. Rep. (CCH) P90,136 (3d Cir. 1998), *rehearing en banc granted, judgment vacated* (Mar. 9, 1998).
53. *Id.* at 90, 318.
54. *Id.*
55. Amicus Curiae Brief of the Securities and Exchange Commission, Klein v. Boyd, 1998 Fed. Sec. L. Rep. (CCH) P90,136 (3d Cir. 1998), *rehearing en banc granted, judgment vacated* (Mar. 9, 1998) (Nos. 97-1143; 97-1261), *available at* http://www.sec.gov/litigation/briefs/klein.txt.
56. *See* In rc Enron Corp. Sec., Derivative & ERISA Litig., 235 F. Supp. 2d 549, 585–86 (S.D. Tex. 2002) ("The majority of [the SEC's] pleading is a submission filed on behalf of the plaintiffs in a case that was pending in the Third Circuit, but which was settled before that appellate court could review the issue en banc.").
57. *See* 17 C.F.R. § 240.10b-5 (2003) (stating in subsection (b) that it shall be unlawful "to make any untrue statement of a material fact or to omit to state a material fact necessary in order to make the statements made, in the light of the circumstances under which they were made, not misleading").
58. *See Central Bank*, 511 U.S. at 191. . . . The SEC in effect severs the maker of the statement from the making of the statement. *See* SEC Brief, *supra* note 1817, at 13. . . .
59. Such a rule still entails limits. *See, e.g.*, Tricontinental Indus., Ltd. v. Anixter, 256 F.Supp. 2d 806, 807 (N.D. Ill. 2003).
60. *See* Amicus Curiae Brief of the Securities and Exchange Commission at 16. . . .

61. 17 C.F.R. § 240.10b-5 (2003).
62. *See, e.g.*, In re ZZZZ Best Sec. Litig., 864 F. Supp. 960, 971–72 (C.D. Cal. 1994); *see also* Prentice, *supra* note 3, at 754 (citing subsections (a) and (c) for the proposition that participation theories are acceptable readings of the statutory text).
63. SEC v. Zandford, 535 U.S. 813 (2002).
64. *See id.* at 819–20, 825. *Cf.* Amicus Curiae Memorandum of the State Attorneys General Relating to Defendant's Motion to Dismiss at 10, In re Enron Corp. Sec. Litig., 235 F. Supp. 2d 549 (2002) (No. H-01-3624). . . . *But* cf. De Leon, *supra* note 5, at 728. . . .
65. *Zandford*, 535 U.S. at 819.
66. *Id.* at 815.
67. *Id.*
68. *Id.* at 820.
69. *Id.*
70. *Id.*
71. *Id.* at 820.
72. *Id.*
73. *Id.* at 819 (quoting subsections (a) and (c) of Rule 10b-5).
74. Amicus Curiae Memorandum of the State Attorneys General Relating to Defendant's Motion to Dismiss at 12. In re Enron Corp. Sec. Litig., 235 F. Supp. 2d 549 (2002) (No. H-01-3624).
75. *Id.* (quoting *Zandford*, 535 U.S. at 816 n.1).
76. *See* Ernst & Ernst v. Hochfelder, 425 U.S. 185, 214 (1976) ("despite the broad view of the Rule advanced by the Commission in this case, its scope cannot exceed the power granted the Commission by Congress under § 10(b)."). The *Hochfelder* Court was addressing an overly broad reading of subsections (a) and (c) when it made this point.
77. *See Zandford*, 535 U.S. at 815. . . . Cf. Tricontinental Industries, 256 F.Supp.2d at 807.
78. *See Zandford*, 535 U.S. at 822. . . .
79. *Cf.* In re Lernout & Hauspie Sec. Litig., 236 F. Supp.2d 161, 173 (D. Mass. 2003). . . .
80. *Zandford*, 535 U.S. at 814.
81. Central Bank, N.A. v. First Interstate Bank, N.A., 511 U.S. 164, 166 (1994).
82. *Cf.* Affiliated Ute Citizens v. United States, 406 U.S. 128, 153 (1972) ("under the circumstances of this case, involving primarily a failure to disclose, positive proof of reliance is not a prerequisite to recovery."). In non-misrepresentation cases involving a failure to disclose, reliance is presumed. *Id.* at 153–54. But such cases involve an obligation to disclose combined with a withholding of material facts that amounts to causation in fact. *Id.* at 154. In misrepresentation cases, the Supreme Court has made clear that reliance is a requirement for private actions. If one

expands the Affiliated Ute theory broadly enough to encompass assistance in a misrepresentation, aiding and abetting liability is readily subsumed within primary liability. This result would be inconsistent with Central Bank.

83. A proposed reason for the broad participation theories of liability in lower courts is an "equilibrium" theory. *See* Langevoort, *supra* note 5, at 887. If accurate, this theory suggests that it is not so much ambiguity that created the circuit split, as a judicial skepticism with *Central Bank*, producing an effort by lower courts to return to the status quo.
84. *See* Musick, Peeler & Garrett v. Employers Ins. 508 U.S. 286, 304 (1993) (Thomas, J., dissenting).
85. *See* supra notes 6–12, 57–60, and accompanying text.
86. *See* 15 U.S.C. 78t(e), (f) (2000).
87. Professor Fisch interprets this post-Central Bank development to support an expansive view of secondary liability. Fisch, *supra* note 54, at 1318. Although, if anything, the congressional choice not to create more expansive private actions supports a narrow reading of the statute, the text means whatever it originally meant respecting private actions, irrespective of Congress's decision to leave that text intact. Were it otherwise, the many instances of congressional silence would invite a constant threat of judicial legislation.

ARTICLE 9.4

Circuit Split or a Matter of Semantics? The Supreme Court's Upcoming Decision on Rule 10b-5 "Scheme Liability" and Its Implications for Tax Shelter Fraud Litigation

Mark S. Pincus

INTRODUCTION

There remains some doubt as to which parties involved in a fraudulent scheme may be held liable for securities fraud under Rule 10b-5. In the 1994 case of *Central Bank of Denver v. First Interstate Bank of Denver*,[1] the Supreme Court recognized a private cause of action against "primary violators" of Rule 10b-5, but not against those who merely aid and abet such Rule 10b-5 violations.[2] Since *Central Bank*, the courts have disagreed about how to distinguish primary violators from "aiders and abettors" under Rule 10b-5.[3]

Although Rule 10b-5 has three provisions,[4] early interpretations of *Central Bank* tended to focus exclusively on Rule 10b-5(b)'s prohibition of material misstatements and omissions.[5] The 2002 case of *In re Enron Corp. Securities, Derivative & ERISA Litigation*,[6] however, sparked new interest in the little-used Rules 10b-5(a) and 10b-5(c).[7]

Since the Supreme Court case described in this section as pending has already been decided, why is this article still important?

Since *Enron*, securities fraud plaintiffs have begun filing separate claims under Rules 10b-5(a) and 10b-5(c), which scholars collectively have referred to as "scheme liability" claims.[8] This emerging theory of scheme liability, which has been called the "new battleground in securities fraud litigation,"[9] raises new questions about the scope of primary liability under Rule 10b-5. Circuit courts addressing the issue have adopted two opposing views on how to distinguish between primary violations and mere "aiding and abetting" under Rules 10b-5(a) and (c).[10] The U.S. Courts of Appeals for the Fifth and Eighth Circuits have adopted a narrow view of scheme liability,[11]While the U.S. Court of Appeals for the Ninth Circuit has adopted a broad view.[12] In March 2007, the U.S. Supreme Court granted certiorari on the Eighth Circuit's decision, which will be argued as *Stoneridge Investment Partners v. Scientific-Atlanta, Inc.*,[13] during the Court's October 2007 Term.[14] The *Stoneridge* case is likely to resolve the circuit split,[15] which may have implications for tax shelter plaintiffs seeking to bring claims under Rules 10b-5(a) and (c).

Part I of this Note discusses the history of tax shelters and litigation arising from them, as well as the evolution of Rule 10b-5 jurisprudence since *Central Bank*. Part II of this Note examines the circuit split as to the dividing line between primary and "aiding and abetting" liability under Rules 10b-5(a) and (c). Part III of this Note argues that, despite differences in language, both views employ similar concepts of primary liability, and tax shelter promoters are likely to be held as primary violators under either view. Part III discusses how to reconcile scheme liability claims under 10b-5(a) and (c) with the more traditional "misrepresentation or omission" liability under Rule 10b-5(b).

I. TAX SHELTERS, RICO, AND SECURITIES FRAUD

Part I discusses the history of tax shelter litigation and the evolution of securities fraud jurisprudence since the Supreme Court decided *Central Bank* in 1994. . . . Part I.C discusses the Supreme Court's holding in *Central Bank* that only primary violators may be held liable under Rule 10b-5 and the lower federal courts' subsequent disagreement about the meaning of this holding. . . .

C. The Great Securities Fraud Controversy: Distinguishing Primary Violators from "Aiders and Abettors" in Rule 10b-5 Lawsuits

The overwhelming failure of RICO claims in tax shelter cases leaves securities fraud as the primary means for investors to establish liability against tax shelter promoters under federal law. The private cause of action[16] for securities fraud is rooted in section 10(b) of the Securities Exchange Act of 1934, which makes it unlawful for "any person, directly or indirectly" to "use or employ, in connection with the purchase or sale of any security . . . any manipulative or deceptive device or contrivance" that contravenes SEC rules and regulations.[17] . . .

[P]laintiffs seeking to establish Rule 10b-5 liability against all parties involved in promoting fraudulent tax shelters face an additional obstacle. Since the Supreme Court decided *Central Bank of Denver v. First Interstate Bank of Denver* [18] in 1994, the courts no longer recognize "aiding and abetting securities fraud" as a valid cause of action under Rule 10b-5.[19] As a result, only defendants deemed "primary violators" of Rule 10b-5 are held liable, while those deemed mere "aiders and abettors" of the 10b-5 violation escape liability.[20] Since *Central Bank*, courts often have disagreed over where to place the dividing line between primary violations of Rule 10b-5 and mere "aiding and abetting."[21] In tax shelter schemes, where promoters had varying roles in the marketing and implementation of the shelter, *Central Bank* and its progeny are important to consider.

1. Central Bank: *No Cause of Action for Aiding and Abetting Securities Fraud*

Before the Supreme Court decided *Central Bank*, almost every federal circuit allowed 10b-5 suits against both primary violators and "aiders and abettors."[22] In fact, liability for aiding and abetting 10b-5 violations had become so firmly ingrained in securities fraud jurisprudence that neither party in *Central Bank* challenged its legitimacy.[23] Instead, the Court sua sponte directed the parties to address whether section 10(b) permitted private 10b-5 suits against aiders and abettors.[24] . . .

In ruling that private plaintiffs may not maintain Rule 10b-5 suits against aiders and abettors, the *Central Bank* Court sparked great controversy over a previously non-controversial issue.[25] The *Central Bank* case transformed the distinction between a "primary violator" and a mere "aider and abettor" from a largely academic exercise into a significant factor in determining Rule 10b-5 liability. *Central Bank*, however, failed to provide meaningful insight into how the distinction between "primary violation" and "aiding and abetting" should be made. Since 1994, the lower federal courts have grappled with *Central Bank's* ambiguous language, often reaching disagreement about its implications for 10b-5 liability. . . .

3. *Scheme Liability Under Rules 10b-5(a) and 10b-5(c)*

The *Enron* decision also took issue with the post-*Central Bank* cases' exclusive focus on misstatements and omissions. Drawing attention to the little-used Rules 10b-5(a) and 10b-5(c), the *Enron* court reiterated the Supreme Court's holding in *Affiliated Ute Citizens of Utah v. United States*[26] that, "while subsection (b) of Rule 10b-5 provides a cause of action based on [misstatements and omissions of material facts], subsections (a) and (c) are not so restricted."[27] Denying that Rules 10b-5(a) and (c) were "impliedly struck down in *Central Bank* merely because [*Central Bank*] addressed only subsection (b) misrepresentation and omission,"[28] the *Enron* court interpreted Rule 10b-5 as authorizing three distinct causes of action: "scheme" liability under 10b-5(a), "misrepresentation or omission" liability under 10b-5(b), and "course of business" liability under 10b-5(c).[29]

Is there a difference between an act that is manipulative and one that is deceptive, and if so, why might this difference be important?

The scope of conduct actionable under Rules 10b-5(a) and (c), however, remains unclear. The language of section 10(b) prohibits "any manipulative or deceptive device or contrivance."[30] Historically, the Supreme Court has held that the term "manipulation" is "virtually a term of art when used in connection with securities markets,"[31] referring to practices "intended to mislead investors by artificially affecting market activity,"[32] such as wash sales,[33] matched orders,[34] or rigged prices.[35] Additionally, the Court has interpreted "deception" as "the making of a material misrepresentation or the nondisclosure of material information in violation of a duty to disclose."[36] However, the Supreme Court also has held that section 10(b) prohibits "all fraudulent schemes in connection with the purchase or sale of securities, whether the artifices employed involve a garden type variety of fraud, or present a unique form of deception."[37] Thus, the Court held, section 10(b) should be "construed "not technically and restrictively, but flexibly to effectuate its remedial purposes.' "[38] The Court's recent repetition of this language in the 2002 case of *SEC v. Zandford*[39] suggests that this expansive view of the securities laws still remains in force.[40]

The lack of post-*Central Bank* case law on 10b-5(a) and (c) liability also leaves the dividing line between primary violations and mere "aiding and abetting" in question. The *Enron* case shed little light on the standard for primary liability under Rules 10b-5(a) and (c). Applying a similar standard for both subsections, *Enron* merely held that, "where a group of Defendants allegedly participated in the scheme to defraud the public and enrich themselves in connection with the purchase and sale of securities," any defendant with the requisite scienter who "actively employed a significant material device, contrivance, scheme, or artifice to defraud" would be primarily liable under Rule 10b-5(a), and any defendant who "actively engaged in a significant, material act, practice, or course of business that operated as a fraud or deceit upon any person in connection with the purchase or sale of any security" would be primarily liable under Rule 10b-5(c).[41]

II. THE SPLIT OVER SCHEME LIABILITY

After the *Enron* decision, securities fraud plaintiffs began filing claims alleging "schemes to defraud" under Rules 10b-5(a) and (c) in addition to the more traditional claims alleging "misrepresentations or omissions" under Rule 10b-5(b).[42] Although the *Enron* court appeared to treat claims for "scheme" liability under Rule 10b-5(a) as separate causes of action from claims for "course of business" liability under Rule 10b-5(c),[43] subsequent courts and scholars have placed both rules under the awning of "scheme liability"[44] and assessed both 10b-5(a) and 10b-5(c) claims under a single standard.[45]

As scheme liability claims have proliferated, controversy has arisen over the proper way to reconcile Rule 10b-5(a) and (c) liability with *Central Bank*. As a result, the distinction between primary violators and "aiders and abettors" under Rules 10b-5(a) and (c) has become a contested issue, leading one commentator to refer to scheme liability as the "new battleground in securities fraud litigation."[46] Whereas the earlier 10b-5(b) cases examined the extent of primary liability for those who participate in another party's fraudulent statement,[47] the new 10b-5(a) and (c) cases generally examine whether primary liability extends to those who participate in a business transaction with knowledge that the other party will use the transaction to misrepresent its financial situation to investors.[48]

Two opposing views have emerged as to the standard for primary liability under Rules 10b-5(a) and (c).[49] The narrow view, embraced by the Eighth

Circuit in *In re Charter Communications, Inc., Securities Litigation* [50] and the Fifth Circuit in *Regents of the University of California v. Credit Suisse First Boston (USA), Inc.*, [51] holds that primary liability under Rule 10b-5 extends only to parties who make material misstatements, make material omissions with a duty to disclose, or participate in the limited range of "manipulative" trading practices defined in *Santa Fe Industries, Inc. v. Green.*[52] The broad view, favored by the Ninth Circuit in *Simpson v. AOL Time Warner Inc.*,[53] holds that defendants who act with the purpose and effect of creating a false appearance of fact are primarily liable, even if those actions do not constitute a misstatement, omission, or manipulative trading practice as defined in *Santa Fe.*[54]

In March 2007, the Supreme Court granted certiorari in the *Charter Communications* case, which will be argued as *Stoneridge Investment Partners v. Scientific-Atlanta, Inc.*[55] In the *Stoneridge* case, which will be argued in the October 2007 Term,[56] the Supreme Court is likely to adopt one of these two views regarding the scope of scheme liability,[57] which could have implications in future tax shelter litigation. Part II.A of this Note discusses the narrow approach to scheme liability favored by the Fifth and Eighth Circuits, while Part II.B of this Note discusses the broad approach favored by the Ninth Circuit.

A. Charter Communications, Regents, and the Narrow View of Scheme Liability

The narrow view of scheme liability holds that primary liability under 10b-5(a) and (c) only extends to those who make misstatements of material fact, omissions when they have a duty to disclose, or engage in one of the manipulative trading practices discussed in *Santa Fe.*[58]

The Eighth Circuit case of *Charter Communications* involved a cable company accused of defrauding its investors by falsely inflating the revenue reported on its financial statements.[59] . . .

According to the Eighth Circuit, *Central Bank's* holding that a private plaintiff ""may not bring a 10b-5 suit against a defendant for acts not prohibited by the text of § 10(b)' included claims under Rule 10b-5(a) and (c), as well as Rule 10b-5(b)."[60] . . . Therefore, held the Eighth Circuit, "any defendant who does not make or affirmatively cause to be made a fraudulent misstatement or omission" or "who does not directly engage in manipulative securities trading practices, is at most guilty of aiding and abetting and cannot be held liable under § 10(b) or Rule 10b-5."[61] . . .

The Fifth Circuit case of *Regents* involved a similar scheme in which Enron arranged to sell certain of its assets to banks on the promise that it would buy the assets back at a premium six months later.[62] . . . Adopting the Eighth Circuit's view that "deceptive" conduct covers only fraudulent misstatements and omissions,[63] the Fifth Circuit refused to hold the banks liable as primary violators.[64] . . .

B. *Simpson* and the Broad View of Scheme Liability

The broad view of scheme liability holds that defendants who act with the purpose and effect of creating a false appearance of fact are primarily liable under Rule 10b-5, even if those actions do not constitute a misstatement, omission, or manipulative trading practice as defined in *Santa Fe*.[65]

Simpson, a Ninth Circuit case, also involved a company accused of inflating its revenues through sham transactions with third parties.[66] . . . Similar to *Charter Communications* and *Regents*, the *Simpson* court assessed whether the vendors who participated in the transactions with the Internet company were liable as primary violators under "scheme to defraud" claims.[67]

Formulating its view on scheme liability, the Ninth Circuit referenced the Supreme Court's holding in *Zandford*[68] that section 10(b) "should be construed not technically and restrictively, but flexibly to effectuate its remedial purposes."[69] Focusing on section 10(b)'s prohibition of "any manipulative or deceptive device or contrivance," the Ninth Circuit broadly defined "deception" as "engaging in a transaction, the principal purpose and effect of which is to create a false appearance of fact."[70] . . .

The Ninth Circuit dismissed the plaintiffs' claims, holding that the plaintiffs failed to allege that either America Online or the vendors had created a false appearance in furtherance of the scheme. According to the Ninth Circuit, "illegitimate transactions in furtherance of a scheme to misrepresent revenues" create a false appearance and are chargeable as primary violations, while actions that merely "facilitate[] or assist[] the fraudulent misreporting of legitimate transactions" do not themselves create a false appearance and therefore only constitute "aiding and abetting."[71] As the complaint failed to allege that the transactions were illegitimate or that "actual advertisements were not purchased and sold" by the vendors, the court held that plaintiffs had not alleged primary violations against America Online or the vendors.[72] According to the court, a false appearance was not created until the Internet company chose to misrepresent the transactions in its financial statements.[73]

The court also set a few guidelines for determining whether a defendant's conduct has "a principal purpose and effect of creating a false appearance of fact."[74] According to the court, "conduct by the defendant that does not have a principal legitimate business purpose"[75] may qualify, while "conduct that is consistent with the defendants' normal course of business" typically would not.[76] Also, "participation in a legitimate transaction, which does not have a deceptive purpose or effect" would not be considered a primary violation, "even if the defendant knew or intended that another party would manipulate the transaction to effectuate a fraud."[77]

III. FILING TAX SHELTER CASES ALLEGING SCHEME LIABILITY UNDER RULES 10B-5(A) AND 10B-5(C)

Part III discusses the impact of the recent scheme liability decisions on tax shelter litigation and contemplates how to reconcile scheme liability under Rules 10b-5(a) and (c) with traditional "misstatement or omission" liability under Rule 10b-5(b). Part III.A argues that, despite their difference in language, the standards for primary liability set forth under both the narrow view of *Charter Communications/Regents* and the broad view of *Simpson* likely cover the same range of conduct. . . . Part III.D suggests that defendants held as primary violators under a theory of scheme liability should be held as primary violators for all misstatements or omissions made in furtherance of the scheme, even if they would not have been held as primary violators for each individual misstatement.

A. Circuit Split or a Matter of Semantics?

The scholarship and case law following *Charter Communications/Regents* and *Simpson* has framed these two views as a circuit split over which conduct is actionable in scheme liability claims brought under Rules 10b-5(a) and (c).[78] Both views certainly employed opposite language while interpreting section 10(b)'s prohibition of "manipulative or deceptive devices or contrivances."[79] Despite this difference in language, it appears that both views may cover the same range of conduct.

Charter Communications and *Regents* employed restrictive language in their approach to scheme liability.[80] Invoking *Central Bank's* holding as a "categorical declaration that a private plaintiff "may not bring a 10b-5 suit against a defendant for acts not prohibited by the text of § 10(b),' "[81] both the *Charter Communications* and *Regents* courts restricted "deceptive" conduct to material misstatements and omissions by those with a duty to disclose, and restricted "manipulative" conduct to the limited number of transactions discussed in *Santa Fe*.[82] According to this view, any defendant whose conduct does not fit into one of these categories "is at most guilty of aiding and abetting" and "cannot be held liable under § 10(b) or Rule 10b-5."[83]

Conversely, *Simpson* employed expansive language in its approach to scheme liability.[84] Although *Simpson* did not challenge the narrow view's definition of "manipulative,"[85] the *Simpson* court seemed to take a broader approach to the term "deceptive."[86] Invoking the holding of *SEC v. Zandford* that section 10(b) "should be construed not technically and restrictively, but flexibly to effectuate its remedial purposes,"[87] the court held that deceptive conduct encompasses "engaging in a transaction, the principal purpose and effect of which is to create the false appearance of fact."[88]

Under closer observation, however, it appears that this "split" simply may be a matter of semantics.[89] Gregory A. Markel and Gregory G. Ballard, two New York securities litigators, believe that the Simpson test covers "active participation in a fraudulent scheme by someone who does not make a misstatement or omission, or engage in a manipulative securities trade."[90] The courts, however, have yet to provide an example of a "deceptive" act that does not involve a misrepresentation or omission, but still would impose primary liability on the actor.

Although *Simpson* may use more expansive language than *Charter Communications*, the conduct prohibited by the *Simpson* standard is actually quite similar. According to *Simpson*, "It is not enough that a transaction in which a defendant was involved had a deceptive purpose and effect; the defendant's own conduct contributing to the transaction or overall scheme must have had a deceptive purpose and effect."[91] Under *Simpson*, a primary violator must affirmatively act in furtherance of the scheme with the purpose of deceiving the plaintiff.[92] Aside from the "manipulative" acts discussed in *Santa Fe*,[93] however, it appears that any act whose "principal purpose and effect" is to "create a false appearance of fact"[94] can be classified as either a material misstatement or omission. Obviously, a securities fraud defendant who intentionally transmits false information to the plaintiff has acted with the "principal purpose and effect" of "creating a false appearance of fact."[95]

The inquiry then must turn to the extent of liability for nonspeaking actors. *Simpson* made clear that a defendant who participates in a transaction and merely is aware that the transaction eventually will be used for a deceptive purpose is considered an "aider and abettor," and therefore would not be liable under 10b-5(a) or (c).[96] This holding appears to be in accord with the holdings in *Charter Communications* and *Regents* that primary liability does not attach without a misstatement of fact or a failure to disclose by one who has a duty to disclose.[97] Without the duty to disclose the true facts to the plaintiff, such as the duty created by a fiduciary relationship,[98] a party's silence would not subject the party to primary liability in 10b-5(a) and (c) lawsuits under either view of scheme liability. . . .

D. Reconciling Scheme Liability with Traditional "Misstatement or Omission" Liability

Charter Communications, *Regents*, and *Simpson* do not indicate how the courts will reconcile claims for scheme liability under Rules 10b-5(a) and (c) with the more traditional "misrepresentation or omission liability" of Rule 10b-5(b). If one assumes that the parameters of scheme liability under both *Simpson* and *Charter* are functionally equal,[99] then one could argue that the only difference between scheme liability and traditional 10b-5(b) liability is that scheme liability covers the "manipulative" trading practices in *Santa Fe* in addition to the misstatements or omissions covered under both theories. As tax shelter cases generally do not allege conduct commonly viewed as "manipulative" by the federal courts,[100] one could also argue that the standard of primary liability would be the same, regardless of whether plaintiffs brought scheme liability claims under 10b-5(a) or (c) or misrepresentation/omission claims under 10b-5(b).

The term "scheme," however, connotes more than just a series of independent misrepresentations or omissions. Although the federal courts never have defined "scheme" as used in Rule 10b-5(a), the Oxford English Dictionary defines "scheme" as "a plan of action devised in order to attain some end."[101] Under this definition, the tax shelters discussed in this Note were fraudulent "schemes" in the true sense of the term. Tax shelter promoters engaged in a premeditated plan of action to market and implement fraudulent tax shelters, devised to achieve their desired end of earning profit. Each promoter was instrumental in designing this plan of action and played a predetermined role in its implementation.

A true scheme, such as the tax shelters discussed in this Note, represents a whole greater than the sum of its constituent parts. The illusion of legitimacy created through the concerted efforts of tax shelter promoters hinged on a series of interdependent misstatements and omissions. Unless promoters properly executed each successive misstatement or omission, the tax shelter plan as a whole was doomed to fail.

Rule 10b-5(b)'s prohibition of material misstatements and omissions[102] seems to apply to single, independent misstatements and omissions, while Rule 10b-5(a)'s prohibition of schemes to defraud seems to apply to premeditated and concerted efforts to perpetrate an overarching fraud through multiple misrepresentations and omissions.[103] Under the narrow conception of 10b-5(b) "misstatement or omission" liability articulated by the Second Circuit's bright-line test,[104] a primary violator's name must be associated with the fraudulent statement at the time it is disseminated.[105] Establishing primary liability under Rule 10b-5(b) against all promoters for the entire operation could be problematic if certain parties' names were not associated with certain specific misstatements. Scheme liability under Rule 10b-5(a) or (c) should differ from Rule 10b-5(b) liability in this critical respect. A party held primarily liable under Rules 10b-5(a) or (c) for furthering a fraudulent scheme should be liable for all misstatements or omissions committed in furtherance of that scheme, regardless of whether the party would be held as a primary violator for each individual misrepresentation or omission. When a party has played enough of an integral role in planning and orchestrating a fraudulent scheme to be held as a primary violator under 10b-5(a) or (c), he should be held as a "creator" of every misstatement, similar to the concept articulated in the *Enron* case.[106] This standard would ensure that each party would be held liable for the wrongful conduct of others who commit fraud in furtherance of the scheme.

In previous scheme liability cases, which dealt with fraudulent financial statements issued on behalf of a corporation, this concept was not much of an issue. In both of these cases, the court found that only one party, the corporation itself, was a primary violator.[107] Although multiple individuals within the corporation may have been responsible for creating or disseminating the fraudulent financial statements, all statements were issued in the name of the corporation, and thus could be imputed to the corporation.[108]

In tax shelter cases, however, the promoters were not acting as agents of a corporation to which all of their conduct could be imputed.[109] Rather, the tax shelter scheme itself, which did not take the form of an identifiable entity, was their "principal." In determining scheme liability for tax shelter promoters under Rule 10b-5(a) and (c), the promoters' relationship should be viewed similarly to a general partnership. By entering into an arrangement to promote, market, and implement a tax shelter, each promoter's actions on behalf of the overall scheme should be considered binding on all other promoters when determining Rule 10b-5(a) and (c) liability. When one promoter makes a misstatement during a sales pitch to an investor, he speaks on behalf of all of the other promoters, even if the investor is unaware of an individual promoter's involvement in the statement. A lawyer who co-plans a tax shelter scheme is equally responsible for misstatements made during the sales pitch by other promoters, even though his true role is concealed to create an illusion of legitimacy in his opinion letters. Under 10b-5(a) and (c), each promoter also should be liable for his co-promoters' actions in furtherance of the scheme. When a banker-promoter performs the orchestrated transactions on behalf of the tax shelter scheme, all other promoters should be held responsible for the consequences, even if they did not take part in the transactions themselves.

CONCLUSION

Regardless of which standard the Supreme Court chooses to adopt in the upcoming *Stoneridge* case, tax shelter promoters are likely to be considered primary violators. However, litigating tax shelter fraud cases may be easier for plaintiffs under Rules 10b-5(a) and (c) than under 10b-5(b). Rather than having to prove that each promoter is responsible for each misstatement made in furtherance of the scheme, plaintiffs can simply demonstrate the existence of a premeditated scheme and prove that each promoter acted in furtherance of that scheme.

END NOTES

1. 511 U.S. 164 (1994).
2. *Id.* at 177. . . .
3. *See infra.* . . . II.A-B.
4. Rule 10b-5(a) prohibits "any device, scheme, or artifice to defraud"; Rule 10b-5(b) prohibits material misstatements or omissions; and Rule 10b-5(c) prohibits "any act, practice, or course of business which operates or would operate as a fraud or deceit upon any person." SEC Rule 10b-5, 17 C.F.R. § 240.10b-5 (2006).
5. [footnote omitted]

6. 235 F. Supp. 2d 549, 589 n.31 (S.D. Tex. 2002).
7. *See* Nicholas Fortune Schanbaum, *Note, Scheme Liability: Rule 10b-5(a) and Secondary Actor Liability After* Central Bank, 26 REV. LITIG. 183, 207 (2007).
8. *See generally* Gregory A. Markel & Gregory G. Ballard, *The Evolution of "Scheme" Liability Under Section 10(b)*, 1571 PLI/CORP 991 (2006); Matthew L. Mustokoff, *"Scheme" Liability Under Rule 10b-5: The New Battleground in Securities Fraud Litigation*, FED. LAW., June 2006, at 20.
9. Mustokoff, *supra* note, at 20.
10. *See infra* Part II.
11. *See infra* Part II.A.
12. *See infra* Part II.B.
13. 127 S. Ct. 1873 (2007).
14. A list of cases to be argued during the October 2007 term appears on the U.S. Supreme Court's website. . . .
15. Sarah S. Gold & Richard L. Spinogatti, *§ 10(b) Secondary Actor Liability: High Court to Resolve*, N.Y.L.J., Apr. 11, 2007, at 3.
16. Although the language of section 10(b) does not expressly create a private cause of action, the Supreme Court has implied one. *See* Superintendent of Ins. of N.Y. v. Bankers Life & Cas. Co., 404 U.S. 6, 13 n.9 (1971) (holding that "it is now established that a private right of action is implied under § 10(b)").
17. Securities Exchange Act of 1934 § 10(b), 15 U.S.C. § 78j(b) (2000).
18. 511 U.S. 164 (1994).
19. *Id.* at 191.
20. *See infra* Part I.C.1.
21. [footnote omitted]
22. *Central Bank*, 511 U.S. at 192 (Stevens, J., dissenting). At the time, eleven circuits allowed private plaintiffs to sue parties who aided and abetted other parties' Rule 10b-5 violations. *Id.* Although the D.C. Circuit had not considered whether private plaintiffs could sue aiders and abettors, it allowed the SEC to bring actions against them. *See id.* at 192 n.1.
23. *Id.* at 194.
24. *Id.* at 194–95.
25. *See* Schanbaum, *supra* note, at 190.
26. 406 U.S. 128 (1972).
27. *Enron*, 235 F. Supp. 2d at 577 (quoting *Affiliated Ute Citizens*, 406 U.S. at 152–53) (internal quotation marks omitted).
28. *Id.* at 589 n.31.
29. *Id.*
30. Securities Exchange Act of 1934 § 10(b), 15 U.S.C. § 78j(b) (1997).
31. Santa Fe Indus., Inc. v. Green, 430 U.S. 462, 476 (1977) (quoting Ernst & Ernst v. Hochfelder, 425 U.S. 185, 199 (1976)).

32. *Id.*
33. *Id.* A wash sale is a "transaction involving no change in beneficial ownership." *Enron*, 235 F. Supp. 2d at 568 n.8 (citing Ernst, 425 U.S. at 205 n.25).
34. *Santa Fe*, 430 U.S. at 476. Matched orders are "orders for the purchase/sale of a security that are entered with the knowledge that orders of substantially the same size, at substantially the same time and price, have been or will be entered by the same or different persons for the sale/purchase of such security." *Enron*, 235 F. Supp. 2d at 568 n.8.
35. *Enron*, 235 F. Supp. 2d at 568 n.8; *Santa Fe*, 430 U.S. at 476.
36. *Enron*, 235 F. Supp. 2d at 568 n.9 (citing Santa Fe, 430 U.S. at 470).
37. Superintendent of Ins. of N.Y. v. Bankers Life & Cas. Co., 404 U.S. 6, 11 n.7 (1971). . . .
38. Affiliated Ute Citizens of Utah v. United States, 406 U.S. 128, 151 (1972).
39. 535 U.S. 813 (2002).
40. *Id.* at 819.
41. *Enron*, 235 F. Supp. 2d at 693.
42. *See* In re Mutual Funds Inv. Litig., 384 F. Supp. 2d 845, 853 (D. Md. 2005) . . .; In re Global Crossing, Ltd. Sec. Litig., 322 F. Supp. 2d 319, 328 (S.D.N.Y. 2004). . . .
43. *See Enron*, 235 F. Supp. 2d at 589 n.31; *see also supra* note 29 and accompanying text.
44. *See* Steiner v. MedQuist Inc., No. 04-5487 (JBS), 2006 WL 2827740, at 20–21 (D.N.J. 2006) (referring to "Rule 10b-5(a) and (c) Scheme Liability"); Mustokoff, *supra* note , at 20 ("Plaintiffs are relying progressively more on the "scheme' liability prongs of Rule 10b-5: subsections (a) and (c).").
45. *See* In re Charter Commc'ns, Inc. Sec. Litig., 443 F.3d 987, 991–92 (8th Cir. 2006) cert. granted sub nom. Stoneridge Inv. Partners v. Scientific-Atlanta, Inc., 127 S. Ct. 1873 (2007) . . .; Simpson v. AOL Time Warner, Inc., 452 F.3d 1040, 1046–48 (9th Cir. 2006). . . .
46. Mustokoff, *supra* note , at 20.
47. *See supra* Part II.
48. *See generally* Regents of the Univ. of Cal. v. Credit Suisse First Boston (USA), Inc., 482 F.3d 372 (5th Cir. 2007); *Charter Commc'ns*, 443 F.3d 987; *Simpson*, 452 F.3d 1040.
49. *See infra* notes 50–54 and accompanying text.
50. *Charter Commc'ns*, 443 F.3d at 997.
51. *Regents*, 482 F.3d at 387.
52. 430 U.S. 462, 476 (1977). These practices include wash sales, matched orders, and rigged prices. For a definition of these enumerated practices, *see supra* notes 33–35 and accompanying text.
53. 452 F.3d at 1048.
54. *See infra* Part II.B and accompanying text.

55. 127 S. Ct. 1873 (2007).
56. A list of cases to be argued during the October 2007 term appears on the U.S. Supreme Court's website. . . .
57. *See* Gold & Spinogatti, *supra* note 15, at 3.
58. The narrow view has also been adopted by the U.S. District Court for the District of Columbia in the case of In re Federal National Mortgage Association Securities. Civ. Action No. 04-1639(RJL), 2007 WL 1378464, at 5 n.3 (D.D.C. May 8, 2007) ("This Court finds that the more restrictive interpretation . . . adopted by the Fifth and Eighth Circuits . . . is in better keeping with the Supreme Court's ruling in Central Bank.").
59. In re Charter Commc'ns, Inc. Sec. Litig., 443 F.3d 987, 989 (8th Cir. 2006).
60. *Id.* (quoting Central Bank of Denver v. First Interstate Bank of Denver, 511 U.S. 164, 173 (1994) (internal citations omitted)).
61. *Charter Commc'ns*, 443 F.3d at 992.
62. Regents of the Univ. of Cal. v. Credit Suisse First Boston (USA), Inc., 482 F.3d 372, 377 (5th Cir. 2007).
63. *Id.* at 388.
64. *Id.* at 390.
65. The broad view also has been adopted by the U.S. District Court for the District of New Jersey in Steiner v. MedQuist, Inc., Civil No. 04-5487 (JBS), 2006 WL 2827740, at 21 (D.N.J. Sept. 29, 2006) ("The Court here finds [the reasoning of the Ninth Circuit] persuasive.").
66. 452 F.3d 1040, 1042 (9th Cir. 2006).
67. *Id.* at 1046.
68. 535 U.S. 813 (2002) (favoring an expansive view of the securities laws).
69. Simpson, 452 F.3d at 1049 (quoting *Zandford*, 535 U.S. at 819) (internal quotation marks omitted).
70. *Id.* at 1048. The *Simpson* court does not elaborate on the definition of "manipulative." This Note assumes that the *Simpson* court accepts the Supreme Court's definition of "manipulative" as expressed in *Santa Fe*.
71. *Id.* at 1052.
72. *Id.* at 1053.
73. *See id.*
74. *Id.* at 1049.
75. *Id.* at 1050. The court gives as an example "the invention of sham corporate entities to misrepresent the flow of income." *Id.* (citing In re Enron Corp. Sec., Derivative & ERISA Litig., 310 F. Supp. 2d 819, 830 (S.D. Tex. 2004) . . .).
76. *Simpson*, 452 F.3d at 1050 (citing *Enron*, 235 F. Supp. 2d at 580) ("Conclusory allegations that are consistent with the normal activity of such a business entity, standing alone, . . . are insufficient to state a claim of primary liability under Central Bank.") (internal quotation marks omitted)).
77. *Id.* . . .

78. Regents of the Univ. of Cal. v. Credit Suisse First Boston (USA), Inc., 482 F.3d 372, 386 (5th Cir. 2007) . . .; In re Fed. Nat'l Mortgage Ass'n Sec., Civ. Action No. 04-1639(RJL), 2007 WL 1378464, at 5 n.3 (D.D.C. May 8, 2007) . . .; Markel & Ballard, *supra* note , at 994. . . .
79. SEC Rule 10b-5(a), 17 C.F.R. § 240.10b-5(a) (2007). *Compare supra* Part II.A (discussing the narrow language employed by *Charter Communications* and *Regents*), *with supra* Part II.B (discussing the broad language employed by *Simpson*).
80. *See supra* Part II.A.
81. *See supra* note and accompanying text; *see also* Central Bank of Denver v. First Interstate Bank of Denver, 511 U.S. 164, 173 (1994).
82. [footnote omitted]
83. *See supra* note 298 and accompanying text; *see also* In re Charter Commc'ns Sec. Litig., 443 F.3d 987, 992 (8th Cir. 2006).
84. *See supra* Part II.B.
85. *See supra* note 70 and accompanying text.
86. Markel & Ballard, *supra* note 21, at 1002 (considering *Simpson's* holding a "broader view").
87. SEC v. Zandford, 535 U.S. 813, 819 (2002) (internal quotation marks omitted); *see also supra* note 69 and accompanying text.
88. Simpson v. AOL Time Warner Inc., 452 F.3d 1040, 1048 (9th Cir. 2006); *see supra* note 74 and accompanying text.
89. *See supra* Part II.A-B.
90. Markel & Ballard, *supra* note 8, at 993.
91. *Simpson*, 452 F.3d at 1049.
92. *See supra* Part II.B.
93. *See supra* notes 61, 63 and accompanying text; *see also Simpson*, 452 F.3d at 1049.
94. *See supra* note 74 and accompanying text.
95. *See Simpson*, 452 F.3d at 1049.
96. *See supra* note 77 and accompanying text.
97. *See supra* note 61 and accompanying text.
98. [footnote omitted]
99. *See supra* Part III.A.
100. [footnote omitted]
101. OXFORD ENGLISH DICTIONARY 616 (2d ed. 1989).
102. *See* SEC Rule 10b-5(b), 17 C.F.R. § 240.10b-5(b) (2007).
103. *See* SEC Rule 10b-5(a), 17 C.F.R. § 240.10b-5(a).
104. [footnote omitted]
105. [footnote omitted]
106. [footnote omitted]
107. *See supra* Part II.A-B.
108. *See supra* Part II.A-B.
109. [footnote omitted]

ISSUE SUMMARY

One thing this chapter demonstrates is that scheme liability, as with many other areas of the law, leads many reasonable people to disagree. That is, there is debate among legal scholars and judges regarding the legality of scheme liability. While many of the opinions in this chapter lean towards skepticism regarding scheme liability's legality, the debate is far from over. In fact, even the Supreme Court is narrowly divided regarding scheme liability's legality. Justices Kennedy and Stevens put forth two opinions included in this chapter that demonstrate how the Court is split regarding when third parties can be held liable for securities fraud. The Court's opinion in *Stoneridge* is certainly not the end of the debate. The law involves a degree of interpretation, which is not to say that the law is inconsistent or lacking in substance. However, the debate regarding scheme liability highlights the fact that the law is rarely "obvious."

What we know is that while it is doubtful that scheme liability will have a significant impact in the future, it is also true that the Enron scandal brought scheme liability to the fore, and the backlash from the Enron case can lead people to question the desirability of scheme liability. If the court says the current laws do not allow for scheme liability, or only in rare cases, it is conceivable that Congress might create laws expanding the scope of scheme liability. This very real possibility makes it important to not only consider whether scheme liability is legal currently, but also whether it is desirable as policy.

ISSUE HIGHLIGHTS

- To bring a successful § 10(b) suit by a private party, the private party must prove that the defendant: (1) made a material misrepresentation or omission; (2) knowingly and intentionally committed misrepresentation or omission; (3) the misrepresentation or omission is related to the purchase or sale of a security; (4) the plaintiff erroneously relied upon the misrepresentation or omission; (5) the plaintiff suffered economic loss due to the misrepresentation or omission; and (6) the misrepresentation or omission is the direct cause of the loss.
- To be held liable under § 10(b), according to the Supreme Court, a third party must be guilty of all of the elements of securities fraud.
- Plaintiffs are increasingly relying upon Rules 10b-5(a) and (c) to try to recover damages from a broader range of defendants under the concept of scheme liability.
- The Securities and Exchange Commission (SEC) favors the application of scheme liability to third parties.

- The Court's opinion in *Central Bank* determined that § 10(b) does not apply to aiders and abettors, but the Court did not clearly establish the difference between aiders and abettors and those involved in scheme liability.
- Lower courts have routinely interpreted *Central Bank* in various, inconsistent ways such that the courts do not have consensus regarding the legality of scheme liability.
- In *SEC v. Zandford*, the Court has upheld Rule 10b-5, including sections (a) and (c), which some scholars argue include the provisions for scheme liability.
- The Enron litigation was the impetus for the increased number of cases alleging scheme liability.
- The Court's opinion in *Central Bank* created controversy surrounding the aider and abettor vs. primary liable party distinction that did not exist before the opinion.
- It is highly likely that scheme liability applies to parties involved in tax shelters.

CRITICAL THINKING

Much of legal reasoning, which includes most arguments about legal issues, involves arguments by analogy. In that American jurisprudence is based on legal precedent, legal arguments tend to make analogies between facts patterns and case specific information to argue when specific precedents apply. It is this process of applying precedent to new situations that builds American law. Accordingly, assessing the quality of legal analogies is key to determining the strength of many legal arguments. As a critical thinker, asking how strong the analogy is between past cases and the issue at hand is a crucial first step towards evaluating the strength of an argument.

The case and articles excerpted in this chapter are no exception. Starting with the Supreme Court case *Stoneridge*, included in this chapter, we see how reasonable people can disagree based on different assessments of the strength of a legal analogy. Much of Justice Kennedy's majority opinion rests on the assessment that the Court's earlier ruling in *Central Bank* bars scheme liability where the third party did not actively make a misrepresentation that was relied upon by other parties. However, in his dissent, Justice Stevens argues that Justice Kennedy misses key points in his application of the legal analogy between *Central Bank* and *Stoneridge*. According to Stevens, the facts of *Central Bank* are too different to apply directly to *Stoneridge*. Depending on how one assesses the analogy between *Central Bank* and *Stoneridge* will determine how one views the Court's ultimate ruling in *Stoneridge*. While the legal analogy is not the only argument presented by the Court, it is the focus of the Court's argument.

Reasoning by analogy, and evaluating the strength of an argument based on the analogies used is not limited to judicial opinions. The articles included in this chapter also engage in reasoning by analogy. McLaughlin's argument involves an assessment of precedents that define key terms to the scheme liability debate. He also argues that many scholars and judges have failed to consider the key precedents in their analysis, and thus have missed the relevant analogies in their arguments. Both Gold and Pincus discuss how there is disagreement in lower courts as to how to properly apply *Central Bank.* In their various approaches to *Central Bank, Zandford,* and lower court opinions, Gold and Pincus engage in reasoning by analogy. Briefly skim the articles you read in this chapter and look for the times when the authors reason by analogy. How strong are the analogies used? Do you agree with the authors regarding the strength of the analogy? If not, how does your disagreement affect your opinion of the authors' conclusions?

Remember, no analogy is perfect. All analogies have flaws and break down eventually under analysis. The point is not to search for the flaw and then simply dismiss the analogy as faulty reasoning. Rather, a critical thinker will determine what the strengths and weaknesses of an analogy are and then evaluate the analogy as a whole. Strong analogies can typically make up for their shortcomings and still function as useful reasoning tools. Analogies with too many weaknesses tend to not provide much support for an argument. Regardless, when evaluating arguments that reason by analogy, start by comparing strengths and weaknesses of the analogy to determine if the analogy is appropriate, and if it supports or hinders the argument. By assessing analogies, you are on your way to becoming a good critical thinker, especially when evaluating legal arguments.

ADDITIONAL READING SOURCES

Andrew Edison, "The *Stoneridge* Case—Much Ado About Nothing?" 9 *J. Investment Compliance*, 5 (2008).

Christine Hurt, *The Undercivilization of Corporate Law*, 33 IOWA J. CORP. L. 361 (2008).

Gideon Mark, "Accounting Fraud: Pleading Scienter of Auditors Under the PSLRA," 39 *Connecticut Law Review*, 1097 (2007).

Gregory A. Markel, and Gregory G. Ballard, "When Can Financial Institutions be Liable for Federal Securities Fraud in Connection with Securities Issued by Others: The Uncertain State of the Law," 4 *Int'l J. Disclosure & Governance*, 106 (2007).

John C. Tanner, Anthony P. Tatum, and Michael J. Cates, "After *Stoneridge*," 55 *Risk Management*, 56 (June 2008).

John C. Tanner, Rebecca M. Lamberth, and John H. Goselin, "Evolving Theories of Scheme Liability: Does Your D&O Policy Cover Guilt by Association?" 52 *Risk Management*, 46 (September 2005).

Johnathan D. Polkes, and Matthew L. Mustokoff, "District Court Weighs Novel Theories of Rule 10b-5 Liability in Mutual Fund Market Timing Litigation," 34 *Sec. Reg L. J.* 4 (2006).

Travis S. Souza, "Freedom to Defraud: *Stoneridge*, Primary Liability, and the Need to Properly Define Section 10(B)," 57 *Duke Law Journal*, 1179 (2008).

For more information check these cites:

http://blogs.wsj.com/law/2007/05/29/scheme-liability-christopher-coxs-litmus-test/

http://www.gaccom.org/index.php?id=50&tx_ttnews%5Btt_news%5D=52&cHash=2fb5a954a8

http://www.metrocorpcounsel.com/current.php?artType=view&EntryNo=6079

http://www.sec.gov/index.htm

http://www.the10b-5daily.com/

ISSUE 10

What Should You Be Able to Keep When You Go Bankrupt?

As the United States is rocked by a housing crisis, ever rising gasoline prices, and stagnating wages, more and more Americans are faced with the prospect of bankruptcy. Accordingly, bankruptcy law and debtors' rights are topics of increasing concern for many Americans. What rights are debtors afforded under bankruptcy laws? What rights should they have? The central focus of this collection of articles is a concern for debtors' rights, both individual citizens as debtors as well as businesses as debtors. Bankruptcy law is intended to allow debtors to continue to function in society while granting them assistance in paying back their debts. Given the dual purposes of aiding debtors and ensuring that creditors receive their money, bankruptcy law seeks to protect two competing groups of people: creditors and debtors. This dual purpose creates tension within bankruptcy law, which makes the issue of debtors' rights all the more salient.

The U.S. Bankruptcy Court's ruling in *Opel v. Daly* serves as useful introduction to the issue of what people can keep when they go bankrupt. As part of his bankruptcy filings, Daly wanted to exclude several tort awards he believed were coming his way from pending litigation. Daly's bankruptcy trustee and the company paying him disability insurance from a previous injury both objected to Daly's desire to retain the tort awards. In their decision, included in this section, the U.S. Bankruptcy Court goes through Daly's various exemptions and considers which awards, and how much of the various awards, he is legally allowed to keep. In their analysis, the court starts to explain what the debtor is allowed to keep and what must go towards paying back his debts.

Michelle White's article compares filing for bankruptcy before and after Congress passed the Bankruptcy Abuse Prevention and Consumer Protection Act of 2005 (BAPCPA). BAPCPA significantly changed the rules and exemptions regarding bankruptcy filings. White analyzes these changes in light of the balancing act in which bankruptcy is intended to engage. This balancing act involves, on the one hand, trying to protect creditors to make sure they receive the money they are owed such that they can continue to lend out money to others. On the other hand, the law also tries to protect debtors who fall on hard times and need help maintaining a reasonable standard of living while they repay their debts. While pre-BAPCPA was debtor-friendly and thus did not quite meet the desired balance, BAPCPA does not serve this balance either, as it is heavily weighted towards creditors. Moreover, BAPCPA creates conditions that punish non-opportunistic debtors who are not trying to cheat the system, while still leaving in ways for opportunistic debtors to manipulate the system to their benefit. Throughout her analysis, White discusses debtors' rights and how BAPCPA affected what opportunistic and non-opportunistic debtors may keep during bankruptcy proceedings.

A developing theme in discussions regarding what rights debtors have in bankruptcy is balancing interests. Furthering this discussion of balance, Joseph Blyskal argues that the purposes of personal injury tort law and bankruptcy law are in conflict when personal injury awards are included as part of the bankruptcy estate. The Bankruptcy Act of 1978 allowed personal injury awards to be included as part of the bankruptcy estate. Since the passage of the Bankruptcy Act of 1978, bankrupt debtors have been essentially stripped of the personal injury tort awards that were intended to make them "whole" again. According to Blyskal, debtors should be allowed to exempt their personal injury awards because failing to do so undercuts the goals of bankruptcy law by robbing the debtors of their chance at a clean start. Moreover, the loss of a personal injury award creates conditions where the debtor is more likely to stay a debtor as well as become a burden on society through increased reliance upon social welfare programs instead of using the personal injury money to care for him or herself. As such, society as a whole benefits when debtors have the right to exempt their personal injury tort awards from their bankruptcy estate.

While individuals are frequently at the center of bankruptcy proceedings, businesses can also declare bankruptcy. When these businesses are involved with providing public services, special issues arise regarding allowing a company to escape some of its debt through bankruptcy while still providing crucial public services. Joseph Smolinsky, using real-world examples, considers what happens when the U.S. Bankruptcy Code conflicts with other federal regulations. Specifically, Smolinsky examines conflicts over when private businesses providing energy to public utilities may get out of long-term power purchase agreements (PPAs) that lock the bankrupt company into agreements to provide energy at a given cost over an extended period of time. Past rulings by the Bankruptcy Court and the Federal Energy Regulatory Commission (FERC) are in conflict as to who has jurisdiction and when businesses may get out of a PPA. Smolinsky explains when debtor businesses are forced to keep their agreements, and when these debtors have the right to drop or renegotiate PPAs as part of a debt settlement.

Continuing the analysis surrounding the purpose of bankruptcy law, Joshua Silverstein argues that bankruptcy law is intended to create a fresh start for debtors, specifically in this case, debtor businesses. In addition, bankruptcy law is intended to help debtors pay back debts to the creditors. This balance is well acknowledged by other authors, including White and Smolinsky. However, Silverstein's analysis adds a twist by focusing on a specific Supreme Court ruling to argue that the Court is in favor of "non-debtor releases." A non-debtor release is when a coliable party, but not the debtor, is released from obligations to pay a debt because the debtor has filed for bankruptcy. Silverstein says the Supreme Court's ruling in *United States v. Energy Resources Co.* upholds as legal non-debtor releases. Furthermore, these releases are necessary to encourage third parties to aid debtors in payments while not creating disincentives for investments. By freeing third parties of their legal obligation to pay, these third parties are freed to help the debtor pay back the creditors while staying in business, and thus non-debtor releases are beneficial to everyone. While non-debtor releases do not refer directly to the rights a debtor has in bankruptcy, these non-debtor releases are connected to debtors' rights as the releases relate to the discharging of a debtor's debt in bankruptcy, not just for the debtor itself but also for coliable parties that could be helpful in paying back debt and keeping businesses from closing forever.

Despite legal rulings, such as *Opel v. Daly* and *United States v. Energy Resources Co.,* and laws, such as BAPCPA, American bankruptcy law is far from a clear, efficient system. Hopefully this set of readings will serve as a useful primer for considering what rights debtors should have under bankruptcy law. While reading the article in this section keep in mind the dual purposes of bankruptcy law: to help debtors get a fresh start, and to help creditors receive payment for their investments.

ISSUE ARTICLES

Robert N. Opel v. Arthur Terry Daly, 344 *B.R.* 304 (2005).

Michelle J. White, "Abuse or Protection?," 29 *REG.* 28 (2006).

Joseph Smolinsky, "Power Agency Fights Court Over Bankruptcy Rights," *International Financial Law Review*.1 (November 2004).

Joseph J. Blyskal III, "Levying Flesh and Charging Society, Creditors, and Insurance Companies for it: The Irony of Including Personal Injury Awards in the Bankruptcy Estate," 23 *Emory Bankruptcy Devlopments Journal,* 677 (2007).

Joshua M. Silverstein, "Hiding in Plain View: A Neglected Supreme Court Decision Resolves the Debate Over Non-Debtor Releases in Chapter 11 Reorganizations," 23 *Emory Bankruptcy Devlopments Journal*, 13 (2006).

ARTICLE 10.1

Robert N. Opel v. Arthur Terry Daly

In 1989, Arthur Terry Daly purchased a disability insurance policy from New York Life Insurance Company (NYL). Daly made a claim in July 1993 against the policy. NYL paid Daly $400 a month for approximately four years before it terminated the policy. On October 20, 1995, NYL filed a complaint in the Eastern District of Pennsylvania against Daly seeking the return of monies paid under the policy. Daly eventually filed for bankruptcy in 2002, with his claim being switched to a Chapter 7 bankruptcy claim in 2003. Robert Opel was appointed soon after as Daly's Interim Trustee. Throughout his bankruptcy proceedings, Daly served as his own attorney, frequently amending the schedules he filed regarding his assets and his exemptions for his bankruptcy filing. Many of the amendments Daly filed pertained to various tort claims to which he was a party.

Should the fact that the debtor acted as his own attorney be relevant in this case?

On October 1, 2003, the Trustee filed a motion to approve a $35,000.00 settlement of Daly's litigation with NYL. Daly elected, yet again, to amend Schedules B & C on October 16, 2003. Daly described eight lawsuits on his Schedule B. Immediately above their descriptions, he included the statement "THE VALUE OF EACH OF THESE CLAIMS IS UNKNOWN; THEY (the claims) ARE IN LITIGATION." In addition, Daly listed "UNKNOWN" in the column labeled "Current Market Value of Debtor's Interest in Property, without Deducting any Secured Claim or Exemption" with regard to the lawsuits. Identical notations were made on Schedule C with regard to the "Value of Claimed Exemption" and the "Current Value of Property Without Deducting Exemption." Daly based these exemptions on "11 USC: 522(d)(5), 522(d)(11)(D), 522(d)(11)(E), 522(d)(10)(C), and/or 522(d)(10)(E)." Opel and NYL filed individual objections to Daly's October 16, 2003 amendment. Daly amended again on December 24, and Opel and NYL again objected.

With regard to the NYL litigation, Daly listed "$675,000" as the "Value of Claimed Exemption" and "$675,000" as the "Current Market Value. . . ." Under the column entitled "Specify Law Upon which Debtor is Relying in Claiming Exemption," Daly lists sections 522(d)(10)(C) and 522(d)(11)(E). Opel and NYL again challenged Daly's amendments.

JUDGE THOMAS DISCUSSION

Subject to a few specific exceptions not relevant here, the filing of a bankruptcy petition creates an estate comprised of "all legal or equitable interest of the debtor in property as of the commencement of the case." . . . This includes a debtor's interest in a cause of action. . . . Section 522(b) permits a debtor to claim certain property interests exempt from administration by the trustee, either under relevant non-bankruptcy law or the federal exemptions listed in § 522(d).

Rule 4003(b) permits a trustee, or other party in interest, to file an objection to the list of property claimed as exempt within thirty days of its filing. The objector must then carry the burden of producing evidence that rebuts the presumption that the claimed exemption is valid. . . .

Both the Trustee and NYL have filed objections to Debtor's latest amendment to his Schedule C. These objections range from technical issues involving procedural deficiencies to issues concerning the propriety of certain exemptions Debtor has claimed in particular causes of action. These objections have presented this Court with a number of issues: . . . (3) whether a debtor may utilize one statutory provision to claim multiple and distinct exemptions in separate causes of actions; (4) whether certain exemptions claimed by Debtor are proper; and lastly (5) whether a debtor's claim that a specific dollar amount of an asset's value is exempted grants him the right to receive all proceeds in excess of that specific dollar amount that may flow from its liquidation. Each of these issues will turn on this Court's interpretation of specific statutory provisions and applicable procedural rules. . . .

III

The Trustee also objects to Debtor's alleged reliance on both state law exemptions and those provided within the Code. In his December 24, 2003 amendment to Schedule C, Mr. Daly indicated in the column entitled "Specify Law Upon which Debtor is Relying in Claiming Exemption" the statutory provisions his exemptions are based. For the most part, Mr. Daly only references the federal exemption provisions outlined in § 522(d). However, with respect to the property identified as "New York Life v. Daly", Mr. Daly declared, in part:

This sum is exempted in its entirety pursuant to **11 U.S.C. § 522(d)(10)(C)** . . . The Court should give Full Faith and Credit to Commonwealth Law, i.e., **42 Pa C.S.A. 8124** entitled **Exemption of Particular Property (C) Insurance Proceeds**. . . .

Doc. 175 at 4 (emphasis in original).

This statement was included under a heading entitled "11 U.S.C. 522(d)(10)(C)."

Under § 522(b),[1] a debtor is required to base any claimed exemption on either the federal exemptions outlined within the statute or some other under relevant non-bankruptcy law. . . . Relying on the First Circuit Court's decision in *John T. Mather Mem'l Hosp. of Port Jefferson, Inc. v. Pearl,* 723 F.2d 193 (1983), the Trustee maintains that a debtor is not permitted to claim exemptions under both the federal scheme outlined in § 522(d) and that which may be provided for under state laws. Debtor counters with the argument that his amendment clearly reflects his election of the federal bankruptcy exemption scheme. Upon review of the document in question, the Court is in agreement with Debtor.

Under the column entitled "Specify Law Upon which Debtor is Relying in Claiming Exemption," Debtor inserted headings reflecting the specific statutory provision relied upon. Debtor included the comment citing to state law under the heading "11 U.S.C. 522(d)(10)(C)." When the document is viewed as a whole, it is evident to this Court that Debtor's statement, "The Court should give Full Faith and Credit to Commonwealth Law, i.e., 42 Pa C.S.A. 8124 . . .," is surplusage and pure argument and not an assertion of a exemption claim under state law. The Trustee's objection is therefore overruled.[2]

IV

The Trustee also objects to Debtor's repeated reliance on § 522(d)(11)(D) for separate causes of actions.[3] Debtor's December 24, 2003 amendment reveals that, with respect to the property described as "Daly v. HSS & Dr. Richman", his claimed exemption is based, in part, on § 522(d)(11)(D). . . . This same statute was also used to claim an exemption in the properties described as "Daly v. Commonwealth" and "Daly v. Phila." . . . According to Mr. Daly's description, "Daly v. HSS & Dr. Richman" concerns a medical malpractice claim for damages comprising "lost wages, medical bills, past and present pain and suffering." . . . The causes of actions labeled as "Daly v. Commonwealth" and "Daly v. Phila." are collectively described as "bad prison conditions, losing clothes, miscellaneous losses."

The Trustee cites the First Circuit Court's holding in *Christo v. Yellin* (*In re Christo*), for the proposition that "the purpose of [section 522(d)(11)(D) . . . is served by limiting it to one exemption, regardless of the number of incidents of bodily injury, because the determination of what is 'reasonably necessary' to support the debtor should not hinge on the number of injuries suffered." *See* 192 F.3d 36, 39 (1st Cir.1999).

The Debtor opposes the Trustee's interpretation of *Christo*. Instead, he understands the First Circuit Court's holding to mean that a "debtor cannot elect to use, i.e. $15,000 for one personal injury, and then another $15,000 for an entirely different personal injury. Nowhere does it state that a debtor may not list or apply alternate exemptions for each claim." . . .

Although the Court respects the decision of the First Circuit Court in *Christo,* it does not control this Court's interpretation of § 522(d)(11)(D). This Court finds little guidance in the reasoning articulated by the majority in *Christo.*

However, this Court does agree with the analysis articulated by Judge Gibson in his dissenting opinion.

Section 522(d)(11)(D) provides:

> (d) The following property may be exempted under subsection (b)(1) of this section:
> (11) The Debtor's right to receive, or property that is traceable to-
> (D) a payment, not to exceed $17,425, on account of personal bodily injury, not including pain and suffering or compensation for actual pecuniary loss, of the debtor or an individual of whom the debtor is a dependent;
> 11 U.S.C. § 522(d)(11)(D).

In *Christo,* the debtor had claimed three separate exemptions for three unsettled personal injury claims stemming from three separate pre-petition accidents. . . . Each personal injury claim was exempted at the maximum amount then allowed under § 522(d)(11)(D), $15,000. . . . This equaled a total exemption of $45,000 under the statute. . . .

Over the dissent of Judge Gibson, the First Circuit Court affirmed the Bankruptcy Appellate Panel's (BAP) holding that a debtor is only entitled to one exemption, up to the statutory limit, for all personal injury claims. This led to the First Circuit Court conclusion "that the phrase 'on account of personal bodily injury' should be interpreted as defining the *nature* of the payment that is exempt and not the *number* of injuries suffered." *See* 192 F.3d at 39 (emphasis in original). The First Circuit Court reached this conclusion in spite of the generally accepted principle that courts should construe the Code's "exemption provisions liberally to reflect their remedial purposes." *See id.* at 39. It concluded "that, in certain situations, there are reasons to afford a more narrow reading" of the Code's exemption provisions. *See id.* (internal quotations omitted). The *Christo* Court provided four reasons for its interpretation of § 522(d)(11)(D):

> First, the language of the exemption in 11 U.S.C. § 522(d)(11)(D) refers to "a payment." While there is some ambiguity, the more natural reading is that there is a single exemption. Second, the overall scheme of exemptions in § 522(d)(11) displays a pattern of allowing one exemption per category. Third, the purpose of exemptions is to provide support for the debtors at a reasonably necessary level. The reasonably necessary level should not, logically, vary to provide more in total exemption amount to someone who is in three minor accidents than one who is in a single catastrophic accident. That is particularly so given that there are the exemptions in §§ 522(d)(10)(A) and (C) for social security and disability benefits. That is, the exemption for "a payment in account of personal bodily injury" is not a proxy for degree of disability. Fourth, the reading of the exemption as limited to one $15,000 exemption more equitably treats similarly situated debtors.
> *See* 192 F.3d at 38–39.

In his dissenting opinion, Senior Circuit Judge Gibson found fault with the majority's reliance on the BAP's "speculative reasoning." . . . Judge Gibson commented that "the BAP's opinion rests on a shaky policy foundation and ignores language in the statute that would allow separate exemptions for separate bodily injury claims." *See id.* at 40. Focusing on the grammatical analysis of § 522(d)(11)(D), Judge Gibson concluded it is equally plausible to interpret "a payment on . . . account of personal bodily injury" to apply to each such payment, as it is to interpret a congressional intent to apply to an exemption of a single payment. *See id.* at 40. Judge Gibson noted:

> The statute simply does not say whether "a payment . . . on account of personal bodily injury" refers to one or more than one such payment. Congress could have specifically stated which of the two meanings it intended, as it did with motor vehicles [(section 522(d)(2))], and as it did by the use of the "aggregate" [(sections 522(d)(1), (3), (4), (5), (6) and (8))]. I can only read the failure to use these restrictive terms as demonstrating an intent from the plain language of the statute that there is no such limitation and more than one such incident may be the subject of exemption.
>
> The legislative history is of no assistance in dealing with this ambiguity. In such circumstances, we should construe the exemption liberally in favor of the debtor. (Citations omitted).
>
> *Id.* at 40–41.

A number of courts have engaged in similar analysis as it pertains to this issue. *See e.g. In re Comeaux,* 305 B.R. 802 (Bankr.E.D.Tex.2003); *In re Marcus,* 172 B.R. 502 (Bankr.D.Conn.1994); *In re Anderson,* 932 P.2d 1110 (Okla.1997). As the *Comeaux* court held, "[i]t seems more plausible to this Court that 'a payment on . . . account of personal bodily injury' would refer to any such payment as might be received, particularly in the light of the repeatedly demonstrated ability of the Congress in § 522 to utilize numeric limits and aggregate monetary caps in order to constrict a debtor's ability to exempt property from the scope of the bankruptcy estate." 305 B.R. at 806–807. As Judge Gibson concluded in his dissent, the absence of this language reflects a legislative intent not to limit debtors to a single exemption claim under § 522(d)(11)(D).

This Court is in agreement with those cases that conclude that nothing forecloses a debtor from properly asserting multiple exemptions under § 522(d)(11)(D) for multiple property interests, which are separate and distinct. The Trustee's objection with respect to this matter is therefore overruled.

V

The Trustee and NYL's final objections focus on whether Debtor may properly assert exemptions in certain causes of actions with respect to §§ 522(d)(10)(E), 522(d)(10)(C) and 522(d)(11)(E).

Among the Trustee's objections, he finds fault with Debtor's reliance on certain exemption provisions as they may pertain to his interests in *Daly v. U.S. Life, Daly v. Allstate Insur. Co.,* and *NYL v. Daly.* One of the Trustee's primary contentions is that it is not proper for Debtor to utilize §§ 522(d)(10)(E), 522(d)(10)(C), and 522(d)(11)(E) as the basis of exempting his interests in causes of actions based on alleged breach of contract violations. This Court, however, takes issue with this argument.

The mere fact that there is a dispute as to the ownership of an asset does not change the nature of the exemption. The only issue the Court must concern itself with is whether an exemption has been properly claimed in any resultant recovery that may arise from the matter being litigated. The legal theories a debtor may rely upon in order to substantiate an ownership interest does not detract from his ability to assert a proper exemption claim based on his respective interest in the asset in dispute.

In reference to the present case, the fact that Debtor may have chosen to employ a breach of contract theory to legitimize his property rights in a particular asset is inconsequential. What is material to this Court's inquiry is whether the substance of any recovery he may reap from these various causes of action may be properly exempted under applicable laws.

Turning to the remaining objections, the Trustee further objects to Debtor's reliance on § 522(d)(10)(E) to exempt his interests in *Daly v. U.S. Life* and *Daly v. Allstate.* In his December 24, 2004 amendment, Debtor describes *Daly v. U.S. Life* and *Daly v. Allstate* as breach of contract actions with regard to accidental death policies issued regarding his mother's life. He claims the total amount recovered under the policies as exempt under § 522(d)(10)(E) to the extent reasonably necessary for his support.[4]

In *Rousey v. Jacoway,* the Supreme Court analyzed § 522(d)(10)(E) and interpreted "on account of" to mean that the debtor's right to receive a payment must be "because of" an illness, disability, death, age or length of service. *See* 544 U.S. 320, 125 S.Ct. 1561, 1566, 161 L.Ed.2d 563 (2005). In addition, this payment must also be a "stock bonus, pension, profitsharing, annuity, or similar plan or contract."

Debtor views these accidental death polices as "contract[s] on the account of death" that are "similar plans or contracts to stock bonus, pension, profitsharing, annuity." In order to be "similar", the policies "must be like, though not identical to, the specific plans or contracts listed in section 522(d)(10)(E), and consequently must share characteristics common to [profitsharing, stock bonus, pension, or an annuity]." *See* 125 S.Ct. at 1568. . . .

Following the Supreme Court's approach in *Rousey,* this Court is not convinced that the accidental life insurance policies at issue share common similarities or characteristics to profitsharing, stock bonus, pension, or an annuity. The insurance policies issued on the life of Debtor's mother is not subject to the exemption provided under § 522(d)(10)(E).

Absent evidence to the contrary, an insurance policy is commonly defined as "coverage by contract whereby one party undertakes to indemnify or guarantee another against loss by a specified contingency or peril." . . . More specifically, "life insurance" is defined as "insurance for payment of a stipulated sum to a designated beneficiary upon death of the insured." . . . By definition, an insurance policy of this nature does not provide a source of income that substitutes for wages in the manner that a profitsharing, stock bonus, pension, or an annuity does.

The Code contains three separate exemptions relating to life insurance policies. *See* 11 U.S.C. §§ 522(d)(7), 522(d)(8) & 522(d)(11)(C). However, a debtor's ability to utilize these provisions is dependent on the "type" of interest being asserted. The fact that the phrase "life insurance" is specifically identified in these provisions, but not identified under § 522(d)(10)(C), demonstrates that a life insurance policy was not contemplated by Congress as the type of "similar plan" anticipated by Congress. . . .

With the exception of § 522(d)(5)'s wildcard provision, the Code does not provide a specific exemption for a debtor's right to receive a payment as a beneficiary under a life insurance policy where the debtor had not been a dependent of the insured. Debtor is therefore unable to sustain an exemption claim in his interest in *Daly v. U.S. Life* and *Daly v. Allstate* under § 522(d)(10)(E).

With regard to Debtor's interest in *NYL v. Daly,* both the Trustee and NYL objection to his use of §§ 522(d)(10)(C) and 522(d)(11)(E) as a means of claiming the property as exempt. Debtor describes his interest in *NYL v. Daly* as a counterclaim for disability benefits arising out of a terminated insurance policy. He believes that his interest is exempt in its entirety under § 522(d)(10)(C) because any resultant recovery would be based on his right to receive "a disability, illness or unemployment benefit" under a disability policy and equal "the net amount payable under any accident or disability insurance." Furthermore, any verdict in his favor would be "the net amount payable under any accident or disability insurance."

Debtor equally relies on § 522(d)(11)(E) as a basis for exempting any monies recovered from his counterclaim in its entirety. He maintains that any resultant recovery would represent his loss of future earnings to the extent it is reasonably necessary for his support. Debtor reasons that these proceeds represent a loss of future earning that will be reasonably necessary to support him for the remainder of his life.

The Trustee argues that since NYL had terminated Debtor's policy prepetition, the *NYL v. Daly* litigation does not represent Debtor's right to receive a disability benefit pursuant to § 522(d)(10)(C). Furthermore, any proceeds derived from the litigation would be a lump sum payment that would not otherwise qualify as Debtor's right to receive a future disability benefit. This Court is not persuaded by the Trustee's argument.

Like § 522(d)(10)(E), a benefit received in accordance to § 522(d)(10)(C) is viewed as a form of income that substitutes for wages. *See Rousey,* 125 S.Ct. at 1569. . . .

It is clear from the Trustee's objection that he raises no issue with the intended purpose of the insurance policy; merely whether Debtor possesses a present right to receive a disability benefit provided for under the policy. The Court takes exception to the Trustee's arguments.

The Court first notes that the pre-petition termination of the insurance policy is immaterial. The sole purpose of Debtor's pre-petition lawsuit is that he is attempting to reap whatever present rights he may possess under the policy to receive a disability benefit and not a right to receive them at some point in time in the future. . . .

Secondly, this Court's reading of § 522(d)(10)(C) is not identical to the Trustee's. Nothing within the unambiguous language of the section indicates a congressional intent to foreclose a debtor's "right to receive" a disability benefit as a lump sum payment versus some type of continual stream of future payments. It is also premature for this Court to assume that any recovery Debtor may receive from the *NYL v. Daly* litigation would naturally take the form of a lump sum payment. The only issue relevant to Debtor's reliance on § 522(d)(10)(C) is whether his recovery actually represents a disability payment. To the extent that it does, the Court finds Debtor's exemption claim to be proper.

The Court finds NYL's argument to be equally unpersuasive. It argues that the Third Circuit Court's decision in *Clark v. O'Neill* (*In re Clark*), 711 F.2d 21 (3d Cir.1983), forecloses him from claiming the *NYL v. Daly* litigation as exempt under § 522(d)(10)(C). More specifically, NYL maintains that *Clark* limits a debtor's ability to assert an exemption in a "right to receive" payments under § 522(d)(10) if they are, in fact, currently being received. This Court, however, takes issue with this argument.

In *Clark,* the Third Circuit Court dealt with the issue of whether a debtor could utilize § 522(d)(10)(E) to exempt his interest in future payments from a retirement plan. Relying on legislative history, the Court noted that the historical purpose of exemption laws has been to "to provide [debtors] with the basic necessities of life so that even if [their] creditors levy on all of [their] nonexempt property, [debtors] will not be left destitute and a public charge." *See id.* at 23. From this passage, the Court reasoned that "the present Keogh payments, to the extent they are necessary for the support of the debtor, is consistent with this goal. The exemption of *future* payments, however, demonstrates a concern for the debtor's long-term security which is absent from the statute." *See id.* (emphasis in original).

Although this Court may be bound to certain aspects of the Third Circuit Court's holding in *Clark,* this Court does not find it to be on point in the present situation. Unlike the debtor in *Clark,* what *is* at issue in *NYL v. Daly* is whether Debtor possesses a present "right to receive" the benefits provided for under the policy. The fact that the policy was terminated pre-petition is immaterial to the inquiry. The sole purpose of Debtor's pending pre-petition counterclaim is to reap whatever present rights he may possess under the policy to receive a disability benefit and not whether he possesses a right to receive them on some future date. These objections are overruled.

Why are the debtor and the trustee in conflict over so many items in this case? Are the trustee's interests always antagonistic toward the debtor's interests?

The Trustee and NYL express concerns whether Debtor may claim *NYL v. Daly* as exempt based on § 522(d)(11)(E). Section 522(d)(11)(E) permits a debtor to exempt a right to receive a payment, or property traceable to a payment, that is "in compensation of loss of future earnings of the debtor or an individual of whom the debtor is or was a dependent, to the extent reasonably necessary for the support of the debtor and any dependent of the debtor."

Having allowed the exemption of this asset under § 522(d)(10)(C), the court need not address the application of this exemption section to the same claim.

Whether or not Debtor's counterclaim has merit is not relevant to a determination as to whether his exemption claims are proper. Issues concerning Debtor's interest in the insurance policy are currently pending in the District Court for the Eastern District of Pennsylvania. In the event the Debtor recovers on his counterclaim, his interest in *NYL v. Daly* is properly exempt under § 522(d)(10)(C).

VI

The final issue affecting the present proceedings was raised *sua sponte* and concerns the legal effect of a debtor exempting the entire reported value of an asset. More specifically, is a debtor limited to the specific dollar amount claimed as exempt, regardless of an asset's reported or court determined value?

Several courts have reflected upon this issue and different conclusions have developed. . . . Each of these decisions are based, to some degree, on the Supreme Court's decision in *Taylor v. Freeland & Kronz,* 503 U.S. 638, 112 S.Ct. 1644, 118 L.Ed.2d 280 (1992). In *Taylor,* the Court was confronted with the issue of whether a debtor is entitled to an improperly claimed exemption that fails to draw an objection. *See id.* at 642, 112 S.Ct. 1644. On her schedules, the debtor claimed an exemption in an award she had expected to win in a discrimination lawsuit against TWA. . . . This property was described as "Proceeds from lawsuit- *[Davis] v. TWA*" and "Claim for lost wages." . . . Both its value and exemption value were listed as "unknown" on the applicable schedules. . . . The Court went on to hold that a party cannot contest the validity of a claimed exemption after the expiration of the objection period. . . .

However, another part of the Supreme Court's decision is more pertinent to this Court's resolution of the pending issue. With regard to the legal significance associated with the debtor's declaration that both the property's value and exemption value were "unknown", the Court noted (or one could say concluded) that the debtor had "claimed the proceeds from her employment discrimination lawsuit as exempt by listing them in the schedule that she filed under § 522(*l*). . . . [The debtor] in fact claimed the full amount as exempt." *See* 503 U.S. at 642, 112 S.Ct. 1644. It is obvious from these statements that the Supreme Court interprets such a declaration, an asset with a listed value as "unknown" and a corresponding exemption value of "unknown", to mean that a debtor has asserted an exemption claim against 100% of the asset's ultimate value.

Post-*Taylor,* the Eleventh Circuit Court addressed a similar fact pattern in *Allen v. Green. See* 31 F.3d at 1098. However in *Green,* the Eleventh Circuit Court was asked to determine the legal significance attached to debtor's exemption of $1.00 in a lawsuit with a listed value of $1.00. . . . As with the trustee in *Taylor,* the trustee in *Green* elected not to object to either the debtor's valuation or exemption. . . . The trustee eventually arranged to settle the lawsuit for $15,000.00, which the debtor consented to and the bankruptcy court approved. . . . The bankruptcy court also denied the debtor's request to receive settlement proceeds in excess of the exempted amount. This ruling was reversed by the district court based on the Supreme Court's holding in *Taylor* and the matter was appealed to the Eleventh Circuit Court. . . . On appeal, the trustee argued the estate was entitled to all but $1.00 of the settlement proceeds since the debtor had only claimed an exemption of $1.00. . . .

In reaching its decision, the Eleventh Circuit Court reviewed *Taylor* and concluded that:

> "an unstated premise of the Court's holding was that a debtor who exempts the entire reported value of an asset is claiming the 'full amount,' whatever it turns out to be.". . . In the present case, Green exempted the full reported value of her lawsuit, and neither the Trustee nor any other interested party objected. The only factual distinction between this case and *Taylor* is that here, instead of reporting her lawsuit as having an "unknown" value, Green reported it as having a value of one dollar . . . Thus, the facts of this case are materially the same as those in *Taylor.* In this case, one dollar exempted is to one dollar reported as, in *Taylor,* "unknown" exempted was to "unknown" reported.
> *See id.* at 1100.

This Court is inclined to follow the Eleventh Circuit's well-reasoned interpretation of *Taylor.* This Court's decision not to follow contrary opinions is predicated on the Supreme Court's statement in *Taylor* that a debtor's declaration that an exemption claim of "unknown" value is asserted against property interest of an "unknown" value is to be interpreted as a debtor's claim that 100% of the value of the property interest is being claimed as exempt. Accordingly, this Court concludes that in those instances where Debtor's exemption schedules reflect an exemption amount equal to the property's listed value amount, he has attempted to exempt 100% of his property interest-regardless of the property's ultimate valuation amount. As such, the Court concludes Debtor's interest in *NYL v. Daly* is exempt in its entirety under § 522(d)(10)(C) to the extent it represents a disability benefit. . . .

For the reasons indicated in the Opinion filed this same date, **IT IS HEREBY**

ORDERED that New York Life Insurance Company's *Motion to Strike Amendments To Claim of Exemptions Filed on December 23, 2003, or in the Alternative Objections of New York Life Insurance Company to the Exemptions Claimed by the Debtor by Amendment Filed on December 24, 2003* (Doc. # 180) is **OVERRULED** in its entirety.

The Court hereby **GRANTS** the Trustee's *Chapter 7 Trustee's Objections to Debtor's Amendments to Schedule C (Property Claimed as Exempt) Filed on December 24, 2003* (Doc. # 178) with respect to Debtor's reliance on 11 U.S.C. § 522(d)(10)(E) to exempt his interest in *Daly v. U.S. Life* and *Daly v. Allstate.* The Trustee's remaining objections are **OVERRULED**. . . .

In accordance with the reasoning articulated in the Opinion issued this date regarding *Chapter 7 Trustee's Objections to Debtor's Amendments to Schedule*

C (Property Claimed as Exempt) Filed on December 24, 2003 (Doc. # 178) and *Motion to Strike Amendments To Claim of Exemptions Filed on December 23, 2003, or in the Alternative Objections of New York Life Insurance Company to the Exemptions Claimed by the Debtor by Amendment Filed on December 24, 2003* (Doc. # 180), **IT IS HEREBY**

ORDERED that the *Second Motion of Chapter 7 Trustee to Compromise Claim of the Bankruptcy Estate* (Doc. # 194) is hereby **DENIED** inasmuch as the claim has been exempted by the Debtor and the Estate has no interest in same.

END NOTES

1. Paragraphs (1) and (2) state, in relevant part: (1) property that is specified under subsection (d) of this section [(federal bankruptcy exemptions)], unless the State law that is applicable to the debtor under paragraph (2)(A) of this subsection specifically does not authorize; *or, in the alternative,* (2)(A) *any property that is exempt under Federal law,* other than subsection (d) of this section, *or State or local law* that is applicable on the date of the filing of the petition. . . . 11 U.S.C. § 522(b)(1) & (2)(A) (emphasis added).
2. Likewise, the Court overrules the Trustee's objection concerning the alleged lack of specificity as to what portion of Federal Bankruptcy Law his exemptions are based. Although the Debtor's amendment is of an unorthodox form, the Court has observed no failure on Debtor's part to clearly specify the various statutory provision to which his various exemptions are based.
3. The Trustee equally applies this analysis to § 522(d)(10)(C). However, based on this Court's review of Debtor's complete list of claimed exemptions, Debtor has only asserted an exemption under § 522(d)(10)(C) with respect to the asset described as "Daly v. NYL." *Compare* Docs. 175, 156, 142 & 139.
4. Debtor has also claimed that his interests are exempt pursuant to § 522(d)(5). The Trustee has not raised an objection to this claim/basis. Section 522(d)(10)(E) provides: (d) The following property may be exempted under subsection (b)(1) of this section: . . . (10) The debtor's right to receive- . . . (E) a payment under a stock bonus, pension, profitsharing, annuity, or similar plan or contract on account of illness, disability, death, age, or length of service, to the extent reasonably necessary for the support of the debtor and any dependent of the debtor, unless- (I) such plan or contract was established by or under the auspices of an insider that employed the debtor at the time the debtor's rights under such plan or contract arose; (ii) such payment is on account of age or length of service; and (iii) such plan or contract does not qualify under section 401(a), 403(a), 403(b), or 408 of the Internal Revenue Code of 1986. 11 U.S.C. § 522(d)(10)(E).

ARTICLE 10.2

Abuse or Protection? "Opportunistic" Debtors Appear to Have Little to Fear from the 2005 Bankruptcy Reforms

Michelle J. White

Last fall, after years of effort and more than $100 million in lobbying expenditures by the large credit card lenders, Congress passed the "Bankruptcy Abuse Prevention and Consumer Protection Act of 2005" (BAPCPA). The new bankruptcy law followed years of rapid increases in the number of bankruptcy filings—from 341,000 in 1985 to 1,263,000 in 1997 (when the earliest predecessor to BAPCPA was introduced in Congress), to more than 1.5 million per year in the years before BAPCPA went into effect. (See Table 1.)

U.S. bankruptcy law was very debtor-friendly prior to BAPCPA. It has become much more pro-creditor today.

It is not surprising that personal bankruptcy law is controversial. Bankruptcy balances the conflicting objectives of helping debtors in financial distress and promoting credit availability by protecting creditors. Bankruptcy law provides debtors with consumption insurance by discharging some or all of their debts when their ability to pay falters. This increases debtors' minimum consumption levels by allowing them to use funds for consumption that would otherwise go to repayment.

What other reasons support bankruptcy laws that are balanced more in favor of debtors?

Preventing debtors' consumption from drastically falling is economically worthwhile because illnesses can turn into disabilities if debtors cannot pay for medical care, debtors and their families may become homeless if they cannot pay rent, and debtors' children may drop out of school in order to work, leading to lower earnings as adults. Debtors may also require charity or public assistance.

However, providing consumption insurance also has costs. Credit availability falls, debtors who repay bear higher interest rates when default rates are higher, debtors may work less because the consequences of job loss or business failure are not as bad, and debtors may file for bankruptcy even when they have not experienced any reduction in consumption. The obligation to repay in bankruptcy and state-sanctioned procedures for enforcing it are intended to reduce those costs.

Suppose debtors who file for bankruptcy are divided into two groups: opportunists and non-opportunists. Non-opportunists who borrow intend to repay their debts and they borrow an amount that they normally could repay.

They file for bankruptcy only if they experience a drop in their incomes or some other hardship—they are the people for whom bankruptcy debt relief was intended. Opportunists, in contrast, plan in advance to maximize their gains from bankruptcy. They often have high incomes and borrow as much as possible. They may have substantial assets, but they shelter the assets from the obligation to repay. They file for bankruptcy even though they have not experienced any drop in their incomes. Famous examples of opportunistic bankrupts include the actor Burt Reynolds (who had $10 million in debt discharged while keeping a $2 million house), corporate raider Paul Bilzerian (who kept a 38,000 square foot house in bankruptcy), actress Kim Basinger, rapper MC Hammer, and boxer Mike Tyson.

Would it be possible to distinguish the opportunist from the non-opportunist filers of bankruptcy? It so, how?

In reality, many debtors are a mixture of both types. For example, optimistic debtors may borrow amounts that they can only repay if they are promoted, when in fact they are in occupations where promotions are rare. Or they may lose their jobs and borrow to support consumption while they search for a new job. If the job search lasts a long time, they may end up in bankruptcy because they accumulate more debt than they can repay. . . .

Although BAPCPA was sold on the grounds that it would discourage opportunism, I argue here that it will mainly affect non-opportunistic debtors. Many of them will find themselves unable to file for bankruptcy even when their incomes have declined substantially and they cannot repay any of their debt.

BANKRUPTCY PRE-BAPCPA

Under bankruptcy law before BAPCPA, there were two separate bankruptcy procedures, Chapters 7 and 13, and debtors were allowed to choose between them. Under Chapter 7, debtors were obliged to repay only from wealth above an exemption level, while post-bankruptcy income was entirely exempt. Under Chapter 13, debtors were obliged to use part of their post-bankruptcy income to repay, but their wealth was entirely exempt. Most unsecured debts were discharged under both procedures.

The peculiar feature of U.S. bankruptcy law that either income or wealth was entirely exempt made filing for bankruptcy very favorable for debtors because they could choose to repay from whichever source they did not have. Even if debtors had both non-exempt wealth and non-exempt income, they could often convert their non-exempt wealth to exempt and then file under Chapter 7. . . .

Exemptions for wealth in bankruptcy were (and still are) set by the states and they vary widely. Most states have a blanket exemption for "household goods" that covers furniture, household equipment, and clothing, plus separate exemptions for particular types of assets, each with a fixed dollar limit. The largest exemption in most states is the "homestead" exemption for equity in owner-occupied homes, which varies from zero in two states to unlimited in Texas, Florida, and several other states. . . . Thus, Chapter 7 wealth exemptions are fixed dollar amounts that differ across individual debtors depending on their state of residence, whether they are homeowners, and other factors. . . .

Non-opportunistic debtors benefit from filing for bankruptcy if the amount of debt discharged in bankruptcy . . . exceeds the cost of filing for bankruptcy . . . plus the value of non-exempt wealth that debtors must give up. . . .

Gaming the System

What about opportunistic debtors? Prior to BAPCPA, they made their bankruptcy decisions in the same way, but they planned in advance to increase their financial gain from bankruptcy. Pre-BAPCPA bankruptcy planning strategies included borrowing more by acquiring additional credit cards and charging more on each card, converting non-exempt assets to exempt by paying down their mortgages or renovating their homes (assuming that the additional home equity would be exempt under the state's homestead exemption), moving to states with higher exemptions, and sheltering non-exempt assets by putting them into "asset protection trusts."

These strategies raised the amount of debt discharged in bankruptcy . . . or raised the amount of wealth that was exempt in bankruptcy . . . , thus increasing debtors' financial gain from filing. . . .

In a study done in the mid-1990s, I used a representative sample of U.S. households—the Federal Reserve Board's Survey of Consumer Finances—to calculate the proportion of U.S. households that would benefit from filing for bankruptcy under Chapter 7. I found that if debtors behaved non-opportunistically, then about 15 percent of U.S, households would gain financially from filing. But if debtors behaved opportunistically by charging more on their credit cards, using non-exempt assets to reduce their mortgages or renovate their homes, or moving to Texas or Florida, then more than half of all households would gain from filing. The more debtors used these strategies, the higher their benefit from filing for bankruptcy was. Thus, pre-BAPCPA bankruptcy gave debtors strong incentives to behave opportunistically.

Now turn to Chapter 13. Prior to BAPCPA, debtors filing under Chapter 13 had to propose a plan to repay some or all of their debt from post-bankruptcy income over a period of three to five years. Only the approval of the bankruptcy judge—not creditors—was required for approval of Chapter 13 repayment plans. Most debtors in Chapter 13 proposed to repay either an amount equal to the value of their non-exempt assets, . . . or a token amount such as 1 percent of debt if they had no non-exempt assets. Bankruptcy judges generally accepted the plans because debtors could otherwise shift their filings to Chapter 7. This meant that the conditions under which debtors gained from filing for bankruptcy under Chapter 13 and Chapter 7 were the same—that debtors' wealth . . . was less than the threshold. . . .

Pre-BAPCPA Chapter 13 also included some special features that were intended to encourage debtors to use it rather than Chapter 7. If debtors were behind on their mortgage payments and lenders were about to foreclose, debtors could delay foreclosure by filing under Chapter 13 (although they were still required to repay the entire amount owed on the mortgage). Some car loans were partially discharged in Chapter 13 because the loan principle could be "stripped down" to the value of the car if the former was greater than the latter. Also, certain types of unsecured debts, such as debts incurred by fraud, could be discharged in Chapter 13.

None of those features were available in Chapter 7. While the special features increased the number of debtors who filed under Chapter 13, they did not generally affect the amounts that debtors repaid on their unsecured debts—most Chapter 13 debtors would pay what they owed on their mortgages or car loans and then stop making payments on their plans. . . .

Opportunists?

But the fact that opportunists gain more from filing for bankruptcy than non-opportunists does not imply that most pre-BAPCPA bankruptcy filers were opportunists. How much opportunism actually occurred prior to the adoption of BAPCPA? Little good research is available on this issue, but the Administrative Office of the U.S. Courts occasionally publishes figures that suggest whether debtors in bankruptcy can repay a substantial amount of their debt.

Table 1 Non-Business Bankruptcy Filings 1980–2005

	Non-Business filings	Percent of U.S. population
1980	287,570	0.13%
1985	341,233	0.14%
1990	718,107	0.29%
1995	874,642	0.33%
2000	1,217,972	0.43%
2001	1,452,000	0.51%
2002	1,539,000	0.53%
2003	1,625,000	0.56%
2004	1,563,000	0.53%
2005	2,000,000	0.68%

Note: Married couples who file for bankruptcy are counted as a single bankruptcy filing, so the number filings is less than the number of people who file for bankruptcy.
Source: www.abiworld.org

Figure 1 Non-Opportunists, Pre-BAPCPA

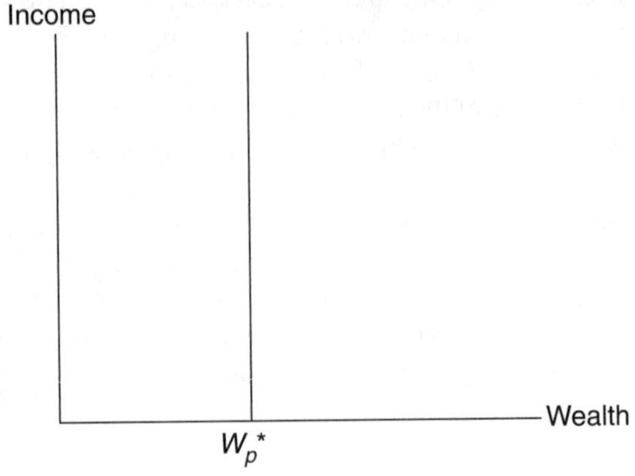

Source: Non-opportunistic debtors benefited under the pre-BAPCPA bankruptcy laws if their income and wealth were to the left of line *Wp**.

Consider "no-asset" Chapter 7 filings, in which debtors repay nothing in bankruptcy because all of their wealth is exempt. No-asset filings constitute nearly three-quarters of all personal bankruptcy filings and 96 percent of Chapter 7 filings. Three percent of no-asset filers have annual incomes of $72,000 or more and the median amount of credit card debt for these filers is $33,500—twice the average level for all bankruptcy filers. Clearly, some of these debtors are opportunists, as they have both high debt and the ability to repay at least part of it. In addition, the top 0.4 percent of no-asset filers have at least $500,000 in credit card debt. But three-quarters of this group of debtors owned failed businesses and most of their debts presumably were business debts. Because their incomes were low, they probably had little ability to repay. There is little information on the fraction of debtors who borrow "recklessly" with little intention to repay.

Thus while some bankruptcy filers behave opportunistically and many run up credit card debt beyond their ability to repay, the proportion of pre-BAPCPA bankruptcy filers who were opportunists appears to have been fairly small. This suggests that the reforms under BAPCPA may have had a broader agenda than just reducing debtor opportunism.

BANKRUPTCY UNDER BAPCPA

BAPCPA retained both the Chapter 7 and Chapter 13 personal bankruptcy procedures, but it abolished debtors' right to choose between them and replaced it with a "means test" for Chapter 7. To qualify for Chapter 7, debtors must demonstrate that their incomes are below a certain cutoff and, if not, they must file under Chapter 13. BAPCPA also changed debtors' obligation to repay in Chapter 13. Instead of debtors proposing their own repayment plans, the new means test determines debtors' "disposable income" and requires that they use all of it for five years to repay.

Also, the special features that previously encouraged debtors to choose Chapter 13 have been abolished. In Chapter 7, the system of wealth exemptions that vary across states remains the same, but BAPCPA introduced new restrictions on when debtors are allowed to use them. Finally, BAPCPA made some types of debts non-dischargeable, greatly raised bankruptcy costs by adding new fees and hurdles to the filing process, and lengthened the minimum period between bankruptcy filings—from six to eight years for Chapter 7 and from six months to two years for Chapter 13.

Consider bankruptcy costs first. Under BAPCPA, debtors must take an approved credit counseling course before filing, and they must take a financial management course before receiving a discharge of debt. They must file about 30 forms with the bankruptcy court that document their real and personal assets, assets claimed as exempt, retirement accounts, debts of all types, income, business income, expenditures, alimony/child support payments, contractual and lease obligations, and information about legal representation. They must also submit copies of their tax returns and wage stubs. (Most of this information was not required pre-BAPCPA.) . . . One bankruptcy guide predicts that the cost of filing under BAPCPA will be around $2,500 for lawyers' fees plus $200–300 in filing fees, compared to less than $1,000 before BAPCPA. . . .

BAPCPA also made some types of debt non-dischargeable in bankruptcy. . . . Those changes mean that the amount of debt discharged in bankruptcy under BAPCPA . . . is smaller than the amount discharged pre-BAPCPA. . . .

Now turn to the new BAPCPA restrictions on debtors' use of wealth exemptions. If debtors move to a new state less than two years before filing, they must use the homestead exemption in their old state. They can no longer gain from moving to Texas or Florida unless they plan for bankruptcy far in advance. Also, debtors can no longer convert non-exempt assets into home equity by paying down their mortgages or renovating their homes, unless they do so at least 40 months or 10 years, respectively, before filing. Otherwise, the additional home equity will not be exempt. Also under BAPCPA, states' general exemptions for household goods are limited to one television, one computer, etc. Overall, the new restrictions reduce the wealth exemption. . . . The reductions in the amount of debt discharged and the wealth exemption and the increase in bankruptcy costs all have the effect of reducing the wealth threshold for filing for bankruptcy under BAPCPA.

Now turn to the means test, which all debtors in bankruptcy must take. The first part of the test determines whether debtors are allowed to file under Chapter 7. . . . Debtors who fail the means test . . . must file under Chapter 13 if they file for bankruptcy at all. The second part of the means test says that debtors who are required to file under Chapter 13 must use their entire disposable income for five years after filing . . . to repay.

Figure 2 Opportunists, Pre-BAPCPA

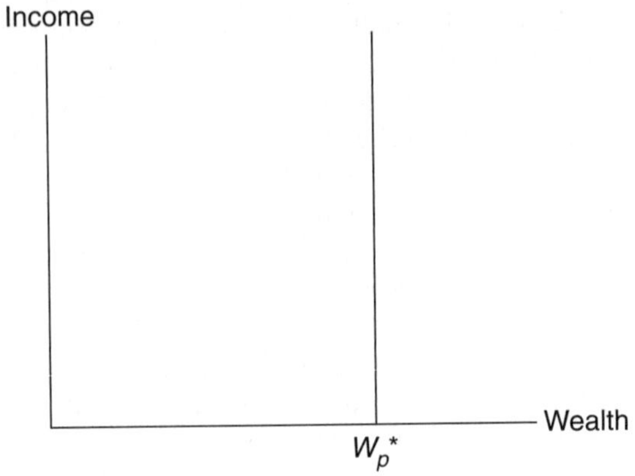

Source: Prior to BAPCPA, opportunistic debtors would strategically manage their assets so as to shift line Wp^* to the right.

What class of filers benefit most from the BAPCA income exemption? Do you think his exemption was a wise inclusion in the new act?

The BAPCPA income exemption . . . is entirely new (prior to BAPCPA, debtors proposed their own income exemptions as part of their Chapter 13 plans). The BAPCPA income exemption equals the sum of a variety of separate allowances for different types of expenditures. One set of allowances, for housing, transport, food, apparel, and personal care, is determined by formula. The housing allowance depends on housing costs where the debtor lives, the debtor's family size, and whether the debtor is an owner or a renter. The transport allowance depends on where the debtor lives and whether the debtor's family owns 0, 1, or 2 cars. Other allowances depend on the debtor's family size and broad categories of income. A second set of allowances covers expenditures that are (mainly) outside the debtor's control, including income tax payments, court-ordered spousal and child support payments, childcare costs, uninsured health care costs, the cost of term life insurance, the cost of telecommunication services, and several minor categories. Finally, a third set of allowances is based on debtors' actual expenditures. These include allowances for spending on health and disability insurance, contributions to the care of elderly or ill family members, additional home energy costs, additional food and clothing expenses up to certain limits, charitable contributions, the costs of protection against family violence, loans to finance contributions to tax-sheltered individual retirement plans and education savings accounts, and all payments on secured debt.

Opportunists and Non-Opportunists

Under what conditions would non-opportunistic debtors gain from filing for bankruptcy under BAPCPA? To decide whether to file under Chapter 7, debtors first must determine whether their incomes satisfy the means test. . . . Assuming that they pass the means test, debtors must go through the same procedure as previously discussed to determine their gains and costs from filing under Chapter 7. . . . The lower block in Figure 3 shows the region where . . . non-opportunistic debtors gain from filing under Chapter 7 and are allowed to do so.

Now consider non-opportunistic debtors' decisions to file under Chapter 13. Under BAPCPA, their gain from filing for bankruptcy is still the amount of debt discharged . . . , but their cost of filing is the sum of bankruptcy costs plus five years of disposable income. . . . [A] further limitation on debtors' use of Chapter 13 is the "best interest of creditors" test, which requires that debtors repay at least as much in Chapter 13 as they would in Chapter 7. This means that debtors must repay at least an amount equal to the value of their non-exempt wealth. . . . The upper block in Figure 3 shows the region where non-opportunistic debtors gain from filing under Chapter 13 because all of the conditions are satisfied, but they are not allowed to file under Chapter 7.

How does the bankruptcy decision differ for opportunistic debtors? As already discussed, BAPCPA closed off many of the strategies that opportunistic debtors previously used to raise their wealth thresholds for bankruptcy, including no longer allowing discharge of some types of debt and preventing some debtors from using high state homestead exemptions. But BAPCPA left some old strategies intact and also opened up some new ones.

Debtors are still allowed to use asset protection trusts to shelter large amounts of wealth in Chapter 7 bankruptcy. (A bill recently introduced in Congress to limit the use of asset protection trusts in bankruptcy is titled the "Billionaire's Loophole Elimination Act.") In about 20 states, married debtors can still shelter the entire value of their homes, as long as they own the homes in "tenancy by the entirety" and only one spouse files for bankruptcy. BAPCPA also provides a generous new exemption in Chapter 7 for up to $1 million in tax-sheltered individual retirement accounts (up to $2 million for married couples who file for bankruptcy). But using that exemption requires that debtors plan for bankruptcy far in advance, as federal law limits the amount that can be contributed to tax-sheltered retirement accounts each year. BAPCPA also exempts debtors from the means test if their debts are not "primarily consumer debts," so that opportunistic debtors can avoid the means test and file under Chapter 7 by setting up a business and acquiring business debt before filing. . . .

Because BAPCPA defines debtors' annual incomes . . . based on their incomes during the six month period before filing, opportunistic debtors can reduce their obligation to repay in Chapter 13 by working less during this period. To illustrate, suppose debtors earn $100 per month less during each of the six months before filing. Doing so costs them $600, but lowers their Chapter 13 repayment obligation by $100 per month for 60 months, or $6,000. Thus, they receive a 10-fold return per dollar of reduced earnings. The high return to working less persists until debtors' income is low enough that they pass the means test and are allowed to file under Chapter 7. Debtors can also

Figure 3 Non-Opportunists under BAPCPA

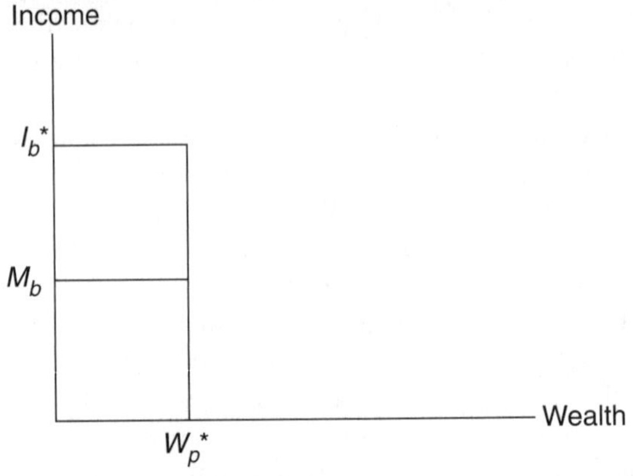

Source: Non-opportunistic debtors benefit from filing for bankruptcy if their wealth/income places them to the left of line W_p*, but they must file for Chapter 13 if they are above M_b.

gain by simply shifting their incomes so that the money is paid outside of the six-month window before bankruptcy.

Opportunistic debtors can also re-arrange their spending so as to raise their income exemption. . . . Under BAPCPA, some of the expenditure allowances are formula-based, which prevents debtors from manipulating them. But others are based on debtors' actual spending levels, so opportunistic debtors can reduce their obligation to repay in Chapter 13 by spending more on those categories. . . .

[T]he BAPCPA means test forces non-opportunistic debtors into Chapter 13 even if they have relatively low incomes, but allows opportunistic debtors with much higher incomes to file under Chapter 7. The main determinant of whether debtors pass or fail the BAPCPA means test is not their "means," but whether they plan for bankruptcy in advance.

Figure 4 shows the income/wealth region where opportunistic debtors gain from filing for bankruptcy. Compared to Figure 3, the lower block in Figure 4 where debtors gain from filing under Chapter 7 is both wider and taller and the upper block where debtors gain from filing under Chapter 13 has nearly disappeared. This is because when debtors behave opportunistically, they qualify to file under Chapter 7 even at high income levels and, as a result, few if any will choose to file under Chapter 13. The wealth threshold for filing under Chapter 7 also shifts out, because opportunistic debtors are more likely than non-opportunists to benefit from the new exemption for retirement accounts.

Finally, how has BAPCPA changed the attractiveness of bankruptcy? We can address this question for non-opportunistic debtors by comparing Figure 1 to Figure 3 and for opportunistic debtors by comparing Figure 2 to Figure 4. To do so, we must re-interpret the wealth and income thresholds as applying to the average debtor of each type. The region in which non-opportunistic debtors benefit from filing for bankruptcy is smaller under BAPCPA than before, i.e., the blocks in Figure 3 are smaller than the area to the left of the wealth threshold in Figure 1. This is because pre-BAPCPA debtors benefited from filing for bankruptcy at any income level, but BAPCPA debtors no longer benefit from filing—even under Chapter 13—if their incomes are above I_b^*. In addition, the combination of much higher bankruptcy costs, narrower discharge of debt, and restrictions on debtors' use of high homestead exemptions imply that the wealth threshold is lower under BAPCPA. Overall, BAPCPA is likely to reduce the number of non-opportunistic debtors who file for bankruptcy.

What about BAPCPA's effect on opportunistic debtors? The comparison between Figure 2 and Figure 4 is more ambiguous. BAPCPA eliminated debtors' automatic right to file under Chapter 7, but it provided many strategies for avoiding Chapter 13 even at high income levels. BAPCPA seems unlikely to prevent determined opportunists from planning for and benefiting from bankruptcy, even if they have high ability to pay.

THE BANKRUPTCY BALANCE

As discussed in the introduction, bankruptcy policy balances conflicting objectives of providing consumption insurance to debtors and protecting creditors. The adoption of BAPCPA shifted the balance toward creditors by raising debtors' cost of filing for bankruptcy and reducing the amount of debt that is discharged in bankruptcy. The changes will have little effect on opportunistic debtors, who can still use pre-bankruptcy planning to avoid Chapter 13 and shelter substantial assets in bankruptcy. But the changes are likely to harm many non-opportunistic debtors simply because they cannot afford the high cost of filing.

Because the pressure to reform bankruptcy law came from the large credit card lenders, consider how the changes under BAPCPA affect them. Credit card lenders compete heavily for new customers—U.S. households receive an average of 45 credit card solicitations per year. Lenders encourage consumers to accept new cards by offering front-loaded rewards such as low annual fees, low introductory interest rates, and frequent flier miles or other benefits. But if customers pay late, use their cards over the credit limit, or make only minimum payments on their balances, then lenders charge high fees ($40 is a common late or over-limit fee) and raise interest rates to extremely high levels (30 percent is a typical rate for high-risk debtors). Over the past decade, competition among credit card lenders has led to reduced fixed charges such as annual fees and increased penalty charges such as late fees and high-risk interest rates.

This pattern of charges increases debtors' borrowing costs when their wealth/incomes turn out to be low, because debtors in this situation are likely to pay late, charge over the limit, and make low monthly payments. Conversely,

Figure 4 Opportunists, offer BAPCPA

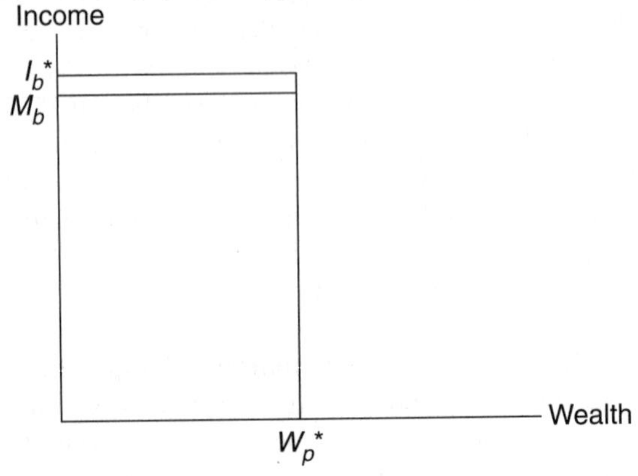

Source: Opportunistic debtors can shift line M_b upward, increasing the area in which they can benefit from filing under Chapter 7.

the pattern of charges reduces debtors' borrowing costs when their wealth/incomes turn out to be high, because in this situation they are likely to repay in full or make high monthly payments. The result is that debtors face high borrowing costs when their ability to pay is low and low borrowing costs when their ability to pay is high.

Prior to BAPCPA, debtors with low ability to pay could easily file for bankruptcy, which allowed them to shift funds from repayment to consumption. But the adoption of BAPCPA means that debtors must pay nearly $3,000 to file for bankruptcy and, once in bankruptcy, they receive less debt relief. As a result, debtors are likely to delay filing or not file at all. This gives lenders longer to collect the high fees and interest charges and, if debtors default but do not file for bankruptcy, then lenders will have more time to collect by garnishing debtors' wages. (Most U.S. states allow lenders to garnish up to 25 percent of debtors' wages following default, but garnishment ends when debtors file for bankruptcy.) In addition, BAPCPA lengthened the minimum period that must elapse between bankruptcy filings, so that fewer debtors are eligible to file for bankruptcy. Thus, for credit card lenders, the adoption of BAPCPA means higher profits.

For debtors, the changes in the pricing of credit card loans increased the variance of consumption so that debtors' minimum consumption levels fell. This change makes bankruptcy-provided consumption insurance more valuable because filing for bankruptcy increases debtors' consumption levels when they are lowest. But BAPCPA'S adoption reduced the amount of insurance that bankruptcy provides because many debtors will not qualify for bankruptcy, will not be able to afford the $3,000 in bankruptcy costs, or will not have enough debt discharged to make filing worthwhile. As a result, more debtors will be subject to wage garnishment, some will quit their jobs to avoid repaying, and some will drastically cut their consumption levels in order to repay. The social costs of debt are likely to increase.

Thus, at a time when changes in the pricing of credit card loans made bankruptcy-provided consumption insurance more valuable to debtors, the adoption of BAPCPA made it less available.

A Better Solution

Overall, U.S. personal bankruptcy law pre-BAPCPA certainly needed reforming. But BAPCPA harms non-opportunistic debtors while doing little to discourage opportunism.

In a recent study with Hung-Jen Wang, I argued that a better approach to bankruptcy reform would be to combine Chapters 7 and 13. Instead of allowing debtors to choose between repaying from only income or only wealth, debtors would be required to repay from both sources, subject to separate exemptions for each. In our simulations, we assumed that the current wealth exemptions would continue and that 93 percent of income would be exempt, i.e., debtors would be required to use 7 percent of their post-bankruptcy earnings over several years, as well as their non-exempt wealth, to repay.

This approach has the advantage of improving the match between debtors' ability to pay and their obligation to repay in bankruptcy, because their ability to pay depends on the combination of wealth and income rather than on just one or the other. It maintains bankruptcy-provided consumption insurance, as debtors with low wealth and low incomes would repay little or nothing. Finally, it deters opportunism, because high income debtors are less likely to file for bankruptcy when they must use some of their future income to repay.

READINGS

"Abuse or Protection: Bankruptcy Reform under BAPCPA," by Michelle J. White. University of Illinois Law Review, forthcoming 2007.

"Bankruptcy by the Numbers: Chapter 13 Disbursements in Fiscal Year 2001: Continued Growth and a New Finding," by Ed Flynn and Gordon Bermant. American Bankruptcy Law Journal, Vol. 22 (Feb. 2003).

"Bankruptcy by the Numbers: Credit Card Debt in Chapter 7 Cases," by Ed Flynn and Gordon Bermant. American Bankruptcy Law Journal, Vol. 22 (Dec. 2003-Jan. 2004).

"Bankruptcy by the Numbers: High-debt Debtors," by Ed Flynn and Gordon Bermant. American Bankruptcy Law Journal, Vol. 22 (March 2003).

"Bankruptcy Reform and the 'Sweat Box' of Credit Card Debt," by Ronald Mann. University of Illinois Law Review, forthcoming 2007.

"The Household Bankruptcy Decision," by Scott Fay, Erik Hurst, and Michelle J. White. American Economic Review, Vol. 92, No. 3 (June 2002).

"It's Time for Means-Testing," by Edith H. Jones and Todd J. Zywicki. Brigham Young University Law Review, 1999.

J.K. Lasser's The New Bankruptcy Law & You, by Nathalie Martin. Hoboken, N.J.: John Wiley & Sons, 2006.

The New Bankruptcy: Will it Work for You? by Stephen Elias. Berkeley, Calif.: Nolo Press, 2006.

"An Optimal Personal Bankruptcy System and Proposed Reforms," by Hung-Jen Wang and Michelle J. White. Journal of Legal Studies, Vol. 29, No. 1 (January 2000).

Paying With Plastic: The Digital Revolution in Buying and Borrowing, by David S. Evans and Richard Schmalensee. Cambridge, Mass.: MIT Press, 1999.

"Taking the New Consumer Bankruptcy Model for a Test Drive: Means-Testing Real Chapter 7 Debtors," by Marianne B. Culhane and Michaela M. White. American Bankruptcy Institute Law Review, Vol. 7, No. 27 (1999).

"Why Don't More Households File for Bankruptcy?" by Michelle J. White. Journal of Law, Economics, and Organization, Vol. 14, No. 2 (October 1998).

"Why It Pays to File for Bankruptcy: A Critical Look at Incentives under U.S. Bankruptcy Laws and a Proposal for Change," by Michelle J. White. University of Chicago Law Review, Vol. 65, No. 3 (1998).

ARTICLE 10.3

Power Agency Fights Court over Bankruptcy Rights

Joseph Smolinsky

From time to time, issues arise before the US bankruptcy court that cause jurists to consider the interplay between the Bankruptcy Code and another Federal statute. The latest of these is the Federal Power Act. The Federal Power Act, among other things, grants the Federal Energy Regulatory Commission (FERC) the exclusive jurisdiction to regulate the transmission and sale of electric energy in interstate commerce. Ferc is also responsible for regulating prices and the terms and conditions for the sale of energy between states and regions.

Before reading the argument of the author, would your tendency be to give power over energy contracts of a party filing chapter 11 to the bankruptcy courts or to the Federal Energy Regulatory Commission?

US courts have been trying to strike a balance between the fundamental principles of the US Bankruptcy Code, which favours reorganization, and the public policy under the Federal Power Act to ensure nationwide availability of reliable and economical power and protect consumers from excessive rates. These independent goals have collided when bankrupt generators have sought to return to profitability by using the Bankruptcy Code to terminate burdensome power purchase agreements, leaving utilities to scramble for replacement power, often at much higher cost.

Efforts to terminate these contracts have been challenged and courts have reached different conclusions about whether it is up to the bankruptcy judge or Ferc to decide whether a power contract can be cancelled in a bankruptcy proceeding. Also at issue is the standard bankruptcy judges must use in their decisions. The outcome of these issues is of interest to the lending community because institutions that finance power projects and utilities wonder about the security of the long-term power purchase agreements (PPAs) that they lend against.

On balance, the bankruptcy court, sitting as a court of equity, is well suited to determine the terms under which a power generator in financial distress can reorganize in an effort to maximize value for its creditors. Rather than place a veto power over a project's survival in the hands of Ferc, the bankruptcy court should, as it always does, consider whether approval of a debtor's business judgment to terminate a PPA would so endanger the power purchaser and its retail consumers as to violate public policy.

Why should the volatility of energy prices be a relevant factor in determining who should have jurisdiction over the validity of energy contracts?

VOLATILITY

Given the recent volatility in energy prices and the liquidity crisis facing the energy industry, power generators and purchasers have found themselves before the bankruptcy court in recent years seeking to restructure their finances. As a result, bankruptcy courts have been faced with debtors' requests to exercise their rights under the Bankruptcy Code to reject or disavow long-term PPAs. In two recent situations arising in the Chapter 11 cases of NRG Energy Inc, Mirant Corporation and their respective subsidiaries, the contract counterparties, both regulated utilities, asserted that only Ferc, and not the bankruptcy court, had jurisdiction over the ultimate disposition of the PPAs. The debtors countered that rejection of contracts is clearly within the exclusive jurisdiction of the bankruptcy courts. Ferc, protective of its mandate, played active roles in these disputes.

For power generators and their lenders and other creditors, this developing law could greatly affect creditor recoveries and limit restructuring alternatives.

REJECTION OF CONTRACTS

Restructuring a business successfully in Chapter 11 often requires not only reducing its indebtedness but also refocusing its business operations to more profitable pursuits. This operational assessment process must include a review of all contractual relationships to determine whether the debtor could improve its future operating margins and profitability by rejecting certain contracts that are no longer in its best interests.

The ability to reject burdensome executory contracts pursuant to section 365 of the Bankruptcy Code is one of the most valuable debtor benefits. It permits a debtor to pick and choose among its unexpired leases and executory contracts. The term executory contract is not defined in the Bankruptcy Code but is generally accepted to mean any contract where both parties have material ongoing obligations. Except for leases of non-residential real property, which are subject to a 60-day deadline (which can be extended by the bankruptcy court), the decision to assume or reject does not have to be made by a debtor until confirmation of a plan of reorganization, unless the bankruptcy court orders otherwise. However, the debtor often seeks to reject unfavourable contracts early on in the bankruptcy case if doing so could result in immediate savings.

A debtor may assume an executory contract (other than an agreement to provide a loan or other financial accommodation) only if, at the time of assumption, two things occur. The company must cure past defaults and show its financial capability to perform the contract fully in the future. Section 365 of the Bankruptcy Code provides a further benefit in that it permits a debtor as part of the assumption process to assign a contract to a third party notwithstanding a prohibition within the contract. Personal service contracts and certain intellectual property licences cannot be assigned without consent.

A bankrupt company alternatively has the power to reject an executory contract if it is burdensome to the estate and if, in the debtor's business judgment, rejection is appropriate. If a contract is rejected, it is not terminated but rather the debtor is deemed to have breached the contract as of a point in time immediately before the bankruptcy filing. This excuses the company from further performance, but also exposes it to a claim for damages by the contract counterparty. This damage claim is treated as a pre-petition general unsecured claim, which could be compromised under a plan of reorganization for cents on the dollar. In contrast, the breach of a previously assumed contract gives rise to an administrative priority claim for damages that is not limited by the Bankruptcy Code. It is the relegation of rejection damage claims to pre-petition general unsecured status that allows a debtor to opt for rejection if a voluntary breach of the contract outside of bankruptcy would not have been considered.

The standard a bankruptcy court will apply in considering whether to authorize a debtor to assume or reject a contract is the business judgment test. It is prevailing law that a debtor's decision to reject an executory contract in its business judgment must be upheld, unless it is the product of bad faith, or of whim or caprice. Most courts will disregard as irrelevant the harm caused to other parties to the contract as a result of a rejection. Some courts, however, have modified the business judgment test to consider a balancing of the harms, but courts have only denied rejection in situations where the debtor's estate would not be aided by rejection and the potential damage to the contract counterparty would be disproportionately greater than the estate's expected benefit.

REJECTION OF PPAs

Contracts in the project finance arena such as PPAs are unique because of their longevity: often 20 years or longer. Also, contract pricing is based on long-term commodity market projections of future prices, which could turn out to be extremely volatile and greatly affected by external forces. As such, these contracts are more susceptible than most to rejection by independent generators in Chapter 11 proceedings.

Mirant and NRG both found their way into Chapter 11 during 2003. Each was a party to one or more PPAs with a regulated utility that each could no longer economically perform under. Both companies recognized that, as part of their overall restructuring efforts, they should take advantage of the Chapter 11 filing to reject certain PPAs. Mirant stated that rejection of its PPA with Potomac Electric Power Co (Pepco) was one of the primary objectives it needed to achieve for a successful reorganization. As described below, Mirant and NRG faced legal snags in implementing these restructuring initiatives as the courts struggled to reconcile the competing interests of the Bankruptcy Code and the Federal Power Act.

NRG

NRG Energy was party through a subsidiary to a four-year PPA with Connecticut Light & Power Company (CL&P), which required NRG to provide a fixed amount of energy to CL&P at a set price from January 1, 2000 until December 31, 2003. Immediately before filing for Chapter 11 relief on May 14, 2003 in the US Bankruptcy Court for the Southern District of New York, NRG provided notice to CL&P that it intended to terminate the PPA. Later that day, NRG commenced its Chapter 11 case and filed a motion to reject the PPA. The next day, in furtherance of their purported regulatory authority, the Connecticut Public Utility Control and the Connecticut attorney-general filed a petition with Ferc to stay the termination, citing harm to CL&P's customers. Ferc issued an order staying the termination on May 16 2003. CL&P thereafter obtained approval of the NRG Court to intervene in the Ferc proceedings.

On June 2, 2003, the Bankruptcy Court authorized the rejection under the business judgment standard but, in doing so, refused to overrule the Ferc stay of contract termination. It further informed NRG that it would have to take steps in another forum to vacate the Ferc stay order, which required continued performance. CL&P appealed the decision and NRG moved in the District Court for declaratory and injunctive relief against Ferc. Ferc responded by issuing a second order requiring NRG to comply with the rates, terms and conditions of the contract pending a Ferc determination of whether NRG's proposed termination was consistent with the public interest.

In addressing NRG's request to enjoin Ferc from conducting further proceedings to enforce the PPA, the District Court held that the issues that were pending before Ferc (whether NRG could cease performance notwithstanding the Federal Power Act guidelines) fell squarely within Ferc's regulatory responsibility. Moreover, the District Court noted that section 8251 of the Federal Power Act provides that orders issued by Ferc are to be reviewed only by the US Court of Appeals. Accordingly, the District Court dismissed the declaratory judgment action and motion for injunctive relief for lack of subject matter jurisdiction. NRG went on to settle its differences with CL&P by stipulation and NRG was able to emerge from Chapter 11 a short time later.

MIRANT

In 2000, Pepco, a regulated utility serving the District of Columbia and Maryland, agreed to sell its power plants to Mirant. Mirant also agreed to replace Pepco as the purchaser under a number of long-term power contracts that Pepco had entered into with other electricity suppliers. Pepco had difficulties assigning to Mirant two of the contracts under which it was an electricity purchaser, so Mirant agreed to enter into a new contract (referred to as a back-to-back agreement) under which it promised to buy electricity from Pepco at the same price that Pepco had to pay under the two agreements it was unable to assign. At the time, the rates under the new contract were reviewed and approved by Ferc. The rates under the back-to-back agreement ultimately proved higher than market rates and Mirant was suffering substantial losses. At the time of the bankruptcy filing, the back-to-back agreement had a remaining term of more than 18 years.

In July 2003, Mirant filed for relief under Chapter 11 in the US Bankruptcy Court for the Northern District of Texas. Mirant had seen the trouble that NRG had caused itself by providing notice of termination to CL&P of its agreement and allowing it to take preemptive action before Ferc by securing orders against NRG directing performance. To avoid the same fate, Mirant filed two motions in an adversary proceeding against Pepco and Ferc: a motion seeking authorization to reject the back-to-back agreement and one asking the Bankruptcy Court to enjoin Ferc or Pepco from taking any action to require Mirant to comply with the back-to-back agreement. The Court granted preliminary injunctive relief against Ferc and Pepco in September 2003.

Before the Bankruptcy Court heard the rejection motion, Pepco sought relief in the District Court, which decided to take jurisdiction away from the Bankruptcy Court and to use its own jurisdiction not only to rehear the motions requesting injunctive relief but also for the rejection motion as well. After extensive hearings and intervention by Ferc, the District Court found in December 2003 that Ferc had exclusive authority to authorize Mirant to stop performing the back-to-back agreement, because Ferc has exclusive jurisdiction over wholesale electricity sales in interstate commerce, and Ferc's exclusive authority may not be undermined through a collateral attack in another forum, such as the Bankruptcy Court.

The District Court further found that the only business justification supporting Mirant's motion to reject the back-to-back agreement was the losses it suffered because the rate approved by Ferc exceeded the market rate—matters directly within the purview of Ferc authority. Based on this analysis, the District Court denied the motion to reject for lack of jurisdiction and overturned the Bankruptcy Court's granting of injunctive relief. Mirant appealed the rulings to the Fifth Circuit Court of Appeals.

The Court of Appeals overturned the District Court's ruling and sided with Mirant. It said in August 2004 that a bankruptcy court's power to authorize the rejection of a PPA, such as the back-to-back agreement, "does not conflict with the authority given to Ferc to regulate rates for the interstate sale of electricity at wholesale".

It found that a rejection of a PPA is a breach of the contract and that the Federal Power Act does not provide Ferc with exclusive authority over the remedies for breach of a Ferc-approved contract. It also noted that elsewhere in the Bankruptcy Code there are express prohibitions or limitations against rejection of government-regulated contracts but that no such exception existed for Ferc. Accordingly, the Court of Appeals reversed the District Court and authorized and directed the District Court (or the Bankruptcy Court to the extent its jurisdiction is reinstated) to consider the rejection motion.

Notwithstanding the finding by the Court of Appeals that the bankruptcy court has exclusive jurisdiction over rejection of the back-to-back agreement, the Court of Appeals recognized the strong public interest in protecting the nation's supply of electricity and directed that the court overseeing the rejection motion impose a more stringent test than the business judgment rule. It instructed the lower court to scrutinize the impact of rejection upon the public interest, as well as ensure that the rejection would not cause any disruption in the supply of electricity to other public utilities or to consumers.

Mirant considered the Court of Appeals decision to be a big victory. However, it remains possible that the court deciding the rejection motion will determine that, to further public interest considerations under the Federal Power Act, the court will apply a stringent Ferc public interest test and only permit rejection if it is in the public interest of both parties.

For example, in the case of NRG, Ferc suggested that, to satisfy the public interest test, CL&P would need to realize full payment for each dollar of damages caused by terminating the contract. If that were the standard applied, it would be difficult for Mirant to show that consumers in Pepco's territory would not be harmed. It is more likely that the court will simply seek comfort that Pepco has access to other sources of electricity, even if this results in a rate increase to Pepco's customers, and otherwise defer to Mirant's business judgment.

In other words, only if rejecting the contract will result in an actual shortage or unavailability of power will the public interest standard supersede the business judgment standard. Also, although not noted by the court or by the parties, Section 202(c) of the Federal Power Act authorizes the US Department of Energy to compel a supplier to provide power in the event of an emergency or a shortage of power and to establish reasonable compensation to the supplier. The court might find that the existence of this remedy can protect the public and allow the business judgment standard to be applied without satisfying additional public interest standards.

Since the Fifth Circuit's decision in August 2004, the District Court has proceeded with the limited issue of whether the District Court should retain jurisdiction to hear all matters with respect to the Pepco dispute and what standard the court should use in approving the request for rejection. At the time of writing, the court has not yet considered the underlying rejection motion or the appropriate standard for review. Given the 18-year remaining term on the back-to-back agreement, the final outcome could be significant for Mirant creditors.

DISAGREEMENT

Both the NRG and Mirant cases suggest that there is no judicial agreement on a bankruptcy court's jurisdiction over the treatment of a PPA. Clearly, the Mirant approach is less rigid, more pragmatic and more oriented toward preserving the going concern value of bankrupt generators. The Mirant approach nevertheless accepts the notion that some safeguards are perhaps necessary to protect a national interest.

We are likely to see other situations in which the jurisdiction of the bankruptcy court is challenged by regulated utilities and Ferc. For debtors who are not as well financed as NRG and Mirant, it might prove difficult to sustain a lengthy campaign against Ferc through the appellate courts to achieve a final order approving rejection. This in itself could jeopardize a project's restructuring efforts. In the near term, these decisions might lead to forum shopping by prospective debtors in the power sector. Ultimately, as with certain other areas where the Bankruptcy Code conflicts with Federal statutory law, there might be legislation or Supreme Court consideration to address the interplay between the Federal Power Act and the Bankruptcy Code. But for now, the power struggle continues.

ARTICLE 10.4

Levying Flesh and Charging Society, Creditors, and Insurance Companies for It: The Irony of Including Personal Injury Awards in the Bankruptcy Estate

Joseph J. Blyskal, III

INTRODUCTION

B. Bankruptcy and the Social and Personal Costs of Injury

Nearly 45.8 million Americans do not have health insurance.[1] The cost of an accidental injury ranges from $800 to $193,800, depending on its locus of occurrence, duration, and severity.[2] Costs of injuries include actual physical loss, lost earnings, medical expenses, and mental suffering.[3] Thus, the uninsured victim of a tort causing personal injury needs as much financial assistance as possible. Financial support for the injured tort victims, especially those without insurance, comes in the form of a monetary recovery intended to replace their losses.[4] . . . However, bankruptcy claims the personal injury recoveries of over 1.5 million Americans each year to repay hungry creditors.[5] . . . The irony is that in nearly forty-seven percent of the bankruptcies filed, illness or injury is the cause of the filing.[6]

There is a problem with including personal injury recoveries in the bankruptcy estate: bankruptcy allows creditors to levy the flesh of innocent debtors. A tort victim loses an arm to a dog bite and in turn brings suit for the injuries. Between filing suit and settlement of the claim, the uninsured victim is forced to file chapter 7 bankruptcy because the victim is uninsured, has incurred countless medical bills, is unable to secure gainful employment as a result of the injuries, and is in need of a discharge from unsecured debt that was incurred at the bequest of all-too-willing creditors.[7] After filing bankruptcy, the debtor receives the right to a $105,000 settlement of the claim.[8] The settlement is intended in part to figuratively replace the arm of the victim and in part to offset the costs of living and medical expenses because the debtor is now relegated to limited-income employment due to her injuries. However, because the cause of action accrued prepetition, the right to receive the settlement funds is no longer the property of the debtor.[9] Rather, the funds are the property of the bankruptcy estate, for the trustee in bankruptcy to collect and divide amongst unsecured creditors.[10] If the debtor lives in a state that permits use of federal bankruptcy exemptions, the debtor may keep $18,450 of the settlement.[11] However, if the debtor lives in a state which does not permit the use of federal bankruptcy exemptions, the debtor may have to forego the entire settlement amount.[12] The debtor is thus left without compensation for the loss of his arm. Instead, unsecured creditors take the figurative arm of the debtor to satisfy the debts. This is an inappropriate debt collection practice. . . .

This Comment will address the implications of including an award for personal injury in the bankruptcy estate and the ironies underlying the practice in light of the competing, yet parallel, goals of tort law and bankruptcy law. I will present the conflict between the policies underlying the formation of the bankruptcy estate and those governing the right to recovery in tort for personal injury, examine the development of the laws governing the bankruptcy estate with regard to personal injury awards, and offer a suggestion for the reformation of the laws governing exemption of such awards from the bankruptcy estate.

Tort law compensates injured tort victims for their loss while bankruptcy law disregards an insolvent tort victim's rights to recovery in favor of compensating financially solvent creditors. Courts have struggled with the conflicting policies underlying tort law and bankruptcy law. Contrary to the purpose of tort law, courts eventually abided by the Bankruptcy Act of 1978 and began including personal injury recoveries in the bankruptcy estate. A debtor may exempt a portion of such an award from the estate, however, such exemptions are limited in amount. In order to protect the interests of an injured debtor in a fresh start after bankruptcy, prevent the social costs of injury from draining public resources, and preserve the credit facilities of credit-granting institutions for future debtors, legislatures need to increase exemption amounts to better reflect the actual loss of injured debtors and bankruptcy judges need to be able to exercise more discretion over the formation of the bankruptcy estate.

I. FLESHING OUT THE POLICIES: THE COMPETING, YET PARALLEL, GOALS OF TORT COMPENSATION AND CREDITOR COMPENSATION

A. Introduction

Tort law and bankruptcy law are competing, yet parallel, systems of compensation.[13] Tort law aims to compensate the victim of a tort for his losses, while bankruptcy law aims to compensate a creditor for its losses.[14] Tort law is primarily concerned with placing an injured victim in the position that he was in prior to being injured.[15] Bankruptcy law is concerned with assisting creditors in collecting outstanding debts and assuring that a debtor has a financial fresh start after bankruptcy.[16] Thus, both tort law and bankruptcy law are concerned with assuring that a debtor can financially support himself.[17] The conflict arises when a debtor is compensated in tort but a bankruptcy creditor lays claim to that compensation to satisfy outstanding debts of that debtor.[18] If a debtor receives the full amount of his tort award, creditors are cheated but the purposes of tort law are fulfilled.[19] However, if a bankruptcy trustee is allowed to distribute the award to unsecured creditors, the creditors are satisfied but the injured debtor remains uncompensated and without a fresh start.[20] . . .

D. Tort Law and Bankruptcy Law as Compensation Schemes

When the author talks about the rights of the parties in conflict, is he leaving out any other interested parties who might also be affected by the handling of tort claims in bankruptcy?

Despite their differences, both tort law and bankruptcy law are in essence schemes of compensation. Tort law seeks to compensate individuals who suffered losses due to the intentional, negligent, or reckless wrongs of another, while bankruptcy aims to compensate creditors who have suffered losses due to the financial negligence or recklessness of a debtor, macroeconomic causes, or other factors that lead the debtor to dire financial straits. Therein lies the fundamental problem addressed in this Comment: the policies underlying bankruptcy and tort compensation schemes are at odds on the issue of who needs the compensation more, tort victims or creditors. In a bankruptcy proceeding where the debtor has the rights to a personal injury action which arose prepetition, tort law dictates that the recovery realized from that action be used to compensate the debtor for the ultimate benefit of society.[21] Bankruptcy law seeks to use the recovery to compensate the creditor.[22] . . . Thus, it is questionable whether the policy of granting a debtor a fresh start after bankruptcy is fully realized when the debtor is the victim of a tort that caused personal injury. Aligning bankruptcy policy with the tort law policy actually will lead to the utility of the fresh start because an injured debtor who receives the recovery that is needed is less likely to be a future credit risk or drain on public funds.

E. The Misalignment of Personal Injury Awards and Bankruptcy Exemptions

Generally, an injured bankruptcy debtor may only exempt a recovery for tangible losses.[23] The debtor may exempt $18,450 on account of "personal bodily injury."[24] In addition, the debtor may exempt the amount necessary for support of a recovery meant to compensate for lost future earnings.[25] However, many statutes do not provide a debtor with an express exemption for funds set aside to cover medical expenses related to personal injury.[26] Furthermore, a debtor typically cannot exempt a recovery for intangible losses such as pain and suffering or punitive damages because of their subjective and hard-to-quantify nature.[27] Because a tort victim may suffer losses that include tangible physical loss, intangible mental loss, medical expenses, loss of earning capacity, and actual loss of future income,[28] an injured debtor will likely suffer economic and noneconomic loss in excess of his exemption amount.[29] . . . The concern over the potential for long-term indebtedness, inability to pay medical expenses, and the risk of unhealthy coping methods as a result of a limited exemption of an injured debtor's recovery for tangible and intangible losses becomes more pronounced and more ironic when considered in the context of the underlying purposes of bankruptcy to compensate creditors and to provide a debtor with a fresh start and an opportunity to stay solvent.[30] As such, the bankruptcy exemptions need to be reformed to advance the policies underlying tort law as opposed to being concerned with compensation of large creditors.

II. THE BANKRUPTCY ESTATE: HOW BANKRUPTCY EXCISES FLESH

A. Introduction

The bankruptcy estate is formed upon the filing of a bankruptcy petition and includes all legal and equitable interests of the debtor as of the commencement of the case.[31] Historically, a personal injury cause of action, and hence recovery, were excluded from the bankruptcy estate on the grounds that personal injury was personal to the debtor and could not be assigned.[32] With the Bankruptcy Reform Act of 1978, the bankruptcy estate was to include causes of action for personal injury.[33] Due to concern over adequately compensating an injured debtor, courts were reluctant to follow that provision.[34] Eventually, every circuit adopted the reading of the Bankruptcy Reform Act of 1978 that included causes of action in the estate.[35] . . .

V. THOSE TOUGH-SKINNED CREDITORS WANT A PIECE OF FLESH, TOO: ADDRESSING THE COUNTERARGUMENTS

B. Counterargument: Creditors Are Entitled to the Largest Estate Possible

. . . Bankruptcy law already recognizes that in some situations it is inequitable to allow a creditor to improve its position at the expense of other parties in interest.[36] An injured debtor that is cheated out of an award meant to ensure that it can support itself may be forced to rely on other means of support after its meager exemption amount is exhausted: "An uncompensated claim for personal injury may seriously complicate the injured's ability to function in the future."[37] As such, the debtor may seek refuge in social welfare programs and may once again become insolvent. Therefore, the inequities to creditors "ought not alter the conclusion" that a debtor is entitled to the proceeds of a personal injury action.[38]

C. Counterargument: Creditors Will Seek to Offset a Low Payout in Bankruptcy by Increasing Interest Rates

It is unlikely that not including a personal injury award in the bankruptcy estate will cause creditors to seek compensation from future debtors to offset this loss. Credit-granting institutions are often held by holding companies engaged in large-scale banking and nonbanking operations.[39] Other assets of those companies will likely offset the credit risk taken by large banks when a bankrupt debtor leaves only a fractional payout to satisfy its debts.[40] . . . In fact, because an injured debtor would be ensured a fresh start and adequate compensation for its injuries if permitted to exempt its award, society and future debtors may be better off because credit institutions would not suffer increased credit risk due to desolate injured debtors and would thus not need to increase interest rates or otherwise guard against higher risk.

D. Counterargument: An Award for Prepetition Personal Injury Is Akin to Prepetition Income and Should Be Included in the Estate

Do you believe that tort compensation should be considered a substitute for lost income?

Tort compensation is often a substitute for earnings lost due to the debtor's injuries.[41] Jury instructions for damages for personal injury specifically reference lost income as an element of tort recovery.[42] Thus, a tenable argument can be made that an award for personal injury compensates the debtor for prepetition lost earnings and therefore should be part of the bankruptcy estate under § 541(a)(6).[43] However, income substitutes as opposed to actual income earned are distinguished in tax law and workers' compensation law.

Monetary awards that substitute for lost income are actually recognized as a special exception from the creditor process in many states and in federal bankruptcy.[44] For instance, an award for workers' compensation that replaces the lost income of an injured worker is exempted from the bankruptcy estate.[45] Such income, had it been earned through employment by the debtor prior to the petition, would normally be included in the bankruptcy estate.[46] However, because the income substitute is awarded as a result of the debtor's injuries, the payments receive special treatment so as to avoid income interruption and the consequent drain on society that an injured debtor would have were it not adequately compensated for injuries.[47] In addition, awards for workers' compensation are exempt from taxation.[48] In fact, the "amount of any damages . . .

received (whether by suit or agreement and whether as lump sums or as periodic payments) on account of personal physical injuries or physical sickness" do not count as gross income.[49] Therefore, any argument that an award for personal injury arising prepetition should be regarded as prepetition income that should be included in the bankruptcy estate fails in light of the wide recognition that income substitutes are exempt from taxes and creditor process elsewhere under the law.

E. Counterargument: Because of the Subjective Nature of Punitive Damages and Pain and Suffering, Such an Award Should Not Be Exempt from the Estate

While damages for lost income are readily calculable and serve a definite purpose, damages for intangible losses are difficult to calculate and serve more amorphous purposes.[50] This has formed the basis for the argument that such awards should not be exempt from the bankruptcy estate.[51] In fact, personal injury awards are often subject to statutory caps already.[52] . . . [T]here is no reason why a creditor as opposed to the debtor should be given a windfall as a result of a large award for pain and suffering or punitive damages.[53] In fact, because tort law aims to compensate victims for their loss[54] and because bankruptcy aims to give a debtor a fresh start,[55] an injured debtor should not be divested of his award for punitive damages or pain and suffering. Punitive damages awards and pain and suffering awards are subjective, personal, and already subject to state tort reform statutes that limit them in amount.[56] In addition, such awards are already judicially tested and peer-approved as they are rendered by a competent jury. To the extent that legislatures have already determined the limits of subjective awards in tort and to the extent that such awards are judicially tested and peer-approved, the debtor should be favored in light of the fundamental principles of compensation and bankruptcy, and such awards should not belong to the estate.

VI. A SOLUTION: SUTURING THE WOUNDS OF INJURED DEBTORS

A. The Need for a Solution

Neither the federal exemption scheme nor the majority of state exemption schemes adequately protect a debtor's interest in a personal injury award. It is unlikely that a lump sum of $18,450,[57] or even less,[58] and payments for lost future earnings[59] will adequately cover the costs of medical treatment, provide the debtor with adequate piece of mind for having to cope with a lost body part, provide support for the debtor's family, and take into account the value of the lost productivity of the debtor.[60] This is especially true for the 45.8 million Americans who do not have health insurance.[61] An injured debtor who is forced to disgorge his personal injury award to his creditors[62] and is permitted only to retain a fraction of the subsequent recovery[63] is likely to need future support in the form of social welfare, additional credit lines, and, in the event they have insurance, continuing insurance benefits to help pay for medical treatment. This means that the debtor becomes a drain on public funds, incurs future debt and perhaps files bankruptcy again, and contributes to the haste with which insurance premiums increase. In short, the injured debtor is forced to repay its debts with money better left to compensating the debtor for his injuries.

The federal bankruptcy exemption or state exemptions do not comport with the principles of compensation underlying tort law.[64] A debtor suffers pain and suffering, physical loss, lost future earnings, loss of productivity, and the cost of medical expenses.[65] A debtor may only exempt the portions of an award for personal injury specified in the federal exemption statute, i.e., that portion that compensates for actual bodily injury.[66] While the debtor may exempt payments made to compensate for lost future earnings,[67] medical devices,[68] and disability or unemployment benefits,[69] to be exempt the payments need to be "traceable to,"[70] "on account of,"[71] or in a form identifiable to one of the categories listed in the statute.[72] Thus, to the extent that a jury award does not allocate a specific amount for each of the categories in an exemption statute, the debtor may be left with a general lump sum award for pecuniary and non-pecuniary losses and thus resigned to a single exemption for loss on account of bodily injury or no exemption at all under § 522(d)(11)(D).[73] While many of the states are more generous than the federal statute, in light of the costs of personal injuries, the statutes still do not adequately account for the losses to a debtor.[74]

Furthermore, the lack of an exemption for personal injury recoveries seems to be at odds with the presence of an exemption for disability benefits.[75] Just like including workers' compensation awards in the bankruptcy estate is inconsistent with the policies underlying workers' compensation,[76] including personal injury recoveries in the bankruptcy estate is inconsistent with principles of tort compensation. . . .

B. Balancing the Needs of Debtors with the Needs of Creditors

There needs to be a balance between the interests of debtors and creditors that favors returning the debtor to solvency, avoiding future loss to creditors, and eventual drain on social resources. This can be accomplished by legislation that honors the principles underlying tort compensation—that an injured individual should be returned to his pre-injury condition and compensated for his losses[77]— and the principles of bankruptcy—that debts should be satisfied and discharged and the debtor should be given a fresh start.[78] The current system of bankruptcy exemptions does not achieve an appropriate balance because it does not honor these policies in a balanced manner.

The current system weighs too heavily in favor of creditors at the expense of injured debtors.[79] In the case of injured debtors, the current system of estate formation and exemptions fails to take into account the interests of debtors and the costs to society and future creditors of stripping the injured debtor of a personal injury award.[80] . . .

On the other hand, entirely excluding a personal injury award from the bankruptcy estate would place it beyond the reach of creditors.[81] Excluding property from the bankruptcy estate rarely is done.[82] Rather, with the Bankruptcy Reform Act of 1978, most property is included in the estate and then an exemption is claimed. . . . Furthermore, allowing a debtor to keep an entire personal injury award without affording creditors a chance to object is inherently unfair. For example, a hospital that provided emergency medical treatment to a bankrupt debtor has an interest in any personal injury award arising from the injury it treated. Allowing a debtor to keep the entirety of a personal injury award of the estate would preclude such a creditor from claiming an interest in the award.[83] Thus, while the current scheme favors creditors, allowing a debtor to keep the entirety of a personal injury award would completely contravene the purpose of bankruptcy to ensure that creditors can collect outstanding debts.[84]

C. A Solution

Modifications to the current exemption scheme will allow bankruptcy law to better protect the interests of debtors, creditors, and society. However, requiring all states to comply with a standard exemption scheme would eliminate states' rights to statutory experimentation,[85] while allowing states the freedom to exempt all or none of a personal injury award has led to the inequities addressed here. Instead, I suggest a presumptive federal exemption for personal injury awards. The federal exemption statute would exempt the entirety of a personal injury award regardless of the type of damages awarded. Each state would still be permitted to enact their exemption statutes for property other than personal injury awards. The debtor would have the opportunity to choose either the state or federal exemptions for property other than personal injury awards but no state would be permitted to exempt out of the federal personal injury exemption. The presumption in favor of the federal exemption for personal injury awards would, however, be rebuttable. Creditors and trustees would have the opportunity to rebut the presumption upon a showing of inherent unfairness to a specific creditor. The only way that a creditor or trustee could raise a successful objection to the use of the mandatory personal injury federal exemption would be to make a showing that the federal exemption would be inherently unfair to a specific creditor in light of the facts of the case, e.g., where there is a creditor like a medical provider that has a vested interest in the personal injury award. Once such a showing is made the court would fashion an appropriate exemption based on the facts of the case. Absent such a showing, there would be a strong presumption in favor of the federal personal injury exemption. Under no circumstances would a general objection on the grounds that the pro rata payout to unsecured creditors as a whole was unfair suffice to overcome the presumption. The objection would need to be based on harm to a specific creditor.

The risk of abuse and inequity under a revised statute could be minimized by the use of certain safeguards that would guarantee that creditors and debtors had incentives to act in the best interest of all parties-in-interest. . . . This would provide the harmed creditor with a substantial portion of the award, and provide the debtor at least a portion of the tort compensation to which he was entitled. Of course, any creditor who sought to displace the mandatory federal exemption with a judicial exemption would only be entitled to receive up to the value of its claim, the remainder of the award going to the debtor.

Any further risk of abuse by creditors could be minimized by giving bankruptcy judges the discretionary authority to overrule any objection and permit the debtor the use of the presumptive federal exemption. The judge also would allow and consider evidence on the issue of an injured debtor's need to be compensated to the fullest extent possible to avoid future loss to itself and society. This evidence could include medical evaluations that show the debtor's need for ongoing treatment, the mental strain of coping with the injury, in addition to any evidence that showed the likelihood or not that a debtor would be forced to rely on social welfare programs and incur more debt for support in light of his injury. If the judge believes that the interests of the debtor and society would be best served by allowing unlimited exemption, the judge could use the federal exemption despite any inequity to a creditor. In short, a hearing should be held on the amount of exemption to which a debtor is entitled.

Finally, to assure that the exemption for personal injury awards is considered in a light favorable to debtors, bankruptcy judges should bear in mind that anything other than an unlimited exemption limits the amount of compensation that a court already determined a debtor was entitled to under tort law. To the extent that a court or jury hearing a personal injury cause of action already determined that a debtor is entitled to a set amount of compensation and punitive damages, a bankruptcy judge should largely defer to the trial court on the issue. Absent clear and convincing evidence that a creditor would suffer irreparable harm, a bankruptcy judge should defer to the judgment of a competent court, jury, or representatives of the parties to a suit for personal injury by honoring the amount awarded or agreed to be paid in settlement of the claim for personal injury. In the event that the federal exemption for a personal injury award is used by the bankruptcy judge, the exemption would only be limited by the statutory caps on pain and suffering and punitive damages in the state where the cause of action accrued. This assures some limit on the debtor's exemption while guaranteeing that he receives what he needs. . . .

A clear and unambiguous statute (if that is possible) would eliminate the need to structure settlements to mimic exemption categories such as lost income or disability payments, afford the debtor the required compensation, and allow creditors the opportunity to object to the exemption by showing evidence that the unlimited federal exemption would harm their interests. In the aggregate, this would achieve an acceptable balance between the interests of the debtor and creditors because it would place the burden on the creditors while providing a presumption that the debtor is entitled to a fully exempted award. Furthermore, because the federal exemption statute would remain unchanged with regard to property other than personal injury awards, creditors would still be entitled to payouts roughly equivalent to those received under the present statute. The only change would be that debtors are favored with regard to personal injury awards.

CONCLUSION

The concept of a fresh start for an injured debtor in bankruptcy is apparitional absent adequate compensation for a personal injury. When an injured individual is not adequately compensated, he cannot bear the costs of injury and in turn the costs to society increase. Monetary awards in personal injury replace human capital so that society does not need to bear that cost. To the extent that bankruptcy takes this human capital to compensate creditors, uninsured debtors are forced to rely on means other than a personal injury award to pay for medical expenses and insured debtors and uninsured debtors alike are resigned to other means to cope with their pain and support themselves and their families and society bears the costs of these alternative means of support. In turn, the costs of healthcare rise, social welfare programs are burdened, and social problems arise if a desolate debtor is forced to turn to crime or drugs to cope with its loss. Absent a solution that takes into account the interests of debtors in being compensated under the principles of tort law, bankruptcy increases the social costs of personal injuries and fails to meet the goal of providing an injured debtor with a fresh start in order to benefit creditors. This is not acceptable because '"it is not, and never has been, the policy of the law to coin into money for the profit of his creditors, the bodily pain, mental anguish or outraged feelings of a bankrupt.'"[86]

END NOTES

1. United States Census Bureau, Income, Poverty, and Health Insurance Coverage in the United States: 2004, at 60 (Aug. 2005).
2. Statistics Department, National Safety Council, Estimating the Costs of Unintentional Injury, 2005, *available at* http://www.nsc.org/lrs/statinfo/

estcost.htm [hereinafter National Safety Council]. Injuries cited include automobile accidents, home injuries, public injuries, and work injuries. *Id.*

3. *See generally* 1 DAN B. DOBBS, THE LAW OF TORTS Ch. 1, §§1–6 (1993).
4. *See id.* § 10.
5. *See generally* Elizabeth Warren & Jay Westbrook, The Law of Debtors and Creditors (4th ed. 2001).
6. *See* Melissa B. Jacoby, *Collecting Debts From the Ill and Injured: The Rhetorical Significance, But Practical Irrelevance, of Culpability and Ability to Pay,* 51 AM. U.L. REV. 229, 235 (2001).
7. *See, e.g.*, In re Dorsey, 120 B.R. 592, 596 (Bankr. M.D. Fla. 1990) (unsecured credit card debt of $ 106,000 despite no identifiable and set income); see also *Legislative Update, Expanding Credit Card Debt: The Role of Creditors and the Impact on Consumers*, 17 AM. BANKR. INST. J., Feb. 1998, 6.
8. *See, e.g.*, In re Hughes, 318 B.R. 704 (Bankr. W.D. Mo. 2004) (annuity payments totaling $ 105,000 for dog bite received as child, victim later filed bankruptcy).
9. *See* 11 U.S.C.A. § 541(a)(1) (West 2005).
10. *See id.*
11. *See id.* § 522(d)(11)(D).
12. *See, e.g.*, ARIZ. REV. STAT. ANN. § 33–1126 (2005) (no exemption for personal injury recovery).
13. *See* discussion *infra* Parts I.B-E.
14. *See* discussion *infra* Parts I.B-E.
15. *See* Dobbs, *supra* note 11, § 10.
16. DAVID G. EPSTEIN ET AL., BANKRUPTCY Ch. 1, § 1–2 (1993).
17. *See* discussion *infra* Parts I.B-E.
18. *See* discussion *infra* Parts I.B-E.
19. *See* discussion *infra* Parts I.B-E.
20. *See* discussion *infra* Parts I.B-E.
21. *See* discussion *supra* Parts I.B and C.
22. *See* discussion *supra* Parts I.B and C.
23. 11 U.S.C.A. § 522(d)(11)(D) (West 2005).
24. *Id.*
25. *See id.* § 522(d)(11)(E). It would seem logical to conclude that the amount prescribed by § 522(d)(11)(D) is intended to preserve the debtor's entitlement to recover his actual physical loss. However, the statute clearly disavows this conclusion. It is unclear what exactly the $ 18,450 is intended to compensate the debtor for if it is not pain and suffering, actual physical loss, or lost future income. There is confusion as to what rationale underlies the personal injury exemption in the federal bankruptcy scheme. *See* Louis J. Papera, *Confusion Over §*

522(d)(11)(D): What Congress Really Meant by Exempting Payments for "Personal Bodily Injury" and Why They Got It Wrong, 16 BANKR. DEV. J. 536 (2000). One author concluded that Congress most likely intended to exempt only recovery for actual physical injury; however, it missed the mark with language that nullifies itself. The author also concluded that the practice of limiting exemptions for personal injury is contrary to the principles of tort law. *Id.*

26. *See, e.g.*, § 522(d) (no exemption for medical expenses); *see also* In re Bippert, 311 B.R. 456, 470 n.24 (Bankr. W.D. Tex. 2004) ("according to the legislative history, it would not be necessary to allow exemption for reimbursement for medical expenses because Congress presumed that medical providers already had a constructive trust on any personal injury award for their expenses, and the constructive trust would not be property of the estate anyway"); Claude v. Claude (In re Claude), 206 B.R. 374, 376 (Bankr. W.D. Pa. 1997) ("The § 522(d)(11)(D) exemption does not cover awards for pain and suffering or reimbursement for actual pecuniary losses such as lost wages or medical expenses.") (citing 4 Collier on Bankruptcy, P 522.09[11], at 522–67 (15th ed., rev. 2003)). However, the logic of Congress is strained when considered in light of continuing medical expenses after the personal injury award is exhausted. A debtor's award would first be diminished by a hospital's claims, the remainder going to the bankruptcy estate less the debtor's exemption, leaving only the set exemption amount to cover any ongoing medical expenses due to the debtor's injury. If the debtor is permanently disabled, ongoing treatment may be costly and the cost of physical therapy and medications and office visits may leave a debtor insolvent again.
27. § 522(d)(11)(D).
28. *See* discussion *supra* Parts I.A-B.
29. *See generally* National Safety Council, *supra* note 2; National Center for Injury Prevention and Control, Cost of Injury in the United States: A Report to Congress (1989), *available at* http://www.cdc.gov/ncipc/pub-res/cost of injury/cost.htm.
30. Epstein et al., *supra* note 16, § 1–2.
31. § 541(a).
32. Bankruptcy Reform Act, § 110(a) (1976) (current version available at 11 U.S.C.A. § 541 (West 2005)).
33. 11 U.S.C.A. § 541(a) (West 2005).
34. *See generally* Sierra Switchboard Co. v. Westinghouse Electric Corporation, 789 F.2d 705, 707 (9th Cir. 1986).
35. *Id.*
36. *See, e.g.*, § 1129(a)(7) (best interests test for confirmation of a chapter 11 plan does not allow a creditor to improve its position over other creditors as compared to a chapter 7 payout plan).
37. In re Schmelzer, 350 F. Supp. 429, 436 (S.D. Ohio 1972).

38. Tignor, 21 B.R. at 222. The question is:

> Who shall benefit from the potential windfall, if a claim for personal injuries can be so characterized. When the question is posed in these terms, it should be clear that we have done no more today than to recognize that the Act, which contains a presumption in favor of the [already financially shaky] bankrupt, was enacted for the protection of debtors, and that its underlying policies favor the bankrupt.

Schmelzer, 350 F. Supp. at 438 (referring to the Bankruptcy Act of 1898). The policies under the current Act are similar to those under the former Act. See In re Luster, 981 F.2d 277, 280 (7th Cir. 1992) ("It is hard to isolate a "bankruptcy policy' distinct from the terms of the 1898 Act and 1978 Code. "Bankruptcy policy' does not exist in the abstract; the term is a shorthand for rules and the implications they create. When construing ambiguities in bankruptcy statutes, courts consider goals that infuse the structure of the laws—goals such as preventing a race among creditors that reduces the total value of the estate, distributing assets according to contractual and statutory entitlements, and providing natural persons with "fresh starts" so that they again can claim the rewards of their labor.")

39. JONATHAN R. MACEY ET AL., BANKING LAW AND REGULATION 119 (3d ed. 2001).
40. *Id.* at 49.
41. *See generally* Stephen D. Sugarman, *Doing Away With Tort Law*, 73 Cal. L. Rev. 555 (1985); *see also* Kenneth S. Abraham, *What is a Tort Claim? An Interpretation of Contemporary Tort Reform*, 51 MD. L. REV. 172, 173–74 (1992) ("[Tort] reforms import into tort law some of the more appealing ... features of non-tort compensation systems—workers' compensation ... and private and social insurance. . . . Indeed, the evolving conception of a tort claim reflects the . . . standardization of recovery that is at the core of health and disability insurance and other non-tort compensation systems.").
42. *See, e.g.*, Eleventh Circuit Pattern Jury Instruction § 1.1, at 455–58 (2005) (negligence).
43. Compensation for the services of the debtor is included in the bankruptcy estate only if the debtor became entitled to it prepetition. 11 U.S.C.A. § 541(a)(6) (West 2000).
44. *See, e.g.*, § 522(d)(11)(E) (lost earnings exemption).
45. *Id.* § 522(d)(10)(C) (exempting disability or unemployment benefits).
46. *Id.* § 541(a).
47. Gagne v. Christians, 172 B.R. 50, 53–55 (Bankr. D. Minn. 1994).
48. 26 U.S.C. § 104(a)(1) (2000).
49. *Id.* § 104(a)(2).
50. Pain and suffering compensates the debtor for the pain of having to cope with an injury while punitive damages aim to deter tortfeasors' bad behavior. RESTATEMENT (SECOND) OF TORTS § 901 (2006).

51. *See, e.g.*, In re Keyworth, 47 B.R. 966 (Bankr. D. Colo. 1985) (punitive damages are exemplary and thus not exempt); *see also* 11 U.S.C.A. § 522(d)(11)(D) (West 2005) (punitive damages and pain and suffering not exempt).
52. *See, e.g.*, Colo. Rev. Stat. § 13–21–102.5 (2005) ($ 250,000 cap on non-economic damages).
53. *See, e.g.*, In re Schmelzer, 350 F. Supp. 429, 438 (S.D. Ohio 1972) ("The question is who shall benefit from the potential windfall, if a claim for personal injuries can be so characterized. When the question is posed in these terms, it should be clear that we have done no more today than to recognize that the Act, which contains a presumption in favor of the [already financially shaky] bankrupt, was enacted for the protection of debtors, and that its underlying policies favor the bankrupt.").
54. DOBBS, *supra* note 3, § 1.
55. EPSTEIN ET AL., *supra* note 16, § 1–2.
56. *See, e.g.*, COLO. REV. STAT. § 13–21–102.5 (2005); CAL. CIV. CODE § 1431.2(b)(2) (2006).
57. 11 U.S.C.A. § 522(d)(11)(D) (West 2005).
58. *See, e.g.*, OHIO REV. CODE ANN. § 2329.66(A)(12) (2006) ($5000 exemption).
59. 11 U.S.C.A. § 522(d)(11)(E) (West 2005).
60. National Safety Council, *supra* note 29. Injuries cited include automobile accidents, home injuries, public injuries and work injuries. *Id.*
61. U.S. Census Bureau, U.S. Department of Commerce, Income, Poverty, and Health Insurance Coverage in the United States: 2004, 60 (2005). . . .
62. § 541(a).
63. *See, e.g.*, *id.* § 522(d)(11)(D) ($ 18,450 federal exemption).
64. *See* discussion *supra* Part I.B.
65. *See* discussion *supra* Part I.A-B.
66. § 522(d)(11)(D).
67. *Id.* § 522(d)(11)(E).
68. *Id.* § 522(d)(9).
69. *Id.* § 522(d)(10)(C).
70. *Id.* § 522(d)(11)(D).
71. *Id.*
72. *See generally* id. § 522.
73. *See, e.g.*, In re Russell, 148 B.R. 564 (Bankr. E.D. Ark. 1992) (debtor could not exempt general jury award as payment on account of loss of future earnings).
74. National Safety Council, *supra* note 29. For instance, the National Safety Council estimates that the cost to society of each personal injury resulting from automobile accidents ranges from $ 19,600 for noncapacitating

evident injuries to $60,500 for incapacitating injuries. *Id.* The federal exemption of $18,450 is meager by comparison. *Id.*

75. *See generally* § 522(d)(10)(C).
76. Gagne v. Christians, 172 B.R. 50, 53–55 (Bankr. D. Minn. 1994).
77. *See* discussion *supra* Part I.A-B.
78. *See* discussion *supra* Part I.C.
79. *See* discussion *supra* Part I.C.
80. *See* discussion *supra* Part I.C.
81. *See* discussion *supra* Parts II. . . .
82. *See* discussion *supra* Part II.
83. *See* discussion *supra* Parts II. . . .
84. *See* discussion *supra* Part I.C.
85. *See generally* Crist v. Bretz, 437 U.S. 28 (1978) (state experimentation cannot be sacrificed for uniformity).
86. In re Tignor, 21 B.R. 219, 222 (Bankr. E.D. Va. 1982) (quoting Sibley v. Nason, 196 Mass. 125, 130 (Mass. 1907)).

ARTICLE 10.5

Hiding in Plain View: A Neglected Supreme Court Decision Resolves the Debate over Non-debtor Releases in Chapter 11 Reorganizations

Joshua M. Silverstein

The conflicting purposes of bankruptcy must be based on what assumptions about the nature of the debtors and that of the creditors?

INTRODUCTION

The ultimate policy of chapter 11[1] of the Bankruptcy Code[2] ("the Code") is the successful reorganization of debtors.[3] A successful reorganization is one that both rehabilitates the debtor and minimizes creditor forfeitures.[4] These two aims, while frequently in conflict,[5] are promoted by the Code's complex array of provisions—provisions that carefully balance the interests of debtors and creditors.[6]

In addition to its specific directives, the Code entrusts bankruptcy courts with "broad equitable powers to balance the interests of the affected parties, guided by the overriding goal of ensuring the success of the reorganization."[7] This equitable authority emanates primarily from § 105(a),[8] which states that "the court may issue any order, process, or judgment that is necessary or appropriate to carry out the provisions of this title."[9] Another source of general equitable power is § 1123(b)(6),[10] which permits a chapter 11 plan to "include any other appropriate provision not inconsistent with the applicable provisions of this title."[11] There is substantial disagreement over the scope of the authority conferred by these statutes.[12] And the controversy is particularly acute in the context of "non-debtor releases."

A key component of debtor rehabilitation is the "fresh start" provided by chapter 11's discharge provision. Under § 1141(d)(1), the confirmation of a plan of reorganization discharges the bankrupt party from all of its pre-confirmation debts (with limited exceptions).[13] The debtor emerges from bankruptcy with only the obligations set forth in its plan.[14] The plan also is binding on all of the debtor's creditors, including those that objected to its approval.[15] Pursuant to § 524 of the Code, the discharge benefits the debtor alone; the liabilities of guarantors, sureties, joint tort-feasors, shareholders, directors, employees, and related companies are not impacted.[16]

Creditors thus generally are free to collect any deficiencies in bankruptcy payments from coliable parties and pursue independent claims against insiders and affiliated entities.[17] However, this is not always so. While the discharge itself does not shield third parties, a substantial number of bankruptcy courts have used the general equitable powers conferred by the Code to extinguish claims against non-debtors—i.e., to grant "non-debtor" or "third-party" releases.[18]

For at least eighteen years, the federal courts have been divided over whether such releases are permissible.[19] The Code does not expressly sanction the issuance of non-debtor releases.[20] However, "pro-release" courts contend that the equitable powers flowing from §§ 105(a) and 1123(b)(6) allow for this type of relief.[21] And they see no explicit prohibition on releases in the Code or elsewhere. "Anti-release" courts, as their label suggests, disagree. Many "anti-release" courts have concluded that non-debtor releases run afoul of § 524(e), which provides that the "discharge of a debt of the debtor does not affect the liability of any other entity on, or the property of any other entity for, such debt."[22] They read this language, and the bankruptcy policies underlying it, to prohibit third-party releases. Other anti-release courts do not believe that § 524(e) constitutes a bar. Instead, they think that §§ 105(a) and 1123(b)(6) simply do not grant sufficient equitable power to permit the release of claims against non-debtors. . . .

[T]he recent scandals rocking Wall Street and the broader American business community are giving rise to precisely the type of mass-tort disputes that have inspired courts to approve of non-debtor releases in the past.[23] The propriety of third-party releases is thus an issue that cries out for Supreme Court guidance,[24] particularly since "the bankruptcy court is quickly becoming the forum for resolution of many of the largest and most complex mass litigations."[25] If the High Court does join the fray, there is a largely overlooked decision from which the Justices should seek guidance—the Court's own ruling in *United States v. Energy Resources Co.* ("*Energy Resources*").[26] *Energy Resources* held that bankruptcy courts may use their equitable powers under §§ 105(a) and 1123(b)(6) to compel the Internal Revenue Service ("IRS") to allocate a chapter 11 debtor's tax payments to those tax liabilities chosen by the debtor.[27] In this Article, I argue that the Supreme Court's holding and rationale in *Energy Resources* demonstrate that the pro-release courts and commentators have the better view of §§ 105(a), 1123(b)(6), and 524(e).[28] I thus conclude that bankruptcy courts have the power to issue non-debtor releases,[29] though only in fairly narrow circumstances.[30]

I. A TAXONOMY OF NON-DEBTOR RELEASES

. . . The focus of this Article is non-debtor releases that extinguish a creditor's direct claims against a non-debtor over the creditor's objection—i.e., involuntary non-debtor releases of direct claims. . . .

IV. UNITED STATES V. ENERGY RESOURCES CO.

B. *In re Energy Resources, Co.*

Energy Resources concerned two bankruptcy proceedings that each addressed whether a bankruptcy court may order the IRS to allocate payments made by a chapter 11 debtor to the debtor's trust fund tax liabilities before its nontrust fund tax liabilities. . . .

D. Consolidated Appeals Before the First Circuit

Energy Resources and *Newport Offshore* were consolidated before the First Circuit. The court of appeals made two rulings. First, it decided that the IRS may "call tax payments within a chapter 11 reorganization "involuntary,' for purposes of applying its own regulations."[31] Second, it held that a bankruptcy court may order the IRS to allocate ""involuntary' payments to a taxpayer's "trust fund' liability first, provided that the court reasonably concludes that this allocation will likely increase the reorganization plan's chances for success."[32] Only the latter ruling is relevant here.

Beginning with the source of the authority to issue tax allocation orders, the court of appeals explained that "Congress has granted bankruptcy courts broad equitable powers, including those powers "expressly or by necessary implication conferred by Congress.'"[33] As support for this proposition, the First Circuit cited § 105(a).[34] The court then observed that an order designating tax payments to trust fund tax debts would satisfy the "appropriate" requirement of that statute in at least some circumstances.[35] For example, responsible persons might agree to contribute funds to their employer's estate in bankruptcy that are necessary for a successful reorganization, but only if they receive assurances from the court that the reorganized debtor will pay its trust fund taxes first.[36]

The court then considered whether any laws prohibit a bankruptcy court from using its equitable power to dictate the allocation of tax payments. It found none.[37] . . .

V. *ENERGY RESOURCES* AND NON-DEBTOR RELEASES

Energy Resources is the Supreme Court's most definitive guidance on the scope of the equitable powers conferred by §§ 105(a) and 1123(b)(6) and the relationship of these statutes to other sections of the Code.[38] Nonetheless, the vast majority of pro-release and anti-release authorities have overlooked the decision.[39] Moreover, those that cited *Energy Resources* did not conduct a sustained analysis of the case and failed to comprehend the full impact of its holding.[40]

In this Part, I contend that *Energy Resources* resolves the split in the courts concerning the propriety of non-debtor releases by providing compelling support for the pro-release position.

First, *Energy Resources* endorsed the broad view of §§ 105(a) and 1123(b)(6)—the view held by pro-release courts and commentators. The decision illustrates that bankruptcy courts may employ their equitable powers for the general purpose of facilitating a reorganization. In other words, bankruptcy courts possess substantive equitable powers; they are not limited to issuing orders that are tethered to specific sections of the Code.

Second, *Energy Resources* demonstrates that shifting the risk of plan failure from non-debtors to creditors—the exact impact of a channeling release vis-a-vis a provisional injunction—comports with equity where such action is necessary to the success of a reorganization. This defeats a critical objection to channeling non-debtor releases—that such relief is inequitable.

Third, *Energy Resources* establishes that the Supreme Court's "plain-meaning" approach to statutory interpretation applies when considering whether a § 105(a) or § 1123(b)(6) order conflicts with another provision of the Code. Thus, because § 524(e) fails, by its precise terms, to proscribe or even address non-debtor releases, the statute places no limit upon a bankruptcy court's equitable power to grant that type of relief.

Do you agree with the reasoning of the court in Energy Resources?

In sum, the *Energy Resources* Court effectively sided with the pro-release authorities on each of the critical issues regarding the validity of third-party releases. These disputes must therefore be resolved in favor of the pro-release position.

[A]s a result, this Article concludes that non-debtor releases are valid under the Bankruptcy Code

A. Energy Resources and §§ 105(a) and 1123(b)(6)

1. The Substantive Equitable Power of Bankruptcy Courts

Pro-and anti-release authorities are divided over the scope of a bankruptcy court's equitable powers. In nearly every pro-release decision, the court implicitly adopted the broad view of § 105(a), finding that the statute, standing alone, confers sufficient power to issue non-debtor releases. Other pro-release authorities concluded that § 1123(b)(6), by itself, permits bankruptcy judges to extinguish claims against non-debtors. In contrast, several anti-release courts and commentators endorsed the narrow view of § 105(a). Pursuant to that interpretation, the statute may only be used to implement other, specific provisions in the Code; it is not a substantive source of power. Therefore, according to the anti-release decisions, because no Code provision can serve as a pathway to grant third-party releases, § 105(a) may not be used to order that type of relief.[41]

Energy Resources ends this debate. There, the Supreme Court embraced the broad view of § 105(a) and an identical construction of § 1123(b)(6). Explaining that these statutes "are consistent with the traditional understanding that bankruptcy courts, as courts of equity, have broad authority to modify creditor-debtor relationships,"[42] the Court made it clear that both §§ 105(a) and 1123(b)(6) are sources of substantive power: the High Court ruled that bankruptcy judges may use these laws to grant relief for the broad aim of promoting a reorganization; § 105(a) and § 1123(b)(6) orders need not be tethered to more specific Code provisions.

To elaborate, *Energy Resources* held that the equitable statutes may be employed to command the IRS to apply chapter 11 payments to a debtor's trust fund tax liabilities before its nontrust fund tax debts.[43] And the Supreme Court ruled that bankruptcy judges may use §§ 105(a) and 1123(b)(6) to grant such relief for the general goal of facilitating a reorganization. . . .

. . . In short, *Energy Resources* constitutes a full endorsement of the broad view of §§ 105(a) and 1123(b)(6), the view defended by pro-release authorities. . . .

Perhaps more importantly, the Supreme Court rejected the narrow view of §§ 105(a) and 1123(b)(6) even though the government presented the same rationale for adopting a restrictive interpretation that anti-release authorities have proffered. . . .

2. The Scope of a Bankruptcy Court's Substantive Equitable Powers After Energy Resources

Despite *Energy Resources's* endorsement of the broad view, one might assert that the substantive authority conferred by §§ 105(a) and 1123(b)(6) is not wide enough to permit third-party releases.

Some courts have stated, for example, that bankruptcy judges are prohibited from using their equitable power to provide relief that is not available under nonbankruptcy law.[44] In other words, while bankruptcy courts may employ §§ 105(a) and 1123(b)(6) to issue orders that do not implement a specific section of the Code, such "untethered" orders may only grant relief that is allowable under other federal or state law. . . . As a result, this objection concludes, nondebtor releases are beyond the bankruptcy court's equitable power.

Energy Resources defeats this argument. There, the Supreme Court held that bankruptcy courts may issue tax designation orders "whether or not the payments at issue are rightfully considered to be involuntary."[45] As noted previously, however, under IRS rules, "involuntary" payments are subject to allocation by the government,[46] a position universally endorsed by the courts.[47] Tax allocation orders thus constitute a permissible remedy in bankruptcy that is unavailable to taxpayers under nonbankruptcy law.[48] Accordingly, lack of availability outside bankruptcy is no objection to an order issued pursuant to § 105(a) or §1123(b)(6). . . .

In short, the limitations that some authorities have placed on *Energy Resources* are simply irrelevant to the validity of non-debtor releases in chapter 11 reorganizations where the modified Master Mortgage test is satisfied.

3. The Equitable Authority of Bankruptcy Courts to Allocate the Risk of Plan Failure

There is one, final anti-release argument based upon the two equitable statutes that must be addressed before I may conclude that §§ 105(a) and 1123(b)(6) provide bankruptcy courts with sufficient power to issue third-party releases. According to this objection, even if the broad view of §§ 105(a) and 1123(b)(6) is correct, non-debtor releases do not comport with equity because they place the risk of plan failure on the releasing creditor rather than the benefiting non-debtor.[49] Therefore, a bankruptcy court's equitable powers only permit the issuance of provisional injunctions; non-debtor releases are prohibited.

However, in *Energy Resources*, the Supreme Court held that bankruptcy courts may use the equitable authority granted by §§ 105(a) and 1123(b)(6) to issue orders that shift the risk of plan default from a third party to a creditor.[50] The High Court also ruled that such orders are permissible whenever it is necessary to the success of a reorganization.[51] *Energy Resources* thus undermines the contention that non-debtor releases improperly shift the risk of plan failure from non-debtors to creditors and demonstrates that this type of relief is entirely equitable.

Tax allocation orders decrease the likelihood that the IRS will receive payment in full because they mandate that liabilities guaranteed by a third party—the liabilities for trust fund taxes—be extinguished first.[52] Should the plan fail after the debtor has paid its trust fund taxes, but before all nontrust fund tax debts are satisfied, the IRS has no alternative source from which to recover its deficiency.[53] In the absence of a tax designation order, however, the IRS may apply the debtor's chapter 11 payments to the nonguaranteed liabilities first. This application protects the IRS because, if the debtor defaults, the responsible person remains liable for any outstanding trust fund taxes. Therefore, tax allocation orders shift the risk of plan failure from the guarantors of the debtor's tax obligations (responsible persons) to the IRS by circumscribing the government's ability to pursue the guarantors in the event of a default.[54]

Non-debtor releases have precisely the same effect in comparison to provisional injunctions—they decrease the likelihood that a creditor will receive payment in full by permanently barring the creditor from pursuing a co-obligor of the debtor rather than merely restraining the creditor from such action temporarily or until the debtor defaults [which is what provisional injunctions do].[55] . . .

In sum, the type of risk shifting endorsed by *Energy Resources* is nearly identical to that which takes place if a non-debtor release is contained in a chapter 11 plan rather than a provisional injunction. And the Supreme Court held that it is appropriate to reallocate risk in this manner when such action is necessary to the success of a reorganization.[56] Therefore, the argument that channeling releases are inequitable must be rejected. A bankruptcy court's power under §§ 105(a) and 1123(b)(6) is not limited to the issuance of provisional injunctions.

Significantly, the Supreme Court ignored the contention of Newport and the Energy Resources trustee that subjecting the IRS to the possibility of plan failure is sanctioned by § 1129(a)(9)(C)[57]—the statute that allowed a reorganizing debtor to pay its taxes within six years from the date of assessment.[58] The Supreme Court apparently found no need to rely upon that provision and instead focused entirely on §§ 105(a) and 1123(b)(6) in assessing whether it is equitable to shift the risk of plan default from a non-debtor to a creditor.[59] This thwarts any counterargument that it is permissible to alter the risk of plan failure only in the tax context where § 1129(a)(9)(C) is applicable.

It is not surprising that the Supreme Court disregarded the respondents' § 1129(a)(9)(C) defense of tax allocation orders. First, debtors are generally permitted to pay their creditors over extended periods of time lasting well beyond six years.[60] Section 1129(a)(9)(C) thus grants the IRS a privilege most other creditors do not receive—all of its claims must be paid within six years of the date the taxes were assessed.[61] In effect, § 1129(a)(9)(C) is intended to reduce the level of risk that may be imposed on the government in a plan of reorganization. It would be strange to interpret a statute designed to provide the IRS with additional protection as authorizing orders that actually lessen the government's chances of recovery. Second, to the extent § 1129(a)(9)(C) does apportion risk to the IRS, it does so in a manner that is entirely distinct from the way that tax designation orders do. The statute permits a chapter 11 debtor to pay the IRS over time. But tax allocations limit the IRS's ability to pursue third parties. Moreover, § 1129(a)(9)(C) shifts risk from the debtor to the IRS. Allocation orders, in contrast, move risk from non-debtors to the government. Accordingly, as the Supreme Court correctly implied, § 1129(a)(9)(C) cannot be read as supporting the bankruptcy court's authority to grant tax designations. The power to shift the risk of plan failure approved of in Energy Resources flows solely from §§ 105(a) and 1123(b)(6).

With the defeat of the final anti-release objection centered on §§ 105(a) and 1123(b)(6), it is now clear that the pro-release authorities are correct about the scope of a bankruptcy court's equitable powers—they are sufficiently broad to permit the granting of channeling non-debtor releases. But §§ 105(a) and 1123(b)(6) may not be used in a manner that conflicts with another provision of the Code. And the most well-accepted argument against non-debtor releases is that they are prohibited by § 524(e). It is to this argument that I now turn.

B. *Energy Resources* and § 524

The majority of anti-release courts, as well as several commentators, believe that the language of § 524(e) prohibits non-debtor releases. Several of these authorities bolster their conclusion by reference to practice under prior laws and to what they perceive to be the policy behind § 524(e)—that bankruptcy only offers protection to debtors willing to submit fully to the jurisdiction of the system. Pro-release courts and commentators counter that the express words of § 524(e) merely identify the impact of the debtor's discharge; the statute says nothing about the power of a bankruptcy judge to extinguish claims via an independent order issued pursuant to § 105(a) or § 1123(b)(6). Given the statute's clear language, previous versions of § 524(e) and any policies underlying that provision are simply irrelevant. Pro-release authorities thus conclude that § 524(e) does not bar third-party releases.

Energy Resources provides the answer yet again. That case establishes that the Supreme Court's "plain-meaning" approach to statutory interpretation applies when considering whether an order issued under the equitable statutes conflicts with a more specific provision of the Code. Therefore, since the clear language of § 524(e) fails to prohibit or even address non-debtor releases, the statute does not bar such relief. . . .

[In *Energy Resources*, the Supreme Court held that], since nothing in the language of §§ 507(a)(8), 523(a)(1)(A), and 1129(a)(9)(C) concerned the allocation of tax payments, those provisions do not forbid tax designation orders.

Comparable reasoning is applicable to the asserted conflict between § 524(e) and non-debtor releases issued under § 105(a) or § 1123(b)(6). Section 524(e) states that the "discharge of a debt of the debtor does not affect the liability of any other entity on, or the property of any other entity for, such debt."[62] Like the specific provisions in *Energy Resources*, this statute says nothing about the allegedly contradictory use of the equitable statutes; § 524(e) makes no mention of third-party releases. Instead, as explained by many pro-release (and even a few anti-release) authorities, the plain language of the legislation simply identifies the impact of the debtor's discharge—the discharge, by itself, does not "affect the liability" of any third party. Section 524(e) leaves open the prospect of orders, independent of the discharge, that otherwise affect the liability of non-debtors. . . .

CONCLUSION

This Article contends that *Energy Resources* vindicates the pro-release position on every major issue concerning the validity of non-debtor releases. Therefore, under existing precedent, bankruptcy courts possess the equitable power to extinguish claims against third parties. While *Energy Resources* resolves the legal dispute, a broader question remains—are non-debtor releases justified on policy grounds? Should courts have the legal authority to grant this type of relief? While the policy debate is generally beyond the scope of my undertaking here, certain aspects of it are worth brief consideration.

Beginning with some pro-release observations, as indicated above, many courts believe that a third-party release can be essential to a debtor's reorganization. Without this relief, for example, corporate insiders might refuse to contribute funds or time to the debtor's plan, making continued operations impossible.[63] Since promotion of reorganizations is the central policy of chapter 11, releases may be defended on the ground that they serve this cardinal goal. In addition, by consolidating adjudication of related claims into a single forum, non-debtor releases "can eliminate piecemeal litigation and curb costs significantly."[64] They might also bring "global peace" to mass tort disputes and allow for timely payments to thousands of injured parties. In short, as one commentator concluded, permitting non-debtor releases gives courts the "flexibility to act in the best interests of all parties concerned."[65]

Turning to the anti-release position, the availability of provisional injunctions casts doubt on the "necessity" of many non-debtor releases. A provisional injunction provides substantially similar relief, but places the risk of plan failure on the benefiting third party. Of course, the non-debtor may hold out for a release to guarantee its future security. But the cases in which a provisional injunction will not suffice should be few and far between. Consistent with this analysis, Professor Brubaker contends that non-debtor releases are seldom necessary to the debtor's reorganization.[66] Such relief is more likely to serve as a form of costless compensation to the third party than as an incentive for funding required to prevent the debtor's liquidation.[67] Indeed, Judith Starr hypothesizes that permitting non-debtor releases creates an incentive for managers to move troubled corporations into bankruptcy where the plan of reorganization might extinguish their personal liabilities.[68] Professor Brubaker also asserts that it "is nearly impossible to verify or disprove in any reliable manner" whether a particular release will mean the difference between a successful reorganization and termination of the debtor's business.[69] And even if such a determination were feasible, he continues, bankruptcy courts are ill-suited to weighing the benefits of a successful reorganization against the burdens imposed by vitiating nonbankruptcy rights through the release.[70] Finally, Peter Boyle suggests that third-party releases may undermine the "integrity of guaranties," which could impact the cost of financing,[71] and limit the usefulness of joint and several liability.[72] Perhaps it was such observations that ultimately convinced the National Bankruptcy Review Commission to counsel that Congress amend the Code to permit only voluntary releases.[73]

It is difficult to assess these policy arguments. Few, other than Professor Brubaker's, have been substantially developed. What is needed at this stage is greater investigation into the empirical details. Whatever the result of that inquiry, the final decision should be made by Congress. Non-debtor releases, even of the channeling variety, are a drastic form of relief. They implicate clashes between critical policies underlying the Bankruptcy Code and other federal and state law. The availability of such relief is an issue best resolved by a legislative body after diligent consideration of the countervailing values.

END NOTES

1. 11 U.S.C. §§ 1101–74 (2000).
2. §§ 101–1330. . . .
3. Pioneer Inv. Serv. Co. v. Brunswick Assoc. Ltd. P'ship, 507 U.S. 380, 389 (1993); NLRB v. Bildisco & Bildisco, 465 U.S. 513, 527 (1984).
4. Pioneer Inv. Serv., 507 U.S. at 389.
5. *See* Energy Res. Co. v. IRS (In re Energy Res. Co.), 871 F.2d 223, 230 (1st Cir. 1989) (observing that the Bankruptcy Code's twin purposes—"ensure fair payment to creditors and provide the bankrupt firm with an opportunity to make a "fresh start'"—are "often conflicting"), aff'd, 495 U.S. 545 (1990).
6. *See* In re Whitfield, 290 B.R. 302, 306 (Bankr. E.D. Mich. 2003) ("The Bankruptcy Code reflects a careful balance of debtors' rights and creditors' remedies."); In re Cason, 190 B.R. 917, 927 (Bankr. N.D. Ala. 1995) ("The Bankruptcy Code as originally enacted carefully balanced creditors' property rights and debtors' fresh start.").
7. Pioneer Inv. Serv., 507 U.S. at 389.
8. *See* Johnson v. Home State Bank, 501 U.S. 78, 88 (1991) ("In addition, the bankruptcy court retains its broad equitable power to "issue any order, process, or judgment that is necessary or appropriate to carry out the provisions of [the Code.]'") (quoting § 105(a)).
9. 11 U.S.C. § 105(a) (2000).
10. United States v. Energy Res. Co., 495 U.S. 545, 549 (1990); United States v. Prescription Home Health Care, Inc. (In re Prescription Home Health Care, Inc.), 316 F.3d 542, 549 (5th Cir. 2002) ("Energy Resources recognized the broad equitable powers accorded bankruptcy courts under 11 U.S.C. § 105(a) and 1123(b)(6).").
11. § 1123(b)(6).
12. *See* 2 Collier on Bankruptcy P 105.01[2], at 105–8 (Lawrence P. King ed., 15th ed. rev. 2004) ("As might be expected with a general grant of power such as section 105, the specific line drawing of the boundaries of that power are not always clear."); *infra* Part II.A.
13. § 1141(d)(1)-(3). . . . And new exceptions to a corporate debtor's discharge were instituted. See id. at § 708, 119 Stat. 126 (adding material to be codified at 11 U.S.C. § 1141(d)(6)).
14. § 1141(a).
15. *Id.*
16. *See* § 524(a), (e). . . .
17. In re Transit Group, Inc., 286 B.R. 811, 815 (Bankr. M.D. Fla. 2002).
18. . . . The terms "non-debtor release" and "third-party release" are used interchangeably in this Article.
19. *Compare* Hat-Hanseatische Anlage v. Sago Palms Joint Venture (In re Sago Palms Joint Venture), 39 B.R. 9, 9 (Bankr. S.D. Fla. 1984) (holding

that § 524(e) bars non-debtor releases), *with* In re A.H. Robins Co., 88 B.R. 742, 754–55 (E.D. Va. 1988) (holding that courts may grant non-debtor releases pursuant to their "equitable and inherent" power under the Bankruptcy Code), aff'd, 880 F.2d 694 (4th Cir. 1989).

20. Class Five Nev. Claimants v. Dow Corning Corp. (In re Dow Corning Corp.), 280 F.3d 648, 656 (6th Cir. 2002). . . .
21. . . . These courts typically mandate that third-party releases satisfy stringent requirements. . . .
22. § 524(e).
23. *See, e.g.*, SEC v. Drexel Burnham Lambert, Inc. (*In re* Drexel Burnham Lambert Group, Inc.), 130 B.R. 910, 918–19 (S.D.N.Y. 1991) (this bankruptcy involved "tens of thousands" of persons with claims against the debtors for securities violations; the plan contained a non-debtor release extinguishing claims against the debtors' officers, directors, and others), *aff'd*, 960 F.2d 285 (2d Cir. 1992); *In re* A.H. Robins Co., 88 B.R. 742, 743–44, 754–55 (E.D. Va. 1988) (indicating that A.H. Robins was forced into bankruptcy because of thousands of tort actions relating to its Dalkon Shield contraceptive device; the company's plan of reorganization contained a non-debtor release extinguishing all claims the injured tort claimants possessed against several third parties), *aff'd*, 880 F.2d 694 (4th Cir. 1989). . . . *In re* Seatco, Inc., 257 B.R. 469, 473 (Bankr. N.D. Tex. 2001) (observing that non-debtor releases have been affirmed "principally in large, complex, mass tort-type bankruptcy cases"). . . . *See generally* Duane Loft, Note, *Jurisdictional Line-Drawing in a Time When So Much Litigation is "Related To" Bankruptcy: A Practical and Constitutional Solution*, 72 FORDHAM L. REV. 1091, 1091 (2004) ("The past five years have seen some of the largest bankruptcies in history—WorldCom, Enron, Federal-Mogul, just to name a few. Collapsing into bankruptcy amid allegations of fraud or mass tort, these companies precipitated waves of litigation in state courts across America." (footnotes omitted)). . . .
24. *See* Kate Inman, *Note, All Debts Are Off?—Can the Bankruptcy Process Be Used to Release the Debts of Nondebtor Parties*, 49 FLA. L. REV. 631, 631 (1997) (observing that the propriety of non-debtor releases is "attractive" for Supreme Court review because of the split in the circuits); Peter E. Meltzer, *Getting Out of Jail Free: Can the Bankruptcy Plan Process Be Used to Release Nondebtor Parties?*, 71 AM. BANKR. L.J. 1, 2 (1997) ("The issue [of non-debtor releases] may attract the attention of the Supreme Court in view of the split in the circuits and the attention of Congress in connection with its ongoing review of the Bankruptcy Code."); *see also* Nat'l Bankr. Review. Comm'n, Bankruptcy: The Next Twenty Years 535 (1997) ("Current law offers little guidance to the parties and the courts on whether nondebtor release provisions

may be included in a settlement or plan of reorganization and subsequently enforced by an injunction.").

25. Ralph Brubaker, *Bankruptcy Injunctions and Complex Litigation: A Critical Reappraisal of Non-Debtor Releases in Chapter 11 Reorganizations*, 1997 U. ILL. L. REV. 959, 965 (1997).
26. 495 U.S. 545 (1990).
27. *Id.* at 548–49.
28. *See infra* Part V.
29. *Id.*
30. . . . The focus here is only on the bankruptcy courts' power to issue third-party releases once jurisdiction is established. . . .
31. *Energy Res.*, 871 F.2d at 227. The IRS asserted that payments under a chapter 11 plan are "involuntary" because they are made pursuant to a court order confirming the plan. *Id.* at 228. The debtors countered that payments are "involuntary" only where they are compelled by a levy, execution, or judicial sale and the more limited role of the bankruptcy court in confirming a plan of reorganization falls short of this standard. *Id.*
32. *Id.* at 227. The First Circuit adopted the following test for bankruptcy court's to use in making this determination:

    Upon consideration of the reorganization plan as a whole, in so far as the particular structure or allocation of payments increases the risk that the IRS may not collect the total tax debt, is that risk nonetheless justified by an offsetting increased likelihood of rehabilitations, i.e., increased likelihood of payment to creditors who might otherwise lose their money. *Id.* at 234. When this standard is satisfied, bankruptcy courts may order an allocation. *Id.*

33. *Id.* at 230 (quoting Johnson v. First Nat'l. Bank of Montevideo, 719 F.2d 270, 273 (8th Cir. 1983)).
34. *Id.* (citing 11 U.S.C. § 105(a) (2000)).
35. *Energy Res.*, 871 F.2d at 230. In addition to § 105(a), the First Circuit observed that "bankruptcy courts have long had the legal power to tell creditors against which of a debtor's several debts they are to apply a particular payment." *Id.* at 231 (citing National Bank of the Commonwealth v. Mechanics' National Bank, 94 U.S. 437, 439 (1876)). But the court's focus appeared to be on § 105(a). *See id.* at 230–32.
36. *Id.* . . .
37. *Id.* at 231–33.
38. The Supreme Court has cited § 105(a) just five times. And only in *Energy Resources* did the Court offer any analysis regarding the scope of a bankruptcy court's powers under the statute. . . . Additionally, the Court has only cited § 1123(b)(6) once—in *Energy Resources*.
39. Only a handful of pro-release and anti-release decisions and articles even cited *Energy Resources*, and most are identified in the next footnote.

40. *See* In re Dow Corning Corp., 255 B.R. 445, 478–79 (E.D. Mich. 2000) (holding that bankruptcy courts have the authority to issue non-debtor releases under §§ 105(a) and 1123(b)(6) because, inter alia, those statutes, pursuant to *Energy Resources*, "provide the bankruptcy courts with broad authority to approve plans of reorganization that include provisions affecting creditors' rights to recover against non-debtors, if the provisions are necessary to carry out the plan") (citing *Energy Res.*, 495 U.S. at 549) (offering no additional analysis regarding *Energy Resources*), rev'd in part, aff'd in pertinent part, 280 F.3d 648 (6th Cir. 2002); Hydee R. Feldstein, *Reinterpreting Bankruptcy Code § 524(e): The Validity of Third-Party Releases in a Plan*, 22 CAL. BANKR. J. 25, 39–40 (1994) (arguing that *Energy Resources* provides that §§ 105(a) and 1123(b)(6) grant substantive powers and thus that these statutes confer the authority to issue third-party releases, but merely quoting several sentences from *Energy Resources* before reaching this conclusion) (citing *Energy Res.*, 495 U.S. at 549); Howard C. Buschman III & Sean P. Madden, *The Power and the Propriety of Bankruptcy Court Intervention in Actions Between Nondebtors*, 47 BUS. LAW. 913, 942 (1992) (concluding that the pro-release decisions are "consistent with the Supreme Court's recent observation regarding the bankruptcy court's "broad authority to modify creditor-debtor relationships,'" but providing no further discussion) (quoting *Energy Res.*, 495 U.S. at 549). . . . The only anti-release authority to consider *Energy Resources* is Professor Brubaker. And his primary discussion of the case is limited to a single footnote where he argues that *Energy Resources* does not support the conclusion that bankruptcy courts may use their equitable powers in a manner that directly contravenes nonbankruptcy law. *See* Brubaker, *supra* note 25, at 1030 n.255. . . .
41. . . . One would presume that the anti-release authorities would reach the same conclusion with respect to § 1123(b)(6).
42. United States v. Energy Res. Co., 495 U.S. 545, 549 (1990).
43. *Id.*
44. *See, e.g.*, Unsecured Creditors' Comm. v. Stern (In re SPM Mfg. Corp.), 984 F.2d 1305, 1311 (1st Cir. 1993). . . .
45. United States v. Energy Res. Co., 495 U.S. 545, 548–49 (1990) (emphasis added).
46. *See* IRS Policy Statement P-5–60(7) (1993), reprinted in 1 INTERNAL REVENUE MANUAL—ADMINISTRATION § 1.2.1.5.14 (CCH Rev. 2000) . . . ; 1 INTERNAL REVENUE MANUAL—ADMINISTRATION § 5.9.15.2(2) (CCH Rev. 2006). . . .
47. 60 Am. Jur. 2d Payment § 69 (2003) ("When a payment is involuntary, IRS policy is to allocate the payments as it sees fit, and this rule has been uniformly followed by the courts in the interest of orderly administration.

A court will not direct the application of funds in any particular manner in such cases.") (footnotes omitted). . . .

48. While court orders allocating involuntary tax payments are not available under nonbankruptcy law, such orders do not actually conflict with nonbankruptcy law because the IRS rules that tax designation orders override lack the force of law. *See* Fargo v. Comm'r, 447 F.3d 706, 713 (9th Cir. 2006) ("The Internal Revenue Manual does not have the force of law and does not confer rights on taxpayers. This view is shared among many of our sister circuits."). . . . And, as the Supreme Court pointed out in *Energy Resources*, nothing in the Internal Revenue Code barred the tax allocation orders at issue in that case. *Energy Res.*, 495 U.S. at 551; *see also* Brubaker, *supra* note 25, at 1030 n.255. . . . The IRS rules at issue are set forth in note 46, *supra*.
49. As noted previously, plans of reorganization containing channeling releases generally do not guarantee that creditors impacted by the release will receive payment in full on their claims. . . .
50. United States v. Energy Res. Co., 495 U.S. 545, 548–50 (1990).
51. *Id.* at 549.
52. *Id.* at 550.
53. *Id.*
54. *See id.* at 548–50.
55. Channeling non-debtor releases may also extinguish independent claims against third parties and transfer the responsibility of payment to the debtor. But generally channeling releases involve a debtor and a third party that are co-obligors. . . .
56. *See Energy Res.*, 495 U.S. at 546, 549.
57. *See* Joint Brief for the Respondents ("Respondents' Brief") at 38, 1990 WL 505637, United States v. Energy Res. Co., 495 U.S. 545 (1990) (No. 89–255); *Energy Res.*, 495 U.S. at 546–51.
58. 11 U.S.C. § 1129(a)(9)(C) (2000). . . .
59. *Energy Res.*, 495 U.S. at 549.
60. *See, e.g.*, In re McCall, No. 93–00632, 1997 WL 428580, at 3, 16 (Bankr. D.D.C. May 27, 1997) (creditors impacted by the channeling release scheduled to receive distributions over eight-or ten-year periods); In re Master Mortgage Invest. Fund, Inc., 168 B.R. 930, 932 (Bankr. W.D. Mo. 1994) (plan provided creditors would be paid over twenty years).
61. § 1129(a)(9)(C). . . .
62. § 524(e).
63. *See* Nat'l Bankr. Review Comm'n, *supra* note 24, at 534–35; *see also* Peter M. Boyle, *Note, Non-Debtor Liability in Chapter 11: Validity of Third-Party Discharge in Bankruptcy,* 61 FORDHAM L. REV. 421, 422, 436 (1992) (suggesting that non-debtor releases may be necessary to "ensure cooperation" of third parties or "generate non-debtor contributions

to the reorganization that the non-debtor otherwise would not have made").

64. Nat'l Bankr. Review Comm'n., *supra* note 24, at 535.
65. Inman, *supra* note 24, at 648
66. Brubaker, *supra* note 25, at 1021.
67. *Id.* at 1023–26.
68. Judith R. Starr, *Bankruptcy Court Jurisdiction to Release Insiders from Creditor Claims in Corporate Reorganizations*, 9 BANKR. DEV. J. 485, 486 (1993) ("Moreover, giving insiders the ability to force a settlement on unwilling creditors, without requiring them to take on the burdens associated with filing for bankruptcy, creates a moral hazard for insiders of troubled companies."). *But see* Inman, *supra* note 24, at 648 (anti-release authorities have "not . . . sufficiently argued . . . that to give courts the power to permanently enjoin suits against non-debtors will provide a mechanism of escape for nondebtors and unfairly prejudice claimants").
69. Brubaker, *supra* note 25, at 1027 & n.48.
70. *Id.* at 1030–32.
71. Boyle, *supra* note 63, at 422, 443.
72. *Id.* at 444.
73. *See* Nat'l Bankr. Review Comm'n, *supra* note 24, at 538 ("The Commission's Recommendation would permit only voluntary releases."); *see also id.* at 534 ("Congress should amend sections 1123 and 524(e) to clarify that it is within the discretion of the court to allow a plan proponent to solicit release of nondebtor liabilities. Creditors that agree in a separate document to release nondebtor parties will be bound by such releases, whereas creditors that decline to release their claims against nondebtor parties will not be bound to release their claims.").

ISSUE SUMMARY

At its core, bankruptcy law is about balance. The authors in this section agree that to function properly bankruptcy law must balance the interests of the debtors in generating a fresh start and the interests of creditors in getting the money they are owed. While there is agreement that balance is necessary, the issue of what constitutes the proper balance is not nearly as clear. Balance is important in bankruptcy law in determining rights, agreements, jurisdiction, and in measuring the success of reforms. The articles presented in this section merely begin to scratch the surface of considerations as to what rights debtors have, and should have, under bankruptcy law. Balance must be reached, not only with respect to how much debtors need to pay back over what time period, but also regarding what assets debtors must use to pay back debts and what assets debtors may keep to help pay for living expenses. This debate over what each side, debtors and creditors, is due is integral to the balance bankruptcy law seeks to achieve.

In light of the readings, what is the proper balance between creditor and debtor rights? What rights should debtors have under bankruptcy laws? Are there important rights that are not protected under bankruptcy law but that should be? Does bankruptcy law favor either creditors or debtors, and if so, is the system in need of repairs? These are all important questions asked and addressed by many of the readings in this section.

The issue of what a debtor may keep is part of an ongoing legal debate that is likely to be of increasing importance over the next few years. As business persons, lawyers, consumers, or citizens, we all need to consider these issues as they are important political and legal topics likely to shape the United States in the coming years. The articles in this section presented important questions regarding bankruptcy law and hopefully stimulated thought regarding what rights debtors should have.

ISSUE HIGHLIGHTS

- Various federal courts are in conflict in their rulings regarding when and how much of a tort award can be exempted from a bankruptcy trust.
- Debtors may exempt multiple claims under § 522(d)(11)(D) for multiple and distinct claims.
- Debtors may exempt a right to a tort award for damages when the award is in compensation for loss of future earnings.
- Debtors have the right to exempt the entirety of a future award by listing the award for the amount of the expected value, even if the actual value turns out to be more than the expected value once it is settled.

- Damage awards typically can be exempt in their entirety to the extent the award is for a disability benefit.
- While bankruptcy law used to favor debtors, since the passage of the Bankruptcy Abuse Prevention and Consumer Protection Act of 2005 (BAPCPA), bankruptcy law has become much more creditor friendly.
- It is not clear to what extent the changes to bankruptcy law codified in BAPCPA encourage opportunistic debtors to try to take advantage of the system, but what is clear is that many honest debtors are worse off after BAPCPA than before.
- Not allowing debtors to exempt all, or enough, of personal injury awards creates a system where debtors are forced into relying upon social welfare programs for subsistence, thus making them a burden on society. If allowed to keep their personal injury awards, these debtors would be able to better care for themselves.
- While companies going through chapter 11 bankruptcy can reject burdensome executory contracts under section 365 of the Bankruptcy Code, it is not clear when companies that provide energy to public utilities may use this right to reject burdensome contracts.
- When a party files for bankruptcy, coliable third parties are not always discharged of their duties to pay, but the courts are split on whether filing for bankruptcy frees third parties of responsibility and if doing so is good for creditors as well as debtors.

CRITICAL THINKING

As was stated earlier, bankruptcy law is largely about balance. This balance is between competing interests for debtors and creditors. Debtors want to clear some of their debt and obtain a fresh start; creditors want to make sure they receive as much of the money they are owed as possible. While bankruptcy law is intended to strike a balance between these competing interests, how do bankruptcy attorneys and trustees decide what is the appropriate balance? Do impressions of responsibility and desert factor in to the decision of what is an appropriate balance?

When faced with difficult decisions, a person's values tend to help decide how that person will answer a dilemma. A value is a positive abstraction that motivates behavior. For example, "freedom" is a value. It is positive, something people would want to support without blushing or risking being unethical (as opposed to a "negative" such as racism or bigotry). Furthermore, freedom is an abstraction because it is something intangible, as opposed to something tangible, or material, such as kittens. Regardless of one's opinion of kittens, they are not abstractions and thus are not values. However, values such as freedom need to be defined because freedom could mean a number of different things to different people.

Focusing on bankruptcy and debtors' rights, two important values are "individual responsibility" and "collective responsibility." Individual responsibility is the belief that people should be responsible for themselves, and as such have a duty to take responsibility for their actions and condition in life. Conversely, collective responsibility is the belief that societal factors impose constraints upon the level of blame that can be properly attributed to individuals, and thus we must all care for one another as part of society we are all responsible for people's social conditions. While it is rare to find advocates of pure individual responsibility or pure collective responsibility, people tend to favor one of these values over the other in a given situation, and this preference tends to motivate how people interpret issues. For example, if you favor individual responsibility, you are more likely to think paying back creditors is more important than providing a fresh start to debtors as the debtor should be held accountable for the debt he or she created. Alternatively, proponents of collective responsibility are likely to argue that societal and economic conditions are pushing people into debt, and therefore we need to help them by relieving some of their debt through bankruptcy and allow them to have a fresh start.

In light of what you now know about values, and especially individual and collective responsibility, return to the articles in this section. Do the various authors prefer either individual or collective responsibility over the other value? If so, does this preference appear to shape a given author's conclusion? Now, think about your own opinions. Do you have a preference for either individual or collective responsibility? Does this preference shape your thoughts on what rights debtors should have under bankruptcy law? In the future, think about what values are implicated in controversies and debates and see if these values are influencing an author's conclusion. By identifying important values and their influence on authors you will better be able to understand how an author reaches his or her conclusion.

ADDITIONAL READING RESOURCES

Anthony C. Coveny, *"Saying Goodbye to Texas's Homestead Protection: One Step Toward Economic Efficiency with the Bankruptcy Abuse Prevention and Consumer Protection Act of 2005,"* 44 HOUS. L. REV. 433 (2007).

Brian A. Blum, *Bankruptcy and Debtor/Creditor: Examples and Explanations* (4th ed. 2006).

Marcia Yablon, "Why Annie Gets to Keep Her Gun: An Analysis of Firearm Exemptions in Bankruptcy Proceedings," 21 *Bank Dev.* J. 553 (2005).

Megan A. Taylor, "Gag Me With a Rule of Ethics: BAPCPA'S Gag Rule and the Debtor Attorney's Right to Free Speech," 24 *Emory Bankruptcy Developments Journal*. 227 (2008).

Neill D. Fuquay, "Be Careful What You Wish for, You Just Might Get it: The Effect on Chapter 11 Case Length of the New Cap on a Debtor's Exclusive Period to File a Plan," 85 *Texas Law Review*. 431 (2006).
Peter Walker, *Bankrupts Behind Bars*, January 2008, at 14.
Satyajit Chatterjee, "The Economic Logic of a Fresh Start," *Business Review Federal Reserve Bank of Philadelphia*, First Quarter 2008, at 1.
Stephen Elias, Albin Renauer and Robin Leonard, *How to File Chapter 7 Bankruptcy* (14th ed. 2007).
Stuart Larsen, "What Every Commercial Landlord Should Know About the Treatment of Leases in Chapter 11 Reorganizations," *Business Credit*, April 2008, at 20.

For more information check these sites:

http://govinfo.library.unt.edu/nbrc/
http://www.debtworkout.com/
http://www.pennlawyer.com/fdcpa.htm
http://www.uslaw.com/library/area.tcl?area_id=11
http://www.washlaw.edu/subject/creditors.html

CONTRIBUTORS TO THIS VOLUME

EDITORS

M. NEIL BROWNE is Distinguished Teaching Professor, emeritus and Senior Lecturer and Scholar at Bowling Green State University. He is the author of 27 books and 150 professional articles in the areas of law, economics, and critical thinking. His current research focuses on the ethical potential and dilemmas of market solutions to allocation and distribution problems.

NANCY K. KUBASEK is a full professor at Bowling Green State University, where she has taught business law and environmental law since 1982. She has published over 75 articles, primarily in law reviews and business journals, and writes the On the Environment column for the *Real Estate Law Journal.* She has written several books, including *Dynamic Business Law, Environmental Law*, 6th ed, and *The Legal Environment of Business: A Critical Thinking Approach*, 5th ed. Active in many professional organizations, she is a former president of the Academy of Legal Studies in Business, the national organization for professors of legal studies in colleges of business, and the Tri-State Academy of Legal Studies in Business, her regional professional association.

AUTHORS

PETER M. AGNETTI received his law degree from St. John's University School of Law in 2006.

JAN M. AMBROSE is a professor at La Salle University.

JOSEPH A. ARNOLD graduated from Seton Hall University School of Law and is an attorney in Philadelphia, Pennsylvania.

NANCY BAUMGARTEN is an attorney in Atlanta with the firm of Dow Lohnes.

DR. JACK N. BEHRMAN is Luther Hodges Distinguished Professor Emeritus at the University of North Carolina's Kenan-Flagler Business School.

JOSEPH J. BLYSKAL III received his law degree from Emory University School of Law in 2007.

BRIAN BORNSTEIN is a professor of psychology at Louisiana State University, Baton Rouge.

DOUGLAS M. BRANSON is the W. Edward Sell Professor of Business Law at University of Pittsburgh Law School.

ANNE CARROLL is a professor at Rider University.

NANCY R. FURNARI is associated with the charitable foundation, The AYCO Co LP.

ANDREW S. GOLD is an associate with Skadden, Arps, Slate, Meagher, and Flom, LLP, and an assistant professor designate at De Paul University College of Law.

EDITH GREENE is a professor of psychology at the University of Colorado at Colorado Springs.

WILLIAM T. HENNESSEY is an attorney with Gunster, Yoakley & Stewart, P.A.

JOHN J. HERMAN received his law degree from Widner University School of Law in 2007.

JULIE K. JONES is an assistant city attorney for the city of Dallas.

TIMOTHY B. LEE is an adjunct scholar at the Cato Institute.

DANIEL A. MCLAUGHLIN is counsel in the New York office of Sidley Austin, practicing primarily securities litigation, class actions, and commercial litigation.

CYNTHIA R. MABRY is a professor of law at Howard University.

EDWARD A. MARSHALL practices law in Atlanta with the firm of Arnall Golden Gregory LLP.

ALYSE MEISLIK is an assistant attorney general in Phoenix.

MARK S. NAGEL is with the Department of Sport and Entertainment Management, University of South Carolina, Columbia.

BRIDGET R. O'NEILL is a partner in the Chicago office of Sydley Austin LLP.

MARK S. PINCUS is a graduate of Fordham University School of Law.

KATY RAND is a member Pierce Atwood's Employment and Litigation Practice Groups.

WILLIAM H. ROGERS is a professor of economics at The University of Missouri at St. Louis.

PAUL H. RUBIN is a research fellow at the Independent Institute and Professor of Economics and Law at Emory University in Atlanta.

FRANK H. SCIALDONE is an associate with Mazanec, Raskin & Ryder in Cleveland.

JOANNA M. SHEPHERD is a professor at Emory University School of Law.

JOSHUA M. SILVERSTEIN is an assistant professor of law at the University of Arkansas at Little Rock.

JOSEPH SMOLINSKY is a partner at Chadbourne & Parker LLP who provides restructuring advice and strategy to borrowers, lenders, investors, and creditors and also represents corporations seeking to reorganize under chapter 11.

WILLIAM CARLOS SPAHT is a graduate of Vanderbilt University Law School.

ALAN STRUDLER is associate professor of legal studies and director of the ethics program at the Wharton School, University of Pennsylvania.

RICHARD M. SOUTHALL is the director of the College Sport Research Institute at the University of North Carolina, Chapel Hill, NC.

MICHELLE J. WHITE is a professor of economics, University of California, San Diego.

CREDITS

1.1 From *Journal of Health Politics, Policy and Law*, 32(5), October 2007, pp. 843–865 (excerpts). Copyright © 2007 by Duke University Press. All rights reserved. Reprinted by permission of the publisher.

1.2 From *Journal of Law and Economics*, by Paul H. Rubin and Joanna M. Shepherd, 50(2), May 2007, pp. 221–238 (excerpted). Copyright © 2007 by University of Chicago Law School. Reprinted by permission of University of Chicago Press, Journals Division and the author.

1.3 From *Risk Management & Insurance Review*, vol. 7, issue 1, Spring 2004, pp. 9 (16 pages). Copyright © 2004 by American Risk & Insurance Association. Reprinted by permission of Wiley-Blackwell.

1.4 From *Law & Human Behavior*, 25(3), June 2001, pp. 217–234 (excerpts). Copyright © 2001 by Springer Science and Business Media. Reprinted by permission via Rightslink.

1.5 From Supreme Court of the United States (538 U.S. 408 (2003)).

2.1 From *HRfocus*, Vol. 84 Issue 10, October 2007, pp. 1–15 (excerpts). Copyright © 2007 by IOMA—Institute of Management and Administration. This text is republished with the express written consent of IOMA; any further use requires the publisher's permission. Please contact IOMA directly at: content@ioma.com or by phone, 973.718.4700; www.ioma.com.

2.2 From *Texas Tech Law Review*, Vol. 34, 2003, p. 1133+ (excerpts). Copyright © 2003 by Texas Tech University School of Law. Reprinted by permission.

2.3 From *Georgia Law Review*, Vol. 35, 2001, pp. 1021 (excerpts). Copyright © 2001 by University of Georgia School of Law. Reprinted by permission.

2.4 Originally published in the *Journal of Law & Sexuality*, by Frank Scialdone, Vol. 11, 2002, pp. 193–207 (excerpts). Copyright © 2002 by the Journal of Law and Sexuality. Reprinted by permission of Tulane University Law School. http://www.law.tulane.edu/tlsjournals/tlas/index.aspx.

2.5 From *Maine Bar Journal*, vol. 22, 2007, pp. 12+ (excerpts). Copyright © 2007 by Maine State Bar Association. Reprinted by permission.

3.1 From *Valparaiso University Law Review*, vol. 36, Summer 2002, pp. 631+ (excerpts). Copyright © 2002 by Valparaiso University School of Law. Reprinted by permission.

3.2 From *Columbia Law Review*, vol. 103, May 2003, pp. 925+ (excerpts). Copyright © 2003 by Columbia Law Review. Reprinted by permission.

3.3 From United States District Court for the Southern District of New York (355 F. Supp.2d, 2005 U.S. Dist., pp. 704).

3.4 From *University of Richmond Law Review*, vol. 37, March 2003, pp. 819+ (excerpts). Copyright © 2003 by University of Richmond Law Review. Reprinted by permission.

4.1 From *Valparaiso University Law Review*, vol. 42, Fall 2007, pp. 341+ (excerpts). Copyright © 2007 by Valparaiso University School of Law. Reprinted by permission.

4.2 From Court of Appeals of South Carolina (327 S.C. 567, 490 S.E.2d 608; 1997, pp. 102+).

4.3 From *American Journal of Law and Medicine*, vol. 24, 1998, pp. 514+ (edited). Copyright © 1998 by American Society of Law, Medicine & Ethics. Reprinted by permission.

4.4 From *Florida Law Review*, vol. 47, January 1995, pp. 147+ (excerpts). Copyright © 1995 by College of Law/University of Florida. Reprinted by permission.

4.5 From *Albany Law Review*, vol. 63, 1999, pp. 537+ (edited). Copyright © 1999 by Albany Law Review. Reprinted by permission.

4.6 From Superior Court of Connecticut by Justice District of Hartford, (July 19, 1994, Conn. Super., pp. 1904+ excerpts).

4.7 From *Sales & Use Tax Alert*, vol. 17, issue 22, December 15, 2007. Copyright © 2007 CCH Incorporated. All Rights Reserved. Reprinted with permission of Sales & Use Tax Alert.

4.8 From *Wisconsin Law Review*, January/February 1988. Copyright © 1988 by Bridget R. O'Neill. Reprinted by permission of the author.

5.1 From Supreme Court of the United States (500 U.S. 20 (1991)).

5.2 From *Alabama Law Review*, by Mary Rebecca Tyre Furman, vol. 52, Summer 2001, pp. 1359+ (edited). Copyright © 2001 by Alabama Law Review. Reprinted by permission.

5.3 From United States Court of Appeals for the Fourth Circuit, (173 F.3d 933; 1999 U.S. App. LEXIS, pp. 6329+ excerpts).

5.4 From *Seton Hall Law Review*, by Joseph A. Arnold, vol. 33, 2003, pp. 1207+ (excerpts). Copyright © 2003 by Seton Hall Law Review. Reprinted by permission.

5.5 From *Berkeley Journal of Employment and Labor Law*, vol. 1, 2003, pp. 71+ (excerpts). Copyright © 2003 by Berkeley Journal of Employment & Labor Law. Reprinted by permission.

6.1 From *Essays on Ethics in Business and the Professions* by Jack N. Behrman (Prentice Hall, 1988), p. 79+ (excerpts). Copyright © 1988 by Jack N. Behrman. Reprinted by permission of the author.

6.2 From *UCLA LAW Review*, vol. 45, December, 1997, pp. 337+ (excerpts). Copyright © 1997 by Alan Strudler. Reprinted by permission of the author.

6.3 From *Arizona Law Review*, vol. 46, Winter 2004, pp. 781 (excerpts). Copyright © 2004 by Alyse Meislik and Arizona Law Review. Reprinted by permission of the journal and Alyse Meislik.

6.4 From United States Court of Appeals for the Ninth Circuit (33 F.3d 1116, 1994).

6.5 From *Indiana Law Journal*, vol. 73, Winter 1997, pp. 187+ (excerpts). Copyright © 1997 by Cynthia R. Mabry. Reprinted by permission of the author.

6.6 From *Regulation*, February 3, 2005. Copyright © 2005 by Cato Institute. Reprinted by permission via the Copyright Clearance Center.

6.7 From *Cato Handbook on Policy*, 6th ed., 2005, pp. 269–273 (excerpts). Copyright © 2005 by Cato Institute. Reprinted by permission via the Copyright Clearance Center.

7.1 From Court of Appeal of Louisiana by Judge Rothschild, (Fifth Circuit, 805 So.2d (2002), pp. 1286+ excerpts).

7.2 From *Real Estate Law Journal*, vol. 33, 2004, pp. 203+. Copyright © 2004 by Thomson Reuters. Reprinted by permission.

7.3 From *Land Economics*, 82(4), 2006, pp. 500–501, 503, 504–507, 511–512 (excerpts). Copyright © 2006 by Board of Regents, University of Wisconsin Press. Reprinted by permission.

7.4 From *Widener Law Journal*, vol. 16, 2006, pp. 165+ (excerpts). Copyright © 2006 by Widener Law Journal. Reprinted by permission.

8.1 From U.S. Supreme Court (545 U.S. (2005) 469).

8.2 From *St. John's Law Review*, vol. 79, Fall 2005, pp. 1259+ (excerpts). Copyright © 2005 by St. John's University School of Law. Reprinted by permission.

8.3 From *Real Estate Law Journal*, vol. 35, no. 4, 2007. Copyright © 2007 by Thomson Reuters. Reprinted by permission.

8.4 From *Sport Marketing Quarterly*, vol. 16, September 2007, pp. 171+ (excerpts). Copyright © 2007 by Fitness Information Technology (FIT), publishing division of International Center for Performance Excellence (ICPE)/School of Physical Education, West Virginia University. Reprinted by permission.

8.5 From *Vanderbilt Law Review*, vol. 60, October 2007, pp. 1599+ (excerpted). Copyright © 2007 by Vanderbilt University Law School. Reprinted by permission.

9.1 From Supreme Court of the United States by Justice Kennedy, (128 S.Ct., 2008, p. 761).

9.2 From *Delaware Journal of Corporate Law*, vol. 31, 2006, pp. 631+ (excerpts; some notes omitted). Copyright © 2006 by The Widener University School of Law. Reprinted by permission.

9.3 From *Catholic University Law Review*, vol. 53, Spring, 2004, pp. 667 (excerpted). Copyright © 2004 by Catholic University Law Review. Reprinted by permission.

9.4 From *Fordham Law Review*, 76, October, 2007, pp. 423+ (excerpts). Copyright © 2007 by Fordham University School of Law. Reprinted by permission.

10.1 From United States Bankruptcy Court (344 B.R. (2005), pp. 304+ (excerpts)).

10.2 From *Regulation*, vol. 29, Fall 2006, pp. 28 (excerpts). Copyright © 2006 by Cato Institute. Reprinted by permission via the Copyright Clearance Center.

10.3 From *International Financial Law Review*, November 2004, pp. 1+. Copyright © 2004 by IFLR Magazine. Reprinted by permission of Euromoney Institutional Investor PLC.

10.4 From *Emory Bankruptcy Developments Journal*, 23, Spring 2007, pp. 677+ (excerpts). Copyright © 2007 by Emory Bankruptcy Developments Journal and Joseph J. Blyskal III. Reprinted by permission of the journal and the author.

10.5 From *Emory Bankruptcy Developments Journal*, Vol. 23, No. 1, Fall 2006, pp. 13+ (excerpts). Copyright © 2006 by Emory Bankruptcy Developments Journal and Joshua M. Silverstein. Reprinted by permission of Emory University School of Law and Joshua M. Silverstein, William H. Bowen School of Law, University of Arkansas at Little Rock.

INDEX